Strategies of Argument

Strategies of Argument

Essays in Ancient Ethics, Epistemology, and Logic

Edited by Mi-Kyoung Lee

OXFORD
UNIVERSITY PRESS

Oxford University Press is a department of the University of
Oxford. It furthers the University's objective of excellence in research,
scholarship, and education by publishing worldwide.

Oxford   New York
Auckland   Cape Town   Dar es Salaam   Hong Kong   Karachi
Kuala Lumpur   Madrid   Melbourne   Mexico City   Nairobi
New Delhi   Shanghai   Taipei   Toronto

With offices in
Argentina   Austria   Brazil   Chile   Czech Republic   France   Greece
Guatemala   Hungary   Italy   Japan   Poland   Portugal   Singapore
South Korea   Switzerland   Thailand   Turkey   Ukraine   Vietnam

Oxford is a registered trademark of Oxford University Press
in the UK and certain other countries.

Published in the United States of America by
Oxford University Press
198 Madison Avenue, New York, NY 10016

© Oxford University Press 2014

All rights reserved. No part of this publication may be reproduced, stored in
a retrieval system, or transmitted, in any form or by any means, without the prior
permission in writing of Oxford University Press, or as expressly permitted by law,
by license, or under terms agreed with the appropriate reproduction rights organization.
Inquiries concerning reproduction outside the scope of the above should be sent to the
Rights Department, Oxford University Press, at the address above.

You must not circulate this work in any other form
and you must impose this same condition on any acquirer.

Library of Congress Cataloging-in-Publication Data
Strategies of argument : essays in ancient ethics, epistemology, and logic / edited by Mi-Kyoung Lee.
pages cm
ISBN 978-0-19-989047-7 (hardback)
1. Philosophy, Ancient.   I. Lee, Mi-Kyoung.
B108.S77 2014
180—dc23
2013033304

1 3 5 7 9 8 6 4 2
Printed in the United States of America
on acid-free paper

For Gisela Striker, beloved friend and teacher

CONTENTS

Preface ix

Notes on Contributors xvii

Part One: Plato

1. The life of Protarchus' choosing: Plato *Philebus* 20b–22c 3
   Verity Harte

2. Fools' pleasures in Plato's *Philebus* 21
   Jennifer Whiting

3. Did Plato's cosmos literally begin? 60
   Sarah Broadie

Part Two: Aristotle's ethics and practical reasoning

4. A swarm of virtues: On the unity and completeness of Aristotle's scheme of character-virtues 83
   Dorothea Frede

5. Justice and the laws in Aristotle's ethics 104
   Mi-Kyoung Lee

6. Aristotle on how to fell a tree and other matters involving experience 124
   Dana Miller

Part Three: Aristotelian logic

7. Deduction in *Sophistici Elenchi* 6 149
   Marko Malink

8. Boethus and finished syllogisms 175
   Jonathan Barnes

9. Alexander of Aphrodisias on Aristotle's theory of the Stoic indemonstrables 199
   Susanne Bobzien

Part Four: Hellenistic ethics

10. Why there are ends of both goods and evils in ancient ethical theory 231
James Allen

11. Ancient goods: The *tria genera bonorum* in ethical theory 255
Brad Inwood

12. The philosophical ambitions of Seneca's *Letters* 281
John Schafer

Part Five: Hellenistic epistemology

13. The epistemology of Ptolemy's *On the criterion* 301
Mark J. Schiefsky

14. The compulsions of Stoic assent 332
Charles Brittain

15. Sextus Empiricus on persuasiveness and equipollence 356
Svavar Hrafn Svavarsson

Bibliography for Gisela Striker 375
Index of Names 379
Index Locorum 385

PREFACE

The original papers in this volume focus on topics in ancient Greek and Roman ethics, epistemology, and logic—and are a tribute to the influence of Gisela Striker, whose work has ranged for over forty years across these areas.

Gisela Striker's career began at the University of Göttingen, where she studied—alongside Dorothea Frede and Michael Frede—with Günther Patzig. She was also a visiting student at Oxford, where she studied with John Ackrill. Her PhD thesis, "Peras und Apeiron" (1969), was on the metaphysics of Plato's *Philebus*. She taught philosophy at Göttingen from 1971 to 1986, writing her *Habilitation*, a landmark study on the "criterion of truth" in Hellenistic epistemology (*Kritêrion tês Alêtheias*, 1978). During her years in Germany, she published many articles in the area of Hellenistic philosophy, was a member of two conferences that inaugurated a revival of interest in Hellenistic philosophy—one in Chantilly (1976) and the other in Oxford (1978)—and was one of the founders of the Symposium Hellenisticum. She is also one of the original members of the advisory board of *Oxford Studies in Ancient Philosophy*. She spent several terms as a visiting professor in the United States: at Stanford (1974), Princeton (1979), and Harvard (1985).

In 1986, Striker accepted a position as professor of philosophy at Columbia University. In 1989, she was appointed George Martin Lane Professor of Philosophy and Classics at Harvard, thereby becoming the first tenured woman in Harvard's Department of Philosophy. Her time at Harvard was interrupted in 1997, when she accepted a position as the Laurence Professor of Ancient Philosophy at Cambridge University (becoming once again the first woman to hold this position). But Striker returned to Harvard in 2000, where she remained until her retirement as professor emerita in 2012, serving from 2002 on as the Walter C. Klein Professor of Philosophy and Classics.

Striker's seminal contributions are clustered in three main areas: Hellenistic philosophy, especially epistemology and ethics; Aristotle's logic, especially his modal logic; and Aristotle's moral and political thought. Her work in Hellenistic philosophy is collected in *Essays in Hellenistic Epistemology and Ethics* (Cambridge, 1996), which includes work in ethics deriving from her Nellie Wallace lectures (Oxford, 1984) and her Tanner Lectures (Stanford, 1987), as well as papers on a wide range of topics in epistemology: Academic and Pyrrhonist skepticism, Epicurean epistemology, and the criterion of truth—including "Sceptical Strategies," the paper on skeptical strategies of argument which inspired the title of this volume. Striker's work on Aristotle's logic recently culminated in a translation and commentary in the Clarendon Aristotle series: *Aristotle's Prior Analytics Book I: Translated with an Introduction and Commentary* (Oxford, 2009). Her other work on Aristotle ranges widely, from his theory of emotions and the significance of his conception of ethics as "political science" to, most recently, her John Ackrill Memorial Lecture (Oxford, 2012), "Two Ways of Deliberating: Aristotle and the Stoics."

As Striker notes in the introduction to her collected papers, *Essays on Hellenistic Epistemology and Ethics*, her essays have been, first and foremost, contributions to the history of philosophy, though she does not distinguish engaging in the history of philosophy as sharply from engaging in philosophy itself as some of her peers have been inclined to do. Many of her papers are attempts to reconstruct the doctrines of philosophers like Epicurus and Chrysippus, which, owing to the lack of evidence and original texts, involves guesswork as well as philological and historical background investigation. She has insisted, in her work and her teaching, on the importance of taking into account unique features of the social, political, and literary contexts in which the ancient philosophers were working; her work is acutely sensitive to the fact that ancient authors were often responding to questions, issues, and problems very different from those that are thought urgent and central today. Even so, her focus on philosophical arguments and theories, and her particular genius at discerning interesting, original, and deep continuities of argument running through the various authors she studies have made her a "philosopher's historian." Her work is thus an inspiration to those who seek to combine exegesis with philosophical thought about the problems studied in ancient as well as modern texts.

Each of the three areas in which Striker has made important contributions is represented in this volume.

The papers by Harte and Whiting focus on the refutation of the hedonist in Plato's *Philebus*, paying special attention to the interplay between particular arguments within the dialogue and how the dialogue as a whole is supposed to work on its audience. In "The Life of Protarchus' Choosing: Plato *Philebus* 20b–22c," **Verity Harte** focuses on the dialogue's treatment of the first of its two major questions: (1) which is the good, pleasure or reason? and (2) if neither is, then which (if either) of the two is responsible for the goodness of the best, that is, the mixed life? In the dialogue, an answer to the first question is given fairly quickly, whereas discussion of the second takes up most of the dialogue. In her paper, Harte addresses a puzzle about the placement and the apparent shortcomings of the argument by which the first question is settled. She argues that the argument has and is presented as having only a limited aim; and that it achieves that aim on a condition whose rejection is designed to motivate the hedonist to think further about the hard questions about pleasure and the good. The argument also sets the agenda for the rest of the dialogue: in particular, while the characters began with three criteria, sufficiency, completeness/perfection, and choiceworthiness, only two, sufficiency and choiceworthiness, are appealed to in the argument—not perfection. Harte says that its omission is significant—and that the rest of the dialogue will take a teleological turn, by offering an argument that reason *is responsible for* the goodness of the mixed life.

Jennifer Whiting seeks, in "Fools' Pleasures in Plato's *Philebus*," to give a unified account of the various forms of falsity that Socrates ascribes to pleasures. She defends Plato against the common charge of equivocation by reading him as presenting a cumulative argument involving different but related senses of "false," one that appeals in the end to the *foolishness* of certain pleasures, which foolishness the subject cannot himself appreciate while he is in their grip. Whiting thus reads the *Philebus* as entertaining the *corrigibility* of self-ascriptions of pleasure in the present tense and as seeking thereby to improve on the anti-hedonist arguments of the *Gorgias*, where Socrates' appeal to the shamefulness of certain pleasures begs the crucial question. Because the appeal to foolishness is content-neutral, whereas the *Gorgias*' appeal to shamefulness was not, the *Philebus* represents an improvement: the diehard hedonist can more easily be brought to worry that he is a fool than that he is a knave. Moreover, in being content-neutral the appeal to foolishness anticipates Aristotle's appeal to the so-called "formal criteria" for something's counting as the good, criteria often taken to be among Aristotle's many debts to the *Philebus*.

In "Did Plato's Cosmos Literally Begin?" **Sarah Broadie** takes up the question of whether modern interpreters are right to read Plato's *Timaeus*—with its thesis that the cosmos had a beginning—as "proto-historical" (i.e., as merely a *façon de parler* that presents the cosmos as though it had a beginning), and so as consistent with a sempiternalist reading of the cosmos. She argues against this, and thinks we should read Plato literally—however unfashionable that might be.

Are Aristotle's virtues of character an integrated whole, as he claims, or are they, in Plato's terms, just like a disparate swarm? The problem is due to the facts that (a) Aristotle enumerates affections without virtues and virtues without affections, and (b) his definitions narrowly confine the virtues to one type of action and affection, so that it is hard to see how they can form an integrated whole. In "A Swarm of Virtues: On the Unity and Completeness of Aristotle's Scheme of Character-Virtues," **Dorothea Frede** argues that certain affections cannot be made the subject of the sort of systematic training and practice that is required by the good life in a community, that there is an affection contained in every disposition even if it is not named, and that the narrowness of the definitions of the virtues is the prerequisite of the right mean between excess and defect: unless the actions and affections are of the same type this conception would be vacuous. She concludes that there are also indications of how to supplement what seems missing so that Aristotle's confidence in the completeness of his catalog of virtues is justified—albeit not by explicit argumentation—because the character-virtues are just those virtues needed for a satisfactory life in a polis.

Mi-Kyoung Lee's paper "Justice and the Laws in Aristotle's Ethics" raises similar questions about the shape of Aristotle's argument concerning virtue by focusing on his claim that justice is identical with "*teleia arête*"—variously rendered "the whole of virtue," "complete virtue," and "perfect virtue." This claim helps us to discern a striking line of argument in Aristotle's account of virtue—namely, that justice in particular is the most important of all the virtues because it encompasses all of them. Lee argues that Aristotle's identification of general justice with virtue "as a whole" strongly implies that Aristotle's virtuous agent, both qua good citizen and qua *phronimos*, will be law-abiding, and that this implication can be defended against both ancient and modern objections by looking at Aristotle's conception of the role and purpose of laws in a well-organized polis. That is, for Aristotle, virtue has to be understood in political and not just individual terms.

What is it to be a rational agent in the sphere of productive activity? In "Aristotle on How to Fell a Tree and Other Matters Involving Experience," **Dana Miller** argues that Aristotle's discussion of practical reasoning in the realm of ethics presupposes a more general account of practical reasoning about how to accomplish ends in non-ethical action. Aristotle does not, however, set out this more general account, with the result that this aspect of Aristotle's thinking is largely ignored. In his paper, Miller seeks to remedy this by posing a practical but non-ethical problem, namely, how to fell a tree, and argues that experience, practical expertise, and deliberation combine to provide the epistemic basis required for successful rational action.

In "Deduction in *Sophistici Elenchi* 6," **Marko Malink** focuses on Aristotle's definition of refutation in the theory of argument presented in his early work, the *Sophistici Elenchi,* which is sometimes considered the ninth book of the *Topics*. This work is seldom studied on its own, because it focuses on fallacious arguments and is therefore viewed as a kind of appendix to Aristotle's general treatment of dialectic and argumentation. But Malink argues that Aristotle's treatment of sophistical and merely apparent refutations has important implications for his conception of what a valid deductive argument is. A refutation, for Aristotle, is a kind of deduction; in particular, it is a deduction whose conclusion contradicts a thesis originally endorsed by one's opponent in a debate. Malink examines in detail the way Aristotle develops this definition of refutation in chapter 6 of the *Sophistici Elenchi*, and explains how this chapter sheds new light on Aristotle's conception of deduction.

Jonathan Barnes' paper "Boethus and Finished Syllogisms" deals with a claim at the heart of Aristotle's assertoric logical theory, that some syllogisms are "perfect," that is, obviously valid or acceptable, and that others are "imperfect" but can be perfected (i) by conversion to one of the perfect syllogisms, (ii) by *reductio ad impossibile*, or (iii) by *ekthesis*. Barnes addresses post-Aristotelian controversies about whether Aristotle was right to regard only some and not all valid arguments as "perfect."

In "Alexander of Aphrodisias on Aristotle's Theory of the Stoic Indemonstrables," **Susanne Bobzien** takes as her starting point Striker's thesis that Aristotle's so-called "hypothetical syllogisms" were his way of expressing valid arguments that are not based on the sort of term-relations characteristic of categorical syllogisms. Bobzien explores the role Alexander played in the development and transmission of Aristotle's and the early Peripatetic hypothetical syllogistic, and in particular in bridging the gap between Aristotelian's term logic and Stoic propositional logic. She argues that in three areas in particular Alexander made a difference. He connected passages from Aristotle's *Topics* and *Prior Analytics* with the Stoic indemonstrables, and consequently appropriated at least four of the five kinds of Stoic indemonstrables as Aristotelian. He developed a specifically Peripatetic terminology in which to describe those arguments—thus facilitating the integration of the indemonstrables into Peripatetic logic. And he made progress towards solving the problem of what place the Stoic third indemonstrables should be given in a Peripatetic setting. Bobzien concludes that Alexander consistently presented passages from Aristotle's logical oeuvre in a manner that makes it appear as if Aristotle was in possession of a Peripatetic correlate to the Stoic theory of indemonstrables.

In the second half of the volume, we turn to Hellenistic ethics and epistemology.

One prominent strategy of argument found in all kinds of ancient ethical theories is the sort of classification and division of goods that is the focus of the papers by Allen and Inwood. In "Why There Are Ends of Both Goods and Evils in Ancient Ethical Theory," **James Allen** adds a new twist to the treatment of ends: he asks why Cicero presents ancient ethical theories under the rubric of "the ends of goods *and evils*." For if an end (*telos*) is something for the sake of which we should do things, then it would seem that bad and evil things should not properly speaking have or belong to ends at all. Allen argues however that the best way of thinking of the question "what are the ends of goods and evils?" is to recognize that "end" here has the earlier senses of (i) a result, and (ii) a standard or criterion by which something is to be assessed. The two senses of "end" are thus connected insofar as a theory of the ends of goods and evils will allow one to judge which things are ends in the sense of being good by means of a criterion, namely, by the ends in the sense of results that typically follow for things of that kind. Allen can then not only explain what "ends" means in Cicero's *De finibus*, but can also make connections with the earlier traditions in thinking about "ends" in the Academy, ones that may go back as far as Plato's *Protagoras* and *Gorgias*.

In "Ancient Goods: The *tria genera bonorum* in Ethical Theory," **Brad Inwood** focuses on the familiar ancient classification of goods into three kinds: goods of the body, goods of the mind, and "external" goods, that is, goods located outside the person. He asks what the argumentative point of this division of goods was, and how this division contributed to ancient ethical theories—and concludes that, in some cases, the pursuit of ever-more-refined classifications became an end in itself. The division can be found early on in accounts of Platonic ethics, in Aristotle and in later Peripatetic ethics, and had an indirect impact on Stoicism. There are indeed texts in Plato and Aristotle that are almost certainly the sources for those attributions. However, whereas in the earlier texts, the division between goods is treated as a matter of common belief, by the later period, the distinction had hardened into doctrine. That is, in the Hellenistic period, the classification of goods came to take too central a place in ethical debates, with the consequence that—in the view of at least some later ancient philosophers—excessive concern with the neat categorizations of the three-way division of goods tended to obscure the discussion of the good. Seneca, for one, reacts strongly and understandably against the Stoic obsession with categories of goods.

Despite the fact that Striker's publications have mostly focused on Greek authors, she has always defended the value and importance of the Roman philosophers of the Hellenistic and post-Hellenistic era, and frequently taught Cicero and Seneca in her seminars. Many of her classics students went on to work on these authors. A particularly successful example of the kind of work this attention inspired is **John Schafer**'s "The Philosophical Ambitions of Seneca's *Letters*," which argues that Seneca's distinction between *decreta* (the doctrinal apparatus of Stoicism with its supporting arguments) and *praecepta* (particular ethical prescriptions, exhortations, and advice) is highly relevant both to his project in the Letters and to his self-appraisal as a philosopher. Schafer presents a Seneca who frankly acknowledges, indeed insists upon, the limitations of his own, largely "perceptive" work, while at the same time skillfully manipulating literary form both to argue for and to instantiate in his audience the moral and intellectual efficacy of his chosen mode of instruction.

Ancient theories of knowledge tend to present themselves as theories about the nature and existence of a "criterion of truth"—that is, something which could serve as a standard or criterion for deciding which impressions (and by extension which beliefs, and theories) are true and which ones are false. In "The Epistemology of Ptolemy's *On the Criterion*," **Mark J. Schiefsky** examines the use that the second century AD ancient Greek mathematician and astronomer Ptolemy makes of the concept of a "criterion" in his *On the Criterion*, a seldom-studied work in epistemology that was evidently intended to be a prolegomena to his scientific works. As Schiefsky argues, Ptolemy's use of the term "criterion" bypasses the Hellenistic uses of the term in the Stoics and Epicureans, and he seems largely unconcerned with skepticism; instead, he returns the term "criterion" to its original meaning as found in Plato and Aristotle, according to which a "criterion" is a means or instrument of judgment. Ptolemy's most original contribution to the history of this concept is his extended development of an analogy between the *kritêrion* and the *dikastêrion* or "lawcourt." He goes on to describe the relative contributions of intellect (*nous*), sense perception (*aisthêsis*), and rational discourse (*logos*) to scientific knowledge. Each has its proper use, and when used properly, they are reliable means for arriving at true judgment and, ultimately, knowledge. On Schiefsky's interpretation, Ptolemy's theory of knowledge fits comfortably with works in epistemology in the Platonic/Aristotelian tradition, such as the *Didaskalikos* of Alcinous and Peripatetic epistemology as described by Sextus Empiricus.

The final pair of papers in this volume has to do with belief, appearances, and assent in Hellenistic epistemology. For philosophers who are optimistic about the possibility of getting at truth, it is important to distinguish carefully between how things appear to one (i.e., mere impressions and non-epistemic appearances) and one's all-things-considered reason-based judgments about how things really are; the key, of course, is to figure out a good and reliable basis for arriving at the latter. **Charles Brittain**'s paper "The Compulsions of Stoic Assent" is on the notion of assent in the Stoic theory of reason, according to which all our judgments are the result of a conceptually distinct act of assent to our impressions, that is, to the perceptual and non-perceptual contents (of varying quality and reliability) we entertain. Brittain argues that even though it is tempting to think that rational creatures are virtually compelled to assent to so-called "kataleptic" ("clear and distinct") impressions and to find such impressions forceful and irresistible, the Stoics did not hold this position; they thought that, while it is natural to assent to kataleptic impressions, there are cases in which we don't assent to them, and indeed some in which it is right not to.

In "Sextus Empiricus on Persuasiveness and Equipollence," **Svavar Hrafn Svavarsson** considers Sextus' suggestion that the skeptic suspends belief because he experiences contrary *logoi* or accounts for appearances (i.e., accounts that purport to establish the truth or falsity of particular appearances) as being equipollent, or equally persuasive or unpersuasive. Svavarsson argues that the immediate effect of equipollence on the skeptic does not consist in his finding contrary accounts equally persuasive in the sense that he is equally persuaded by both accounts. Although this can happen, the effect of equipollence consists in the skeptic's being unable to determine by which account he ought to be persuaded, irrespective of which account *in fact* persuades him. For Sextus suggests—as Svavarsson argues—that what appears to the skeptic to be the case may appear so to him precisely because he is persuaded at some point by one account of its being the case rather than by another account for its contrary. Such accounts include philosophical arguments. Any account could persuade the skeptic and thus affect his way of life without forestalling his suspension of belief.

The range and richness of the papers offered here is a small testament to that of Gisela Striker's work. It is a great pleasure to present this collection of papers to Gisela Striker—teacher, mentor, colleague, and friend to the contributors of this volume.

NOTES ON CONTRIBUTORS

James Allen is Professor of Philosophy, University of Toronto.

Jonathan Barnes is Professor Emeritus, Universities of Oxford, Geneva, and Paris–Sorbonne.

Susanne Bobzien is Senior Research Fellow, All Souls College, Oxford University.

Charles Brittain is Professor of Classics and Philosophy, Cornell University.

Sarah Broadie is Professor of Moral Philosophy and Wardlaw Professor, University of St. Andrews.

Dorothea Frede is Professor Emeritus of Philosophy, University of Hamburg and University of California at Berkeley.

Verity Harte is Professor of Philosophy and Classics, Yale University.

Brad Inwood is University Professor of Classics and Philosophy, Canada Research Chair in Ancient Philosophy, University of Toronto.

Mi-Kyoung Lee is Associate Professor of Philosophy, University of Colorado at Boulder.

Marko Malink is Associate Professor of Philosophy, University of Chicago.

Dana Miller is Associate Professor of Philosophy, Fordham University.

John Schafer is Assistant Professor of Classics, Northwestern University.

Mark J. Schiefsky is Professor of the Classics, Harvard University.

Svavar Hrafn Svavarsson is Professor of Philosophy, University of Iceland.

Jennifer Whiting is Chancellor Jackman Professor of Philosophy, University of Toronto.

PART ONE

Plato

1

THE LIFE OF PROTARCHUS' CHOOSING
PLATO *PHILEBUS* 20B–22C

Verity Harte

The *Philebus* is something of a rarity among Platonic dialogues. First, it is a dialogue about which there is a rare, near universal consensus as to its dating—it is late (a thought supported by its unusually extensive allusions to a very great number of other Platonic works). Second, for a late Platonic dialogue, it is unusual in having Socrates as principal speaker, and in what we might think of as typical "Socratic" form; the *Philebus* contrasts in this respect with, for example, the *Sophist*, *Statesman*, or *Laws*, although it is like the *Theaetetus*. Last and most important for my purposes, then, the *Philebus* is a dialogue that, unlike the *Theaetetus*, and despite its "Socratic" renaissance, not only poses a question, but also gives it an answer. In fact, it does this not just once, but twice.

Its questions are highly specific: of two rival candidates—pleasure, championed by Protarchus, taking over from Philebus, and reason, championed by Socrates himself—the question is first, which (if either) is the good or, more specifically, which (if either) is that "state or disposition of soul capable of providing the *eudaimōn* human life" (*Philebus* 11d4–6)? Having arrived at a verdict on this question—that it is neither pleasure, nor reason, but some combination of both—the dialogue goes on to formulate a second, related question, namely, which (if either) of our rivals is responsible for the goodness of this victorious mixed life? The verdict on this second question is given at the end of the dialogue, in an elaborate prize-giving. On a previous occasion I have examined the details of this second verdict within the context of the dialogue as a whole.[1] My focus here is the dialogue's early, and curiously abrupt, arrival at the first verdict.[2]

---

[1] Harte (1999).
[2] In both cases, I use the term "verdict" advisedly. The dialogue's questions and answers are frequently posed in explicitly legal terms and with considerable interest in the parallel between legal judgments, cognitive judgments, and the judgment we are invited to decide upon here regarding our two contenders.

In outline, my aim is, first, to identify, and then, hopefully, to resolve various problems regarding the timing and means by which Socrates and Protarchus arrive at this first verdict. In doing so, I hope to provide evidence for the view that the *Philebus* is not, as it might appear, a poorly structured ragbag,[3] but a dialogue as carefully written as any.

INTRODUCING THE FIRST VERDICT AND ITS CONTEXT

I begin by introducing the argument by which the first verdict is arrived at, and setting it in context.

The *Philebus* begins in the middle of things. It is clear that a conversation of some kind has already taken place, in which Philebus and Socrates have disputed the rival claims of pleasure and reason. The title for which pleasure and reason have been disputing is less clear. Philebus is reported as holding that enjoyment, pleasure, and the like are "good for all creatures" (11b4–5), but this is neutral between the claim that pleasure is *a* good and the claim that pleasure is *the* good, into which it is subsequently resolved.[4] Socrates' counterclaim is carefully nuanced: first a comparative claim—that for those capable of it, reason and its kin are "at least better and more to be valued than pleasure"; then a superlative, but restricted in scope—they are "the most beneficial of all things," for all things capable of them (11b7–c2).

This conversation, whatever its object, has clearly run aground—at least, Philebus has baled out. Hence the dialogue begins with an elaborate handover, in which Protarchus agrees to accept custody of Philebus' thesis, and in which the rules of engagement are set. Significantly, these rules include formal provision for what should happen in the event that some third candidate should emerge victorious over both pleasure and reason—the very result that the argument on which I will focus produces. Indeed, the anticipation of this argument is more than merely formal. Socrates' phrasing is, in retrospect, pretty informative. He asks:

> SO. What if some other [state or disposition[5]], better than these, should emerge? If it turns out to be more akin to pleasure, then, while both [lives,[6] viz. that of pleasure and that of reason] are defeated by the life securely having these

---

[3] See, for example, the memorably scathing words of no less august a figure than Jowett (Introduction and Analysis to *Philebus*, in his [1871]): "diminution of artistic skill....want of character....a laboured march....a degree of confusion and incompleteness in the general design."

[4] First implicitly at 13b7, explicitly at, e.g., 60a7–b1.

[5] Supplying ἕξις καὶ διάθεσις as per 11d4, tracked through feminine articles of d8.

[6] Supplying βίοι for masculine plural ἀμφότεροι 11e2, by comparison with βίου, e2.

[sc. (the states or dispositions of) pleasure and reason[7]], won't the [life[8]] of pleasure surpass the [life] of reason?

PRO. Yes.

SO. But [if it turns out to be more akin to] reason, won't reason conquer pleasure and [pleasure] be defeated? (11d11–12a4)

Two features of the language are especially worthy of note. First, this is the first time in which the candidates—pleasure and reason—have been presented as competing in the form of representative *lives*. Prior to this, the talk has been of pleasure and reason as such, or, in the immediately preceding passage, of states or conditions of the same. Second, the hypothetical claimant on first prize is envisaged as having a rather specific character. It is not just any old life, but a life secure in its possession of our two rival candidates—pleasure and reason. On both points, we have here a rather careful anticipation of the argument to come, in which Protarchus will be invited to consider three lives—the life of pleasure, the life of reason, and a life in which both are together—and in which the life that has both will emerge victorious over the others.

There is a way to go, however, before we get to this argument. Notice that the tone of Socrates' descriptions of the contest is rather martial in character. This combative spirit threatens to undo progress right from the start. For no sooner has their conversation begun in earnest than Socrates and Protarchus get into a fight. Protarchus initially disputes Socrates' claim that pleasure is something complex, that one pleasure may differ from or even be opposed to another in the same way as one shape may be opposed to another. And he downright objects to the provocative way in which Socrates frames the question that such complexity gives rise to. And he does so with reason, since Socrates asks what he takes to be the common characteristic among the good *and bad* sorts of pleasures, in light of which he calls all of them "good" (13b3–5). As Protarchus points out, no self-respecting defender of hedonism will allow his opponent to *start* from the contention that some pleasures are bad (13b6–c2).

A truce is called by their agreement that both pleasure and reason are on a par as regards possible complexity and that they themselves are contending, not for the love of victory, but as allies in search of truth (14b5–7). This truce is followed by the first of the *Philebus*'s apparent digressions from the seemingly user-friendly topics of the good, pleasure, and reason to the seeming obscurities of Platonic metaphysics. We are led from a general discussion of problems of simplicity and complexity—or one and many—through a focus on the way in which these problems arise, in particular, for

---

[7] Supplying these, in one formulation or another, as natural referents of ταῦτα, 11e2, picking up on τούτων, 11d11.

[8] Supplied for masculine articles of 11e2 and 12a1, as per n6 above.

certain imperishable *henads* (or "units"), to the outline and illustration of a method of investigation which is supposed to resolve them.

It is from this labyrinth that the argument to the first verdict promises rescue, not to mention a breath of fresh air. Not without justification, Protarchus and Philebus have had difficulty seeing the relevance of much of the abstruse talk of method to the matter under dispute. But Protarchus does get the point at last and he does not like what he sees. The question before them, he says, is whether or not there are kinds of pleasure and of reason, and, if so, how many and what they are like (19b2–4). Protarchus balks at the question and insists that Socrates must decide whether or not such a division of the competitors is in fact necessary (20a5–8).

Cue sudden Socratic inspiration. And in less than two Stephanus pages their question is answered. The argument goes like this.

Socrates begins by gaining agreement on what, with characteristic understatement, he terms "minor matters" (20c8). Three features are agreed to be characteristic features of the good: the good is complete or perfect (τέλεον); it is sufficient (ἱκανόν); and it is such that "everything that recognizes it pursues it, having no interest in anything else save what is accomplished together with goods" (20d8–10), a formula later captured by the notion of being choiceworthy (αἱρετός, e.g. 22b1). These characteristics subsequently function as necessary conditions to test candidates for the good. It is not clear whether they are also taken to be jointly sufficient to identify the good.

Having identified these characteristics of the good, Socrates next proposes a method of proceeding. Two lives are distinguished: a life in which there is pleasure, but no reason; and a life in which there is reason, but no pleasure. These two lives are to be put to the test on Protarchus (21a4).

The life of pleasure gets the most extensive discussion. Protarchus is first asked whether he would agree to live his whole life through enjoying the greatest pleasures, and he says that he would and that he would have no need of anything further; and, a fortiori, no need of any of the family of reason. Socrates then highlights three consequences of the absence of reason, memory, and so on, consequences concerning the present, past, and future respectively. Without reason, Protarchus would not recognize whether or not he is enjoying himself (21b6–9). Nor, without memory, would he remember that he once did enjoy himself (21c1–4). Finally, being deprived of reckoning (λογισμός), he would be unable to reckon that he will enjoy himself at some future time (21c5–6). Such a life, Socrates proposes, is not a human life, but the life of a mollusk or sea-lung. Asked now whether such a life is choiceworthy, Protarchus declares himself speechless (21d4–5).

The discussion of the life of reason is much swifter. Protarchus is invited to consider whether anyone would accept a life consisting of the various faculties of reason, but without any pleasure or pain. Protarchus immediately answers that neither this nor the life of pleasure seems to him choiceworthy.

Protarchus is then asked to consider one final life—discussion of which is the least elaborate of all. He is simply asked what he makes of a life in which pleasure and reason are both mixed together and declares that everyone would choose this life over either of the others.

Socrates proceeds to draw conclusions. Of the three lives considered, he says, two—the life of pleasure and the life of reason—have been shown not to be the good. He thus declares it sufficiently shown that Philebus' goddess, pleasure, is not the same as the good. And nor is Socrates' reason, Philebus adds, in one of his rare contributions to the discussion.

This is the end of the argument by which their first verdict is agreed. The dialogue does not end here, of course. A new contest is forged, whose discussion prompts a second, lengthy digression into general metaphysics, with the production of a fourfold division of beings, followed by a lengthy examination of different sorts of pleasure, and a shorter examination of different sorts of reason or knowledge, as a backdrop to a dramatic enactment of the mixing of the victorious, mixed life and the giving of prizes. Nor is this the last we hear of the argument to the first verdict. For it is explicitly reprised at the end of the examination of pleasure and reason and before the mixing of the victorious life (59e7–61a3), and an opportunity to correct it is offered and declined (60d3–e7).

In all, then, the argument by which the first verdict is arrived at seems of central importance to the dialogue as a whole. And this impression is reinforced by the weight it is given in the dialogue's own signposting as to its structure. Not only does the argument answer the central question from which the dialogue begins, but, as we have seen, the way in which it does so is anticipated at the beginning of the dialogue and reprised en route to its end.

PROBLEMS OF THE FIRST VERDICT

For all its apparent importance, however, there are several puzzling aspects of the argument to the first verdict, regarding both its position in the dialogue and the argument itself.

First, the argument is oddly placed. The argument comes after the dialogue's first lengthy discussion of method. But there is not obviously anything in the argument itself that could not have been stated beforehand, right from the start. So, why put it here? This oddity of the argument's placement is certainly not hidden. In fact, it is positively flaunted by the use of a favorite Socratic device: the argument is portrayed as one of

Socrates' arguments '*ex machina*'; a fortuitous, sudden, divinely inspired gift of memory of arguments heard long ago, perhaps in a dream (20b).

The explicit reason for the argument's intrusion is to relieve us of the task that the discussion of method has threatened. Socrates proposes that this argument will allow us to avoid the need for a division of pleasure into kinds (20c4–6). But if this helps with the first puzzle, it raises a second. For, despite the divine inspiration of Socrates' sudden memory, the argument turns out oddly redundant. It achieves its apparent goal of settling the dialogue's question, and yet the dialogue does not finish. Worse still—from the point of view of the argument's explicit intended achievement—the dialogue will go on to draw distinctions between kinds of pleasure the need for which this argument was meant to forestall.[9]

Of course, the dialogue goes on to do this in answering a *second* question, and one might think that this fact is enough to defuse the puzzle here. But the second question is not just another question; it arises out of and depends upon the answer to the first question. So it is at least ironic that an answer to the second question should involve (among other things) the very task from which the answer to the first was meant to relieve us.

Last and by no means least of the puzzles: the argument of the passage seems pretty poor. It is, in the first place, very uneven. The life of pleasure gets fairly detailed treatment. The treatments of the life of reason and of the mixed life, by contrast, are cursory at best: in each case, a simple question and answer. There is no reason given, save Protarchus' fiat, to explain why it might be that the life of reason without pleasure and pain is not to be chosen. And the mixed life is scarcely described: it is a life in which there is both pleasure and reason, and that is all we are told. And yet this is enough for Protarchus to decide that everyone will choose this life over either of the others and, more worryingly, for it to be treated as though it has won outright in the discussion that follows.

This brings us to a second troubling feature of the argument: its unusual form with its total reliance on Protarchus' choices. The passage is methodologically unusual and in a way that is not really captured by those who see it as a resurrection of Socratic method. Frede describes the argument as the dialogue's only elenchus.[10] But this is not a typical elenchus, if by that we mean a procedure that exposes inconsistencies in an interlocutor's beliefs.[11] At best, the examination of the life of pleasure could be read this way, but even here, only if we supply the relevant beliefs. Our best clue as to the form of the passage lies in Socrates' invitation at 21a4: "Then shall we put these to the test on

---

[9] This drawing of distinctions is hardly a thorough division, it is true. But it was not from *thoroughness* of division that Socrates promised to rescue us, but from the need for division at all.
[10] Frede (1997) 176.
[11] Here I agree with Delcomminette (2006) 171.

you?" Two rather different images are implied by the verb (βασανίζω): the torture of the lives before Protarchus to provide him evidence from them or the use of Protarchus as a touchstone with which to test their metal. The touchstone motif goes along with the thought that the good is the sort of thing that, once recognized, would be chosen by everyone. But it does not follow from this that all choices are equal, and the trouble about Protarchus is that he has a stake in the outcome.

In places, then, the argument is excessively thin and it is oddly reliant on Protarchus' partisan opinion. And finally, even where there is at least some measure of argument, and which Protarchus might justly be expected to answer, in the examination of the life of pleasure, the argument looks vulnerable to (and has been subject to) serious objection.

In sum, the interpretation of the passage faces the following dilemma: if the argument is good, it is hard to explain its apparent sidelining within the dialogue overall (despite the noise that is made about its importance); and if the argument is bad, it is hard to explain its appearance at all (especially with fanfare).

In the remainder of the paper, I will take up these problems and puzzles and attempt to steer my way through the dilemma.

THE EXAMINATION OF THE LIFE OF PLEASURE

I begin with the examination of the life of pleasure, where there is at least some argument to go on. The argument has been subject to two rather different sorts of objection, each directed at the legitimacy and strength of its claim to be a strike against hedonism.

First is what I shall call the *Instrumentalist Objection*.[12] This is the charge that Socrates' putative victory over the hedonist is hollow, since the hedonist need concede no more than that the inclusion of reason is of instrumental value in the service of pleasure. Sure, Protarchus would like to have the faculties of reason in the life of his choosing—so as to maximize his pleasures. Such value as reason has is derivative of the value of pleasure.

The second objection is what I shall call the *Recalcitrant Objection*.[13] The objection turns on the unusual form of the argument—it depends on the choice of Protarchus. And its success might seem correspondingly fragile. If Protarchus cannot bring himself to choose the life of a mollusk or sea-lung, another, more robust hedonist might say that names can never hurt him.

---

[12] The charge is levelled by both Gosling (1975) 183–4 and Frede (1997) 180–1.
[13] The objection is raised and addressed by McCabe (2000) 128–34.

These objections are serious, because each has the consequence that the hedonist's central thesis—that pleasure is the good—is left entirely untouched. But it is just this claim that the argument targets. Fortunately, the argument can, I think, be defended, more or less directly, against each of these objections.

Consider, first, the *Instrumentalist Objection*. In places, Socrates' choice of language certainly invites and might be taken to support such an objection.

Having been asked whether he would agree to live his whole life through enjoying the greatest pleasures, and whether he would think himself in need of anything further (21a8–12), Protarchus is asked to consider whether he would need any aspect of thinking, understanding, or "reckoning" or "calculating what's needed" (λογίζεσθαι τὰ δέοντα, 21a14–b1). At least he is asked it this way in Burnet's edition (1901); but the text is disputed. Frede excises "τὰ δέοντα" as a corruption with Badham (1878) and Diès (1941), and one that gives away what she takes to be the punch line of the argument rather too soon.[14] Whatever exactly he is asked, Protarchus is in any case confident that, with enjoyment, he would have everything.

Socrates next draws his attention to three consequences of the absence of reason: concerning the present, that he would be ignorant of whether or not he is enjoying himself (21b6–9); concerning the past, that he would not remember that he once did enjoy himself (21c1–4); and concerning the future, that "being deprived of calculation (or: reckoning, λογισμός), [he][15] would be unable to calculate that [he] will enjoy [himself] in the future" (21c5–6). Use of the term λογισμός, a term associated with arithmetical calculation, invites the thought that the use of reason in this case at least is for the calculation of how to acquire the maximum future pleasures. And this thought is encouraged by a translation like Frede's: "being unable to calculate, you could not figure out any future pleasures for yourself."[16] But we are not forced to adopt such a construal. Socrates may simply point to the lack of ability to *predict* future occasions of pleasure.[17]

Whatever Socrates' choice of language may suggest, there is one rather simple reason why the argument may be saved from the *Instrumentalist Objection*. It is preempted by the way in which the argument is set up. The objection holds that the hedonist will agree to incorporate reason, but only for instrumental reasons—to maximize pleasure. But, in the context of this argument, this rationale for the inclusion of pleasure is

---

[14] Frede (1997) 25, note *ad loc*.

[15] Socrates puts his question directly in the second person, of course.

[16] Frede (1993) tr. *ad loc*. ὡς χαιρήσεις, 21c6, might be translated as purposive (in particular as regards the manner of the future enjoyment), but such a translation is by no means obvious or required.

[17] See, e.g., the translation *ad loc* in Gosling (1975).

directly ruled out. For this argument supposes, ex hypothesi, that the life of pleasure under consideration is one in which Protarchus has the *greatest* pleasures (see 21a9, b3-4) and has them *throughout* the life (see 21a8, b3). The life under consideration is thus already maximal in terms of pleasure. A fortiori, the inclusion of reason cannot be intended to maximize pleasures.[18]

The point may be spelled out. It is possible to think of reason as being itself a source of pleasure and as a means to secure or increase other pleasures. But for the argument at hand, these ways of thinking of reason are irrelevant. Take, for example, the case of reasoning about the future. It is, of course, true that in the life envisaged we would not be able to reason out ways to ensure we get the maximal possible future pleasures. But, given the argument's hypothesis, this does not mean that we will be deprived of the maximal possible future pleasures. We will get them in any case, without the labor of reasoning for them. Hence, the inclusion of reason is not required for the maximization of pleasures.[19]

Of course, this raises the question of why Protarchus *does* agree to the inclusion of reason,[20] and, in particular, why he does not simply refuse the hypothesis, and simply deny that a life without reason could be maximal in terms of pleasure.[21] I shall say more about this question later, in considering the argument's scope and context. For now, it brings us neatly on to the second *Recalcitrant Objection*. Protarchus' sudden

---

[18] The point is made by Irwin (1995) 334 and Cooper (2003) 121.

[19] A variant of the *Instrumentalist Objection* is made the basis of an alternative reading of the argument by Evans (2007), who takes Protarchus' rejection of the life of pleasure without reason to be based on his recognition of a human limitation requiring the involvement of reason in a human life, and not on the value of reason as such (350–1). However, as Evans notes (351–2), on this reading, the argument does not secure the conclusion that Socrates explicitly gives it, not only at 22b3–4, which Evans discusses (359), but also, in anticipation of the argument, at 20b8 and c2.

[20] Protarchus could simply miss the point, but this seems a counsel of despair.

[21] I assume that he does not in fact refuse the hypothesis, nor is he *directly* invited to do so. Contrast here Lear (2004) 54–7. Where she takes Socrates' question, at 21b3–4, directly to invite Protarchus to reject the supposition that the life illustrated would involve the greatest pleasures, and to do so for reasons consistent with his hedonism, I take Protarchus' assent to the question to underline the argument's hypothesis and, in so doing, to flush out the hedonist's present reliance on purely quantitative variations among pleasures and give him reason to think more seriously about kinds of pleasure and about the relation between reason and pleasure. Delcomminette (2006) 172–82 also appears to adopt a reading according to which the hypothesis is rejected or at least undermined by the life's absence of reason. However, all such readings—according to which the life of pleasure without reason turns out not to contain pleasure or not the very greatest pleasures—face the difficulty that such an interpretation will not generate Socrates' conclusion for the hedonist: that pleasure is not the good.

capitulation prompts the worry that there might be another more stubborn hedonist waiting in the wings.

The objection is one that is raised and, to a large extent, answered by M.M. McCabe.[22] As she points out, Socrates' points about present, past, and future implicitly highlight the sort of psychological continuity we expect of human *lives*. Socrates concludes the examination of the life of pleasure with the claim that it is not a human life at all, but the life of a sea-lung or mollusk. He then asks Protarchus whether he thinks that a life of this sort is choiceworthy—not for sea-lungs or mollusks, but for us humans. Protarchus' answer is striking: the argument has rendered him speechless (21d4–5). This is not just the embarrassment of one beaten in argument by Socrates. If, on pain of absurdity, Protarchus were to choose such a life, then speechless is just what his choice would make him;[23] a fact of which the conspicuous silence of the recalcitrant Philebus is a vivid reminder.

Notice that on this (which I take to be broadly McCabe's) view, the unusual form of the argument is its strength, not its weakness.[24] For the fact that a stubborn hedonist might simply make this choice and opt to be like a mollusk shows the choice to be evidently absurd. And it is an absurdity that arises directly from the position and not from any fancy argumentative footwork against it.[25]

We are, however, once again forced to confront the hypothesis: that the life under consideration is maximal in terms of pleasure. We are forced to do so, because the success of this answer to the *Recalcitrant Objection* depends, first, on the assumption that Philebus espouses a particularly extreme sort of hedonism. Second, and more importantly, it depends on the assumption that Protarchus must agree that hedonism of this extreme sort can give us a life with the greatest of pleasures.

Let us take stock. We have candidate answers to each of the two objections to the treatment of the life of pleasure, *granted its hypothesis*. But we have yet to see why Protarchus should grant the hypothesis. And we have not yet considered the more

---

[22] McCabe (2000) 128–34. In what follows, I am heavily indebted to her discussion.

[23] This is not at all to deny that Protarchus is invited to *make* the choice from *outside* the perspective of such a life and not from the perspective of an occupant (as rightly emphasized by Irwin (1995) 333 and Lear (2004) 54–5). Indeed, in this case, choice is only possible from such a perspective.

[24] For interesting reflection on the force of appeals to human nature in this and other Greek philosophical arguments, see Nussbaum (1995), though I am not persuaded by her proposal that the argument turns in part on Protarchus' perceived lack of continued personal identity if transformed into the subject of such a life.

[25] This is not to say that we have yet been given an *explanation* of the evident absurdity. For some suggestive discussion, see Bobonich (2002) 153–79, with whom I agree that the move made here "is only a starting point for the hard philosophical work done in the rest of the dialogue," a provisionality which, I argue, is clearly marked in the frame of this argument.

general objections as to the shape and form of the passage as a whole. For answers to these questions, I turn to the passage's aims and context.

THE FIRST VERDICT AS A WHOLE AND IN CONTEXT

Return to Socrates' sudden inspiration. What he remembers is arguments to the effect that neither pleasure nor reason is the good, but some third thing (20b7–9). And he takes the promise of such arguments to be this:

> SO. And yet, if this were to become clearly apparent to us now, then pleasure would be displaced from victory—for the good would no longer turn out to be the same as it, isn't that so?
> PRO. Yes.
> SO. And, in my judgment, we will no longer need in addition a division of kinds of pleasure. (20b9–c5)

This characterization of what the arguments would show—that the good is not the same as pleasure—is exactly what Socrates takes the subsequent examination of lives to have shown, in conclusion. He says:

> It seems to me to have been sufficiently stated that we do not need suppose that *Philebus' goddess* and the good are the same. (22c1–2)[26]

The argument's object is thus presented as the limited, negative object of establishing that pleasure and good are not the same, where this thesis is understood as having a particular association with Philebus' understanding of pleasure. This limited object immediately helps with the question of why the treatments of the life of reason and of the mixed life are comparatively uneven. We do not need to suppose that this is to give Socrates' candidate an unreasonably easy ride; nor to suppose that Protarchus' choosing too quickly does him in. Instead we may recall the nuance with which Socrates' claim was recorded right at the beginning. We do not need to spend a great deal of time showing (or, for that matter, denying) that Socrates' candidate is not identical with the good. Socrates never claimed that it was, but only that it was a better good than pleasure for those capable of it.

The limited object can help us further. Return to the unquestioned hypothesis—that the life of pleasure without reason that is described to Protarchus is a life consisting of

---

[26] Emphasis to reflect the effect of γε, c1.

the greatest pleasures throughout. It is a moot question, at this point in the dialogue, whether Protarchus has the resources to question such a hypothesis and deny that a life deprived of reason could be maximal in terms of pleasure. Is Protarchus in a position to claim that there are certain sorts of pleasures—those of reason, for example—that are simply *better* than others? What would this mean? Well, if the good is pleasure, then something is *better* if and only if it is *more pleasant*. But what does it mean to be *more pleasant*? Protarchus is clearly happy with the idea that pleasure is something that can be *maximized*—and thus that some pleasures are quantitatively greater than others. But it would be simply question-begging for him to claim that, as it happens, it is the pleasures involving reason that are quantitatively greater than the rest. And it is unclear that he can lay claim to any other sort of salient variation among pleasures. Protarchus, after all, has resisted the idea that there are different kinds of pleasure, and, even more strongly, that any kinds there might be could make a difference as regards value.[27]

He has done so, we may note, in the terms of the Phileban identity the first verdict will challenge. What he said was this:

> Do you think that anyone who supposes that pleasure is the good will agree to allow you to say that some sorts of pleasures are good, and certain other sorts are bad? (13b6–c2)

Thus the defense of the Phileban identity has left Protarchus in a bind. The examination of the life of pleasure succeeds in its limited object, given its hypothesis. And Protarchus is not in a position to question its hypothesis if he sticks to his guns about pleasure and kinds.

Is the passage disappointing if it has only a limited object? Well, it would be if the dialogue finished here. But the dialogue does not. And it would be if that were all that the passage accomplished. But it is not. For, just as the dialogue does not end here, so its limited argumentative object is not the only thing the passage achieves.

First, the argument's success against its limited object precisely serves to motivate Protarchus in the direction of an examination of pleasure and its kinds of the sort the dialogue will turn to later. This motivational role of the argument helps with the passage's puzzling placement. And it is underscored by a striking feature of the way the passage is written. This is its use of marked parallels between the terms of the discussion and the terms in which the discussion itself takes place.

---

[27] This is a little complicated. He is committed to all kinds of pleasure that there might be being good. It would be open to him to think them good to differing extents. But the question is whether he has to date the resources to support anything beyond mere quantitative variation.

Return to the way in which Socrates frames the argument. If the argument succeeds in displacing pleasure from victory, he says, "we will no longer need in addition a division of kinds of pleasure" (20c4–5). And he concludes that the rejection of Philebus' identity has been "sufficiently stated" (22c2).

Sufficiency, we may recall, is one of the three criteria agreed as marks of the good, and it is the main one tested in the examination of the life of pleasure. The test for sufficiency is captured by the idea that if a life has the good in it—the life of pleasure or reason—then we will not need anything in addition. This verb (προσδέομαι) is used to introduce the examination of lives (20e6) and forms the question that drives the examination of the life of pleasure (21a11). And it is the very same verb with which Socrates makes his claim that, given this argument, there will not be any additional need of a division of kinds of pleasure.

There are, then, two parallel questions about sufficiency, about whether there is need for anything more. As far as the dialogue's overall discussion goes, the question is whether the argument we have been given is sufficient to defeat the view that pleasure is the good or whether we need in addition to embark on a division of pleasure. Within the argument, the question for Protarchus is whether, if he has the maximal possible pleasure, where pleasure is considered invariant with respect to value save quantitatively, this would suffice to make this life the good life, or does he need reason in addition? And the answers to these questions are designed to stand or fall together. If Protarchus takes the life of pleasure to suffice (to be the good life), then the argument suffices to defeat him (to defeat the view that pleasure is the good) without the need for, and because he has no room for, the sort of view of pleasure that would motivate a division of pleasure. But if Protarchus accepts that maximal pleasure, considered as invariant with respect to value save quantitatively, does not suffice to make the life of pleasure the good life, then this argument too does not suffice to address the various new questions now provoked, nor to defeat the view that pleasure is the good and give a positive answer to the dialogue's original question. For it is now open to Protarchus to reconsider the question of the greatest pleasures. In this way, the limited object of the argument acts as a control on the question of whether we will need in addition a division of pleasure. And it provides the reluctant hedonist with a motive for thinking we do.

Motivating Protarchus is not, however, the only thing the passage can be seen to achieve over and above its limited argumentative object. It also sets the agenda for the inquiry it motivates him to follow. One rather obvious way in which it does so is in the questions that are raised by the examination of the life of pleasure. These include the question of what should count as the greatest of pleasures (and what greatness amounts to)—a question the dialogue will later explore in contrasting intense pleasures, inevitably mixed up with pain, with true, pure pleasures; and the question of the relation between reason, memory, and expectation as to the future and the experience of pleasure—a question explored, above all, in the dialogue's discussion of false pleasure.

Examination of these questions would require us to look at pretty much the whole of the rest of the dialogue. I do not propose to attempt this here. Instead, I want to concentrate on a less obvious way in which our passage sets the agenda for the inquiry to follow, and one which relies once again upon its context and framing.

Recall that Socrates began the argument of the passage by proposing for agreement three criteria of the good: it is complete or perfect (τέλεον), sufficient (ἱκανόν), and choiceworthy (αἱρετός). I have already drawn attention to the way in which the sufficiency criterion is applied both within the discussion and to the terms of the discussion itself. There is another example of this sort of parallel, this time one of omission.

When we examine the details of the examination of the lives of pleasure, of reason and of them both together, we find that only two of the criteria are directly appealed to: sufficiency—as we have seen; and choiceworthiness, mentioned directly at 21d3, e4, and 22a5. The criterion of completeness or perfection, however, is not mentioned during the course of the examination. Further, its absence is made pointed by the way in which the passage concludes. At the end of the examination of all three lives, Socrates invites Protarchus to state the outcome, which he does, like this:

> Three lives having been put forward, [it follows] for two of them that they are neither sufficient nor choiceworthy for any person or animal. (22a9–b2)

This summary confirms that only two of the criteria have been appealed to in the course of the argument. Socrates then continues:

> Isn't it then already clear, regarding these [two lives] at least, that neither of them has the good? For it was to be sufficient and complete and choiceworthy for every plant and animal capable of living in this fashion throughout its life. (22b3–6)

Socrates mentions all three criteria. But this does not mean we were wrong to suppose that the argument has used only two of them.[28] Socrates' remark is an accurate reflection of what they required of the good. And we do not need to have gone through all three of the criteria for it to be true that the lives of pleasure and of reason have failed this test. (If we know that something is not sufficient and is not choiceworthy,

---

[28] Contrast Cooper (2003) 119–20. Contrast also Delcomminette (2006) 167, who has a different view both of which criteria are explicitly used and of the implications of their not all being so.

then we also know that it is not sufficient, choiceworthy, and perfect.) What Socrates' remark does do—especially following Protarchus' accurate summary—is draw our attention to the fact that the completeness criterion has not been considered.

There is a rather pleasing irony to the parallel suggested by this failure to consider the completeness criterion: the examination of the lives—of the surviving mixed life, in particular—is as incomplete as their discussion turns out to be. But I think there is also more to be said about the significance of the omission of the completeness criterion, although it will be brief and at this stage somewhat speculative.

If we were reading Aristotle's *Nicomachean Ethics*—which borrows heavily from this passage of the *Philebus*[29]—it would be tempting to translate the omitted criterion, not as "complete" or "perfect," but as "final,"[30] a translation that immediately brings to the fore a teleological framework. Even if it lacks the technical sense the term may come to have in Aristotle, it is not without teleological connotations in the *Philebus* at least. At the time that the first verdict is drawn, no teleological framework has yet been established within the dialogue. But its establishment is among the first jobs of the newly formulated contest to which the first verdict gives rise.

This newly formulated contest asks which of our two candidates—pleasure or reason—should be declared responsible for the goodness of the victorious, mixed life. Socrates immediately embarks on the second of the dialogue's adventures into general Platonic metaphysics, in which he divides everything there is into four kinds: unlimited, limit, mixed, and cause. Our missing criterion—being complete, perfect, or final—is one of the hallmarks of the successful complex items that are found in the mixed kind[31] and of which the mixed life is taken to be an example. The existence of such good, successful mixtures is credited to the teleological operation of reason, to which responsibility is given for the way in which these things are ordered for the best.

Now, it is not my intention to explore these matters here.[32] But two points may be noted. First, we ought to be somewhat surprised at the second contest's implicit assumption that a life mixed of pleasure and reason has not only beaten the alternatives—the life of pleasure and the life of reason—but won outright. Given the brevity of its treatment, and its lack of completion, this is hardly something the interlocutors

---

[29] The relation between Aristotle's *NE* and this passage of the *Philebus* is the subject of two excellent recent discussions in Cooper (2003) and Lear (2004).

[30] Cf. Lear (2004) 53, who explicitly rejects this translation for the *Philebus* passage in contrast to its meaning in Aristotle. Of course, the translation of the term in the context of Aristotle's *NE* is itself a controversial matter, but for reasons that need not concern us here.

[31] See, e.g., 26a4. And notice 31a8–10, where τέλος is among the ordered features denied to pleasure, as a generic unlimited, and 66b2 where τὸ τέλεον is among the identifying marks of the second prizewinners.

[32] There are related discussions in Harte (1999) and Harte (2002) §4.3.

could claim to have shown. Second, once the mixed life is identified as a mixture—in the terms of the fourfold division—and hence as something whose value is the responsibility of reason, why is the second contest not already over? After all, this second contest concerned precisely the identification of what is responsible for the goodness of the victorious, mixed life.

The answer, I suggest, is the dialogue's implicit acknowledgment that it has not even completed its first contest as yet. The progress towards the dialogue's second verdict is as much a continuation and expansion of the inquiry into what gets first prize as an inquiry into which of pleasure and reason comes second. And it is, I would argue, a progress that is organized around the omitted teleological criterion—aimed at revealing pleasure's status as a teleologically dependent item, the mixed life's nature and constitution if it is to be good, and the organization by reason that makes it so.

I want to close by linking this teleological turn of the dialogue with an example of an aspect of the *Philebus*'s character that I have mentioned, but not thus far explored: its habit of alluding, more or less directly, to other Platonic works.[33] The dialogue's teleological turn is anticipated and, it is tempting to suggest, highlighted by a rather striking cluster of reminiscences of a foundational passage in Platonic teleology: the fictional autobiography of Socrates which he provides in Plato's *Phaedo*. The first such reminiscence comes when prior to Socrates' sudden inspiration and faced with the implication drawn from their discussion of method, Protarchus suddenly "comes over all Socrates," for a moment. Faced with Socrates' claim that, not only must he consider whether, how many, and of what sort are the kinds of pleasure and reason, but we will not be worth anything until we have answered this question about *everything*, Protarchus' reply is both worthy of and reminiscent of Socrates:

> While it's a fine thing for a prudent man to know everything, a second sailing,
> I think, is not to be mistaken about oneself. (19c2–3)

The phrase "second sailing" has a history in Plato and one pertinent to our theme. In the *Phaedo*, Socrates describes a *second sailing* in his account of the history of his investigations into the nature of causal responsibility (τὸ αἴτιον, αἰτία) (*Phaedo* 99c9–d1). It is an investigation of this sort that is launched in the *Philebus* following the drawing of their first verdict (and the arguments prompted by the exchange following Protarchus' modest refusal). In this second contest, Socrates goes on to provide a teleological account of causal responsibility in which the goodness of mixtures is

---

[33] This is a feature of the dialogue, the extent of which was first drawn to my attention by Myles Burnyeat (pers. comm.); aspects of it are now explored in Burnyeat (2004).

the responsibility of reason (νοῦς). Just this model of causal responsibility—that reason (νοῦς) arranges things for the best—was the Anaxagorean model of Socrates' *first Phaedo* sailing, for which he held out great hope.

What should we make of this complex allusion, if that is what it is? I suggest that it draws attention once again to an elaborate parallel at work in the *Philebus* between the terms of the discussion and the discussion itself. The striking omission from consideration of the teleological criterion from the *Philebus*'s first verdict has a methodological payoff for the dialogue's discussion: it indicates the (teleological) direction the inquiry must take. According to the *Phaedo*, this is exactly what we should expect to be the payoff of getting a theory of causal responsibility (αἴτια), especially a teleological one: it directs our inquiry (cf. *Phaedo* 97c6–d4).

Not only that: this structure, an orientation for the purposes of good organization has the sort of structure for which we may very well be looking not only for the inquiry to come, but also for the answer to its question: what state or disposition of soul is capable of providing the *eudaimōn* human life? Certainly, this seems to be part and parcel of what is involved in the good turning out to be something τέλεον, and it goes along with the dialogue's gloss on its being choiceworthy. To be choiceworthy, we may recall, is to be such that "everything that recognizes it pursues it, having no interest in anything else save what is accomplished together with goods" (20d8–10). Once recognized, that is, the good acts in such a way as to provide an orientation and structure for all one's desires. Finally, as his use of a cognitive word here might suggest, and as the *Philebus* likes frequently to remind us,[34] the nature of this good organization is something that it will be the responsibility of our own reason to investigate and discover both in the remainder of the dialogue and in life.

Acknowledgments

It is a great pleasure to include this paper in a volume in honor of Gisela Striker, a friend and colleague, and early advocate of the philosophical interest of the Philebus beyond the metaphysical passages on which she did her own, sterling early work. Versions of this paper were given to the Cambridge Philological Society (May 2005), to the Eighth Symposium of the International Plato Society in Dublin (July 2007), and to a conference at Cornell (October 2008). I am grateful to my audience on all three occasions and to my commentator at Cornell, Kristen Inglis. In addition, work on this paper was much helped by opportunities to try out thoughts on this passage on the participants

---

[34] In the vicinity, see, e.g. the play on Socrates' νοῦς, at 22c3, c5, e3, in setting the terms of the second contest.

in two graduate seminars: in Cornell, in Spring 2002; and in King's College London, 2004–5. Particular thanks, in addition, to Peter Adamson, Joachim Aufderheide, Tad Brennan, Charles Brittain, Amber Carpenter, Matt Evans, Era Gavrielides, Carl Ginet, Terry Irwin, MM McCabe and Tom Tuozzo.

References

Altham, J.E.J and Harrison, R. eds. (1995) *World, Mind, and Ethics: Essays on the Ethical Philosophy of Bernard Williams.* Cambridge: Cambridge University Press.
Badham, C. (1878) *The Philebus of Plato.* London: Williams and Norgate. Second Edition.
Bobonich, C. (2002) *Plato's Utopia Recast: His Later Ethics and Politics.* Oxford: Clarendon Press.
Burnet, J. (1901) *Platonis Opera II: Parmenides, Philebus, Symposium, Phaedrus, Alcibiades I, II, Hipparchus, Amatores.* Oxford: Clarendon Press.
Burnyeat, M.F. (2004) "Fathers and Sons in Plato's *Republic* and *Philebus*," *Classical Quarterly* 54.1: 80–7.
Cooper, J.M. (2003) "Plato and Aristotle on 'Finality' and '(Self-)Sufficiency,'" in Heinaman ed. (2003): 117–47.
Delcomminette, S. (2006) *Le Philèbe de Platon: Introduction à l'agathologie platonicienne.* Philosophia Antiqua 100. Leiden: Brill.
Diès, A. (1941) *Platon oeuvres complètes IX.2: Philèbe.* Paris: Les Belles Lettres.
Dixsaut, M. ed. (1999) *La fêlure du plaisir: Études sur le philèbe de platon 1: Commentaires.* Paris: Vrin.
Evans, M. (2007) "Plato's Rejection of Thoughtless and Pleasureless Lives," *Phronesis* 52.4: 337–63.
Frede, D. (1993) *Plato Philebus.* Translated, with Introduction and Notes. Indianapolis: Hackett.
Frede, D. (1997) *Platon Philebos.* Übersetzung und Kommentar. Göttingen: Vandenhoeck & Ruprecht.
Gosling, J.C.B. (1975) *Plato Philebus.* Translated with Notes. Clarendon Plato Series. Oxford: Oxford University Press.
Harte, V. (1999) "Quel prix pour la vérité? (64a7–66d3)," in Dixsaut ed. (1999): 385–401.
Harte, V. (2002) *Plato on Parts and Wholes.* Oxford: Clarendon Press.
Heinaman, R. ed. (2003) *Plato and Aristotle's Ethics.* UCL Keeling Series in Ancient Philosophy. Aldershot: Ashgate.
Irwin, T. (1995) *Plato's Ethics.* New York: Oxford University Press.
Jowett, B. (1871) *The Dialogues of Plato.* Oxford: Clarendon Press.
Lear, G.R. (2004) *Happy Lives and the Highest Good.* Princeton: Princeton University Press.
McCabe, M.M. (2000) *Plato and his Predecessors.* Cambridge: Cambridge University Press.
Nussbaum, M.C. (1995) "Aristotle on Human Nature and the Foundations of Ethics," in Altham and Harrison eds. (1995): 86–131.

2

FOOLS' PLEASURES IN PLATO'S *PHILEBUS*

Jennifer Whiting

It seems to me that as far as thinking about philosophical problems is concerned, historians of philosophy are doing much the same as specialists in systematic fields. In trying to make sense of the arguments and theories of older philosophers, we cannot help but think about the problems they were thinking about—problems which are often versions or interesting variants of questions that are discussed in contemporary systematic debates. One polemical way of describing the difference... would be to say that it's a matter of taste: historians tend to be those who prefer to read, say, Hume rather than the latest issue of a philosophical journal, or who prefer to do ethics with Aristotle (to borrow a phrase from Sarah Broadie) to doing it with the latest school of consequentialists or deontologists. Their prejudice is that there may often be more to be learned from these authors than from our technically more sophisticated contemporaries. It seems highly implausible to suggest that the historian is thinking about Hume or Aristotle *rather than* ethics or epistemology, and if she does she will not get very far.

One might object that this will not eliminate the difference between the exegetical exercise of figuring out what Aristotle was saying about virtue, for example, and a straightforward discussion of questions of desert or moral responsibility. But the line between exegesis and argument is less clear than these labels suggest. The historian who wants to understand a classical author will have to rely on her own sense of what is philosophically plausible, what counts as a strong or a weak argument, and in this respect she will of course be guided by her training as a philosopher, which can only be that of a contemporary philosopher....

But what can historical exegesis contribute to present-day philosophical debate? I would like to argue that the historian's contribution consists in keeping available the thought of past philosophers as a resource that would otherwise be lost or inaccessible.
—Gisela Striker, Preface to *Essays on Hellenistic Epistemology and Ethics* (1996)

Rarely has the line between exegesis and "systematic" argument been less distinct than in debates about the conception of false pleasure in Plato's *Philebus*. Philosophers seeking to make "systematic" sense of the very idea make liberal use of the *Philebus*, especially its infamous reference to the allegedly false pleasure experienced by someone who pictures himself in the future, getting lots of gold and many consequent pleasures, and also (presumably as a result) "beside himself with delight."[1] But different philosophers read this example in different ways. And recent exegetes have (as we shall see in §4) followed their different leads. Matthew Evans (2008) follows what he calls the "Old School" lead of Bernard Williams (1959), while Verity Harte (2004) claims to follow what Evans calls the "New School" lead of Sabina Lovibond (1989–90). But Williams and Lovibond make only passing reference to the *Philebus*; neither pretends to serious exegesis or attempts to read this example as part of the sequence in which it is merely the first step. It is thus no surprise that exegetes following these leads have lost sight of important aspects of Plato's thought, aspects best recovered through the sort of historical and philosophically astute exegesis so wonderfully displayed in Striker's own work. We do better to read the *Philebus* in the light of Plato's *Gorgias* (which is generally agreed to be earlier) and some passages from Aristotle's account of *phantasia* that are close in spirit (and sometimes even in letter) to the *Philebus* itself. For this context reveals both the flawed argument on which the *Philebus* aims to improve and the means by which it seeks to do. Or so I argue.

The flawed argument is the one Socrates ran in the *Gorgias* against the professed hedonism of Callicles. The *Philebus*'s means for improving on it are two. One is an appeal to the *foolishness*—as distinct from the *shamefulness*—of certain pleasures, an appeal designed to avoid the sort of reliance on contested values that taints the *Gorgias* argument. The other is a proto-Aristotelian understanding of Socrates' talk of false pleasures as "ridiculous imitations of true ones" (40c4–6).

One natural way to take this talk is to take "false" (*pseudês*) to function here in its alienans capacity, as in talk of a "false friend." But there are reasons to resist doing so. For one, doing so is in tension with a highly plausible reading according to which the *Philebus* seeks (in ways explained below) to improve on the *Gorgias* by producing a *genuine* pleasure that a hedonist subject might himself take to detract, even ceteris paribus, from the goodness of his life. More importantly—and less controversially— seeing the alienans use here would undermine the analogy between false pleasure and false belief on which the immediate argument turns. For Socrates—who seeks here to persuade his hedonist interlocutor Protarchus that some pleasures are false and hence bad—responds to Protarchus' skepticism about the possibility of false pleasure by appealing to what Dorothea Frede calls "the facticity claim" and its parallel applicability to pleasure and belief: just as "whoever judges anything at all (even if it is not about anything existing in the present, past or future) *is always really judging*," so too

---

[1] *Philebus* 40a9–12. Translation from Frede (1993). Others (except where indicated) are my own.

"someone who has any pleasure at all, however ill-founded it may be, *really does have pleasure*" [40c8–d10]).² So here at least the pleasures that are supposed to be false are meant to be *genuine* pleasures and their falsity seems to lie in the falsity of their *propositional content*.

I say "here at least" because the *Philebus* argument proceeds in four stages and Socrates does seem in the third to use "false" in its alienans capacity. Many commentators are troubled by the apparent equivocation. Most seem to assume that Socrates *should* use "*pseudês*" in the same sense throughout. And most focus primarily on the first stage, taking the sense there to indicate the sense that must—on pain of equivocation—be present in what follows. The charge of equivocation is common: Gosling accuses Plato of "rank equivocation."³

Dorothea Frede is a notable exception in suggesting that Socrates may *legitimately* use "false" in different senses. She characterizes the various senses as follows (with my italics):

1. Pleasures are false because *the state of affairs which is enjoyed is not real*. Such falsity presupposes that certain pleasures…have propositional form and content…
2. Pleasures are called false, when they are *inflated in size*.… What is false here is not the pleasure itself, that is, *what* it was taken to be, but rather the *size or worth attributed to it*.
3. Freedom from pain is sometimes *falsely called pleasure*, although it is not a pleasure at all. In this case, there is no false pleasure but a confusion about what pleasure *is*.
4. Pleasures are called false because they contain an admixture of pain. In this case, *falsity consists in impurity*.⁴

These characterizations are controversial. There is even a question about whether "mixed" pleasures are supposed to be false. For although Socrates does not call them "false," he does call "true" the pure pleasures to which they are opposed. But the point here is that, however many senses there are, Frede sees no problem of equivocation: she reads Socrates as giving a generic account of pleasure as a kind of process of restoration and then simply describing *various* "ways in which something can go wrong with processes of restoration."⁵

---

² Frede (1993) 39, n. 2. Because so much of the secondary literature uses "belief" for what Plato calls "*doxa*," I use "belief" where Frede uses "judgment."
³ Gosling (1975) 212, who takes Socrates to move from speaking of pleasures as false in the sense that their propositional content is false to speaking of pleasures in the alienans sense.
⁴ Frede (2000) 234–5 (cf. Frede [1997] 242).
⁵ I explain the restorative account in §1. Note that it is *not obvious* that Socrates treats *all* pleasures as involving a process of restoration: this may apply only to body-involving pleasures. For

Frede's suggestion is salutary. But I think she goes too far in taking Socrates to present what is effectively a *list*. What matters here is not that Socrates' use of "*pseudês*" be absolutely univocal, but rather the coherence of his overall argument. And for that it may suffice if he employs a core notion of falsity departures from which are justified in their respective contexts and contribute to the argument *as a whole*.[6] So, for example, it is not necessarily a problem if, in moving from the first to the second stage, Socrates moves from speaking of pleasures as false in the sense that they have false propositional content to speaking of pleasures as false in the sense that they appear to be larger or smaller than they really are. For there is an intuitive sort of unity provided by the common use of "*pseudês*" to characterize things as *lying* or *deceitful*. Pleasures that seem larger or more significant than they really are can be said to resemble false propositions insofar as they threaten to deceive us about some way the world really is: a pleasure that appears larger or more significant than it really is threatens to deceive us about *itself*.[7] And it need not be a problem if Socrates then in the third stage speaks of pleasures as false in the sense that they are merely apparent pleasures mistaken by their subject for genuine ones. For as long as the non-alienans use is *also* in play—especially where the falsity of pleasure is assimilated to the falsity of belief—Socrates can perhaps allow that *some* self-ascriptions of pleasure in the present tense are mistaken and still come up with an example of a genuine pleasure his hedonist interlocutor will think he is (even ceteris paribus) better off without.

In sum, we need not choose between absolute univocity and a mere list: Plato may aim to provide Socrates with a coherent story involving different *but related* senses of "false." So I propose to examine Socrates' various "models" of false pleasure by attending to the role each plays in the overall sequence. Note that I speak of "models" here so as to avoid begging questions about whether what we find here are different examples of the same kind, different kinds of false pleasure, or something else instead. And I shall pay special attention (as Galen apparently did) to what Socrates says as he transitions from one model to another.[8]

---

further discussion of this, and powerful argument that it is part of the *point* of the *Philebus* that no *generic* account of pleasure *can* be given, see Fletcher (2012) (from whose author I have learned much).

[6] I see here misguided assumptions about what is required for the consistency of Plato's argument similar to those I see in readings of Plato's *Republic* and diagnose in Whiting (2012).

[7] The second stage is in fact best read this way, since there is otherwise a puzzle, clear from Frede's characterization, about why it is the *pleasures themselves* (and not the subjects' estimates of their sizes) that are called "false."

[8] Galen, in *De libris propriis* 13, lists among his works on Plato one (now lost) on the transitions in the *Philebus*: *Peri tôn en Philêbô(i) metabaseôn*.

But first let me explain the dialectical situation and the distinction between forms of pleasure on which Socrates' arguments turn (§1). I shall then—after a brief digression that prepares the way for my reading of the third model (§2)—say a bit about the *Gorgias* background (§3), turning finally to the sequence as such (§§4–8) and the light it might shed (§§9–10) on the interpretive controversies surrounding the infamous example at the heart of Socrates' first model.

1. THE *PHILEBUS*: A BRIEF INTRODUCTION

The *Philebus*, whose official topic is the human good, begins in medias res. Protarchus has just taken over from Philebus, who has apparently been defending the life of pleasure, though there is little sign from here on that he has any interest in doing so. This may be significant. For the dialogue seems focused more on the difficulties involved in *defending* the life of pleasure than any difficulty involved in *living* it. Someone who simply loses himself in first-order pleasures—without stepping back and taking a kind of second-order satisfaction in what a great thing it is, perhaps even the essence of *eudaimonia*, to be enjoying such pleasures—may escape Socratic refutation. But that is no guarantee against serving as an object lesson for would-be hedonists who are sufficiently reflective to ask themselves whether pleasure *really is* the human good.

Socrates is defending the life of intelligent activity, including not only knowledge and true belief but also memory. When Protarchus says that he would gladly live his whole life enjoying the greatest pleasures and would need nothing further in addition, Socrates asks whether Protarchus would *really* be content with such a life, since, lacking intelligence, he would not even realize that he was enjoying himself when he was in fact doing so.[9] Nor, lacking memory and the power of reasoning, would he be able to remember that he had previously enjoyed himself or calculate how to do so in the future. He would be living the life not of a human being but of a jellyfish or some testacean (21c–d). Protarchus quickly concedes that a life of pleasure involving these forms of intelligence is more choiceworthy than a life of pleasure that lacks them. It is not entirely clear how to interpret Protarchus' concession, but he may be supposing (contrary to their explicit hypothesis) that adding memory of past pleasures, awareness of present ones, and planning for future ones would yield new forms of pleasure such that any life to which they were added would be *more pleasant* with than without them. So it is tempting to see second-order pleasures lurking here, setting us up for the arguments that follow.

---

[9] Cf. *Gorgias* 474b, where Socrates suggests that Polus, too, fails to know his own mind.

Socrates himself makes a parallel concession: that there are some forms of pleasure such that a life of intelligent activity that includes them is more choiceworthy than a life of intelligent activity devoid of them (21a8–22b1). So they agree early on that the human good is some form of life that combines pleasure and intelligent activity, and spend the rest of the dialogue debating the relative merits of pleasure and intelligent activity *within* the best combination, with Socrates mainly attacking pleasure's claim to superiority. Socrates launches his attack by positing (with Protarchus' consent) two forms (*eidē*) of pleasure and pain: those experienced by the soul together with the body (henceforth "body-involving") and those experienced by the soul itself and apart from the body (henceforth "purely psychic") (32b–c). Socrates then seeks to persuade Protarchus that some pleasures are bad by persuading him that purely psychic pleasures can be false in a way such that any life to which they are added is less rather than more choiceworthy.

Pleasure and pains of the *first form* are common to rational and non-rational animals, including the simple sea creatures mentioned at 21c–d. They involve departures from and returns to harmonious conditions that are natural to the organisms subject to these pleasures and pains, departures and returns that are (as we learn at 43b–c) large enough for their subject to *sense*. *Aisthetically* registered departures from these conditions constitute pains; *aisthetically* registered returns, pleasures. The pains of hunger and thirst and their corollary pleasures are the obvious paradigms. But there are other paradigms, such as the pleasures of warming up (when chilled) or cooling down (when overheated), all suggesting a connection between these pleasures and the survival—and to that extent the *good*—of their subjects.

We might thus speak of these pleasures as "tracking" the good of their subjects. But they do so in ways that do *not require* their subjects to *conceive of* the natural harmonious conditions or the returns to them *as good*: it is (as Harte suggests) *de re* and not *de dicto* that these pleasures track the relevant goods.[10] What we find here are thus sensory mechanisms (of a sort plants are generally thought to lack) for achieving and maintaining the subject's good. But these mechanisms, although they presuppose subjects that are conscious in the sense of being subjects of sensation, do not require *self*-consciousness: they do not require the subject to take itself—nor even to be capable of taking itself—to be experiencing pleasure or pain. So they include the sort of pleasures and pains the simple sea-creatures at 21c–d are supposed to experience without realizing, *when* they are doing so, *that* they are doing so.

Pleasures and pains of the *second form* are said to belong to the soul itself, apart from the body (32c3–5). Socrates introduces them by appeal to the expectation of

---

[10] Harte, personal communication; cf. n. 40.

body-involving pleasures and pains (*to toutôn tôn pathêmatôn prosdokêma*): he says that the anticipation preceding the pleasant *pathêmata* is itself pleasant while that preceding the painful *pathêmata* is itself painful (32b9–c2). Since Socrates seems at this point to be *identifying* body-involving pains and pleasures with the relevant departures and restorations, I take *toutôn tôn pathêmatôn* to refer to body-involving pleasures and pains construed *experientially*: the idea seems to be that pleasures and pains of the *second* form are taken—at least in the first instance—in *experiences* of pleasure and pain that belong to the first form.[11] "In the first instance" because purely psychic pleasures admit of iteration and may be taken not only in body-involving pleasures but also in other purely psychic ones. An Epicurean, for example, might now enjoy *anticipating* the higher-order pleasure she *will* someday take in *recollecting* all the pleasures she *now* enjoys, including any higher-order pleasure she *now* takes in how many and how great her base-level pleasures (whether body-involving and/or purely psychic) currently are and/or have been.[12] And it is precisely such pleasures I see in play in the second part of Socrates' infamous example.

Pleasures and pains of the second form are experienced only by animals endowed with powers of memory that, by putting their currently empty subjects in touch with *past* experiences of being filled, allow these subjects to form both desires for and hopes (or expectations) of being refilled in the future.[13] Socrates seems to think the requisite powers of memory widespread (36b8–9): there are few animals as benighted as the sea-creatures singled out at 21c. But Socrates seems also to take human powers of *logos* to give rise to a distinctive form of *anticipatory* pleasure, one in which the anticipatory pleasure *itself* is appropriately described as false in some sense yet to be explained.

We shall return to purely psychic pleasures. The crucial point here is to see how the restorative account of body-involving pleasures opens the door to a possibility to which Socrates at least *seems* to appeal in his discussion of the third model: the possibility of merely apparent pleasures that might be mistaken by their subject for genuine ones. For any subject in a neutral bodily state—one involving neither any departure from nor any return to its natural harmonious condition—will be experiencing neither pleasure nor pain, at least not of the restorative kind. But it seems possible that a subject endowed with the forms of *nous* that give rise to self-ascriptions of pleasure might mistake its current bodily state for a pleasant or painful one. It may be, for example,

---

[11] Cf. Harte's very different reading, discussed in n. 29.
[12] I speak of "base-level" and "higher-order" pleasures—rather than "first" and "second-order" ones—precisely so as to accommodate such iteration.
[13] I oversimplify in speaking of subjects that are *empty* rather than *being emptied*. But see 42c–43d and 53c–55b, which should be compared to *Gorgias* 492e3–494e7 (where Socrates assimilates the souls of the foolish [*ho anoêtoi*] to leaky jars).

that he has just endured a period of intense pain and thus experiences the neutral state as pleasant; or, conversely, that he has just been enjoying especially intense pleasures and so experiences the neutral state as painful. And Socrates seems to appeal to this possibility with a view to allowing that at least some present-tense self-ascriptions of pleasure made "from the inside" are *corrigible*.

But taking Socrates to allow such corrigibility is controversial, not just because of well-entrenched Cartesian assumptions (the "charitable" application of which might however be dismissed as anachronistic), but also because of common-sense views expressed in the *Philebus* itself. For Socrates appears in his presentation of the first model to be committed to the *incorrigibility* of such ascriptions. So his presentation of the third model seems to contradict his presentation of the first.

Frede seeks to render these presentations consistent by arguing that, despite appearances, Socrates is concerned in the third model not with self-ascriptions of present pleasure made (as we might say) "from the inside," but rather with *theoretical identifications* made "from the outside" by a certain kind of "ascetic," one who takes freedom from pain, and so the neutral state, to *be* pleasure (or at least one kind of it).[14] In other words, Frede denies that Socrates means to refer to the sort of case where a subject, after prolonged suffering, is in fact in a neutral state but says of this state, spontaneously and without any theoretical axe to grind, "Now *this* is what I call pleasure." She takes Socrates to speak rather of a theoretician who identifies pleasure with freedom

---

[14] These so-called "ascetics" should be distinguished from the "harsh" scientists introduced at 44b. The latter seem to hold an eliminativist view according to which there is no such thing as pleasure: they recognize only *two* conditions—pains and processes of escape from pain—and say that what people call "pleasures" are really just processes of escape from pain. But Frede's "ascetics" allow *three* conditions. And there is no evidence that they deny that the *process* of returning to a natural harmonious condition is—like the *state* of not being pained—pleasant. Their asceticism seems to consist in taking this state to involve a form of pleasure *preferable to* the form involved in processes of return. This is presumably why what we find in 43d are not (as many translations suggest) identity statements. The question at 43d4–5 is whether or not being pained is *ever* (*pote*) the same with enjoying (though Taylor [1956] alone, among translations I checked, renders the "*pote*"). Moreover, what we find at d10 is an adjective, not a substantive: the point is not (as Frede has it) that the ascetic identifies *pleasure* with freedom from pain, but rather that he treats not being pained as *pleasant*, which leaves it open that escaping from pain is *also* pleasant. These things are clearly different: I cannot *be escaping* from pain unless I still have *some* pain, which is precisely the problem with the sort of kinetic pleasure the harsh scientists privilege on account of its intensity: such pleasure is inextricably bound up with pains, whose necessary presence makes such pleasures such *seem* larger and/or more valuable than they *really* are. For discussion of these issues in connection with the distinction between Cyrenaic and Epicurean hedonism, see Striker (1993), especially n. 11 on the apparent coincidence of the distinction between "kinetic" and "katastematic" pleasures with the *Philebus* distinction between "mixed" and "unmixed" pleasures.

from pain and then applies his (in Socrates' view *mistaken*) theory to particular states, determining on *its* basis whether or not someone's state *is* a state of pleasure.[15]

Frede may be right. But I am more inclined to go the other way and argue that the first model, despite appearances, involves no commitment to incorrigibility on *Socrates'* part. This is largely because I think we can make better sense of the overall sequence—especially the role played in it by the third model—if we read the third model as appealing to the sort of corrigibility to which the restorative account of body-involving pleasures opens the door. But I have independent reasons for thinking that Frede's reading of the first model—which motivates her revisionary reading of the third—is weak. So let me explain briefly why I am inclined to go the other way.

2. THE CONSISTENCY OF SOCRATES' VIEWS ON CORRIGIBILITY (CONTRA FREDE)

Frede's reading of the third model seems to be motivated primarily by her belief that Socrates is firmly committed, in his presentation of the first, to incorrigibility. But this motivation is suspect. The crucial passage is at 36e5–8, where Socrates starts by stating what he takes *Protarchus* to be saying:

> SOC: So you are saying, then, that neither in a dream nor in sleep, nor in forms of madness or insanity, is there anyone who at some time takes himself to be enjoying <something> but is in no way enjoying <anything>; nor again <anyone who> thinks he is in pain but is not in pain.

Protarchus replies: "we all suppose, Socrates, that all these things are so." But it is not clear whether what we all suppose is supposed to be (*a*) that there *is* no one who takes himself to be enjoying when he is not or (*b*) that this sort of thing *does* sometimes happen.

Fortunately, we need not resolve this issue. For what matters is whether *Socrates* commits himself to what "everyone" is supposed to say. And the answer is arguably "no." For he replies with the following question:

> But <do we suppose so> correctly? Or is it necessary to examine whether these things are said correctly or not?

---

[15] Frede (1993) 50. A subject could of course apply this in a theoretical way to her own experiences, thus treating them in the way a third person might do. But she would then, absent *physiological* signs of some restorative process, be required to correct or suspend self-ascriptions of present-pleasure made "from the inside."

It is true that Socrates does not register explicit dissent from Protarchus' claim about what we all suppose. But by asking whether "we" all suppose so *correctly*, and whether *that* is not what they should be asking, Socrates effectively *sidesteps* the question whether everyone, *himself included*, in fact supposes this. So even if the point here *is* that present-tense self-ascriptions of pleasure are incorrigible, these lines provide little reason to read the third model in a way that avoids taking *Socrates* to allow the corrigibility of some such ascriptions.

But Frede's reading of the third model may rest partly on how she reads the remainder of the first. For in explaining why she takes 36e5–12 to reveal Socrates' commitment to incorrigibility, Frede says that "the 'facticity' of pleasure is granted immediately."[16] It would however be a mistake to take the assertion of facticity as evidence of—or worse yet as tantamount to—a commitment to incorrigibility. For the facticity claim is entirely compatible with corrigibility. Even if it were possible for it to seem to a subject in a neutral state that she was experiencing body-involving pleasure, this would in no way impugn the virtual tautology embodied in the facticity claim. For it would provide no counterexample to the claim that "whoever has any pleasure at all, however ill-founded it may be, really does have pleasure." Given the "restorative" account of bodily pleasure and the hypothesis that she is *mistaking* a neutral (bodily) state for a pleasant one, the subject is *not* in fact experiencing the (bodily) pleasure she takes herself to be experiencing. She may of course be experiencing a purely psychic pleasure. But that (as I explain in §7) is a different issue.

The case where someone mistakes a neutral state for a pleasant one is clearly a case involving a mistake about the *first* form of pleasure, the form *identified* with something like a *perceptually registered process of return* to some natural harmonious condition: if there is no process of return occurring—or there is such a process but it is not *aisthetically* registered—then there is no such pleasure. Someone who mistakes a neutral state for a pleasant one is presumably someone whose experience is (as we now might say) "*as of* being replenished." It *feels good* in just the way it tends to feel good when one *is* being replenished, only there is in this case no replenishment going on: what we have here is something like *perceptual illusion*. And this, as we shall see, fits nicely into the sequence of models as I understand it. For not only is the first model introduced by the possibility of someone mistaking a distant statue for a man (or vice versa); the second model features mistakes a subject might make when she views (so to speak) her own pleasures and pains either from a distance or alongside of one another, mistakes explicitly assimilated to various forms of perceptual illusion. So it would be no surprise to find the third model turning to the possibility of merely apparent pleasures

---

[16] Frede (1993) 39, n. 2.

that are mistaken by their subjects for genuine ones; it would in fact be more surprising to find Socrates turning suddenly to theoretical identifications made by "ascetic" philosophers.

Nor is the theoretical-mistake reading plausible. To see why not, compare this reading of the passage where it seems most natural to read Socrates as affirming corrigibility with the mistaken-self-ascription reading of that passage. After agreeing (as at 32e) that there is a neutral state between pleasure and pain, and so the possibility of a intermediate life like the one earlier ascribed to the gods (43d), Socrates says that if someone were to believe or to say that the intermediate life was either pleasant or painful, he would do so *incorrectly*. When Protarchus assents, Socrates points out that there are in fact people who both say *and believe* this (44a). The dialogue—which I render in English in a way as close as possible to the Greek, so as to highlight the apparent force of the repeated "*tote*"—continues as follows:

SOC: Do [these people] really think they are experiencing pleasure then [*tote*] whenever they are not suffering pain?
PRO: They *say* so, at any rate.
SOC: So they *think* then [*tote*] that they are experiencing pleasure.
PRO: That seems likely.[17]

The second "*tote*" seems especially telling: the idea seems to be that when these people *say* they are experiencing pleasure, they *then*—at that very time—*think* they are doing so. And it is difficult to see the point of Socrates' question unless he is asking whether those who claim in the theoretical mode that freedom from pain is pleasant—indeed the most pleasant state there is—really practice what they preach. For there would be little point to asking whether these people believe their theory *when they are theorizing*. The question is whether these "ascetics" really think *then*, when they are simply free of pain, that they are enjoying themselves *then*. And the question is pointed only if (as Protarchus seems to think) common sense takes present-tense self-ascriptions of pleasure to be incorrigible. But it does not follow that Socrates himself holds the common-sense view. For he often reverses common sense, as for example in *Gorgias* 479e–481c, which culminates in Callicles' claim that if what Socrates says is true, then "this human

---

[17] The question is clearly what these people think about their *own* experiences, the subjects of "*oiontai*" being by default the subjects of the present infinitive "*chairein*," which (together with repeated use of "*tote*") suggests the simultaneity of the ostensible pleasures and their subjects' thoughts and assertions about them.

life of ours will be turned upside down and everything we do will evidently be the opposite of what we should do."

This point is worth stressing lest anyone take hedonism itself to presuppose a commitment to the incorrigibility of present-tense self-ascriptions of pleasure. For no particular claim about the nature of pleasure is presupposed by the hedonist thesis that pleasure is the good. And it would be anachronistic—or at least heedless of Plato's text—to claim that no self-respecting hedonist will worry about ending up with merely apparent pleasures, especially not if he thinks he cannot distinguish them "from the inside" from real ones. We must keep in mind the version of hedonism against which Socrates is *actually* arguing.

Protarchus, who readily accepts the restorative account of body-involving pleasures, seems from the outset to take the fact that all animals pursue pleasure as *evidence* that pleasure is *the good*, not just for other animals but also for human ones. So he seems at least tacitly committed to objectivism both about the human good and about pleasure. He takes pleasure to be the good for every living creature, whatever (if anything) any given subject happens to think. And he denies (at least in the case of body-involving pleasure) that what constitutes an experience as pleasure is even partly the fact that its subject takes it to be one.[18] These commitments help to explain why Protarchus does not resist the restorative account when Socrates proposes it, and why he does not renege on it when it starts to cause trouble for his account of the human good. They also underlie the vulnerable points pressed by Socrates. For Protarchus has reason to worry not just about the possibility of mistaking neutral states for pleasures and so settling for neutral states in lieu of genuine pleasures, but also about whether pleasure—or a certain sort of pleasure—is in fact the highest good.

It is the latter worry that Socrates exploits in the "denouement" of his argument. But we will be in a better position to appreciate that when we come to it, if we have the *Gorgias* background in mind. So let me turn briefly to it.

3. THE *GORGIAS* BACKGROUND AND THE EMENDATIONS THAT OBSCURE IT

The relevance of the *Gorgias* background, and with it the role played by foolishness in the *Philebus*, are obscured by the widespread tendency of modern editors to adopt emendations proposed by Cornarius in 1561, and so to substitute "*agnoia*" (or "ignorance") in five places where all extant manuscripts of the *Philebus* have "*anoia*" (or

---

[18] Contra Mooradian (1996), who reads Protarchus as defending a Protagorean view; and Harte (2004), who says in n. 6 that her reading is similar to his.

"foolishness").[19] This might seem trivial, but it is not: Socrates' infamous disavowals of knowledge were *not* professions of foolishness. Foolishness involves the *illusion* of knowledge, which is clearly in play in 48c–49e, where four of the five substitutions are proposed. The case against these substitutions is thus strong. So too is the case against the first. For the overall argument of the *Philebus* is framed by two passages where there is no controversy about the text and the emphasis on foolishness is clear.

The first such passage is at 12c8–d6, on the dialogue's second Stephanus page, where Socrates (in a passage reminiscent of *Gorgias* 497e3ff.) contrasts the pleasures of the intemperate agent with those of the temperate one (who takes pleasure in exercising temperance itself) and those of the foolish agent with those of the wise one (who takes pleasure in exercising wisdom itself). Although he allows in each case that *both* agents experience pleasure, Socrates suggests that only a *fool* would claim that their respective pleasures are *similar* (12c8–d6). And his talk here of "someone acting foolishly, full of foolish opinions and hopes" (*ton anoêtainonta kai anoêtôn doxôn kai elpidôn mes-ton*) clearly foreshadows the crucial discussion of false anticipatory pleasures, which is where (at 38a8) the first of Cornarius' five proposed substitutions appears. So there is no reason for this substitution and positive reason *against* it.

The remaining four substitutions (at 48c2, 49c2, d9 and 49e6) all occur in the discussion of the mixed pleasures, where Socrates turns from tragic to comic mixtures. Here again the issue seems to be foolishness rather than mere ignorance. He is discussing a special sort of failure of self-knowledge, one where someone thinks he is in some way better—or better off—than he in fact is. (The comparative aspect is relevant here.) Socrates gives three examples. A person may think that he is *richer* than he in fact is; or *larger and more handsome*; or *more virtuous* and especially *wiser*. And as Frede notes, "would-be beauty, wealth, or wisdom are the laughingstock in comedy."[20] Of course would-be wisdom (*doxosophia*) is (as Socrates points out) dangerous and hateful when found among the powerful; but it also (he says) makes those who are weak and unable to avenge themselves "ridiculous" (*geloion*). Given this context, there is little reason to substitute "*agnoia*" for "*anoia*" throughout this exchange.[21] There is in fact reason

---

[19] The exceptions are French: see Pradeau (2002) 268–9, n. 149; and Delcominnette (2006) 363, n. 25 for further references. Karel Thein, to whose writings and conversation I am much indebted, is another.

[20] Frede (1993) 57, n. 1.

[21] The main reason for emendation is apparently to fit the talk of *gnôthi sauton* at 48c10, *to mêdamê(i) gignôskein hauton* at 48d1–2, and (especially) *tôn agnoountôn hautous* at 48d9. But this is not a good reason: the point of the passage is to distinguish *foolish* failures of self-knowledge from other (more dangerous) forms: *anoia* figures here as one species of *agnoia*, which genus is thus mentioned as they home in on this species.

against doing so: ignorance, simply as such, is lamentable, not laughable: it is the pretence of wisdom, at least among those without power, that has comic potential.

This brings me to the second frame passage, roughly four Stephanus pages from the end, where Socrates represents *nous* and *phronêsis* as answering the question whether they would need (in order to partake of the best sort of life) to associate with "the strongest and most intense pleasures, in addition to the true ones." *Nous* and *phronêsis* are represented as saying that these pleasures, which are "forever involved with foolishness" (*met' aphrosunês*),

> are a tremendous impediment to us, since they infect the souls in which they dwell with madness or even prevent our own development altogether.... (63d2–64a1)

Here again foolishness is clearly in view. So the frame passages, especially taken together, make a powerful case for retaining the manuscript readings.

The case is even stronger given that retaining them allows us to make good sense of the *Philebus*'s extensive allusions to the *Gorgias*—especially in the denouement, where Socrates appeals to the restorative account of pleasure widely acknowledged to approximate the account of pleasure assumed by Callicles in the *Gorgias*. Callicles identifies pleasure with the *process* of coming to be filled (with for example food or drink); and he compares the *state* of being full to the condition of a stone or a corpse, a condition that (like the neutral states in the *Philebus*) admits of no pleasure (*Gorgias* 494a6ff.). Appetites for food, drink, et cetera are thus *conditions* for experiencing the sort of processes that *constitute* pleasure. The greater the appetites, the greater the pleasures and so (according to Callicles) the greater the happiness. Socrates thus asks Callicles "whether a man who has an itch and scratches it and can scratch to his heart's content, scratch his whole life long, can also live happily." After chiding Socrates for his "nonsense" and being urged by Socrates not to succumb to shame, Callicles agrees that "even the man who scratches would have a pleasant life" and so a happy one. Socrates then asks:

> What if he scratches only his head—or what am I to ask you further?... And isn't the climax of this sort of thing, the life of a catamite, a frightfully shameful and miserable one? Or will you have the nerve to say they are happy as long as they have what they need to their heart's content [*ean aphthonos echôsin hôn deontai*] (*Gorgias* 494c6–e6)[22]

---

[22] Translation by Zeyl, in Cooper and Hutchinson (1997). Cf. *Philebus* 40a10, where the subject pictures gold coming to him *aphthonon*.

Callicles responds by asking *Socrates* whether *he* isn't ashamed to bring the discussion to such a point. And when Socrates lays the blame on those (like Callicles) who refuse to distinguish good kinds of pleasure from bad, Callicles says, "well, to keep my argument from being inconsistent if I say (pleasures) are different, I say they are the same."

This "refutation" is notoriously flawed by its question-begging appeal to the shamefulness of certain pleasures. Any hedonist as shameless as Callicles claimed to be could simply—and should simply—have taken the pleasures of the catamite on board, saying calmly, "whatever turns him on." And Plato, I think, was well aware of this. That, I submit, is partly why he wrote the *Philebus*: to give Socrates a chance to improve on the anti-hedonist argument he ran in the *Gorgias*. And the improvement consists largely in replacing the *Gorgias* appeal to shamefulness with an appeal not just to the *falsity* of certain pleasures but to the *foolishness* of the sort of pleasure specifically championed by Callicles and featured prominently in the *Philebus*'s denouement.

This is at 46dff, where Socrates is discussing mixed pleasures, whose very existence depends on some admixture of pain (in this case bodily). Socrates describes a subject whose enjoyment of scratching is so intensely pleasant that it "causes him to leap about, produces [in him] all sorts of colors, contortions and panting, and finally results in a complete frenzy and foolish shouting [*pasan ekplêxin kai boas meta aphrosunês energazetai*]" (47a6-9)." This

> causes him *to say about himself* and others to say as well that he is almost dying of these pleasures. And the more intemperate and foolish [*akolastoteros kai aphronesteros*] he happens to be the more he will always pursue these <pleasures> by any means possible; and he calls these greatest, and counts as most *eudaimôn* of all creatures the man who lives always enjoying them to the greatest extent possible. (47b2-7)

Note the use of "*aphrosunê*" and "*aphronesteros*," which tie this to the first frame passage (12c8-d6). Note also Socrates' use of the present-tense indicatives, which suggest someone making self-ascriptions of *present* pleasure—someone saying of himself, at the time when he is enjoying such pleasures, that he is "almost dying of them," that "they are the greatest," et cetera. Note finally that the subject does not simply *enjoy* such pleasures and *affirm* that he is doing so; he goes on to identify a life filled with the maximum possible enjoyment of such pleasures as the *most desirable life*: this is his conception of *eudaimonia*. Moreover, the subject seems not just to *believe* that his highest good lies in the maximization of such pleasures: he seems also to take a kind of higher-order *enjoyment* in the fact that he experiences (when he does) so many such pleasures. Such *enjoyment* may of course involve propositional falsity, but the base-level pleasures that give rise to it need not. For the pleasures of scratching have no propositional content, which may help to explain the presence earlier in the sequence of the second model, where (as we shall see) pleasures without propositional content may give rise to false beliefs.

In sum, the denouement features a Calliclean hedonist's answer to the *Philebus*'s main question. The character featured here sincerely thinks, at least when he is enjoying such pleasures to the hilt, that nothing further can be added to improve his life so long as he can go on like that—itching and scratching—forever. But whatever *he* thinks, we readers are surely supposed to think this foolish, involving not simply ignorance but the *illusion of knowledge*.

Of course the subject might *later* come to think this foolish if he could *later* be induced to reflect back on his present experience, perhaps by reflecting on the similarity of his present behavior to that of some third party whose sincere present-tense expressions of intense pleasure *he* sees as manifestly foolish. The question is whether he could ever, *when in the grip of such foolishness*, make any such comparison. And the answer, I fear, is not. For the intensity of his pleasure stands in the way, which is surely why Socrates focuses at 45c on the intensity, not the overall magnitude, of his pleasure.

But it does not follow that subjects whose pleasures are less intense could not be induced, even while in the grip of illusion, to ask whether their present experiences might not be in some way illusory. They could perhaps be induced to consider forms of blindness they have seen in others and to ask whether they themselves might *now* be suffering some such blindness. For even if the problem with illusions is that their subject's present attitudes prevent her from seeing them *directly* for what they are, it may be possible to get her to worry *indirectly* that things are not really as they presently seem to her to be. And we should be able to induce such a worry in any domain in which the subject allows facts about how things *really* are, facts at least partly independent of how things *seem* to her. We can now see why Protarchus' objectivist commitments, stressed at the end of §2, are so important. For it is precisely by appeal to them that Socrates seeks to induce in Protarchus a *series* of such worries, to which I now turn.

4. THE FIRST MODEL (36C–41B): THE PROTO-ARISTOTELIAN SETUP

When Protarchus resists the "facticity argument" for the existence of false pleasures on the ground that the alleged falsity belongs not to the pleasure but rather to some belief on which the pleasure depends, Socrates responds by comparing the human soul to an illustrated book in which perception and memory function together as a kind of "scribe," who writes in our souls *logoi* that are then illustrated by a "painter," whose operations include those of what we would call "imagination" and what Aristotle calls "phantasia." These *logoi* presumably include both words (such as "man" and "statue") and statements (or propositions) employing these words. Socrates says that when what "this experience" (*touto to pathêma*, construed as the joint operation of memory and perception) writes is true, then belief and *logoi* resulting from it (*ap' autou*) turn out to be true; and when what it writes is false, belief and *logoi* opposite to true ones come about.[23]

It is important in reading this passage to note both the immediate context, in which memory and perception are said to lead to belief *or to the attempt to arrive at a belief* (*to diadoxazein encheirein*, 38b12–13), and the example contained in it: that of the subject who sees, not at all clearly, something in the distance and is *trying to work out* whether it is a man or a statue (presumably a statue *of a man*, since this makes the best sense of the subject's uncertainty). For this suggests that the point is *not* (as often supposed) that whenever what the scribe writes is true, both true belief and true propositions *in fact* come about, but rather that whenever what the scribe writes is true, belief and propositions, *when they do come to be in us*, turn out to be true. (And even this may be true only for the most part.) This leaves it open that some of the propositions actually formed are objects of propositional attitudes other than belief, most notably hope and fear, to which Socrates explicitly assimilates pleasure, presumably so as to address Protarchus' objection that the falsity in question depends on some *belief*. For just as we can hope for (and indeed strive to bring about) states of affairs we believe highly unlikely to occur, and can fear (and work to prevent) the same, so too we can take pleasure in contemplating states of affairs we do not believe ever are, have been, or will be occurring. That should be clear from Socrates' later discussion of the pleasures and pains experienced in watching tragedy and comedy.

That Socrates seeks to establish the possibility of non-doxastic propositional attitudes on which to model pleasure seems clear from his claim that it may take the subject some time to work it out and finally *to say* to himself—and perhaps also aloud to another—that what appears in the distance is (or is not) a man (38c–e). It follows from this that the subject might fail ever to say any such thing, even to himself. He may be distracted and move on before working it out, or decide in the face of uncertainty

---

[23] This translation-cum-paraphrase of 39a4–7 is meant to bring out three things: (1) the contrast between the singular "*doxa*" and the plural "*logoi*," which may indicate a distinction between the state of believing and the various propositions believed; (2) Socrates' choice to speak here not in terms of *falsity* (to which he moves cagily, by way of inference, at 40b7) but rather in terms of *opposites of true* belief and *logoi*; and (3) the way the natural construal of "*en hêmin gignomenoi*" as a circumstantial participle supports my reading.

to suspend judgment. He may say, "It *appears* to be a statue, but I know there are some excellent mimes around here, so it *might* be a man: I just don't know." This is one of the *Philebus*'s several points of contact with the Aristotelian account of *phantasia* and the primary basis for my proto-Aristotelian reading of the first model. Aristotle may even have this passage in mind when he says, in discussing truth and falsity in perception and imagination, "it is not when we are actively and precisely engaged with what is perceived that we say that it *appears* to us to be *a man*; but rather when we do not perceive clearly" (*DA* 428a12–15).

The Aristotelian view I see germinating in the illustrated book passage is encapsulated in *De Anima* 431a8–17:

> Perceiving, then, is like *simply saying or thinking* [*tô(i) phanai monon kai noien*].[24] Whenever <the perceptible object> is pleasant or painful <the soul>, as if asserting or denying, pursues or flees <it>. And to feel pleasure or pain is to act with the perceptive mean towards the good or bad as such.... But to the thinking soul images [*phantasmata*] are like perceptions [*aisthêmata*]. And whenever it <the thinking soul> says or denies[25] <that something is> good or bad, it pursues or avoids <that thing>.[26]

The idea is that animal perception *in general* involves propositional contents that the subject of perception does not strictly speaking assert or deny. In many cases the animal tends to experience pleasure when it perceives the sorts of things that are *in fact* good for members of its kind and pain when it perceives the sorts of things that are *in fact* bad for members of that kind; so it pursues and avoids these objects *as if* affirming or denying that they are good. For Aristotle agrees with Socrates' claim, at *Philebus* 20d7–10, that "every creature that recognizes [the good] hunts and strives for it, wishing to capture it and keep it for itself." But the sort of recognition involved here—*to gignôskein*—does not usually involve the animal's conceiving of the object *as good*. Only rational animals pursue their good *by* pursuing objects under, as we now say, "the guise of the good."[27]

---

[24] *Tô(i) phanai monon kai noien*: I take this to involve grasping, without yet asserting or denying, the propositional content of some appearance, as in the *Philebus* example of someone trying to work out whether what he sees in the distance is a man or a statue.

[25] I take *ê apophêsê(i)*, in light of *hoion kataphasa ê apophasa*, to indicate that *phêsê(i)* here means "assert" (and not "simply say").

[26] Translation from Whiting (2002), where the passage is discussed in detail. See also Charles (2006) and Moss (2010). The best account of the affinities between the *Philebus* and the Aristotelian view is in Lorenz (2006).

[27] The phrase is due to Velleman (1992), who criticizes the view; for admirable defense of it, see Boyle and Lavin (2010).

Other animals simply feel a natural affinity, mediated by pleasure, for objects that are *in fact* good for them.[28]

Of course rational animals sometimes respond immediately to their "aisthetic" experience, pursuing or fleeing objects *as if* asserting or denying that they are good. But rational animals typically move beyond such responses in both theoretical and practical spheres. As in Aristotle's example of the subject to whom the diameter of the moon appears to be the length of a foot although she believes the moon is larger than the earth (*DA* 428b2–5), so too an object or activity can appear good to some subject although he believes it is not. Rational animals are able not only to suspend judgment about the propositional contents of any appearances to which they are subject; they can even deny the contents of these appearances. But when a rational animal pursues some object insofar as the object *appears* good, this is still a case of the sort of perceptively mediated and hedonically charged motivation characteristic of animals as such. For such appearances, whether strictly perceptual or the offspring of *phantasia*, have hedonic aspects that distinguish them from mere beliefs. And these aspects play important roles in the motivational economies of their subjects: they can even move akratic subjects to act *against* their *considered beliefs* about what is best.

In sum, appearances—especially when they present objects and activities as good—are powerful but potentially misleading agents. And they can give rise to pleasure even in the absence of belief in their propositional content. We should keep this in mind as we interpret the first model and its place in the sequence that follows.

5. THE FIRST MODEL CONTINUED: CONTROVERSIES SURROUNDING THE INFAMOUS EXAMPLE AT 40A9–C6

We should also keep in mind that anticipatory pleasures exemplify the first model but do not exhaust it. For excessive focus on the anticipatory example tends to distort readings of this model. Socrates clearly assumes the existence of past- and present-tense analogues, asking only *after* he likens the human soul to an illustrated book whether Protarchus takes the illustrated book phenomena to apply *only* to past and present events and *not also* to future ones—a sensible question if the "painter" illustrates only those *logoi* provided by perception and memory, for the future is not as yet an object of either perception or memory. But Protarchus says immediately that we experience these phenomena in relation to *all* times, indeed *especially* in connection with

---

[28] I see here roots of the Stoic theory of *oikeiôsis*, about which I have learned much from Striker, especially (1983) and (1991). Themistius too seems to have read Aristotle in this way: see, for example, *In libros Aristotelis de anima paraphrasis* 47a23–5 (quoted in Whiting [2008], 123).

future: "especially" since (as Socrates goes on to say) "these things are hopes [or expectations, *elpides*] and we are <all> always, throughout our entire lives, full of hopes" (39d1–e5, which is foreshadowed in the first frame passage).

Socrates then claims (with Protarchus' assent) that "that there are in each of us *logoi* that we call '*elpidai*'" and continues as follows:

> And <isn't it the case that> there are *also* [*kai dê kai*] those painted images [presumably of the contents of the foregoing *logoi*]? And <that> someone envisages [*tis hora(i)*] often coming to himself lots of gold *and many consequent pleasures* [*kai ep' autôi pollas hêdonas*]; and he *also* [*kai dê kai*] sees himself painted, *enjoying himself immensely* [*eph' hautôi chaironta sphodra*]. (40a9–12)

I take this passage to describe someone—presumably a hedonist—who takes anticipatory pleasure not only in the "many pleasures" he now pictures himself *experiencing in the future*, but also (*kai dê kai*) in the higher-order satisfaction he now pictures himself *then* enjoying, when he contemplates all the base-level experiences of pleasure he *then* enjoys. In sum, I see here two distinct forms of *anticipated* pleasure in which the subject now takes the sort of *anticipatory* pleasure this example is meant to illustrate—that is, the sort of anticipatory pleasure constituted by the subject's picturing his own future experiences of pleasure (both base-level and higher-order).[29] But this does not resolve the interpretive controversies, to which I now turn.

---

[29] Harte (2004) reads this differently. She relies on the fact that "*hedonai*" can—like "pleasures"—be used not only to refer to *experiences* of pleasure but also to refer to the *activities* in which experiences of pleasure are taken, as in talk of wining and dining as "my pleasures." This allows her to treat the "many pleasures" that follow the gold not as *experiences* of pleasure but rather as the *activities* in which the subject anticipates taking such pleasure. She then suggests that the *anticipatory* pleasure (construed experientially) is taken *directly* in the *activities* in which the anticipated pleasures (construed again experientially) are supposed to be taken—directly, for example, in the subject's *then wining and dining*. This leads her to treat the *anticipatory* pleasure as simply an "advance installment" of the *anticipated* one. So she sees only one pleasure here, the anticipated pleasure, which is temporally extended in ways not always recognized: it may begin in the subject's current anticipation of these activities and live on beyond the activities themselves in his memories of having engaged in them.

I have trouble accepting this, but not because I have the sort of difficulty Evans has making sense of an advance installment of something that never comes to be—I am too familiar with advance installments of nonexistent books for that. I do not understand how the advance installment of a body-involving pleasure can be (as Socrates' initial account of the two forms of pleasure seems to require) purely psychic. Nor do I see how Socrates' setup allows Harte to handle the present-tense case. For it not clear what the present-tense analogue of the "advance installment" of an anticipated pleasure would be: we seem to be left simply with the present enjoyment of the activity itself (which will in some cases be body-involving rather than purely psychic). But Socrates sets us up (at 21b–c) to expect a kind of psychic pleasure associated with realizing,

Evans divides interpretations into two schools. According to "Old School" readers, the idea is essentially that the anticipatory pleasure is false because the anticipated pleasures *fail to come about*: the subject either fails to get the gold or gets it but fails to experience as a result the pleasures (whether base-level or higher-order) he pictured himself enjoying. The falsity of the anticipatory pleasure—whether the subject *believes* the anticipated pleasures will come about or simply *hopes* or *imagines* they will—lies here in the falsity of its propositional content.[30]

According to "New School" readers the idea is rather that the anticipated pleasures come about but are defective in ways that render false any anticipatory pleasure taken therein. The defect lies according to Evans in the *non-goodness* of that in which the *anticipated* pleasures are taken. And the idea seems to be that this defect renders the anticipated pleasures false in a way that in turn "infects" any *anticipatory* pleasure taken therein.[31] So the *anticipated* pleasures are the primary locus of falsity. There is however a question whether their falsity lies simply in the falsity of their propositional content or whether something more is involved.

Evans' presentation of the New School view suggests that the appeal to value is meant to shift the locus of falsity from the beliefs on which a pleasure depends to the pleasure itself. But a mere appeal to value cannot do that: it is open to Socrates'

---

when one is enjoying something, that one is doing so, a pleasure distinct from that taken in (for example) enjoying one's food and drink. So even if Harte's reading of the infamous example is compatible with Socrates' immediate presentation, her reading seems to me neither required by it nor supported by the way the example fits into the overall sequence.

I should perhaps note that Harte's reading is aimed in part at avoiding saddling Plato with confusions ascribed to him by twentieth-century commentators, confusions summarized in Appendix A of Gosling and Taylor (1982). I am not myself so concerned to acquit Plato, in part because the confusions are subtle and it is not clear to me that Plato succeeded entirely in avoiding them, in part because it is not clear to me that Plato would himself agree that there is any confusion here. For even if one *can* picture past pleasures without taking pleasure in doing so (as for example when one remembers with pain pleasurable athletic feats one will never again perform) and even if one *can* picture future pleasures without taking pleasure in doing so (as for example when one anticipates with pain giving into temptations of pleasure one would prefer to resist) Plato might claim that he is speaking of what are perhaps the more usual cases where picturing such activities is *itself* pleasant.

[30] Although some Old School readers assume that the subject must *believe* these things will come about, I do not think this essential. Evans says that on such views "what makes a pleasure false is either its having false content or its sharing its content with some false belief" (p. 92), which leaves room for a subject whose anticipatory pleasure involves *hoping* or *imagining* that such things will come about and is false when they do *not* come about.

[31] The idea behind such "infection" is presumably that the falsity of the *anticipated* pleasures renders *them* non-good (something hedonists will surely resist), and that their non-goodness gives rise in turn to the falsity of any *anticipatory* pleasure taken therein (again something the hedonist may resist).

interlocutor to object that the pleasures in question are called false by association with some false belief, in this case a belief about what is *good*, which is the real locus of falsity. Nor (as we have seen) is it necessary to introduce talk of what is good in order to answer this objection. As long as we are willing to allow that a pleasure can depend on an *appearance* whose propositional content the pleasure's subject does *not endorse*, we can allow that the falsity of a pleasure is not simply a function of its dependence on a false *belief*. That was the point of Socrates' appeal to hopes and fears. So what is going on here? Why suppose *any* connection between the falsity of a pleasure and the goodness of that in which it is taken?

The best and most common reason for seeing an appeal to value is to explain the puzzling claim made by Socrates in the wake of his example: the claim, accepted without hesitation by Protarchus, that because good agents are loved by the gods, the things inscribed (*ta gegrammena*) in their souls are for the most part *true*, while bad agents suffer the opposite, with the result that the pleasures painted (*hêdonai... ezôgraphêmenai*) in *their* souls are generally *false*. It follows, Socrates says, that "wicked people (*ho ponêroi*) enjoy many false pleasures while the good among us enjoy true ones"; and so, that "there are in human souls pleasures that are quite ridiculous imitations of true ones" (40b2–c6; Frede's translation). But this lopsided distribution of false pleasures is difficult to explain simply by appeal to propositional falsity. For why should good agents be better than bad ones at *predicting* what their future will *in fact* hold? Or even simply at *hoping* for things they will *in fact* get?

Some Old School commentators are satisfied to explain the lopsided distribution by taking the gods' attitudes to be part of the truth-making mechanism: Evans (for example) suggests that the gods are assumed to reward good agents by making their future-directed beliefs (or hopes) come true and to punish bad agents by making their future-directed beliefs (or hopes) prove false.[32] It is, alas, not out of the question that

---

[32] Socrates' claim is so puzzling that Frede has proposed, seriatim, three different explanations, starting in her (1985) with a version of the present view, one according to which the gods' affections are supposed to provide for the truth of falsity of beliefs that would otherwise be in logical limbo, awaiting future events to make them true or false. Frede (1997) 256–8, says that that was "in Ermanglung einer besseren Erklärung" and that the most plausible explanation is that those who are loved by the gods tend to be successful because they have correct (*richtige*) *logoi* and pictures in their souls and so do not harbor insane or unrealistic hopes (*unsinnige Hoffnungen*). To the extent that the emphasis here is on foolishness, not moral defect, this explanation seems to differ from the one in Frede (1993), where we find what is perhaps the baldest extant statement of a New School reading: "It is not likely that Plato is merely referring to the common (but also much disputed) Greek wisdom that those whom the gods love prosper in life. He must also be implying that the *moral content* of foolish pleasures is mistaken, that they represent a skewed view of life" (p. 44, n. 2). Note by the way that this "moral" sense is not reflected in Frede's original list (quoted at the outset): it seems to be *yet another way* pleasures can go wrong.

Plato has some such view in mind, either as Socrates' own or (as seems more likely) one that Protarchus and many of Plato's readers can be counted on to accept. But many commentators find such accounts unsatisfactory. And this leads some to suggest that the talk of pleasures as false should be understood not in terms of these pleasures resting on false beliefs or empty hopes, but rather in terms of their being taken in activities or objects that are *bad* (or at least *not good*). For this would provide a neat explanation of the puzzling claim: the pleasures of good agents are for the most part true because *what it is* for a pleasure to *be true* is for it to be taken in something *good*, while the pleasures of bad agents are for the most part false because *what it is* for a pleasure to *be false* is for it to be taken in something *bad* (or at least *not good*).[33]

But even if a New School reading would explain the puzzling claim, we should not rush to embrace this reading. For it rests largely on a conjecture aimed primarily at explaining this claim but not independently supported by Plato's text. The text may even tell *against* a New School explanation of the puzzling claim. For Socrates says explicitly that the falsity of a pleasure is the *only* ground for calling a pleasure "*ponêra*." And when Protarchus objects (at 41a1–4) that this is "the opposite of the truth"—that it is "not at all because they are false that we regard pleasures or pains as bad, but because there is some other large and great *ponêria* involved"—Socrates holds his ground. So if *anyone* makes the sort of appeal to value associated with New School views it seems to be *Protarchus*; Socrates himself explicitly rejects any such appeal. And Socrates' explicit rejection seems to me significant. For what we find here is a curious reversal of the position Socrates assumed in Plato's *Gorgias*, where Socrates appeals (in his attempt to undermine Callicles' professed hedonism) to the *shamefulness* of certain pleasures—most notably those enjoyed by catamites.

This reversal on Socrates' part seems to me one among other signs that we should read the *Philebus* with the *Gorgias* in mind. Another, even stronger sign is the way Socrates' reversal is mirrored by a no less curious reversal on Protarchus' part *within* the *Philebus* itself. For the mirroring seems unlikely to be accidental. Though Protarchus starts off (at 13b6–c2) vehemently resisting the idea that some pleasures are bad, he changes his tune when Socrates appeals to the facticity of doxa to establish the facticity of pleasure: Protarchus now claims that the hedonic analogue of false belief involves some other form of *ponêria* (besides that of falsity). And it is now Socrates who, reversing the position he assumed in the *Gorgias*, vehemently resists: he insists that the *only* way pleasures can be *bad* is by being *false*; and he says that they can talk later about other forms of badness, *if it still seems fit to them to do so* (41a5–6). He then turns

---

[33] This is of course more plausible if we assume that the subject *conceives* of that in which the relevant pleasures are taken *as good* (or at least *non-bad*), which seems to be Lovibond's view (but not Harte's). See §9.

immediately to his second model, which involves pleasures that are false, as he *himself* says, "in another way" (*kat' allon tropon*, 41a8).

Many commentators are critical of what they see here as an abrupt transition to Socrates' second model. They worry that Protarchus is not fully persuaded that pleasures can be false in the propositional sense, and see Socrates as turning prematurely to a *different kind of falsity*, one consisting in something's having a *misleading appearance*. But Socrates himself *advertises* that he is turning to pleasures that are false "in *another* way," which suggests that he is up to something far more interesting—namely, continuing to address Protarchus' reservations about the idea that pleasures can be false while seeking simultaneously to induce in Protarchus and other hedonists the worry that they might take their own pleasures to be smaller or larger than they *really* are, and so be *fooled* into accepting smaller pleasures in lieu of larger ones.

6. THE SECOND MODEL: PERCEPTUAL ILLUSION AND THE TRANSFER OF FALSITY FROM PLEASURE TO BELIEF (41B–42C)

Socrates describes what we find here as the "opposite" of what we found in the first model, where pleasures seemed to be "infected" by the falsity of their attendant beliefs (42a5ff). In this case, the pleasures *themselves* are supposed to be false in ways such that *they* may give rise to false beliefs.[34] And though we might be tempted to read Socrates as turning to the question whether the sort of propositional falsity Protarchus has just conceded is what makes pleasures *bad*, it is better (in light of the reservations Protarchus expresses at 41b3) to read Socrates as seeking to reassure Protarchus that pleasures can themselves be false by presenting an *even stronger argument* than the one afforded by his first model, an argument that does not require the pleasures in question to inherit their content directly from the beliefs or other propositional attitudes whose contents they are supposed to share.

This is especially plausible given the way Socrates assimilates the sort of falsity involved here to the sort involved in perceptual illusion, a move for which the man/statue example has prepared us. Socrates points here to two different sources of perceptual illusion, both visual. One is being too close or too far from the target; the

---

[34] Gosling and Taylor (1982, 474) see that this is Plato's idea, but dismiss it as "incoherent" on the ground that the overestimation is itself a belief. They reject the obvious way of achieving coherence—i.e., by allowing the possibility of false propositional content without affirmation of it—on the ground that it fails to provide a *general* account of the overestimation of future pleasures. But this initial model may *not* be intended to provide a *general* account; there are other, different models to come.

other is seeing the target in the company of other objects whose presence somehow distorts the appearance of the target, making it seem larger or smaller than it really is. Socrates suggests that we are vulnerable in both ways when we view (so to speak) our own pleasures. Especially large or intense pleasures—whether present, remembered, or anticipated—can make moderate ones seem small. And pains—again present, remembered, or anticipated—can make even small pleasures seem not just larger but of greater worth than they in fact are.

Appearances of worth come to the fore in the denouement. But there, the subject comes to have the relevant *belief*: the pain of itching leads him not just to *enjoy* scratching immensely, but to *affirm* that there is no greater pleasure—indeed no greater happiness—to be had. Here, however, the point may be—as in the man/statue case—that *if* the subject *does* form the relevant belief, then any falsity in her belief will be due not to some prior belief but to some deceptive feature of the appearance itself.[35]

Consider someone in significant but not extreme physical pain. The pleasure she *now* experiences when she receives an analgesic may *seem* in her present circumstances far greater than the pleasure she recalls having experienced in the distant past when she had in fact been in far greater pain and so in fact (as she would now say if she could, per impossible, compare the pleasures side by side) experienced greater pleasure from a significantly higher dose of analgesic. But as with her past experience, so too with her present one: as the memory of *it* fades with time, it too may come to *seem* to her smaller than it now seems, so small then that she will then be willing, when suffering significant pain, to forgo an analgesic for the sake of some pleasure that *then* seems—perhaps because of some long-standing and thus especially intense desire—greater to her than it will *in fact* seem when it eventually comes to pass, at which point she may say, "I cannot believe I forewent the analgesic for *that*." And at that point the remembered pleasure of receiving the analgesic may suddenly seem to her far greater than it did at the time when she chose to forgo the analgesic for the sake of the alternative pleasure (which suddenly seems to her smaller in retrospect than it did in prospect).

My example is designed to highlight the absence of any need for propositional falsity at the base-level, which is important if Socrates aims to reassure Protarchus that a pleasure can be false in a way that cannot be explained by appeal to the idea that it shares

---

[35] The point must be made with care. There is no doubt that in Aristotle's example of the subject to whom the diameter of the moon appears to be a foot in length, the subject's beliefs (about for example feet, their sizes, the size of the earth etc.) contribute to the appearance, which is in this respect theory-laden. But it does not follow that the appearance derives its content from a false belief whose content it *shares*. The point is that there is a kind of falsity in the appearance that is not *simply* the effect of—and so not to be explained *simply* by appeal to—the subject's prior beliefs.

its propositional content with some false belief. In this case, the base-level pleasures and pains do not themselves have propositional content: they are mere sensations that may however give rise to appearances that do have such content—for example, appearances of being larger or smaller than other sensations to which they are compared. The subject *need not* endorse these appearances; but she *may* do so, in which case she may (as Protarchus readily agrees) come to have false beliefs. Protarchus' ready agreement is significant. It suggests that he thinks there are some facts at least partly independent of how things seem to a subject at a particular time about the psychological states the subject experiences at that time. In other words, he allows at least some respects in which self-ascriptions of pleasure in the present tense *are* corrigible: I may for example be mistaken about the *size* of my present pleasure, especially its *relative* size.[36]

Any hedonist who thinks (like Protarchus) that there are facts about the respective sizes of her present (or past) pleasures and pains—facts at least partly independent of how things now seem (or then seemed) to her—may be cautious about appearances of pleasure and pain. She may say to herself things like "The pleasure to be had from this here analgesic certainly *seems* (from this vantage point) great: but will it *really* be so great? Let me consider it from a different point of view." This is how the *Protagoras*-Socrates envisages the reflective hedonist coming to prefer the art of measurement to the power of appearance and to regard as our salvation any art that would allow her to measure past, present, and future pleasures (*Protagoras* 356–7). And the *Philebus*-Socrates too compares the visual distortions effected by spatial distance to the hedonic distortions effected by temporal distance.

The comparison is especially clear in his transition to the third model. After reminding Protarchus that the falsity in the first model seemed to stem from false beliefs, Socrates says explicitly that it is now the other way round:

> SOC: Now [the condition of falsity] applies to *pleasures and pains themselves*; it is because they are alternately looked at from close up or far away, or simultaneously put side by side, that the pleasures seem greater compared to pain and more intensive, and pains seem, on the contrary, moderate in comparison with such pleasures....But if you take that portion of them by which they appear greater or smaller than they really are, and cut it off from each of them *as a mere appearance and without real being*, you will neither admit that this appearance is right nor dare say that anything connected with this portion of pleasure or pain is right and true. (42b2–c3)

---

[36] This falls short of allowing corrigibility about the *nature* of my present experience: Protarchus may still insist that I cannot be mistaken in taking it to be *pleasure* that I now feel. I read the third model as addressing this.

Socrates then turns to the third model, promising to reveal pleasures and pains "even falser" than those just discussed.

7. THE THIRD MODEL: MERELY APPARENT PLEASURES? (42C–44B)

We can make good sense of the idea that the pleasures of the third model are "even falser" than those of the second by taking the *whole* pleasure—and not simply *some portion* of it—to be illusory. And the restorative conception, to which Socrates explicitly points in introducing this model, seems to require this, at least as far as body-involving pleasures are concerned. A subject who is in a neutral state, undergoing neither any departure from nor any return to her harmonious nutritive state, might picture herself, ravished with hunger, enjoying a fine meal. And she might do so in any tense: she may seem to herself (truly or falsely) to be *remembering* some such experience; she may *anticipate* (truly or falsely) enjoying some such experience in the future, and even take herself (truly or falsely) to be enjoying some such experience at present.[37] I may, for example, hallucinate that I am enjoying a cold beer after a round of summer tennis when I am in fact lying in my straitjacket, properly hydrated and mineralized, in the climate-controlled wing of my local psych ward. But anyone committed to the restorative account of such pleasures must deny that I am experiencing any *such* pleasure. So this model seems (pace Frede) to entail the corrigibility of sincere self-ascriptions of pleasure *even in the present tense*.

It is true that I will in the case just described be enjoying *the present appearance* of now enjoying such a pleasure, which is analogous both to enjoying *the memory* (or apparent memory) of having enjoyed some such pleasure in the past and to enjoying *anticipating* (whether correctly or not) enjoying some such pleasure in the future. And there will be *some* genuine pleasure in each of these cases. But it would be a mistake to take the presence of *this* pleasure as showing that the third model is, after all, committed to the incorrigibility of present-tense self-ascriptions of pleasure. The incorrigibility claim is a claim about *particular* pleasures: if I take some *particular* experience of mine to be pleasant, the claim is that *that* experience is pleasant. And the possibility of mistaking a neutral state for a pleasant one conflicts with this *even if* we allow that a subject who mistakes the neutral state for a pleasant one thereby experiences pleasure

---

[37] Plato presumably chose to illustrate this model by appeal to anticipatory pleasures because they are *more often false* than their analogues: false memories are presumably less common than false anticipations but more common than the present-tense analogues (which would seem to involve something like especially vivid daydreaming or outright hallucination). Still, an adequate interpretation *must* accommodate these analogues.

of the *second* form, and so really has *that* pleasure, no matter how ill-founded *it* may be. In other words, the incorrigibility claim is not adequately provided for by saying that the subject in question, in falsely taking herself to experience a pleasure of the *first* form, thereby secures for herself a pleasure of the *second*. For this clearly involves a *mistake* that could in principle be *corrected*, however disinclined the subject may be to have that happen.

So there *are* genuine pleasures here, but these are purely psychic and have *other* pleasures (whether real or merely apparent) as their ostensible objects. We may thus be back to something like an Old School version of the first model. In cases where a merely apparent body-involving pleasure is mistaken for a genuine one, any psychic pleasure that thereby comes about may be described as false in the sense that *its* propositional content is false because there are in such cases *no base-level pleasures* available to qualify as false. But the hedonist may well take such psychic pleasures, in spite of their falsity, to increase her hedonic yield, in which case this model fails to provide the sort of example Socrates seeks of a *genuine* pleasure his hedonist interlocutor *might* be prepared to concede she is better off without.

This may explain the ensuing discussion of mixed pleasures. To the extent that Protarchus continues to harbor reservations about the first model and the third model fails to provide the requisite example, the burden of the argument falls so far on the second. But pleasures that appear larger (or smaller) than they really are, while they may give rise to false beliefs, are not clearly false in a way that renders *them* bad simply as such. A hedonist might even think that the larger they seem, the better, since the larger they seem, the larger the higher-order pleasures to which they give rise. Still, the possibility of such pleasures may worry a hedonist who fears that such pleasures will give rise to false beliefs that might lead her to choose smaller base-level pleasures where there are larger ones to be had. But such pleasures are not *themselves* counterexamples to the claim that pleasure is *the good*. Similarly, the merely apparent pleasures of the third model may worry a hedonist who fears that she might settle for faux pleasures in lieu of genuine ones; but neither do they provide the sort of example Socrates needs. So the discussion of mixed pleasures is crucial.

8. "MIXED" PLEASURES (44B–50C): IMPURITY AS A *FORM*—OR SIMPLY A *CAUSE*—OF FALSITY?

Since Socrates does not explicitly call mixed pleasures "false," it is perhaps best to see the impurity here not as *constituting* falsity but as *giving rise to* it—specifically to the sort of falsity constituted (as in the second and third models) by a misleading appearance, which may (but need not) give rise to a false belief. Here, however, the appearance that threatens to give rise to false belief seems to be not of some pleasure's existence or (relative) magnitude, but rather of its *worth*.

In the second model, pleasures and pains *appear* to their subjects larger or smaller than they *really* are both because they are viewed alongside one another (pains, for example, making pleasures appear larger than they really are) and because of variations in the temporal distance from which they are viewed (distant pains, for example, appearing smaller than they will appear when actually present). Here too we find something similar: pleasures that appear not just larger but *of greater worth* than they really are because they are accompanied by pains that make them especially intense, their greater intensity endowing them with an appearance of greater worth. More importantly, the pains in question are not simply part of the scenery: they are conditions for the very existence of the relevant pleasures. So the subject cannot (as in the second model) seek to correct the appearances by changing her point of view and experiencing the pleasure in different company or further away (so to speak) from the pain in question: in this case the pain must be *present* if the subject is to experience the relevant sort of pleasure. Scratching is paradigmatic: there would be no pleasure in scratching if there were no itch to begin with, and the intensity of the pleasure is roughly commensurate with the intensity of the itch alleviated by the scratching, which would otherwise be hedonically neutral (or even, perhaps, painful).

We might thus distinguish the point of the second model from the present point by taking the point of the second to be that pleasures in general *admit of* various forms of illusion (about, for example, their respective sizes) while taking the present point to be that mixed pleasures in particular *lend themselves* to such forms of illusion. But there seems also to be a shift in the *nature* of the illusion. In the second model, Socrates focuses on illusions of *size*; here he seems to focus on illusions of *value*. For his description of the leaping madman suggests that the mistake is not (or not simply) that the itch makes the pleasure of scratching *seem larger* than it really is. The more serious problem is that the itch makes the pleasure of scratching *seem good* to its subject in ways it is not: the subject calls such pleasures "greatest and counts as most *eudaimôn* of all creatures the man who lives always enjoying them to greatest extent possible" (47b6–7).

I think it is meant to be clear from outside—both to Socrates' interlocutor and to Plato's readers—that this is *foolish*. Absent the pain of the itch, the subject would not be tempted to identify his good with the pleasure of scratching. The itch distorts the subject's "vision," leading him to see *as good*—indeed his *highest* good—something whose candidacy for the highest good he would in other, epistemically more favorable circumstances dismiss as ridiculous. Absent any itch, he would not seek one out so as to put himself in a position to achieve such a good, perhaps at the expense of other pleasures to whose attractions he might (absent any itch) be more alive—or so, I think, it is supposed to seem to us *from the outside*. But the fact that his "vision" is thus distorted is something the subject is not himself in a position to see, at least not *while* he suffers the itch.

Here again the point is about foolishness, not mere ignorance. The subject of mere ignorance can be painfully aware of her ignorance and seek to correct it; but the fool seems to himself to be wise about the very matters with respect to which he is ignorant. Such apparent wisdom—which Socrates calls "*doxosophia*"—is one of the three failures of self-knowledge discussed in the wake of the leaping madman example. It is the one Socrates describes as "ridiculous"—at least when it appears in those who are weak and unable to take revenge when they are being laughed at.[38]

These references to *illusions of wisdom, wealth*, and *beauty* extend the sequence inaugurated, in the first model, with the man/statue example. The sequence continues with *illusions of size* (in the second) and *illusions of pleasure* (in the third). So it is natural, insofar as wisdom, wealth, and beauty are supposed to be *goods*, to read the fourth stage as focused on the possibility of mistaking a merely apparent *good* for a genuine *good*. Perhaps the admittedly genuine pleasure of scratching is a merely apparent good, something that, because of the company it necessarily keeps, appears to its subject good although it is not. Or perhaps it is a merely remedial (or conditional) good that is mistaken for a non-remedial (or non-conditional) one. Whatever the exact nature of the mistake—and the text may well underdetermine this—we seem at last to have the sort of example Socrates needs if he is to defeat the hedonist on her own turf: a genuine pleasure the hedonist can perhaps be brought to see—at least from *some* point of view—she is better off without.

9. THE FIRST MODEL REVISITED: MISTAKING APPARENT *GOODS* FOR GENUINE *GOODS*

It should now be clear that the first model can be read as introducing a mistake like that of mistaking a statue of a man for a genuine man. Suppose that some pleasure—whether past, present, or future—presents the activity in which it is taken as good in ways the activity is not. In such cases, the *presentation* involved in the pleasure will not be what *it* appears to be—namely the presentation (speaking now *de re*) of a *genuine good*. But this presentation may from its subject's present point of view be indistinguishable from presentations of genuine goods in much the same way that false beliefs

---

[38] Another allusion to the *Gorgias*, specifically to Callicles' tirade against philosophy at 484cff. See also *Philebus* 58a7–b3, which refers not just to Gorgias himself but to a view of his featured at *Gorgias* 452e.

are from their subject's present point of view indistinguishable from true beliefs. For just as false beliefs are by their very nature presentations of their contents *as true*, so too false pleasures of the relevant kind are by their very nature presentations of their contents *as good*.

If so, the false pleasures of the first model may be ridiculous imitations of true ones not in the sense that they appear to be *pleasures* although they are not, but in the sense that they present as good activities that are *not* in fact good, with the result that these pleasures cannot be distinguished "from the inside" from pleasures that present as good activities that *are* in fact good. This explains how we can be fooled by false pleasures into settling for merely apparent goods when there are genuine goods to be had or settling for lesser goods when there are greater ones to be had. And it seems plausible to suppose that the scratching subject whose present pleasure is so intense that he would settle to scratch like that for the rest of his life makes some such mistake.

This reading makes good sense both of the facticity argument's assimilation of false pleasure to false belief and of the way the statue/man example is used to introduce the first model. It also makes good sense of this model as part of the overall sequence. The second and third models clearly involve something like perceptual illusion: pleasures appearing to their subjects larger or smaller than they really are, and non-pleasures appearing to their subjects to be pleasures. For a hedonist interlocutor, each will of course involve an illusion of *goodness*, pleasures appearing larger—*and so better*—than they really are; and non-pleasures appearing as pleasures—and *so as goods* –when they are not. The same goes, I think, for mixed pleasures: an inferior pleasure may—thanks to the company it necessarily keeps—appear to be good in ways it is not. This suggests that the first model too may be supposed to involve illusions: cases where pleasures masquerade as *presentations of goodness* when they in fact present no such thing.

This comes close to the idea Aristotle expresses in *Nicomachean Ethics* 6.2, where he says that the good is in the practical sphere what the true is in the theoretical sphere, an idea towards which I take the *Philebus* to be working. This is why what we find in the first model is not simply an Old School view that happens to involve false *beliefs* about what is *good*, but something closer to the sort of New School view Evans ascribes to Lovibond: the point is that appearances can, even absent belief in their contents, play the explanatory role—and sometimes also what appears "from the inside" to be the justificatory role—of beliefs. And when the appearances are false, the genuine pleasures they help to constitute are themselves false in the way that hopes and fears can be. Someone who is afraid of things that are not in fact bad can be genuinely afraid: it is just that her fears are not warranted by their objects; and someone who hopes for things that are not in fact good, can genuinely hope; its just that her hopes are not warranted by their objects. And so it is with subjects who enjoy apparent goods that are not in fact good.

Here, however, we should note that the view in question is not well captured by Evans' characterization of New School views as those that take the falsity of a pleasure to consist in the failure of its object to be good. For there is an important feature of Lovibond's view that Evans fails to capture. In what appears to be her formulation of the central issue, Lovibond asks:

> Does the inadequacy of [a pleasure's] cognitive base "infect" a pleasure in respect of its essence (cf. Plato, *Phlb.* 42a7–9), causing it to be *something less than a genuine pleasure* (*Phlb.* 40c1–6....)? Or is there a *"first-person privilege"* here such that no one can qualify my sincere self-ascription of pleasure at a particular moment—not even, perhaps, myself at a later moment?[39]

And Lovibond (who is Evans' primary example of a New School reader) goes on to speak of "the idea of "false pleasure" (in the Platonic sense of *specious* pleasure)" (p. 226, her italics). So she sees the issue as at least in part one about the corrigibility (or lack thereof) of first-person present-tense ascriptions of *pleasure*. But such corrigibility, to the extent that it is associated with the *speciousness* of a pleasure, threatens to deprive Socrates of the sort of example he seeks—namely, a *genuine* pleasure the hedonist *himself* will think he is better off without.

Note, however, that the quotation from Lovibond suggests two ways a New School view might go, each of which is problematic in a way such that together they present would-be New School readers with a dilemma. If the falsity of the anticipated pleasures renders them "specious," the resulting view will be close to Williams' Old School view: there will be no genuine *anticipated* pleasures to count as false and any *anticipatory* pleasure taken therein will be false in the propositional sense. This is the first horn, on which the main advantage of the New School view is lost; it will no longer afford a neat explanation of Socrates' puzzling claim that bad agents are prone to experiences false pleasures in a way good agents are not.

The alternative is to allow that the anticipated pleasures are genuine while taking their falsity to consist in the failure of their objects to *warrant* the pleasure taken therein, and then to explain the falsity of *anticipatory* pleasures by appeal to the falsity of the *anticipated* pleasures in which they are taken. But this way of developing the New School view is questionable insofar as it requires the anticipated pleasure either to have its *own* propositionally false content or to depend on some *belief* whose propositional

---

[39] Lovibond (1989–90) 214–15.

content is false. For either way, Socrates' appeal to anticipatory pleasure risks losing its dialectical grip. This is the second horn (itself disjunctive): *either* the anticipatory pleasure depends on some belief to which the alleged falsity of the pleasure can then be assigned *or* the anticipatory pleasure is supposed to derive its falsity from the very sort of falsity whose possibility Protarchus questions—that is, the *propositional* falsity of the *anticipated* pleasure. And the latter is no less a non-starter than the former. For in the latter case, it is not clear how the appeal to *anticipatory* pleasures is supposed to remove Protarchus' original doubts about the possibility of a pleasure that is false in the propositional sense. It is one thing to argue that anticipatory pleasures (and their analogues) can be false in the propositional sense because their ostensible objects fail to exist (which takes us back to the first horn). But the idea that anticipatory pleasures (and their analogues) can be false in the propositional sense because anticipated pleasures and their analogues can be false in this sense is, in this dialectic, a non-starter.

Lovibond seems to be aware of this dilemma. For she seeks to avoid the first horn by explicitly straddling the line between affirming and denying the corrigibility of present-tense self-ascriptions of pleasure, saying (for example) that "even by the exacting standards of hindsight, a pleasure-episode which we [as its subjects] now condemn as specious *cannot be dismissed as nothing*" (228, my italics). And she seeks to avoid the second horn by insisting that the subject consider matters not from a third-person, theoretical point of view but rather "from the inside": she would require Protarchus to ask about his *own* apparent pleasures—past, present, and future—whether they are *really* pleasures by asking whether their objects are *good* in ways presupposed by the pleasures that he seems to himself to take in them. And though we might be tempted to assimilate this to Old School views in which anticipatory pleasures and their analogues are false because the relevant anticipated pleasures and their analogues fail to exist, this would be a mistake: Lovibond's view differs from Old School views in allowing the existence of an *apparent pleasure* that "cannot be dismissed as nothing." It also differs, given its emphasis on the corrigibility of self-ascriptions of pleasure made "from the inside," from New School views as characterized by Evans.

Lovibond's view might thus be called "Reform School." And this seems apt. For she emphasizes the developmental role played by pressing a certain evaluative response "on the learner, *as her own response*, in the teeth of the behavioral evidence [viz. that the learner seems to herself to be responding differently]." Such pressure is aimed "at making actual what is at present only ideal, namely, the spontaneous occurrence in the learner of what we consider to be the appropriate response" (p. 219). But this requires the learner to engage in some *de dicto* (and not simply *de re*) pursuit of her own good.[40]

---

[40] There is nothing like this in Harte, who relies on the biological basis afforded by the "restorative" model (which is not obviously transferable to purely psychic pleasures) and insists (in correspondence) that it is only *de re* that pleasures can be said to track their subject's good.

And this is just what the illustrated book's restriction to "our souls" (38b2) would lead us to expect—namely, that the first model is about a form of hedonic falsity associated with a subject's *self-conscious* pursuit of the good (considered as such).

10. THE PUZZLING CLAIM REVISITED (40B)

Let us now revisit the puzzling claim from which New School readings seem to derive their support. One way to understand this would be to say that the sorts of objects and activities that wicked subjects are disposed to picture themselves enjoying—for example, gold and the sorts of "pleasures" (in the sense of pleasant activities) afforded by it—are not in fact good. So any apparent experience of pleasure taken in such things (whether these things are past, present, or future) will be false in the sense that it fails to be warranted by that in which it is taken and the subject can perhaps be brought to question (in something like the way Lovibond suggests) whether what he experiences is *really pleasure*. But this requires us to deny that good agents who picture themselves enjoying such things experience in so doing the sort of true pleasures Socrates seems to suggest they experience. There is however a more interesting and genuinely Socratic way to understand this claim. We need simply invoke an idea he expresses in the *Euthydemus, Meno*, and perhaps elsewhere—that is, the idea that so-called goods such as wealth and health are good *only for virtuous agents*.[41]

If the *Philebus*-Socrates is assuming this "conditionality thesis," then he can allow (with common sense) that vicious subjects who picture themselves in the future getting lots of gold and many consequent pleasures are no less likely to get these things than virtuous agents are likely to get what they picture themselves getting in the future; and he can allow that vicious subjects are no less likely than virtuous agents, when the time comes, to seem to themselves to be enjoying what they expected to enjoy and to be doing so in more or less the ways they expected to enjoy them. But the vicious agent's base-level experience will be false in a way the virtuous agent's experience is not. For given the conditionality thesis, gold and other such things will be good for virtuous agents in the way presupposed by these agents' apparent enjoyment of them but not for vicious agents in the way presupposed by *their* apparent enjoyment of them. The vicious agents' enjoyment of such things will involve illusions of value in a way in which the virtuous agents' enjoyment of them does not: so the vicious agent's anticipated pleasures will be false either in the propositional sense or in the sense that they are merely apparent pleasures (a possibility provided for if we read the third model in the way I suggest). In the latter case, the vicious agent's so-called enjoyment of these

---

[41] For more on this, see Whiting (1996).

things may involve the sort of unwitting "misery" that Socrates ascribes to Archelaus at *Gorgias* 471ff. And we will have something close to Lovibond's Reform School view. But as in real-life reform schools, the errors in play may be such that their subjects cannot be brought to recognize them as such without undergoing a radical shift in point of view.

The suggestion that Socrates operates here with the conditionality thesis up his sleeve is of course speculative. But it is not easily ruled out by either of two objections likely to be raised against it. The first is that whatever Socrates might think, we cannot explain Protarchus' ready agreement with the puzzling claim by supposing that *he* accepts this idiosyncratic thesis. But this objection is less devastating than it might first seem and not just because Socrates *often* puts forward claims that he himself understands in one sense but surely expects his interlocutor to understand in another: see *Apology* 30b2–3, where the conditionality thesis itself may be in play. If there is any truth in my story, the *Philebus* may provide another case where Socrates utters what might be called a "generic truth" that he understands in one way but allows his interlocutor to accept in the interlocutor's preferred terms.

This strategy of argument helps also with the second objection—namely, that seeing the conditionality thesis behind the puzzling claim fails to do justice to the role allegedly played by the gods. For the gods are supposed to make it the case that the pleasures painted in the souls of good agents tend to be true while the pleasures painted in the souls of bad agents tend to be false, but the appeal to the conditionality thesis leaves the gods out of the loop.

Obviously any assertion Socrates makes about the gods is slippery and liable to be understood both by Socrates' interlocutors and by your average contemporary-of-Plato reader in ways different from those in which Socrates himself may be supposed to understand it. But there is—even apart from this—good reason to suppose that the exact mechanisms involved in the divine dispensation of false pleasures are left open. For gods, being gods, can presumably effect the differential distribution of false pleasures in any number of ways. And making the hopes or expectations of good agents come true while those of bad agents prove false by making sure that good agents in fact get gold when they hope or expect to (or enjoy it in the ways they hope or expect to) while making sure bad agents fail to get gold when they hope or expect to (or at least fail to enjoy it in the ways they hope or expect to) is only one among other possible ways, one that might involve a laborious form of micromanaging. If gods are (as the *Euthyphro*-Socrates seems to think) by nature good, it would surely be more efficient for them to ordain matters so that wealth and other so-called goods are genuinely good only for virtuous agents, however good such things might *seem* to vicious ones. Call this divine justice or a cruel joke (or both): we can at least imagine the *Gorgias*-Socrates supposing divine rewards and punishments to be implemented in this way.

11. CONCLUSION

I have argued that the main point of the *Philebus*'s substitution of the appeals to falsity and foolishness for the *Gorgias*'s appeal to shamefulness is twofold: to relieve *Socrates* of any need to appeal to contested values and to allow his interlocutors and readers to run his arguments with their *own* values (whatever, if any, they happen to be). Falsity and foolishness are *topic-neutral* in a way shamefulness is not. They are, more importantly, *ethically neutral*: even a knave might worry about being a fool. So even if Protarchus' bias against foolishness rests to some extent on considerations that are (whether consciously or not) non-hedonic, it is not open to the sort of tarring with the brush of mere conventionalism to which Callicles subjected Socrates' talk of shame.

The appeals to falsity and foolishness are thus of *general* strategic value. They allow any given interlocutor or reader to plug his or her own values into Socrates' argument and to reflect on the dangers of falsity or foolishness with respect to *whatever* it is that he or she happens to value, *including pleasure itself*. A hedonist would have reason to worry if she thought it possible to overestimate the size or value of some pleasures, or worse yet to mistake a non-pleasure for a pleasure. So it is no surprise that Socrates appeals, in seeking to defeat the hedonist on her own turf, to such possibilities. He seeks to induce in Protarchus and other hedonists the worry that misleading appearances will lead them to act in ways such that their yield of base-level pleasures is smaller—or perhaps of lesser worth—than it would otherwise be. But even if, in acting in such ways, the hedonist's *higher-order* pleasures prove indistinguishable from her point of view from those she would have had if her base-level pleasures really were as large or as significant as they seemed to her to be, she might still be worse off *by her own theoretical lights* than she would have been if these base-level pleasures really were that large or that significant. For had these appearances not misled her, she might have had the same degree of higher-order pleasure but even more base-level pleasure, and so (by the criteria set down at 20d) a more complete—and more choiceworthy—overall package. But she herself would be in no position to recognize this, at least not "from the inside."

What the hedonist needs are the sort of distancing techniques on display in the *Philebus* itself. Each of Socrates' models invites the interlocutor—and thereby the reader—to imagine herself in a situation that involves a kind of foolishness on her part such that she could not, when she is in the relevant situation, see for what it is: this is something she can appreciate only from some other point of view, either

her own point of view at some other time or the point of view of someone else. The reader is first asked (at least indirectly) to imagine herself in the future in a way such that what happens later might reveal her present pleasures to be *foolish*. The reader is then asked (again indirectly) to imagine herself in situations where she is subject to the distorting effects of something analogous to perceptual illusion and is thereby *fooled* into some attitude (whether doxastic or not) she would not otherwise adopt. There are two versions of this mistake: one in which she is fooled into thinking her base-level pleasure larger than it really is and one in which she is fooled into taking a neutral state to be a state of pleasure. Finally, she is asked (even if only implicitly) to imagine herself in the shoes of someone else, someone whose current foolishness *she* can see from the outside even though the imagined subject cannot himself see it. This may—if she is sufficiently reflective—lead her to worry that the joke may be on *her*: that she too may unwittingly display the faults at which she laughs when she sees them in others. In each of these cases, the reader is supposed to imagine the subject in question experiencing pleasure which *she now* (the reader, that is) is in a position to recognize as in some sense foolish even though the *imagined subject*—whether it is another person or simply the reader herself at a different time or in a different situation—cannot.

This may in fact be the point of having Philebus sit by, so manifestly content with his *own* condition, while Socrates demonstrates to *others* what is wrong with it. It may even be why the dialogue is named for a character who scarcely speaks. It may be called after Philebus because the joke is on him: he is the one who is shown to be a fool. The dangers of foolishness are of course no less pressing for present-day philosophers than they were for Plato's contemporaries. So if more historical exegesis can preserve for us insights into such dangers—or can remind us of ways in which appeal to such dangers can advance ethical argument—then more power to historical (but not therefore non-philosophical) exegesis.

Acknowledgments

Work on this paper was generously supported by SSHRC and I have benefited from discussing versions of it with audiences at Stanford, Harvard, Oxford, Chicago, and Boston University. I am also grateful to Brad Inwood for his constant support; to Mitzi Lee for several rounds of very helpful comments; and to Verity Harte, not just for extended conversation and the opportunity to discuss the penultimate version with her seminar at Yale, but for detailed written comments (to which note 29 does not begin to do justice). But I am most grateful to Gisela herself, for all I have learned from her since 1985, when I had the good fortune to attend her first seminar at Harvard, on Hellenistic ethics.

Works Cited

Boyle, M. and Lavin, D. (2010) "Goodness and Desire" in Tenenbaum (2010).
Charles, D. (2006) "Aristotle's Desire" in Hirnoven, Holpainen, and Tuominen (eds), *Mind and Modality: Studies in the History of Philosophy in Honour of Simo Knuuttila* (Leiden: Brill).
Cooper, J. and Hutchinson, D. (1997) *Plato: Complete Works* (Indianapolis: Hackett).
Delcomminette, S. (2006) *Le Philèbe de Platon: Introduction à l'agathologie platonicienne* (Leiden: Brill).
Evans, M. (2008) "Plato on the Possibility of Hedonic Mistakes," *Oxford Studies in Ancient Philosophy* **35**: 89–124.
Fletcher, E. (2012) *Plato on Pleasure, Intelligence and the Human Good: An Interpretation of the Philebus* (University of Toronto dissertation).
Frede, D. (1985) "Rumpelstiltskin's Pleasures: True and False Pleasures in Plato's *Philebus*," *Phronesis* **30**: 151–80.
Frede, D. (1992) "Disintegration and Restoration: Pleasure and Pain in Plato's *Philebus*" in Kraut ed., *The Cambridge Companion to Plato* (New York: Cambridge).
Frede, D. (1993) *Plato: Philebus* (Indianapolis: Hackett).
Frede, D. (1997) *Platon Werke: Übersetzung und Kommentar (Band III 2) Philebos* (Göttingen: Vandenhoeck & Ruprecht).
Frede, D. (2000) "The Hedonist's Conversion: The Role of Socrates in the *Philebus*" in Gill and McCabe eds., *Form and Argument in Late Plato* (Oxford: Clarendon Press) 225–60.
Gosling, J. (1975) *Plato: Philebus* (New York: Oxford).
Gosling, J. and Taylor, C.C.W. (1982) *The Greeks on Pleasure* (New York: Oxford).
Harte, V. (2004) "The *Philebus* on Pleasure: The Good, the Bad and the False," *Proceedings of the Aristotelian Society* **104**: 111–28.
Lorenz, H. (2006) *The Brute Within: Appetitive Desire in Plato and Aristotle* (New York: Oxford).
Lovibond, S. (1989–90) "True and False Pleasures," *Proceedings of the Aristotelian Society* **90**: 213–30.
Mooradian, N. (1996) "Converting Protarchus: Relativism and False Pleasures of Anticipation in Plato's *Philebus*," *Ancient Philosophy* **16**: 93–112.
Moss, J. (2010) "Aristotle's Non-Trivial, Non-Insane View that Everyone Always Desires Things under the Guise of the Good" in Tenenbaum (2010).
Pradeau, J.-F. (2002) *Philèbe* (Paris: Flammarion).
Striker, G. (1983) "The Role of Oikeiôsis in Stoic Ethics," *Oxford Studies in Ancient Philosophy* **1**: 145–67; reprinted in Striker (1996).
Striker, G. (1991) "Following Nature: A Study in Stoic Ethics," *Oxford Studies in Ancient Philosophy* **9**: 1–73; reprinted in Striker (1996).
Striker, G. (1993) "Epicurean Hedonism" in Brunschwig and Nussbaum (eds) *Passions and Perceptions* (New York: Cambridge): 3–17; reprinted in Striker (1996).
Striker, G. (1996) *Essays on Hellenistic Epistemology and Ethics* (New York: Cambridge).
Taylor, A. E. (1956) *Plato: Philebus and Epinomis* (London: Thomas Nelson and Sons).
Tenenbaum, S. (ed). (2010) *Desire, Practical Reason, and the Good* (Oxford: Oxford University Press).
Thein, K. (2000) "Entre *anoia* et *agnoia*. La nature humaine et la comédie dans les dialogues de Platon" in M.L. DesClos ed., *Le rire des Grecs. Anthropologie du rire en Grèce ancienne* (Grenoble: Jérôme Millon) 169–180.

Thein, K. (unpublished) "Foolishness, Pleasure and Imagination in Plato's *Philebus* and Other Dialogues."

Velleman, D. (1992) "The Guise of the Good," *Nous* **26**: 3–26; reprinted in D. Velleman *The Possibility of Practical Reason* (Oxford: 2000).

Whiting, J. (1996) "Self-Love and Authoritative Virtue: Prolegomenon to a Kantian Reading of *Eudemian Ethics* 8.3" in Engstrom and Whiting (eds). *Aristotle, Kant and the Stoics: Rethinking Happiness and Duty* (New York: Cambridge).

Whiting, J. (2002) "Locomotive Soul," *Oxford Studies in Ancient Philosophy* **22**: 141–200.

Whiting, J. (2008) "The Lockeanism of Aristotle," *Antiquorum Philosophia* **2**: 101–36.

Whiting, J. (2012) "Psychic Contingency in Plato's *Republic*," in Barney, Brennan, and Brittain (eds.) *Plato and the Divided Self* (New York: Cambridge).

Williams, B. (1959) "Pleasure and Belief," *Proceedings of the Aristotelian Society*, supplement **33**: 52–72; reprinted in B. Williams *Philosophy as a Humanistic Discipline* (Princeton: Princeton University Press, 2006).

3

DID PLATO'S COSMOS LITERALLY BEGIN?*

Sarah Broadie

1. IN THE BEGINNING?

In several places in the *Timaeus-Critias* Timaeus clearly speaks as if the Demiurge made this cosmos "once upon a time."[1] The phrase may not be quite right, since chronological—that is, measurable—time (*chronos*) is itself a designed feature of the organized world. *Chronos* was brought into being along with the visible system of circulating celestial bodies (*Timaeus* 37a6–39e4). Even so, the account of cosmopoiesis displays a succession of constructive phases starting with the Demiurge's "taking over" the pre-cosmic materials to use in fashioning the cosmos (30a3–6; 68e1–4). And in more than one place Timaeus says simply that the cosmos will come to be or has come to be, as if its not being and its being are related as before and after (34a8–9; *Critias* 106a3–4).[2] The picture, then, is of a proto-historical inauguration.

The debate, almost as old as the *Timaeus* itself, on whether Plato means this "literally" has been governed by its connection with the question of the sempiternity of the world (i.e., its everlastingness in both temporal directions).[3] The view that the cosmos is sempiternal had many adherents from the early Academy onwards, and the

---

* I am delighted to have this opportunity of marking my appreciation of Gisela Striker's always seminal and incisive contributions to our discipline.

[1] This chapter is based on material drawn from Broadie 2012 and Broadie 2010. My discussion here of the "literalism" of the beginning does not rely on passages from any Platonic dialogue besides the *Timaeus*.

[2] At *Critias* 106a1–b7 Timaeus rounds off his cosmological speech. Clay in Cooper, 1997, 1293, mistranslates the crucial lines a3–4 as: "I offer my prayer to that god [i.e. the cosmos] who had existed long before in reality, but who has now been created in my words"; likewise Apelt 1919, 189 and H. D. P. Lee 1971, 129. The Greek says: "I offer my prayer to the god who has come into being (a) long ago in reality and (b) just now in my words." *tô(i)....theô(i) gegonoti* is equally qualified by *prin men palai pot' ergô(i)* and by *nun de logois arti*.

[3] "Sempiternalism" here will refer not to the view that nature has always existed and will always exist in one or another shape or form, but to the view that the world in its present form is everlasting in both temporal directions. For a survey of the exegetical debate in antiquity and discussion

Platonists among them—Xenocrates is named in this connection—reconciled their commitments by supposing that the *Timaeus* account is couched as a proto-historical narrative because the author thought it was easier to teach cosmology that way (*didaskalias charin*; Aristotle, *On the Heaven* I. 10, 280a1).[4] This sort of interpretation implies that the proto-historicity is nothing but a presentational device, so that recasting the work in sempiternalist form should leave all its serious content unaffected.

Postulating a beginning opens the gate to more than one charge of arbitrariness, and arbitrariness about a fundamental fact of the cosmos seems at odds with the Timaean principle that the cosmos is as perfect as possible (*Timaeus* 28c2-29a6; cf. 92a4-9). There is the well-known objection: if God brought order to matter when previously it was disordered, why did God not do this before?[5] There is also the fact that the Timaean story implies that for some finite number n the finished cosmos is currently n years old. Since the value of n must be some number rather than another, even if we cannot know which, the supposed fact of the matter on any given number of years belongs among things that are arbitrary and unbeautiful. Why n rather than n plus 1 or n minus 10,000?[6] Further: the Timaean time-system is supposed to be the crowning glory of the immortal, age-free, divine cosmos, rendering its life as like as possible to the true eternity of Now without Was and Will be (37c6-d7); but can that make sense if time's actual effect is to maintain the cosmos at an ever-changing interval from its birthday?[7] Why would any rationalist philosopher seriously take on such a commitment unless under pressure, as Plato was not, from Judeo-Christian scriptural

---

of the textual evidence in the *Timaeus-Critias*, with references to modern scholarship, see Sorabji 1983, 268-76; also Sedley 2007, 98-107. For a useful discussion see Gregory 2007, 147-51.

[4] On the attribution to Xenocrates, see Vlastos 1939, in Allen 1965, 383, n.1. Aristotle does not state that these Platonists were interpreting the *Timaeus* (as distinct from some separate account of their own), but scholars seem to be united in inferring a reference to that work. The evidence is discussed by Cherniss 1944, 421-3 and Baltes 1976-8, vol. 1, 18-22.

[5] The seed of this argument is in Parmenides B8, 8-10; cf. Aristotle, *On the Heaven* I, 283a11. As Tarán 1971, 379, and Sedley 2007, 105; 144-6, point out, in antiquity this type of objection survived the riposte that until God ordered matter, there was no "before" in terms of chronological or measurable time. But in fact this objection casts doubt not on the perfection of the cosmos so much as on the divine status of its maker, the thought being that a god is too perfect to jump into action.

[6] This difficulty arises from the assumption of a proto-historical moment when the making of the cosmos was complete. If, as in contemporary cosmology, we hold that the cosmos is still undergoing physical development (e.g. expansion) there is nothing arbitrary about calculating a beginning as many years ago as necessary for the cosmos to have reached the present stage.

[7] But this particular ever-changing interval seems to be exactly what Timaeus implies (by contrast) at 38a3-4, where he says that it does not belong to *intelligible* reality to become either older or younger than itself through time. As X lives on, it becomes older than it was at some previous time t, so that at t it was younger than it would be later; cf. *Parmenides* 151e3-152e3; 141a5-d3. But this is possible only if X at each moment has existed a finite time.

revelation? If we assume that the cosmic beginning in the *Timaeus* is not meant literally, these awkward questions disappear.

On the other hand, sempiternalist interpreters face a major question for which there is no satisfactory answer. If the proto-historicism of Timaeus's account is only a device of presentation, why doesn't Plato make Timaeus explain this? It would have been an easy thing to do. A few words to this effect could easily have been added to Timaeus's general remarks about the epistemic character and possible failings of his discourse at 29c1–d3, especially c4 ff., where he asks his interlocutors to excuse him if his *logoi* are not "completely consistent with each other and exact." Throughout the dialogues Plato, it seems to me, is in general anxious—indeed sometimes laboriously so—to explain where explanation is both necessary and possible.[8]

One might also point out that we are not in position to take it for granted that Plato could have counted on the immediate recipients of the *Timaeus* to understand its proto-historicism as a mere device of presentation. The fact that some in the early Academy did understand it in that way is not particularly strong evidence that Plato would have reckoned, when writing the work, that such an essential point could need no explanation. Aristotle, a sempiternalist who interprets the Timaean beginning literally (*On the Heaven* 280a28–31; 300b17–18) states that "everyone" (*hapantes*) up to his time of writing holds that the *ouranos* (i.e., the astronomical system or world system as it is today) had a beginning (279b12). Even if one allows for a degree of exaggeration by Aristotle here,[9] his remark indicates that the intellectual context in which the *Timaeus* was composed was one in which it would have seemed natural and unexceptionable to understand the present cosmos as having once begun.[10] Since Plato knew that context at least as well as Aristotle did, we have all the more reason to be puzzled by his failure to indicate his real view, if his real view was that there was no beginning. At that time the theory of sempiternity was the new kid on the block; so if Plato in fact endorsed it when writing the *Timaeus* one would have expected him to show this by some clear sign even if he chose to narrate the cosmology in proto-historical style.[11] Plato could easily have made Timaeus begin with words such as these: "But since it is an old tradition among the Greeks, and perhaps among all who inquire about such

---

[8] At 29b4–5 Timaeus refers to discourses, his own included, as *exêgetai* ("revealers," "expounders") of their subject matters. Expounders are surely not supposed to speak in riddles themselves. For discussion of the word *ad loc.*, see Burnyeat 2005, and Betegh 2010.

[9] At any rate Cherniss 1944, 415, does not dispute this statement of Aristotle's.

[10] Thus Aristotle goes to considerable trouble in many places to maintain the contrary view: *Physics* VIII. 1; *On the Heaven* I, 270a12–b25; I. 10–12; II. 1; *Generation and Corruption* II. 10–11; *Metaphysics* XII. 6.

[11] It is also possible that sempiternalism did not arrive on the block until after Plato had brought out the *Timaeus*.

things, to speak of this cosmos as having come to be, I too in the account I am about to give shall often fall in with this familiar way of speaking, even though doing so might seem rather childish—because it is hard for mortals through a long stretch of discourse on the one hand to express thoughts, and on the other hand to receive them, in terms which, though accurate, are strange and unaccustomed." But Plato has done nothing of the sort.[12]

It would be unreasonable for a modern scholar to argue that if we today should be swayed by this evidence against a sempiternalist reading, the same evidence ought to have stifled the sempiternalist reading of Plato's contemporary Xenocrates—which it manifestly failed to do. Xenocrates was a Platonist who evidently was convinced, by Aristotle's arguments or by other arguments, that *the truth* about this cosmos is that it is sempiternal. He therefore had a motive, and from his own point of view a good reason, to see sempiternalism in the *Timaeus*. But this is not a motive or reason that should guide the modern interpreter of Plato.[13]

I cannot help thinking that modern sempiternalist interpreters may to some extent be inspired by one or both of two things: first, the desire to put Plato in the same camp as some of the greatest and most sophisticated Platonists of antiquity, especially Plotinus and Proclus; and second, a related sense that it would have been naive and crude of Plato to be serious about the idea that the cosmos had a beginning.[14] The crucial question, however, is whether the proto-historical picture does philosophical work for Plato which cannot be done (or could not have been done by him) using a sempiternalist account. If the answer is "Yes," the proto-historicism is surely more than a presentational device. One can equally ask whether the proto-historical picture and

---

[12] Not that he is generally reticent about themes being unaccustomed; see 48d5 on the Receptacle and 53c1–2 on the particle-geometry. Aristotle is often castigated for uncharitableness because he sticks to a literal reading whereby order replaced pre-cosmic disorder, instead of understanding the disorder counterfactually as the way things would have been without the Demiurge (*On the Heaven* I. 280a1–2; 300b17–18). But the reproach is deserved only if it was unreasonable or disingenuous of Aristotle to expect Plato to have planted a clear warning that the "before and after" were not to be taken seriously, if that was the intention. If I am right, such an expectation on Aristotle's part would have been perfectly reasonable and fair.

[13] On Xenocrates and his philosophy, see Dillon 2003b, ch. 3, especially 89–136.

[14] This despite the considerable roll-call of literalist interpreters in antiquity; see Sedley 2007, 107, n. 30. Anti-literalist interpreters are also, of course, inspired by discrepancies between the surface account in the *Timaeus*, especially what it says about the creation of soul, and accounts in the *Phaedrus* and the *Laws*; cf. Cherniss, 1944, 427–30. Since I focus here only on the *Timaeus*, I shall not discuss these arguments. A satisfactory "literalist" exegesis would, in my view, be one that attributes to Plato a serious *cosmological* reason for the proto-historicism. Thus consistency with dialogues that are not primarily cosmological may not be a crucial consideration. In any case, taking the cosmic beginning non-literally leaves untouched some of the difficulties of reconciling the *Timaeus* with other dialogues; see Vlastos 1965, 414–7; Sedley 2007, 104, n. 23.

the sempiternalist one are substantially equivalent. If they are not, then either Plato is gravely conflicted or confused, as well as misleading (he means to present a sempiternalist system, but does so under the guise of a substantially different account as if there were no significant difference), or he is serious about the proto-historicism and we need to understand why.

The question about Timaean proto-historicism is often phrased as the question whether Plato meant it "literally." Just now, however, I have slipped into speaking of Plato's "seriousness" in this connection, although "serious" and "literal" are certainly not synonymous. In fact, it is not easy to find the right terms for stating the issue. Perhaps the best way to do it is by distinguishing the content of the Timaean cosmology from Plato's presentation of the content. Obviously, to insist in a general way on separating content from presentation would be a very bad rule to bring to the writings of Plato, of all philosophers. Even so, this distinction seems to me to provide a useful tool for the limited purpose of formulating the question of how to understand Timaeus's proto-historicism. It is no good putting this in terms of Plato's "seriousness," since the fact that something is solely an aspect of presentation would not undermine its seriousness: for example, even if the proto-historicism is only a didactic device, it has the serious purpose of communicating more effectively.

But "literal" too is not fully adequate. To explain why not, let me return to Aristotle. When he asserts in *On the Heaven* I. 10 that Plato in the *Timaeus* says that the cosmos had a beginning but will have no end (280a30–32), Aristotle is not primarily engaging in Plato-exegesis; he is addressing the first-order question whether the world could have a beginning but no end. He does not ask himself *why* Plato has Timaeus present the cosmos in this way. Aristotle is only interested in (a) whether this represents Plato's actual view in the *Timaeus*, and (b) whether the view can be true. And he is only interested in question (a) because the answer to it forms part of the dialectical context in which he develops his own answer to question (b): Plato is one of the predecessors whose views he surveys before starting his own positive discussion. One reason for surveying contrary views, Aristotle says, is that ignoring them could undermine the credibility of his own sempiternalist position: it might seem to have been reached by default (*On the Heaven* I, 279b4–12). Now, he could incur the same charge of not taking contrary views seriously if he were to accept too easily the claim put about by some of the Platonists that the Timaean "beginning" is only a matter of presentation. Aristotle makes it clear that he *would* be accepting this too easily if he accepted their attempt to justify their claim: for their justification fails, as he explains at *On the Heaven* I, 279b33–280a10.[15] Giving this explanation leaves Aristotle free to pursue

---

[15] They had argued that the proto-historicism should be taken no more seriously than the "first this, then that" of a geometrical construction; e.g.: "First extend to D the side AB of the triangle

his own first-order inquiry, citing the *Timaeus* as a contrary view which his method requires him to confront openly.

The point of these remarks is to bring out the business-like first-order nature of Aristotle's interest. His question is simply whether or not it is true, or even possible, that the cosmos had a beginning but will have no end. That being so, if one looks at Timaeus's proto-historicism from Aristotle's corner, the matter presents itself in the flattest and baldest terms: the Timaean account is interesting only because, in Aristotle's view, it contradicts the sempiternalism that for him is the true theory. It is reasonable to call this a "literal" interpretation of the proto-historicism. However, for us—whose chief concern is not with the actual temporal structure of the physical world, but with Plato's meaning—such a flat and literal interpretation is disappointing and unacceptable. Plato could not have meant to be simply telling his readers: "The cosmos has not always existed; for some unknown number n, it has fully existed for only n years." If we find this an unsatisfying interpretation of what Plato is about, it may seem that the only remedy is to maintain that, despite appearances, the position of the *Timaeus* is a sempiternalist one after all. It may seem as if the only way to escape the flatness of literalism is to suppose that Plato in the *Timaeus* is a secret sempiternalist. But these are not the only options. There is also the possibility that Timaean proto-historicism is in a genuine sense emblematic and indeed mythic, but stands for something important *about the cosmos* that cannot, or cannot at all easily, be signified in a more direct way. If this is the case, then the proto-historicism cannot be brushed aside to reveal an underlying sempiternalist cosmology. In short, we need to allow for the possible combination "not just flatly literal, nor just presentational, but an intrinsic aspect of the *content* being presented."

The possibility of this third option invites an investigation along the following lines: first, we try to identify any important lesson conveyed by casting the cosmology in its actual proto-historical form, and then, if such a lesson emerges, we consider whether it would still be preserved in a sempiternalist cosmology (even if such a framework would make the message more difficult to read). If the answer is that such a lesson or lessons would be preserved, then the proto-historicism is optional, and we

---

ABC, then intersect AD at B with a line parallel to AC." The proof (that the internal angles are equal to two right angles) depends on the simultaneity (or timelessness) of the relationships. Aristotle points out that the cases are not parallel: the original triangle ABC is still present when the new lines are drawn. They are an addition, not a replacement (otherwise there would be no proof). By contrast, the pre-cosmic disorder of the *Timaeus* cannot be simultaneous with the order caused by the Demiurge, because order and disorder are contraries. The others might have replied that the disorder is really to be envisaged as only counterfactual; but presumably they failed to make this point (the example of geometrical construction is irrelevant to it), and there is no reason why Aristotle should have made it on their behalf.

are free to think of it as a pedagogical device: sempiternalist interpreters of the *Timaeus* would not be missing anything philosophically significant. If, on the other hand, the lesson would not be preserved, the proto-historicism is intrinsic to what is being presented. If this were the result, we should have to respect it even if doing so meant tolerating some incoherence in Timaeus's narrative. The reason for mentioning incoherence here is that some interpreters uphold the sempiternalist reading on the ground that adopting it eliminates various incoherences thrown up by the proto-historical appearances of the actual discourse.[16] But we are only entitled to prefer sempiternalism for this sort of reason after we have checked to see that the proto-historical aspects are not doing important philosophical work that could not be done without them. The interpreter would have to weigh the value of the philosophical work in question against the disvalue of the incoherences, such as they are.

I shall take up the task of identifying the lesson of Timaeus's proto-historicism in Section 4 below. First, however, we must look more closely at the different proto-historical structures appearing in his narrative.

2. PROTO-HISTORICAL STRUCTURES

It will be useful to distinguish different ways in which Timaeus's account shows a proto-historical "before and after." There are at least three kinds of proto-historical feature, and they should be considered separately.

(PH1) There is the way in which a divine agent is shown introducing order into something previously unordered. Thus we are told more than once that the fashioning of the cosmos began when Demiurge "took over" the pre-cosmic materials, as if they are already there before he starts to initiate the cosmos (30a4; 68e3). We are also shown a prior pre-cosmic moment when the god transformed rudimentary versions of those materials into full-blown versions by giving them beautiful geometric structure at the level of minute particles (53a8–b5; 69b3–4; c1).

(PH2) There is the way in which the work of making the cosmos, body and soul, and mortal animals is shown proceeding in successive stages. We could also think of the pre-cosmic geometrization as the first stage in the making of the cosmos itself. It is perhaps arbitrary whether a building project starts when construction begins or when the materials are brought to a suitable state of perfection as materials. Note that a literal

---

[16] Classic criticisms of some sempiternalist arguments of this kind are Vlastos 1939 and Vlastos 1965. See also Cherniss 1944, 424–5; Tarán 1971, 374–5; Dillon 1997, 39–40, for sempiternalist arguments based on the "cosmic soul before cosmic body" order of creation (*Timaeus* 34b10–35a1). In my view, these arguments (which focus on an instance of PH2) fail through ignoring the variety of ways in which one item can be said to be "prior" to another.

reading of PH1 examples does not commit one to a literal reading of PH2. It is possible to conceive of a moment when lack of order was made to give way to complete or finished order without necessarily supposing that the transition occurred in a plurality of successive stages.[17]

(PH3) There is the way in which the history of the complete cosmos, stocked with all its contents including the mortal animals, is shown as having started at a moment long ago from *now*: a moment that marks the beginning of the duration of the world stretching from its inception to the present day. In the *Timaeus-Critias* we first encounter the PH3 structure as encompassing the dramatic "today" when the characters Socrates, Timaeus, Critias, and Hermocrates are assembled against the background sweep of a past stretching away from their present, through their "yesterday,"[18] back to the cosmic beginning which Timaeus expounds "today." However, when recipients of Plato take a view for or against interpreting the Timaean system as covertly sempiternalist, they are obviously considering the matter from their own real-world temporal perspective; and they are equally obviously considering whether Plato means (or "literally" means) to convey that the physical world in which he and they live or lived was divinely fashioned *once long ago* in relation to Plato and themselves.

The PH3 structure is distinct from PH1 and PH2 in that neither separately nor together do the latter entail PH3. This is because features 1 and 2 merely order things in a narrative, whereas feature 3 locates things in the past relative to the thinker's *now*.[19] One could construct a "cosmogonic" story with features 1 and 2, and simply leave the matter at that. One might have shown how a cosmos as perfect as possible would come to be *if* such a thing did or were to come to be. Relations of succession depicted in such an account would be internal to a suppositional cosmogony left unconnected with our world today, or "this All," as Timaeus calls it. Thus doing actual-world cosmogony—whether Timaeus is doing it in the dialogue-world or Plato in the real world—means using PH3 and not just PH1 and PH2.

Features PH1–3 in combination give the full Timaean proto-historicist picture: the picture of the cosmos (1) brought into being from unordered matter; (2) brought into

---

[17] Cf. Harte 2002, 215, n. 99; she attributes the point to Burnyeat (conversation).

PH2 does seem to assume some kind of beginning to the stage-by-stage process. This is because a point comes when the work done in stages is complete, and it is hard to conceive, or anyway to imagine, how a purposeful series of stages would reach completion unless it had started. However, the beginning of a stage-by-stage process need not be understood in PH1 terms, i.e. as the transition from a situation in which matter preexisted in an unordered state. One can conceive that God created the world both ex nihilo and by stages. Thus PH1 and PH2 are logically independent of each other.

[18] For "yesterday" see 17a2; 19a7; 20b1; c6; 25e2; 26a3; 7; b4; c8.

[19] According to McTaggart's distinction, PH1 and 2 are B-series concepts, while PH3 is A-series.

being by stages; and (3) seen as long ago completed, as from the perspective of the present. Our main question is whether Timaean proto-historicism is merely presentational. Now, no substantial content (as distinct from expository clarity and rhetorical effect) is lost if PH2 seriality is removed. A similar claim can be upheld for PH1 considered on its own, although this case is more complicated.[20] So I leave these aside and turn forthwith to PH3. By examining the meaning and implications of this structure in its Timaean context, I shall give reason for concluding that the *Timaeus* is committed, substantially and not just presentationally, to a proto-historic beginning of the cosmos.

3. NATURE AND ITS DIVINE ORIGIN

Let us begin with two questions: (a) the relation of PH3 to PH1 and PH2, and (b) any immediate implications of PH3 concerning the past-wards duration of the cosmos.

(a) I pointed out in the last section that PH1 and PH2 do not entail PH3, either separately or together. What about entailments in the reverse direction? Well, what is essential to PH3 is the idea that once the cosmos had been fully constructed, a new phase set in, namely its post-construction existence: the existence of that which (given an intelligent Constructor) the act or acts of construction were for. This is the literally temporal existence that is or constitutes the duration of the world. PH3 implies only that the construction has been completed and the construct has continued in existence. Logically, then, it does not matter whether or not the constructive activity went through successive stages (PH2); nor does it matter whether or not it involved a transition from pre-cosmic disorder (PH1). So PH3 is neither entailed by nor (in itself)[21] entails PH1 and 2.

(b) It seems clear that PH3 in itself is compatible with the view that the cosmos has existed from everlasting, that is, that any given stretch of past time was preceded by an equal stretch of past time. This is because we can think in a purely aspectual way of the cosmos's status as divine construct. The thought is that at any given moment of its temporal existence the cosmos is a having-been-created thing, and the truth of this leaves it open whether or not there was a first moment of time, or whether or not there is a past-wards limit L, finitely remote from the present, such that every moment of past time lies between the present and L. So PH3 seems to allow for the theory that the cosmos is everlasting in both temporal directions (since the future-wards case is not in doubt in the Timaean context). And this appearance is reasonable as long as we consider the PH3 structure in an abstract and schematic way. But, as we shall see presently,

---

[20] The arguments for these claims are in Broadie 2012, section 7.2.
[21] The reason for this qualification will become clear.

the case changes once PH3 is more concretely understood as applying to a cosmos that fits the Timaean specifications.

Now for the main question: what is the point of the PH3 structure in the *Timaeus* cosmology? It is already clear that PH3 conveys the identity of god-constructed cosmos with this world that is going on round us today. Coming at this point from a slightly different angle, we can further describe the PH3 structure as Plato's way of showing how the divinely originated cosmos is also a *natural* world that proceeds in accordance with natural processes and natural causal connections. The reason for the emphasis is to bring out the fact that the natural workings are not themselves the actions or activities of originating gods. PH3 puts nature (including ourselves) in the foreground and transcendent divine origination firmly in the background, keeping them both separate and connected. As we shall see, it is not clear that there is any better device for this purpose than PH3.

We from our perspective may well find it prima facie easier (whatever we ultimately believe) to make sense of or imaginatively realize the natural world's separateness from, rather than its closeness to, a divine origin. This is surely due to the fact that we are so used to thinking of God as incorporeal and transcendent. To us the separateness is so obvious that the problem is in how to connect nature with a divine origin at all. But Plato cannot so easily take for granted the separateness of the two, because divinity and corporeity are not mutually exclusive for him. The Timaean cosmos is itself a sense-perceptible god full of visible astral gods (*Timaeus* 34b1–9; 39e3–40d5; 41a3–7; 92c6–7). The outlook that makes this a possible view belongs to the same culture that made possible previous philosophies such as those of Empedocles and Diogenes of Apollonia according to which the corporeal materials of the world, or natural forces operating in matter, are divine and intelligent and are working their regular purposes out through the patterns of nature all around us. Plato's cosmic god is a new scion of the same teleological stock as these older divine principles, and the latter are culturally real enough to Plato to give him the task of deliberately excluding them from his system.[22] Although this effort of deliberate exclusion is responsible for several major features of the Timaean cosmology, here I shall focus on just one of those features, the PH3 structure. This (a) shows the incorporeal, trans-natural, origin of nature as always already *having* played its part, and thereby (b) makes salient and distinct *what* was originated, namely the ordinary course of nature as it is today.[23]

---

[22] The pre-Socratic "teleological materialisms" are closely studied by Sedley 2007.

[23] I am aware that this formulation will be questioned by interpreters who hold that the separateness of the Timaean Demiurge from both the body and the soul of the cosmos (he is shown as making each of them) is merely presentational. In Broadie 2012, I argue for taking the separate Demiurge "literally."

Let us now look more closely at the "ordinary course of nature" side of this picture, starting with the all-encompassing living being that is the cosmos. The soul and body of this supreme animal were designed and constructed by the supreme and invisible Demiurge, but the motions of the visible celestial system belong to the stars that constitute that system, and these astronomical movements manifest the activity of the cosmic soul itself. The cosmic animal is a *natural* being—one that has the status of a great god because its life is intelligent, immortal, completely self-sufficient, and all-containing, but nonetheless natural because once it has been made by the Demiurge, being assigned its proper motion by him (34a1–5), it works on its own physical and psychological principles.[24] With mortal animals inside the cosmos it is even clearer that they have been constructed to live their own lives in accordance with their own natures and that of the environment. Divine proxies for the supreme Demiurge[25] fashioned the mortal bodies with their complex respiratory and metabolic systems, but it is clearly the mortal animals *themselves* that will be breathing in and out and undergoing the stages of the metabolic cycle. The gods fashioned the organs of vision, hearing, and speech, but it is of course for the animals to engage in these activities *themselves*. Similarly, the gods designed and constructed the original organs of animal reproduction, but again it is the mortal animals *themselves*, male and female, that are to play their respective roles of insemination, conception, gestation of the fetus. In short, the animals will be living their own lives. Plato's detailed treatments of the structure, materials, and physical workings of various animal organs proclaim the wisdom of divine craftsmanship, but also the mundane biological reality of the natural systems themselves.

How is it to be shown that the mundane biological reality of mortal animals has a source that is not merely divine (ageless, immortal, prior to perishable things—all of which is true of the great cosmic animal), but transcendently so? The obvious way is in terms of the PH3 structure. For the present purpose, however, the *Timaeus* gives this structure a particular interpretation which we have not yet discussed. So far, we have said only that PH3 in the *Timaeus* shows the present-day cosmos as having been divinely originated long ago. As long as we consider only the immortal cosmos and the astral gods, it seems clear that "having been divinely originated" can be understood as purely aspectual,[26] and

---

[24] Pace Tarán 1971, 376–8, Vlastos 1965, was correct in arguing that there is no contradiction in holding that souls are both self-moving and brought into being by the Demiurge. They are self-moving in that once in existence they essentially move of themselves. But this does not mean that they are self-moving in the sense of being wholly responsible for the fact that they move at all. They owe this fact, of course, to their own nature, but also to whatever made them, given that they were made.

[25] Because he can make only immortal beings, 41c2–6.

[26] The use of "aspectual" in this exposition is meant to convey a conceptual structure. It does not depend on the textual claim that *Timaeus* verb-formations representing divine demiurgic action encode a perfective aspect.

that "long ago" can be interpreted as "infinitely long ago," that is, so as not to rule it out that the world has existed from everlasting. But when it comes to mortal animals, the *Timaeus* gives us a version of PH3 in which (a) there is a *first* or *prototype* generation directly minted by divine demiurgy, and (b) this gives rise to subsequent generations by natural reproduction.[27] The prototypes belong with, because they head the series of, the post-origin generations, and they do so through biological propagation. But their primacy connects them equally with the transcendent source. They were divinely made in immediate accordance with the transcendent intelligible paradigm (28c2–29b1; 39e3–40a2), and through them, because of natural reproduction, the paradigm is somehow reflected in their wholly natural descendents.[28]

What about the immortal parts of nature: the cosmic god and the astral gods? Being immortal they neither beget nor are biologically begotten; hence the notion of a divinely crafted ancestral prototype cannot apply to them. But the world they constitute is incomplete without the mortal kinds. Once those cosmic and celestial gods have been brought into being the mortal prototypes must be brought into being forthwith. The lives of the cosmic and celestial gods cannot have run from everlasting if the series of mortal generations has not run from everlasting. And as far as I can see the latter is ruled out by the assumption of mortal *prototypes*. Perhaps it is possible to conceive of the prototypes as standing at the head of an infinite number of generational removes from their biological descendants, so that the ancestry stretches back through endless time. But in the absence of any obvious model showing how this is possible, it seems clear that the *Timaeus* story as actually presented implies a finite number of generations between now and the prototypes for any given mortal kind, and thereby implies that for some unknowable finite number n the cosmos is now in its nth year. And I do not see clearly how the story is not thereby committed to PH1, the proto-historical transition from the pre-cosmos to the cosmos. Can we think (1) that, for some finite n, the cosmos is now in its nth year, without being committed to the thought (2) that we are now in the nth year measured from a past-wards limit on the series of moments at which it was true to say "The cosmos (complete with the chronological system) is having-been-originated" (this being understood aspectually, as above)? And can we be confident that Plato and those around him would have been able to think (1) and (2) without also thinking (3) that there was a *when*[29] when the cosmos had not yet come to be, so that it came to be having not been? But any ancient Greek who thinks

---

[27] I am leaving aside the complication that female humans and brutes are reincarnations of ethically inferior members of the first generation: 42b5–c4; 90e6–91a1; 91d5–92c3.

[28] The brief discussion of reproduction runs from 90e6 to 91d6.

[29] They need not and should not think of this *when* as in the time series of measurable periods: cf. Vlastos 1939.

(3) will surely also think (4) that *when* the cosmos had not yet come to be, there nevertheless existed the materials out of which it was constituted; since there would be no question of supposing that it came to be but not out of anything.

I have argued that Plato's reason or motive for picturing the cosmos and the systems within it in terms of the general structure PH3 is to mark vividly the difference between, on the one hand, the moment of divine origination and, on the other hand, the natural workings of the order that was originated, while at the same time making it intelligible that they are linked. I then argued that realizing the PH3 structure for mortal animals in terms of prototypes makes it difficult if not impossible for him to escape the implication that the world has existed for an unspecifiable finite time. Even if this implication is unsettling,[30] the strangeness has to be balanced against the importance of what is achieved by securing that connection between a natural order and a divine origin.

There may have been a difference, of course, between the way in which Plato thought he needed to present this idea to others, and some more sophisticated grasp of it which he kept to himself. The next section provides the basis for an answer to that question. First, however, I must briefly take note of a major incoherence in the Timaean account: the PH3 picture of divine origination, as developed above, is out of kilter with the Receptacle-motif (48e2–53a7). The Receptacle, along with the relevant Forms, is a metaphysical principle of the four corporeal materials considered in their pre-cosmic state, or in abstraction from their use in demiurgic construction of the cosmic animal and mortal animals. Now, it seems clear that the Receptacle's contribution (hence also that of those Forms) is not something that was fully completed "once upon a time long ago"; this principle, rather, is an ongoing metaphysical condition of the empirical existence, movements, and transformations of fire and water, et cetera throughout the duration of the cosmos. Nor is there any suggestion in the text that the Receptacle ever had a beginning. Thus the Receptacle-motif speaks strongly for a sempiternalist interpretation of that aspect or level of nature which the motif is employed to explain, namely the four inanimate materials considered in themselves. The PH3 structure (with mortal prototypes) is, by contrast, Timaeus's framework for demiurgic fashioning *from* the materials.[31]

---

[30] It is unsettling because of the lack of transparency. Compare this case with (a) the Biblical account which is designed to enable us to calculate the world's finite age from the ages of known persons in the human generations from Adam, and (b) contemporary cosmology which has various ways of calculating the current age of the universe.

[31] Obviously, this paragraph raises a huge array of issues. I have tried to deal with a number of them in Broadie 2012, ch. 6.

The discrepancy between this "continual" metaphysical generation of the materials and the "once upon a time" demiurgic construction of animals may be one of those "glaring inconsistencies" which some scholars think Plato has deliberately strewn about in the *Timaeus* to indicate (as if he had no other way of doing so) that the "once upon a time" demiurgy is a facade that fronts an across-the-board sempiternalist position. Whether this is a reasonable hypothesis depends on whether Plato could in his own mind have combined thoroughgoing sempiternalism with the philosophical point which (I have argued) the PH3 picture is meant to convey. If, instead, this point would have been very hard or impossible to preserve in sempiternalist terms, then we are on weak ground for concluding that Plato was "really" a sempiternalist throughout the *Timaeus* or that the internal discrepancies show anything more than human failure to gain complete control over all parts of a huge and difficult subject-matter.[32]

4. COULD PLATO HAVE MANAGED WITHOUT PH3?

The question now is whether it is reasonable to suppose that a uniformly sempiternalist author of the *Timaeus* could have maintained a clear connection between nature and its divine origin while at the same time marking the clear difference between the two. Thoroughgoing sempiternalism would entail that if there is a transcendent origin, no generation of mortal animals is more closely related to it than any other. Consequently, thoroughgoing sempiternalists (these are the ones under consideration now) who want to keep the connection with the transcendent origin are committed, I think, to regarding divine demiurgy in the light of the paradigm as equally operative in the coming to be of mortal animals at every stage. And how, if one holds this, can one also coherently hold that mortals in each generation are also genuinely natural causes of their own offspring? Perhaps a reconciliation can be effected, but our question should be whether *Plato* in his place in history could have effected it.

---

[32] Given what I have called the "major incoherence" summarized in the previous paragraph, it turns out that Timaeus really does have reason to beg his audience not to be surprised if his exposition shows some failures of consistency and exactness (29c4–d3). Whether or not Plato was fully aware of the problem which the Receptacle poses for a uniform PH3 reading of the whole cosmology, he was not deterred from *resuming* (all flags flying, moreover) the PH3 framework after concluding his lengthy discussion of the corporeal materials as such. This discussion, 47e3–68d7, whose launch is marked as a new beginning (48a7–b3 and d2–3), is sandwiched between two stretches governed by PH3 (they also, of course, feature plenty of PH2). These run from 29d7 to 47e3 (mainly on demiurgic construction of immortal animals and immortal souls), and from 68ae1 to the end (demiurgically constructed mortal animals, with a portion on aging, diseases, and physical and moral regimen).

The difficulty of doing so will become clearer if we locate the *Timaeus* in a larger philosophical context. The *once and for all* picture of divine origination is a form of deism.[33] Timaean deism has the Demiurge making the cosmic animal which then exists under its own steam and by the laws of its own nature. The living activity of the cosmic soul in this account seems a good illustration of "under its own steam." The Demiurge is said to delight when he observes the cosmic animal "in motion and alive" (37c6), that is, living its own life and, since its life is its existence, exercising its own existence now from itself. The passage may hint that the Demiurge is pleased not only by its excellence but also because it is, as it was meant to be, independent (except for the fact that it exists at his pleasure; he could destroy it if he wished, 41a7–b2). Another very obvious deistic touch: once the Demiurge has set up the immortal souls of mortals and commissioned his ancillaries to construct the mortal bodies, he is depicted as withdrawing (42b5–7). Presumably the account allows us to imagine the ancillaries as likewise withdrawing when the immortal souls start to live in and through the bodies constructed for them.

Now, how easy is it to replace this deistic sort of account with one that understands divine origination as "never over," but even so preserves the distinction as well as the connection between the natural and the divine, coherently allowing that natural things in the world today operate by their own powers and activities? The history of Western philosophy shows that this is no mean challenge.[34] The pressure towards asserting that the divine activity is immediately necessary to retain the creaturely world in being at every moment of its history, so that all stages, early or late historically speaking, equally radiate from the same transcendent source, can easily end in a vision of nature as an attribute or offshoot or phase of the divine, or in an occasionalism that altogether denies causal powers to natural beings.[35] Obviously there have been philosophers more than happy to surrender to one or another of these resulting visions. However, our concern at the moment is with the difficulty of resisting them if what one wants is to

---

[33] "Deism" is the label of contemporary philosophers of theology for the view that once God made the world, the world continued to exist without being constantly created, or recreated, or conserved, or sustained in being by God. Contemporary discussions of deism assume a monotheistic framework, so in that respect it is anomalous to apply the category to the system of the *Timaeus*.

[34] The technicality, sophistication, and ingenuity of recent responses, informed by the subtle and vigorous medieval and 16th and 17th century debates, are on display in Freddoso 1991, McCann and Kvanvig 1991, and Kvanvig 2007. See also Oakes 1977 and Quinn 1979. On some related discussions in late antiquity and mediaeval Islamic philosophy, see Sorabji 1983, Part IV; for the ancient sources see Sorabji 2004, vol. 2, chs. 8–9. On continuous creation in Neoplatonism, see Phillips 1997. On the debates from the medieval to the early modern period, see S. Lee 2008.

[35] We may view Aristotle's rejection of the early Platonistic view on the role of the Idea of Man in human genesis as the ancestor of later defenses of "second causes" as against occasionalism.

maintain a clear distinction between the operation of nature and the operation of the divine cause of nature. Even today, philosophers of theology are not agreed on exactly how to understand the lien between the world and God in a way that avoids deism (and in general any position that makes God seem causally too remote from the operations of creatures) while at the same time avoiding pantheism or occasionalism; nor is there even agreement on whether a coherent position on the matter is even possible.[36]

One prop for the view that Plato in the *Timaeus* is a crypto-sempiternalist has been the assumption that he could *easily* have replaced the deistic or PH3 parts of the actual text with sempiternalist versions, but chose not to do so for purely didactic reasons. Although this assumption deserves to be examined critically, it tends to be taken for granted by its adherents. One cannot help suspecting circular reasoning. If some interpreters do not bother to look and see whether the proto-historicism, or some form of it, carries an irreplaceable meaning for the *content* of the cosmology, this is probably because they are already from the outset convinced that the proto-historicism is a childish surface-phenomenon. From their standpoint it is settled and obvious (a) that the account as actually given can be exchanged for an "adult" sempiternalist version without loss or distortion of content; and (b) that it would have been feasible for Plato *first* to formulate for himself the grown-up sempiternalist doctrine, and *then* to trick it out in proto-historicist clothing. But if instead one scours the different proto-historical features for philosophical meaning, between them they yield the idea that nature has a divine origin, yet is not itself part of or an attribute of or consubstantial with or a phase of the divine origin, any more than the divine origin is part of nature. The question then becomes: could *this* idea, content unchanged, be presented in terms both sempiternalist and coherently available to Plato? The considerations brought forward from the later history of philosophy show that it hardly could. Someone may suggest that Plato was an *in*coherent crypto-sempiternalist. But why is this kinder than allowing that his non-sempiternalist deism, shown in his reliance on the PH3 structure, is serious and sincere? I conclude that Xenocrates's anti-literalist interpretation did the author of the

---

[36] See the last paragraph of Kvanvig 2007, for a marked lack of complacency on this score. In outline, a solution, if there is one, will probably turn on a distinction of roles according to which God's task is to be constantly or in a single act creating the entire universe anew by his will alone ex nihilo, whereas the task of every finite natural substance is to engage in an existence defined by exercises of powers of a totally different metaphysical order. If the kinds of task are different enough, the distinct reality and powers of finite substances would not seem to compete with, nor therefore to be inconsistent with, the total immediate dependence of everything in nature on the infinite God. Such a highly developed theological perspective, in which the divinity's status as the power of creating ex nihilo places it beyond competition with any finite power, was nowhere near being available to Plato.

Timaeus no favors, and that Aristotle's literalism was not only not uncharitable, but literally correct (even though hermeneutically inadequate in its literalism).[37]

Assigning to the divine world-maker continuous engagement with the world may be conceptually easier in some sectors than in others. For example, it may be relatively easy to assert that divine providence, in the sense of concern about the ethical faring of mortals, never sleeps and is interested down to the last detail. But this in itself has little to do with cosmology or cosmogony. It may also be comparatively easy to hold that the world-maker is the constantly operative cause of celestial motion. Then if one sees the incessant movement of the heavens not as an adjunct to their created being but as of its essence, it is easy to move to the anti-deistic conclusion that a distinct divine power is constantly maintaining them in existence even today. I do not mean to assert that Plato could not or did not have such thoughts about the heavens.[38] But try extending this picture to the detail of the mortal realm, so that a divinity crafts each animal as it comes into existence. The result is absurd if it implies, as it certainly seems to, that intra-mundane causation, that is, parental procreation, is not responsible for the process. And the very hard work of showing how to avoid this implication still lay in the future. Thus notwithstanding passages in Plato that may suggest the idea of continuous divine creation, there is good reason to accept that when in the *Timaeus* he focuses on the divine origination of mortals—and on this as much as on the divine origination of the heavens—he relies, not merely seems to rely, on a proto-historical (namely, PH3) way of thinking.

When sempiternalism took over among Plato's younger associates, he may well have been a working philosopher still, and able to interact with its proponents. This may well have been so when Xenocrates put forth the statement that the proto-historicism of the *Timaeus* was only a pedagogical device. So why did no one manage to get from Plato an answer on whether the Timaean cosmology was really sempiternalist? For it is hard to believe that there would have been no record of the answer had he given one. Thus we have to suppose that if Plato was active during those developments he chose not to discuss the question.[39] Now, if the others were debating on whether to understand the

---

[37] With Xenocrates there are different possibilities. He may simply have missed the philosophical point of the Timaean PH3 structure. Or he may have seen and sympathized with this point (strict separation of nature's divine origin from its everyday natural workings) but underestimated the difficulty of combining it with his own Platonistic sempiternalism. Or he may not have cared about maintaining the strict separation. Xenocrates wrote separate works on physics and on metaphysical subjects, but we cannot infer from this that he cared about an ontological separation of natural operations from divine ones.

[38] E.g. at *Laws* X, 896e8–899b9, the Athenian argues that the major processes of the universe are going on under the guidance of perfectly virtuous souls, i.e. gods.

[39] Dillon 1989, 72: "What is disturbingly plain.... is that the Master himself managed to avoid giving any definitive account of what he meant to his immediate followers. How he managed to avoid this, I do not know, but I see no other explanation of the phenomena."

Timaeus in a flatly literalist way (i.e., the salient question being whether the Timaean cosmos has a temporal beginning and no temporal end), Plato may have had reason to feel that he should not take sides on this. That would be so, if, as I have argued, he had adopted the PH3 structure to express something serious that had nothing directly to do with theories about the temporal profile of the cosmos. There is also the real possibility that the PH3 structure was his best or even his only tool for expressing the intended relation between nature and its divine origin. Centuries of discussion of the nature of such a relation and its problematic demands of connection and distinctness have furnished us with terms which Plato did not have, such as "transcendent" and "naturalistic." Thus we can explain the conceptual aim of the Timaean PH3 structure in more abstract terms, and we can try ways of implementing that aim that do not depend on the structure. But with Plato perhaps the situation was this: he could not endorse the anti-literalist interpretation of Xenocrates since this would have entailed abandoning what the PH3 structure stands for; nor, however, could he endorse Aristotle's bald literalism since this by itself misses the point of PH3. If this was so, Plato's rational course was silence.

5. CONCLUSION

This chapter has centered on the question: what is Plato aiming at in presenting the Timaean cosmology in proto-historical terms?

By way of reply, I have argued that with the proto-historicism (or at least one form of it) Plato is making a point of considerable philosophical significance. This point has to do with his subject matter, the cosmos; it is not a manner or mode of presentation that could be replaced while leaving philosophical and cosmological content the same. Therefore the proto-historicism is not solely the pedagogical device that so many interpreters have claimed it to be. For something cannot be "only a pedagogical device" unless eliminating it would leave the content unchanged in important respects.

However, what counts as an "important respect" is not a matter on which everyone can be expected to agree. Interpreters would be less disposed to see the proto-historical framework as contributing anything significant to the content to the extent that, for whatever reason, they have invested heavily in the sempiternalist interpretation of the *Timaeus*. This would have been the situation of any ancient thinkers who (1) thought that they had good independent grounds (cosmological, theological, metaphysical, logical) for affirming the sempiternity of the universe, and (2) regarded Plato as the voice of truth in metaphysics and cosmology. It would also be the situation of any modern interpreters who (whatever their own first-order views about the universe) (1) believe that according to "real Platonism" the cosmos proceeds timelessly from its transcendent origin, and therefore is sempiternal, and

(2) believe that the author of the *Timaeus* was a "real Platonist." Such interpreters have to decide whether the reasonableness of this pair of commitments outweighs the arguments in this chapter.

References

Allen, R. E. ed., 1965: *Studies in Plato's Metaphysics*, London.
Apelt, O., 1919: *Platons Dialoge* Timaios *und Kritias übersetzt und erläutert*, Leipzig
Baltes, M., 1976–8: *Die Weltentstehung des Platonischen Timaios nach den antiken Interpreten*, Leiden.
Betegh, G., 2010: "What Makes a Myth *Eikôs*?" *One Book, The Whole Universe* eds. R. Mohr and B. Sattler, Las Vegas, 213–24.
Broadie, S., 2010: "Divine and Natural Causation in the *Timaeus*: The Case of Mortal Animals," *La Scienza e le Cause a partire dalla* Metafisica *di Aristotele*, a cura di F. Fronterotta, Bibliopolis, C. N. R., Istituto per il Lessico Intellettuale Europeo e Storia delle Idee, 73–92.
Broadie, S., 2012: *Nature and Divinity in Plato's* Timaeus, Cambridge.
Burnyeat, M., 2005: "EIKÔS MYTHOS," *Rhizai 2*, 143–65.
Cherniss, H., 1944: *Aristotle's Criticisms of Plato and the Academy*, Baltimore (reprinted 1962, New York).
Cooper, J. ed., 1997: *Plato, Complete Works*, Indianapolis.
Dillon, J., 1989: "Tampering with the *Timaeus*: Ideological Emendations in Plato," *American Journal of Philology* **110**, 50–72.
Dillon, J., 1997: "The Riddle of the *Timaeus*: Is Plato Sowing Clues?" in *Studies in Plato and the Platonic Tradition* ed. M. Joyal, Aldershot, 25–42.
Dillon, J., 2003: *The Heirs of Plato: A Study of the Old Academy*, Oxford.
Freddoso, A., 1991: "God's General Concurrence with Secondary Causes: Why Conservation Is Not Enough," *Philosophical Perspectives* **5**, 553–85.
Gregory, A., 2007: *Ancient Greek Cosmology*, London.
Harte, V., 2002: *Plato on Parts and Wholes*, Oxford.
Kvanvig, J., 2007: "Creation and Conservation," *Stanford Encyclopedia of Philosophy*, http://plato.stanford.edu/entries/creation-conservation/.
Lee, H. D. P., 1971: *Plato,* Timaeus *and* Critias, *translated with an introduction and appendix on Atlantis*, Harmondsworth.
Lee, S., 2008: "Occasionalism," *Stanford Encyclopedia of Philosophy*, http://plato.stanford.edu/entries/occasionalism.
McCann, H. and Kvanvig, J., 1991: "The Occasionalist Proselytizer: A Modified Catechism," *Philosophical Perspectives* **5**, 587–615.
Oakes, R., 1977: "Classical Theism and Pantheism: A Victory for Process Theism," *Religious Studies* **13**, 167–73.
Phillips, J., 1997: "Neoplatonic Exegeses of Plato's Cosmogony (*Timaeus* 27C–28C)," *Journal of the History of Ideas* **35**, 173–97.
Quinn, P., 1979: "Divine Conservation and Spinozistic Pantheism," *Religious Studies* **15**, 289–302.
Sedley, D., 2007: *Creationism and Its Critics in Antiquity*, Berkeley.
Sorabji, R., 1983: *Time, Creation and the Continuum: Theories in Antiquity and the Early Middle Ages*, London.
Sorabji, R., 2004: *The Philosophy of the Commentators 200–600 AD*, London.

Tarán, L., 1971: "The Creation Myth in Plato's *Timaeus*," in *Essays in Ancient Greek Philosophy* eds. J. Anton and G. Kustas, Albany, 372–407.

Vlastos, G., 1939: "The Disorderly Motion in the *Timaeus*," *Classical* Quarterly *33* (02): 71–83; reprinted in Allen 1965, 379–99; and in D.W. Graham (ed.), *Studies in Greek Philosophy*, vol. 2, Princeton: Princeton University Press, 1995.

Vlastos, G., 1965: "Creation in the *Timaeus*: Is it a Fiction?" in Allen 1965, 401–19; reprinted in D.W. Graham (ed.), *Studies in Greek Philosophy*, vol. 2, Princeton: Princeton University Press, 1995.

PART TWO

Aristotle's Ethics and Practical Reasoning

4

A SWARM OF VIRTUES
ON THE UNITY AND COMPLETENESS OF ARISTOTLE'S SCHEME OF CHARACTER-VIRTUES

Dorothea Frede

1. INTRODUCTION: THE PROBLEM

The notoriously sketchy state of Aristotle's extant works leaves his readers with many open questions. The *Nicomachean Ethics* is no exception, though it contains, at least in outline, a well worked-out ethical system, with its depiction of the good life as both its basis and its capstone. There is the separation and cooperation of the virtues of character and intellect as its condition, and there is the analysis of friendship and pleasure as encompassing explanations of what ties human beings to each other and turns life not only into a satisfactory project but also into an enjoyable one. But though the *EN* contains a brilliant sketch and represents the most detailed account of a "morality of happiness" that has survived antiquity,[1] there are lots of issues that Aristotle more hints at than explains, so that his interpreters are forced to take refuge in creative speculation.

One of those open questions is whether Aristotle regards his list of character-virtues as complete, and if so, why he does so.[2] Kant's complaint that Aristotle has not provided a principle of justification for his list of ten categories should be familiar to every student of the *Critique of Pure Reason* (A 81/B 107). A philosopher worth his salt, so Kant insists, ought to provide some kind of principle of deduction as to why there should be ten categories—no more and no less. If Kant does not raise the same complaint

---

[1] For an overall characteristic of Aristotle's ethics cf. J. Annas (1993), chs. 1 and 2, whose title is referred to here. Needless to say, this article cannot pretend to respond to the ever-increasing literature on Aristotle's ethics.

[2] Aristotle often addresses "ethical virtue" in the singular as if it forms a unity, and in VI 13, 1144b32–1145a6 he denies that virtues are acquired piecemeal, so that some could be absent. There is no further explanation for that claim, beyond the general presupposition that the good life is a unity—to be hit or missed like the bull's eye by an archer (I 1, 1094a22–24).

against Aristotle's list of character-virtues then this must be due to the fact that he was less familiar with Aristotle's ethics than with his metaphysics. But Kant or no Kant, this question should vex the student of Aristotle's ethics: if Aristotle's list is supposed to be complete, what constitutes its unity? Does it not rather, to speak with Plato, contain a loosely connected "swarm of virtues"?[3] This should be a challenge not only for our assessment of Aristotle's conception of character-virtues, but it seems especially relevant at a time and age when virtue-ethics of an Aristotelian pedigree has had a kind of comeback.

Nothing in Aristotle's enumeration of the character-virtues in *EN* II 7 provides any clue as to how he arrived at that list, beyond the fact that he seems to refer to a table of virtues and vices displayed in his lecture room (1107a33–4: *ek tês diagraphês*).[4] This fact suggests some canonical status of the list, but that is all the information we get. It certainly would be wrong to claim that Aristotle's list is a mere expansion of Plato's four cardinal virtues. It has at least undergone substantial revision. For, first of all, he does not treat wisdom as a character-virtue, but as an intellectual virtue and therefore discusses it separately in his systematic treatment of the different kinds of intellectual capacities in book VI. Second, justice is not a regular member of the list in II 7, on the ground that it is "not spoken of in a simple way" (1108b7–9). Though the different types of justice remain character-virtues they are treated separately in book V. Hence, the explanation that Aristotle followed Plato and added a few extra popular virtues does not do justice to his elaborate system. The assumption that Aristotle picked "commonly accepted" positive character-traits that happened to fit his schema of a right mean between a vice of excess and a vice of deficiency is more promising. But again, his resorting to some traditional canon cannot explain how Aristotle arrived at his catalog. For, as a perfunctory look at the enumeration in II 7 shows, there was no ready-made set of triads of virtues and vices. In many cases Aristotle admits that there is no name for one of the extremes or even for the middle. And in the case of physical pleasures he grants that the lack of susceptibility to pleasure is rarely found in human beings. So

---

[3] Cf. *Meno* 72a. If that question has been touched in the secondary literature at all, no definite principle of their selection and order has been suggested. Gauthier/Jolif (2002), I 2, 154–55 hold that the table of virtues contains an enumeration rather than a classification. A more systematic organisation is suggested by Irwin (1999), 199. But no one seems to have repeated the effort of Häcker (1863) to work out a real *Einteilungsprinzip*.

[4] The list of virtues and vices in *EE* II 3, 1220b38–1221a12 is even longer; but this is an issue not to be discussed here. Susemihl excised two pairs, *karteria* and *phronesis*, because they are not discussed in what follows; he suspects that in the *EE*, too, Aristotle had meant to treat *phronesis* as an intellectual virtue rather than as a character-virtue, and that *karteria* was conceived of as the counterpart of *akrasia*.

the triads of virtues and vices are not something Aristotle could just pick up as a generally shared wisdom, but are clearly his own invention.[5]

Before going into any further speculation on the reasons that led to this catalog it is necessary to recall the items on the list in chapter 7: There we find: (1) courage with respect to fear and confidence, with rashness as the excess, and cowardice the defect, (2) moderation with respect to certain pleasures, with intemperance as excess and the rarely found defect of insensibility, (3) liberality in handing out money on a small scale with the defects of prodigality and stinginess as the extremes; (4) and magnificence in expenditure on a large scale as opposed to vulgarity and shabbiness. A similar dichotomy exists with respect to the disposition towards honor: (5) magnanimity is concerned with honor on a large scale, with empty vanity and undue humility as its vices, (6) love of honor on a small scale, a virtue without a name, with over- and under-ambitiousness as its vices; (7) there is the virtue of even-temperedness with respect to anger, with irascibility as excess and in-irascibility as its defect. Finally, there are no less than three attitudes with respect to social conduct: (8) there is truthfulness in the sense of projecting the right image of oneself, as opposed to boastfulness and mock-modesty, (9) there is wittiness as opposed to buffoonery and boorishness, (10) and there is friendliness in dealing with others in the general run of life, as opposed to obsequiousness on the one hand and cantankerousness on the other.

This leaves us with a list of ten, just as in the case of the categories. But given that Aristotle was no Pythagorean and the number ten was not sacred to him, the sheer number is no satisfactory explanation for this catalog.[6] What rules out any such number-theory, anyway, is the fact that justice is not part of that catalog. Though its discussion is postponed, because there is more than one kind of justice, at least the particular kinds of

---

[5] In his classical article on *eudaimonia* J. L. Ackrill (1974) treats the question of the criteria determining right action and moral virtue as one of the open questions that ultimately lead into a blind alley or into a circle: Good is what the good man is like. To break the impasse some "noetic" insight into human nature as a whole will have to be assumed, of the sort Aristotle assumes for the comprehension of first principles in general. Some such comprehension of the perfect human life seems presupposed in Burnyeat's explanation of how to become good (1980). Broadie (1991), 103–123, gives a more piecemeal account of how goodness is achieved through education. For a discussion of the catalog of virtues cf. Gottlieb (2009), esp. I, 2 and 4. But Gottlieb's examination of possible further virtues, including Christian and modern kinds, does not sufficiently focus on the criterion of the types of actions and emotions that constitute definite dispositions.
[6] It would be very unsatisfactory to claim that he made the subdivisions of the attitude towards money and towards honor in order to reach the number ten, or that he did so by introducing no less than three different social virtues.

justice are treated as character-virtues.[7] So, all in all there are eleven and not ten triads of virtues and vices.[8]

If Aristotle is silent about the criteria that determined his choice of virtues, he is also silent about the rationale of the order in which he is discussing them. There is at best a rough orientation suggested by the objectives in question: courage and moderation deal with physical pain and pleasure respectively, magnanimity on a large and small scale with money, ambition on a large and small scale with honor, equanimity with anger, and the three social virtues with agreeable attitudes towards others in everyday life. But this is clearly not a schema that follows the customary division into goods of the soul, the body, and external goods. Nor does Aristotle separate the virtues concerned with affections from those concerned with external goods; otherwise the virtue dealing with anger would have been grouped with those concerning fear and pleasure of the body. So it does not seem that Aristotle had an overall fixed order in mind, but started out with courage and moderation as the two virtues that are tied to bodily pains and pleasures and therefore involve the non-rational parts of the soul as the best-known types, and then worked his way through the rest as he saw fit.

But even if there is no stringent order, the question of whether he regarded his catalog as complete is all the more pertinent. An indication that he did, is contained not only in his summary at the end of book VI,[9] but also in the preface to his detailed discussion of each of the character-virtues that starts in book III: "Let us now take up the virtues again, and discuss them one by one. Let us say what they are, what sorts of things they are concerned with (*peri poia*), and how (*pôs*) they are concerned with them. It will also be clear at the same time how many of them (*posai*) there are" (5, 1115a4–5). So, Aristotle appears to be confident that his specifications of "the sort of things the virtues are concerned with and how" will provide an answer to the question of their number. There is no reason to read this statement, as some interpreters do, in a non-standard way, so that Aristotle only wants to emphasize the numerousness of virtues rather than their precise number. This is indicated inter alia by the fact that Aristotle takes care to assign separate virtues and vices to liberality and magnanimity, to concern for liberal and honorable deeds large and small, because he assumes that they are based on different dispositions. Such meticulousness suggests that he is, indeed, concerned with completeness.

---

[7] While universal justice presupposes all virtues and therefore all types of right means, particular justice in the sense of distributive and retributive justice presupposes a specific intermediate.

[8] Later traditions attribute twelve character-virtues to Aristotle, but they include modesty, a condition which Aristotle explicitly excludes, because susceptibility to shame is not a virtue.

[9] Cf. n. 2. Diogenes Laertius V 31, however, claims for Aristotle that there was no mutual dependence among the virtues (*mê antakolouthein*), so that someone could be a *phronimos* and just, but either immoderate or uncontrolled.

But what are the "kinds of things" the character-virtues are concerned with? Their general definition might provide a clue: "Virtue is, then, a disposition concerned with choice, lying in a mean relative to us, this being determined by a rule/reason (*logos*) and in the way the man of practical reason (*ho phronimos*) would determine it. Now it is a mean between two vices, that which depends on excess and that which depends on defect; and again it is a mean because the vices respectively fall short or exceed what is right in both affections and actions, while virtue both finds and chooses what is intermediate" (II 6, 1106b36–1107a6). At first sight this definition is not very informative concerning the completeness-question, because of the fact that choice, reason, and the *phronimos*' special virtue belong to the field of intellectual- rather than that of character-virtue. Therefore it seems better to focus on the actions (*praxeis*) and affections (*pathê*)[10] and their connection with what is intermediate.

2. THE RIGHT MEAN AND ITS CONSTITUENTS

To determine the precise nature of the intermediate is actually a much harder task than the simple formula of a right mean between excess and defect suggests. First of all, the question of what kind of quantification Aristotle has in mind poses grave difficulties.[11] Second, the depiction of the character-virtues and of the way they are acquired shows that (1) the activities that lead up to and that result from the virtues and (2) the affections that are involved in them are quite different and play different roles, despite the fact that Aristotle treats *praxeis* and *pathê* as complements and often mentions them in one breath.[12] It is advisable, therefore, to take a preliminary look at the determination of *praxeis* and *pathê* separately and then see how they fit together.

When Aristotle describes the way in which character-virtues are acquired he first mentions activities that are typically mastered by practice. He compares this acquisition to that of technical skills. Just as a builder or a cithara-player learns how to build a house or

---

[10] Because of the affinity to *paschein*, preference is here given to the by now old-fashioned translation of *pathos* by "affection" that is lost in the more fashionable "emotion." That Aristotle's *pathê* are not confined to passive impressions, but imply a particular desire or aversion, would be confirmed by a careful analysis of the items on his list in II 5 and the extensive discussion of the *pathê* in *Rhetoric* II 5–11.

[11] Important questions, such as to the feasibility of the model of a "right mean," will have to be bypassed here. Cf. the critique of Urmson's attempt (1973) to provide a quantitative interpretation in a literal sense by Hursthouse (1980/81). For an extended discussion of the need to combine qualitative and quantitative criteria in the determination of the right mean cf. Rapp (2006).

[12] The thorny question will have to be passed over whether *pathos* is used only for the affections or whether it also refers to the counterpart of *praxeis*: e.g. being treated generously, as seems sometimes presupposed.

to play the cithara by doing it in the right way, so the just, the courageous, and the moderate person becomes so by acting justly, courageously, and moderately. If one wonders who or what guarantees that the practice leads to the appropriate rather than an inappropriate result, there is at least an indication in the text: in the arts or crafts there are standards set by the state of the respective art or craft, and ultimately by the telos each serves. In the case of moral actions the state of the art is set by the community and its laws, with the good life as the ultimate aim.[13] Thus, there are certain authorities that see to it that the right actions are practiced, and practiced in the right way, in analogy to teachers in the art of building and in the art of cithara-playing. But this hardly explains why character-virtues should not be intellectual virtues. For, though house-building and cithara-playing require practice, that is, a certain know-how that cannot be acquired by the study of instruction-books alone, no such skilful know-how is required for virtuous activities. Instead, the reason why the character-virtues involve non-rational forces lies in the fact that they concern the appetitive and desiderative part of the soul (*to epithymêtikon kai holôs orektikon*, I 13, 1102a30). There is no counterpart to this element in the analogous cases of building and cithara-playing, where affections have no significant role to play.[14] But just, moderate, or courageous actions are not just a matter of the intellect, nor of a skilful performance; they presuppose certain affections, which, if properly trained, are under rational guidance by, but not reducible to, reason. This aspect is, then, concerned with the affective side of the character-virtues that provides the incentive to act in a particular way.

That the affective element constitutes the chief difference from the practice of the *technai* is obvious already in its introduction in II 1: "By doing the acts that we do in our transactions with other men we become just or unjust, and by doing the acts that we do in the presence of danger, and *being habituated to feel fear or confidence*, we become brave or cowardly. The same is true with appetites and anger; some men become temperate and good-tempered, others self-indulgent and irascible, by behaving in one way or the other in the appropriate circumstances" (1103a16–20). This quote is just one of many expressions of Aristotle's conviction that character-virtues are equally concerned with actions and affections and that every qualification that applies to the *praxeis* applies to the *pathê* as well (II 2, 1104b14; 5, 1106b17 ff.; 1107a4–5 *et pass.*).[15] Because the affective aspect plays such an important role in moral behavior, the appropriate training from early infancy on is crucial: it concerns, most of all, the right affective disposition—and its acquisition and possession seems not to depend on

---

[13] Cf. Striker (2006) on the connection between ethics and politics.

[14] A certain "taste" is undeniably a component in both cases, but they do not provide the all-important incentives for artistic or technical production.

[15] The relationship between activities and affections is the topic of a careful study by Kosman (1980).

rational insight only but equally on habituation.¹⁶ Thus a proper "sentimental education" is an important part of the right moral upbringing. As Aristotle explains concerning the training of our affections that makes or breaks the affective dispositions: "For the person who flies from and fears everything and does not stand his ground against anything becomes a coward, and the person who fears nothing at all but goes to meet every danger becomes rash, and similarly the person who indulges in every pleasure and abstains from none becomes self-indulgent, while the person who shuns every pleasure, as boors do, becomes in a way insensible. Moderation and courage, then, are destroyed by excess and defect, and preserved by the mean" (II 2, 1104a20–2).

In order to find out the reasons for Aristotle's canon of character-virtues it would seem natural, then, to consult his list of affections that he regards as typical for human beings and to see what kinds of "firm dispositions" he regards as desirable in each case. Taken as such, affections are natural phenomena, as Aristotle quite emphatically asserts. We are neither praised nor blamed for simply "having" them: "For these reasons the *pathê* are not faculties; for we are neither called good nor bad, nor praised nor blamed, for the simple capacity of feeling affections" (4, 1106a6–8). Virtues and vices, by contrast, consist in the *acquired dispositions* with respect to the *pathê*, that is, whether we feel them as we should, to the degree we should, and at the occasion we should. And such dispositions are not provided by nature, they are a matter of education and practice, as Aristotle never tires of repeating.

Now Aristotle provides a fairly extensive list of the affections in II 4, 1105a21–23: "By affections I mean appetite (*epithymia*), anger (*orgê*), fear (*phobos*), confidence (*tharsos*), envy (*phthonos*), joy (*chara*), love (*philia*), hatred (*misos*), longing (*pothos*), zealousness (*zêlos*), pity (*eleos*), and in general what is connected with pleasure and pain." As the formulaic end "and in general…" indicates, this list does not pretend to be complete.¹⁷ There are other, similar lists, in other Aristotelian works. The list in the *De anima* contains affections roughly of the same kind but less in number,¹⁸ and so does the list in the *Rhetoric*.¹⁹

---

[16] Aristotle is rather silent concerning the actual process of moral education that leads from early infancy to adulthood. A detailed analysis of the gradual acquisition of the character-virtues is provided by Sherman (1999).

[17] It does not contain shame *aidôs*, righteous indignation (*nemesis*), or schadenfreude (*epichairekakia*), both of which are mentioned at the end of ch. 7 and further discussed at the end of book IV.

[18] *De an.* I 1 403a17–18: anger, even-temperedness, fear, pity, confidence, joy, love, and hatred. All these are there said to be connected with specific states in the body.

[19] The *Rhetoric*'s list is at first quite short, II 1: "Anger, pity, fear and whatever else is of that sort, and their opposites." But the subsequent detailed discussion contains many more affections (chs. 2–11). Some of these are not on the list in *EN* II 5—and some of those in the *EN* are not discussed in the *Rhetoric*. The differences seem mainly due to the context: the kinds of affections that a

But as a comparison of the list of affections in *EN* II 5 and the list of virtues in II 7 shows, the affections cannot be the determinant factors of Aristotle's canon of character-virtues. For not all affections are treated as constitutive of virtues and vices. In fact, more than half of the affections are not included. There is no particular disposition mentioned that is concerned with joy, there is none related to hatred, longing,[20] or zealousness,[21] and, somewhat to our surprise, there is none that is concerned with pity. Given that neither the list of affections nor the specifications of the respective virtues and vices provide adequate information about the reason for Aristotle's choice of his catalog of virtues, we should look, first of all, for clues as to why several of the affections are not mentioned as the subject matter of virtues.

In some cases the answer is easy to find: envy is clearly not the kind of feeling that constitutes a proper attitude in any form. A morally well-educated person does not feel envy at his neighbor's good fortune, whether deserved or not, and the same applies to Schadenfreude about his misfortune. There is no right mean between defects and excesses that would constitute the right affective dispositions in their case. The feeling of hatred is a somewhat different matter. Aristotle repeatedly asserts that loving and hating the right actions is the sign of good moral upbringing.[22] But hatred against a person is another matter. In *Rhetoric* II 4 hatred is defined as the "wish that the person should not exist at all" (1382a15). To entertain such a wish against a certain person at a specific occasion may be appropriate, but there is no *disposition* with respect to hatred that could and should be cultivated from childhood on by the requisite kinds of activities. How odd that would be is nicely illustrated in the famous cartoon in Punch (fig. 4.1).

Aristotle is surely right in not accepting any such practices in his program of moral education. Both a systematic training and the corresponding permanent affective

rhetorician must know how to stir up or appease are not necessarily those that are relevant in ethical concerns.

[20] According to Plato, *Crat.* 420a, *pothos* is always longing for someone absent; but by many authors the word is used for longings of all kinds, for things absent or lost, as well as desire and love. It is not on any of Aristotle's other lists of affections, with the exception of *MM*.

[21] Emulation—*zêlos*—has its own chapter in *Rhetoric* II 11. It is called a pain at seeing the presence of good things in person like ourselves, which we do not have ourselves. It carries positive value because it is an incentive to acquire the good things ourselves. The "good things" cover a large variety of goods: wealth, an abundance of friends, but also virtues of all kinds that one might try to acquire.

[22] Cf. *EN* I 11, 1100b35; III 11, 1118b25; IV 8, 1128a28 *et pass*. In the *Rhetoric* Aristotle indicates that hatred is not concerned with individuals but with types: everyone will hate a thief and a sycophant (1382a6–7). But the right response in this case is a matter of justice, not of activities specifically assigned to hatred.

STUDY OF A PRUSSIAN HOUSEHOLD HAVING ITS MORNING HATE.

FIG 4.1 From C. Graves, *Mr. Punch's History of the Great War*, London 1919, 27.
Source: © Punch Limited

disposition of hate towards persons that one should, at the occasion one should, for reasons one should, and so on, would be an absurdity.

These cases provide important clues as to why not all kinds of affections are the subject matters of virtues: Just as some actions are bad per se, without a right mean, so are their respective affections. More importantly: there are affections that are not the appropriate subject matter of a systematic acquisition by the respective activities from early on. Though Aristotle says very little about these affections, he provides at least some clues as to why they are not to be systematically cultivated by character-training.

3. AFFECTIONS WITHOUT A VIRTUOUS DISPOSITION

That there are bad actions and affections that do not allow for a "right middle" is explained by Aristotle in II 6, 1107a8: Their very names indicate that they are bad affections, as in the case of Schadenfreude, shamelessness, or envy, and the same applies to certain activities such as adultery, theft, and murder. As far as their moral evaluation is concerned the particular circumstances make no difference. Why this should be so is illustrated by Aristotle in a rare display of his wry sense of humor with respect to adultery: it does not matter with what woman one commits adultery or at what occasion or in what way. But amusing as this case may be, and plausible as it is that some terms per se signify bad affections or bad actions and dispositions so that the model of a "right mean" between excess and defect does not apply to them, this is not really the phenomenon that we are interested in here.

Most significant is the case where Aristotle does accept an intermediate between two extremes for the affections, but denies the existence of a corresponding virtue, that is, an acquired good disposition. At the end of his catalog of character-virtues in book II (7, 1108a30–b6) Aristotle mentions certain affections that are related to virtues without actually constituting such dispositions. Thus he explains that shame (*aidôs*) is an affection without a corresponding virtuous disposition, despite the fact that it *is* the appropriate affection for a person who has committed a shameful act and that there is both excess and defect with respect to that affection: "There are also means in the affections and concerned with the affections; since shame is not a virtue, and yet praise is extended to a man capable of shame (*aidêmôn*). For even in these matters one man is said to be intermediate, and another to exceed, as for instance the bashful person who is ashamed of everything; while the person who falls short or is not ashamed of anything is shameless and the intermediate is shameful" (1108a30–35). But why, then, should there be no appropriate character-disposition with respect to shame?[23] The brief discussion at the end of book IV shows why Aristotle assigns only a limited positive value to this affection, without postulating a corresponding disposition. As he explains, a morally mature person should have no need to feel shame: "The affection is not, however, becoming to every age, but only to youth. For we think that young people should be prone to shame because they live by affection and therefore commit many errors, but are restrained by shame;…but an older person no one would praise for being prone to the sense of disgrace, since we think he should not do anything that need cause this affection" (9, 1128b15–21).

While it is a good thing to be capable of shame before the personality has matured, it is not so for a grownup. For such a person will not commit disgraceful acts. This means that "practicing" in the case of such actions does not make sense. There is no type of action to be performed systematically in order to acquire the right middle of shamefulness. For it would presuppose the practice of shameful acts until one gets the right attitude towards them as part of one's moral education. That this is the salient point can be concluded from Aristotle's verdict concerning such a "virtue": "To be so constituted as to feel disgraced if one does such an action, and for this reason to think oneself good, is absurd; for it is for voluntary actions that shame is felt, and the

---

[23] Aristotle does not seem to be worried by the fact that *aidôs* in ordinary Greek is used in different ways, so that it means shame as well as respect and self-restraint, as witnessed in Plato's dialogues. The *Protagoras* treats *aidôs* in the sense of respect or awe; the *Charmides* at first presupposes calmness, then shame, and finally self-control in the sense of self-knowledge. Aristotle here as elsewhere confines himself to shame with respect to disgraceful acts.

good man will never voluntarily do bad actions" (1128b26–29). For this very reason Aristotle does not even want to consider shame as good in a qualified sense, as a kind of preventive force, in the case of an adult: "Shame might be said to be conditionally (*ex hypotheseôs*) a good thing; if a good man did such actions, he would feel disgrace; but the virtues are not subject to such a qualification. And if shamelessness—not to be ashamed of doing base actions—is bad, that does not make it good to be ashamed of doing such actions" (1128b29–33).

The case of righteous indignation, *nemesis*, which Aristotle mentions at the end of book II as the attitude towards one's neighbor's undeserved good luck, and somehow pairs together with envy at his good fortune, and with Schadenfreude at his bad luck, seems to be different. The three affections do have some affinity because they are all concerned with one's neighbors' good or bad fortune. But they do not really form a proper triad, for there is not too much and too little of the same objective. Thus righteous indignation is not the right mean between envy and Schadenfreude and this triad is not taken up again in the detailed discussion of the character-virtues and character-vices in book IV.[24] In the case of righteous indignation, *nemesis*, one may wonder, however, why Aristotle does not assign to it a virtuous disposition of its own, with an excess and a defect.[25] After all, one can habitually feel too much and too little righteous indignation at one's neighbors' ill-deserved good fortune, even if these defective states are nameless. For namelessness does not prevent Aristotle in other cases from postulating a mean disposition between excess and defect. If he does not assign a virtuous disposition to righteous indignation, it must be due to his conviction that the systematic *practice* of right indignation from early on concerning one's neighbor's undeserved good fortune cannot be part of the good life. As a witty student once suggested in discussion of this issue, such practice is one of the favorite pastimes of most Americans, and I guess that this preoccupation is not limited to the United States. But however this may be, Aristotle for good reasons would not have approved of such

---

[24] The common denominator is the neighbor's good or bad fortune, whether deserved or undeserved. Contrary to his promise in II 7, 1108a6 Aristotle does not return to this topic later in the *EN*, as he does in the case of shame. He must have realized that righteous indignation, envy, and Schadenfreude don't make a triad of the right kind and therefore dropped the issue. This does not mean that there cannot be fixed dispositions with respect to these affections—the *phthoneros*, the *epichairekakos*, and the *nemesêtikos* are persons with those dispositions. But not only are they not related to *nemesis* as vices to the right mean, but the *nemesêtikos* is not a type of person Aristotle wants to recommend.

[25] Cf. the list in *EE* II 3, 1221a3 and the discussion in III 7; *Rhetoric* II 6, 1384b4–5 and ch. 9, 1386b10–15, where Aristotle calls *nemesis* the counterpart of pity and both together as "feelings associated with a good character," but does not call them virtues. Feelings like righteous indignation may be tied to virtues like justice, although it is not the affection that is specific to it, and the same may be true of other "unaffiliated" affections.

practices, even if the feeling of righteous indignation at certain occasions is justified, because habituation would imply the cultivation of systematic observation and judgment of one's neighbors in a critical spirit rather than that of mutual *eunoia*.

Reflections of this kind explain why there are no dispositions concerning many of the affections on Aristotle's list of virtues, such as—besides those mentioned already—joy, longing, zealousness, and pity. These are just not affections that could be trained systematically from early on by appropriate activities. In some cases the actions themselves should be avoided, as in the case of shame; in other cases the objects and occasions are too wide-ranging and unspecific to allow for a systematic training, as in the case of joy, zealousness, or longing.[26] But if it is for these reasons that Aristotle does not attribute virtues and vices to these affections, why did he not make it explicit? He may well have regarded his treatment of shame as a sufficient indication of how to deal with analogous cases. Given his usual explanatory parsimony, this is indeed quite as much information as one can expect to get from him.

4. THE NARROW CONFINEMENT OF THE CHARACTER-VIRTUES

Taking seriously the demand for a specifiable systematic training from early on not only explains why Aristotle does not assume the existence of right dispositions for many of the affections he lists, but also suggests explanations for certain peculiar features in his depiction of the character-virtues. Thus, most readers who have bothered with the nitty-gritty of the details will have been puzzled by the narrow limitations that Aristotle imposes on the character-virtues. By "narrow limitations" I mean, for instance, that courage is limited to the military virtue of facing death and injury in battle, while the fear of other evils, such as poverty, illness, and the lack of friends, is excluded.[27] In the latter cases he wants to speak of "courage" only in an extended sense: "Poverty and disease we, perhaps, ought not to fear, nor in general the things that do not proceed from vice and are not due to a person himself. But not even the person who is fearless of these is courageous. Yet we apply the word to them also in virtue of a certain similarity" (III 6, 1115a17–19). The rationale for the limitation of courage proper is indicated in the clause that such happenings are not in our power. In the case of misfortunes such as poverty or illness there are no specific actions to

---

[26] A survey of the use of *pothos* and *zêlos* by different authors shows that their objects differ widely, and the same holds for *chara*.

[27] C.C.W. Taylor (2006) reproaches Aristotle with blindness in that respect (e.g. concerning courage 176–79). Aristotle admits that occasions for the proper exercise of courage are much rarer than for that of moderation (III 12, 1119a25–27), but does not therefore widen its scope.

be done, and hence there is also no systematic practice of such actions that would lead to a right intermediate disposition. They should not be feared in advance but endured, once they happen, but neither of the two attitudes is to be called courage proper. The same consideration must be behind Aristotle's denial that courage applies to death at sea: "Yet, at sea also, and in disease, the brave man is fearless.... While we show courage in situations where there is the opportunity to display strength and to die is noble, in these forms of death, i.e. at sea and in disease, neither of these conditions is fulfilled" (1115b35–b6). The point of the distinction is that aboard ship there is nothing to be *done* by a passenger, however courageous he may be otherwise, except endure what cannot be avoided, just as there is nothing to be done in face of disease. Patience, it should be pointed out, and endurance in the sense required here, are typically Christian virtues; they have no place in the Greek schema of virtues, and certainly not in Aristotle's action-centered conception of character-virtues.

The question why pity does not constitute a character-virtue can be answered on similar lines: fearing misfortunes for our neighbors who don't deserve them is no more specific than fearing misfortunes for oneself. There are neither particular occasions nor particular activities that would lead to a right middle disposition between excess and defect, although there is, of course, the possibility of feeling too much and too little at the misfortunes of others, once they occur, just as there is in our own case. But there is no right median disposition to be acquired that would apply to all possible misfortunes. That one should help others in need is, of course, a demand that Aristotle endorses. But that action falls under a different kind of virtue: liberality is the readiness to help a friend in need, and its analysis is concerned largely with the material aspect of helping others, rather than with the affective attitude towards them.

Different kinds of support for others are dealt with under the title of "friendship"; for friendship encompasses all sorts of relationships and all sorts of actions. The width of this conception explains, then, why Aristotle is somewhat vague about the status of friendship: He calls it "either a virtue or a virtue-like state" (VIII 1, 1155a3–5). Which of the two it is, and whether it is a character-virtue or a character-cum-intellectual virtue is left open, just as it is left open whether the mutual well-wishing (*eunoia*) is a kind of affection or a rational attitude with an affective part. *Philia* in the sense of friendliness is listed in the catalog of affections in II 5 and accepted as a virtue in II 7, but it concerns the attitude of the socially agreeable person (1108a26–28) and is not to be confused with friendship proper. In the discussion of friendship *philêsis* and *philein* play an important role, but they are not treated as affections of which there is excess and defect. Most important, there are different *types* of friendship with different motivations: there is friendship for the sake of what is mutually expedient, there is friendship for pleasure, and there is friendship for the other person's sake, which is at the same time the friendship for the sake of virtue. So friendship is not a unitary relationship and its affective aspects, as far as they are recognizable at all, have different bases and different aims.

The justification of the narrow confinement of the character-virtues in Aristotle may seem unsatisfactory, because it puts him at odds with the traditional, much broader, conception of the virtues. That courage—*andreia*—was ordinarily not confined to facing up to death and wounding in battle only is witnessed by Plato's discussion in the *Laches*—and it would be confirmed by other literary witnesses as well.[28] Likewise, moderation—*sôphrosynê*—was not normally tied exclusively to the physical pleasures of food, drink, and sex, as it is in Aristotle. Not only is Plato, once again, a fair witness to this fact in the *Charmides*, but as Helen North's magisterial study on *sophrosyne* (1967) has shown, it can be a stand-in for nearly all virtues, because it really means "being of a sound mind." If Aristotle sets aside that tradition, he must have had compelling reasons for doing so.

His reason for confining each of the moral virtues to *one* particular kind of affection and to *one* particular type of action is indeed not hard to find: otherwise his postulate of a right disposition to act and to be affected would be hopelessly vague. Even if the right mean is not to be determined by arithmetical means, but is a "mean relative to us," so that it may vary with the persons involved and the specific circumstances, it presupposes a clearly defined and comparable subject matter. Otherwise the assumption of excess and defect would be quite vacuous. Whether someone possesses too much or too little or just the right kind of readiness to face up to danger can be determined only if that readiness or unreadiness is of the same type and concerned with the same objective, that is, with frightening things of the same sort. For this very reason Aristotle confines moderation not only to the pleasures of the body, but exclusively to those of food, drink, and sex, to the exclusion even of pleasures of the eyes and ears. Given that the latter are tied to experiences of a higher sort, Aristotle clearly thinks that they are not on the same footing with the pleasures of the body that humans share with animals. They are therefore not concerned with the same "mean affective state" and are not overdone or "underdone" in the same way and by the same kind of activities as in the case of moderation proper.

This exclusiveness of the definition of the virtues has the consequence that many moral attitudes are not contained within Aristotle's narrow margins, but seem to be

---

[28] Cf. *Laches* 191d–e. Plato enumerates there the same cases we find in Aristotle: danger at sea, illness, poverty, and adds even the ability to withstand the lures of pleasure. Though *andreia* may usually be associated with behavior in battle, Aristotle not only admits that that there is a wider use (1115a19: "Yet we apply the word to them"), but in the *Politics* attributes a special form of courage to women, which is clearly not tied to valor in battle (III 4, 1259b31–1260a25).

left "homeless." What about the moderate, immoderate, or deficient enjoyer of beautiful sights, sounds, or other such things?[29] Aristotle does not tell us where these virtues and vices belong, nor does he even say that they *are* virtues and vices. A hint at a solution concerning such cases can be elicited, however, from the discussion of *akrasia*—the lack of self-control. Though *akrasia* proper is limited to the pleasures of the body, Aristotle grants that there is also the possibility of *akrasia* with respect to honor, money, reputation, love, and—above all—with respect to anger (*EN* VII 4, 1148a22–b14). For these types Aristotle suggests that they should be called *akrasia* with the qualification "in respect of" (*peri ti*) and with the proviso that they are based on some "analogous similarity." This principle can, then, be generalized in such a way that it is possible to tie each of the "homeless" virtues and vices to one of the standard virtues and vices on Aristotle's list, with the proviso that they resemble that virtue in a certain respect, as we found in the discussion of courage. Courage in the face of misfortune is then courage "with a special qualification"—and with a different middle and different extremes than courage in battle. This device makes the list of Aristotelian virtues and vices expandable, not ad infinitum, but at least in those cases where there is a legitimate basis for such an expansion. Thus it seems indeed that we are confronted by a "swarm of virtues," all of which, however, must be derivable from the ten/eleven tribes of virtues on Aristotle's list in II 7.

5. VIRTUOUS DISPOSITIONS WITHOUT AFFECTIONS?

But if the determination of the right disposition towards actions and affections is the salient point in Aristotle's conception of character-virtues as means between extremes, this seems to make the fact that most of the virtues he discusses have no particular affection assigned to them all the more perplexing. For this actually applies to the majority of the virtues in his catalog in II 7, and their detailed discussion in the subsequent books confirms that this is no mere omission. So this fact calls for some elucidation.

As even a perfunctory look shows, Aristotle's list of the triads of virtues and their corresponding vices in II 7 indeed contains few references to the affections enumerated in II 5. Only courage, moderation, and even-temperedness are determined by their characteristic affections. In all other cases no special affection is mentioned: not for liberality on the large or on the small scale, not in the case of honor, large or small, and also not in the case of the "social virtues" of forthrightness, wittiness, and friendliness. Furthermore, no specific affection is assigned to particular justice in book V,

---

[29] Cf. III 10, 1118a1–10. He reminds us of Plato's "sightlover" in *Republic* V 475d.

that is, to the right attitude in the case of distributive and retributive justice. Though Aristotle assumes a readiness to both distribute and accept a fair share of public goods and to make retribution in case of damage, there is no particular affection specified for this most central social virtue. Instead, all these virtues are defined only on the basis of their specific actions and their objects. Liberality on the small scale, for instance, consists in assisting others to the degree one should and in the way one should. Magnificence on the large scale manifests itself in great expenditure for the general public. Honor, large and small, should be pursued neither too little nor too much, and by the appropriate kinds of action.

The question therefore seems pertinent of what justifies the assumption that all character-virtues involve a specific affection, beyond those where Aristotle explicitly says so. There are two reasons that can be only indicated here. First, in his definition of the character-virtues at II 6, 1107a3–8 Aristotle includes both *praxeis* and *pathê* without indicating that the latter do not apply to all virtues. Second, the affections have an important role to play because they provide the necessary incentives to become active. For this very reason all moral virtues remain tied to the non-rational part of the soul, even if they fully agree with reason.[30]

Thus, we are back with the question why no affections are referred to in the case of many virtues. The solution that suggests itself is that in each case there is a certain "love" or "desire" that is at least implied in the name of the virtue. Thus, each of these virtues will be based on a certain affective predilection: love of giving, love of honor, love of forthrightness, love of wittiness, love of friendly behavior, and finally, love of justice, each of which prompt a person to become active. These affections could easily be assigned a name that forms a compound with "*philo-*" as a prefix or *-philia* as a suffix. The seeming lack of proper affections in the specifications of these virtues would then be due, once again, to their "namelessness" in ordinary Greek. Not all of them are in fact nameless, for Aristotle mentions *philotimia* and *philomatheia* in III 13, 1117b29 as "pleasures of the soul," in contradistinction to those of the body, and indicates that there are others of that kind, so that everyone enjoys the sorts of things towards which he is *philikos*. *Philotimia* is actually included on the table in II 7, 1107b31, but not in the lists of natural affections earlier.[31]

---

[30] This is not the place for a discussion of Aristotle's moral psychology. Because he does not draw clear borders between the contributions to decisions and actions of *pathos*, pleasure, pain, and desire, a clarification of their interdependence would require a thorough study of its own.

[31] Aristotle may assume there is a natural susceptibility towards the objects of all virtuous dispositions, such as love of honor, liberality, and social agreeableness. Nevertheless, it seems significant that Aristotle never uses the word *pathos* in connection with these virtues, while he does so in the case of the right and wrong attitude towards anger (*orgê*) (IV 11, 1125b30). In the

There is something that is right about this explanation of how all virtues involve affections, but also something that is wrong. Aristotle certainly ascribes to each virtue its own kind of pleasure or pain as motivating forces. That those pleasures and pains are intimately tied to the virtues is emphasized throughout book II. In chapter 3 Aristotle mentions their existence as an important "sign" (*sêmeion*) of the existence of virtuous or vicious dispositions: "For character-virtue is concerned with pleasures and pains: it is on account of pleasure that we do bad things, and on account of pain that we abstain from noble ones. Hence we ought to have been brought up in a particular way from our very youth, as Plato says, so as both to delight in and to be pained by the things we ought; for this is the right education" (1104b8–14). And soon afterwards Aristotle specifies virtuous behavior in terms of pleasure and pain: "but it is on account of pleasures and pains that humans become bad, by pursuing and avoiding these—either the pleasures and pains they ought not or when they ought not or as they ought not, or by going wrong in one of the similar ways" (1104a21–24). This distinction justifies the claim that ethics in its entirety is in a way concerned with pleasure and pain and that it extends to political science as a whole (1105a10–12). Pleasure and pain therefore serve as a kind of litmus test of whether someone really possesses a certain virtue: only if the agent enjoys doing the right activity does s/he possess the virtue in question.

So, if all virtues and vices are characterized by their respective pleasures and pains, and these pleasures and pains are or are based on affections, what, then, is wrong with the principle that all virtues and vices are characterized by their affections? There is a distinction to be observed here that Aristotle must have been aware of, though he does not make it explicit. His initial list of affections at II 5 concerns only natural kinds, that is, those we have by nature and that as such are neither good nor bad. So perhaps the affections in case of the other virtues are "acquired tastes," because they develop only gradually as the result of the requisite habituation in a social setting. Because arguments *ex silentio* are notoriously weak this explanation must remain somewhat speculative. For Aristotle may well think that there is at least a natural affective or desiderative predisposition, a natural *philia* towards liberality, honor, pleasant social behavior, and most of all towards justice, because there is a natural striving for self-perfection in human beings that will be fulfilled under the right conditions. But given his silence, it must remain an open question whether there is in all of us a natural propensity to act generously, to strive for honor and so on, or whether that kind of "love" is culturally induced in Aristotle's eyes. There is also the possibility that he assumes a combination

---

discussion of the social virtue of friendliness Aristotle in fact denies that there is a *pathos* and love (*stergein*) of the persons at stake at all—in contradistinction to the case of true friendship, IV 6, 1126b22–25.

of both factors, that is, a natural inclination to honor and liberality on the one hand and a specific form that is due to the moral education received on the other.[32]

If Aristotle presupposed such a combination, that would explain why he pays so little attention to a further difference that should be at least mentioned here, concerning the pleasures and pains involved in moral conduct. As a closer look at the relevant texts shows, there are two kinds of them: there are pleasure and pain as the *objects* of moral actions, and there are the pleasures or pains of *acting* in the right or wrong way. That Aristotle was aware of the difference at least in some cases is obvious from pronouncements as the following: "For the person who abstains from bodily pleasures and delights in this very fact is temperate, while the man who is annoyed at it is self-indulgent, and the person who stands up against things that are terrible and delights in this or at least is not pained is brave, while the person who is pained is a coward" (II 3, 1104b5–8). In both cases there are two different types of pleasures and pains at work: there is fear of physical pain that is to be endured in the case of courage, and there is the moral pleasure, or at least the moral satisfaction, of acting in the right way. The avoidance of an unsuitable pleasure of the body provides the "moral pleasure" of acting with moderation. Now the question is whether Aristotle assumed there is such a division for all virtues, that is, whether he presupposed that there is one kind of affection that is the object of every virtue, and another kind that is part of the performance of the right activities.[33] In the case of propensities like love of honor or generosity the distinction between object and performance is harder to specify than in that of courage and temperance, so that may be the reason why Aristotle does not pursue the question of their underlying affections.

6. CONCLUSIONS

It may not be obvious what this last complication has to do with the topic of this discussion, that is, whether Aristotle regards his list of virtues as complete or not. There is indeed a connection, which can here only be indicated in brief without the full discussion it would need and deserve. If all virtues have a natural basis in our affective nature one might think that Aristotle assumes there is a definite set of character-virtues and

---

[32] Given that Aristotle holds that we are all by nature more prone to take rather than to give (IV 1, 1120a17–18), he may regard a natural affection for generosity at least as a rare thing.
[33] On the distinction between pleasure as the subject matter and as the integral part of an activity, cf. Frede (2009). For a brief indication of the difference cf. Broadie (1991), 90–95. In the former case all pleasures are at the same time desires and all pains are aversions; in the latter case this is not so. For while doing a virtuous activity properly and enjoying it, there is nothing further to be desired. In case of the pain of doing an improper action or of performing it badly, there must be the wish to stop—but that is different from the aversions in the case of fear, anger, or hatred.

that he has done justice to all of them, including the varieties that are due to the kinds of qualifications mentioned above. But if some of the virtues are the products of social conditioning, then the list of character-virtues could vary, depending on a society's particular values that are part of that education in what is deemed to be the life of a "decent citizen." Now, Aristotle once mentions that there is a natural root for all character-virtues. Thus in book VI he introduces the notion of "natural character-virtues": "For all think that each type of character belongs to its possessor in a sense by nature; for from the very moment of birth we are just or fitted for moderation or brave or have the other moral qualities" (13, 1144b3–6). These are not sufficient, Aristotle continues, unless we also acquire the corresponding intellectual capacities because naturally good leanings can lead us astray. Unfortunately, he does not elaborate on the conception of natural virtues and their extent; it seems like an afterthought that he introduces as a proof that character and practical reason are necessary complements throughout.

Instead, Aristotle leaves it to the reader's ingenuity to draw the right conclusions. This very fact confirms the suspicion fostered by the various uncertainties and open questions that Aristotle was not much vexed by the question that forms the topic of this essay, namely whether his catalog of virtues and vices is complete.[34] If his insouciance in that respect is due to his reliance on the criterion, mentioned earlier, that every desirable character trait must be the result of publicly organized practice, such reliance would be rather unsatisfactory as far as the completeness and the unity of the virtues are concerned. Not only would the criterion seem overly pragmatic: what can be acquired by joint practice and seems desirable, constitutes what is right. It also does not explain how the character-virtues form a unity so that Aristotle's injunction is justified that the good person must have them all. But where should such a unity come from? Though this point cannot be argued here in full, the guarantee of the unity of the virtues is derivable from the conception of the good life as such. That this is not as empty a postulate as is sometimes assumed becomes obvious if we recall that according to Aristotle it is the concern of the "most architectonic science" of the human good that he attributes to the statesman (EN I 2, 1094a22–b11). Because the lawgiver knows what that good is, it is his task to see to it that the citizens learn all the things that are necessary to guarantee a life in fulfillment of their intellectual and moral potential. Given that the polis—at least in its ideal form—provides the perfect condition of human life, Aristotle's list of virtues must be the result of his reflection on all the good character-states that are essential for

---

[34] Aristotle nowhere explains why it should be necessary to separate virtues dealing with honor on a large scale from those on a small scale, or why the same should apply to handing out money. He may simply take it for granted that his conception of a right mean with deficiency and excess would make that separation necessary.

human life, both public and private. This explains his confidence that he has not overlooked any of the major virtues that constitute the good life.

It is indeed hard to find virtues that are not somehow accountable on Aristotelian terms. We may miss honesty, industriousness, reliability, and patience. But Aristotle would file honesty under either justice or forthrightness. Industriousness and reliability are not virtues in their own right; instead, they are part and parcel of the pursuit of every virtuous activity. And the same goes for patience in the sense of putting up with adversity where necessary. Humility and turning the other cheek, however, were not part of the ancient set of virtues, and Aristotle would have seen no reason for including them. That the ancient set of virtues differs from the Christian ones is witnessed by the fact that anger is treated as the legitimate subject-matter of a virtue: If someone insults you without provocation, you ought to react in the way you should, to the degree you should, concerning the person you, and at the time, you should. No more and no less.

The question of the completeness of the Aristotelian set of virtues depends, of course, on the *form of life* that is deemed satisfactory by all those concerned. And with changing times, the requirements may change—to a certain degree. For, if Aristotle is right, there is a basic human potential that does not change, as well as basic human needs that always need to be fulfilled. There would, then, be a catalog of "core-virtues" and a catalog of extensions. The specification of the different kinds of desirable character-traits may depend not only on the linguistic conventions of each culture but also on its overall character. While Aristotle regards "being active" in accordance with our best potential as a central feature of human nature, we might feel prompted to speak of a "suitable occupation," and while Aristotle regards friendship as an essential element in human life, we may rather speak of satisfactory personal relationships. But clearly not all differences can be attributed to difference in terminology alone. For human life has undergone fundamental changes since Aristotle's time and its focus on life in the small and well-ordered polis. This is one of the reasons why the emphasis on honor, large and small, and liberality, large and small, at first sight strike us as quaint, just as do the social virtues that Aristotle regards as important. Our society has become a mass-society and our world has become a "work-world," so that its successes and failures are largely measured in those terms. This would suggest that a catalog of contemporary virtues and vices, if it could be drawn up at all, would look considerably different from Aristotle's list. And yet there will no doubt be also similarities to the Aristotelian virtues, for any such theory that does justice to human nature will have to be concerned with those actions and affections that are part of it, just as it will have to do justice to the need for a life that consists of worthwhile activities. And given the diversity and multiplicity of activities and the respective affections, a contemporary catalog should contain quite a swarm of virtues, whose unity is based on the fact that they are the constituents of a fulfilling human life in the Aristotelian spirit.

Acknowledgments

Previous versions of this chapter were given as part of the Grey lectures at the University of Cambridge in 2009 and at the colloquium in honor of Gisela Striker at Harvard University. The final version benefited greatly from the discussion at both occasions, and also from extensive written comments by Michael Pakaluk.

Bibliographical References

Ackrill, J. L. 1974: Aristotle on *Eudaimonia*. *Proceedings of the British Academy* **60**, 339–59; repr. in: (ed.) Rorty (1980), 15–34.
Annas, J. 1993: *The Morality of Happiness*. Oxford: Oxford University Press.
Broadie, S. 1991: *Ethics with Aristotle*. Oxford: Oxford University Press.
Broadie, S. & Rowe, C. 2002: *Aristotle Nicomachean Ethics*. Translation, introd. & commentary. Oxford: Oxford University Press.
Burnyeat, M. F. 1980: Aristotle on Learning how to be good. In: (ed.) Rorty (1980), 69–92.
Frede, D. 2009: Nicomachean Ethics 11–12: Pleasure. In: (ed.) Natali (2009), 183–207.
Gauthier, R. A. & Jolif, J. Y. 2002^2: *Aristote, L'Éthique à Nicomaque*. Louvain-la-Neuve.
Gottlieb, P. 2009: *The Virtue of Aristotle's Ethics*. Cambridge: Cambridge University Press.
Häcker, K. F. 1863: *Das Einteilungs- und Anordnungsprinzip der moralischen Tugendreihe in der Nikomachischen Ethik*. Berlin: Nauck.
Hursthouse, R. 1980/81: A false doctrine of the mean. *Proceedings of the Aristotelian Society* **80/81**, 57–72; repr. in (ed.) N. Sherman, *Aristotle's Ethics: Critical Essays*. Lanham, MD, 105–20.
—— 2006: The central doctrine of the mean. In: (ed.) R. Kraut, *The Blackwell Guide to Aristotle's Nicomachean Ethics*. Oxford: Blackwell, 96–115.
Irwin, T. 1999^2: *Aristotle Nicomachean Ethics*, transl. with introd., notes, and glossary. Indianapolis: Hackett Publishing Co.
Kosman, L. A. 1980: Being properly affected: virtue and feelings in Aristotle. In (ed.) A. O. Rorty, 103–116.
Natali, C (ed.) 2009: *Aristotle's Nicomachean Ethics Book VII. Symposium Aristotelicum*. Oxford: Oxford University Press.
North, H. 1967: *Sophrosyne: Self-Knowledge and Self-Restraint in Greek Literature*. Ithaca, NY: Cornell University Press.
Rapp, C. 2006: What use is Aristotle's doctrine of the mean? In: (ed.) B. Reis, *The Virtuous Life in Greek Ethics*. Cambridge: Cambridge University Press, 99–126.
Reis, B. (ed.) 2006: *The Virtuous Life in Greek Ethics*. Cambridge: Cambridge University Press.
Rorty, A. O. (ed.) 1980 *Essays on Aristotle's Ethics*. Berkeley: University of California Press.
Sherman, N. 1989: *The Fabric of Character*. Oxford: Oxford University Press.
—— 1999: The habituation of character. In (ed.) N. Sherman, *Aristotle's Ethics: Critical Essays*. Lanham MD: Rowman & Littlefield, 231–60.
Striker, G. 2006: Aristotle's ethics as a political science. In: (ed.) Reis (2006), 127–41.
Taylor, C. C. W. 2006: *Aristotle Nicomachean Ethics Books II–IV*. Oxford: Oxford University Press.
Urmson, J. O. 1973: Aristotle's doctrine of the mean. *American Philosophical Quarterly* **10/3**, 223–30.

5

JUSTICE AND THE LAWS IN ARISTOTLE'S ETHICS

Mi-Kyoung Lee

1. INTRODUCTION

It is commonly supposed, by readers and admirers of Aristotle's ethics, that the laws of the state have very little to do in his conception of the behavior and the deliberation of the truly virtuous person. The laws play a merely contingent role, both epistemically and motivationally, in the psyche and actions of the virtuous person: (1) epistemically, the virtuous person is perfectly capable of figuring out what the right thing to do is, and does not need the law to tell her, and (2) motivationally, the virtuous person does not need the threat of punishment to get her to do the right thing; unlike the immature person or ordinary sinner, she does the right thing for the right reason, that is, because it is the right thing to do, not because otherwise she might lose her good reputation or be punished.

That this is Aristotle's view is strongly suggested by his way of distinguishing between the fully virtuous and less than fully virtuous by saying that the former are those who know what the right thing to do is and why, whereas the latter are those who merely follow rules set down by others, for example by one's parents, or by the laws of the state. Aristotle quotes Hesiod to help him make the point:

Far best is he who knows all things himself;
Good, he that hearkens when men counsel right;
But he who neither knows, nor lays to heart
Another's wisdom, is a useless wight.
(*EN* I 4. 1095b10–14, trans. Ross rev. Brown)

The point is that the merely "good" man lacks understanding, but at least can be credited with "hearkening when men counsel right"—that is, of following the instructions of others, thus approximating the behavior and actions of the fully virtuous person who is "far best." Later, at the very end of the *Nicomachean Ethics*, Aristotle returns to this thought—now explaining that the law is a good way of training the people of a state for virtue, presumably via appeals to their sense of shame and nobility, and incentives of reward and punishment (*EN* X 9. 1179b31–1180a5).

These passages and others seem to suggest that Aristotle thinks that the virtuous person really has no need of the law, either to tell her what to do, or to get her to do what she already knows she must do. The function of the law is, rather, to educate, train, and if necessary coerce that part of the populace in whom the virtues have been imperfectly and insufficiently inculcated. It is, even so, a rough and imperfect tool—perhaps adequate for the masses, in the absence of anything better, but not the ideal method for moral instruction. It follows, or so it seems, that Aristotle's moral theory can be understood independently of his theory of the aims and content of the laws of the state.

I want to argue that this is a mistaken view about the shape and ambitions of Aristotle's ethics, for he thinks that there is an essential connection between virtue and the law. In this paper, I will take up and develop an argument made by Gisela Striker, namely that the virtuous person deliberates by thinking about what the law requires her to do.[1] The law spells out in detail what the right thing to do is, and the virtuous person is someone who correctly grasps what the law requires of her, and does it for the right reasons. For the virtuous agent decides what to do by considering what is legislated for citizens in her society for the common good.

Now, it's certainly true that Aristotle thinks that the virtuous person is not motivated by the threat of punishment and the sanctions attached to any law. Her actions flow from her good character—not from her fear of punishment. It's also true that the virtuous person doesn't need the law to direct her actions, because she has *phronêsis*, that is, practical wisdom. For example, if she sees someone in need of her help, she doesn't have to be told to give assistance; if she makes a promise, she doesn't need reminding by the law that she ought to keep it. So the laws are not needed to tell the virtuous person what to do, and it also does not motivate her to do what she should do. The reason why every virtuous person is necessarily obedient to the laws is instead the following:

(1) Every virtuous person is just.
(2) Being just means being concerned to promote the common good.
(3) ∴ Every virtuous person is concerned to promote the common good.
(4) What will promote the common good is spelled out by laws (at least, by good laws in a well-ordered state).
(5) ∴ Every virtuous person is obedient to the laws.

---

[1] Striker 2006: 134.

Clearly, if we are to be persuaded by this line of thought, we will want to hear more about two related ideas. The first is the idea that a just person is necessarily a lawful and law-abiding citizen. The second is the idea that the virtuous person necessarily cares about the common good. In the rest of this paper, I will explore these two ideas. I hope to show that justice and its concern for the common good is central to Aristotle's conception of the virtuous agent, and that justice, in turn, cannot be understood apart from the various laws that states devise for the common benefit.

2. THE JUST PERSON IS A LAWFUL PERSON

Let us start with the first idea, that being a just person means being a lawful and law-abiding citizen. At the outset I should acknowledge that in English, it sounds odd to call someone "just"; we think that institutions, laws, distributions, and states of affairs can be "just," meaning above all that they are fair and equitable, but if you say that a person is "just," it's not quite clear, in English, what you mean. In Greek, when Aristotle talks about a man being "just" (*dikaios*), he means, as we shall see, that the person is law-abiding and that his relations with other people are as they should be, because he does what he should for other people, and has a concern for the good of others or for the common good. Thus, it might be better to translate "just man" here by "good man" or even "morally good person," in order to capture the idea that one is "just" insofar as one's relations with others are as they should be. Indeed, it has been suggested that for Aristotle, *dikaiosunê* "justice," not *aretê* "virtue," is the concept that corresponds most closely to our concept of moral goodness or moral rightness.[2]

In fact, Aristotle acknowledges that in Greek, there is an ambiguity between two senses of the word "just," roughly corresponding to the idea of fairness and to the idea of moral goodness; as we might put it, there are in fact two distinct, but related, concepts of justice in Aristotle.

> Both the lawless man [ὁ παράνομος] and the grasping and unfair man [ὁ πλεονέκτης καὶ ἄνισος] are thought to be unjust [ἄδικος], so that evidently both the law-abiding [ὁ νόμιμος] and the fair man [ὁ ἴσος] will be just. The just [τὸ δίκαιον], then, is the lawful [τὸ νόμιμον] and the fair [τὸ ἴσον], the unjust [τὸ ἄδικον] the unlawful [τὸ παράνομον] and the unfair [τὸ ἄνισον].[3] (V 1. 1129a32–b1)

---

[2] Irwin 1986; Striker 2006: 135.
[3] All translations of Aristotle's *Nicomachean Ethics* are from the Oxford translation by Ross revised by Brown (Oxford World Classics 2009).

The term "unjust" (*adikos*) sometimes describes (1) someone who is "lawless," a law-breaker, and sometimes describes (2) someone who is "grasping and unfair." Conversely, to call someone just is to say either (1) that he is lawful and law-abiding, or (2) that he is "fair." Aristotle goes on to identify justice in the sense of lawfulness with the whole of virtue, and justice in the sense of being fair-minded with just a part of virtue, because it is an individual virtue of character, coordinate with courage, moderation, generosity, wittiness, and so forth (*EN* V 2. 1130b10–16). These two concepts of justice are traditionally called "general justice" and "special justice." Special justice is the virtue that belongs to people who care above all about the fairness of social and political institutions, arrangements and distributions of benefits and harms. Aristotle clearly has in mind a virtue that would belong to magistrates, statesmen, and especially judges—but presumably this is a virtue that all citizens in a good state should be expected to have. Special justice is a virtue that is conceptually secondary to a prior concept of fairness, understood as equality in distributions of goods, or equality in rectification of harms. General justice, by contrast—which is the subject of this paper—is a broader umbrella concept, which includes special justice, but goes beyond a concern for fairness, and has to do with correctness in one's relations with other people quite generally.

So Aristotle describes general justice as the virtue of being a law-abiding person (the *nomimos*) who cares about the norms of society and obeys the constraints that are imposed on his or her behavior; general injustice refers to the person (the *paranomos*) who shows disrespect for the laws and norms of society, both written and unwritten. The law lays down constraints on behavior in many areas—for example, it requires you to pay your taxes, perform military service, keep your hands off your neighbor's property, support your parents in their old age, and so on. The just person obeys those constraints whereas the unjust person does not. (It is worth keeping in mind that Greek *nomoi* include laws both written and unwritten—and the latter includes customs, conventions, and norms widely endorsed and followed.)

When Aristotle defines general justice in terms of lawfulness, he is insisting upon two things. First, his definition shifts the focus away from the motivational set of the agent, back to the behavior and actions of the agent described in terms of action-types. A person is just *because* he does the things required by the laws of society; he is unjust *because* he breaks those laws.[4] Second, Aristotle is insisting that justice has to do with one's relations with other people—it is above all a *social* virtue, spelled out in terms of laws that sometimes require one to confer benefits on other people. That justice has to do with one's relations with other people, and that it requires obedience to the laws,

---

[4] Hence, general justice corresponds roughly to what Sachs calls the "vulgar conception of justice" in Plato's *Republic* IV 442d–443a (Sachs 1963).

are deeply familiar ideas in Greek thought. That it requires obedience to the laws is familiar for example from Antiphon's *On Truth*:

> Justice is a matter of not transgressing what the laws prescribe in whatever city you are a citizen of. (Oxyrynchus Papyrus XI no.1364, ed. Hunt, col. 1 line 6– col. 7 line 15 = Antiphon DK 87B44, trans. McKirahan)

The idea that justice has to do with one's relations with other people and more specifically that it requires one to benefit others besides oneself, is familiar from Thrasymachus in Plato's *Republic*, for example, who says that justice is "the advantage of the stronger." As he explains, the laws are the product of existing power relations in a state, and hence serve the advantage of those who are in power. That is, the just person always benefits someone else rather than himself (*Republic* I. 338d–339a).

Aristotle endorses this familiar conception of justice when he says that justice is lawfulness. In his view, justice has to do with proper relations with and fulfillment of obligations to others. It is a social virtue that belongs to people insofar as they live with, cooperate with, and rely on others. Furthermore, it is a virtue that is characterized above all by its benefits for a group of people—maybe *only* for other people and not for oneself, as Thrasymachus says so memorably.

3. OBEDIENT TO *ANY* LAW?

Aristotle thinks that the just person is lawful and law-abiding. But does obedience to the laws necessarily make one virtuous?[5] It would only if the laws were good laws. After all, if one lived in a state where the laws were unjust, or badly conceived, then it would seem to follow that the virtuous agent would have the obligation *not* to follow the laws of that state. So when Aristotle says that "all lawful acts are in a sense just acts," does he mean *everything* that *any* law sets out is just? And that there are no unjust laws? Is he a conventionalist about justice and the law?[6] On the one hand, there is a close connection between *nomos* and *doxa*, such that a *nomos* is a norm or expectation generally accepted and endorsed by a group of people. Now in English usage of the term "law," it is conceivable that there could be a law that is unknown or not accepted by anyone. By contrast,

---

[5] The following discussion is greatly indebted to Kraut 2002: Ch. 4, esp. 103–25, which defends the cogency of Aristotle's discussion of general justice.

[6] One might think of Cleitophon's interpretation and defense of Thrasymachus' conception of the laws in Plato's *Republic* I 340b: justice is what the stronger believes to be to his advantage. Kraut 2002: 104 cites for comparison Hobbes' claim that no sovereign power can be guilty of injustice, because injustice consists in the violation of a covenant, and no sovereign makes a covenant.

there couldn't be a *nomos* which no one believes or endorses; *nomoi* are norms which a group of people regard as valid and binding, and includes customs, norms, and unwritten laws. Furthermore, the conceptual connection between *nomos* and *dikaios* is so tight that Myles Burnyeat has gone as far as to say that a law cannot be unjust;[7] a law may be badly formulated, or ill-conceived, but cannot be *adikos*.

I am skeptical about the idea that Aristotle is a conventionalist about law, and also about Burnyeat's specific claim that laws in Greek can't be unjust. For Aristotle holds that laws can be unjust. For example, in *Pol.* III 11. 1282b8–13, he says that the laws must suit the regime, and since there have been both correct and deviant regimes, "it is clear that laws that accord with the correct constitutions must be just, and those that accord with the deviant constitutions not just."[8] So he clearly doesn't think that laws are just simply because they are the law.

Rather, when Aristotle offers two arguments that obedience and lawfulness is indeed a virtue (*EN* V 1. 1129b11–25), he is thinking of obedience to laws that meet a certain minimum standard of correctness. Here is the first argument he offers:

> Since the lawless man was seen to be unjust and the law-abiding man just, evidently all lawful acts are in a sense just acts; for the acts laid down by the legislative art are lawful, and each of these, we say, is just. Now the laws in their enactments on all subjects aim at the common advantage either of all or of the best or of those who hold power, or something of the sort; so that in one sense we call those acts just that tend to produce and preserve happiness and its components [i.e. virtues] for the political society. (V 1. 1129b11–19)[9]

He argues that acts are lawful when they are laid down *in accord with the lawgiver's art* (*nomothetikê*), and hence are in accord with the *right* laws; when they are lawful in *this* sense, they are just. This would imply that a law that was not in accord with *nomothetikê* would not be a good law. What then is the lawgiver's art? It is, in the first instance,

---

[7] I have heard Burnyeat say this at Princeton in the early 1990s; he apparently has an unpublished paper on this which I have not seen.
[8] See also *Pol.* II 8. 1268b38–1269a3 where he says that the laws of archaic societies are "simple and barbaric," though he does not use the word "unjust" for them. Kraut 2002: 104 also mentions the distinction made in *EN* V 7 between legal or conventional justice and natural justice, where the latter seems to imply a basis for evaluating the justice or goodness of laws.
[9] Ἐπεὶ δ' ὁ παράνομος ἄδικος ἦν ὁ δὲ νόμιμος δίκαιος, δῆλον ὅτι πάντα τὰ νόμιμά ἐστί πως δίκαια· τά τε γὰρ ὡρισμένα ὑπὸ τῆς νομοθετικῆς νόμιμά ἐστι, καὶ ἕκαστον τούτων δίκαιον εἶναί φαμεν. οἱ δὲ νόμοι ἀγορεύουσι περὶ ἁπάντων, στοχαζόμενοι ἢ τοῦ κοινῇ συμφέροντος πᾶσιν ἢ τοῖς ἀρίστοις ἢ τοῖς κυρίοις [κατ' ἀρετὴν] ἢ κατ' ἄλλον τινὰ τρόπον τοιοῦτον· ὥστε ἕνα μὲν τρόπον δίκαια λέγομεν τὰ ποιητικὰ καὶ φυλακτικὰ εὐδαιμονίας καὶ τῶν μορίων αὐτῆς τῇ πολιτικῇ κοινωνίᾳ.

the "controlling part" of political science, which is the same as practical wisdom (*EN* VI 8. 1141b23–5).[10] But Aristotle does not now immediately move to the realm of ideal legislation, by saying for example that an act is just if it is in accord with the laws that an ideal legislator would legislate; instead, he simply says, "Now the laws in their enactments on all subjects aim at the common advantage either of all or of the best or of those who hold power, or something of the sort; so that in one sense we call those acts just that tend to produce and preserve happiness and its components [i.e. virtues] for the political society" (V 1. 1129b14–19).

I take Aristotle to be arguing as follows:[11]

(1) The laws in their pronouncements about everything—that is, the laws, both written and unwritten—aim at (i.e. try to attain, but may fail to secure) the common advantage of a political community—whose membership may be more or less inclusive (inclusive in democracies and, perhaps, Aristotle's ideal city-state, exclusive in oligarchies and tyrannies).[12]

That the laws should aim at the common advantage can be true of legislation for a wide variety of political systems, ranging from more democratic to more aristocratic forms. But the common advantage he's talking about is presumably not mere expedience, but genuine common benefit—ruling out cases like the law instituted by the Thirty confiscating the property of metics to finance the Spartan garrison, which was perhaps

---

[10] There, Aristotle is concerned to defend his claim that practical wisdom and political wisdom "are the same state of mind, but their essence is not the same." He thinks the widely held opinion that practical wisdom requires one to mind one's own business is wrong; instead, practical wisdom requires one to recognize the extent to which one's own good depends on the good of others. As he says, "yet perhaps one's own good cannot exist without household management, nor without a form of government. Further, how one should order one's own affairs is not clear and needs inquiry" (*EN* VI 8. 1141b34–1142a11; see also *Pol.* III 4. 1277b25–30). See also Reeve 1992: §§12, 20, 32; Schofield 2006: 318–21.

[11] It is somewhat uncertain how exactly to construe the sentence: *koinêi* can go either with all four disjuncts ("the common advantage either of all or of the best or…", with Ross and Kraut) or just with the first ("either the common advantage of all or the advantage of the best or…", with Irwin 1988: 424–5), and some manuscripts omit *kat' aretên* in the third disjunct; for helpful discussion, see Kraut 2002: 113n24. Kraut I think correctly notes that, however one construes the text, Aristotle's meaning is clear: "however narrowly or broadly the political community is defined, justice in the broad sense produces and preserves happiness for the whole of it."

[12] One can either read Aristotle as saying, as here, that the laws are comprehensive, and address all matters, or as saying that the laws, in all the matters that they deal with, aim at the common advantage.

expedient for the Thirty who were in power, but not to the common advantage of the political community. That is, he thinks that

(2) The common advantage of a political community consists of the happiness and its parts (i.e. the virtues) for the members of that community.

For this reason, it follows that

(3) Lawful acts—those in accord with laws that aim at the common advantage, that is, the production and preservation of happiness and its parts for the members of the political community—are therefore the ones we call just.

From the nature of the law and its orientation towards the happiness and virtue of the members of a political community he infers that lawful actions are just and virtuous. The argument, then, is that law-abiding behavior is just and virtuous because the aim of legislation is to promote the common good for the political community (as Aristotle frequently maintains elsewhere, cf. *EN* VIII 9. 1160a13–14, *Pol.* III 6. 1279a17–19, III 12. 1282b16–18, III 13. 1283b35–42). The lawbreaker's actions are unjust because they are inimical to the general happiness of a polis; he engages in anti-social behavior, and is a threat to the well-being of his fellow citizens.

Aristotle offers a second reason why law-abidingness is a virtue: it is precisely because the laws legislate virtue:

> And the law bids us do both the acts of a brave man (e.g. not to desert our post nor take to flight nor throw away our arms), and those of a temperate man (e.g. not to commit adultery nor to gratify one's lust), and those of a good-tempered man (e.g. not to strike another nor to speak evil), and similarly with regard to the other virtues and forms of wickedness, commanding some acts and forbidding others; and the rightly-framed law does this rightly, and the hastily conceived one less well. (*EN* V 1, 1129b19–25)[13]

According to this argument, the laws provide moral instruction and guidance, by prescribing forms of behavior that will promote virtue—or, more realistically (since then the task would presumably be endless), as here, by prohibiting forms of behavior

---

[13] προστάττει δ' ὁ νόμος καὶ τὰ τοῦ ἀνδρείου ἔργα ποιεῖν, οἷον μὴ λείπειν τὴν τάξιν μηδὲ φεύγειν μηδὲ ῥιπτεῖν τὰ ὅπλα, καὶ τὰ τοῦ σώφρονος, οἷον μὴ μοιχεύειν μηδ' ὑβρίζειν, καὶ τὰ τοῦ πράου, οἷον μὴ τύπτειν μηδὲ κακηγορεῖν, ὁμοίως δὲ καὶ κατὰ τὰς ἄλλας ἀρετὰς καὶ μοχθηρίας τὰ μὲν κελεύων τὰ δ' ἀπαγορεύων, ὀρθῶς μὲν ὁ κείμενος ὀρθῶς, χεῖρον δ' ὁ ἀπεσχεδιασμένος.

that are incompatible with virtue and common happiness. That the aim of politics is "making the citizens be of a certain kind, viz. good and capable of fine deeds" (*EN* I 9. 1099b29–32; see also I 13. 1102a7–12) is emphasized throughout the *Nicomachean Ethics*. He returns to the thought that laws will provide moral education in *EN* X 9, where he compares the state to a father educating his children.[14] Insofar as the laws aim to make citizens good, lawful acts will be virtuous.

But now we can reformulate the earlier question about obedience to the law: given the fact that many or perhaps most laws fall short of what ideal *nomothetikê* would legislate, doesn't this imply that many or perhaps most laws are bad ones, and hence shouldn't be obeyed? There is, of course, nothing sacrosanct about the particular laws that a particular state happens to have—and Aristotle is neither a relativist nor a reactionary with respect to the laws. For example, in *Politics* II 8 he acknowledges that sometimes laws need to be changed.[15] And as Richard Kraut has argued, even though Aristotle states in *Politics* III 4 that civic virtue consists of the ability to both rule and be ruled—and that it more specifically charges each citizen with the "preservation" (ἡ σωτηρία) of the constitution of the state to which he belongs (*Pol.* III 4. 1276b27–30; cf. Kraut 2002: 363–84)—even so, there are limits to what the good citizen will do. For example, in *EN* III 1, Aristotle says that there are some things that no one should contemplate doing, even if ordered by a tyrant. He also seems to think that under some circumstances, the good citizen ought to act to overthrow the constitution—for example, a tyranny (*Pol.* IV 10). Furthermore, Kraut argues persuasively that it is compatible with "preserving" the constitution that one act to meliorate its defects; in particular, if one lives in a democracy, which Aristotle regards as a deviant constitution, the good citizen will do what he can to prevent the more extreme and unstable forms of democracy from arising. Such a citizen might, for example, advocate proposals for a mixed constitution—tempering a democracy with elements of an oligarchic constitution (see e.g. *Pol.* IV 13–14; cf. Kraut 2002: Ch. 12). All of these indicate that Aristotle fully recognizes that some laws and constitutions are defective and require change.

If, then, what makes laws good is that they aim at the common good, then this is the proper criterion for judging which laws are good and which are not. And it is possible for the lawgivers to miss the mark in one of two ways (Young 2006: 182). First, the lawgivers could hold a mistaken conception of happiness, but craft the laws well so that they do a good job of promoting this mistaken conception of happiness.

---

[14] For an idea of what laws and customs that educate citizens for virtue will look like, see *Politics* VII 13–17 and VIII.

[15] De Romilly 1971 atttributes to Aristotle an anti-progressivist conservative thesis *against* changing the law on the basis of *Pol.* II 8, but see Brunschwig 1980.

Second, the lawgivers could hold a correct conception of happiness, but fail to implement that conception well in the laws. Hence, drafting the laws of a state is presumably no easy matter. It is the job of *nomothetikê*, or the art of legislation, to formulate laws that correctly identify what is good for a community of citizens and that promote it well. Aristotle goes on in the *Politics* to argue that correct identification of the end and nature of the polis is what distinguishes the correct forms of constitution from the deviant ones (*Pol.* III 6, 7, 9); thus, for example, oligarchies are deviant because they are conceived along the lines of a commercial enterprise, not a polis (*Pol.* III 9). And existing laws count as lawful and just to the extent that they conform to or approximate what ideal legislation aims at, that is, to the extent that they aim at the happiness and well-being of the citizens.

Aristotle is therefore able to accept and reject laws as being good, or well-formulated, from an objective point of view. And he recognizes that the laws of a corrupt state will not be an infallible guide to virtuous action. Only from the perspective of *nomothetikê*, the lawgiver's art, is it possible to determine which laws are just and which are not. But the question "how do you decide which laws of your state are correct and should be obeyed?"—that is, the question of individual action—is not a question that he is interested in answering, not here and maybe not ever. He may think that citizens of a state are obliged to obey its laws as long as they meet to some minimal degree the standard set out here: that of producing and preserving happiness and the virtues for a political community.[16] Perhaps Aristotle thinks that there are so many commonalities among different law systems, such as laws against violence and theft (see *EN* V 7 on the prevalence of what he calls "natural" as opposed to "legal" or "conventional" justice), that he is generally satisfied that most legal systems meet this minimum standard.[17] In any case, his project is not to offer guidance to individuals for deciding which laws to obey and when, but rather to describe the science whose subject matter is the correct administration of the state. He is interested in giving guidance to the legislator who is trying to determine what the aim of the best state and laws should be, and this is clearly his focus throughout the *Nicomachean Ethics* and the *Politics*. Hence, the real burden on Aristotle is to spell out what kind of laws would promote the common good best

---

[16] Kraut discusses the difference between the equitable juror or judge who tries to rectify deficiencies in a law, and the citizen who decides that a law is unjust and hence does not require compliance (Kraut 2002: 111–18, esp. 110–11), as well as Aristotle's views on the obligation of citizens to "preserve the constitution" and civil disobedience (2002: §10.6–10.8, esp. 379–84).

[17] Aristotle's claim that "Practically the majority of the acts commanded by the law are those which are prescribed from the point of view of virtue taken as a whole" may perhaps imply that this can be found in most existing laws (*EN* V 2. 1130b22).

under what conditions—which is, as he tells us in the last chapter of the *Nicomachean Ethics*, his next task for the *Politics*.

4. THE VIRTUOUS PERSON IS JUST AND ACTS FOR THE COMMON GOOD

Let us turn to the second idea we wanted to explore, the idea that every virtuous person is necessarily just, that is, possesses the virtue of general justice and hence a concern for the common good. While we may accept Aristotle's definition of justice as a virtue motivated by concern for the common good, and we might grant that the laws of a good state should promote the common good, still we might wonder why Aristotle's happy and virtuous person necessarily has to be a just and law-abiding citizen—that is, why she should care about promoting the common good.

Let's begin by examining Aristotle's argument for identifying general justice with the whole of virtue. It is worth quoting the argument in full:

> This form of justice, then, is complete virtue, although not without qualification, but in relation to our neighbour [αὕτη μὲν οὖν ἡ δικαιοσύνη ἀρετὴ μέν ἐστι τελεία, ἀλλ' οὐχ ἁπλῶς ἀλλὰ πρὸς ἕτερον]. And therefore justice is often thought to be the greatest of virtues, and "neither evening nor morning star" is so wonderful; and proverbially "in justice is every virtue comprehended." And it is complete virtue in its fullest sense because it is the actual exercise [χρῆσις] of complete virtue. It is complete because he who possesses it can exercise his virtue not only in himself but towards his neighbour also; for many men can exercise virtue in their own affairs, but not in their relations to their neighbour. This is why the saying of Bias is thought to be true, that "rule will show the man"; for a ruler is necessarily in relation to other men, and a member of a society. For this same reason justice, alone of the virtues, is thought to be "another's good," because it is related to our neighbour; for it does what is advantageous to another, either a ruler or a co-partner. Now the worst man is he who exercises his wickedness both towards himself and towards his friends, and the best man is not he who exercises his virtue towards himself but he who exercises it towards another; for this is a difficult task. Justice in this sense, then, is not part of virtue but virtue entire, nor is the contrary injustice a part of vice but vice entire [αὕτη μὲν οὖν ἡ δικαιοσύνη οὐ μέρος ἀρετῆς ἀλλ' ὅλη ἀρετή ἐστιν, οὐδ' ἡ ἐναντία ἀδικία μέρος κακίας ἀλλ' ὅλη κακία]. (V 1. 1129b25–1130a10)

Aristotle claims that "this form of justice [i.e. general justice], then, is complete virtue, although not without qualification, but in relation to another" (V 1. 1129b25–7). To put it another way, justice is coextensive with "the whole of virtue," though not identical. If one has general justice, one necessarily also has all of the special character-virtues all together, and conversely, if one has the special virtues, one necessarily also has general justice. Though "general justice" and "virtue" may refer to the same dispositions and activities, in definition they are different: by calling someone who has one of the special character virtues "just," one is calling attention to a particular aspect of her virtue, namely, her "relation to others." General justice, then, picks out the social or other-regarding aspect of virtue, as the term "virtue" does not. As Hardie puts it, "As states or dispositions they are the same, but the terms 'justice' and 'injustice' convey, as 'virtue' and 'vice' do not, a relationship between a man and his neighbours (1130a8–13)" (Hardie 1968: 185).

In addition, Aristotle says that general justice "perfects" the other virtues, by extending their exercise beyond oneself. Justice is "complete" or "perfect" virtue, where the virtues have been activated not just in a limited sphere of action having to do with one's own affairs, but in every sphere, including one's relations to other people. One may demonstrate courage in attending to one's own affairs and interests, but that is incomplete and imperfect unless one is capable of doing so when it comes to matters that affect one's neighbors as well. That is why those who have been given the opportunity to govern and administer the affairs of an entire state, not just their own affairs, have been given the widest possible scope and latitude in which to "perfect" their virtue—or indeed to perfect their vices.

Thus, anyone who has general justice must also have all the specific virtues, for possession of the specific virtues is in a sense a necessary condition of achieving general justice. For one always exercises general justice in some special area (e.g. in matters where one's temper might be provoked or where one's judgments about liberality are required), and in order to exercise general justice in that area one must have the special virtue relevant to that area—for example, one's feelings of fear, anger, or about money must be as they should be. Thus, being just is not a matter of passively and blindly following the laws—it includes the proper cultivation of character and *phronêsis* of someone who has all the particular virtues, all together. Having the character virtues means that one's appreciation of what the right thing to do is—especially when others are involved—is not impeded or occluded by one's desires and emotions.

Of course, many of the other specific virtues are also essentially other-oriented, such as generosity, the virtues having to do with honor, and the conversational virtues, as Broadie notes (2002: 34–5). So what then is distinctive about the other-regarding aspect of justice? To call an action just is specifically to call attention to the fact that it fits in with what the agent owes to others, to do and not to do, whereas to call it generous is to call attention to the presence or absence of a certain type of special motivation and to note that the agent was or was not incorrectly guided by that kind of motivation. When we describe someone as generous, we mean that his impulse to give to others is as it should be; his desires to help others are in the right balance between giving too little and too much (presumably at the cost of attending to his own needs or doing so even when it is not helpful or useful). To call someone "generous" is to praise his emotional dispositions and state (with respect to the other-regarding desire to give to others) for being properly modulated, such that he is not put off by his own stinginess or wastefulness from doing the right thing. But to call a generous person just is to say that his generous impulses and actions are what they should be with respect to other people—he helps other people in the right way, that is, in accordance with the laws and customs that promote the good of the whole. Hence, a generous person is just (or "morally good" as we would say) when his charitable giving is in line with our social expectation that each of us should try to help friends and fellow citizens whenever we can, either for their sake, or for the common good.

Similarly, "courageous" and "just" pick out different aspects of the same disposition. When we say that someone is acting courageously (e.g. by defending himself or standing at his post in battle), we are pointing to his emotional dispositions and state, and saying that his sense of fear and confidence are properly modulated, and do not prevent him from seeing and acting on the right thing to do. We say this in abstraction from how his actions affect other people—hence, one can act courageously even when no one else is involved. But when we say that he is just, we're drawing attention to the fact that his courageous action is what it should be with respect to other people—namely, his actions are in accordance with laws that promote the good of others—say the good of the soldiers in his platoon, that of the whole army, and ultimately that of the community he is defending. Thus, the courageous person is just when, for example, he stands at his post, even at peril to life or limb, precisely because the law and the common good require it of him.

If this is correct, then we might venture further and make a distinction between the disposition to act in conformity with what the laws prescribe, and the disposition to act out of respect for the law and its intent. Someone who is mindlessly obedient to the law acts in conformity with the law simply because this is what the law requires. But if she not only (a) acts in conformity with the laws and norms generally accepted by the community, but also (b) acts out of respect for other citizens and for the laws governing them, then she is just. She acts in conformity with the law not simply to avoid censure or punishment, nor because she is in the habit of acting in a generous, mild, or temperate fashion, but because she endorses those laws and what they demand of her and others.[18]

---

[18] That is, general justice is, as Broadie puts it, "a sort of meta-excellence: one that has its own sort of motive and gives rise to some actions of its own [i.e. lawful ones], but is not expressed in any area that is special or exclusive to itself" (Broadie 2002: 35).

Now Aristotle doesn't precisely say this in the *Nicomachean Ethics*—he doesn't use the Kantian language of "acting out of respect for the law." What he does say, instead, is that it is distinctive of the virtuous agent that she aims at the fine or the noble (*to kalon*), and that she chooses to do virtuous action "because it is fine" or "for the sake of the noble."[19] Thus, for example, courage is described as "a mean with respect to things that inspire confidence or fear, in the circumstances that have been stated; and it chooses or endures things because it is noble to do so, or because it is base not to do so" (*EN* III 8. 1116a10–12).[20] It is remarkable and odd, given its evident importance, that Aristotle nowhere explains in the *Nicomachean Ethics* the concept of the fine and noble. I think this is because Aristotle doesn't think of it as a technical notion, but one that is familiar and obvious from common use. He discusses its common use—the grounds on which an action or person is commonly taken to be "fine"—in *Rhetoric* I 9 and in *Eudemian Ethics* VIII 3. From these and other passages, it is clear that someone who cares about what is fine is not exclusively concerned with her own self-interest (*Rhet*. I 3. 1358b38; II 12. 1389a32–5; II 13. 1389b35; *EN* II 3. 1104b31; IX 8. 1169a6). Rather, what is characteristic of fine actions is that they benefit others (*Rhet*. I 9. 1366b3–4, *EN* IV 1. 1120a11, 1121a27–30, IV 2. 1123a31–2).[21]

Take for example Aristotle's distinction between "civic" (*politikê*) courage and real courage: "Citizen-soldiers seem to face dangers because of the penalties imposed by the laws and the reproaches they would otherwise incur, and because of the honours they win by such action.... This kind of courage is most like to that which we described earlier [i.e. real courage], because it is due to virtue; for it is due to shame and to desire of a noble object (i.e. honour) and avoidance of disgrace, which is ignoble" (*EN* III 8. 1116a18–21, 27–9). The citizen soldier is motivated by something noble—namely, fear of disgrace, and love of honor. While this person is better than someone who follows the general's commands simply to avoid punishment, he falls short of the really courageous person, who acts "for the sake of the noble," for the courageous person is

---

[19] A point I owe to Gisela Striker.

[20] See also III 8. 1115b12, 1116a28, b2–3, 1117b9, 14. The other virtues are also all described as present when the agent acts "for the sake of the fine or noble," including temperance (III 11. 1119a18: "If something is pleasant and conducive to health or fitness, he will desire this moderately and in the right way; and he will desire in the same way anything else that is pleasant if it is no obstacle to health and fitness, does not deviate from what is fine, and does not exceed his means"; and also b16), generosity (IV 1. 1120a12, 23), magnificence (IV 2. 1122b6: "In this sort of spending the magnificent person will aim at what is fine, since that is a common feature of the virtues"; see also 1123a24), and justice (V 9. 1136b22).

[21] Here I have found Irwin 2007: 206–9 very helpful. I am in agreement with his explanation of the connection between virtue, the fine, and the common good; for a different view, see Rogers 1993 and Lear 2004 on *to kalon*. Lear thinks that calling an action *kalon* is to draw attention to the teleological features of an action, e.g. the presence of order and symmetry and form in it.

not thinking of himself at all, but of the good of the community, and what will happen to it if he does not act. By contrast, the citizen-soldier is thinking of the wrong thing, namely glory if he acts well, and disgrace if he does not. Gaining glory for oneself is of course a noble and admirable thing, in Aristotle's view (in comparison for example to living an obscure and undistinguished life), but to act for the sake of the noble is to act not because glory will follow but because it is required for the good of his fellow soldiers, and the whole community. In other passages, Aristotle frequently describes those who do things "for the sake of friends and fatherland" as "choosing what is fine."

In a discussion of self-love, Aristotle again emphasizes that the true self-lover acts for the sake of the noble, where this means acting for the common good, or the good of others:

> It is true of the good man too that he does many acts for the sake of his friends and his country, and if necessary dies for them; for he will throw away both wealth and honours and in general the goods that are objects of competition, gaining for himself nobility (περιποιούμενος ἑαυτῷ τὸ καλόν); since he would prefer a short period of intense pleasure to a long one of mild enjoyment, a twelvemonth of noble life (καλῶς) to many years of humdrum existence, and one great and noble action (μίαν πρᾶξιν καλὴν καὶ μεγάλην) to many trivial ones. Now those who die for others doubtless attain this result; it is therefore a great prize (μέγα καλὸν) that they choose for themselves. (IX 8. 1169a18–26)

Here, Aristotle describes doing things for the sake of friends and fatherland as "choosing what is fine."

We can now see why Aristotle thinks that the virtuous person is necessarily someone who cares about the common good—it is already built into the virtues that the virtuous person acts for the sake of the fine, where that means, in this context, acting for the common good. General justice, then, is the virtue of someone who acts out of respect for the common good. Since the laws are supposed to spell out what is required for the common good, the virtuous person is necessarily lawful.

Now one might object to the thesis that when Aristotle says that the virtuous person acts for the sake of the noble, that what he means is that the virtuous person acts for the sake of the common good. This has been labeled by Kelly Rogers the "altruistic interpretation" of *to kalon*, and she rejects it, on the grounds that it is not part of the concept of the fine that it just *means* "for the common good." Although it may be correct that "fine" does not *mean* "for the common good," nevertheless, in the context of what people regard as most admirable in fellow members of their community, "acting for the sake of the fine" does refer to acting for the sake of the common good. It is misleading to call this the "altruistic" interpretation, since this equates Aristotle's idea that justice is acting for the *common* good with Thrasymachus' idea that justice is acting for someone *else's* good. It would be more accurate to call this the political sense of the term "*to kalon*."

Irwin, who is the most prominent advocate of this reading, agrees that "for the sake of the fine" does not mean "for the common good" (2007: 207); rather, the fine is what is admirable—and things can be admired for many reasons, such as for being aesthetically beautiful, or for being impractical and hence tokens of luxury (e.g. long hair for men). What is fine is either that which *is* admired by people, or that which is most deserving of admiration—that is, that which is most worthwhile, as we might say, or of supreme value. It is in this stricter sense of "most deserving of admiration" that actions aiming at the common good are "fine": political communities organized around the principle of mutual and shared happy lives regard these actions as most deserving of admiration and praise (*EE* VIII 3. 1248b17–25; cf. *EN* I 12. 1101b31–2; VIII 1. 1155a28–31; *Rhet.* I 9. 1366a33–6, 1367b28). And they are deserving of such praise because they benefit many rather than one, as Aristotle explains at the beginning of the *Nicomachean Ethics*:

> For even if the end is the same for a single man and for a state, that of the state seems at all events something greater and more complete whether to attain or to preserve; though it is worth while to attain the end merely for one man, it is *finer and more godlike to attain it for a nation or for city-states*. (*EN* I 2. 1094b7–10)[22]

Thus, to say that attainment of the final good for an entire city-state is "fine" or noble is to say that it is admirable, and it is admirable because it is simply better and more worthwhile to bring about the good for a whole community than for a single individual. *Politikê*, the science of producing the good for all the members of a city-state, is the highest science because its end—the common good—is the noblest and finest end of all. Thus, what is regarded as *most* noble and admirable by political communities is in fact what promotes the common good.

It is a commonplace in classical Greek oratory and in Herodotus that the law directs people to do what is noble, and the two most typical examples of what is noble are (1) fighting for one's country, and (2) respecting one's parents (i.e. caring for and supporting them financially in old age). Both are examples of virtuous actions which benefit others. They are noble because they are actions that are highly worthy of praise, and

---

[22] εἰ γὰρ καὶ ταὐτόν ἐστιν ἑνὶ καὶ πόλει, μεῖζόν γε καὶ τελειότερον τὸ τῆς πόλεως φαίνεται καὶ λαβεῖν καὶ σῴζειν· ἀγαπητὸν μὲν γὰρ καὶ ἑνὶ μόνῳ, κάλλιον δὲ καὶ θειότερον ἔθνει καὶ πόλεσιν.

what makes them praiseworthy is the fact that they require one to set aside self-interest narrowly construed and act for the good of others.

Aristotle thinks that it is the job of the laws to set fine or noble ends for the citizens. Examples of noble ends set by the state include funding the construction of a new warship or financing a theater production for the enjoyment of one's fellow citizens (Striker 2006; see e.g. *EN* IV 2. 1122b19–23). The laws thereby get people to do actions that promote the common good and happiness and to love doing what is fine and noble. Furthermore, they also encourage virtuous behavior, and hence virtue, in the citizens of a state.

> The character, then, must somehow be there already with a kinship to virtue, loving what is noble and hating what is base. But it is difficult to get from youth up a right training for virtue if one has not been brought up under right laws. (X 9. 1179b29–32)[23]

> This is why some think that legislators ought to stimulate men to virtue and urge them forward by the motive of the noble, on the assumption that those who have been well advanced by the formation of habits will attend to such influences. (X 9. 1180a5–8)[24]

These passages make it clear that Aristotle thinks that the laws are supposed to educate people by causing them to learn to love doing what is fine.

In a passage where Aristotle is distinguishing the true self-lover from the rank egoist, Aristotle describes the common benefit that results when everyone is eager to do fine actions:

> …Hence he will count as "self-lover" the most—not the same kind people speak of censoriously, but different by as much as living by reason differs from living by emotion, and desiring the fine, on the one hand, from desiring what appears to bring advantage on the other. Those, then, who are exceptionally eager for fine actions are welcomed and praised by everyone; and if everyone vied for what is fine, and strained to do the finest things, not only would everything be as it should on the communal level but as individuals too each person would be possessed of the greatest goods, given that excellence is such a thing. Thus the good person

---

[23] δεῖ δὴ τὸ ἦθος προϋπάρχειν πως οἰκεῖον τῆς ἀρετῆς, στέργον τὸ καλὸν καὶ δυσχεραῖνον τὸ αἰσχρόν. ἐκ νέου δ' ἀγωγῆς ὀρθῆς τυχεῖν πρὸς ἀρετὴν χαλεπὸν μὴ ὑπὸ τοιούτοις τραφέντα νόμοις.

[24] διόπερ οἴονταί τινες τοὺς νομοθετοῦντας δεῖν μὲν παρακαλεῖν ἐπὶ τὴν ἀρετὴν καὶ προτρέπεσθαι τοῦ καλοῦ χάριν, ὡς ἐπακουσομένων τῶν ἐπιεικῶς τοῖς ἔθεσι προηγμένων.

should be a self-lover, since by doing what is fine he will both be better off himself and benefit others, but the bad one should not; for he will harm both himself and those round him through following worthless attractions. (trans. Rowe, *EN* IX 8. 1169a3–15)

Aristotle claims that (1) by doing what is fine, each person is better off (because he acts virtuously) and also benefits others (because actions are *kalon* which benefit others), and (2) if the competitive impulse is harnessed so that everyone is eager to do fine things, then the whole group or community will be better off—presumably because the whole community is better off when its members are in competition so to speak to see who can do the most for others. Institutions that encourage this kind of competition in virtue benefit the community as a whole.[25]

Thus, good laws will be crafted in such a way that they endorse and recommend certain actions because they promote ends that are fine and supremely worthwhile, and will attach sanctions to noncompliance. Some people will obey such laws only out of fear of punishment. But others will do it because these actions are fine—that is, they promote the common good. But one can see that acting for the common good need not imply some kind of pure and selfless altruism or benevolence. It is entirely consistent with acting for the common good that one should do so because this indirectly benefits oneself, and that one should look forward to the praise and honor that will be one's just desert. Acting for the sake of the fine thus seems to me less like altruism and more like civic-mindedness, with its respect for one's fellow citizens and its willingness to participate fully in the cooperative ventures that constitute the city. And it would help to explain why Aristotle so frequently associates justice with civic or political friendship; each is necessary for, and fosters, the other. That it is natural to human beings to act in these ways is, I believe, part of what Aristotle means when he says that man is a "political animal."[26]

5. CONCLUSION

I will conclude by making two broad points about what I hope to have shown. First of all, it is unfortunate that justice is, of all the virtues and ethical concepts in Aristotle, the most neglected. This is partly due to the very rough and disjointed state of the book on justice in the *Ethics*, a book that is clearly an early draft in need of revision. It

---

[25] Cf. Demosthenes, *Against Leptines* 20.5: Demosthenes says that if you give people rewards for virtuous behavior, they will vie with each other to see who can do the most for the city.
[26] *Pol.* I 2. 1253a7–18, III 6. 1278b15–30; *EN* VIII 12. 1162a16–19, IX 9. 1169b16–22, *EE* VII 10. 1242a19–28.

may also be due to current fashions in virtue ethics, which in centralizing the concept of virtue have tended to marginalize that of justice, with its Kantian overtones of duty and obligation. In any case, this often means that readers assume that Aristotle's ethics can be described purely in terms of his moral psychology and theory of the individual virtues. But when Aristotle describes general justice as the same as the whole of virtue, he clearly means that virtue and justice are, for him, two ways of talking about the same thing. This shows that his theory of justice is, in fact, central to his project in the *Ethics*.

Second, the law plays a much more interesting role in Aristotle's theory than one might have thought. Particular laws will provide the starting points in the practical reasoning of virtuous agents. Further investigation of this will show, I believe, that what makes virtuous agents possess understanding of these starting points—what allows them to apply the law not blindly but with understanding—is the fact that they are capable of taking the point of view of the legislator—of reasoning about the common good, and how it can be achieved, from an impartial perspective (e.g. *EN* VI 8, *Pol.* III 4). It is, in any case, the point of view of the legislator that is Aristotle's primary concern. There are of course large questions about what the common good is, and how Aristotle thinks it can be achieved—but those require further study, especially of the *Politics*.

Acknowledgments

I was very fortunate to study with Gisela Striker, who was my undergraduate and graduate teacher and advisor at Columbia and Harvard. I offer this paper to her with affection and gratitude for her advice and support over the years. Her work has been a continual source of inspiration to me, including, most recently, her paper Striker 2006 "Aristotle's Ethics as Political Science," some of whose arguments I take up and develop in this paper. Versions of this paper have been presented to audiences at the University of Colorado at Boulder, the University of Colorado at Denver, Berkeley, Davis, Northwestern, Harvard, and Yale. I am very grateful to those audiences for their comments and criticisms, especially Dorothea Frede, Verity Harte, Richard Kraut, Rob Metcalf, Gisela Striker, and Jan Szaif, as well as to Dominic Bailey, Peter Hunt, Dana Miller, and Robert Pasnau for very helpful comments on this paper.

Bibliography

Broadie, Sarah. 2002. "Philosophical Introduction," in Sarah Broadie and Christopher Rowe (eds.), Aristotle, *Nicomachean Ethics: Translation, Introduction, and Commentary*. New York: Oxford University Press.

Cooper, John. 1990. "Political Animals and Civic Friendship," with comments by J. Annas in G Patzig (ed.), *Aristoteles' Politik*. Göttingen: Vandenhoeck & Ruprecht.

de Romilly, Jacqueline. 1971. *La loi dans la pensée grecque: des origines à Aristote.* Paris: Belles-Lettres.

Irwin, T.H. 1985. "Aristotle's Conception of Morality" in John Cleary (ed.), *Proceedings of the Boston Colloquium in Ancient Philosophy,* vol. 1. Washington, DC: University Press of America.

——. 1988. *Aristotle's First Principles.* Oxford: Clarendon Press.

——. 2007. *The Development of Ethics: A Historical and Critical Study,* vol. 1: *From Socrates to the Reformation.* New York: Oxford University Press.

Keyt, D. 1989. "Injustice and Pleonexia in Aristotle: A Reply to Charles Young," *Southern Journal of Philosophy* **27** (suppl.): 251–7.

——. 1991. "Aristotle's Theory of Distributive Justice," in D. Keyt and F. D. Miller (eds.), *A Companion to Aristotle's Politics.* Malden, MA: Blackwell; extensively revised version of "Distributive Justice in Aristotle's *Ethics* and *Politics,*" *Topoi* **4** (1985) 23–45.

Kraut, Richard. 2002. *Aristotle: Political Philosophy.* Oxford: Oxford University Press.

Lear, Gabriel Richardson. 2004. *Happy Lives and the Highest Good: An Essay on Aristotle's Nicomachean Ethics.* Princeton: Princeton University Press.

Rawls, John. 1955. "Two Concepts of Rules," *Philosophical Review* **64**: 3–32; also available online at http://www.hist-analytic.org/Rawlsonrules.htm.

——. 1999. *A Theory of Justice,* revised edition. Cambridge: Harvard University Press (1st edition 1971).

Rogers, K. 1993. "Aristotle's Conception of Τὸ Καλόν," *Ancient Philosophy* **13**: 355–71. Reprinted in L. Gerson (ed.), *Aristotle: Critical Essays* (London: Routledge, 1999), 4.337–55.

Sachs, David. 1963. "A Fallacy in Plato's Republic," *Philosophical Review* **72**: 141–58.

Striker, Gisela. 2006. "Aristotle's Ethics as Political Science," in B. Reis (ed.), *The Virtuous Life in Greek Ethics.* New York: Cambridge University Press.

Williams, B. 1980. "Justice as a Virtue." in A.O. Rorty (ed.), *Essays on Aristotle's Ethics,* Berkeley: University of California Press; reprinted in *Moral Luck* (New York: Cambridge University Press, 1981).

Young, Charles M. 1989. "Aristotle on Justice," *Southern Journal of Philosophy* **27** (suppl.): 233–49.

——. 2006. "Aristotle's Justice," in R. Kraut (ed.), *The Blackwell Guide to Aristotle's Nicomachean Ethics.* Malden, MA: Blackwell.

6

ARISTOTLE ON HOW TO FELL A TREE AND OTHER MATTERS INVOLVING EXPERIENCE

Dana Miller

I have a problem. A large, tall tree whose branches loom over my driveway, the electric lines, and the telephone line, is dead. Dead organisms disintegrate. The disintegration of this organism will almost certainly end my power supply and possibly crush me as I walk or drive underneath it. What to do? Cut it down. But how? This question is important to me because my well-being may depend on it. Philosophers, especially ancient philosophers, claim to tell us things that will serve our well-being. What, then, does Aristotle tell me that will help answer my question?

It was as evident to Aristotle as it is to us that the answer to the question about how to fell my tree must refer to certain facts about the world, represented to me as beliefs, and to a form of reasoning based on these beliefs. Aristotle has views about both the source of these beliefs and the form of reasoning I should use. The intent of this paper is to examine these views. The reason for this examination is that Aristotle's response to practical questions, such as the one asked, has been little treated and has epistemic importance. It has been little treated because Aristotle himself, like most philosophers, says almost nothing directly about such questions. His response has epistemic importance because it is Aristotle's explanation of how we interact with the world to achieve goals. In Aristotle's view, the relevant sources of our beliefs are experience (ἐμπειρία) and expertise (τέχνη). The interworkings of these two cognitive states, and the form of reasoning used—what he usually calls "deliberation" (βούλευσις, τὸ βουλεύεσθαι)—provide our epistemic footing for productive action. I shall begin the paper with an investigation of Aristotle's account of experience and expertise and then discuss the relevant form of reasoning.

Before continuing I must mention a terminological difficulty created by different uses of the term "practical." In the ethical treatises, the *Politics*, and elsewhere Aristotle distinguishes between "productive" action (ποίησις) and "practical" action (πρᾶξις), the latter involving moral action, the former the making or doing of things.[1] But, to quote

---

[1] For a discussion of the distinction see, e.g. Siwecki 1934: 175–189.

John Cooper, Aristotle "never attempts to discuss moral reasoning as such, but always instead focuses on practical reasoning in general, treating moral reasoning as a species of this wider genus."[2] What Cooper calls "practical reasoning in general" has, for Aristotle, two distinct species, or application in two distinct realms: the "productive" and the "practical." This exposes the terminological difficulty mentioned above. In reference to Aristotle, does "practical" refer only to the moral realm, or is it broader? Cooper's genus of practical reasoning, that is, the form of reasoning we use to determine means with respect to ends, whether in moral or productive action, fits well with much contemporary philosophical usage. For example, Hilary Bok gives the following account of practical reasoning: "The purpose of practical reasoning is to determine the will, to answer the question 'What should I do?' Its aim is to ascertain what we have reason to do or not to do, to determine the relative importance of these various reasons for action, and thereby to arrive at a decision that we can regard as justifiable." And in a footnote, "A professional assassin trying to figure out from which vantage point to try to shoot her target, an executive trying to determine how best to advance her career…are all engaging in practical reasoning as I understand it."[3] But it is also common in philosophy to use "practical" in a sense restricted to ethics, although this often conflicts with the broader use of "practical" in common parlance. In an attempt to minimize confusion and to preserve Aristotle's distinction mentioned above, in what follows I shall call the form of reasoning employed to accomplish goals such as felling a tree or treating an illness (Aristotle's common example) "productive reasoning." In so doing I retain the claim that productive reasoning does not differ essentially from reasoning in the moral domain, inasmuch as both share the same, as it were, genus for Aristotle. A straightforward defense of this claim lies in the fact that Aristotle explicitly models his account of reasoning in the ethical realm on how workers in the various expertises proceed in producing the products of their expertise. If these two forms of reasoning were essentially different, one could not explicate the other.[4] Furthermore, Aristotle uses the term "deliberation" for reasoning both in the productive context, such as money-making (*EN* 3.3 1112b4), and the moral context.

I return to the specifics of my tree problem. The goal I intend to achieve is clear: to fell the tree. But the tree, once cut, should fall in a way that leaves the power and phone lines intact as well as myself. The tree must not merely fall, but fall in a certain direction. The problem before me, then, is how to fell the tree such that it falls in the intended direction. I look up at the tree and notice that most of its branches are on the

---

[2] Cooper 1986: 1.
[3] Bok 1998: 62.
[4] On the issues involved in the analogy between moral (or, "practical") wisdom and expertise see Broadie 1991: 190–198.

side that overhangs the wires and that it leans in that direction. From this I infer that the tree will tend to fall exactly where I do not want it to fall. How, then, shall I achieve my goal? If I have experience in doing this sort of thing, I know how I have successfully handled similar cases in the past. If I have expertise, I should have some additional knowledge that consists, as Aristotle says, in a grasp of relevant universals and causal relations. Ideally, I should have both. But if I have neither, I would be quite unable to discover how to proceed, and if I were to proceed anyway by guesswork, I would be a fool, very likely a dead fool.[5] Mere knowledge of the form my goal-directed reasoning should take would avail me nothing without the content provided from experience and expertise. Therefore, with the specter of being a dead fool before my eyes, I shall begin with Aristotle's account of experience and expertise, since they provide the beliefs on the basis of which productive reasoning can proceed.

EXPERIENCE AND EXPERTISE

Aristotle does not provide me with any facts about tree-cutting.[6] He does, however, explain where these facts, or beliefs about these facts, can be obtained. They are provided by perception, experience, and practical expertise. I will pass over the much discussed subject of perception in Aristotle and begin with experience. Aristotle's conception of experience is not easily grasped, in part because Aristotle does not quite mean by "experience" what we usually mean.[7] He says that "the many memories of the same case [πράγματος: or, thing, event] bring to completion the capacity of a single experience" (*Met.* A.1 980b29-981a1); and "experience is from a memory of the same <case> happening many times, for memories that are many in number are a single experience" (*AnPo.* 2.19 100a4-6). It is not immediately obvious what he means by saying that experience is constituted of many memories and what "a single experience" means. Every event is different. Take, for example, driving to work. Let us say that I drive to work five times a week, fifty weeks a year. I take the same road and leave about the same time in the same car. My memory has stored many cases of driving

---

[5] I could, however, just get lucky. Aristotle allows that production can also occur by chance (*Met.* Z.7 1032a28-30; cf. *Rhet.* 1.5 1362a2).

[6] It should be noted that Aristotle would probably consider tree-cutting to be "banausic" or menial work, of which he takes a very dim view with respect to the achievement of human excellence, and especially social excellence (cf. e.g. *Pol.* 8.9 1328b37-41, *Pol.* 9.1 1337b8-11). This axiological judgment, which would presumably cover tree-cutting, is not relevant to this paper.

[7] In fairness to Aristotle, what we mean by "experience" is also not fully obvious. Everson 1997: 227 notes: "*empeiria* is much closer to 'concept' than to 'experience,' by which it is standardly translated." For recent discussions of experience in Aristotle see: Gregoric, Grgic 2006; LaBarge 2006.

to work; I have "many memories" of these cases. But each case is significantly different. Last time there was a traffic jam at Exit 20; the time before that there was that lunatic in the blue SUV; the time before that all traffic was stopped for some dignitary; and so on. I mostly remember the differences. This would be true of multiple cases of making, say, bookshelves. Last time the boards warped; the time before that the countersink cut too deeply. But Aristotle claims that all these many memories can be unified somehow such that they constitute one experience. It is true that I would say that I have a "lot of experience" driving this road at this time to this location. But this is not quite what Aristotle means. Experience, he says, is a kind of "capacity" (δύναμις: *Met.* A.1 981a1) that is actualized as "conceptions" (ἐννοήματα),[8] and these conceptions are the source of the universals grasped by expertise (*Met.* A.1 981a5–7). I certainly have quite a few "conceptions" about driving to work. For example, my many memories of driving by Exit 20 generate in my mind the "conception" "always stay as far left as possible" when passing it. When memories of repeated cases or events unite to generate a specific "conception," this indicates the presence in the mind of a "single experience" to which I can refer in my thinking. When I consider Exit 20 while driving, I bring to mind what has happened before, frequently or less so, and gauge what to expect and how best to deal with it. The "conception" that is generated in my mind articulates a common feature that my mind finds in these memories, such as, "at Exit 20 entering cars suddenly slow right-lane traffic." The forming of such a "conception" is what Aristotle means when he refers, in *Met.* A.1, to "the completion of the capacity of a single experience," where the single experience is many similar memories united in the mind according to some common feature.

The capacity of the mind, or soul, that makes possible the unification of singular cases provided by sense-perception is what Aristotle calls φαντασία. *Phantasia* is a sub-part of the non-reasoning part of the soul which is the sensory capacity. The sensory capacity unites the soul's perceptual capacities and its capacity to retain and represent sense-based information as images.[9] Though lacking reason, many animals possess *phantasia* which enables them to perform complex activities (*DeAn.* 3.3 429a4–6).[10] Memory and, in

---

[8] I will use "conception," not "belief," in an attempt to designate the particular term that Aristotle employs. Even so, I think "belief," in its contemporary usage, would be accurate as well.

[9] There is now a great deal of new discussion of *phantasia* in Aristotle. A strong case is made for its non-rational but cognitive role in thought, motivation, and action (see, most recently and most thoroughly Moss 2012, which appeared well after this paper was completed, and Johansen 2013: 199–220). For simplicity, in my brief discussion of *phantasia* I follow the literature in attributing to *phantasia* these roles. However, I agree with the view of Gregoric 2007: 205–207 *et passim* that many of these roles are in fact performed by the higher-order sensory capacity that unifies the operations of the various perceptual capacities and *phantasia*.

[10] "[T]he sensory capacity of the soul is in fact a single thing which is only conceptually divided. Hence, it can discharge certain activities that go beyond either of its two conceptually distinct parts taken separately. That is to say, on account of being a unified whole, the sensory capacity

humans, higher thinking have as their objects *phantasia*'s representations (*DeAn.* 3.7 431b2, 432a7-10; *Mem.* 1 449b30-a7).[11] Emotions, as well, are a response to, or affirmation of, how things get represented to us in *phantasia* (see, e.g. *Rhet.* 2.5 1382a21-22 for the case of fear; likewise desire: *DeAn.* 3.10 433b28-29). When many memories constitute a single experience, the human mind possesses a particular "conception" from the compiled representations which, as a group or series, "give us something like a standardized picture of a state of affairs in general."[12] For example, when I call to mind many cases of passing by Exit 20, I see, as it were, images that highlight a particular fact, namely cars entering recklessly on the right, while other facts particular to each case remain in the background, such as, three days ago the car entering was a black BMW and it was raining.

A "single experience" is (completed by) a particular "conception." The repetitions of daily life furnish us with a great many "single experiences" which constitute many "conceptions."[13] These "conceptions" are what we might call basic beliefs which we consider when we think about world, and the mind grasps them as image-like representations. An example given by Aristotle is deliberation about the future. "When a person calculates and deliberates about future events in relation to present ones, <he does so> as though seeing <them> in representations (φαντάσμασι) or thoughts in the soul. And when he determines that, 'There is the pleasant or <there is> the painful,' at that moment he flees or pursues, and so in action generally" (*DeAn.* 3.7 431b6-10). To explicate this, take the following example: I am sitting in an empty subway car at 3 AM and, calculating the probability, as we would say, of being robbed or worse, I deliberate about whether to remain sitting or to go to a different car or to get off at the next

---

can discharge complex non-rational activities that combine perception and imagination, such as 'experience' (ἐμπειρία). This allows us to speak of a higher-order cognitive power emerging from the unity of the sensory capacity of the soul, and this power is in charge of the complex non-rational activities" (Gregoric 2007: 57).

[11] "Representations (φαντάσματα) are like objects of sensation to the thinking soul. When it affirms or rejects a good or a bad, it avoids or pursues, for which reason the soul never thinks without representations" (*DeAn.* 3.7 431a14-17). See D. Frede 1992: 290; also Lorenz 2006: 160: "It is at least part of the idea that thinking anything at all, anyhow for thinkers like us, requires visualizing the objects of thought by means of sensory imagination. The visualizations in question are *phantasiai*."

[12] D. Frede 1992: 293. Also Lorenz 2006: 136: "There is, then, good reason to accept that Aristotle conceives of *phantasia* so that it is cognitively powerful enough to enable a subject to apprehend what one might, speaking loosely, refer to as situations—performing an action, say, or enjoying an experience. It is, of course, a further step to accept that *phantasia*, on Aristotle's view, also enables subjects to apprehend *prospective* situations (e.g. eating the stag over there)" (a claim for which Lorenz argues later).

[13] In view of the fact that we remember the same events differently depending on our aims and concerns, our representations of these events will vary accordingly. It should follow that more than one "experience" and more than one "conception" can be based on the same events.

station and take a cab. To reckon a probability and to consider the possible benefits and harms of options for future action I must appeal to experience. That is, I consider the various representations (φαντάσματα) that I project on the future,[14]—namely the ones that align with my "conceptions." Once I determine that remaining seated has a high probability of "the painful," while taking a cab should be pleasant, I flee.[15] In Aristotle's account, we make an inference (συλλογισμός) about the future outcome of an action that we consider taking at the present (*DeAn.* 3.11 434a11). The inference consists in choosing between presentations to the mind in *phantasia* of probable scenarios. When we judge that a good future result of the action is likely, we do it. We would be unable to reach this decision without considering the "conceptions" that are experience. We engage in this kind of thinking all the time. As Hume pointed out, we cannot function in the world without it. Without the mind's natural disposition to draw inferences from past experience, "we should be entirely ignorant of every matter of fact beyond what is immediately present to the memory and the senses. We should never know how to adjust means to ends or to employ our natural powers in the production of any effect. There would be an end at once to all action."[16]

This being, very briefly, Aristotle's account of experience, what does he mean by "experience is knowledge (γνῶσις)[17] of particular <cases>"[18] (*Met.* A.1 981a15–16)? From the context, which states that many memories constitute one experience, it is clear that Aristotle is not identifying experience with sensation, which is also "of the particular" (see, e.g. *AnPo.* 1.18 81b6 and *passim*). Here Aristotle is explaining why it is the case that a person who has experience, but cannot give a general account of why some type of action should succeed, will be more effective than someone who can give such an account but lacks experience (*Met.* A.1 981a13–15; cf. *EN* 6.7 1141b16–21).

---

[14] D. Frede 1992: 280 notes that Aristotle in *DeAn.* 3.3 uses *phantasia* in several related senses: "as a necessary condition of thought" and as "mere after-images of sense-perception." In the case of future projections these two senses evidently merge.

[15] In such a case we are using what Aristotle calls "deliberative *phantasia*" (*DeAn.* 3.11 434a7–10). On this see Moss 2012: 137–152.

[16] Hume 1955: section 5, 58–59.

[17] γνῶσις is a broad term in Aristotle, the exact sense of which needs to be derived from context. I therefore use "knowledge" in a very broad sense which includes simple recognition. Labarge 2006 prefers the less prejudicial "cognition."

[18] There is a debate over what, precisely, is meant by "particulars" here. Cooper 1986: 30 argues that only "specific types" are meant, not individual things, for example, the "particular fact that chicken [meat] is light." Devereux 1986: 488, on the other hand, points out passages where Aristotle "at the very least means to include individuals among the things he here calls 'particulars.'" Aristotle's account of experience accords better with Devereux's broader understanding of "particular": "The content of the knowledge [of particulars] is in a way general, but also particular insofar as it involves reference to one or more individuals" (489).

If there were an expertise that consisted merely in the grasp of certain universals and their relations but lacked input from experience, such an expertise would often fail to accomplish anything because it would lack knowledge of particulars, and "all actions and productions are concerned with what is particular" (*Met.* A.1 981a17–18).[19] The example Aristotle gives of "knowledge of particulars" is the following. "It belongs to experience to have the supposition (ὑπόληψις)[20] that in this <particular> illness this <treatment> helped ailing Callias and also Socrates and many <other> particular <cases>" (*Met.* A.1 981a7–9). The knowledge of particulars in this case involves a supposition that a particular treatment has helped particular people suffering from a particular illness. Experience is not just a conception formed from recollection of observed facts (e.g. Socrates is coughing; his wife is cooking; the room is hot; a dog outside is barking; it is past noon). It is ordered sets of particular facts, derived from memory's recall of the representations of *phantasia* and selected according to some organizing principle, being placed into comparison with other ordered, selected sets, where the comparison is based on similarity (e.g. Socrates is coughing; Socrates drinks whipped egg yokes; Socrates stops coughing; Callias, pretty much the same).[21] In so doing a person "has a supposition"[22] that unites these particular facts as a kind of generalization which serves as a basis for inference to a probable future particular (e.g. this treatment will quite probably help Crito). This apparently being what "knowing particulars" means here, having experience of particulars is a different mental state from having sensory awareness of particulars. What experience "knows" about a particular is its similarity relation to other particulars and ordered sets of particulars relative to some framework. Experience, then, in Aristotle's understanding of the term, is the beliefs ("conceptions," "suppositions") that the mind generates as it observes similarities among specified cases stored in memory and represented in *phantasia*. Experience is knowledge of particulars inasmuch as it situates particulars within this organized

---

[19] Cf. *Pol.* 2.8 1269a12; see also *Rhet.* 2.19 1393a17–18: "Particular things [i.e. facts about particular things] are more authoritative than universals with respect to employment."

[20] The word ὑπόληψις is broadly used by Aristotle (see *De An.* 3.3 427b24–27). "[A]lthough Aristotle sometimes uses it [*sc.* hupolambanein] as a synonym for 'opine' (*doxazein*), its official use is to mark out the genus of cognitive attitudes of which understanding [*episteme*] and opinion are two species" (Barnes 1994: 201). The ὑπόληψις in the case of experience is the grasping of a "conception" (ἐννόημα: *Met.* A.1 981a6).

[21] Cf. Gregoric, Grgic 2006: 10: "It seems that experience requires that the observed and stored facts be retrieved in connection with the thing that these facts are about. That is, the facts have to be minimally organized in one's mind around the object that these facts are about."

[22] Gregoric, Grgic 2006: 17–18, 24, argue that experience generalizes over observed cases and that these generalizations serve as universals, but ones that are not viewed by the mind as explanatory. If this is right, the supposition proper to expertise would grasp the relevant universal as explanatory, as part of a causal account, while the supposition proper to experience would not.

cognitive framework. When we refer a particular case to experience, we cognize this case as sharing commonalities with other cases. Since we remember what was done in those cases and how things transpired, we have a guide for action in this case as well (cf. *EN* 10.9 1180b16–20). Therefore Aristotle holds that we can act effectively on the basis of experience alone: "With respect to doing (πράττειν) it appears that experience does not differ at all from expertise" (*Met.* A.1 981a12–13).

Experience, however, is clearly limited in its scope by what a person has stored in her memories and by what sorts of suppositions she derives from these remembered facts. The fewer cases a person has witnessed, the less reliable and nuanced her suppositions will be. The more cases she has witnessed, the more reliable and nuanced her suppositions will be, the more inclusive of possible contingencies. Experience, as the accumulation of an individual's "single experiences," is "personal" in this sense. The suppositions and conceptions that constitute my experience will differ to some degree from yours. Gisela Striker 2006: 138–139 distinguishes between the notion of experience as "systematic empirical observation that forms the basis of skills and theories and can be passed on to others" and "personal experience that will help one to find the appropriate response in a given situation," experience that "each person has to acquire for himself." She argues that "when Aristotle says, as he does with respect both to medicine and to ethics, that experience without theory is better than theory without experience, he is clearly thinking of personal experience." As I understand Aristotle, experience, as he uses the term, is necessarily "personal" in this sense, and the suppositions which constitute experience lack universality. The lack of universality entails, in Aristotle's view, that these suppositions cannot serve as causal explanations of what occurs, since only universals "make known the explanatory cause" (*AnPo.* 1.31 88a5–6). Experience, therefore, is epistemically deficient. On the other hand, since experience results from our own direct cognitive interactions with the changing world around us, it constitutes our immediate knowledge of the world and how to act productively in it. I know from experience that doing this particular action will cause this kind of effect, though I may not know, or be able to say, why it does. On this point Striker 2006: 139 observes that, for Aristotle, "although experience may rank below scientific knowledge in the order of understanding, it also vastly exceeds the scope of what we can explain, and even what we can clearly articulate."

Aristotle thinks that the epistemic deficiency of experience is overcome by the acquisition of expertise, because expertise is based on the grasp of universals through induction. He says:

> It belongs to experience to present the supposition that in this <particular> illness this <treatment> helped ailing Callias and also Socrates and many <other> particular <cases>, but it belongs to expertise <to present the supposition> that

<this treatment> helped all persons having this illness and are of this type <of constitution> marked off as a single class—as, for example, <it helped> phlegmatic or bilious people who had high fevers. (*Met.* A.1 981a7–12; cf. *Rhet.* 1.2 1356b28–32)

When a person who has experience thinks about how to treat a new case, she refers to a supposition derived from past similar cases and decides to use the same treatment in the present case. A person who has the relevant expertise, medicine, will classify the incoming patient as having a certain type of constitution and refer to the supposition that a particular kind of treatment helps the type of person who suffers from a particular illness. The experienced person "knows the that, but not the reason why," while the physician knows "the reason why, that is, the cause" (*Met.* A.1 981a29–30). The physician, as possessing the expertise, understands the causal relations between various universals: the kind of treatment, the kind of illness, and the kind of constitution the patient presents. The healer, who possesses only experience, lacks such understanding. Universals guide the physician in reasoning about what treatment to give while the memory of similar particular cases guides the person with experience. Both may apply the same treatment with the same results, but the possessor of expertise does what she does from a stronger epistemic position. The scope of her reasoning extends beyond what she has observed. As Aristotle might say, she is closer to knowing the truth.[23]

I said above that productive reasoning requires beliefs about the world in order to proceed. These beliefs are provided by perception, experience, and expertise. Perception makes known to us singular facts about the world and ourselves. For example, as I look at it, this tree has more branches on its left side. Experience, as Aristotle understands it, enables the mind to situate a particular fact within a generalized framework of similar observed facts and sets of facts. For instance, experience provides the "supposition" that this tree, like other standing objects I have observed to be weighted to one side, will fall towards the weighted side when nothing obstructs. The suppositions of experience are often sufficient for guiding action, but their effectiveness may be increased by a knowledge of relevant universals which serve as causal explanations. For example, dead trees occasionally have rotten cores. Core strength keeps the tree upright even when its center of gravity does not lie on its perpendicular axis. A rotten tree is not held up by its core but by the remaining wood outside the core. Therefore

---

[23] "The experienced," Aristotle says, meaning, I take it, people who possess both experience and expertise, "judge each work correctly, and they understand the means through which or how they are accomplished, and what sorts of <actions> are in agreement with what" (*EN* 10.9 1181a19–21). There is, of course, a great deal more to say about experience, expertise, and "scientific" knowledge. For a useful discussion see M. Frede 1996.

when such a tree is cut, it will fall before a saw reaches the core during a back-cut (experience notes that the consequences of this can be dire). These beliefs, and others like them, provide a basis from which I may begin to reason, or as Aristotle would say, deliberate, about how to fell my tree.

DELIBERATION AS PRODUCTIVE REASONING

Aristotle's most careful and direct account of deliberation occurs in his ethical works where his focus is on how we reach decisions concerning actions that bear on our living well or the reverse. Aristotle's intent in these works is not to explicate productive reasoning. This raises the worry that what Aristotle says about deliberation in the ethical treatises cannot inform us about productive reasoning. This worry is directly connected to the difficulty over the use of the term "practical" discussed at the beginning of this paper. There I endorsed the claim that productive reasoning and moral reasoning are species of a broader genus, roughly speaking, which might be called "practical reasoning in general." This claim is supported by Aristotle's account of deliberation in the *Nicomachean Ethics* where we find two versions of it, each adapted to its context: version (a) in *EN* 3.3, in the context of voluntary action and its contribution to decision, and version (b) in *EN* 6.2-9, in the context of a treatment of the intellectual virtues. In (a) deliberation is considered broadly as the kind of thinking we do when we have to figure out how to accomplish some action that we judge we need to do. But in (b), more narrowly, it is the kind of thinking that a morally wise person (a person who is φρόνιμος) does in achieving what is best, in a moral sense of "best," and this is distinguished from the kind of thinking that a person does who has an expertise, such as medicine or carpentry. In (a), then, deliberation is treated as the genus that is done both in the operation of the expertises (*EN* 3.3 1112b2-8) and in voluntary action in general that proceeds from a decision, while in (b) we learn that moral wisdom (φρόνησις) and expertise are two distinct kinds of intellectual capacities, since production (ποίησις) is different from action (πρᾶξις: *EN* 6.4 1140a2, 16–17; cf. *Pol.* 1.4 1254a5; *Met.* E.1 1025b22–24), and deliberation is discussed chiefly with respect to the role it has in moral action. In (b), therefore, Aristotle treats deliberation as it occurs in a specific domain, while in (a) deliberation is used in both the productive and the moral domains. The account of deliberation in (a), then, has application to productive reasoning. Nevertheless, the effect of Aristotle's claims in (b) can be that one may wonder whether (b) denies that deliberation is operative in expertise.[24] This, however, would

---

[24] One might also point to *Phys.* 2.8 199b28: "Expertise, however, does not deliberate." Here, however, the deliberation denied to expertise is one that determines an end, since Aristotle says

misinterpret Aristotle's argument. In (b) Aristotle does not deny that expertise requires deliberation. His point is that since moral action differs from production, the subjects deliberated on will also differ in relevant ways. For instance, if I possess the appropriate expertise, I can deliberate successfully on how to fell a tree on my irritating neighbor, but this kind of deliberation would not be undertaken by a morally wise person. In what follows I shall use "deliberation" in its broad sense when discussing *EN* 3.3.

I shall begin with *EN* 3.3 where we have an account of deliberation in the broad sense that includes productive reasoning. Here deliberation is taken to be the thinking process by which we arrive at "decision" (προαίρεσις) that leads to action. The action in which deliberation results is the means to an end or goal. We do not, therefore, deliberate about ends, since an end must be presupposed for any deliberation about means. If a rational thinking process cannot, because of the subject matter, arrive at a decision, this process is not what Aristotle means by deliberation. It follows that the English term "deliberation," as commonly used, does not fully correspond in meaning with Aristotle's βούλευσις. For example, Aristotle says that Spartans would not deliberate about what is the best form of government for Scythians (*EN* 3.3 1112a28–29), but this is the sort of thing that contemporary academics do all the time. Aristotle's point is that the conclusions that Spartans might reach cannot result in action, as in a change in Scythian law. Therefore he would say that Spartans and academics may discuss, but do not deliberate, about such matters. Deliberation results in action. For the same reason Aristotle says that we do not deliberate about chance occurrences (e.g. finding buried treasure) or "what happens differently at different times" (e.g. rainstorms) (*EN* 3.3 1112a26–27). Aristotle excludes cases where we cannot bring about an effect by our decision to act and cases in which the causes of effects lie beyond our understanding.

Aristotle determines the scope of deliberation by a three-stage argument: (1) by listing the subjects which we do not, in his view, deliberate about, (2) by stating the subjects about which we do deliberate, and (3) by giving a brief account of the actual process of deliberation. I have just given the general sense of (1). To this should be added the claim that we do not deliberate about the subject matters of the "exact and self-sufficient sciences"; these are not subjects about which we are in doubt and so no deliberation is needed (*EN* 3.3 1112a34–b2). On (2), Aristotle says that deliberation is "about what is in our power" (περὶ τῶν ἐφ' ἡμῖν) and what "can be done" (τῶν πρακτῶν)[25] (*EN* 3.3 1112a30–31), and about "that which comes about through us, not

---

"the that-on-account-of-which is in the τέχνη" (b30). In the *EN* we find that deliberation is not about ends at all.

[25] The term πρακτά is used in 3.3 in a sense that ignores the distinction Book 6 makes between ποίησις and πρᾶξις and is therefore broader. Making money, medicine, and navigation are πρακτά that we deliberate about (*EN* 3.3 1112b4–5).

always in the same way" (*EN* 3.3 1112b3). Aristotle's examples are matters that fall under the expertises of medicine, money-making, and "navigation more than athletic training in as much as there is less exactitude <in navigation than in athletic training>" (*EN* 3.3 1112b4–6). In short, we deliberate "in cases where things occur for the most part and yet it is not evident how they will turn out and in cases <in which something> is indeterminate" (*EN* 3.3 1112b8–9). What Aristotle has told us thus far can be made clearer by taking one of his examples, money-making, which is productive of wealth. Say I want to invest $10,000 in the stock market in order to make some money through dividends and a rise in stock price. This is something that "can be done," and it is also something that is "in my power," provided I have the money. Investing, however, is not an "exact science." Although making money in this way "occurs for the most part," the outcome of my investment is far from evident, and the future dividends and stock price are quite "indeterminate." Being "in doubt" about what stock to buy and even whether I should buy a stock now, given market fluctuations, I deliberate. I think everyone would agree with Aristotle that we would, and should, deliberate in such a case, but he has not told us how to go about it or what sort of factors we should consider. This lack is partially filled by what follows. We do not deliberate about the ends (for example, whether or not to make money), but about "the things that promote the ends" (*EN* 3.3 1112b12),[26] that is, the various kinds of means that can be employed to achieve the ends. This point is restated as the claim that we deliberate about "the how and <the> through what <the end> will come about" (*EN* 3.3 1112b15).

At this point in Aristotle's account we come to (3), the process of deliberation (*EN* 3.3 1112b15–20). The process consists of three stages: (i) having a clear conception of the end or goal that one wants to achieve and setting this as a basis for deliberation; (ii) investigating what is the immediate, direct means to achieve the end, and if there are more than one possible immediate means, which among them are best; in the case that the means discovered in (ii) is insufficient to achieve the end, then (iii), investigating further what means will bring about the means determined in stage (ii), and then what will bring about this mediate means, and so on, until one conceives a series of means that concludes with the discovery of a first action to take. Presumably at each step in (iii), one repeats the method used in (ii), namely investigating whether there is one means to achieve the step, or many, and if many, which is best. Once the final stage is completed, a decision is made to act, that is, to do the first action of the series of actions that one has set out in one's mind.[27]

---

[26] τὰ πρὸς τὰ τέλη. In Broadie's 1987: 237 translation: "the things by the realization of which the end(s) would be realized."

[27] Actually, because "decision" is understood by Aristotle to be a particular kind of impulse (ὄρεξις), the act follows immediately. There is no notion of a third factor, such as a will, that must be engaged to implement the decision in action. In light of *Met.* E.1 1025b22–24, where Aristotle

On stage (i) Aristotle says merely that "they lay down some end" (*EN* 3.3 1112b15), "they" referring to people who deliberate, such as the physicians, rhetoricians, and politicians mentioned at *EN* 3.3 1112b13–14. Elsewhere Aristotle tells us more about (i) and I shall return to it below. On (ii) Aristotle says: "When it appears that <the end could> come about through several <means>, they look out for the one <means among them> through which <the end will come about> in the easiest and best way" (*EN* 3.3 1112b16–17). It can occur that there is only one possible means. If this is the case, and this means is sufficient to achieve the end, then the deliberator can stop deliberating without moving on to stage (iii). Aristotle leaves unexplained the commonsensical criteria "easiest and best" for choosing among immediate means to the end. It is evident that a means that is best may not be easiest, and conversely that a means that is easiest may not be best. We should also like to know more about the sense in which a means is judged to be best (κάλλιστα). For example, let us say that I identify three possible means to making money with my $10,000. I can put it into a CD with a 3% interest and the certainty of not losing my investment. I can invest in the stock market with moderate risk, getting a 6% dividend (for the time being) and hopefully an increase in stock price, or with significant risk I can put money in my friend's start-up robotics company with the hope of significant long-term gain. Which of these means is best? The higher the risk, the more the potential for gain. A difficult weighing of options is needed here. The criteria "easiest and best" seem insufficient.

Aristotle has the following to say about stage (iii).

> But when the <end> is accomplished through one <means>, <they look out for> how <the end> will come about through it, and through what <action> this <means will come about>, <and so on> until they come to the first cause, which <cause> is last in the process of discovery. For the person who deliberates seems to investigate and analyze in the way just mentioned, as if <it were> a diagram … <where it is> also <the case that> the last in the process of analysis is the first in the process of generation. (*EN* 3.3 1112b17–24)

A great deal of interpretive effort has been spent on Aristotle's comment that deliberation resembles the mathematical method of analysis.[28] I think, however, that the

---

distinguishes between productive and moral (πρακτική) knowledge, saying that "the starting point (or, principle) of productive <action> is in the doer, that is, intelligence or expertise or some power" while the starting point of moral action is in the agent as "decision," Aristotle may think that when a strict distinction is made between production and moral action, "decision" occurs only in the latter case. For the role of *phantasia* and the apparent good as the "starting point" for moral action, see Moss 2012.

[28] For a discussion of the method of analysis and reference to this passage in the *EN*, see Menn 2002: 208.

analogy is a remark meant merely to help make the point that stage (iii) is an investigation that works through a series of actions until arriving at the discovery of an action that we must decide to do first. Stage (iii) does not seem mysterious. We do such thinking very frequently. Still, how we work backwards through the series is by no means as self-evident as Aristotle's sketch might suggest. For example, in the money-making example above, after long deliberation I decide that the best option is a stock investment. The action to bring about this means is choosing a stock to invest in. But there are thousands of stocks. Which of them will be "easiest (if relevant) and best" to choose? This choice confronts me with the difficult risk versus gain assessment problem again. Therefore, to determine which stock to choose, I have to consider the next member backwards in the series: the means of determining which stock is best, as, for example, company reports, analysts' assessments. But as all of these have dubious value, I must discover a means to determine which of these means are best. And so on. My point is that although Aristotle's proposed series of deliberative steps is reasonably clear and accords with what we in fact do, he omits from consideration most of the difficulties that confront deliberative reasoning, leaving a multitude of problems to solve under the expression "best." This is not to say that he intimates that deliberation should be an easy matter. Deliberation can be arduous and time-consuming (*EN* 6.9 1142b5), as we should expect since we deliberate only about matters of which we lack exact knowledge, which occur only for the most part, and concerning which we are in doubt.

A clear example of deliberation as productive reasoning in all three of its stages is given in *Metaphysics* Zeta 7. In the context of an argument to show that form is not generated and a discussion of kinds of coming to be, Aristotle says that coming to be in the case of production consists of two processes, thinking (νόησις), which corresponds to the account of deliberation in *EN* 3.3, and production or doing (ποίησις), where one carries out what has been determined in the former. Because the argument is about form, Aristotle gives as examples cases of expertise, since expertise involves knowledge of universals. The reasoning process for a person possessing the expertise of medicine is said to be the following: "Because this is health, if <the patient> is to be healthy this must be the case, for example an evenly balanced state [of the primary qualities, heat, cold, wet, dry], but if this <evenly balanced state is to occur>, then heat <must be applied>, and he continues thinking the same way until he comes to that last <step> which he himself is able to make" (*Met.* Z.7 1032b6–9); in taking this step the physician begins the process of "doing," that is, producing health. Alexander's commentary on the passage provides the following useful clarification:

> First he [Aristotle] divides coming to be into thinking and doing, and says that "of the comings to be, one is called thinking while the other doing" (*Met.* Z.7 1032b15–16). Thinking proceeds from the starting-point, that is the form, but

doing proceeds from the conclusion of the thinking. For example, the builder considers the form of the building, that it is this kind of covering [or, shelter], and that if this is going to come about, walls must come to be, but if it is necessary for walls to come to be, a foundation must come to be, and if there is to be a foundation, it is necessary to dig. So the builder then begins to dig, and having completed the digging, makes a foundation, then walls, then a roof. The coming to be, or process, from the starting-point of the form until the digging is called "thinking"—the digging being the end [or, goal] of the thinking and the starting-point of the coming to be of the building—while the coming to be, or process, from the digging until the roof is called "doing." (*In Met.* 490.33–491.5)[29]

In the *Metaphysics* passage and Alexander's example, stage (i) in the productive reasoning of someone who possesses the appropriate expertise consists in recognizing the end or goal to be accomplished, for example health or a building suitable for shelter. The possessor of the appropriate expertise knows the form of health, or the building; she knows what health, or a building is. Knowledge of the form is the starting point of her reasoning. For example, the definition of health presumably includes the fact that there be a proper balance of the hot, the cold, the wet, and the dry in an organic body. Thus the physician, on the basis of her knowledge of the form—knowledge which she cannot lack qua physician ("the form is in <her> soul" [*Met.* Z.7 1032b23])—can begin to reason about the means required to achieve health. Putting aside for the moment, with Aristotle, the complications of the particular case and circumstances and the other truths about health entailed by the definition, productive reasoning can proceed to stages (ii) and (iii). In *EN* 3.3 Aristotle says that the deliberator employs the criteria of what is "easiest and best" to establish a series of actions that will achieve the end in view. I noted above that these criteria are not sufficiently informative. In the present passage about productive reasoning the criteria are definitions and causal relations. These criteria are informative. With respect to causal relations, the possessor of expertise, qua possessing expertise, has an account of the causal relations between the relevant universals. She therefore appeals to her expertise to determine necessary and sufficient causal conditions for bringing about each of the means in the series which she expresses as inferences: if there is to be a roof, there must be walls; if walls, there must be a foundation.[30] With respect to definitions, Aristotle says a bit later in the

---

[29] Alexander gives the building example because Aristotle mentions building in passing at *Met.* Z.7 1032b13–14.

[30] C.f. "A person acts from a starting point. If there will be a cloak, necessarily this must be first, and if this, <then> this, and this he does immediately" (*De Motu* 7 701a20–22).

passage that at each step the physician poses, as it were, to herself the question: what is health? What is it to be in an evenly balanced bodily state? What is it to be warmed? And so on (*Met.* Z.7 1032b19–20). In this example, the physician first asks herself what is it to be warmed and then determines a suitable cause that will produce the warmth required, namely rubbing (friction). Here Aristotle gives us an example of stage (ii) of the reasoning process, that is, the determining of the single, best, and easiest action needed to achieve the end, health. Alexander gives us an example of stage (iii), that is, when there are several actions that must be taken: build walls, build foundation, dig trench. In both stages the productive reasoner appeals to the knowledge of the universals belonging to her expertise and constructs an inferential chain that is completed in a first action that must be taken: to rub or to dig.

Insofar as the series of actions to be taken is reasoned out by reference to definitions and causal relations, the possessor of expertise is a paradigm of productive reasoning. Aristotle seems to suggest that the expertise will enable its possessor to determine without significant difficulty what means to use in what order. In real cases, however, this seems less likely to occur. "Matters surrounding actions and things that bring advantage have nothing steady about them" (*EN* 2.2 1104a3–4).[31] Real cases present many particular circumstances which may make the expertise's recommended means impracticable. For example, expertise informs the physician that the patient must be heated, but this particular patient has a severe skin disease that makes it impossible to employ any of the recommended heating methods. Expertise alone, as a knowledge of universals, is not sufficient to deal with real cases. Since "all actions and productions are concerned with what is particular" (*Met.* A.1 981a16–17), and "no expertise looks into (σκοπεῖ) the particular" (*Rhet.* 1.2 1356b28–29), but we have knowledge of particulars through experience and perception, experience (and obviously perception) is also needed for actions and productions. It would seem, then, that a more complete account of productive reasoning would be given when its stages are explained by appeal to both expertise and experience. For example, we are told that the builder asks herself, "What is a wall?" as she reasons. She knows the form of walls, which knowledge probably includes their function and how they fulfill this function. But the form does not instruct the builder how to build a wall, what cement to use, what materials are best in the circumstances (e.g. stone block, or solid cement block, or cinder block, or bricks), what quantity to purchase, what tools to use and how to use them, and what problems one may expect to arise. As anyone knows who reasons about producing

---

[31] See also *EN* 2.2 1104a6–9: "The account of what is particular even more lacks exactness, for it neither falls under expertise nor under any set of rules, but on each occasion those who act must examine the <circumstances> regarding the occasion."

things, these issues must be addressed before the production process begins, and frequently revisited during production as unforeseen circumstances arise. A person who has experience in building many walls will be able to do this, even without an articulate understanding of the form. For these reasons Aristotle's account of productive reasoning seems to need supplementation.

I think Aristotle's response to this objection—beyond the point that in the *Metaphysics* passage expertise is merely used as an example for a different claim— would be that he is providing an outline of how productive reasoning proceeds, and that the outline consists in the starting points for individual steps in the "thinking" process. For example, the starting point for building a wall is the form of wall to which a builder, qua possessing expertise, refers in her reasoning. With the definition, or grasp of the concept, in place, the productive reasoner must continue from here, aided by her experience and expertise, to determine how the wall is to be built, what materials are required, what tools to use, and so on. Furthermore, Aristotle does not claim that a person who only has experience, but no expertise, would be incapable of reasoning out how to build a wall or treat an illness.[32] The reasoning, however, of such a person would refer only to a cognitive framework of similarity to past cases, and this might or might not be an appropriate paradigm for the present one. In short, I am claiming that Aristotle's account of productive reasoning takes the role of experience for granted. Aristotle thinks, as do we, that a person who possesses both the relevant experience and expertise will reason best about how to achieve productive ends.

Before returning to my tree problem I want to discuss a possible objection to Aristotle's account of expertise and its relation to productive reasoning. When distinguishing expertise from moral wisdom (φρόνησις), Aristotle defines the former as "a productive [mental] disposition (ἕξις) accompanied by a true account…concerning what can occur otherwise," while the lack of expertise (ἀτεχνία) is a "productive disposition accompanied by a false account" (*EN* 6.4 1140a20–23). It should be evident that there is a good deal of space between possessing and not possessing expertise. On the one hand, Aristotle seems to be speaking of an ideal expert who can not only reason effectively to produce the end but can also give a true causal account of why the means produces that end based on the true definition of the end. On the other hand, the person who lacks expertise is said not only to lack such an account but also to have a false account. One might ask, who are these people? I may know a fair number of the universals involved with carpentry and be able to employ them in building some structure, but I certainly do not have a "true account," and if an account were demanded

---

[32] In *Met*. E.1 1025b22–24, where Aristotle distinguishes between ποίησις and πρᾶξις, he says "of things that are produced the starting point, [i.e.] intelligence or expertise or a capacity, is in the producer." Ross 1988: *ad loc*. 1.354 takes the capacity referred to here to be experience.

of me, much of the account I gave would likely be wrong. Do I therefore possess none of this expertise? I also know a number of excellent professional carpenters who could not meet Aristotle's standard. If we are going to be charitable to Aristotle, we should allow that he recognizes there to be a vast middle ground between these two extremes. Justification for such charity appears in statements about expertise such as the following: "For those things which we must produce by learning how to do so, these we learn in producing them, for example, we become house builders in building houses" (*EN* 2.1 1103a32–34). Presumably this means that with each new house that a builder builds she increases her knowledge of the universals and causal principles involved with house building through reflection on experience.[33] This seems right, but there is no evident completion of this process. Every time someone builds a house she deepens her experience and she may grasp new universals. If asked for an account, the account might be "truer." Aristotle, I think, would grant that most of us who attempt to achieve some end by production occupy the middle ground between his two extremes and that this middle ground is one in which we appeal both to experience and to universals and, further, one in which we may be able, at best, to give an account that is more true than false. The existence of this middle ground suggests that the distinction between experience and expertise is not as clear-cut as Aristotle seems to claim. It is very unlikely that a person who possesses a great deal of experience in producing a certain kind of product would be unable to cite relevant universals when asked why she does such and such. What she may not be able to do is give a systematic causal account, linking the universals into a scientific explanation. In other words, she may not satisfy Aristotle's extreme requirements for possession of an expertise. But in the middle ground, where most of us find ourselves, experience generates a degree of expertise, and expertise deepens experience. This, of course, did not escape Aristotle: "Expertise comes about when from many conceptions belonging to experience a single universal supposition about similar <cases> comes about" (*Met.* A.1 981a5–7). Quite naturally for us humans the grasp of a universal gradually emerges through induction as our experience increases. And the experiential framework of the practitioner becomes clearer and more steady as her mind becomes better acquainted with universals.

---

[33] Here is an example of a reflection on experience from the possibly spurious *Mechanics* (1.26 857a5–6): "Why is it more difficult to carry long wooden planks on the shoulder from the end rather than at the middle, though the weight is the same?" The explanation refers to universals about counterbalancing. One could, of course, note this fact of experience and not ask oneself why it occurs.

SOLUTION TO THE TREE PROBLEM AND CONCLUSION

The middle ground between expertise and the absence of it is where I stand, epistemically speaking, with regard to the tree. The tree, as I said in the beginning, leans towards the electric and telephone wires along the driveway. The end, to which I deliberate, is felling the tree in the opposite direction. Therefore I must deliberate about how to achieve this. To fell a tree, it must be cut. The common means used to do this is a chainsaw. The use of a chainsaw involves a good deal of experience, but not the grasp of many universals. If I do not have experience using a chainsaw, I should stop this project immediately. Let us suppose that I have this experience. How should the cut be made? Here there is a universal to appeal to. A method derived from "single experiences" exists. Assuming that I know this method, I know that I must cut a large notch (depending on the width of the tree) in the tree's trunk on the side towards which I want the tree to fall; then I must do a back-cut parallel (in most versions of the method) to the ground that is an inch or two above the bottom of the notch on the opposite side. The purpose of the method (a causal account appears) is to create a hinge that allows one to control the tree's fall. At this point, however, I must take cognizance of the particular facts of the case. Gravity (the tree's weight) is drawing the tree in the wrong direction. To deal with this problem I appeal to my experience. My memory of past cases, which include a number of disasters and close encounters with death, gives me the "supposition" that the hinge must be thick and also that using the method alone is insufficient: gravity always wins the day. What action (means) must I take to counteract gravity? Experience tells me, on the basis of past cases, what actions work, while my possession of some expertise tells me why these actions will work. Because there is a hinge, the tree can be swung to a position where gravity will work for me, not against me. But how will I manage to pull a large tree to a perpendicular position? Past cases, observations, and expertise tell me that I can put a rope high in the tree for leverage, attach the rope to a hand winch, which itself is secured to the base of another tree at a distance greater than the height of the tree to be felled (to prevent the operator [me] from being crushed), and then, through a rather complex dance of back-cutting, running back and forth, and winching, I can slowly pull the tree to the required position. Of course, each one of these steps may have its own set of particular facts that must be considered as I attempt to carry out my plan, and I know that events may well turn out otherwise than expected (rule of thumb: always leave a cleared path for escape). In my productive reasoning I set all of these steps in order in my mind until I discover the first action that must be taken: buy gas for my chainsaw.

Following Aristotle's account of productive reasoning I first determine a goal, which in this case is evident. The goal should fall under a form, the grasping of which begins the process of reasoning. The form would seem to be a particular kind of human activity, namely "tree-cutting." To know the answer to the question, What is tree-cutting? one must know a good number of universals. To answer the question, How shall I cut down this particular tree? one must also have a lot of experience. The same would be true of money-making and other productive activities. The unpacking of this knowledge follows Aristotle's description of stage (iii), quoted above (*EN* 3.3 1112b17–20). In the present case, the "one means" is cutting the tree such that it falls in the right direction. The described epistemic resources which constitute experience and some level of expertise make it possible to reason out what are the further means required to accomplish this immediate means; the series of actions determined is lengthy. Without these epistemic resources no amount of reasoning could reveal how to achieve the end. Productive reasoning, therefore, assumes experience and expertise to get off the ground.

Aristotle's account of productive reasoning, as I have attempted to explicate it, corresponds rather well with how we actually reason in the domain of production and, unsurprisingly, with contemporary accounts of the same.[34] Productive reasoning is essential for survival, and even more for human flourishing. One might therefore wonder why Aristotle does not treat it directly, but only appeals to it as a species of reasoning that parallels moral (practical) reasoning, which he does treat. He does not, in his writings, submit productive reasoning itself to a close examination, and he does not investigate, beyond what I have cited, the cognitive mechanisms that generate experience and the expertise employed in real-life situations in the minds of real-life people. He is the first to put these subjects forward for scrutiny, but leaves them largely unexplored. The reason for this, I think, is that Aristotle considers these matters to be sufficiently self-evident starting points for the treatment of subjects that he finds actually in dispute. Productive reasoning and experience seem to be among the things that he considers "better known and more evident to us" "from which" paths of inquiry lead (*Phys.* 1.1 184a16–17). We might agree with him that there is self-evidence here. Even so, we now realize that many pressing epistemological questions lie unanswered behind this veil of self-evidence. For example, philosophers, cognitive scientists, and neuroscientists recognize that the broad term "experience" covers a great many factors

---

[34] See, e.g., Goldman 1970: 104 on practical deliberation: "Often the agent must perform a sequence of acts in order to put himself in a position for performing the desired act.... Once he is in a position to perform the desired act, he must still know what lower acts to perform, including certain basic acts. Thus there will be a chain of practical inferences leading from a desire to perform the original act to a desire to perform some basic act." See also Bengson and Moffett 2011, esp. their chapter "Nonpropositional Intellectualism," 161–195.

in our cognitive abilities that we are still striving to understand.[35] Cognitive scientists seek to understand how experience and expertise alter, as distinct from enrich, our perception of objects.[36] We want clear, unambiguous answers to questions such as: "How can a system organize its experience so that it has some basis for action even in unfamiliar situations? How can a system determine that rules in its knowledge base are inadequate? How can it generate plausible new rules to replace the inadequate ones?"[37] Without answers to questions of this kind we now recognize that we cannot fully understand the various cognitive mechanisms by virtue of which we manage to make our way in the world. Such questions seem not to have occurred to Aristotle, but if they had, there is no reason to think that he would not have seen them as belonging to inquiry into what is "more evident and better known in nature" (*Phys.* 1.1 184a20–21) and therefore subjects for further investigation.

Acknowledgments

My thanks first and foremost to Gisela Striker whose wisdom in things both practical and theoretical made this paper possible. Then to Mitzi Lee for her suggestions and editorial labors, and to my colleague Brian Johnson for his comments on an earlier draft.

References

Barnes, J. 1994. *Aristotle: Posterior Analytics* (Oxford: Clarendon Press).
Bengson, J., Moffett, M. edd. 2011. *Knowing How: Essays on Knowledge, Mind, and Action* (Oxford: Oxford University Press).
Bok, H. 1998. *Freedom and Responsibility* (Princeton, NJ: Princeton University Press).
Broadie, S. 1987. "The Problem of Practical Intellect in Aristotle's Ethics," *Proceedings of the Boston Area Colloquium in Ancient Philosophy* **3**: 229–52.
———. 1991. *Ethics with Aristotle* (Oxford: Oxford University Press).
Cooper, J. 1986. *Reason and Human Good in Aristotle* (Indianapolis, IN: Hackett).
Devereux, D. 1986. "Particular and Universal in Aristotle's Conception of Practical Knowledge," *Review of Metaphysics* **39**: 483–504.
Everson, S. 1997. *Aristotle on Perception* (Oxford: Clarendon Press).
Frede, D. 1992. "The Cognitive Role of *Phantasia* in Aristotle," in edd. Nussbaum, Rorty, *Essays on Aristotle's* De Anima (Oxford: Clarendon Press): 279–95.

---

[35] See, for example, Lipton (1993): "Since our principles of induction are neither available to introspection, nor observable in any other way, the evidence for their structure must be highly indirect. The project of description is one of black box inference, where we try to reconstruct the underlying mechanism on the basis of the superficial patterns of evidence and inference we observe in ourselves. This is no trivial problem" (15). See also the astonishing Kahneman 2011 on the distinct mental systems we employ in daily life.
[36] The area of research is called "perceptual learning." See, e.g. Kellman, Garrigan (2009).
[37] Holland et al. (1989): 3–4.

Frede, M. 1996. "Aristotle's Rationalism," in edd. Frede, Striker, *Rationality in Greek Thought* (Oxford: Clarendon Press): 157–73.

Goldman, A. 1970. *A Theory of Human Action* (Princeton, NJ: Princeton University Press).

Gregoric, P. 2007. *Aristotle on the Common Sense* (New York: Oxford University Press).

Gregoric, P., Grgic, F. 2006. "Aristotle's Notion of Experience," *Archiv für Geschichte der Philosophie 88.1*: 1–30.

Holland, J.H., Holyoak, K.J., Nisbett, R.E., Thagard, P.R. 1989. *Induction: Processes of Inference, Learning, and Discovery* (Cambridge: MIT Press).

Hume, D. 1955. *An Inquiry concerning Human Understanding* (New York: Liberal Arts Press).

Johansen, T.K. 2013. *The Powers of Aristotle's Soul* (Oxford: Oxford University Press).

Kahneman, D. 2011. *Thinking, Fast and Slow* (New York: Farrar, Straus, and Giroux).

Kellman, P.J., Garrigan, P. 2009. "Perceptual Learning and Human Expertise," *Physics of Life Reviews 6.2*: 53–84.

LaBarge, S. 2006. "Aristotle on *Empeiria*," *Ancient Philosophy 26*: 23–44.

Lipton, P. 1993. *Inference to the Best Explanation* (London: Routledge).

Lorenz, H. 2006. *The Brute Within: Appetitive Desire in Plato and Aristotle* (Oxford: Clarendon Press).

Menn, S. 2002. "Plato and the Method of Analysis," *Phronesis 47*: 193–223.

Moss, J. 2012. *Aristotle on the Apparent Good: Perception,* Phantasia, *Thought, and Desire* (Oxford: Oxford University Press).

Ross, W.D. 1924. *Aristotle's* Metaphysics (Oxford: Clarendon Press).

Siwecki, J. 1934. "πρᾶξις et ποίησις dans *l'Éthique Nicomachéenne*," in *Charisteria Gustavo Przychocki a Discipulis Oblata* (Varsovi: Gebethner & Wolff): 175–89.

Striker, G. 2006. "Aristotle's Ethics as Political Science," in ed. Reis, *The Virtuous Life in Greek Ethics* (New York: Cambridge University Press): 127–41.

PART THREE

Aristotelian Logic

7

DEDUCTION IN *SOPHISTICI ELENCHI* 6

Marko Malink

Aristotle's logical theory is centrally concerned with deductions (συλλογισμοί). A deduction, for Aristotle, is "an argument in which, certain things being assumed, something else than what has been assumed results of necessity through what has been assumed." This definition is from the opening chapter of the *Topics*. Similar definitions are given at the beginning of the *Prior Analytics*, *Sophistici Elenchi*, and *Rhetoric*. In none of these passages, however, does Aristotle explain in any detail what the definition and its individual parts mean. Instead, his most extensive discussion of the definition of deduction is to be found in chapter 6 of the *Sophistici Elenchi*. Although this chapter has received relatively little attention in the recent scholarly literature it has important implications concerning the nature of deductions—or so I will argue. My aim here is to explore what we can learn from the chapter about Aristotle's conception of deduction.

The *Sophistici Elenchi* deals with apparent refutations, that is, with arguments which appear to be refutations but are not refutations. In chapters 4 and 5 of the treatise, Aristotle identifies thirteen kinds of apparent refutations. In chapter 6 he states that these thirteen kinds can ultimately be reduced to one of them, namely to *ignoratio elenchi* (see Section 1 below). In order to prove this, he argues that all apparent refutations violate some condition laid down in the definition of refutation. Since refutations are a kind of deduction, his argument also appeals to the definition of deduction (Section 2). Aristotle explains why various apparent refutations violate some condition in this latter definition. In doing so, he appeals to two conditions which are not explicitly included in the standard definition of deduction quoted above. Thus Aristotle extends the standard definition by two new conditions which he does not state elsewhere (Section 3).

One of these new conditions concerns the premises of deductions. Aristotle requires that premises be simple predicative sentences consisting of a single predicate and a single subject (*SE* 6 169a6–18). He thereby excludes complex premises such as "If it is day, the sun is above the earth." The other new condition to which Aristotle appeals in *Sophistici Elenchi* 6 concerns the linguistic form of deductions more generally. He introduces it in connection with arguments such as (i) and (ii):

(i) Every robe is a cloak.
Every cloak is useful.
Therefore, every robe is useful.

(ii) Every robe is a cloak.
Every mantle is useful.
Therefore, every robe is useful.

The latter argument differs from the former in that the second occurrence of the term "cloak" has been replaced by its synonym "mantle." Clearly (i) is a deduction, that is, a valid deductive argument. But although "cloak" and "mantle" are synonyms, Aristotle denies that (ii) is a deduction (*SE* 6 168a26–33). In his view, (ii) violates a condition laid down in the definition of what a deduction is. This shows that, contrary to what is sometimes thought, Aristotle took deductions to be of an essentially linguistic nature. He does not say which condition it is that is violated by (ii). I will argue that the condition in question ultimately relies on schemata of deductions such as the following:

(iii) Every C is B.
Every B is A.
Therefore, every C is A.

For Aristotle, I argue, (i) is a deduction because it conforms to the schema in (iii), whereas (ii) fails to be a deduction because it does not conform to this or another schema of deduction. Of course, schemata of deductions formulated by means of schematic letters such as "A," "B," and "C" do not occur in the *Topics* and *Sophistici Elenchi*. Aristotle introduces them only later, in the *Prior Analytics*, and it is unlikely that they were available to him at the time he wrote the former two works. Nevertheless, by denying that (ii) is a deduction Aristotle is gesturing toward a schematic account of deduction in the *Sophistici Elenchi* (Section 4). Finally, I will argue that, by Aristotle's lights, the argument of *Sophistici Elenchi* 6 goes some way towards establishing the correctness of his extended definition of deduction (Section 5).

1. THE THESIS OF *SOPHISTICI ELENCHI* 6

In the opening sentence of the *Sophistici Elenchi*, Aristotle states that the treatise is concerned with certain fallacies called sophistical refutations:

> Let us now discuss sophistical refutations, i.e., what appear to be refutations but are really fallacies instead.[1] (*SE* 1 164a20–2)

---

[1] περὶ δὲ τῶν σοφιστικῶν ἐλέγχων καὶ τῶν φαινομένων μὲν ἐλέγχων, ὄντων δὲ παραλογισμῶν ἀλλ' οὐκ ἐλέγχων, λέγωμεν. I read καὶ in this sentence as epexegetical, following Forster (1955: 11), Barnes (1984: 278), Dorion (1995: 119), Schreiber (2003: 192), Fait (2007: 99), and Hasper (2012: ad loc.).

Table 7.1 Aristotle's classification of apparent refutations

Due to language (SE 4):	*Outside of language* (SE 5):
homonymy	accident
amphiboly	*secundum quid*
composition	*ignoratio elenchi*
division	consequent
accent	begging the question
form of expression	non-cause as cause
	many questions

Sophistical refutations are arguments which appear to be refutations but are not refutations. They are apparent refutations. In chapters 4 and 5 of the treatise, Aristotle identifies thirteen kinds of apparent refutations. He classifies six of them as being "due to language" (παρὰ τὴν λέξιν) and seven as being "outside of language" (ἔξω τῆς λέξεως), as shown in Table 7.1. Aristotle takes this to be an exhaustive classification of all apparent refutations.[2]

A special role in the classification is played by *ignoratio elenchi*; for Aristotle will argue in chapter 6 that all thirteen kinds of apparent refutations can be reduced to *ignoratio elenchi*. He characterizes this kind of apparent refutation as follows:

> Those [apparent refutations] which arise because it has not been defined what a deduction is or what a refutation is come about due to (παρά) falling short of the definition [of deduction or refutation].[3] (*SE* 5 167a21–2)

This passage refers to the definitions of deduction and refutation. As we will see shortly, refutations are a special kind of deduction, namely deductions which refute a given thesis. The definition of deduction is therefore included in the definition of refutation, and falling short of the former entails falling short of the latter. Thus, Aristotle's characterization of *ignoratio elenchi* in effect relies on the condition of falling short of the definition of refutation.[4] More precisely, an apparent refutation falls under the heading

---

[2] See *SE* 4 165b23–30, 166b20–7, 8 170a9–11.

[3] οἱ δὲ παρὰ τὸ μὴ διωρίσθαι τί ἐστι συλλογισμὸς ἢ τί ἔλεγχος παρὰ τὴν ἔλλειψιν γίνονται τοῦ λόγου. I omit ἀλλά after ἔλεγχος, following Barnes (1984: 282), Dorion (1995: 238), Schreiber (2003: 212), and Fait (2007: 12).

[4] The phrase ἔλλειψις τοῦ λόγου at 167a22 may be taken to mean either "defect in the definition of refutation" (e.g., Forster 1955: 29, Edlow 1977: 19 n. 17; Schreiber 2003: 88), or "falling short of the definition of refutation" (Dorion 1995: 238–9). The translation given above prefers the latter

of *ignoratio elenchi* just in case it comes about due to falling short of the definition of refutation.

What is it for an apparent refutation to come about due to falling short of that definition? First of all, the argument which constitutes the apparent refutation should violate one of the conditions laid down in the definition of what a refutation is. But in addition, the preposition "due to" (παρά) introduces a causal aspect. Elsewhere Aristotle indicates such an aspect by speaking explicitly of a cause of apparent refutations:

> If the refutation is merely apparent, the cause (τὸ αἴτιον) will be either in the deduction or in the contradiction [...], while sometimes it is in both. (*SE* 10 171a5–7)

The cause referred to here seems to be a cause which explains, or contributes to explaining, why a given argument is an apparent refutation. Now, apparent refutations are arguments which appear to be refutations but are not refutations. So we may distinguish between a cause which explains why the argument is not a refutation, and a cause which explains why it appears to be a refutation. In scholastic terminology, these causes are called *causa non existentiae* and *causa apparentiae* respectively.[5] The passage just quoted seems to refer to the former cause.[6] In the case of *ignoratio elenchi*, it is doubtful whether an argument's not satisfying the definition of refutation can constitute a *causa apparentiae*, but it clearly can constitute a *causa non existentiae*.[7] I will have more to say about the way in which it is a *causa non existentiae* for an apparent refutation. For now, it suffices to note that every apparent refutation which falls under the heading of *ignoratio elenchi* is required to meet two conditions: first, that it violate the definition of refutation; and second, that this violation constitute a *causa non existentiae* for the apparent refutation.

---

option (cf. the phrase ὑπερβολή τε καὶ ἔλλειψις τοῦ μέσου at *NE* IV.8 1128a3–4, which refers to an excess and a deficiency as compared with the mean). On the first option, Aristotle states that in instances of *ignoratio elenchi*, the interlocutors implicitly rely on a deficient definition of refutation, and therefore take an argument which is not a refutation to be a refutation. In this case, too, the apparent refutation can be taken to come about due to falling short of the *proper* definition of refutation.

[5] See Ebbesen 1987: 115–17, Fait 2007: xix–xx. The former cause is also called *causa defectus*.
[6] Thus, τὸ αἴτιον at 171a6 is translated as "cause of falsity" (Forster 1955: 57), "reason of the falsity" (Barnes 1984: 290), or "cause de l'erreur" (Dorion 1995: 144 and 272).
[7] Fait 2007: xx.

Let us now turn to chapter 6 of the *Sophistici Elenchi*. There Aristotle argues that all thirteen kinds of apparent refutations introduced in chapters 4 and 5 can be reduced to one of them, namely to *ignoratio elenchi*:

> We should either classify apparent deductions and refutations as just described [in chapters 4 and 5], or else reduce them all to ignorance of what a refutation is, and make this our starting point; for it is possible to analyze all the aforesaid modes of apparent refutations into the definition of refutation. (*SE* 6 168a17–20)

Aristotle's thesis is that every apparent refutation which falls under one of the thirteen kinds is an instance of *ignoratio elenchi*. Since the classification into the thirteen kinds is meant to be exhaustive, his thesis is that all apparent refutations fall under the heading of *ignoratio elenchi*. Given Aristotle's characterization of *ignoratio elenchi*, this implies, first, that every apparent refutation violates the definition of refutation.[8] In other words, the definition of refutation is extensionally correct with respect to the class of apparent refutations, in the sense that no apparent refutation satisfies the definition. We may call this the thesis of extensional correctness. Second, Aristotle's thesis implies that for every apparent refutation, its violating the definition of refutation is a *causa non existentiae* for it. In other words, the violation is a cause which explains why the argument in question is not a refutation. Call this the causal thesis.

The causal thesis implies, or presupposes, the thesis of extensional correctness. One might think that the latter thesis also implies the former, on the grounds that every violation of the definition of refutation constitutes a *causa non existentiae*. I will argue below, in Section 5, that this is not so, and that Aristotle had in mind a more specific notion of *causa non existentiae* which does not include any arbitrary violation of the definition of refutation. But for now, let us have a look at the definitions of refutation and deduction employed by Aristotle in his argument for the thesis of chapter 6.

2. DEFINING REFUTATION AND DEDUCTION

In the first chapter of the *Sophistici Elenchi*, Aristotle defines refutation as follows:

> A refutation is a deduction (συλλογισμός) together with the contradictory (μετ' ἀντιφάσεως) of the conclusion. (*SE* 1 165a2–3)

---

[8] Dorion 1995: 89.

This means that a refutation is a deduction whose conclusion is the contradictory of a thesis endorsed by one's opponent in a debate; the purpose of the deduction is to refute that thesis.[9] Thus, every refutation is a deduction.[10] Since the definition of refutation relies on the notions of deduction and contradiction, let us consider these in turn. In the first chapter of the *Sophistici Elenchi*, deduction is defined as follows:

> A deduction is from certain things which have been assumed, in such a way as to necessarily lead to the assertion of something else than what has been assumed, through what has been assumed.[11] (*SE* 1 164b27–165a2)

This is a version of Aristotle's standard definition of deduction, which is also found at the beginning of the *Topics*, *Rhetoric*, and *Prior Analytics*.[12] The definition imposes at least three conditions on deductions:[13]

C1   The conclusion follows necessarily from the premises (*necessitas consequentiae*).

C2   The conclusion is not identical with any of the premises.

C3   The conclusion follows through the premises.

Condition C2 is comparatively straightforward. The precise import of conditions C1 and C3 is less clear, and we will consider them later.

As for the notion of contradiction, Aristotle does not explicitly define it in the *Sophistici Elenchi*; but he does so in the *De Interpretatione*, as follows:

> Let a contradiction (ἀντίφασις) be this: an affirmation and a denial which are opposite. I speak of sentences as opposite when they (C4) affirm and deny the same thing of the same thing—(C5) not homonymously, (C6) together with all other such conditions that we add to counter the troublesome objections of sophists. (*Int.* 6 17a33–7)

---

[9] See Crivelli 2004: 140. Elsewhere, Aristotle simply says that a refutation is a "deduction of the contradictory" (*SE* 6 168a36–7, 9 170b1–2, *AnPr.* II.20 66b11).

[10] *SE* 10 171a2–3, see also 6 168b4–5.

[11] ὁ μὲν γὰρ συλλογισμὸς ἐκ τινῶν ἐστι τεθέντων ὥστε λέγειν ἕτερον ἐξ ἀνάγκης τι τῶν κειμένων διὰ τῶν κειμένων.

[12] *Top.* I.1 100a25–7, *Rhet.* I.2 1356b16–18, *AnPr.* I.1 24b18–20.

[13] In addition, the plural phrase "from certain things" seems to indicate a fourth condition, to the effect that deductions have more than one premise (see Frede 1974: 20, Striker 2009: 79–80). Unlike C1–3, this condition plays no role in *SE* 6, and can therefore be set aside for present purposes.

Contradictions consist of an affirmation and a denial. Affirmations and denials are linguistic expressions.[14] They are sentences. An affirmation is a sentence affirming something of something, and a denial is a sentence denying something of something. That which is affirmed or denied is called the predicate of the sentence; that of which it is affirmed or denied is called the subject of the sentence. Like sentences, their subjects and predicates are linguistic expressions.[15]

Aristotle's C4 seems to require that in a pair of contradictory sentences, the same predicate is denied and affirmed of the same subject. This means that the same linguistic expression serves as the predicate in both sentences, and likewise for the subject.[16] In addition, Aristotle requires that the predicates (and subjects) of the two sentences not be merely homonyms (C5). Finally, he mentions "all other such conditions that we add to counter the troublesome objections of sophists" (C6). He does not specify these conditions in the *De Interpretatione*; but he does specify them in the *Sophistici Elenchi*, in an extended definition of refutation that he gives in chapter 5:

> A refutation is a contradictory[17] (C5) of one and the same item, not merely of the name but of the object, (C4) and of a name which is not synonymous but the same name[18]—(C1) a contradictory which follows necessarily from the premises granted, (C2) without including in the premises the original point to be proved—(C6) a contradictory in the same respect and relative to the same thing and in the same manner and at the same time. (*SE* 5 167a23-7)

The additional conditions mentioned in *De Interpretatione* 6 are specified at the end of the passage.[19] The passage also shows that Aristotle endorses C4 and C5 in the *Sophistici Elenchi*. In his formulation of C4, he makes it clear that the subjects (and predicates) of a pair of contradictory sentences are required to be the same linguistic

---

[14] Affirmations and denials are λόγοι (*Int.* 5 17a8–9). A λόγος, in turn, is a "significant spoken sound" (φωνὴ σημαντική, *Int.* 4 16b26). Thus, affirmations and denials are significant spoken sounds (*Int.* 5–6 17a23–6), and hence linguistic expressions.

[15] See Crivelli 2012: 113–15.

[16] See Ammonius, who takes Aristotle at 17a33–7 to require that the predicate of both sentences be the same term (ὅρος), and likewise for the subject (Ammonius *In Int.* 84.13-27). It is clear that Ammonius regards terms (ὅροι) as linguistic expressions (see, e.g., *In Int.* 7.32–3, 10.1–17).

[17] This is to say that a refutation is a deduction whose conclusion is the contradictory of the opponent's thesis.

[18] ἔλεγχος μὲν γάρ ἐστιν ἀντίφασις τοῦ αὐτοῦ καὶ ἑνός, μὴ ὀνόματος ἀλλὰ πράγματος, καὶ ὀνόματος μὴ συνωνύμου ἀλλὰ τοῦ αὐτοῦ. This is one of the few places where Aristotle uses συνώνυμος to mean "synonymous," picking out expressions that differ in linguistic form but have the same meaning (see Bonitz *Index Arist.* 734b54–8, Dorion 1995: 239, Schreiber 2003: 212, Fait 2007: 120).

[19] See Weidemann 2002: 200–1.

expression. Even if they are synonyms, the sentences will not be contradictory. For example, "A mantle is useful" and "A cloak is not useful" are not contradictory, even if "mantle" and "cloak" are synonyms.

In C5 Aristotle requires that in addition to being the same linguistic expression, the subjects (and predicates) of the two sentences signify the same object. He thereby excludes homonymous subjects (and predicates). For example, the sentences "Ajax fought against Hector" and "Ajax did not fight against Hector" are not contradictory if "Ajax" is taken to signify Ajax the Greater in one of them and Ajax the Lesser in the other.

In sum, the three requirements imposed on contradictions in refutations can be stated as follows:

C4   The predicate of the refutation's conclusion is the same linguistic expression as the predicate of the opponent's thesis—and likewise for the subject.

C5   The predicate of the refutation's conclusion signifies the same object as the predicate of the opponent's thesis—and likewise for the subject.

C6   The refutation's conclusion and the opponent's thesis affirm and deny the predicate of the subject in the same respect, relative to the same thing, in the same manner, and at the same time.

In his formulation of C4 and C5 in *Sophistici Elenchi* 5, Aristotle draws a clear distinction between names (ὀνόματα) and objects (πράγματα). Thus he distinguishes between linguistic and non-linguistic items. This distinction is not prominent in Aristotle's discussion of deductions in the other works of the *Organon*; indeed, it is often thought that Aristotle is unclear or confused about it. But the distinction is prominent in the *Sophistici Elenchi*, as is shown, for example, by the following passage from the first chapter:

It is not possible to discuss by bringing in the objects (πράγματα) themselves, but we use names (ὀνόμασιν) as symbols instead of objects [...]. Names are finite and so is the number of phrases, while objects are infinite in number. Necessarily, then, the same phrase and a single name signifies many [objects]. (*SE* 1 165a6–13)

Since the number of linguistic expressions is finite and the number of objects is infinite, there are cases in which one expression signifies many objects. This potential ambiguity of linguistic expressions constitutes a cause (αἰτία, 165a4, 165a18) of apparent refutations, especially of those under the heading of homonymy and amphiboly.

Hence it is important for Aristotle in the *Sophistici Elenchi* to attend to the distinction between linguistic and non-linguistic items. In this context, his endorsement of C4 shows that he takes contradictions, and hence refutations, to depend essentially on the linguistic items involved. As we will see, his argument in chapter 6 shows that he holds a corresponding view about deductions, too.

3. TWO ADDITIONAL CONDITIONS ON DEDUCTION

As we saw above, Aristotle's thesis in chapter 6 implies the thesis of extensional correctness, that every apparent refutation violates one of the conditions in the definition of refutation. Aristotle's proof of this latter thesis relies on conditions C1-6, which are stated in chapters 1 and 5. In addition, however, the proof relies on two other conditions that are not stated in chapters 1-5. Both of these conditions concern deductions. One occurs in Aristotle's discussion of apparent refutations due to many questions. The other occurs in the discussion of apparent refutations due to composition, division, and accent. I will first briefly consider the former condition; the bulk of this and the next section will then be devoted to the latter.

In the course of establishing the thesis of extensional correctness, Aristotle argues that apparent refutations due to many questions violate the definition of what a premise is:

> Those apparent refutations which arise because several questions are made into one consist in our failure to articulate the definition of premise. For a premise is concerned with one item about one item. [...] If, then, a single premise is a premise which claims one item of one item, a premise, without qualification, will be the putting of a question of that kind. (*SE* 6 169a6–12)

According to this passage, premises are questions which ask whether a single item holds of a single item. The first of these items is the predicate of the premise, or what is signified by the predicate. The latter item is the subject or what is signified by it. Each of these items is required to be one, not many. Questions that meet this requirement may be called simple predicative questions.

Apparent refutations due to many questions contain would-be premises which fail to be simple predicative questions, and therefore violate the definition of what a premise is (169a12–18). For present purposes, it is not necessary to consider why these apparent refutations violate the definition of premise. What is important is the fact *that*, for Aristotle, they violate it. From this Aristotle infers that they violate the definition of refutation, and that they fall under the heading of *ignoratio elenchi*. Thus he seems to regard the condition that premises be simple predicative questions as part of the definition of deduction and refutation. Call this condition C7.

In the *Prior* and *Posterior Analytics*, premises are taken to be declarative sentences rather than questions. Specifically, they are taken to be simple declarative sentences, in which something is affirmed or denied of something.[20] According to the *De Interpretatione*, every single affirmation and denial affirms or denies a single item of a single item.[21] In view of this, C7 may be extended as follows:

C7   The premises of every deduction are simple predicative questions or simple declarative sentences.

This condition excludes declarative sentences that are not simple. For example, it excludes compound sentences composed of two or more simple ones, such as "If it is day, the sun is above the earth" or "Either it is day or it is night." Given C7, such sentences cannot, by definition, serve as premises of deductions.[22] In his formulation of C4 and C5, Aristotle implicitly assumed that the conclusion of any refutation is a simple declarative sentence. He now makes the same assumption for the premises of any deduction.

Alexander and other commentators in antiquity thought that C7 is already implicit in Aristotle's standard definition of deduction. This definition states that "a deduction is from certain things which have been assumed." Alexander and others took the word "assumed" (τεθέντων) to imply that the premises are simple declarative sentences.[23] However, their view is open to question, and it is rejected by Ammonius (*In AnPr.* 27.6–14, 28.13–20). If Ammonius is right, then C7 adds new content to Aristotle's standard definition of deduction. Nevertheless, the passage from *Sophistici Elenchi* 6 shows that Alexander is correct in thinking that Aristotle regarded C7 as part of the definition of what a deduction is.

Let us now turn to the other additional condition imposed on deductions in chapter 6. Aristotle introduces it in his discussion of the six kinds of apparent

---

[20] Cf. *AnPr.* I.1 24a16–17, *Int.* 5–6 17a20–6; see also Alexander *In AnPr.* 11.6–9, Barnes 2007: 135.
[21] *Int.* 8 18a12–13, 10 19b6–7, 11 20b12–15.
[22] Barnes (2007: 135–6) argues that one and the same sentence can be analyzed as having the form of a simple and of a compound sentence. In this case, C7 may be taken to require that premises of deductions *be analyzed* as having the form of simple declarative sentences (or simple predicative questions).
[23] See Alexander *In AnPr.* 17.5–10, 348.29–32, 350.16–18, *In Top.* 8.8–14. Alexander says "predicative" (κατηγορικός) instead of "simple declarative" (ἁπλοῦς ἀποφαντικός or ἁπλῆ ἀπόφανσις); the two expressions are equivalent, see Ammonius *In Int.* 73.35–74.1, *In AnPr.* 17.26–9, Bobzien 2002: 364 n. 18.

refutations that he classifies as being due to language: homonymy, amphiboly, form of expression, division, composition, and accent. The first three kinds are due to an ambiguity of linguistic expressions (παρὰ τὸ διττόν, 168a24). That is, they are due to the fact that different occurrences of the same linguistic expression in them signify different things. By contrast, the other three kinds of apparent refutations are not due to an ambiguity. Instead, Aristotle claims, they are due to the fact that two distinct, though similar, linguistic expressions in them signify different things.[24] For example, consider the following apparent refutation due to accent, in which the two expressions οὗ ("where") and οὐ ("not") signify different things (SE 21 177b37–178a3):

A1 A house is where you lodge (τὸ οὗ καταλύεις οἰκία).
"You do not lodge" is a denial (τὸ οὐ καταλύεις ἀπόφασις).
Therefore a house is a denial (ἡ οἰκία ἄρα ἀπόφασις).

This argument is a merely apparent deduction because it lacks a single middle term. For the predicate of the first premise (τὸ οὗ καταλύεις) is not the same linguistic expression as the subject of the second premise (τὸ οὐ καταλύεις). Likewise, apparent refutations due to composition and division are caused by the distinctness of linguistic expressions.[25] In order to show that these three kinds of apparent refutations violate a condition in the definition of refutation, Aristotle writes:

> Composition and division and accent arise because the phrase is not the same, or because the name which is different is not the same. For this also would be required, just as it is required that the object be the same, if a refutation or deduction is to be effected. For example, if a mantle is under consideration, you must not deduce a conclusion about a cloak but about a mantle. For the former conclusion is also true, but it has not been deduced, and there is a further need for a question whether it signifies the same thing in response to the one who asks the reason why.[26] (SE 6 168a26–33)

The apparent refutations under consideration in this passage violate the definition of refutation because certain linguistic expressions in them are not the same. If this defect

---

[24] SE 6 168a26–8; see Dorion 1995: 245, Schreiber 2003: 57–8, Fait 2007: 125.
[25] Aristotle has in mind here distinctness in oral language, not necessarily in written language (SE 20 177b1–9; see Kirwan 1979: 43–4, Schreiber 2003: 60–76, pace Hasper 2009: 137–46).
[26] ἡ δὲ σύνθεσις καὶ διαίρεσις καὶ προσῳδία τῷ μὴ τὸν αὐτὸν εἶναι τὸν λόγον ἢ τὸ ὄνομα τὸ διαφέρον. ἔδει δὲ καὶ τοῦτο, καθάπερ καὶ τὸ πρᾶγμα ταὐτόν, εἰ μέλλει ἔλεγχος ἢ συλλογισμὸς ἔσεσθαι, οἷον εἰ λώπιον, μὴ

occurs in the supposed contradiction, the apparent refutation will typically violate C4 (the condition that the predicate of the refutation's conclusion be the same linguistic expression as the predicate of the opponent's thesis, and likewise for the subject). However, when this defect occurs within the supposed deduction, as it does in A1, then the apparent refutation is not excluded by C4.

Aristotle seems to describe such a defective deduction in the second half of the passage just quoted. There he indicates an example which involves the words "mantle" and "cloak." For Aristotle, these two expressions signify the same object (*Top.* I.7 103a9–10, 25–7). They are synonyms. It is not entirely clear what role these synonyms play in Aristotle's example. Two different interpretations have been proposed in the secondary literature. On one interpretation, the pair of synonyms occurs in the supposed contradiction; on the other, it occurs in the supposed deduction. According to the former interpretation, the opponent's thesis contains the word "mantle." Aristotle's point would be that this thesis cannot be refuted by means of a deduction whose conclusion contains the word "cloak" instead of "mantle" (Poste 1866: 19, Schreiber 2003: 90). Even if this deduction is flawless, it would not constitute a refutation of the original thesis. For example, if the opponent's thesis is "A mantle is useful," it cannot be refuted by means of a deduction whose conclusion is "A cloak is not useful." The person mentioned at the end of the passage who "asks the reason why" would be the opponent asking why one should think that his thesis has been refuted by the deduction.

However, this interpretation is in tension with Aristotle's remark "for the former conclusion (κἀκεῖνο) is also true, but it has not been deduced." As I have translated it, the pronoun κἀκεῖνο refers to the incorrect conclusion containing the word "cloak" instead of "mantle." Accordingly, the remark states that this conclusion has not been deduced.[27] This is incompatible with the interpretation under consideration, on which the incorrect conclusion containing "cloak" has been properly deduced, but merely fails to contradict the opponent's thesis. Hence, commentators who endorse this interpretation take κἀκεῖνο to refer to the correct conclusion containing "mantle."[28] They take the remark to say that, given the truth of the premises, the conclusion containing "mantle" would be true as well as the other one, but that that conclusion has not been deduced (simply because no attempt was made to deduce it).

ἱμάτιον συλλογίσασθαι ἀλλὰ λώπιον. ἀληθὲς μὲν γὰρ κἀκεῖνο, ἀλλ' οὐ συλλελόγισται, ἀλλ' ἔτι ἐρωτήματος δεῖ εἰ ταὐτὸν σημαίνει, πρὸς τὸν ζητοῦντα τὸ διὰ τί.

[27] I take it that in the phrase ἀληθὲς μὲν γὰρ κἀκεῖνο, ἀλλ' οὐ συλλελόγισται, the pronoun κἀκεῖνο is the grammatical subject of οὐ συλλελόγισται. *Pace* Forster (1955: 37) and Colli (1955: 660), who translate ἀλλ' οὐ συλλελόγισται as "but the reasoning is not complete."

[28] Poste 1866: 19, Schreiber 2003: 90. See also the translation of 168a30–1 in Barnes 1984: 284: "if the point concerns a doublet, then you should deduce about a doublet, not about a cloak. For the former conclusion also would be true, but it has not been deduced."

Now, this reading of κἀκεῖνο is less natural than the other. For the pronoun ἐκεῖνο typically refers to the item that is more distant in the preceding text. According to this rule, κἀκεῖνο should refer to the conclusion containing "cloak" instead of "mantle."[29] On this reading, Aristotle's point is that the conclusion containing "cloak" cannot be properly deduced from the premises adduced because the premises contain the word "mantle" instead of "cloak." This is the traditional interpretation of the passage given by Michael of Ephesus and the anonymous paraphrase of the *Sophistici Elenchi* edited in *CAG* 23.4.[30] The author of the paraphrase, who is believed to be Sophonias, gives the following example:

A2 Every mantle is preventive of frost and heat.
    Everything preventive of frost and heat is useful.
    Therefore, every cloak is useful.

According to this interpretation, the pair of synonyms occurs not in the supposed contradiction, but in the supposed deduction. Because "mantle" and "cloak" are two distinct expressions, A2 fails to be a deduction, and hence does not constitute a refutation of the thesis "A cloak is not useful." The person mentioned at the end of the passage who "asks the reason why" is the opponent asking why the conclusion of A2 follows from the premises adduced.

In view of the problems the other interpretation has with the pronoun κἀκεῖνο, the traditional interpretation of the example at 168a30–3 seems preferable. Still, both interpretations of 168a30–3 are perfectly in accordance with Aristotle's intentions in the passage at 168a26–33 as a whole. The first sentence of the passage indicates that Aristotle is concerned with the identity of certain linguistic expressions in

---

[29] This interpretation of κἀκεῖνο is preferred by Michael of Ephesus *In SE* 57.25–31, Anonymus *In SE* 18.16–17, von Kirchmann (1883: 12), Rolfes (1918: 13), Forster (1955: 37), Colli (1955: 660), Dorion (1995: 133), and Hasper (2012: ad loc.). Of course, it is not impossible that κἀκεῖνο refers to the correct conclusion containing "mantle." But such an interpretation also leads to a problem with the καί in κἀκεῖνο. The καί implies that the conclusion which is not referred to by ἐκεῖνο is true, and that its truth can be taken for granted in the context under consideration. Given the preceding sentence, the conclusion which is salient in the context is the correct conclusion containing "mantle"; for this conclusion is recommended by Aristotle while the other is dismissed. If ἐκεῖνο referred to the correct conclusion, καί would imply the truth of the incorrect conclusion dismissed in the preceding sentence. In this case, the connection to the preceding sentence would be less smooth than on the other interpretation, on which καί implies the truth of the correct conclusion containing "mantle."

[30] Michael of Ephesus *In SE* 57.15–31, Anonymus *In SE* 18.8–18; the interpretation is also given by von Kirchmann (1883: 12) and Rolfes (1918: 13).

refutations. The second sentence states that this identity is required "if a refutation or deduction is to be effected." The fact that deductions are mentioned here strongly suggests that Aristotle is concerned with the identity of linguistic expressions not only within the contradiction of a refutation, but also within the deduction. Thus, even if it were the case that the subsequent example about "mantle" and "cloak" focuses on defective contradictions such as "A mantle is useful" versus "A cloak is not useful," the passage as a whole would still take into account defective deductions such as A2.

It seems clear, then, that in 168a26–33 Aristotle denies A2 the status of a deduction.[31] Given this, he should also deny the status of a deduction to arguments that have a pair of synonyms instead of a single middle term, such as the following:

A3   Every robe is a cloak.
      Every mantle is useful.
      Therefore, every robe is useful.

The fact that Aristotle rejects A2 and A3 shows that he takes deductions, like contradictions, to depend for their success on the identity of the linguistic expressions involved. Deductions are not preserved by substitution of synonyms. For example, A4 below is a correct deduction; but when the second occurrence of "cloak" in it is substituted by "mantle," the result (i.e., A3) is not a deduction.

A4   Every robe is a cloak.
      Every cloak is useful.
      Therefore, every robe is useful.

These results are in tension with some claims that Alexander of Aphrodisias makes about Aristotle's views on deduction. Alexander claims that unlike the Stoics, Aristotle

---

[31] Here I am in agreement with Crivelli (2012: 139 and 147 n. 5). At the end of *SE* 6, Aristotle claims that all apparent refutations due to language have their defect in the contradiction (169a18–21; see Michael of Ephesus *In SE* 65.25–66.1). However, this claim is simply not true (Poste 1866: 115–16, Dorion 1995: 250, Fait 2007: 130–1). Elsewhere Aristotle recognizes apparent refutations due to language whose defect is only in the deduction; for example, he recognizes them under the heading of accent (see A1 above; *SE* 21 177b37–178a3) and under the heading of homonymy (see A5 below; *SE* 10 171a9–11, *AnPo*. I.12 77b27–33). Thus, it makes sense for him to address such apparent refutations at 168a26–33.

does not attend to linguistic expressions in his account of deduction. Discussing certain arguments which the Stoics called "subsyllogistic," he writes:[32]

> They [the Stoics] do not call such arguments deductions since they attend to language and expression, whereas Aristotle, where the same object is signified, looks to what is signified and not to the expressions. (Alexander *In AnPr.* 84.15–17)

Accordingly, Alexander attributes to Aristotle the following view:

> A deduction has its being not in the words but in what is signified by the words. (Alexander *In AnPr.* 372.29–30)

> As we said, a deduction comes about through what is signified by the words, not through the words. (Alexander *In AnPr.* 373.16–17)

According to Alexander, Aristotle took deductions to depend not on words, but only on what is signified by words. On this view, given that synonyms signify the same object, deductions should be preserved by substitution of synonyms, contrary to what we saw with A3 and A4.[33]

Alexander's claims may be motivated, in part, by the fact that Aristotle often does not pay attention to the precise linguistic formulation of deductions. In the *Sophistici Elenchi*, however, the distinction between linguistic expressions and what is signified by them is of importance, and in this context Aristotle's rejection of A2 and A3 makes it clear that he did take deductions to depend on the identity of the linguistic expressions involved. Thus, Alexander does not, in the above passages, adequately represent Aristotle's views on deduction.

Given that A2 and A3 are not deductions, the definition of deduction should contain a condition that is violated by them. It is not immediately clear what kind of condition this might be. In what follows, I will argue that none of the three conditions we have seen so far (C1–3) is, by itself, sufficient to exclude A2 and A3. Thus, the definition of deduction needs to be extended by an additional condition which excludes these two arguments.

---

[32] On subsyllogistic arguments, see Barnes 2007: 314–21.
[33] Moreover, Alexander claims that "He has a dagger" is the same premise (πρότασις) as "He has a poniard" (*In Top.* 12.11–15). Thus, he should also hold that "Every mantle is useful" is the same premise as "Every cloak is useful." Again, this would make it difficult to explain why A3 is not a deduction while A4 is.

4. SYNONYMS IN DEDUCTIONS

Among the conditions laid down in the definition of deduction, the most important is C1, that the conclusion follow necessarily from the premises.[34] However, Aristotle does not explain what this condition means. Rather, he treats the relation of following necessarily as an undefined primitive in his logical writings.[35] It is therefore not always obvious which arguments he takes to satisfy C1 and which not. Nevertheless, many cases are reasonably clear. For example, an argument such as A5, which involves a homonymous middle term, presumably does not satisfy C1:[36]

A5   Homer's poem is a circle.
      Every circle is a figure.
      Therefore, Homer's poem is a figure.

It is less clear whether arguments such as A2 and A3, which involve a pair of synonyms, satisfy C1. But there is reason to think that Aristotle took them to satisfy C1. This can be seen as follows. Aristotle states that in arguments such as A2 and A3 "there is a further need for a question whether it signifies the same thing in response to the one who asks the reason why" (168a31–3). By this he seems to mean that if the opponent asks why the conclusion follows from the premises in these arguments, one should ask him whether "cloak" signifies the same thing as "mantle." The implication is that if the answer is affirmative, there will be a genuine deduction. Thus, Aristotle seems to hold that A2 and A3 can be turned into genuine deductions by adding a premise to the effect that "cloak" signifies the same thing as "mantle"; but as long as such a premise is missing, they are not deductions.

Now, Aristotle holds that some arguments satisfy C1 although premises are missing in them.[37] He gives an example of such an argument in *Prior Analytics* I.32:

A6   A substance is not destroyed by the destruction of what is not a substance.
      If the things out of which something is composed are destroyed, then what consists of them must also perish.
      Therefore, any part of a substance is a substance.

---

[34] This is the first condition to which Aristotle appeals in his proof of the thesis of *SE* 6 (168a19–23).

[35] See Lear 1980: 2–14.

[36] In addition to violating C1, Aristotle seems to think that arguments which contain a homonymous subject or predicate violate C7 (*SE* 17 175b39–176a18; see Bobzien 2005: 258–64 and 2007: 301–12).

[37] *AnPr.* I.32 47a22–35. See Alexander *In AnPr.* 21.28–30, 344.9–345.12, 346.27–8, Philoponus *In AnPr.* 320.16–322.18, 323.18–27, Frede 1974: 20–3.

Aristotle comments on this argument as follows:

> When these [i.e., the two premises of A6] have been assumed, it is necessary that any part of a substance be a substance; yet it has not been deduced through what has been assumed, but premises are missing.[38] (*AnPr.* I.32 47a26–8)

A6 satisfies C1: its conclusion follows necessarily from the premises. Nevertheless, A6 fails to be a deduction (47a31–5), because one or more premises are missing in it. Aristotle does not specify which premises are missing in it. Alexander suggests that it is a premise such as "A whole is composed of its parts."[39] In any case, whichever premise or premises are missing in A6, their truth does not seem to be more obvious than the truth of the premise which is missing in A2 and A3, that "cloak" signifies the same thing as "mantle." Hence, given that A6 satisfies C1, it is natural to conclude that A2 and A3, too, satisfy it.

If the two arguments satisfy C1, they may still violate C3, the condition that the conclusion follow through the premises.[40] What does it mean to "follow through the premises"? In the *Topics*, Aristotle takes this condition to exclude arguments that contain superfluous premises (*Top.* VIII.11 161b28–30). But in the *Prior Analytics*, he also seems to take it to exclude arguments in which premises are missing. In the first chapter of the *Prior Analytics*, he explains the import of C3 as follows: "no further term is needed from outside in order for the necessity to come about" (24b20–2). This can be taken to mean that all premises necessary to deduce the conclusion are present.[41] If so, then given that a premise is missing in A2 and A3, these two arguments violate C3.

However, C3 does not explain why a premise is missing in the two arguments, nor does it imply that one is missing in them. Consequently, C3 alone does not suffice to establish that they are not deductions. In general, it is not at all clear whether and, if so, which premises are missing in a given argument. For example, Aristotle regards A4 as a deduction, in which no premise is missing. But the Stoics deny this, and insist that a premise is missing in order for A4 to be a deduction (e.g., a premise such as "If every robe is a cloak and every cloak is useful, then every robe is useful").[42]

---

[38] τούτων γὰρ τεθέντων ἀναγκαῖον μὲν τὸ οὐσίας μέρος εἶναι οὐσίαν, οὐ μὴν συλλελόγισται διὰ τῶν εἰλημμένων, ἀλλ' ἐλλείπουσι προτάσεις. In this passage, ἐλλείπειν can be taken to mean "be missing" (Mueller 2006: 30, Ebert & Nortmann 2007: 78, Striker 2009: 52). For this meaning of ἐλλείπειν, see Bonitz *Index Arist.* 238b5–11.

[39] Alexander *In AnPr.* 347.5–7. For alternative suggestions, see Ebert & Nortmann 2007: 800–5, Striker 2009: 214.

[40] Aristotle expresses this condition in various ways: διὰ τῶν κειμένων *SE* 1 165a2, *Top.* I.1 100a26–7; διὰ ταῦτα *Rhet.* I.2 1356b16, *AnPr.* I.1 24b20; τῷ ταῦτα εἶναι *Rhet.* I.2 1356b17, *AnPr.* I.1 24b20, see also *SE* 6 168b24, *Top.* VIII.11 161b30.

[41] See Frede 1974: 22, Ebert & Nortmann 2007: 227, Striker 2009: 81.

[42] See Mueller 1969: 179–80, Frede 1974: 4–5 and 10, Barnes 1990: 114–6.

Conversely, someone might hold that no premise is missing even in A2 and A3: based on Alexander's contention that "a deduction has its being not in the words but in what is signified by the words," she might argue that these two arguments satisfy C3, and are deductions without the addition of further premises.

How can Aristotle defend his view that premises are missing in A2 and A3? A promising strategy would be to appeal to the schemata of deduction that he introduces in the *Prior Analytics*. These schemata contain schematic letters like "A" and "B" in place of concrete expressions like "mantle" and "useful." A typical example is the following:

A7 Every C is B.
    Every B is A.
    Therefore, every C is A.

Aristotle takes the schemata introduced in the *Prior Analytics* to be applicable to a wide range of deductions. In fact, he claims that any deduction whatsoever "comes about through" one of these schemata (*AnPr.* I.23 40b20–2, 41b1–5). Thus, Aristotle might argue that due to the distinctness of the expressions "mantle" and "cloak," A2 and A3 do not fit the pattern of A7 or of another schema of deduction, and therefore fail to be deductions. To make them fit a schema of deduction, a premise such as "Every cloak is a mantle" would need to be added. Aristotle's opponent, however, may still disagree. She might contend that whether or not an argument fits a schema of deduction should be determined not with respect to linguistic expressions, but with respect to what is signified by them.[43] Since "mantle" signifies the same thing as "cloak," she might argue, A2 and A3 both fit the pattern of A7, so that no premise is missing in them.

At this point, it is instructive to consider a parallel disagreement between two more recent logicians, namely Bolzano and Tarski. Bolzano (1837) would accept that in arguments such as A2 and A3 the conclusion is logically derivable from the premises, whereas Tarski (1936) would deny this.[44] Bolzano takes his relation of logical

---

[43] Such a view is sometimes attributed to Aristotle himself. For example, Morison (2012: 182) argues that when Aristotle formulates schemata such as A7, he "articulates the *semantic* content of the premisses and conclusion in question. He does not give any hints as to how they should be expressed in Greek." Similarly, Barnes (1996: 187) holds that "when Aristotle says 'If A is predicated of every B,...' he is not offering a schema in accordance with which categorical sentences may be regimented. Rather, the schema indicates the semantic structure which an appropriate categorical sentence must display." This is in tension with Aristotle's denial that arguments such as A2 and A3 are deductions. However, it is beyond the scope of this paper to enter into a detailed discussion of Morison's and Barnes's views.

[44] This disagreement between Bolzano and Tarski has been pointed out by Siebel (1996: 204–7 and 2002: 593–4).

derivability to obtain not between sentences, but between certain non-linguistic items signified by sentences (see 1837: §155). He calls these items "sentences-in-themselves," and they can be thought of as the propositional content of sentences. Two distinct sentences may signify the same sentence-in-itself. For example, "Every cloak is useful" and "Every mantle is useful" signify the same sentence-in-itself, say: EVERY GARMENT IS USEFUL. Consequently, the three sentences in A3 signify exactly the same three sentences-in-themselves as those in A4:

A8   EVERY ROBE IS A GARMENT.
     EVERY GARMENT IS USEFUL.
     EVERY ROBE IS USEFUL.

In A8, the third sentence-in-itself is logically derivable from the first two. Now, Bolzano does not explain how his relation of logical derivability can be extended from sentences-in-themselves to linguistic sentences. But it is natural to assume that a given sentence is logically derivable from a plurality of sentences if and only if the sentence-in-itself signified by it is logically derivable from the sentences-in-themselves signified by the members of that plurality.[45] If this is correct, then there is no difference in logical derivability between A3 and A4: in both arguments, the conclusion is logically derivable from the premises. Likewise for A2.

Unlike Bolzano, Tarski takes his relation of logical consequence to obtain between sentences, that is, between expressions of a given language. In order to decide whether the conclusion of an argument is a logical consequence of the premises, he proceeds in two steps. First, the argument is transformed into an argument form. This is done by replacing every non-logical expression in it by a variable, in such a way that all occurrences of the same non-logical expression are replaced by the same variable, and different expressions are replaced by different variables (1936: 8). Tarski does not, in his 1936 paper, explain how the distinction between logical and non-logical expressions might be drawn. Still, it is clear that A4 contains exactly three non-logical expressions, namely "robe," "cloak," and "useful." When A4 is transformed into an argument form, each of these expressions is replaced by a distinct variable. The resulting argument form contains three distinct variables, much like A7 (except that A7 employs schematic letters instead of variables). By contrast, the argument in A3 contains a fourth non-logical expression, namely "mantle," so that the resulting argument form contains four distinct variables.

As a second step, Tarski determines whether the resulting argument form is valid (he does so by means of his notion of satisfaction). If it is valid, the conclusion of the

---

[45] Siebel 1996: 196–7 and 2002: 586.

original argument is a logical consequence of the premises. Now, the argument form obtained from A4, which contains three distinct variables, is valid. On the other hand, the argument forms obtained from A2 and A3 contain four distinct variables and are not valid. Hence, for Tarski, the conclusion of A2 and A3 is not a logical consequence of the premises.

Aristotle's denial that these two arguments are deductions is in line with Tarski's approach. Of course, Aristotle did not have Tarski's conception of an argument form. Instead, he employed schemata of deductions in the *Prior Analytics*. Moreover, Aristotle and Tarski do not agree on exactly which schemata, or forms, should be regarded as valid. They do, however, seem to agree that deduction, or logical consequence, depends on the identity of the linguistic expressions involved and on their being arranged in certain patterns. Thus, Aristotle may be taken to reject A2 and A3 on the basis of a condition closely akin to Tarski's account, such as the following:

C8 Any deduction can be obtained from a schema of deduction by replacing every occurrence of a given schematic letter by the same linguistic expression.

Clearly, A4 can be obtained by such a substitution from the schema in A7. By contrast, A2 and A3 cannot be obtained in this way from this or another schema of deduction. Hence, given that C8 is part of the definition of deduction, the latter two arguments are not deductions.

C8 does for deductions what C4 does for contradictions, namely to require that linguistic expressions be arranged in certain patterns. In C4 the pattern is given by the subject-predicate structure of simple sentences; in C8 it is given by Aristotle's schemata of deductions. It must be acknowledged, however, that C8 is a rather strong condition. Aristotle is far from explicitly formulating it in the *Sophistici Elenchi*. In fact, he would arguably not be in a position to do so in this treatise. Schemata of deductions formulated by means of schematic letters are introduced in the *Prior Analytics*, but they are absent from the *Topics* and *Sophistici Elenchi*. It is generally agreed that these two works were written before the *Prior Analytics*, and it is unlikely that the concept of a schema of deduction was already available to Aristotle at the time he wrote them. Nevertheless, by denying that A2 and A3 are deductions he is gesturing toward a schematic account of deduction in *Sophistici Elenchi* 6. Had he been pressed to explain why these two arguments are not deductions, I submit, he would ultimately refer to a condition very much like C8.

5. CAUSES OF (NOT) BEING A REFUTATION

As we have seen, apparent refutations due to composition, division, and accent fail to be refutations because certain linguistic expressions in them are not the same. If this defect occurs in the supposed contradiction, then C4 is violated; if it occurs in the supposed deduction, C8 is violated. However, these apparent refutations not only fail to be refutations because of the distinctness of certain expressions, they also fail to be refutations because these expressions do not signify the same object.[46] For example, consider the apparent refutation due to accent given in A1 above: it fails to be a deduction not only because the expressions "where you lodge" (τὸ οὗ καταλύεις) and "You do not lodge" (τὸ οὐ καταλύεις) are distinct, but also because they do not signify the same object. If this kind of defect occurs in the supposed contradiction, then C5 is violated. If the defect occurs in the supposed deduction, as it does in A1, then the apparent refutation will presumably violate C1 (just as arguments that involve homonyms, like A5, violate C1).

Given this, every apparent refutation due to composition, division, and accent violates either C1 or C5. These two conditions suffice to prove that those apparent refutations violate the definition of refutation. Conditions C4 and C8 are not needed, nor are they used elsewhere in chapter 6 to establish that other apparent refutations violate the definition of refutation. Consequently, the latter two conditions are not necessary to establish the thesis of extensional correctness, that every apparent refutation violates the definition of refutation.[47]

---

[46] See Schreiber 1983: 89–90, Fait 2007: 126–7. Aristotle can be taken to express this view at SE 7 169a25–9 (see Fait 2007: 126) and SE 20 177a33–5, 177b1–4 (see Dorion 1995: 341–2 n. 295).

[47] If A2 and A3 counted as apparent refutations, C8 would be needed to establish that they violate the definition of refutation. However, these two arguments are presumably not apparent refutations, since they do not *appear* to be refutations in the appropriate way. Because the synonyms "mantle" and "cloak" are very different linguistic expressions, A2 and A3 lack the deceptive appearance typical of the thirteen kinds of apparent refutations introduced in SE 5 and 6. Aristotle takes the thirteen kinds to provide an exhaustive classification of apparent refutations (cf. n. 2 above); but A2 and A3 do not seem to fall under any of them. A similar point can be made for arguments that violate C4 without violating C5. One might object that arguments such as A2 and A3 would count as apparent refutations if the synonyms in question are sufficiently similar in linguistic form, e.g. if they were similar in the same way as οὐ and οὗ are similar to each other (I am grateful to Pieter Sjoerd Hasper for pointing this out to me). One might argue that such arguments are apparent refutations for the same reason for which A1 is. However, such arguments seem to be of little use for the purposes of a sophist. Now, the *Sophistici Elenchi* seems to be concerned only with those apparent refutations that would typically be used by sophists. Given this, arguments of the kind in question are not under consideration in the *Sophistici Elenchi*. Thus, C4 and C8 are not needed to establish that all apparent refutations that are under consideration in the *Sophistici Elenchi* violate the definition of refutation.

Why, then, does Aristotle introduce C4 and C8 in *Sophistici Elenchi* 5 and 6? He does not need them to establish the thesis of extensional correctness. But given that he does not introduce them without reason, a natural explanation is that he needed them to establish the causal thesis: that for every apparent refutation, its violating the definition of refutation is a *causa non existentiae* for it, that is, a cause that explains why it is not a refutation. On this view, the violation of C1 or C5 is not a *causa non existentiae* for apparent refutations due to composition, division, and accent. It does not constitute a specific defect characteristic of these apparent refutations, and therefore does not provide the proper explanation of why they are not refutations. Rather, such a defect is constituted by the non-identity of certain linguistic expressions, that is, by the violation of C4 or C8.

If this is correct, then Aristotle's argument in chapter 6 crucially relies on the assumption that each of the conditions C1-8 is part of the definition of refutation, and in particular that C1-3 and C7-8 are part of the definition of deduction. This assumption is not uncontroversial. Those who follow Alexander and Bolzano would deny that C4 and C8 are part of the definition of refutation or deduction. Others might reject other conditions. For example, the Stoics would reject C7, the condition that the premises of deductions be simple predicative sentences. Also, the Stoics would reject C2, the condition that the conclusion be not identical with any of the premises.[48] In view of this, Aristotle's appeal to C1-8 may seem unwarranted and ad hoc. Thus, Poste criticizes Aristotle's argument in chapter 6 as follows:

> We only give a semblance of unity to the theory of fallacies by lumping them all together under the definition of confutation, for the elements of that definition are obtained by no systematic subdivision, and form, as far as appears, a purely arbitrary and incoherent agglomeration. (Poste 1866: 116)

In the remainder of this paper, I want to indicate a possible way for Aristotle to reply to this objection. I will argue that the proof of the causal thesis in chapter 6 itself provides such a reply.

Aristotle's proof of the causal thesis aims to show that for any apparent refutation, there is a condition among C1-8 such that the violation of this condition constitutes a *causa non existentiae* for it. In other words, for any argument that is an apparent refutation, there is a condition among C1-8 such that the argument's violating that condition is a cause of its not being a refutation. Given this, it is natural to say that for any

---

[48] See Alexander *In Top.* 10.6-12, *In AnPr.* 18.14-18, Ammonius *In AnPr.* 27.35-28.8, Frede 1974: 23.

argument that is an apparent refutation, its violating C1–8 is a cause of its not being a refutation.[49] Violating C1–8 is such a cause inasmuch as violating a specific member of C1–8 is such a cause. Since "violating" here simply means "not satisfying," we have: for any argument that is an apparent refutation, its not satisfying C1–8 is a cause of its not being a refutation.

Now, Aristotle holds that if not being A is a cause of not being B, then being A is a cause of being B:

> For example, why does the wall not breathe? Because it is not an animal. For if this were a cause of not breathing, then being an animal would have to be a cause of breathing: i.e. if the denial is a cause of not holding, then the affirmation is a cause of holding. Thus if the hot and cold elements' being imbalanced is a cause of not being healthy, their being balanced is a cause of being healthy. (AnPo. I.13 78b15–20)

If not being an animal were a cause of not breathing, then being an animal would be a cause of breathing. (Aristotle denies that being an animal actually is a cause of breathing, 78b21–3.) If the hot and cold elements' not being balanced is a cause of not being healthy, then their being balanced is a cause of being healthy. Likewise, if not satisfying C1–8 is a cause of not being a refutation, then satisfying C1–8 is a cause of being a refutation.

There is a question as to what it means to say, in this context, that being A is a cause of being B. Jonathan Barnes takes it to mean that for anything that is B, its being A is a cause of its being B. More precisely, everything that is B is A, and its being A is a cause of its being B. Likewise for the negative case. Thus, Barnes (1994: 157) takes Aristotle to state the following principle in the passage just quoted:

> If for anything that is not B, its not being A is a cause of its not being B,
> then for anything that is B, its being A is a cause of its being B.

As we saw above, for any argument that is an apparent refutation, its not satisfying C1–8 is a cause of its not being a refutation. This does not imply that the same is true for any item that is not a refutation. What about arguments that do not appear to be refutations, or items that are not arguments at all? What is a cause of their not being a refutation? Perhaps for some of them such a cause consists in not satisfying one of the

---

[49] Part of the reason why this is natural is that none of the conditions C1–8 is superfluous, but each of them is used by Aristotle in his proof of the causal thesis.

conditions C1–8. For others such a cause may consist in not satisfying another, additional condition. Assuming that the number of these additional conditions is finite, let C1–n be the conjunction of C1–8 and the additional conditions. So, for anything that is not a refutation, its not satisfying C1–n is a cause of its not being a refutation. It follows by Aristotle's principle that for anything that is a refutation, its satisfying C1–n is a cause of its being a refutation.

Satisfying C1–n is a cause which explains why a given argument that is a refutation is a refutation. Now, Aristotle holds that causal explanation is closely connected to definition and essence. Consider, for example, the following passage from the second book of the *Posterior Analytics*:

> In all these cases it is clear that what it is and why it is are the same. What is an eclipse? Privation of light from the moon by the screening of the earth. Why is there an eclipse? or Why is the moon eclipsed? Because the light leaves it when the earth screens it. (*AnPo.* II.2 90a14–18)

The answer to the question what an eclipse is is the definition of eclipse, that is, a specification of its essence. The answer to the question why the moon is eclipsed is a cause of its being eclipsed. According to Aristotle, the two answers are identical: the definition of eclipse is identical with a cause of the moon's being eclipsed.

As we saw above, Aristotle suggests that for anything that is healthy, its having the hot and cold elements balanced is a cause of its being healthy. At the same time, he takes "balance of hot and cold elements" to be the definition (ὁρισμός) of health.[50] Thus, the answer to the question what health is is the same as the answer to the question why anything that is healthy is healthy.

For anything that is a refutation, the answer to the question why it is a refutation is that it satisfies C1–n (n ≥ 8). This answer should be the same as the answer to the question what a refutation is. So we may conclude that C1–n constitute the definition of refutation. Consequently, C1–8 are part of the definition of refutation, and, in particular, C1–3 and C7–8 are part of the definition of deduction.

If this line of reasoning is correct, then Aristotle's proof of the causal thesis in *Sophistici Elenchi* 6 provides the resources for establishing that C1–8 are part of the definition of refutation. Thus, chapter 6 not only adds two new conditions, C7–8, to the definition of deduction, it also goes some way towards justifying that these conditions, along with C1–3, should in fact be included in the definition of deduction. One might even speculate that it was through the argument of *Sophistici Elenchi* 6 that Aristotle

---

[50] *Top.* VI.6 145b7–8, see also VI.2 139b20–1, *Phys.* VII.3 246b4–5.

was led to include C7 and C8 in this definition. The latter of these two conditions relies on the concept of a schema of deduction—a concept that is otherwise absent from the *Topics* and *Sophistici Elenchi*, but constitutes one of Aristotle's significant achievements in the field of logic. This concept, then, might have an origin in Aristotle's reflection on the specific defects of apparent refutations due to composition, division, and accent. But whether or not this is so, I hope to have shown that Aristotle's discussion of apparent refutations in *Sophistici Elenchi* 6 sheds new light on his account of what a genuine refutation and deduction is.

Acknowledgments

This paper is dedicated to Gisela Striker. It owes much to her excellent work on Aristotle's logic and the various kinds of συλλογισμός discussed by him.

Earlier versions of this paper were presented at the Humboldt-Universität zu Berlin, the University of Chicago, the Chicago Area Consortium in Ancient Philosophy, and at the Universität des Saarlandes in Saarbrücken. I would like to thank the audiences for their helpful comments, especially Jonathan Beere, Agnes Callard, David Ebrey, Pieter Sjoerd Hasper, Gabriel Lear, Christian Pfeiffer, Christof Rapp, and Jacob Rosen.

References

Barnes, J. (1984): *The Complete Works of Aristotle: The Revised Oxford Translation, vol. 1*, ed. J. Barnes, Princeton: Princeton University Press.
— (1990): "Logical Form and Logical Matter," in: A. Alberti (ed.), *Logica, mente e persona. Studi sulla filosofia antica*, Firenze: Olschki, 7–119.
— (1994): *Aristotle's Posterior Analytics*, 2nd edn., Oxford: Clarendon Press.
— (1996): "Grammar on Aristotle's Terms," in: M. Frede & G. Striker (eds.), *Rationality in Greek Thought*, Oxford: Clarendon Press, 175–202.
— (2007): *Truth, etc. Six Lectures on Ancient Logic*, Oxford: Clarendon Press.
Bobzien, S. (2002): "The Development of Modus Ponens in Antiquity: From Aristotle to the 2nd Century AD," *Phronesis* 47, 359–94.
— (2005): "The Stoics on Fallacies of Equivocation," in: D. Frede & B. Inwood (eds.), *Language and Learning: Philosophy of Language in the Hellenistic Age*, Cambridge: Cambridge University Press, 239–73.
— (2007): "Aristotle's *De Interpretatione* 8 Is about Ambiguity," in: D. Scott (ed.), *Maieusis: Essays in Ancient Philosophy in Honour of Myles Burnyeat*, Oxford: Oxford University Press, 301–21.
Bolzano, B. (1837): *Wissenschaftslehre*, 4 vols., Sulzbach: Seidel.
Colli, G. (1955): *Aristotele: Organon*, Torino: Einaudi.
Crivelli, P. (2004): *Aristotle on Truth*, Cambridge: Cambridge University Press.
— (2012): "Aristotle's Logic," in: C. Shields (ed.), *The Oxford Handbook of Aristotle*, Oxford: Oxford University Press, 113–49.
Dorion, L.-A. (1995): *Aristote: Les réfutations sophistiques*, Paris: Vrin.

Ebbesen, S. (1987): "The Way Fallacies Were Treated in Scholastic Logic," *Cahiers de l'Institut du Moyen Age Grec et Latin* 55, 107–34.
Ebert, Th. & Nortmann, U. (2007): *Aristoteles: Analytica Priora. Buch I*, Berlin: Akademie Verlag.
Edlow, R. B. (1977): *Galen on Language and Ambiguity*, Leiden: Brill.
Fait, P. (2007): *Aristotele: Le confutazioni sofistiche*, Roma: Laterza.
Forster, E. S. (1955): *Aristotle: On Sophistici Elenchi, On Coming-To-Be and Passing-Away, On the Cosmos*, transl. of *On the Cosmos* by D. J. Furley, Cambridge, MA: Harvard University Press (Loeb Classical Library).
Frede, M. (1974): "Stoic vs. Aristotelian Syllogistic," *Archiv für Geschichte der Philosophie* 56, 1–32.
Hasper, P. S. (2009): "Logic and Linguistics: Aristotle's Account of the Fallacies of Combination and Division in the *Sophistical Refutations*," *Apeiron* 42, 105–52.
(2012): "Aristotle's *Sophistical Refutations*: A Translation," *Logical Analysis and History of Philosophy* 15, Special Issue: Fallacious Arguments in Ancient Philosophy, ed. by C. Rapp & P. S. Hasper.
Kirwan, C. (1979): "Aristotle and the So-Called Fallacy of Equivocation," *Philosophical Quarterly* 29, 35–46.
Lear, J. (1980): *Aristotle and Logical Theory*, Cambridge: Cambridge University Press.
Morison, B. (2012): "What Was Aristotle's Concept of Logical Form?," in: B. Morison & K. Ierodiakonou (eds.), *Episteme, etc. Essays in Honour of Jonathan Barnes*, Oxford: Oxford University Press, 172–88.
Mueller, I. (1969): "Stoic and Peripatetic Logic," *Archiv für Geschichte der Philosophie* 51, 173–87.
(2006): *Alexander of Aphrodisias: On Aristotle's Prior Analytics 1.32–46*, London: Duckworth.
Poste, E. (1866): *Aristotle: On Fallacies or the Sophistici Elenchi*, London: Macmillan.
Rolfes, E. (1918): *Aristoteles: Sophistische Widerlegungen*, Leipzig: Meiner.
Schreiber, S. (2003): *Aristotle on False Reasoning: Language and the World in the Sophistical Refutations*, Albany: SUNY Press.
Siebel, M. (1996): *Der Begriff der Ableitbarkeit bei Bolzano*, Sankt Augustin: Academia Verlag.
(2002): "Bolzano's Concept of Consequence," *The Monist* 85, 580–99.
Striker, G. (2009): *Aristotle: Prior Analytics, Book I*, Oxford: Clarendon Press.
Tarski, A. 1936: "Über den Begriff der logischen Folgerung," *Actes du Congrès International de Philosophie Scientifique* 7, 1–11; republ. in: K. Berka & L. Kreiser (eds.), *Logik-Texte*, 4th edn., Berlin: Akademie Verlag, 1986, 404–13.
von Kirchmann, J. H. (1883): *Aristoteles' sophistische Widerlegungen*, Leipzig: Dürr.
Weidemann, H. (2002): *Aristoteles: Peri Hermeneias*, 2nd edn., Berlin: Akademie Verlag.

8

BOETHUS AND FINISHED SYLLOGISMS

Jonathan Barnes

1. AMMONIUS

According to Aristotle, the four canonical syllogisms of the first figure—Barbara, Celarent, Darii, Ferio—are τέλειοι or finished (*APr* A 26b28–30). The four canonical syllogisms of the second figure, and the six of the third, are all ἀτελεῖς or unfinished (28a4–7, 15–16).[1] And "all the unfinished syllogisms are finished by way of the first figure" (29a30–31).[2]

When in his commentary on the *Prior Analytics* Ammonius comes to discuss the several clauses in Aristotle's definition of what a syllogism is, he says that

> some people, with their eye on what Aristotle himself says (namely, that the syllogisms in the second and third figures are unfinished) have claimed that he puts in the clause "by their being so" on account of the second and third figure syllogisms, meaning to expel them from the company of syllogisms. (*in APr* 31.25–29)

Those anonymous exegetes supposed that an unfinished syllogism was not (yet) a syllogism, and inferred that, according to Aristotle, the items in the second and third figures are not syllogisms.

Ammonius rejects that interpretation: he recognizes that Aristotle takes second and third figure arguments to be genuine syllogisms, and he holds that Aristotle is

---

[1] As for the non-canonical syllogisms of the first figure (Baralipton, Barbari, and the rest), Aristotle does not expressly say whether they are finished or unfinished; but he was taken, no doubt rightly, to have thought them to be unfinished (see e.g. Alexander, *in APr* 69.26–29; Boethius, *syll cat* 823A).

[2] On the finishing of syllogisms see Striker, "Perfection"; cf. Patzig, *Aristotle's Theory*, pp.43–87; Barnes, *Truth, etc.*, pp.378–386.

right to do so. But he does not agree with Aristotle's view of their status. Earlier in the commentary he had explained that

> by finished Aristotle means a syllogism which is self-sufficient and lacks nothing for its being, and by unfinished one which lacks something.... We shall see when we come to the passage in which he speaks about finished and unfinished syllogisms that perhaps none is unfinished—Aristotle thinks that some are unfinished but in truth all are finished. (*in APr* 14.28–33)

Ammonius thinks that Aristotle's definition is a definition of finished syllogisms (see *in APr* 27.14–16); and of the second and third figure syllogisms, he observes that

> they do not lack any term: rather, in them the terms are confused. So you may actually grasp from what Aristotle himself says that these syllogisms are not, as he thinks, unfinished (after all, their terms are finished)—it is simply that in them the terms are jumbled. (*in APr* 33.18–21; cf 32.33–37)

Ammonius agrees with the anonymous exegetes that all syllogisms are finished syllogisms; he disagrees with them inasmuch as he holds that second and third figure arguments are finished; and he infers that Aristotle is mistaken when he states that second and third figure syllogisms are unfinished.

Ammonius takes a syllogism to be finished provided that there are no terms missing from its premisses. Thus he takes the word "τέλειος" or "finished" in the sense of "complete," and he holds that all syllogisms are complete syllogisms. The second and third figure syllogisms lack no terms: they are all finished.

Ammonius takes himself to be correcting Aristotle.

But when Aristotle said that second and third figure syllogisms are unfinished, he did not mean that they are incomplete, or that their premisses lack a term or two:

> I call finished a syllogism which needs nothing apart from the assumptions in order that its necessity be apparent, and unfinished a syllogism which needs one or several items—items which are necessary given the terms taken but which are not assumed as premisses. (*APr* A 24b22–26)

Aristotle uses the word "τέλειος" in the sense of "perfect": a finished syllogism is one the necessity, or validity, of which is evident; and an unfinished syllogism stands in need of something—of a conversion or two or else of a *reductio ad impossibile*—in order that its validity be grasped.³

Ammonius does not misunderstand Aristotle's account of finish (see *in APr* 31.38–32.3; 32.33–33.1); but he thinks that it is a mistaken account. He does not deny that the syllogisms which Aristotle calls unfinished need to be worked over—unjumbled—in order for their validity to be grasped; but he thinks that that is not a matter of finish. According to Ammonius, all syllogisms are finished but some are jumbled. According to Aristotle, all syllogisms are complete but some are unfinished. The two agree that all syllogisms are complete but some are imperfect. Ammonius has not corrected Aristotle: he has changed the terminology. Neither the Ammonian notion of completeness nor the Aristotelian notion of perfection is pellucid.⁴ But there is nothing of interest in Ammonius' putative correction of Aristotle.

And yet Ammonius took himself to be rehearsing a generally accepted view—a view which had been championed by Boethus, who "proved that all the syllogisms in the second and third figures are finished," and by Porphyry and Iamblichus and Maximus. Themistius defended Aristotle against Maximus, and the disputants asked the emperor Julian to arbitrate. Julian decided for Maximus; and Syrianus and Proclus and Hermias later took the same line. What is more, "it appears that Theophrastus, Aristotle's pupil, held the opinion contrary to his on the matter." (See Ammonius, *in APr* 31.11–15.)

It is a striking story.⁵ And puzzling, for two reasons. First, it is hard to believe that Theophrastus and Boethus and all those later lights wasted their breath on such a silly business. Secondly, Alexander breathes no word of the "contrary opinion" in his commentary on the *Analytics*—neither does Philoponus, and neither does Boethius. The silence is strange.⁶ As for Theophrastus, Porphyry, Iamblichus, Syrianus, Proclus, and Hermias, no other text supports Ammonius—and in the case of Theophrastus, scholars have doubted his claim.⁷ But Ammonius did not invent the story.

---

³ "τέλειος" means sometimes "complete" and sometimes "perfect" (see *Met* Δ 1021b16–1022a3). In *APr* it means "perfect" (see Striker, "Perfection," pp.207–208). In this paper I use "finished" in order to preserve the ambiguity.
⁴ No ancient text offers much by way of elucidating the notions, and nothing will be offered here.
⁵ Parts of it are also told in an Aristotelian scholium, 156b43–47, and by David, *in APr* xi 1. According to the *Suda*, Julian wrote *About the three figures* (s.v. Ἰουλιανός): his written judgement on the dispute?
⁶ Lee, *Syllogistik in der Spätantike*, p.132, suggests, implausibly, that it would have been out of place to discuss the question in a commentary on Aristotle.
⁷ See Huby, *Theophrastus*, pp.67–68.—Bocheński, *Logique de Théophraste*, pp.64–65, accepts the story, supposing that Aristotle himself came to hold that "the first figure is not the only perfect one": the supposition was canonized by Moraux, *Aristotelismi* I, p.173; but there is nothing to be said for it. Patzig, *Aristotle's Theory*, p.71, suggested, implausibly, that once Theophrastus had added the five supplementary syllogisms to the first figure, he might have thought that "if the

2. THEMISTIUS

Themistius' defence of Aristotle has survived in an Arabic translation.[8] The translation bears the title: *Treatise of Themistius in reply to Maximus on the reduction of the second and third figures to the first*. (At the end the translator refers to it as the *Treatise of Themistius in reply to Maximus and Boethus on the reduction of the second and third figures to the first*.) Themistius says that

> I offer this to your judgement, my noble sir, in order that you may judge it and see if you find any part of it acceptable. (180.10–12)

(Is Julian the noble sir to whom Themistius submitted the piece and who found it wanting?[9])

> I have set down in the most concise way I could—and in the space of a single day, and a day when I was in particularly poor health—the doubts I have concerning the extraordinary book in which Maximus proposes to prove that the predicative syllogisms of the second and third figures are finished in themselves, and that they require neither proof nor reduction to the first figure. (180.5–10)

Themistius means to refute Maximus; but he insists that "my refutation of Maximus is no more than a defence of Aristotle" (180.15–16).

The structure of the defence is reasonably clear: first, Themistius tries to establish a certain primacy for the first figure (180.5–184.37); next, he criticizes the view which Maximus set out in his extraordinary book (184.38–190.38); third, he turns to Boethus, since Maximus drew heavily on him (190.39–193.20); and a coda explains why, even though the syllogisms in the second and third figures reduce to those in the first, all three figures are useful (193.21–194.26). The essay is always difficult and frequently baffling. In part the difficulties are due to the vicissitudes of its history; but some of them at least derive from the nature of the piece: Themistius is presenting one side of a case, and he supposes that we are familiar with the other side.

---

first figure contains imperfect syllogisms, then the other two figures could be put on a level with it."—See further below, n32.

[8] The text was edited by Badawi, *Aristote chez les Arabes*, pp.309–325, and translated into French in his *Transmission*, pp.180–194. Marwen Rashed, who is preparing a new edition, has with great generosity allowed me to make use of his provisional text: my English translations are versions of his French (but references are by page- and line-numbers of Badawi's translation).

[9] The Arabs knew a "letter to Julian" written by Themistius (Badawi, *Transmission*, p.117); but that can scarcely have been the same as the essay against Maximus.

The view which Themistius defends, and which he takes to be Aristotle's, may be outlined like this. The four syllogisms of the first figure are finished: their validity is evident, and whether or not it can be proved, it does not need to be proved. No other syllogisms are finished: their validity is not evident—it needs to be proved. It can only be proved by way of the first figure; for the first figure is prior to and explanatory of the other two figures, and a proof must proceed from the prior to the posterior and from the explanatory to the explained. The best form of proof is reduction by way of conversion; but where that cannot be done, a *reductio ad impossibile* is legitimate (provided that the *reductio* invokes the first figure).

3. MAXIMUS

Maximus purports to show that "the predicative syllogisms of the second and third figures are finished in themselves, and that they require neither proof nor reduction to the first figure".[10] What is the scope of Maximus' claim? Ammonius' thesis holds of every syllogism, supplementary as well as canonical, modal as well as non-modal. Does Maximus' claim have the same universal application, or was it restricted—perhaps to non-modal syllogisms, or to the fourteen canonical non-modal syllogisms? The text gives no formal answer to the question; but Themistius' discussion mentions only the fourteen syllogisms of *APr* A 4–6.

In any event, Maximus' claim was certainly quite different from Ammonius' view. For Maximus urges that second and third figure syllogisms do not need to be proved, that they are finished not only in the sense of being complete but also in the sense of being perfect. That is a strong thesis, and it is something which Aristotle expressly denies. It was the thesis which Julian approved; and Ammonius' account of the matter is mistaken—not because Maximus rejected the thesis which Ammonius ascribes to him; but because Ammonius has confused that commonplace thesis with something far less tedious.

Second and third figure syllogisms "are finished in themselves, and ... require neither proof nor reduction." Several paraphrases are possible, of which the most plausible (I think) is this: "Second and third figure syllogisms are perfect—that is to say, they don't need to be proved (and in particular, they don't need to be reduced to the first figure)." So there are two claims, the first stronger than the second. For it is one

---

[10] On Maximus see Santos, "Maxime." He is not known primarily for his logical interests: he wrote a commentary on the *Categories* (Simplicius, *in Cat* 1.13–16), to which the *Suda*, s.v. Μάξιμος, presumably refers when it lists a ὑπόμνημα εἰς Ἀριστοτέλην—if the singular noun may be trusted, then Maximus wrote no other commentary; and in any event there is no reason to posit a commentary on *APr*.

thing to say that a syllogism does not need to be proved, another to say that it does not need to be proved by way of reduction to the first figure.

In an obscure paragraph, Themistius recognizes that there are two distinct theses in play:

> What he must show[11] is this: that the moods of the last two figures are no less[12] clear or less evident than the moods of the first figure. For that is the only way in which our man can refute what the old philosophers said. And if he cannot do that, then he must look for some other way of showing that the last two figures are valid without in any way appealing to the first figure. (184.38–185.1)

Maximus must show that Cesare and Darapti and the rest are no less evident than Barbara and her three colleagues: if he can do that, then he will have shown that all the moods are finished. But if he can't do that, then he must prove the validity of Cesare and Darapti and the rest without appealing to the first figure. In other words, Maximus needs to show that the second and third figures moods are evident and do not need proof, or else (failing that) that they do not need reduction to the first figure.[13]

4. BOETHUS

At the end of his discussion of Maximus, Themistius says that

> this, then, is what we find dubious in the method which he has recently dreamed up. But since Boethus tried to establish it by several arguments, we must now examine what he said. (190.38–191.1)[14]

---

[11] The Arabic has "what we must show," which makes no sense.
[12] The Arabic has "no more"—again, a nonsense.
[13] Themistius seems to say at one point that Maximus "has shown adequately that the first figure is the most complete and the most perfect" (181.4–6—"most complete and most perfect" will be the translator's version of a single Greek word, "τελειότατος"): did Maximus argue that, although all syllogisms are finished, some are more finished than others? The idea that there are degrees of finish, absent from Aristotle, crops up occasionally in later texts (see e.g. Alexander, *in APr* 77.6–9, 26–28; 113.7–9; Philoponus, *in APr* 114.16–20; cf Patzig, *Aristotle's Theory*, pp.48–49). But I incline to think that it is no part of Maximus' view.
[14] At 190.38–39 the Arabic gives this: "So much for our doubts concerning the method which Boethus has dreamed up": Rashed excises "Boethus," so that the subject of "dreamed up" is Maximus.

And so Boethus becomes the chief opponent in the third part of the essay.[15] Boethus and his several arguments were mentioned earlier: having remarked that Maximus must show that the syllogisms of the second and third figures are no less evident than those of the first, or at least that they can be proved without reduction to the first figure, Themistius adds that

> some of the later Peripatetics[16] have taken this view, and Boethus, in Book II of his *On Demonstration*, undertakes to establish it by several considerations. (185.3-5)

The Boethan title suggests something comparable to Aristotle's *Posterior Analytics*, which antiquity sometimes referred to as his *On Demonstration*. Such a work has seemed an unlikely place in which to find a discussion of finished and unfinished syllogisms;[17] but ancient titles were generous (consider, say, Galen's *On Demonstration*).

Themistius claims that Maximus adopted a "method" from Boethus. But he never says that Maximus owed everything to Boethus; and two significant differences have been discovered between the two men.

First, consider the sentence I have just quoted: "Some...have taken this view, and Boethus...undertakes to establish it." What is "this view"? The text does not determine an answer; but it is natural to suppose that it is the view that second and third figure moods can be proved without reference to the first figure. So whereas Maximus held that second and third figure moods do not need proof of any sort, perhaps Boethus had argued, less audaciously, that they do not need reduction to the first figure? That notion gets some support from the sentence with which Themistius introduces his discussion of Boethus' ideas:

> But since Boethus tried to establish <his thesis> by several arguments, we must now examine what he said to see if it is truer than what Aristotle says and if he can validate the other two figures by way of the arguments he has used without invoking the first figure. (190.38-191.3)

Certainly, Boethus thought to show that the second and third figure syllogisms can be proved valid without invoking the first figure. But is that all he thought to show? The

---

[15] On Boethus see Moraux, *Aristotelismo* I, pp.149-184; on Boethus and logic see Patzig, *Aristotle's Theory*, pp.69-78; Moraux, *Aristotelismo* I, pp.170-175; Striker, "Perfection," pp.214-219; Barnes, *Truth, etc.*, pp.373-378, 394-395; Barnes, "Peripatetic Logic," pp.10-21; Schneider, "Boéthos."
[16] The Arabic has "old Peripatetics."
[17] Lee, *Syllogistik in der Spätantike*, p.10, wonders, implausibly, if the title does not mean "demonstration of the validity of syllogisms."

next passage, which carries the second of the supposed differences between Boethus and Maximus, suggests that it was not.

This is the text:

> I think that Boethus, because he treated the matter exhaustively, claimed that the moods in the second figure which do not need demonstration are three and not four. (186.8–10)

Maximus thinks that no mood needs proof: Boethus thinks that at least one mood does need proof.

Themistius' remark has been overlooked or discounted; and after all, he says, "I think that..."—perhaps he means that something in Boethus' book implies or suggests that he took only three of the four second figure moods to need proof? and perhaps in reality there was no such implication or suggestion? But that is implausible; and what Themistius means is this: "It was, I think, because Boethus—unlike Maximus—treated the matter exhaustively that he held that three rather than four moods are finished."

Which was the odd mood out? Themistius does not identify it; but what he later says about Boethus and the second figure suggests that it was Baroco—and no one, I imagine, will doubt that it was. What about the third figure? Themistius does not say anything pertinent. But if Boethus held that Baroco was unfinished, he can scarcely have held that Bocardo was finished; for what marks off Baroco from the other three second figure moods is the fact it cannot be proved by conversion—and the same fact marks off Bocardo from the other five third figure moods. In that case, Boethus thought that of the fourteen canonical syllogisms, twelve are finished and two are unfinished.

Or perhaps he thought that four are unfinished? In the second figure, Aristotle proves the validity of Cesare and Camestres by E-conversion, and of Festino by I-conversion. In the third figure, Disamis and Datisi and Ferison are proved by I-conversion, Darapti and Felapton by A-conversion ("AaB" converts to "BiA"). The difference between A-conversion and the other two operations struck the ancient logicians, who came to refer to A-conversion as "accidental." Thus Darapti and Felapton, as well as Baroco and Bocardo, might be set off from the other moods—and Boethus might have thought that they too were unfinished. But Themistius tells us that Boethus applied his method to Darapti, which he took to be finished (192.15–29); and although there is no information about Felapton, I suppose that it was treated in the same style as Darapti.

So Boethus urged that no syllogisms need to be reduced to the first figure, and that twelve syllogisms are finished. Maximus urged that no syllogisms need to be reduced to the first figure, and that all fourteen syllogisms are finished. Themistius rejected both positions. Was he the first to do so? At the end of his discussion of Boethus, Themistius says this—according to the received text:

> It is in this way that we must validate conversions, and not in the way taught by Boethus and Herminus and Alexander and all those who, among our predecessors, have tackled these puzzles. (193.9–11)

That is nonsense; and there can be little doubt but that Themistius in fact claimed Herminus and Alexander as his own precursors, and not as partisans of Boethus. It is tempting to infer that Herminus and Alexander had somewhere discussed and criticized Boethus' views on finish. But the temptation is to be resisted: here, Themistius is referring to Boethus' views on conversion, and not to his views on finish; and the text, however it may be repaired, will not say that Alexander and Herminus had argued against Boethus' claim that there are twelve rather than four finished syllogisms.

Another text is pertinent. In his *institutio logica* Galen remarks that

> some of the Peripatetics, Boethus among them, call arguments which depend on leading assumptions not only unproved but also primary, whereas they are not prepared to call primary those unproved syllogisms which depend on predicative propositions. Of course, in another way such syllogisms are prior to the hypotheticals inasmuch as the propositions from which they are constructed are certainly prior. (vii 2)

Arguments which "depend on leading assumptions" are, as the context shows, hypothetical syllogisms. So according to Galen, Boethus and some other unnamed Peripatetics held a double thesis: (i) unproved hypothetical syllogisms are primary, whereas (ii) unproved predicative syllogisms are not primary. A syllogism is "unproved" provided that it does not need to be proved—or in other words, provided that it is finished.[18] An item is primary (with regard to a given group of items) if and only if nothing (in the set) is prior to it.[19] One syllogism is prior to another if and only if it can be used to prove the other and the other cannot be used to prove it. Thus Boethus held that some predicative syllogisms are finished and that all predicative syllogisms can be proved.

How proved? The sentence "Of course...," which is a comment by Galen and not a continuation of his report, indicates that thesis (ii) holds inasmuch as certain hypothetical syllogisms are prior to the finished predicative syllogisms. Although Galen goes on

---

[18] See Sextus, *PH* II 156; *M* VIII 223; Alexander, *in APr* 6.22; Apuleius (?), *int* ix [205.21–206.6]; [Galen], *hist phil* XIX 239.
[19] So several members of a group may each be primary.

to say that the question of priority is of no importance, he implies that it was frequently debated; but apart from a casual reference in Alexander (*in Top* 218.3–5) nothing more is heard of it.[20] In particular no text hints at the way in which Boethus thought to prove the validity of predicative syllogisms by way of hypothetical syllogisms.

However that may be, Boethus stayed his view with "several arguments": what were they? and how did Maximus exploit them in support of his own thesis?

5. ECTHESIS

When Themistius turns from Maximus to Boethus and says that we must see "if he can validate the other two figures by way of the arguments he has used without invoking the first figure," the first thing he mentions is ecthesis:

> We say, then, that Boethus, although he gives preference to ecthesis over reduction, is not in a position altogether alien to Aristotle—if he differs from him, it is because he does not use ecthesis all by itself. (191.4–6)

By "reduction" here, Themistius means—as he usually does—reduction by means of conversion (and not *reductio ad impossibile*). So he claims that Boethus prefers ecthesis to proof by conversion, and that—unlike Aristotle—he uses ecthesis in conjunction with something else.[21]

Themistius proceeds to criticize Boethus' way of dealing with the second figure. The text is opaque, and in part corrupt; but it suggests that Boethus used ecthesis in conjunction with *reductio ad impossibile*—and if that is so, it is not difficult to divine what he must have said. Take the premisses of Cesare

BeA, BaC.

Then hypothesize that

AiC.

---

[20] On the question see Frede, "Stoic vs Aristotelian," pp.122–124.
[21] At *in APr* 100.14–18, where he is discussing Aristotle's ecthetic proof of Darapti, Alexander notices that some people think that if they take a perceptible individual, then with regard to it they will have predicates for the subject which are either connected or separated. "It is possible that Alexander has Boethus in mind" (Barnes *et al, Alexander*, p.174 n.37).

That is to say, there is at least one individual which is both A and C. Take an individual—any individual you like—of the kind and call it 'α'. So

α is A and α is C.

Since BeA, it follows that

α isn't B,

and since BaC, it follows that

α is B.

There is a contradiction—and we may infer that the hypothesis is false, and hence that

AeC.

The argument shows that Cesare is valid. It uses ecthesis and *reductio ad impossibile*. It does not use conversion (unlike Aristotle's proof), nor does it appeal to any mood of the first figure[22] (or to any other syllogistic mood).

The existence of such an argument shows that Cesare does not need to be reduced to the first figure. Something similar can be done for the other syllogisms of the second and third figures—and also for the syllogisms of the first figure. Boethus doubtless recognized the fact, and inferred that no syllogisms need to be reduced to the first figure. It does not of course follow that all syllogisms are finished.

Aristotle, who recognizes ecthesis as a method of proving validity, has no reason to quarrel with Boethus: Boethus shows that second and third figure syllogisms do not need to be reduced to the first figure in order that their validity be grasped; Aristotle proves that second and third figure syllogisms can all be reduced, by conversion or by *reductio ad impossibile*, to the first figure. There is no incompatibility between those two positions.

Themistius' attitude to ecthesis is uncertain. He knows that Aristotle used it; but he thinks that Aristotle preferred proof by conversion—for two reasons:

> first, because reduction by conversion invokes items which are more evident, as any true knowledge must do; and secondly, because ecthesis, like induction, concerns itself with particulars and is closer to perception than to syllogism. (189.36–40)

---

[22] Ecthesis "does not lead to first-figure syllogisms and hence is not a method of reduction to the first figure" (Striker, "Perfection," p.208 n.9).

And insofar as Themistius claims that "the methods <by which second and third figure syllogisms are proved> cannot fail to invoke the first figure" (185.1–3), he implicitly holds that ecthesis is not a method of proof. No doubt ecthesis is a valid argumentative procedure, which can be used to establish the validity of syllogisms; but it is not a method of demonstrative proof—for it does not proceed from the prior to the posterior, from the more evident to the less, from the *explanans* to the *explanandum*.

Themistius is not the only person who has thought that ecthesis, understood as a method which "sets out" individuals rather than classes, depends upon perception and so is not a proper logical procedure. But that is mistaken. The individuals which ecthesis sets out may or may not be perceptible items—you may set out the number 57 just as properly as the llama Lorenzo. And even when the individuals are perceptible items, perception plays no part in their setting out. You say: "AiC—so there's at least one individual which is both A and C. Suppose that α is such a one...": you can say all that with your eyes shut.

6. THE GENERATION OF SYLLOGISMS

Immediately after his reference to Boethus' *On Demonstration* Themistius states that

> it is there that <Maximus> took his claim to the effect that since certain conjugations are not found by conversion, then they cannot be finished by way of the first figure or be reduced to the conjugations of that figure. (185.5–8)

The argument runs, I suppose, like this: "Some second and third figure conjugations cannot be discovered or 'generated' by conversion from first figure conjugations; a mood can be reduced to the first figure only if its conjugation is generated by conversion from a first figure conjugation: therefore some second and third figure moods cannot be reduced to first figure moods." Maximus found the argument in Boethus' book, and it is natural to infer that it is one of the "several arguments" with which Boethus supported his thesis. But when Themistius comes back to the "several arguments," he writes as though he has not yet discussed any of them; so perhaps Maximus found the argument in one argumentative context and adapted it to another.

Themistius probably had the argument in mind earlier in the essay when he remarked that

> if we are among those who, like Eubulides and Menelaus, reject the conversion of propositions, then we are obliged to deny that the two later figures are derived from the first. (180.23–26)

Eubulides and "Menelaus" rejected Aristotle's conversion rules[23]—and Themistius is thinking in particular of E- and I-conversions.

Then consider the four first-figure moods. Barbara generates nothing. Celarent generates Cesare: Celarent is

AeB, BaC :: AeC.

Convert the first premiss and you get

BeA, BaC :: AeC,

which is Cesare. Thus Celarent generates or produces or is the cause of Cesare. (And also of Camestres, if conversion of the conclusion is allowed.) In the same way Darii generates Datisi (and Disamis with conversion of the conclusion); and Ferio generates Festino and Ferison. Not all first figure moods are generative, and not all second and third figure moods are generated. But this much is true: a mood M is proved from M* by conversion of a premiss if and only if M is generated from M* by conversion of a premiss.

So Maximus' argument claims that a second or third figure mood can be reduced to the first figure by means of non-accidental conversion if and only if it can be generated from a mood of the first figure by non-accidental conversion. That is true; and it follows that some second and third figure syllogisms cannot be reduced to the first figure by non-accidental conversion. But that is a commonplace, accepted by all parties; and it is hard to see how it can have functioned as an argument, or part of an argument, in favour of Maximus' thesis.

Or perhaps that was not Maximus' argument? When Themistius presents his argument for the primacy of the first figure, he begins like this:

> We establish that the second and third figures derive from the first by using a plain and indubitable principle, namely that each of the premisses of the first figure, when it converts from itself, produces each of the two other figures: of the two premisses, the first (the major) when converted produces the second figure and the second (the minor) when converted produces the third figure. (180.17–23)

---

[23] See Barnes *et al*, *Alexander*, pp.85 nn.11 and 12.—"Menelaus" presumably hides "Menedemus."

Conversion, here, is not the conversion of propositions but what was called the conversion of terms. (Conversion of terms is the interchange of subject and predicate in a predicative proposition, so that "AxB" converts to "BxA": see Alexander, *in APr* 29.23-29.) Eubulides and "Menelaus" did not reject the conversion of terms—there is nothing to reject.

As for generation, it is the generation of the figures, not of the moods—as Themistius insists:

> Neither I nor Alexander claims that each of the first figure syllogisms generates each of the second and third figure syllogisms: what we claim is that the first figure generates the other two.... The claim that the two figures are generated from the first figure is not made by Aristotle, nor by Theophrastus, nor by Eudemus—it is a thing of the more recent Peripatetics. (184.13-16, 24-27)

"A figure is simply a certain communality between two propositions" (184.29-30). The first figure is defined by the communality of the conjugation {AxB, ByC}: convert the terms of the first proposition and you get {BxA, ByC}, which shows the communality of the second figure; convert the terms of the second proposition and you get the third figure conjugation {AxB, CyB}.[24]

Conversion of terms is symmetrical: x converts from y if and only if y converts from x. Hence the fact that a first figure conjugation converts to a second figure conjugation cannot show that the first figure generates the second rather than vice versa. Themistius recognized the point. He argued that the first figure is naturally prior to the other two; and that conversion from it to them is therefore generative.

Look again at Maximus' argument. If it appeals to the conversion of propositions, it is futile. Suppose, then, that it appeals to the conversion of terms. Then the conjugation of Celarent, {AeB, BaC}, yields the conjugation of Cesare, {BeA, BaC}; and various other second and third figure conjugations are similarly generated. But not all of them—the conjugations of Camestres and Baroco, and of Disamis and Bocardo cannot be generated.

True—but how can that have anything to do with finish, or with Maximus' thesis? More generally, how can the "generation" of the figures, or of the conjugations, or of the moods, have anything to do with any logically interesting issue?

---

[24] On the generation of the figures see Lee, *Syllogistik in der Spätantike*, pp.120-124; cf. Striker, "Perfection," p.215 n.20; Barnes *et al*, *Alexander*, p.109 n.41.

7. CONVERSION

Another line of argument turns about the non-accidental conversion of propositions. Maximus accepted the Aristotelian conversion rules—and yet he denied that they allow the reduction of second and third figure moods to the first figure (185.30-33). How can that be?

Aristotle denied that "AeB" and "BeA" have the same sense, and he doubtless took the same view of "AiB" and "BiA": a conversion may not be a syllogism, and perhaps it is not exactly an inference—but it does take you from one proposition to another.[25] According to Themistius, Maximus holds that "converted negative propositions have the same sense" (185.38-39).[26] And it seems that such a thesis might be used to support Maximus' account of finished syllogisms.

For consider Cesare:

BeA, BaC :: AeC.

Since "BeA" expresses the same proposition as "AeB," Cesare is the same syllogism as this:

AeB, BaC :: AeC

—and that is Celarent. In a similar way, Camestres—

BaA, BeC:: AeC.

—is the same as Celarent. Similar remarks apply to all second and third figure syllogisms, save Baroco and Darapti and Felapton and Bocardo. So six of the syllogisms which Aristotle takes to be unfinished turn out to be identical to finished syllogisms—and therefore to be finished.

Whatever may be thought of that argument, it was not advanced by Maximus; for Themistius criticizes him in this vein:

> How can he decree that converted negative propositions have the same sense when he also thinks that the second mood of the first figure and the first mood of the second figure are different? ... And how does the second mood of the first

---

[25] See *APr* B 53a11-12; and 59a10-11 (on particular affirmatives): cf. Barnes, *Truth*, pp.304-305; Frede, "Stoic vs Aristotelian," p.114 (at *APr* B 58a27-29 Aristotle says that "AeB" and "BeA" "are the same proposition"; but that, as Frede remarks, is a slip).

[26] Since Themistius refers a few lines later, at 186.9, to Boethus, it is generally supposed that Boethus had advanced the synonymy thesis and that Maximus had borrowed it from him: so Frede, "Stoic vs Aristotelian," p.114. But the sentence at 186.9 seems to me to be parenthetical.

figure differ from the two syllogisms in the second figure if their conclusion is the same? (185.38–40, 186.3–5)

Maximus held that Celarent and Cesare are two distinct moods even, though that "AeB" expresses the same proposition as "BeA." Themistius thinks that that is incoherent: if you accept the synonymy thesis, then you should say that there are not fourteen canonical moods but eight, and that four of the eight are finished. After all,

> if the proposition is the same even when the terms are interchanged, then the conjugation is the same and it will be said to be in each of the two figures—or rather, the figure too will be the same. (185.40–43)

Is Themistius right?

Maximus might have replied along the following lines. It is true that "AeB" and "BeA" have the same sense; and it follows that the conjugations {AeB, BaC} and {BeA, BaC} have the same sense. But it does not follow that they are one and the same conjugation, so that Celarent and Cesare are one and the same mood. For although {AeB, BaC} and {BeA, BaC} agree in sense, they differ in structure: the former is, and the latter is not, a special case of the structure {AxB, ByC}—and that is the structure which defines the first figure and distinguishes it from the other two.

Suppose, for the sake of argument, that that is a coherent position: how does it help Maximus? Well, he must urge that if two syllogisms have the same sense, then—whether or not they have different structures—either both are finished or both are unfinished. And since it is agreed that Celarent is finished, it follows that Cesare is finished. Then Maximus will need to explain how and why it is sense which determines finish; and that is a subject on which both he and Boethus before him had something to say.

8. THE *DICTUM DE OMNI ET NULLO*

According to Aristotle,

> it is plain that all the syllogisms in this figure [i.e. in the first figure] are finished; for they are finished by way of what we assumed at the start. (*APr* A 26b28–30)

That sentence puts together what Aristotle had said of the individual first figure moods at 25b39–40, at 26a24 and at 26a27–28. By "what we assumed at the start" he means what came to be known as the *dictum de omni et nullo*:

> We say that something is predicated of every so-and-so when none of it can be taken of which the other is not said. Similarly for of none. (24b28–30)

The interpretation of the *dictum* and the link between it and finish are disputed matters;[27] but it is plain that the *dictum* is supposed to answer the questions "What is it for something to hold of each of the so-and-sos?" and "What is it for something to hold of none of the so-and-sos?"; and it is plain that those answers are supposed to underwrite or to explain our grasp of the validity of finished syllogisms.

Boethus and Maximus must surely have had a view about the Aristotelian *dictum*. In principle, they might have held that it underwrote all the moods, not just those of the first figure; or that it was entirely worthless, to be replaced by something completely different. Or they might have taken an intermediate position, thinking that what was needed was something similar to but more puissant than Aristotle's *dictum*.

They did not take the first line. For Themistius says that

> one should not try to prove the first figure by their method: rather, we see that the thing is self-evident by way of the methods used by the old thinkers. (186.18–20)

The methods used by the old thinkers are, or at least include, an appeal to the Aristotelian *dictum*: Maximus and Boethus proposed a different method. And their method somehow turned about the notion of parts; for Themistius has just said that

> the eristics fall upon us once they see that one thing may hold of another without the other being a part of it—as colour holds of man but man is not a part of colour. (186.14–18)[28]

The fact that "one thing may hold of another without the other being a part of it" establishes that the method of the eristical Boethus and Maximus is unworkable—so the method must have invoked parts.

How did it do so? and did it do so in the form of a new *dictum*? The evidence is thin; but it suggests that Boethus had elaborated a *dictum*. Themistius remarks that

> since Boethus now turns to the third figure, let us see how he falls into error over the number of the syllogisms inasmuch as he understands the expression "in every" differently from the way in which Aristotle does in the *Analytics*. (192.9–12)

---

[27] See Barnes, *Truth, etc.*, pp.386–419.
[28] The Arabic has: "one thing may be part of another without holding of it"; but the illustrative example shows what Themistius actually said (or at least, what he meant to say).

Boethus understood universal affirmatives in an un-Aristotelian way—that is to say, he did not construe them according to Aristotle's *dictum de omni*. His alternative way of understanding them was, implicitly if not explicitly, a rival *dictum*. And the rival *dictum* explains why Boethus got the number of syllogisms wrong: it yielded, or seemed to Boethus to yield, more than four finished syllogisms.[29]

Themistius then explains how Boethus dealt with Darapti, which is

AaB, CaB :: AiC.

He said[30] that we show that the third figure is demonstrative by reference to Boethus' account of the first conjugation in this figure, in which each of the two extremes is predicated of all the middle term: according to him, when two things hold of something it is perfectly plain that each of them is in the other as in a part. But we need to show how he uses "in every." If I use it simply in the sense of "of every," then even if we grant the claim, it is neither perfectly plain nor immediately evident (192.15–22).

According to Themistius, Aristotle's *dictum* does not show Darapti to be finished (that is what he means when he says "if I use it simply..."), and in fact Aristotle offers a proof, by accidental conversion (and indicates that a *reductio ad impossibile* and an ecthetic argument will also serve). What is Boethus' *dictum*? and how was it supposed to work? Themistius does not say, and we must guess. The *dictum*, I think, must have been something like this:

X holds of every Y if and only if Y is a part of X.

X holds of no Y if and only if X and Y are wholly separated one from the other.

According to the *de omni* part of that, the premisses of Darapti state that B is a part both of A and of C. It follows that A and C have a part in common, or overlap. And in that case at least one item is both A and C—or AiC. (It is tempting to add a clause *de aliquo* to the *dictum*:

X holds of some Y if and only if there is an overlap between X and Y.

---

[29] The phrase "the number of syllogisms," which the Arabic transmits, is either a mistake for, or must be understood as, "the number of finished syllogisms."
[30] "He said": surely not Boethus, who is named in the next clause—so Maximus? And yet, given the larger context, "he" can only refer to Boethus.

But there is no trace in the ancient texts of anything like that.)

What about, say, Celarent, or

AeB, BaC :: AeC?

By the first premiss, A and B are wholly separated. By the second premiss C is a part of B. So A must be wholly separated from C—or AeC. And so on.

But are there not decisive objections to the business? First, the purpose of a *dictum* is to show how certain moods are finished. Yet haven't I just used the *dictum* to prove the validity of Darapti and of Celarent? And how can you show that a mood doesn't need proof by producing a proof of it? Secondly, isn't the Boethan *dictum* false? Themistius thinks so; and when he says that colour holds of man although man is not a part of colour, he seems to have a point.

Before saying something about those objections, I shall turn again to Maximus.

9. MEREOLOGY

Boethus' hypothetical *dictum* is mereological; and whether or not Maximus adopts it, his thesis certainly rested upon a mereological account of predicative propositions. There is nothing astonishing in that: Aristotle himself frequently hints at such a thing by use of the words "whole" and "part" in his characterisation of universal and particular propositions;[31] and the idea of mereological "separation" was exploited by Theophrastus and Eudemus in their non-Aristotelian proof of E-conversion.[32]

Having announced that the error of the eristics is based on a misprision about parts, Themistius goes through Maximus' treatment of the second and third figure moods. He begins like this:

> He says: "When the middle term holds of each of one of the two terms and of none of the other, then if one of the terms is wholly included in it and is wholly separated from the other, then it separates them wholly one from the other by reason of its position relative to each of the two (for something which separates wholly separates each of the parts)." (186.22–26)

---

[31] See Striker, "Perfection," pp.216–217; Mignucci, "Theory of Predication"; Barnes, *Porphyry*, pp.148–150.
[32] See e.g. Alexander, *in APr* 31.4–10: other references in Barnes *et al, Alexander*, p.86 n.13; commentary in Mignucci, "Theophrastus' Logic"; Huby, *Theophrastus: Logic*, pp.54–55.—Perhaps that is why Theophrastus got into Ammonius' story? (Above, n.7.)

That deals with Cesare and Camestres together. Maximus' treatment of Cesare is also set down in a scholium on the *Prior Analytics* (which derives, in one way or another, from Themistius):

> Maximus said that all the syllogisms are finished. For example, we say that B holds of none of the As and that B holds of every C; and it is concluded that A holds of none of the Cs. For since B holds of every C and of no A, A is separated from B. Therefore A will certainly be separated from C as well, and will hold of none of it. And we had no need of a reduction to the first figure. (schol in Arist, 157a13–18)[33]

Since BeA (which is one of the premisses of Cesare), A is wholly separated from B. Since BaC (the other premiss), C is a part of B. If A is separated from B, it is separated from every part of B. Since C is a part of B, A is separated from C—hence AeC (which is the conclusion of Cesare).

Maximus treated the other moods of the second and third figures in the same way: the conjugation is translated into mereological terms, a mereological conclusion is inferred—and translated back into "normal" predicative form. Themistius had more than one objection.

First, he claims that Maximus' procedure is not what it seems. Of its application to Cesare he says:

> That is a cheat: he thinks he has shown something, but if you reflect you will find that, even though he denies it, he is obliged to use conversion.... When he says that A is separated from B and from all its parts, that is no use at all unless he grants its conversion, namely that B in the same way is separated from A. (186.26–20, 35–37)

As the scholiast puts it,

> how can you say that if B holds of no A then A is separated from B unless you know that universal negative propositions convert from themselves? (157a18–21)[34]

---

[33] The scholiast writes "M, N, Ξ," which for the sake of homogeneity I have translated as "A, B, C."
[34] The scholiast goes on to say that "perhaps Maximus and Themistius can be brought into agreement: Maximus says that all syllogisms are finished because each has its necessity within it; Themistius considers the clarity or lack of clarity of the necessity and says that some are finished and others not" (157a24–28). That supposes that Maximus held not the thesis which Themistius ascribes to him but rather something like the Ammonian view.

The mereological translation of "BeA" is "B is separated from A." Maximus needs "A is separated from B"; so despite what he says, he cannot dispense with a conversion—in which case he reduces Cesare to Celarent.

But the mereological translation of "BeA" is, indifferently, either "B and A are wholly separated one from the other" or "A and B are wholly separated one from the other." The two translations have the same sense; and if you know that Mr. and Mrs. Wisty are separated, you don't need to call upon a logical conversion in order to learn that Mrs. and Mr. Wisty are separated—for that Mrs. and Mr. Wisty are separated is precisely what you already know.

Secondly, Themistius urges that the mereological translations are not, or not always, true; for "one thing may hold of another without the other being a part" (186.15). If X holds of Y, it does not follow that Y is a part of X. And Themistius seems also to believe that if Y is a part of X, it doesn't follow that X holds of Y. At least, that seems to be supposed by this passage:

If animal holds of no grammar and of every man, then grammar holds of no man. There he can say: since animal is separate from grammar, it is so in all its parts. But you can see that when you say that, you convince no one that grammar holds of no man. (187.1–3; cf. 192.33–40)

The text is obscure; but the point appears to be this. Maximus' translations require him to reason as follows: "Animal holds of no grammar; so grammar is separated from animal and from all its parts. But animal holds of every man, so that man is a part of animal. Hence grammar is separated from man, and grammar holds of no man—and so no man is grammatical." That is absurd. Hence the translations do not go through.

Themistius' argument is a sophism. It takes the premiss, "Animal holds of no grammar," to mean that no grammatical science is an animal (which is true); and it takes the conclusion, "Grammar holds of no man" to mean that no man is grammatical (which is false). Thus it construes the term "grammar" in two different ways and commits a fallacy of equivocation.

Nonetheless, isn't Themistius right about the relation between "X holds of Y" and "Y is a part of X"? Animal holds of man—but a man isn't a part of an animal. Arms are parts of human bodies—but human body does not hold of arm. True—but that is not how the mereological translations work. Every man is an animal: being an animal holds of every man; and, equivalently, the class of men is a part of the class of animals. X holds of every Y if and only if the class of Ys is a part of the class of Xs. To be sure, the equivalence holds only if "part" is taken to include "improper" parts. (Suppose not. If Y is a proper part of X, then X is not a proper part of Y. So if X holds of every Y if and only if Y is a proper part of X, then if X holds of every Y, Y does not hold of every X.)

Thirdly, Themistius urges that even if Maximus' procedure works for Camestres and for Baroco (187.30–32), it is inferior to Aristotle's procedures since it does not apply as widely as they do (187.35–38). That is doubly odd. First, if Themistius really means to allow that Maximus' method works for some second figure moods, then must he not allow that some second figure moods are finished? The text is not crystalline; but Themistius does appear to accept that Maximus succeeds with Camestres. Secondly, Themistius compares Maximus' method with the Aristotelian procedures of conversion and *reductio ad impossibile*. In so doing, he implicitly construes it as a method of proof, whereas in fact it is quite the opposite—a method which purports to show that proof is not needed.

Nevertheless, isn't Themistius' comparison fundamentally correct? Isn't Maximus' method in fact a method of proof? (And if it is, then Themistius may allow that it works for Camestres without conceding that Camestres is a finished syllogism.) Here is a formal version of Maximus' treatment of Cesare:

1	(1) BeA	premiss
2	(2) BaC	premiss
1	(3) A and B are wholly separate	1, transl
1	(4) A is separate from every part of B	3
2	(5) C is a part of B	2, transl
1,2	(6) A is separate from C	4,5
1,2	(7) AeC	6, transl

Isn't that an argument which establishes the validity of Cesare, comparable to the argument which Aristotle uses to the same end? Isn't the difference between Aristotle and Maximus not that Aristotle offers a proof and Maximus does not, but that Aristotle's proof invokes the first figure whereas Maximus' proof does not? And doesn't the same go for Boethus' treatment of Darapti?

There is a *tu quoque* answer to those questions. If you wonder how Aristotle's *dictum* is supposed to underwrite, say, Celarent, you are likely to come up with an argument—and an argument which looks for all the world like a formal proof. Maximus and Boethus may be in a leaky boat, but they have Aristotle as a fellow-sailor: their treatment of Cesare is, in that respect, indistinguishable from Aristotle's treatment of Celarent.

A second answer is suggested (unintentionally) by Themistius. Maximus does indeed offer an argument for the validity of Cesare. But the argument, though effective, is not demonstrative—it is not a proof. It is not a proof because it does not satisfy the Aristotelian conditions on proof. It does not appeal to items which are prior to and explanatory of its *probandum*: perhaps it establishes that Cesare is valid—it does not prove that Cesare is valid. What is more, it enables you to grasp the validity of Cesare without having a proof of it—and hence it serves to show that Cesare is finished.

A third answer calls upon the syllogistic diagrams devised by Euler and Venn and Lewis Carroll and the rest. Such diagrams might represent a particular affirmative proposition, "AiB," by two overlapping circles, one of them enfolding the As and the other the Bs: the two circles have a part in common. Similarly, "AeB" might be pictured by two non-overlapping circles: the As and the Bs are wholly separated. The diagrams are naturally described in mereological terms; and it has more than once been remarked that the mereological formulations used by Boethus and Maximus could be read as descriptions of such syllogistic diagrams.[35] A diagram can scarcely count as a proof of the validity of a syllogism; but it can serve to make its validity evident: if you scrutinize the diagram you can see that the syllogism which it represents is valid. Neither Boethus nor Maximus is reported to have drawn diagrams; but perhaps their mereological translations enable you to see the validity the syllogisms which they describe in much the same way as the diagrams do?

10. CONCLUSION

Julian voted for Maximus—and by implication for Boethus. Was he right?[36]

Themistius asserts and Boethus denies that there are primary or unprovable predicative syllogisms. If you insist upon a strictly Aristotelian notion of proof, which requires that the premisses explain the conclusion, then perhaps you will side with Themistius—though it is not very clear (to me at least) what would count as an explanation of the validity of a syllogism. If you are content with a more relaxed notion of proof—I mean, with the common or garden notion—then Boethus is right.

Themistius asserts that four syllogisms are finished, Boethus holds that twelve are, Maximus contends that all fourteen are. Themistius' case rests, implicitly, on the Aristotelian doctrine that if something can be proved, then you know it only if you have a proof of it. The doctrine is false. But it does not follow that the assertion which Themistius founds upon it is false. The difficulty, I think, is not one of deciding among the three litigants: it lies in the nature of the case. Is this or that syllogism finished? Can

---

[35] See e.g. Lee, *Syllogistik in der Spätantike*, p.129 n.20; Striker, "Perfection," p.217.
[36] According to Patzig, *Aristotle's Theory*, p.70, Julian took the part of Maximus because Maximus was one of his lieutenants and he himself was ignorant of logic. According to Striker, "Perfection," p.218, "it seems obvious that the Emperor Julian was right to decide... in favor of Maximus."

you apprehend its validity without having a proof of it? Why ever think that there is any general answer to such a question?

Bibliography

Badawi, A. *Aristote chez les Arabes* (Cairo, 1947)
——. *La transmission de la philosophie grecque au monde arabe*, Études de philosophie médiévale 56 (Paris, 1987²)
Barnes, J. *Porphyry: Introduction* (Oxford, 2003)
——. *Truth, etc.* (Oxford, 2007)
——. "Peripatetic Logic: 100BC-200AD," in R.W. Sharples and R. Sorabji (edd), *Ancient Philosophy 100BC-200AD* (Oxford, 2008)
Barnes, J., S. Bobzien, K. Flannery, and K. Ierodiakonou (eds.), *Alexander of Aphrodisias: On Aristotle*, Prior Analytics *1.1-7* (London, 1991)
Bocheński, I. *La logique de Théophraste*, Collectanea Friburgensia 32 (Fribourg en Suisse, 1947)
Frede, M. "Stoic vs Aristotelian Syllogistic," *Archiv für Geschichte der Philosophie* **56**, 1974, 1-32 [= Frede, *Essays in Ancient Philosophy* (Oxford, 1987), pp.99-124]
Huby, P.M. *Theophrastus of Eresus: Sources for his Life, Writings, Thought and Influence— Commentary volume 2: Logic*, Philosophia Antiqua 103 (Leiden, 2007)
Lee, T.-S. *Die griechische Tradition der aristotelischen Syllogistik in der Spätantike*, Hypomnemata 79 (Göttingen, 1984)
Mignucci, M. "Aristotle's theory of predication," in I. Angelelli and M. Cerezo (edd), *Studies on the History of Logic* (Berlin, 1996), pp.1-20
—— "Theophrastus' logic," in J. van Ophuijsen and M. Raalte (edd), *Theophrastus: Reappraising the Sources* (Leiden, 1998), pp.39-65
Moraux, P. *L'aristotelismo presso i Greci* I (Milan, 2000)
Patzig, G. *Aristotle's Theory of the Syllogism* (Dordrecht, 1968)
Santos, F.D. "Maxime d'Éphèse," in R. Goulet (ed), *Dictionnaire des philosophes antiques* IV (Paris, 2005), pp.313-22.
Schneider, J.-P. "Boéthos de Sidon," in R. Goulet (ed), *Dictionnaire des philosophes antiques* II (Paris, 1994), pp.126-30
Striker, G. "Perfection and reduction in Aristotle's *Prior Analytics*," in M. Frede and G. Striker (edd), *Rationality in Greek Thought* (Oxford, 1996), pp.203-19

9

ALEXANDER OF APHRODISIAS ON ARISTOTLE'S THEORY OF THE STOIC INDEMONSTRABLES

Susanne Bobzien

In her important 1979 paper "Aristoteles über Syllogismen 'aufgrund einer Hypothese,'"[1] Gisela Striker provided an in-depth analysis of these vexing and perplexing Aristotelian arguments. She showed that they were Aristotle's way of providing a logical vehicle for inferences based on other than term-logical relations; that the "hypothesis" that gives them their name is best understood as a rule that is not based on a relation of terms,[2] rather than as a premise; and that in those arguments "the thing taken instead" (τὸ μεταλαμβανόμενον) is an assertion that is used instead of the *demonstrandum*.[3] It was upon reading this paper that I realized that the (then) prevalent interpretation of later ancient texts on hypothetical syllogisms as presenting the Stoic theory of indemonstrables needed a thorough revision. For it is possible to show that, starting from Aristotle's "syllogisms based on a hypothesis," a specifically Peripatetic (and from the third century CE also partly Platonist) development can be traced through the centuries up to the late ancient passages on hypothetical syllogistic in Philoponus and Boethius. Although the Stoic indemonstrables undoubtedly played a role in this development, the various theories of hypothetical syllogisms over the centuries are all Peripatetic (and sometimes a little Platonist) in form, function, and terminology.[4] The present paper looks at Alexander of Aphrodisias' role in this development.

Alexander's commentaries on Aristotle's *Organon* are valuable sources for both Stoic and early Peripatetic logic, and have often been used as such—in particular for early Peripatetic hypothetical syllogistic and Stoic propositional logic.[5] By contrast,

---

[1] Striker [1979]. See now also Striker [2009], 174–8, 201, 237–238.
[2] Striker [1979], 46.
[3] Ibid., 43.
[4] Here I am in agreement with Maroth [1989]. The arguments the Stoics called hypothetical syllogisms were completely different from those the Peripatetics called hypothetical syllogisms: see my [1997].
[5] E.g. Mueller [1969], Frede [1975], Goulet [1978], Barnes [1984], [1985], Mignucci [1993], Ierodiakonou, [1990], Bobzien [1996], Speca [2001].

this paper explores the role Alexander himself played in the development and transmission of those theories. There are three areas in particular where he seems to have made a difference: (1) First, he drew a connection between certain passages from Aristotle's *Topics* and *Prior Analytics* and the Stoic indemonstrable arguments, and, based on this connection, appropriated the Stoic indemonstrables as Aristotelian. (2) Second, he developed and made use of a specifically Peripatetic terminology in which to describe and discuss those arguments—which facilitated the integration of the indemonstrables into Peripatetic logic. (3) Third, he made some progress towards a solution to the problem of what place and interpretation the Stoic third indemonstrables should be given in a Peripatetic (and Platonist) setting.[6] Before I discuss these points in detail, here are some general remarks about Alexander and the context in which his contribution to the development of a Peripatetic theory of hypothetical syllogistic should be seen.

Alexander, like his older contemporary Galen and the Middle Platonists, was faced with the Stoic five kinds of indemonstrables and with a rudimentary early Peripatetic theory of four types of hypothetical syllogisms, both seemingly covering the same logical ground.[7] The Stoic theory and the terminology that came with it was generally known and taught, and parts of it at least had become standard logic and standard terminology, learned, used, and/or referred to by members of all philosophical schools in the first and second century CE.[8] The early Peripatetic "theory" was known to Galen, and the fact that some fragments of it are also preserved in Alexander, and in some later texts, suggests that later Peripatetics were familiar with it. Galen, despite displaying a preference for the Peripatetic-Platonist approach to logic, remains eclectic in his *Institutio Logica* and does not officially side with any school.[9] By contrast, and not surprisingly, Alexander always defends the Aristotelian or Peripatetic line and habitually attacks the Stoics. Yet this had not been the manner of all Peripatetics: in the first century BC, Boethus appears to have adopted the Stoic indemonstrables wholesale, terminology and all (Galen, *Inst.Log*.7.2, see below, Section 2.2). Propriety in matters of logic—as in other areas of philosophy—seems

---

[6] For Alexander's view on the so-called "wholly hypothetical syllogisms" see Bobzien [2000].
[7] For the Stoic indemonstrables, see e.g. Frede [1974], Bobzien [1996]. For the early Peripatetic theory, see Barnes [1985], Bobzien [2002a], [2002b].
[8] Cf. e.g. S.E.*P.H*.II.157–59; Gal.*Inst.Log*.6.6; Cic.*Top*.12.53–14.57, *Fin*.IV.19.54–5; Plutarch, *De E apud Delphos* 386E–387C; Philo *De Plantatione* 115; Alcinous, *Didasc*.ch.6; Apul.*Int*.191.6–11, 201.4–11, 209.9–14, 212.10–12; Aulus Gellius, *N.A*.XVI.8.1–8; Boethus Perip. acc. to Gal.*Inst.Log*.7.2; Lucian *Vitarum Auctio* 24; [Galen] *Hist.Phil*.15.
[9] Bobzien [2004].

to have developed, together with a more historico-philologically orientated study of the texts of Plato and Aristotle, only after the turn of the millennium. The competition between the philosophical schools (and various other factors, no doubt) led to the desideratum that each of the founding philosophers have a view or dogma (if not a theory) on every philosophical subject matter—including those which had seen the light of day only after their death. These include prominently fate, the criterion of truth, and propositional logic, all three standard philosophical topics in the second century CE, and all three introduced into philosophy only in Hellenistic times, and not originally part of Plato's or Aristotle's philosophy. Thus, Alexander, or some recent predecessors of his, patched together a "theory of fate" for Aristotle from several of Aristotle's writings, and in [Plutarch] *On Fate* we find a similar patchwork for Plato.[10] In Ptolemy, we find a Peripatetic "theory of the criterion,"[11] in Alcinous (*Didasc.* ch.4) a Platonist one, pieced together from excerpts from Plato's dialogues. Similarly, as this paper intends to show, Alexander, or some recent predecessors,[12] purposely credited Aristotle with a theory that corresponds to Stoic propositional logic (i.e. with a hypothetical syllogistic).

Unlike in the case of fate, we have no extant separate treatise by Alexander on hypothetical syllogistic.[13] We have to rely on some remarks and brief discussions in his commentaries on Aristotle's *Prior Analytics* and *Topics*. Alexander likely also considered some material relevant to hypothetical syllogistic in his lost commentaries on the *Categories* and *De Interpretatione*.[14] So there is no evidence that Alexander ever attributes a worked-out theory of hypothetical syllogisms to Aristotle. Rather, what is remarkable is that Alexander persistently (if not always consistently) interprets and presents passages from Aristotle's *Organon* in a light that makes it appear as if Aristotle was in the possession of a Peripatetic correlate to the Stoic theory of indemonstrables.

---

[10] Cf. Alexander *On Fate* 165.14–171.17; [Plutarch] *On Fate* 568b–574e.
[11] See Mark Schiefsky, this volume.
[12] In what follows, I suppress the adjunct "or some recent predecessors"; but readers should keep in mind that it is virtually impossible to decide whether a certain innovation is Alexander's or whether he adopted it from lost Peripatetic commentators of the previous generation.
[13] The view until recently held by the majority of scholars that Ibn Sina (Avicenna) provides evidence for the existence of a treatise by Alexander on hypothetical syllogisms has been laid to rest by Street [2001].
[14] Thus, in Ammonius' and Al-Farabi's *De Interpretatione* commentaries we find classifications of hypothetical propositions or premises, and Al-Farabi's short *Categories* commentary contains a classification of consequence (ἀκολουθία) and conflict (μάχη).

1. THE CONNECTION OF PASSAGES FROM ARISTOTLE'S *ORGANON* WITH THE STOIC THEORY OF INDEMONSTRABLES AND THE APPROPRIATION OF THE LATTER AS ARISTOTELIAN

Alexander draws two connections between Aristotle's logic and the Stoic indemonstrables: first, a connection with Aristotle's "syllogisms from a hypothesis," and second, a connection with two of Aristotle's *topoi*.

1.1 Aristotle's Syllogisms from a Hypothesis and the Stoic Indemonstrables

There are four passages germane to the first connection, all in Alexander's *Analytics* commentary.[15] In each of the four passages, Alexander either states or implies that the indemonstrables are a subclass of Aristotle's "syllogisms from a hypothesis." In one, in addition, he actually undertakes to show this. First, his mere claims and suggestions that there is a connection (italics mine):

(1) To those "by means of another hypothesis," as he (i.e. Aristotle, *An.Pr.*41a40f)[16] said, presumably also belong the arguments which are the only ones that the more recent <philosophers> want to call syllogisms. These are *the arguments that come to be by means of the mode-forming <premise>, as they say, and the co-assumption, the mode-forming premise being either a conditional or a disjunction or a conjunction.* (Alex.*An.Pr.*262.28–31)[17]

(2) ...or, after he (i.e. Aristotle) has said which of the hypotheticals clearly fall under the presented method (these are both the <arguments> through the impossible, and the <arguments> in accordance with that-which-is-taken-instead (μετάληψις)—which include *all of the so-called indemonstrables*—and the arguments in accordance with a quality)...(Alex.*An.Pr.*326.3–5)

(3) (i) Having talked about the <arguments> from agreement and the ones that lead to the impossible, Aristotle says that there are many other arguments that also conclude from a hypothesis; he defers speaking about these with

---

[15] Alex.*An.Pr.*262.28–265.5, 326.4–5, 386.27–30, 389.31–390.1, 3–6. Potentially relevant: *An. Pr.*325.37–326.1 and 386.22–3.
[16] Mueller [2006] 136 n.33 reads εἶπον instead of Wallies' εἶπεν, at 262.28 and takes Alexander to refer to the earlier passages Alex.*An.Pr.*262.9 and 262.28–264.31.
[17] For reasons of word limit, and with some regret, I refer the reader to the *TLG* (*Thesaurus Linguae Graecae*) for the Greek text from Alexander.

more care.... (ii) He would mean *the hypothetical <arguments> by means of that-which-connects, which is also called a conditional, and the co-assumption, and the ones by means of that-which-divides, i.e. disjunction, and perhaps the ones by means of the negation of a conjunction.* (Alex.*An.Pr.*389.31–390.1, 390.3–6)

(4) The <arguments> which prove something by leading to the impossible, too, are "from a hypothesis".... <This is> so also in the case of *the hypothetical <arguments> by means of that-which-connects, and* similarly <in the case of *the hypothetical arguments> by means of that-which-divides.* That which has been posited is not accepted by means of syllogisms but because of the hypothesis; the syllogism is of something else.[18] (Alex.*An.Pr.*386.22–23, 27–30)

It appears that the clauses in italics were all used by Alexander to denote the same types of argument. He refers to them in different ways, but his glosses in passage (3) make it clear that he intends the same argument types each time. The Stoic terminology in (1), (2), and (3) ("mode-forming," "co-assumption," "conditional," "disjunction," "negation of a conjunction," "indemonstrable") and the reference to the more recent philosophers suggest that these are the arguments the Stoics call indemonstrables. (The terminology is discussed in detail in Section 2.) On this assumption that Alexander intends the same types of argument each time, taken together the passages suggest he envisages a classificatory scheme of Aristotle's syllogisms from a hypothesis as sketched in Figure 9.1.[19]

If Alexander did not envisage a scheme similar to this, he worked with several incompatible schemes. (Aristotle's text is far from clear on the logical relation between the different types of syllogisms he mentions.)

Taken literally, Alexander's classification of the Stoic indemonstrables seems clearly anachronistic. At the time the Stoics introduced them, Aristotle had been dead for some time. Should we say that in classifying the Stoic indemonstrables as Aristotelian, Alexander confuses Peripatetic hypothetical syllogisms with Stoic indemonstrables?[20] I believe this puts things the wrong way. Rather, Alexander assumed that humans generally make use of certain ways of arguing or patterns of inference

---

[18] For the details of these arguments, see Striker [1979].
[19] Types with correlates in Aristotle in bold. For syllogisms from a hypothesis, see Arist.*An. Pr.*A.23, A29, A44; "through the impossible": 41a22–37, 45a23–b15, 50a29–38; "from agreement: 50a16–28, 33–5; "with *metalêpsis*" and "with quality": 45b15–19; "others": 41a37–41, 45b15–16, 50a39–b2.
[20] As suggested by Speca [2001] 52–3, 56.

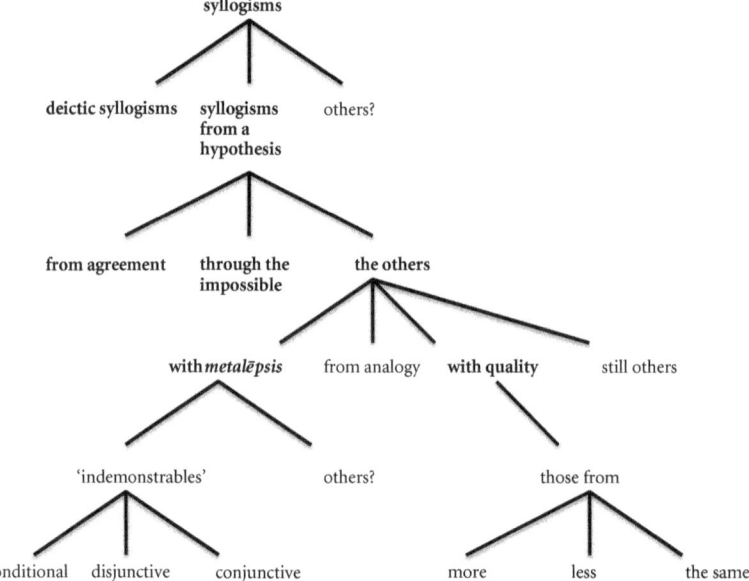

FIG 9.1 Alexander's classificatory scheme of Aristotle's syllogisms from a hypothesis.
Notes on Figure 9.1: Types with correlates in Aristotle are in bold. For syllogisms from a hypothesis see Arist.*An. Pr*.A.23, A29, A44; "through the impossible": 41a22–37, 45a23–b15, 50a29–38; "from agreement: 50a16–28, 33–5; "with *metalêpsis*" and "with quality": 45b15–19; "others": 41a37–41, 45b15–16, 50a39–b2. With respect to "still others," Alexander says: "Those with some other kinds of hypothetical premises which have been discussed elsewhere"; we don't know where Alexander discussed these. With respect to "others" under those with *metalêpsis*: From passage (2) it's unclear whether Alexander thought the so-called indemonstrables exhausted the syllogisms with *metalêpsis*.

(e.g. we argue from "if Diotima is breathing, then Diotima is alive" and "Now Diotima is breathing" to "Diotima is alive"), and they are justified in doing so, since the resulting arguments are valid; and that both Aristotle and the Stoics theorized about such arguments: the Stoics in a way that is at least partially wrong, and Aristotle in the right way—just that, unfortunately, Aristotle did not leave in writing a full theory of such arguments. And, as elsewhere, where Aristotle has not left a worked-out theory or terminology, Alexander supplies one in—what he takes to be—the Aristotelian spirit. Several factors suggest that this was Alexander's approach. Like Galen, he polemicized against what he regarded as Stoic "formalism," that is, their way of determining what kind of argument or proposition something is by its linguistic form, rather than by its meaning;[21] in his view, the Stoics

---

[21] E.g. Alex.*An.Pr*.373.18–20, 28–35.

systematized the inference patterns at issue in the wrong way and, in the wake of this, allowed useless arguments to count as syllogisms. However, Alexander never doubts that *there are* underlying syllogisms which the Stoics get wrong, and which Aristotle and the Peripatetics get right. Similarly, he thinks the Stoics thought—wrongly—that the "indemonstrables" were indemonstrable, whereas Aristotle did not make this mistake. Again, Alexander believes that the Stoics—wrongly—thought that the indemonstrables were syllogisms because they are evidently valid basic (non-demonstrable) arguments, whereas he (in agreement with Aristotle, or so he assumes) holds that they are syllogisms because they demonstrate that something does or does not hold (of something). That is why he usually calls them "so-called indemonstrables" (cf. e.g. passages (2), (6), (7), (10)).

Thus we are made to believe that the arguments the Stoics call "indemonstrables" belong to a class of syllogisms which Aristotle was aware of, but did not himself fully develop. Alexander fits them into an Aristotelian classification of syllogisms. As part of this classification, they then automatically sport a number of properties, that is, all those which the more generic types of syllogisms of the classificatory scheme share: being Aristotelian syllogisms, they demonstrate that something holds or does not hold (of something);[22] they have more than one premise and no redundant premises. (Stretching his master's stance to the limit, Alexander also assumes that the so-called indemonstrables come about through the three figures of the categorical syllogisms and are brought to completion through the first figure (cf.Arist.*An.Pr.*A23.)) As the syllogisms are hypothetical syllogisms, the search concerns that-which-is-taken-instead (τὸ μεταλαμβανόμενον cf.Arist.*An.Pr.*A29 and below, Section 2.2), and "they cannot be led back from the things hypothesized" (cf.Arist.*An.Pr.*A44).

By integrating the "indemonstrables" into a presumed Aristotelian taxonomy and describing them in Peripatetic terms,[23] Alexander makes it look plausible that they are of Aristotelian origin and thus appropriates them.

In the long passage *An.Pr.*262–5, Alexander goes beyond merely *stating* that the arguments the Stoics call "indemonstrables" are Aristotelian syllogisms from a hypothesis; he also undertakes to *show* they are. He proceeds as follows: he provides examples of several indemonstrables, and, by describing them in the way Aristotle describes *his* example of a syllogism from a hypothesis demonstrates that they fit Aristotle's description of the "other" syllogisms from a hypothesis (Arist.*An.Pr.*A44). In particular, he

---

[22] It is unclear whether they are meant to fit Aristotle's *definition* of the syllogism.
[23] For Alexander's use of terminology, see also Section 2.

focuses on the following points: (i) that the second premise must be proved[24] by a categorical syllogism; (ii) that the conclusion (the thing-to-be-proved) is established by means of (διά) the hypothesis, that is, the first premises; (iii) that this hypothesis in turn needs no proof, and in fact cannot be proved.[25]

Alexander's argument is unimpressive. First, he presupposes that the second premise of the indemonstrables is a "categorical statement," with distinct subject and predicate terms. Thus he excludes existential statements such as "providence exists." Aristotle's syllogisms from a hypothesis may have excluded such cases,[26] but the Stoic indemonstrables certainly did not. Second, Alexander presupposes that the mode-forming (τροπικά) premises (which he reinterprets as hypotheses) are posited as "well-known" (γνώριμα). Again, most Stoics would not have agreed, though Aristotle would.[27] So we have the choice of either charging Alexander with a *petitio principii*, or saying that at most he has shown that the indemonstrables, *if* understood in a Peripatetic way, tally with Aristotle's theory of syllogisms from a hypothesis. Either way, the Stoics would have no reason to think that *their* indemonstrables have anything to do with Aristotle's logic. Presumably this does not matter for Alexander. He gives the Peripatetics some reasons for believing that the (inference patterns that lie behind the) Stoic indemonstrables are the sort of thing Aristotle had in mind as some of the "other syllogisms from a hypothesis." From a Peripatetic perspective, they do fit, give or take, the general conception of the "other syllogisms from a hypothesis" that can be extracted from the Aristotelian passages.

1.2 Aristotle's *Topics* and the Stoic Indemonstrables

Alexander draws a second connection between Aristotle's logic and the Stoic indemonstrables on pages 165–6 and 174–5 of his *Topics* commentary. Here he connects the Stoic indemonstrables with some *topoi* from Aristotle's *Topics*. The first passage on which Alexander comments is from *Topics* II.4:

(5) One must examine, regarding the point at issue, [i] what is such that if it is, the point at issue is, or [ii] what is by necessity, if the point at issue is: [i] if one wants to establish something, one must examine what there is such that if *it* is, the point at issue will be (for when the former has been proved to hold, the point at issue will also have been proved to hold); [ii] if, on the other hand, one wants to refute

---

[24] "To prove" is here used not as strictly as in Arist.*An.Post.*
[25] Cf. Alex.*An.Pr.*264.32–265.13. Still, if it *had* to be proved, this, too, would have to happen by means of a categorical syllogism (Alex.*An.Pr.*263.22–5).
[26] See my [2002a].
[27] The—probably—Stoic accounts of "argument" in S.E.*PH.*2.136 and *M.*7.301–2 suggest that *some* Stoics thought the premises in an argument must be agreed upon by the discussants.

something, one must examine what it is that is if the point at issue is (for when we prove that what follows from the point at issue is not, we will have destroyed the point at issue.) (Arist.*Top*.111b17–23)

Alexander describes this *topos* as "twofold, since it can both establish and refute from a consequence."[28] He considers each subtype of the *topos* separately, starting with a paraphrase of point [i] from Aristotle's text. Then he continues:

(6) for if the antecedent, then also the consequent, in accordance with the first so-called indemonstrable, which establishes from a consequence… (Alex.*Top*.165.12–13)

and adds an example. Moving to the second subtype, he again starts with a paraphrase of point [ii] from Aristotle's text. Then he continues

(7) for if the consequence <does> not <hold>, nor <does> the antecedent, in accordance with the second so-called indemonstrable, which refutes from a consequence… (Alex.*Top*.166.11–13)

Again he adds an example. It is unclear, how exactly Alexander envisages the relation between the "twofold" Aristotelian *topos* and the first two indemonstrables. He certainly believed that the two so-called indemonstrables are somehow related to the two ways of the *topos*: The *topos* is said to be "establishing and removing from consequence," and the first so-called indemonstrable is said to be "establishing from consequence"; the second to be "removing from consequence." Moreover, he seems to think that the so-called indemonstrables *explain* the corresponding sub-*topos* ("for if…"). However, the exact purpose of the explanation is hard to gauge. Alexander talks about *the* so-called[29] first and second indemonstrables. He seems to regard the so-called indemonstrables as patterns of inference or argument forms or schemata. His formulations ("for if…, then also…"; "for if…, neither…") suggest that these patterns can be used as justifications of the two sub-*topoi*. Thus Alexander considers these patterns called "so-called indemonstrables" as logically prior to the *topos*. This, again, suggests that Alexander thinks of certain inference-patterns similar to *modus ponens* and *tollens* as existing valid patterns; patterns Aristotle was aware of and which

---

[28] Ὁ μὲν τόπος ἐστὶν ἐξ ἀκολουθίας. διπλοῦς δ'ἐστί· καὶ γὰρ κατασκευαστικός ἐστι καὶ ἀνασκευαστικός. Alex.*Top*.165.6–7.
[29] The Stoics called indemonstrables the individual actual arguments that satisfied the descriptions of first, second, etc. indemonstrable. See my [1996] Section 1.

the Stoics wrongly thought of as being indemonstrable. This is confirmed by another passage from Alexander's *Prior Analytics* commentary (Alex.*An.Pr.*336.13–20), in which Alexander couches two arguments in a Peripateticized version of the Stoic mode-arguments,[30] and then adds:

(8) The establishing is in accordance with the second indemonstrable and the refuting is in accordance with the first.[31]

Here again the Aristotelian methods of establishing and refuting are said to be "in accordance with" (κατά) the indemonstrables. The latter are hence considered as logically prior.

The second passage on which Alexander comments is from Aristotle's *Topics* II.6:

(9) In the case of things of which hold one and only one of two <predicates>, as for instance of a human being holds either illness or health, if we are well-equipped to argue about the one, that it holds or does not hold, we will also be well-equipped with regard to the remaining one; this converts with regard to both; for [iii] when we have proved that the one <predicate> holds, we will also have proved that the other does not hold; and [iv] when we prove that the one does not hold, we will have proved that the remaining one holds. (Arist.*Top.*112a24–31)

In this case, the connection Alexander draws between the Aristotle passage and the indemonstrables is more complex. He starts with describing the *topos* as "establishing or refuting from a conflict" (τόπον ἐκ μάχης κατασκευαστικόν τε καὶ ἀνασκευαστικόν, Alex.*Top.*174.7). The parallel to his treatment of the previous *topos* is obvious. Taking his comments on the two passages (Alex.*AnPr.*165–6 and 174–5) together, we can see what Alexander did: He combined the Stoic pair of logical expressions "consequence" and "conflict" with the Peripatetic pair of "establishing" and "refuting." It seems that this combination of the pairs of terms is not known before Alexander. We find it in some later texts, with slight variations that reflect further developments.[32] So here Alexander may have been innovative. At any rate, in this passage we have evidence of one important step towards the incorporation of Stoic logic into Peripatetic and Platonist syllogistic.

---

[30] λογότροποι, see DL.7.77.
[31] διὸ ἡ μὲν ἀνασκευὴ κατὰ τὸν δεύτερον ἀναπόδεικτον ἔσται, ἡ δὲ κατασκευὴ κατὰ τὸν πρῶτον (Alex.*An. Pr.*336.18–20).
[32] Galen used this pair of terms for a Peripatetic logical distinction; but he didn't make the connection with the *Topics*; or if he did, (in his lost commentaries?) this didn't survive.

After this description of the *topos* Alexander interprets Aristotle's passage in the light of an Aristotelian logical distinction that originates with the *Categories*. The distinction is that of contraries without intermediates, contraries with intermediates, and contradictory opposites (which are not contraries and have no intermediates). In *Categories* 10, Aristotle classifies these as three different kinds of opposites (ἀντικείμενα), and explains each one.[33] Here Alexander draws another important connection: the Aristotelian kinds of *opposites* are understood as three different types of *conflict*. Thus a Peripatetic logical distinction and a Stoic logical term are linked.[34]

Alexander suggests that in the cases of contraries without intermediates and of contradictories, the *topos* under discussion can be used both for establishing and for refuting. The connection between Aristotle's *topos* and the contraries without intermediates is obvious, and Alexander appears merely to spell out what Aristotle would have taken for granted. (Like Aristotle, Alexander only talks about contraries without combination, i.e. contrary pairs of *terms*, not contraries with combination, i.e. contrary pairs of *sentences*.)

The case of contradictories is also—if somewhat forced—dealt with within term logic: it holds of *everything*, if you have proved that something is affirmed of it, then you have refuted that that thing is negated of it, and vice versa. The *topos* under discussion can thus be used both for establishing and for refuting in the case of contradictories, too (Alex.*Top*.175.2-10). I am unsure whether this interpretation of the *topos* would have found Aristotle's approval.

Alexander's introduction of the opposites with intermediates into the *topos* would most probably not have found Aristotle's approval. Aristotle starts from a certain *relation of terms* (contraries without intermediates) and explains what inferential moves of establishing and refuting one can make *given this relation*. Alexander, by contrast, seems to have focused on two general *inference patterns* that involve conflict. The text suggests that these two patterns are along the lines of "If A and B conflict, then if we have A, we have refuted B" and "If A and B conflict, then if we don't have A, we have established B." Starting from these patterns, Alexander investigates the

---

[33] Arist. *Cat*.11b17-23, 11b38-12.a25, 13a37-b35 (cf. Amm.*Cat*.95.8ff). Aristotle talks of contradictory opposites as "things opposed as affirmation and negation"; Alexander uses the expression from the *De Interpretatione*, ἀντίφασις. Aristotle describes the contraries (ἐναντία) without middle as τούτων οὐδέν ἐστιν ἀνὰ μέσον, those with middle as τούτων ἔστιν τι ἀνὰ μέσον. Alexander and later commentators tend to use the terms ἔμμεσα and ἄμεσα. Aristotle does not say that contradictory opposites have no middle, but such a description is in keeping with *Cat*.13a37-b35.
[34] He illustrates the cases of contraries with examples from Arist.*Cat*.10 and adds further examples from other Aristotelian works.

above-mentioned three Aristotelian types of opposites, as to whether they "fit" *them*. He concludes that contradictories and contraries without intermediates fit both patterns, but contraries with intermediates fit only the pattern for refuting. Once more, Alexander appears to regard the patterns of inference as independent of and prior to the specific *topos* under discussion, and as having wider application than the *topos*. The passage in Aristotle's *Topics* betrays no such assumption of underlying independent inference patterns. Again, Alexander's specific interpretation of an Aristotelian passage facilitates his drawing a connection with the Stoic indemonstrables: the fourth and fifth indemonstrables show markedly clearer similarities to Alexander's two inference patterns than to Aristotle's *Topics* passage.

Alexander introduces the indemonstrables at the very end of his comments on the *Topics* passage:

(10) And the proof that is fitting for the <contraries> without intermediates is rather the one by means of the so-called fifth indemonstrable, which is the one that concludes from that-which-divides and the contradictory to one of the <components> in that-which-divides the remaining <component>. But for the contraries with intermediates the <proof> by means of the fourth <so-called indemonstrable is fitting>, which is the one that refutes from that-which-divides and one of the <components> in that-which-divides the other <component>. (Alex.*Top*.175.21–6)

In this passage, Alexander does not mention the Aristotelian contradictories at all. His correlation of the two types of contraries with the fourth and fifth types of indemonstrables seems unique. We discuss his correlation of the fourth indemonstrables with the contraries with intermediates in Section 3.2. Here we note that what he says about contraries *without* intermediates is unexpected, given his earlier remarks on the contraries. We would have expected him to say that both the fourth and the fifth indemonstrable fit the case of contraries *without* intermediates. Yet he correlates only the fifth with these.[35]

We disregard this problem and focus on Alexander's positive input. He reports the Stoic description of the fifth indemonstrables almost correctly, with the exception of some terminological modification (for which see below and Section 2.2).

---

[35] We note that to his credit, Alexander makes his statement sound tentative, using the expression "rather" (μᾶλλον). Of course, the idea that both patterns fit, but one may fit somewhat better than the other is also not terribly attractive.

But the use he makes of this description is distinctly un-Stoic. The *Stoic* theory of indemonstrables is a theory of basic formally valid arguments to which all more complex formally valid arguments can be reduced, but which themselves need no proof.[36] The Stoics would simply say that everything with the form described is a fifth indemonstrable. This includes arguments from false premises and arguments that in the disjunction have the same component assertible twice. Alexander despises this focus on the mere validity of arguments, since it produces useless argument forms.[37]

What interests *Alexander* is how one can produce proofs by using valid inference patterns. Proofs need to have true premises. Alexander (in line with Aristotle's *Topics*) considers first what *types* of complex premises are such that their instances are always true. In the case at issue, the relevant types must all fit the general pattern of dividing premises/propositions. They turn out to be those types of dividing hypothetical premises in which the two components express opposites: the dividing premises/propositions are always true if they express contraries with intermediates; or contraries without intermediates; or contradictories. Second Alexander considers by addition of what true categorical premises/propositions one can then establish or refute something.

The Stoic fourth and fifth indemonstrables are thus reinterpreted as general inference patterns and put to a distinctly Peripatetic use within Peripatetic logic: they provide the general pattern for proofs that refute or establish something from a conflict (μάχη) of things. Three of Aristotle's types of opposites are interpreted as three different types of conflict; each can be used for producing proofs. Thus, again, the indemonstrables are treated as logically prior to the *topos* at issue.

The details of this use of the Stoic indemonstrables are messy. Alexander's commentary on the *topos* (Alex.*Top*.174–6) before the introduction of the indemonstrables is done in terms of term-logic. Where Alexander introduces the descriptions of the indemonstrables, he leaves out all nouns that would allow us to pin them down as Stoic or as Peripatetic:

… the so-called fifth indemonstrable, which is the one that concludes from that-which-divides and the contradictory to one of the <components> in that-which-divides the remaining one.

---

[36] Cf. my [1996] Section 1.
[37] Cf. e.g. Alex.*An.Pr*. 18.12–22.

The Stoic version would be:

> ... the fifth indemonstrable, which is the one that concludes from a *disjunctive assertible* and the contradictory to one of its *disjuncts* the remaining *disjunct*.[38]

The Stoic relation of the disjunctive assertible and the assertibles that are used as disjuncts is such that the truth-value of the disjunctive assertible depends on the truth-values (and modal relations) of the assertibles used as disjuncts. At the other extreme, we would have a Peripatetic version that does not acknowledge the existence of molecular propositions:

> ... the so-called fifth indemonstrable, which is the one that concludes from a *dividing hypothetical premise* and the contradictory to one of the *terms in the dividing hypothetical premise* the remaining *term as holding of the object in question*.

Various intermediate versions can be constructed. Since in our passage Alexander is commenting on the *Topics*, it is more likely here (than in his commentary on the *Prior Analytics*) that he considers "naked" relations between terms rather then the relation between sentences or premises that contain two terms and share one term. But this is merely conjectural.

What matters are the following points: with the chosen formulations, Alexander does not commit himself to the elements of propositional logic in Stoic logic. Nothing suggests that that-which-divides is such that its truth-conditions depend on the truth (and modal relations) of some truth-bearers that function as its components. There is in fact no evidence that that-which-divides is thought to have logically independent components that are truth-bearers. Historically, the passage Alex.*Top*.174–6 is important, since it is the earliest one that connects the fourth and fifth Stoic indemonstrables with Aristotle's *Topics* (and the only one in Alexander). Moreover, it is the earliest that connects the Stoic indemonstrables with Aristotle's theory of opposites. Later commentators take up both points and improve on them.

To sum up this section: Alexander has given the first two and the last two types of Stoic indemonstrables a home in Aristotelian dialectic. He has appropriated them as Peripatetic tools, in the form of argument patterns, for establishing or refuting theses. He has identified particular Aristotelian *topoi* which correspond to them, or which

---

[38] E.g. DL.7.81, SE.*PH*.2.158, Gal.*Inst.Log*.6.6.

are "cases" or "examples" of them. Moreover, he has connected two of the indemonstrables with Aristotle's theory of opposites from the *Categories*. Thus, in a second and third way, the indemonstrables (four of them, more precisely) have been anchored in Aristotle's logic.

2. THE DEVELOPMENT AND USE OF A SPECIFICALLY PERIPATETIC TERMINOLOGY FOR THE STOIC "INDEMONSTRABLES"

The greater awareness of the differences in the views of the various philosophical schools together with the philologically and historically more thorough study of the original texts of Aristotle and Plato in the second century CE (in contrast with the first BCE) is reflected in Alexander's choice and use of terminology.[39] Thus, not only does he, in his comments on hypothetical syllogistic, bring together material from Aristotle, early Peripatetics, Stoics, and later Peripatetics (including himself); he also preserves and juxtaposes elements of at least four different (though partly overlapping) sets of terms:

(a) Although Aristotle had no terminology for hypothetical syllogisms (as he had no theory of such syllogisms), his general theory of logic, the terminology he used for syllogisms from a hypothesis, and the terminology used in the *topoi* discussed in Section 1.2, taken together, provided Alexander with a basic stock of useful expressions.

(b) The early Peripatetics had made some rudimentary advancement towards a theory of hypothetical syllogisms and appear to have introduced some basic vocabulary that went beyond Aristotle's.[40]

(c) The Stoics had a complete set of technical terms for their syllogistic.[41] When Stoic syllogistic became *the* logic of hypothetical syllogistic in the first century BCE, many Stoic terms became part of the common terminology used in logic, although we witness some modifications.[42] Some Peripatetics of the first BCE seem to have adopted together with parts of Stoic theory also parts of Stoic terminology.[43]

(d) In the second century CE, there is demand for a distinctly Peripatetic (and also for a distinctly Platonist) theory of hypothetical syllogistic. One way of marking

---

[39] This section requires knowledge of ancient Greek. It can be skipped.
[40] Cf. my [2002a], [2002b], [2004] for details.
[41] Cf. my [1996].
[42] Cf. Section 2.1 for some examples.
[43] Galen is a witness to this development, see my [2004].

out a distinct theory is by introducing a distinct terminology. This seems to be precisely what Alexander did. His surviving commentaries provide evidence that he deliberately replaced terms from the Stoic theory of indemonstrables by terms that are either taken from the closest Aristotelian or early Peripatetic correlates, or are coined with an eye to expressions from Aristotelian and early Peripatetic logic. For this purpose Alexander uses primarily two devices. First, he glosses one term with another, using phrases of the form "*x*, that is, *y*" (in Greek "*x* καὶ *y*," where καί is used epexegetically). He generally puts first the less familiar term (that is, the Aristotelian, early Peripatetic, or newly coined one), and explains it with the one more familiar in his time, usually either the Stoic one, or the common term that had been developed from the Stoic one. Second, Alexander explicitly distances himself from the Stoic, or Stoic-derived common, terminology; he does this in particular where he thinks that the descriptive component of the term is inaccurate.

Alexander's use of the sets of terms (a) to (d) is not systematic. Nor is it random. Naturally, he employs Aristotle's own terms when he presents or paraphrases Aristotle's views. Where necessary, he explains them in terms of common or later Peripatetic terminology.[44] Equally naturally, he uses Stoic terminology mainly when presenting and criticizing Stoic theory.[45] He sometimes makes use of Stoic terms that have become common coinage where there is no Peripatetic substitute or where he explains the early Peripatetic equivalents or newly introduced Peripatetic terms. However, he also sometimes uses more recent Peripatetic terms without glossing them in this way. This last fact suggests that these more recent Peripatetic terms were at the time already established to some degree among the Peripatetics, or at least among his students.

If Alexander's strategy as described in (d) was successful, we should have the Stoic theory of indemonstrables not only Peripatetically modified and firmly grounded in Aristotle's logical system, but also cleverly terminologically disguised in a way that would suggest to someone historically not on the ball that there had always been a worked-out Aristotelian theory that covered the same logical ground as the Stoic indemonstrables. I now consider Alexander's choice of terminology for hypothetical syllogistic in detail.

2.1 Propositions or Sentences and Their Components

Alexander uses the Peripatetic term πρότασις, rather than the Stoic term ἀξίωμα ("assertible"), for propositions (or meaningful sentences). Like Aristotle and the

---

[44] So for instance at Alex.*An.Pr.*11.18, 262.32 κατηγορικός.
[45] So for instance ἀξίωμα, Alex.*An.Pr.*177.31, 179.32, 180.2; τὸ λῆγον at Alex.*An.Pr.*177.21, 178.28.

early Peripatetics, he also uses πρότασις for "premise." To denote simple propositions, Alexander uses the adjective "categorical" (κατηγορικός), not the Stoic "simple" (ἁπλοῦς).[46] Thus Alexander uses an Aristotelian term, but with a different meaning than Aristotle himself; and he is aware of this.[47] (This option must have seemed preferable to using a Stoic term.) Instead of the Stoic expression "mode-forming propositions" (τροπικός, i.e. those which can be used as a complex premise in a Stoic syllogism) Alexander uses the Peripatetic "hypothetical proposition" (ὑποθετικὴ πρότασις, which for the early Peripatetics seems to have meant "hypothetical *premise*" and not "hypothetical *proposition*").[48] There seems to be only one passage where Alexander indubitably uses ὑποθετικὴ πρότασις for hypothetical propositions (Alex.*Top*.191.18); in other passages it is unclear whether the intended meaning is proposition or premise (e.g. Alex.*An.Pr*.11.17–20, 17.7–8, 324.7, 327.2–3), and when Alexander reports Aristotle, it is likely intended as premise.

For the various *kinds* of mode-forming propositions, Alexander appears to introduce his own terms. In later antiquity, the Stoic terms for conditional and disjunctive assertibles (τὸ συνημμένον ἀξίωμα and τὸ διεζευγμένον ἀξίωμα) were shortened to τὸ συνημμένον and τὸ διεζευγμένον and took on a life outside Stoic logic, as independent noun phrases, not as elliptic for conditional assertible and disjunctive assertible. They were used by Peripatetic, Platonist, and other non-Stoic philosophers who would call propositions προτάσεις, not ἀξιώματα. Aristotle had no terms for such non-simple propositions. The early Peripatetics—if we trust Galen[49]—had words for the two types of relations between things that are signified or expressed by hypothetical προτάσεις: συνέχεια and διαίρεσις; and they referred to the corresponding types of hypothetical premises as προτάσεις κατὰ συνέχειαν and κατὰ διαίρεσιν. In Alexander we occasionally find τὸ συνημμένον in non-Stoic contexts (Alex.*Met*.318.23). Much more frequently, we find that-which-connects (τὸ συνεχές—not ἡ συνεχὴς πρότασις!). Alexander glosses this expression several times with τὸ συνημμένον (e.g. Alex.*An. Pr*.262.7, 390.4–5 and text (3)(ii)). Thus we can safely assume that Alexander took the latter term, τὸ συνημμένον, to be generally understood, and the former, τὸ συνεχές, as in need of explanation. In Alexander's commentaries, τὸ διεζευγμένον occurs on its own, without explaining another term, only in Stoic context. In non-Stoic contexts Alexander uses it to gloss that-which-divides (τὸ διαιρετικόν; e.g. Alex.*An.Pr*.20–1). The two terms τὸ συνεχές and τὸ διαιρετικόν don't occur before Alexander in logical context. Thus it seems likely that Alexander himself coined the two expressions in parallel to the

---

[46] We find this also e.g. in Gal.*Inst.Log*.2.2, 6.2. Alcin.*Didasc*.11.15.
[47] See e.g. Alex.*An.Pr*. 11.18, καλουμένης κατηγορικῆς.
[48] See my [2002a] and [2002b].
[49] See my [2002b].

original Stoic ones τὸ συνημμένον and τὸ διεζευγμένον, and intended them as a replacement for the latter. They could be understood as being truly Peripatetic, since they are formed in analogy with the early Peripatetic ἡ κατὰ συνέχειαν ὑποθετικὴ πρότασις and ἡ κατὰ διαίρεσιν ὑποθετικὴ πρότασις. For the Stoic third type of mode-forming assertible and how Alexander dealt with it, see Section 3 below. Here we only mention the following. The Stoics, in line with their propositional-logical approach, called these kinds of propositions conjunction-negating assertible (ἀποφατικὸν συμπεπλεγμένον ἀξίωμα) or negation of a conjunction (ἀποφατικὸν συμπλοκῆς/συμπεπλεγμένου, S.E.*P.H.*2.158 *M.*8.226, D.L.7.80): negation has the largest scope and thus the category of assertibles to which these belong is (non-simple) negations. We have a compound proposition, compounded from a negation and a conjunction by prefixing the negation particle to the conjunction. By contrast, Alexander (like Galen and most later ancient authors) called their equivalents a negative conjunction (ἀποφατικὴ συμπλοκή, below passage (11)). This, once more, suggests that the propositional-logical element from Stoic logic is lost. The negative conjunction is just another type of hypothetical premise/proposition from which inferences can be drawn.

The Stoic terms for the components in a conditional, that is, the antecedent and the consequent, were τὸ ἡγούμενον and τὸ λῆγον. Alexander instead uses the Aristotelian pair τὸ ἡγούμενον and τὸ ἑπόμενον. However, Aristotle himself used this latter pair of expressions mostly for terms rather than propositions.[50] Thus we have another case where Alexander chooses an Aristotelian term but doesn't keep to Aristotle's main use of it.

2.2 Syllogisms and Their Components

The picture is similar for syllogistic. We saw that Alexander associated the Stoic indemonstrables with Aristotle's syllogisms from a hypothesis. This fact is reflected in his terminological choices. Where Alexander uses the name "indemonstrable," he usually does so only with the addition "so-called" (λεγόμενον). His reason for this is not just that the name is Stoic, but more importantly, that he thinks it to be inaccurate. The Stoics, and at least one Peripatetic, Boethus, believed the indemonstrables to be indeed indemonstrable, that is, not in need of proof since self-evident.[51] The Peripatetics regarded some categorical syllogisms as indemonstrable, usually those of the first

---

[50] E.g. Arist.*An.Pr.*43b17.

[51] Gal.*Inst.Log.*7.2. Maroth maintains that Galen reports a discussion *within* the Peripatetic school, in which Boethus defended the priority of the hypothetical before the categorical syllogisms (Maroth [1989] 246–7). However, in Galen the terminology and preceding context are Chrysippus' logic, and (*pace* Maroth) we have no evidence of the use of the pair of terms "categorical syllogism" and "hypothetical syllogism" before the second century CE.

figure. Alexander—purporting to follow Aristotle—accepts nothing but the first figure categorical syllogisms as indemonstrable.[52] Hence for the types of arguments the Stoics call indemonstrables a different name is not just desired but philosophically required.

As the generic term Alexander uses "hypothetical syllogism." This may have been used already by earlier Peripatetics, or was in any case easily coined by taking Aristotle's phrase "syllogisms from a hypothesis" as model. Alexander does not doubt that the arguments the Stoics call "indemonstrables" (and the later so-called "mixed" hypothetical syllogisms in general) are syllogisms. His justification of this fact is Aristotelian, however, not Stoic.[53]

Alexander calls the first premises of the hypothetical syllogisms, generically, "hypothetical premises."[54] It is less clear whether he had a way of referring to the specific kinds of premises. For the second premise, which the Stoics called co-assumption (πρόσληψις), Alexander considers τὸ μεταλαμβανόμενον and τὸ προσλαμβανόμενον. He takes these to be synonyms, the first being the term Aristotle and some early Peripatetics used, the second having been used by some early Peripatetics, perhaps in addition to the first (*An.Pr.*19.4–5, 262.6–9). However, whereas in Aristotle μεταλαμβανόμενον is used to indicate that the premise is that-which-is-taken-instead,[55] (instead of the conclusion, as that which is to be proved by a categorical syllogism, that is),[56] Alexander interprets it as meaning "changed assumption," in the sense that in the hypothetical proposition/premise, the component proposition *p*, say, is taken as being hypothesized only, whereas in the "changed assumption," *p* is taken to state that something is the case, it has thus changed—changed in its status of force, as we might say.[57] This may show awareness at Alexander's time of what is called the "Frege point" in contemporary philosophy.

Moreover, unlike the Stoics, Alexander at least sometimes takes πρόσληψις (and also μετάληψις) to be the *act* of taking a proposition as the additional premise, and τὸ προσλαμβανόμενον and τὸ μεταλαμβανόμενον as the *result* of this act. For the Stoics the πρόσληψις is an assertible (an incorporeal entity),[58] taken as premise, never the act of taking the assertible as premise. (Similarly, Aristotle and Alexander sometimes use "syllogism" for the *act* of deducing ["deduction"], whereas for the Stoics it always denotes the argument itself, i.e. a composite of sayables [λεκτά].)

For the five individual types of "indemonstrable" syllogisms, there appears to have been no set of Peripatetic expressions on offer which Alexander could have adopted wholesale. To denote them, Alexander uses two different sets of descriptions, each

---

[52] E.g. Alex.*An.Pr.* 24.2–12.
[53] Cf. e.g. Alex.*AnPr* 265.1–24.
[54] Cf. Alex. *An.Pr.*17.8–9, 326.6–7, *Top.*63.25, 191.18.
[55] Μεταλαμβάνω in its meaning of "to take instead of," cf. Striker [1979] 43.
[56] See my [2002a].
[57] Alex.*An.Pr.*263.26–33; μεταλαμβάνω used in its meaning of "to change."
[58] E.g. D.L.7.76.

corresponding to one way he connected them with Aristotle's *Organon* (see Section 1). The first, found in Alexander's *Analytics* commentary, is based on his terms for conditionals and disjunctions (cf. Alex.*An.Pr.*390.3–5, 386.27–8, passages (3) and (4) above):

- the hypothetical syllogisms/arguments by means of that-which-connects, which is also called a conditional, and the co-assumption (οἱ διὰ τοῦ συνεχοῦς, ὃ καὶ συνημμένον λέγεται, καὶ τῆς προσλήψεως ὑποθετικοὶ <συλλογισμοί/λόγοι>)
- the hypothetical syllogisms/arguments by means of that-which-divides, which is also called disjunction, and the co-assumption (οἱ διὰ τοῦ διαιρετικοῦ, ὃ καὶ διεζευγμένον λέγεται, <καὶ τῆς προσλήψεως ὑποθετικοὶ συλλογισμοί/λόγοι>)

These are descriptions in the style of the early Peripatetics,[59] each describing the two premises through which the syllogism comes about. In a second passage we find abbreviations of these descriptions: "the hypotheticals by means of that-which-connects" and "the hypotheticals by means of that-which-divides" (οἱ διὰ τοῦ συνεχοῦς ὑποθετικοὶ <συλλογισμοί/λόγοι> and οἱ διὰ τοῦ διαιρετικοῦ ὑποθετικοὶ <συλλογισμοί/λόγοι>). Whether these may actually have functioned as *names*, rather than mere descriptions, of these types of syllogisms is unclear. I have not found them in any author other than Alexander. In any event, these descriptions (or names) are clearly in the Peripatetic tradition, based on Aristotelian and early Peripatetic terms and descriptions of what was to come to be the hypothetical syllogisms.[60]

Alexander's second set of descriptions, the one in his *Topics* commentary, is based on his terminology for the relevant *topoi*. Alexander describes the relevant first *topos* as τόπος ἐξ ἀκολουθίας κατασκευαστικός τε καὶ ἀνασκευαστικός (Alex.*Top.*165.6–7, 174.5–6); the first resulting syllogism as the first so-called indemonstrable, which is ἐξ ἀκολουθίας κατασκευαστικός; and the second resulting syllogism as the second so-called indemonstrable, which is ἐξ ἀκολουθίας ἀνασκευαστικός. He describes the second relevant *topos* as τόπος ἐκ μάχης κατασκευαστικός τε καὶ ἀνασκευαστικός (Alex.*Top.*174.6–7); the first corresponding syllogism as the fifth so-called indemonstrable, which is ἐκ διαιρετικοῦ καὶ τοῦ ἀντικειμένου ἑνὶ τῶν ἐν τῷ διαιρετικῷ τὸ λοιπὸν συνάγων; and the second corresponding syllogism as the fourth so-called indemonstrable, which is ἐκ διαιρετικοῦ καὶ τοῦ ἑτέρου τῶν ἐν τῷ διαρετικῷ ἀναιρῶν τὸ ἕτερον.[61] Thus it is possible that the fifth was considered as ἐκ μάχης κατασκευαστικός, and the fourth as ἐκ μάχης ἀνασκευαστικός, although Alexander does not explicitly say so. In any case, Alexander's description, even though it follows the Stoic standard definition, has taken on a Peripatetic coloring: we have

---

[59] Cf. Alex.*An.Pr.*262.31–2 μίκτους ἐξ ὑποθετικῆς προτάσεως καὶ δεικτικῆς together with my [2002a].
[60] See also Alex.*An.Pr.*19.4 ὁ <ἐκ ἀντιφάσεως> διαιρετικὸς συλλογισμός and Alex.*Top.*11–12, 175.
[61] Elsewhere he classifies a different kind of argument as fifth indemonstrable, see Section 3.

Table 9.1 Expressions relevant to hypothetical syllogistic

Aristotle	Early Peripatetics[a]	Stoics	Alexander
proposition/statement	proposition	simple assertible	categorical proposition
?	?	mode-forming proposition	hypothetical proposition
-	?	conditional assertible	that-which-connects
-	?	disjunctive assertible	that-which-divides
-	?	conjunctive assertible	conjunction?
-	?	negation of conj.	assertible negative conjunction?
antecedent	antecedent	antecedent	antecedent
consequent	consequent	'ending'	consequent
'following'	connection	to follow	consequence
?'conflict'	division	to conflict	conflict
(syllogism from hypoth.)	syll. from hypothesis	indemonstrable syllogism	hypothetical syllogism/ so-called indemonstrable syllogism
-	in acc. w. connection	first indemonstrable	hyp.syll. through that-which-connects / establishing from consequence
-	in acc. w. connection	second indemonstrable	hyp. syll. through that-which-connects / removing from consequence
-	?	third indemonstrable	(See Section 3)
-	in acc. w. division	fourth indemonstrable	hyp.syll. through that-which-divides / establishing from conflict
-	in acc. w. division	fifth indemonstrable	hyp. syll. through that-which-divides / removing from conflict
that-which-is-taken-instead	that-which-is-taken-instead	co-assumption	changed premise
-	that taken in addition	co-assumption	that taken in addition
-	proving premise	(co-assumption)	categorical premise
(hypothesis)	hypothetical premise	mode-forming assumption	hypothetical premise

[a] Maroth's conjecture that the early Peripatetics used the word hypothetical (ὑποθετικός) for propositions and syllogisms ([Maroth 1989] 33, 34) is based on the wrong assumption that Alcinous is the same person as Galen's teacher Albinus and seems unfounded. Cf. [Bobzien 2002a]

διαιρετικόν instead of διεζευγμένον. Moreover, instead of the Stoic τὸ ἀντικείμενον τοῦ λοιποῦ ἔχων συμπέρασμα we have the Peripatetic ἀναιρῶν τὸ ἕτερον; that is, instead of being formulated in terms of contradictoriness, the conclusion is formulated in terms of refuting. Alexander is our earliest source for these features, and they all recur, further refined, in later Aristotle commentators. The fourfold descriptions of the "indemonstrables" in terms of the two pairs of expressions "consequence" and "conflict" and "establishing" and "refuting" seem to be echoed in one text only, namely Alcinous' *Handbook of Platonism (Didasc.* ch.6). Alcinous' dates are uncertain, but he is likely to have been either a contemporary of Alexander or a generation or so later.

I conclude the present section with a table of the various expressions relevant to hypothetical syllogistic found in Alexander (or which he is likely to have known), sorted according to ascription and/or likely origin (Table 9.1).

Table 9.1 shows that Alexander has succeeded in building up a vocabulary for hypothetical syllogistic that is in its entirety non-Stoic and based on Aristotelian and early Peripatetic terms.

3. THE PROBLEM OF THE NEGATIVE CONJUNCTIONS AND THE THIRD INDEMONSTRABLES

Historically perhaps the most fascinating aspect of Alexander's appropriation of the Stoic indemonstrables for Peripatetic purposes is his treatment of the third indemonstrables and their mode-forming premises, the conjunction-negating assertibles. We know from Galen that there was a debate about the usefulness and validity of the Stoic third indemonstrables, and also that they had no early Peripatetic correlate.[62] Galen himself rejected negative conjunctions with a contingent relation between the conjuncts (e.g. "Theo walks and Dio talks") as unsuitable for producing syllogisms. But he considered negative conjunctions with partially incompatible conjuncts (i.e. those which cannot be true together, e.g. "Theo is in Athens and Theo is on the Isthmus") suitable for syllogistic. He took them to express a relation of incomplete conflict and called them quasi-disjunctions (παραπλησία διεζευγμένοις), despite their linguistic form of a negative conjunction.[63] Later commentators on Aristotle reserved the "third mode of the hypothetical syllogism," as they called it, for contraries with intermediates, and expressed their first premises grammatically as disjunctions.[64]

There are no signs that Alexander was acquainted with Galen's suggestions or with the alternatives chosen by the later commentators. Still, he was aware that there was a

---

[62] Pace Barnes [1985]; cf. my [2002a], [2002b].
[63] Cf. Gal.*Inst.Log.*5.1.
[64] E.g. Philop.*An.Pr.*245.3–23; [Ammon].*An.Pr.*68.23–41; see also my [forthcoming].

problem with the third type of indemonstrables and that there was a debate about it. We have no evidence that Alexander himself had a firm view on the matter. However, he is a valuable witness for the transitional period in which some Peripatetics, and presumably some Platonists, attempted both to retain all five Stoic types of indemonstrables, and to pass them all off as Peripatetic (or Platonist), as far as their origin, character, and justification are concerned. The four Early Peripatetic hypothetical syllogisms are thus augmented by a fifth. I consider the relevant passages in Alexander's commentaries in turn.

3.1 The *Prior Analytics* Commentary

In the above-discussed passage (3)(ii) Alexander lists three types of hypothetical arguments that Aristotle could have meant by "the other arguments that conclude from a hypothesis":

(3)(ii) He would mean the hypothetical <arguments> by means of that-which-connects, which is also called a conditional, and the co-assumption, and the ones by means of that-which-divides, that is disjunction, and perhaps the ones by means of the negation of a conjunction. (Alex.*An.Pr.*390.3–6)

The first of these would encompass the first and second Stoic indemonstrables, the second the fourth and fifth Stoic indemonstrables, and the third the third Stoic indemonstrables. Two things are noteworthy in (3)(ii): First, for the conditional and disjunction, Alexander first uses his Peripatetic term and then glosses it with the Stoic one; but he presents only one expression (the Stoic "negation of conjunction") for the third case. This suggests that either there was no terminological Peripatetic counterpart available to Alexander, or, if there was, it was referred to with the same or a similar expression as the Stoic one.[65] Second, this case is added with the tentative "and perhaps" (ἢ καί). Thus Alexander seems to have some reservations as to whether Aristotle would have had arguments with negative conjunctions in mind.

The long passage *An.Pr.*262.28–265.5 (discussed in part in Section 1.1), in which Alexander attempts to show that the Stoics indemonstrables are Aristotelian syllogisms from a hypothesis, both confirms these points, and makes them clearer. At the beginning

---

[65] I assume that the early Peripatetics didn't have an expression for a counterpart to the third indemonstrables, since they didn't have such a counterpart; and that the Peripatetics in the first century BCE (e.g. mentioned by Galen *Inst.Log.*7.2) may have taken over Stoic terminology with Stoic theory.

of the passage Alexander lists in Stoic terminology the three mode-forming premises used for the five indemonstrables: "the mode-forming <premise/assertible> being either a conditional or a disjunction or a conjunction"[66] (*An.Pr.*262.31). Then he shows that the syllogisms with conditional premise and those with disjunctive premise fit Aristotle's description of syllogisms from a hypothesis: the former correspond to the first and second indemonstrables, the latter to the fourth and fifth ones. (Here again, he glosses his own expressions τὸ συνεχές and τὸ διαιρετικόν with the Stoic τὸ συνημμένον and τὸ διεζευγμένον.) Third, he turns to the syllogisms from a negative conjunction. I quote the passage in full:

(11) But (15) also in the case of the <mode> from a negative conjunction <can it be shown that it belongs to Aristotle's syllogisms from a hypothesis>, *if, that is, this mode differs from the previously discussed ones, and is not the same as that by means of a conditional which begins with an affirmation and ends in a negation, such as "if A, then not B."*[67] For in the case of these <syllogisms>, too, if the co-assumption requires proof, it is to be proved by means of a categorical syllogism. For example: "it is not both the case that living pleasantly is the goal (20) and virtue is choiceworthy by itself. But virtue is choiceworthy by itself. Hence it is not the case that living pleasantly is the goal." For that which has been co-assumed, i.e. "virtue is choiceworthy by itself," is proved through a categorical syllogism. For example, ... (25) ... "Hence virtue is choiceworthy in itself." *But if the same thing were assumed hypothetically in the following form: "if pleasure is the goal, then it is not the case that virtue is choiceworthy in itself," then the consequence would be proved through a syllogism of this kind:* .... (Alex.*An.Pr.*264.14–31)

Alexander here considers two possibilities for the syllogism from a negative conjunction: either (i) it is different from the conditional and disjunctive hypothetical syllogisms or (ii) it is the same as one of the conditional modes. Alexander does not commit himself to either possibility. Instead, he demonstrates that either way the syllogism

---

[66] τοῦ τροπικοῦ ἢ συνημμένου ὄντος ἢ διεζευγμένου ἢ συμπεπλεγμένου (Alex.*An.Pr.*262.31). One might expect "negative conjunction" rather than "conjunction" here. However, since for Alexander the negative conjunction is a type of conjunction (whereas the Stoics have "negation of a conjunction," classified as negation), from Alexander's perspective, what he says is correct, if unspecific.
[67] Or: "if the first, then not the second"—the description of the conditional is entirely in Stoic terms, hence so might have been the illustration.

could be seen as a case of an Aristotelian syllogism from a hypothesis—showing which is after all the purpose of *An.Pr.*262-4. It is likely that both options (i) and (ii) were discussed in Alexander's time. (i) implies the introduction of a Peripatetic correlate to the third indemonstrables without the claim of Peripatetic ancestry; (ii) enables the Peripatetics to argue that the hypothetical syllogism with a negative conjunction is one of those syllogisms the Peripatetics already accepted (namely a type of conditional hypothetical syllogism); it is just worded differently (and wording matters to the Stoics, but not the Peripatetics).[68] Since Alexander does not commit himself to either view, and is rather tentative in his statements about them,[69] it seems that at the time there was no Peripatetic standard solution to the problem available. This notwithstanding, passage (11) sports some interesting features:

We consider option (ii) first: the indemonstrable mode from a negative conjunction (or negation of a conjunction, as the Stoics would say) is the same as a mode by means of a conditional. Alexander's description of the mode as "that by means of a conditional which begins with an affirmation and ends in a negation" suggests that he assumes that there are several different modes of the hypothetical syllogisms with a conditional hypothetical premise. Alexander here uses the Greek word "mode" (τρόπος) not in the Stoic, but in an Aristotelian or Peripatetic sense: one syllogistic figure has several modes. The conditional and disjunctive hypothetical syllogisms would be (the equivalent to) figures, in parallel to Aristotle's categorical syllogistic. Alexander's specification "such as 'if A, then not B'" suggests that option (ii) might assume there to be eight different modes in the "conditional figure": four of type *modus ponens*, four of type *modus tollens*, obtained by drawing out all possible combinations with affirmative and negative antecedent and consequent propositions. In Alexander's time, there was a similar Peripatetic use of "mode" and "figure" for wholly hypothetical syllogisms.[70] Moreover, we know of such a classification of *modus ponens* and *modus tollens* arguments from Boethius and from the anonymous Scholium Waitz.[71] These two later texts don't discuss hypothetical syllogisms with a negative conjunction as hypothetical premise. So conceivably there was a faction of Peripatetic logicians that integrated the third Stoic indemonstrable into Peripatetic hypothetical syllogistic by equating it to the mode of the form "if A, not

---

[68] A third possibility, one actually taken by later commentators, would be to add it and equate it with something else from Aristotle's logic, such as the case of contraries with intermediates.
[69] Cf. the "ifs" at Alex.*An.Pr.*264.15 and 264.26.
[70] See my [2000].
[71] See my [2002c].

B; A; therefore not B."[72] Note that the classification of "if A, then not B" as mode of a *conditional* hypothetical syllogism differs from that of the early Peripatetics, who would have considered "if A, then not B" as a—non-standardly expressed—dividing (or *disjunctive*) proposition.[73]

What about option (i)? Which faction of Peripatetics (or other philosophers) believed that the hypothetical syllogisms with a negative conjunction differ from the ones with a conditional or with a disjunction that Alexander discussed beforehand? They would be either the first century BCE Peripatetics who adopted the Stoic indemonstrables; or alternatively, philosophers like Galen, who classified the negative conjunctive hypothetical propositions as among those that indicate a kind of conflict (μάχη), and thus among the other group of hypothetical syllogisms which the early Peripatetics distinguished. In the latter case, these hypothetical syllogisms, while being an independent kind, could still be subsumed under the early Peripatetic categorization of "connection" and "division," which Galen called ἀκολουθία and μάχη, and thus, if desired, could be reclaimed as Peripatetic in origin.

3.2 The *Topics* Commentary

One of the *Topics* passages discussed above in Section 1.2 shows in a different way that Alexander had not yet found a place for the third indemonstrables:

(10) And the proof that is fitting for *the contraries without intermediates* is rather the one by means of the so-called fifth indemonstrable, which is the one that concludes from that-which-divides and the contradictory to one of the <components> in that-which-divides the remaining <component>. But for *the contraries with intermediates* the <proof> by means of the fourth <indemonstrable is fitting>, which is the one that refutes from that-which-divides and one of the <components> in that-which-divides the other <component>.

We saw in Section 1.2 that Alexander uses the pattern of the fourth and fifth indemonstrables to describe how, by using them, one can obtain proofs. We noted that we would have expected him to say that the contradictories without intermediates fit the pattern of the fifth *and the fourth* indemonstrables.

---

[72] Later commentators on Aristotle generally use the expression "mode" (τρόπος) differently: i.e. to denote the (by then) five different forms of hypothetical syllogisms: e.g. Philop.*An.Pr.*244.1–246.14, Anon.*Log.etQuadr.*38, Heiberg. (On *Log.etQuadr.*38 cf. Barnes [2002].)

[73] See my [2002a], [2002b].

Now let us take a closer look at Alexander's suggestion that the contraries with intermediates are such that the pattern of the fourth indemonstrables is fitting for them. The connection appears to be roughly this: when two terms are contraries with intermediates, then they are in conflict (μάχη), since they cannot both hold of the same thing. The hypothetical premises or propositions that express conflict are the dividing (or disjunctive) ones. The inference patterns built on dividing (or disjunctive) hypothetical premises/propositions are those of the fourth and fifth indemonstrables. The pattern of the fifth indemonstrables does not "fit" the contraries with intermediates, since one cannot, for example, infer from the conflict of black and white that if this is not white, than it is black. It could be gray or yellow. But the pattern of the fourth indemonstrable does "fit": we can safely infer from the conflict of black and white that if this is white it is not black. So far, so good.

We are left with two problems. Alexander's omission of the fact that the pattern of the fourth indemonstrables also fits the contraries *with* intermediates (and contradictories, of course). And the difficulty that the hypothetical propositions in the fourth and fifth indemonstrables are expressed in disjunctions, whereas disjunctions are not a suitable way for expressing the conflict of contraries with intermediates. We just don't say "this is either black or white" when we wish to express that particular kind of conflict.

The third indemonstrable is not at all considered by Alexander in the passages quoted from his *Topics* commentary (nor anywhere else in the commentary), although it would lend itself perfectly to arguments using contraries with intermediates. Some later Peripatetics or Platonists solved both of Alexander's problems, by assigning both the pattern of the fourth and the fifth indemonstrables to the contraries without intermediates, and by assigning the pattern of the third indemonstrable to contraries with intermediates.[74] The negative conjunction with component sentences that share the same subject term is the perfect grammatical vehicle for expressing contraries with intermediates. ("This is not both black and white. But it is black. Hence it is not white.") Alexander equipped these later philosophers with the connection of Aristotle's classification of opposites (from the *Categories*) with (i) the passages from Aristotle's *Topics* and with (ii) the Stoic indemonstrables. He thus laid the foundation for this later, more coherent, theory.

4. CONCLUSION

Alexander is the first known ancient author who *both* suggested that Aristotle was aware of the inference patterns the Stoics encapsulated in their theory of indemonstrables, *and*

---

[74] See my [forthcoming].

attempted to provide evidence for this fact by drawing a connection between the indemonstrables and selected passages from Aristotle's *Organon*. Furthermore—presumably in order to support his view that Aristotle had considered such inference patterns, and to establish a Peripatetic theory of them (a hypothetical syllogistic)—Alexander introduced a logical vocabulary that is based on Aristotelian and early Peripatetic terminology. He modified Aristotelian and early Peripatetic terms and their use in such a way that they fit a theory of syllogisms derived from the Stoic indemonstrables. The resulting elements of a hypothetical syllogistic are Peripatetic both in spirit and in nomenclature. Alexander did not manage to integrate the third Stoic indemonstrables into the Peripatetic system. But he provided the foundations for what later became the standard way of doing so.

The *importance* of Alexander in the development of a Peripatetic (and Platonist) propositional logic is thus twofold: first, he no longer condones the eclectic method used by earlier Peripatetics, who unabashedly (and sometimes without acknowledgment) took over parts of Stoic logic to complement Aristotelian logic. Instead, now, elements of Stoic logic that are integrated into Peripatetic theory have to be *shown* to have their origin in some Aristotelian (or early Peripatetic) thought. Second, Alexander paved the way for a full Peripatetic/Platonist hypothetical syllogistic by drawing a number of important, if sometimes somewhat far-fetched, connections between Stoic logic and Aristotle's *Organon*; connections on which later Aristotle commentators were able to build.

Acknowledgments

I am indebted to Fabio Acerbi and István Bodnár for helpful comments on a draft of this paper and to Geoffrey Moseley for catching a number of errors at the proof stage.

References

Barnes, J. [1984] "Terms and Sentences: Theophrastus on Hypothetical Syllogisms," *Proceedings of the British Academy 69*, 279–326.
Barnes, J. [1985] "Theophrastus and Hypothetical Syllogistic," in J. Wiesner (ed.), *Aristoteles—Werk und Wirkung*, vol. 1 (Berlin: De Gruyter), 557–76.
Barnes, J. [2002] "Syllogistic in the anon Heiberg," in K. Ierodiakonou (ed.), *Byzantine Philosophy and Its Ancient Sources* (Oxford: OUP), 97–137.
Bobzien, S. [1996] "Stoic Syllogistic," *Oxford Studies in Ancient Philosophy 14*, 133–92.
Bobzien, S. [1997] "The Stoics on Hypotheses and Hypothetical Argument," *Phronesis 42(3)*, 299–312.
Bobzien, S. [1999] "Stoic Logic," in K. Algra et al. (eds), *The Cambridge History of Hellenistic Philosophy* (Cambridge: CUP), 92–157.

Bobzien, S. [2000] "Wholly Hypothetical Syllogisms," *Phronesis 45*, 87–137.
Bobzien, S. [2002a] "The Development of *Modus Ponens* in Antiquity," *Phronesis 47*, 359–94.
Bobzien, S. [2002b] "Pre-Stoic Hypothetical Syllogistic in Galen" in V. Nutton (ed.), *The Unknown Galen, Bulletin of the Institute of Classical Studies*, Suppl. vol. (London: Institute of Classical Studies), 57–72.
Bobzien, S. [2002c], "A Greek Parallel to Boethius' *De Hypotheticis Syllogismis*," *Mnemosyne 55*, 285–300.
Bobzien, S. [2004] "Hypothetical Syllogistic in Galen—Propositional Logic off the Rails?" *Rhizai: Journal for Ancient Philosophy and Science 2*, 57–102.
Bobzien, S. [forthcoming], "The Making of a Platonist Hypothetical Syllogistic."
Frede, M. [1974] *Die stoische Logik* (Göttingen: Vandenhoeck & Ruprecht).
Frede, M. [1975] "Stoic vs. Peripatetic Syllogistic," *Archiv für Geschichte der Philosophie 56*, 99–124.
Goulet, R. [1978] "La classification des propositions simples," in J. Brunschwig (ed.), *Les Stoïciens et leur Logique* (Paris: Vrin), 191–222.
Ierodiakonou, K. [1990] "Rediscovering Some Stoic Arguments," in P. Nicolacopoulos (ed.), *Greek Studies in the Philosophy and History of Science* (Dordrecht: Kluwer), 137–48.
Maroth, M. [1979], "Die hypothetischen Syllogismen," *Acta Antiqua 27*, 407–36.
Maroth, M. [1989], *Ibn Sina und die peripatetische "Aussagenlogik"* (Leiden: Brill).
Mignucci, M. [1993], "The Stoic *Themata*," in K. Doering / Th. Ebert (eds.) *Dialektiker und Stoiker* (Stuttgart: Franz Steiner), 217–38.
Mueller, I. [1969] "Stoic and Peripatetic Logic," *Archiv für Geschichte der Philosophie 51*, 173–87.
Mueller, I. [2006], *Alexander of Aphrodisiac: On Aristotle's* Prior Analytics *1.23–31* (London: Duckworth).
Schiefsky, M. [This volume].
Speca, A. [2001] *Hypothetical Syllogistic and Stoic Logic* (Leiden: Brill).
Street, T. [2001] "The 'Eminent Later Scholar' in Avicenna's Book of the Syllogism," *Arabic Sciences and Philosophy 11*, 205–18.
Striker, G. [1979] "Aristoteles über Syllogismen 'aufgrund einer Hypothese,'" *Hermes 107*, 33–50.
Striker, G. [2009] Aristotle, *Prior Analytics: Book I* (Oxford: OUP).

PART FOUR
Hellenistic Ethics

10

WHY THERE ARE ENDS OF BOTH GOODS AND EVILS IN ANCIENT ETHICAL THEORY

James Allen

I

In a burst of creative energy in 45–44 B.C. Cicero wrote a series of books dedicated to the main philosophical issues of his day in order to make Greek philosophy available to a wider Roman public. Not the least valuable is the *De finibus bonorum et malorum*, *On the ends of goods and evils*, often called simply the *De finibus* or *On Ends* for short, whose five books expound and criticize the ethical theories of Epicurus, the Stoa, and the so-called Old Academy of Antiochus.

The notion of the end or *telos*, the Greek term that Cicero translates as *finis* (*Fin.* 1. 42, 3. 26), as that for whose sake other things are to be done which is not itself to be done for the sake of anything else, is familiar to every student of ancient philosophy.[1] It appears to find its first clear expression in Plato's *Gorgias* (499e; cf. *Tim.* 90d),[2] is ubiquitous in Aristotle, and was embraced by Epicurus, the Stoics, and Pyrrhonian skeptics among others.[3] Together with those of the highest good and happiness, it belongs to a system or network of concepts that furnished the major schools with a common framework. It would hardly be surprising, then, if Cicero had undertaken to examine the views of the most important schools about the end so conceived.[4] As the central organizing principle of both a well-conducted life and the theory of how to lead such a

---

[1] Cicero gives "that for the sake of which" as the meaning of "finis" (*Inv.* 1. 6; cf. *Part. orat.* 3, 9). At *Fin.* 4. 19, he compares the end of prudence or the *ars vitae* to the ends belonging to each of the different arts.

[2] "Perhaps the earliest clear instance of τέλος in the sense "purpose" "end of action," so common in later works from Aristotle onwards" (Dodds 1959, 317).

[3] Epicurus *Men.* 128, 131; R.S. 22, 25 (he wrote a book Περὶ τέλους Diogenes Laertius 10. 27) For the Stoics see SVF 3. 2; 3. 16 = LS 63 A; the Pyrrhonists, Sextus Empiricus *PH* 1. 25, 215, 231; DL 9. 107–8.

[4] Cicero refers to the περὶ τελῶν σύνταξις and five books περὶ τελῶν in letters to Atticus (Schiche 1915, xi–xiii). There is some disagreement about whether the plural, *De finibus*, should refer

life, the end is, as he observes, as important a topic as there is in philosophy (*Fin.* 1. 11; cf. 5. 15; *Acad. pr.* 132).[5]

The problem, however, is that the book's full title is *De finibus bonorum **et malorum***, *On the ends of goods **and evils***. If the *telos* is that for the sake of which, anything viewed as an end in this way must also be regarded as good (cf. Aristotle, *EE* 2. 10, 1227a18–22). Nothing evil can be an end for those who so conceive it. What sense, then, can we make of an end on the side of evils?

Moved by considerations like these, the eminent sixteenth-century scholar Scaliger the elder (1484–1558) accused Cicero of getting the title of his own book wrong.[6] It seems incredible that Cicero should make an error of this magnitude, and it was a bit much of Scaliger, you might think, to undertake to teach the Romans how to write Latin. The last observation is due to John Davies (1679–1732), the eighteenth-century Cambridge scholar, who was the first person I know of to come to Cicero's defense.[7] Yet Scaliger's view was still being cited with sympathy occasionally in the twentieth century, which shows, if nothing else, just how difficult scholars have continued to find the problem.[8]

Though not a puzzle on the solution to which our understanding of the *De finibus* let alone of ancient ethics more generally hangs, the problem is a vexing one. If the end of evils is not, as it evidently cannot be, a goal or that for the sake of which, what is it and what is its relation to the end in the more familiar sense? What is more, the question is not simply how there can be an end on the side of evil as well as one on that of good. There is already something puzzling about talk of an end of goods.[9] It is not as

---

to the diverse views held by different schools about the end or, in the first instance, the two ends, one of goods, the other of evils, that belong to a single system. In Cicero's hands it can do both: *Acad. pr.* 132 (the former); 114 and 129 (the latter).

[5] Cicero also surveys views about the end in the *Academica priora* to demonstrate the extent and seriousness of the disagreement prevailing among philosophers (129, 132). A lost work of Galen's, apparently called *The kinds of life consistent with each telos*, may have been about the ends of the different schools (*Lib. propr.* XV. 4). Clement of Alexandria's survey of philosophical views about the end furnishes a late and partial parallel (*Stromateis* 2. 127 ff.). See Döring 1893, 165–203, at 180–95; Warren 2002, 19–23. Before Cicero's time, the Stoics Chrysippus and Hecaton composed books entitled "On ends" or "On the end" though it is not clear that their purpose was to survey views of the end (DL 7. 87, 102). See Döring 1893, 165–6; Glucker 1978, 54; Lévy 1992, 348; Hadot 1994, 336–56, at 359.

[6] "Omnis.... finis est in genere bonorum. Quocirca non decuit M. Tullium vocem hanc tam ad mala, quam ad bona retulisse in suorum librorum inscriptione"(*Exercitationes exotericae de subtilitate* CCL). Scaliger's complaint was an *obiter dictum*; the grounds for suspecting the title were set out in more detail by his younger contemporary and acquaintance, Muretus (1526–1585), (*Variae Lectiones* XVII. 1).

[7] In his edition of the *De finibus* (Cambridge, 1728, 2 ed. 1741).

[8] Lörcher 1911, 221 n. 2, Martha 1928–30 I, vii–viii.

[9] Cf. Philippson 1913, 598–617, at 612, who objects that it does not make sense to speak of the goal of the goods, but rather of the good as goal (cf. Aristotle *EN* I 7, 1097a18–19).

if we are accustomed to finding the phrase "end of goods" by itself in the authors to whom we usually turn for enlightenment about ancient ethics, and it is not obvious what it could mean.[10] To understand what is meant by "ends" in the formula, then, we must discover what the relation that obtains between one end and goods and another and evils could be.

II

The obvious way to put doubts about Cicero's testimony to rest is by finding the formula in other authors. To this end, Davies cited occurrences in Seneca and Apuleius,[11] and Madvig drew attention to a passage from Augustine.[12] These are of course Latin authors postdating Cicero, so the possibility that they borrowed the formula from him cannot be excluded. Early in the twentieth century, however, Robert Philippson drew attention to evidence that is not open to the same objection, namely, a passage referring to ends of goods and evils in the *Rhetorica* of Philodemus, a Greek author a little older than Cicero, many of whose works survive on papyri buried in Herculaneum by the eruption of Mount Vesuvius.[13]

> Yet since nothing is at all praiseworthy or worthy of reproach by itself, but comes to be so insofar as it agrees with the *end* of goods on the one hand, or with the *end* of evils on the other, someone who has not come to know these by a process of judicious assessment will also not be able to determine the things said with a view to praises by *reference* to them [the ends]. (IV col. XXXVIIa, 4–17; Sudhaus, I 218).[14]

---

[10] Though as it happens, the phrase "end of goods" appears twice early in the *Magna Moralia*, the first time as an emendation inspired by the second occurrence (I.2 1184a14; I.3 1184b8). Though one cannot be certain, it does not seem as if "end of goods" is being used as a technical term in the *MM*. A possible parallel is furnished by *EE* VIII 3 1248b18, which can be understood in two ways: "all goods have ends, which are to be chosen for their own sake" (Dirlmeier 1963, ROT (Solomon), and perhaps, to judge by their punctuation, Walzer and Mingay) or "of all the goods those are ends that are worthy of choice for their own sake" (Décarie 1978; Woods 1992).
[11] Seneca, *Ep.* 78. 25; Apuleius, *Apology* 15, 10.
[12] 1876, lxi n. 1: *De civitate Dei* 19.1, the source for which is thought by Madvig and others to be Varro.
[13] 1913, 612–13; cf. Philippson 1939, 1104–1192, at 1135.
[14] Οὐ μὴν ἀλλ' ἐπεὶ
πρᾶγμα καθ' ἑαυτὸ τοῖς
ὅλοις οὐ[θ]έν [ἐσ]τιν ἐπαι-
[νε]τὸν ἢ ψεκτὸν ἀλλὰ
[γε]ίνεται τὸ μέν, καθό-

The formula also appears in another Herculaneum papyrus (PHerc 1012, col XIII) containing a work by another Epicurean, Demetrius of Laconia, who was probably slightly younger than Cicero,[15] and is found in Eusebius in a passage falsely attributed to Plutarch, according to which Aristippus of Cyrene held that the end of goods is pleasure, that of evils, pain (Eusebius, *Praeparatio Evangelica* 1.8.9 = Diels, *Doxographi graeci*, 581, 21–582, 1 = Mannebach fr. 159A = Giannantoni IV A 166).[16] Though ps.-Plutarch is presumably a late author of little distinction, the chances that he was influenced by a purely Latin tradition are slim.

So far as I have been able to discover, Greek testimonies containing the whole formula, "ends of goods and evils," end here. I shall adduce evidence from other passages in which ends figure on the side of evil as well as that of good and argue that, properly interpreted, they point the way to an explanation of the meaning of the formula, but it must be conceded that there is a gap between the evidence and the conclusion that I shall defend, and the argument that fills this gap will inevitably be conjectural.

III

For the time being, however, these testimonies, scant and obscure though they may be, are enough to put to rest the suspicion that the formula and the problems that it presents were of Cicero's making, and this in turn should encourage us to use—with

σον ὁμολογεῖ τῶι τέλει
τῶν ἀγαθῶν, τὸ δέ, κα-
θόσον τῶι τῶν κακῶν,
ὁ μὴ ταῦτ' ἐγνωκὼς ἐπι-
λελογισμένως οὐδὲ κα-
τὰ τὴν ἀναφορὰν τὴν
ἐπ' αὐτὰ δ[ι]ορίζειν δυνή-
σεται τὰ λαμβανόμενα
πρὸς τοὺς ἐπαίνους,...

The context is criticism of the so-called rhetorical sophists. Human beings are exhorted to good by praises and deterred from evils by reproaches, but these sophists, Philodemus complains, actually succeed in making people worse. They prefer Clytemnestra to Penelope and Paris to Hector. Even when they do praise good people, it is only those conventionally regarded as good. Whence the need for a sound understanding of the ends of goods and evils.

[15] Puglia 1988; Crönert 1906, 117 ad col. 57.

[16] As Giusta 1964, 1. 217–18 n. 2 observes, this shows that Cicero's formula had a Greek source. Liscu 1939, 28–39, and Hartung 1970, 114 ff., seem not to have been aware of the Greek evidence. The latter holds that the relation expressed in the formula "end of goods" does not and cannot occur in Greek; on his view, both *bonorum* and *malorum* are supplements added to *finis* by Cicero (128–30).

caution—the evidence furnished by his writings, in which ends of goods and evils are pervasive.

Two things stand out in his testimony.

(i) He feels compelled to use several Latin terms to help him convey the idea; apart from *finis*, he speaks of the *summum*, the *ultimum*, and the *extremum*, and he seems to regard them as all but synonymous (esp. *Fin.* 1. 42, 3. 26; 5. 15, 23).
(ii) The idea of the end—or the *summum* or *ultimum* or *extremum*—as that to which other things are *referred* recurs again and again (*Acad. post.* 19; *Acad. pr.* 129; *Fin.* 1. 11, 29, 42, 5. 15–17, 23).

I shall begin with a thought suggested by the second of these points before returning to the first.

The idea of ends as items to which goods and evils are referred, or by being referred to which they qualify as good and evil, is also prominent elsewhere, among other places as we have seen, in the Philodemus passage (cf. Aristotle *EN* 7. 11, 1152b1–3). Consider, for example, a passage in Plato's *Protagoras*, which is especially important because it belongs to an author who is both influential and, relative to those cited so far, ancient (354b–d). The context is Socrates' famous argument that weakness of the will is impossible (349a6 ff.). His case is dialectical, directed to the many, who, he maintains, believe *both* that weakness of the will is a matter of going against one's better judgment as a result of being overcome by pleasure *and* that good, ultimately and in the last analysis, is pleasure, and evil pain. The second of these beliefs, he argues, makes nonsense of the first. To go for the pleasant is thereby to go for the good and to fail to go for the good is thereby to fail to go for the pleasant. It must rather be that one goes wrong, not by preferring the pleasant to the good in moments of weakness, but rather by mistakenly taking something other than the pleasant, and therefore other than the good, to be pleasant, and therefore good.[17]

In the passage that matters for our present purpose, Socrates prepares the way for this argument by asking the many whether they can name a *telos* other than pleasures and pains *by looking to which* they call some pains good and some pleasures evil (354 b8, d2, 8). Some translators give "end" for *telos*, but others, unsurprisingly, resort to "criterion" (Croiset and Bodin 1948; Guthrie 1956; Lombardo and Bell 1992) or "end or standard" (Jowett 1892). Rendering *finis* or *telos* in the same way elsewhere, especially in Cicero's formula, *fines bonorum et malorum*, would make good sense. And in 1882 Rudolf Hirzel maintained that the term *telos* did have this meaning as one of its

---

[17] Cf. Allen 2006, 6–31.

senses.[18] His main evidence was not Plato, whom he does not mention, but a passage about the Cyrenaics in Sextus Empiricus' survey of views about the criterion of truth, where Sextus observes that what the Cyrenaics say about ends is analogous to what they say about criteria (*M* 7. 199–200).

> Some affections are pleasant, others are painful, and others are intermediate; and the painful ones are, they say, evils whose end is pain, the pleasant ones are goods whose unmistakable end is pleasure, and the intermediates are neither goods nor evils whose end is neither good nor evil, this being an affection between pleasure and pain. Thus the affections are the criteria and the ends of things, and we live, they say, by following these and attending to the evident (ἐνάργεια) and to approval (εὐδόκησις), to the evident with regard to other affections and to approval in relation to pleasure.[19]

According to Hirzel, a *telos*, as the Cyrenaics conceive it, is that whereby we recognize what is a good and what an evil, a standard or measure, that is, something very much like a criterion.[20]

Hirzel went on to argue that the use of *telos* in this sense was an innovation of the Cyrenaics, and that it reached Cicero through the Academy, where it was introduced by Carneades, who, as a native of Cyrene, would have picked it up there in his early years. Now this seems to be open to question even before we consider evidence from other sources. Nevertheless if Hirzel's main idea, that the formula "ends of goods and evils" means something like the standards or criteria with reference to which goods are good and evils evil, is sound, it would matter less that his views about the provenance of this sense of *telos* were questionable.

This idea has problems of its own, however. To show that ends, pleasure and pain in this case, serve as criteria of value and action in Cyrenaic ethical theory or elsewhere does not establish that there was a sense of *telos* meaning standard or criterion.[21] There is a substantial gap in Hirzel's argument. As he presents it, the postulated sense hangs in midair, unsupported by relations to other more familiar senses. Nevertheless, I believe that he was onto something, namely the idea that the *function* of ends of goods and evils is to serve as standards. And this function of a *telos*, even if it is not

---

[18] Hirzel 1882, 663–668; endorsed by Antoniadis 1916, 35–7.
[19] Translation Tsouna 1998, 156, lightly modified. An alternative translation takes the crucial phrases to be a non-restrictive relative clauses, i.e. "painful [affections] are evil, whereof the end is pain" (Bury 1933–49, Bett 2005).
[20] Hirzel 1882, 665.
[21] Cf. Diano 1933, 167–169 at 168.

the meaning of the term "telos," furnishes us with an important clue. To understand the formula "ends of goods and evils" we need to discover a sense of *telos*, such that, by being ends (τέλη) in this sense, a suitably related pair of items can serve as standards or criteria of good and evil.

IV

Reconceived as a view about the function of ends of goods and evils, Hirzel's position is no longer incompatible with the principal alternative interpretation of the formula, which, in one form or another, is the view supported by most scholars who have looked into the question.[22] This interpretation takes its start from the first of my two observations about Cicero's talk of ends of goods and evils, that is, the fact that he appeals constantly to the notions of the *summum*, the *extremum*, and the *ultimum* to explain that of an end. There is an especially clear statement by Rackham in his Loeb edition of the *Academica*, where he says in a note on *Acad. pr.* 129: "*finis* has come to be almost a synonym for 'summum', highest in the scale, losing the sense of object aimed at."[23]

If this view is on the right lines, it seems that a solution to the problem is to hand. The genitive plurals *bonorum* and *malorum*, taken together with the substantive adjectives, *summum, extremum,* and *ultimum*, are partitive genitives, and the objects designated by the adjectives, *summum, extremum,* and *ultimum* are the highest, furthest, or most extreme members of the classes of goods and evils to which "bonorum" and "malorum" refer. The same will be true of the Greek counterparts of these formulas.

The idea of the highest of the goods has a distinguished history: "what is the highest of the goods achievable by action?" is one way in which Aristotle poses the central question of practical philosophy (*EN* 1. 4, 1095a16). The idea of the highest, or at any rate the most extreme or ultimate member of the class of evils, presents no more of a problem than that of the highest of the goods, though in each case it raises an important question of interpretation.[24]

If *finis* is functioning as a synonym or near synonym of *summum, ultimum,* or *extremum* in the formula, presumably we are to take "goods" and "evils" as partitive

---

[22] Muretus, 146–7; Davies 1741, Diano 1933, cf. Diano 1946, 110–11, Madvig 1876, lxi n. 1; Mannebach 1961, 110–11; Philippson 1913, 612–13; Schäublin et al. 1995, 280–1 n. 331; Reid 1885, 309 n. 23 ad *Acad. pr.* 114; Lieberg 1958, 3–11 at 5; Giannantoni 1990, vol. 4 179.

[23] P. 634; cf. his introduction to the *De finibus* ed. 2. 1931 vii–viii.

[24] Is the question "what is the highest good?" a request to select from a list of the goods considered severally, health, wealth, good looks, and the like; or a question to be answered by an appeal to a maximally inclusive aggregate of the items on the list; or, as Aristotle and other ancient philosophers seem to have done, one properly answered by identifying the cause and principle of the goods (*EN* I 12, 1102a3–4; *EE* I 8, 1217b2–5, 1218b7–12). Cf. Broadie 2005, 41–58.

genitives and the items designated by *finis* as, so to speak, the end members or outermost bounds of the classes of goods and evils to which they belong. And if this is right, it is possible to see how ends in this sense could serve as standards or criteria of goods and evils. This interpretation receives some support from Cicero, where the terms *finis, summum, extremum*, and *ultimum* are, as we have seen, constantly conjoined and freely interchanged. Indeed it may well be Cicero's understanding of the formula.[25] If it were his invention, this might be enough. But, as we have seen, it is not, and I believe that better interpretation is available.[26]

The main reason is the discordant clash between the postulated sense of "end" and the familiar not to say dominant sense as that for the sake of which. To be sure, for Aristotle, as for Plato at least in the context of the *Gorgias*, the end conceived as that for whose sake *is* the highest good, but this is a substantive point of considerable importance, not a piece of elegant variation (see esp. *EN* 1. 7 1097a22). What is more, the formula "ends of goods and evils" conveys the idea less well than the alternatives. As superlatives, the adjectives *summum, extremum*, and *ultimum* (and their Greek counterparts) invite us to read "goods" and "evils" as partitive genitives and to see the classes of goods and evils to which they refer as ordered or ranked by degree of goodness or evil, so that the items designated by the adjectives turn out to be their highest or most extreme members. *Telos*, trailing associations with choice and action from the more familiar sense, does not lend itself to these purposes nearly as well. It is not by accident that generations of scholars have been puzzled by the formula.

V

Another relevant piece of evidence that is sometimes cited by proponents of the view that the formula "ends of goods and evils" means the highest or most extreme members of the classes of goods and evils is supplied by a further sense of *telos* recognized by the Stoics.[27] In this sense, the end is the last or most extreme of the objects of appetite (ἔσχατον τῶν ὀρεκτῶν), to which all the other are referred (SVF 3. 3). The same idea shows up in Cicero as the *rerum expetendarum extremum* (*Acad. post.* 19; *Fin.* 5. 37), the *ultimum rerum appetendarum* (*Fin.* 4. 32; cf. 1. 11), or the *terminatio rerum expetendarum* (5. 27). I take it, however, that it is not an extreme or limit

---

[25] Cf. Oxford Latin Dictionary s.v. *finis* 15. As has been observed, Latin *finis*, which counts among its primary senses "limit" or "boundary" (cf. *finire* to bound, limit) may lend itself better to this interpretation than Greek *telos*.

[26] Antoniadis 1916, 35 goes so far as to maintain the interpretation that I reject is "grammatisch ganz unmöglich."

[27] Diano 1933.

in degrees of quality that is at issue, but rather something that comes very close to the *telos* conceived in the familiar way. The implied principle according to which the objects of appetite are ordered here seems to be the *for-the-sake-of* relation. An item comes before another in the sequence if it is for its sake but not the other way round. The relation is transitive: everything for the sake of a second thing will also be sought for the sake of everything for whose sake the second item is sought. The extreme will be the last in the order, that for whose sake everything else is sought—whether mediately or immediately—which is not itself for the sake of anything further, i.e., the end.[28]

A class of things to be avoided or shunned—the φευκτά—ordered by a mirror image relation and whose extreme member is that with a view to shunning which we shun everything that we shun is easy to conceive, as, to be sure, is one ordered by degrees of the quality opposite to desirability. But though this is true, the formula is not "ends of things to be pursued and shunned" but "ends of goods and evils," which remains to be explained.

VI

The suggestion that I shall defend takes the familiar sense of "end" as that for the sake of which to be dominant but not basic. If it is on the right lines, it is a mistake, though a natural and understandable one, to try to derive the sense of "end of evils" directly from the dominant sense of the term. A more promising approach, I suggest, is to look to the proximate roots of the dominant sense.[29] The essential clue, on which we have already touched, is the close relation between the end as that for the sake of which and action and choice. The connection is pervasive in Aristotle, but it is also conspicuous in the *Gorgias*, where the end as that for whose sake makes its first clear appearance. There Socrates invites Callicles to agree that the good is the end of all *actions* and that for the sake of which all other things should be *done* (499e).

In Homer the verb *telein* is transitive; it takes an object, which can also be expressed as a grammatical subject when the verb is in the passive voice.[30] Two types of case are especially illuminating for our present purpose. In the first, where the object is a deed or an undertaking, for example, the task (ἔργον) of dispatching the disloyal retainers in

---

[28] Aristotle sometimes brings the notion of a *telos* into connection with those of an extreme (*eschaton*) and a limit (*peras*). At *Met.* α 2, 994a8ff. he argues that the end for the sake of which is an extreme and a limit and not capable of being pushed back to infinity; to hold otherwise is to abolish the nature of the good, as no one would undertake anything if he did not expect to come to a limit (cf. Δ 17, 1022a6-8; *EE* II 1, 1219a10-11; *EN* I 2, 1094a18-21).

[29] Holwerda 1963, 337-63 contains a huge and hugely helpful collection of testimonies.

[30] Cf. Ambrose 1965, 38-62 on whose exceptionally illuminating paper I draw in what follows.

the *Odyssey* (22. 479; cf. Gorgias, *Helen* 8), it means to bring fully to an end. In the second, where the object is a handiwork, for example, a bed, or an item viewed as something brought gradually into being, such as the day, it means to bring fully into being. Compare the English verbs "finish" or "complete" and the way we speak of completing or finishing a chore, say, or a statue. The two meanings are obviously complementary. Often enough the end or terminus of a doing or process will be the completion or final coming into being of that which it was the process of making or bringing about. And the noun *telos* has a similarly related pair of senses: completion, for example, of some tripods (*Il.* 18, 378); the end or terminus, for example, of a war, of a voyage, or that consisting in death.[31] And lexicographers give a prominent place to "fulfillment," "consummation," or "realization" among the senses of *telos*.[32]

The same thought seems to lie behind the adjective τέλειος, perfect or complete, and variants of it. Something is τέλειος when it has been brought to or reached the end by which it is completed or realized, or alternatively, the process or undertaking of which it is the product has attained this end. Latin conveys the same idea with *perfectum*, the perfect passive participle of *perficio*, to do completely. That is perfect which has been done completely or all the way through to the end. A natural extension allows us to apply the term to items that are not the product or outcome of a process or undertaking, God, say, or a syllogism in the first figure, things which are perfect without ever having been perfected.

VII

The way for the sense of *telos* as that for the sake of which was, then, well prepared. For in paradigm cases of action it will be the fulfillment or consummation of the action that both brings it to a close and was the reason or that for whose sake the agent undertook it in the first place. But though this use is thoroughly entangled with human or divine designs and expectations, there is still a gap between the idea of fulfillment or consummation, on the one hand, and that of goal or that for the sake of which, on the other. Some fulfillments, for example, of certain prophecies, are, of course, to be dreaded.

Consider also an old use of *telos* of which Hesiod furnishes an especially striking example.[33] Dilating on the perils of sailing, he says the *telos*, of goods or evils, is with

---

[31] Cf. Ambrose 1965, 38–62, at 47.

[32] LSJ, Chantraine 1968 s.v. τέλος.

[33] Cf. Mimnermus 2.5.7: the dark goddesses of death stand by, one holding the *telos* of grievous old age, the other that of death; [Euripides] fr. 1110 Nauck, Antiphon 5. 89, Semonides 1. 12 (references from Holwerda 1963, 351 ff.; add Gorgias, *Palamedes* 36. See also Fischer 1965, 11 ff).

the gods, meaning that they have control of the outcome, or that, as we would say, our fate is in their hands (*Op.* 669). These ends are, to be sure, the outcomes intended by the gods, but this is not the point of view from which they are being regarded here or what is conveyed by calling them "ends," as we can see from a remark expressing similar apprehensions, but reflecting a different understanding of the workings of fate, that is attributed to Democritus (DK 269): "Action begins in daring, but chance has control over the end."[34]

This suggests that the idea of a *telos* contains different moments, one or the other of which may predominate when they coincide. This is the point of Aristotle's citation of the "laughable" line of an unnamed poet "he has the end for the sake of which he was born," that is, death (*Physics* 2. 2 194a 31–2). The context is a defense of the assertion that it falls to the natural scientist to know "the for the sake of which and the *telos* and as many things as are for their sake" (194a27). When there is an end (*telos*) to a continuous process of change, Aristotle continues, this is both the terminus (ἔσχατον) and that for the sake of which," that is, an end in both these senses. The poet's line is laughable because it is not every end, in the sense of a terminus, that is an end, in the sense of that for the sake of which, but only the best.

Consider the matter from another angle. One could imagine a development in the meaning of *telos* that began with the bare sense of end or terminus, without necessarily implying that the end in question is a fulfillment or consummation, and led via a focus on cases in which it is a consummation or fulfillment, to the sense consummation or fulfillment. The evidence, such as it is, counts against this. But be this as it may, there was a widespread and well-attested sense of *telos*, meaning simply the end or terminus of a process, a doing, an event or series of events without regard to whether it is good or bad, intended or not. The end of the war or battle, which is already in Homer (*Il.* 16. 630), but found also in authors like Herodotus (9. 2; cf. 1. 82, 155), the end of the day, the end of the events, or, and especially, the end of life, which is found in Sophocles (*Oed. Col.* 1721), Euripides (*Hipp.* 867; *Electra* 956), and Gorgias (*Palamedes* 35) among others,[35] and can be expressed by the very same phrase, *telos biou*, that, for example, Aristotle (*Pol.* 1337b36), Plutarch (*Comm. not.* 1070 F), and Clement (*Strom.* 21. 130, 2) will use of the goal of life.[36] The end in cases like these is, however, often not just the bare termination, but the result, issue, event, or outcome, and lexicographers recognize such a sense of *telos* too. Thus the end of the war is not just the cessation of hostilities, but the condition that results from the war. Homer can speak of the "equal

---

[34] τόλμα πρήξιος ἀρχή, τύχη δὲ τέλεος κυρίη.
[35] βιότοιο τελευτὴ (Homer *Il.* 7.104, 16, 787); τελευτὴ τοῦ βίου (Herodotus 1. 30).
[36] Ambrose 1965, 60 n. 2.

issue" (ἴσον ... πολέμου τέλος) of a conflict (*Il.* 20.101).[37] The issue or result in such cases can be good or bad, foreseen or not, intended or not.

There are two ways of thinking about an end as a terminus and two kinds of ends depending on which applies, in connection with the second of which the idea of a result or issue is likely to be especially prominent. An end may be a more or less arbitrary cutoff. Although there are views according to which death, of the right sort, is the consummation or fulfillment of life—the heroic view that a glorious death in battle is the highest fulfillment that life has to offer; the view in the *Phaedo*, that the philosophical life is preparation for death—the more usual view sees death as an arbitrary cessation of life, life that could have continued going on just as it had been. The other kind of end is that by ending in which, bringing about or terminating in which, the process or doing or event or sequence of events whose end it is qualifies as what it is in some important respect. This brings us back to the idea of fulfillment or consummation. Some of these consummations will be goals, both desired and sought, others merely welcome, still others neither.

VIII

The respect that matters now is, of course, being good or evil. "It is the outcome or issue of an action, which makes it good or bad." This is a very crude statement of a view that is capable of considerable refinement. Such a view is found in the passage of the *Protagoras* to which we turned because of its use of the term *telos* (354a ff.). The broader context, it will be recalled, is the case for hedonism. Socrates' immediate object is to forestall an objection, namely, that we rightly call some pleasures evil and some pains good. The evil pleasures are the ones that we go for in alleged episodes of weakness of will; the good pains, things like surgery or physical exercise. Socrates argues that the many at least can give no reason why these pleasures are evil except that they—the pleasures—*result or issue* in pain or the loss of pleasures; and no reason why the pains are good except for the pleasures that *result or issue* from them and the pains from which they protect us. The many, then, have no recourse but to say that good is pleasure and evil pain (354e8).

The verb translated as "result-in" is ἀποτελευτάω (353e8; 354b7; cf. τελευτάω 355a5; cf. *Lysis*, 220b).[38] The *telos* looking to which one calls some pains good and some pleasures evil takes up talk of *resulting-in*. Translators who resort to "criterion" or "standard"

---

[37] Ambrose 1965, 52.
[38] Cf. Plato, *Symp.* 181e, where Pausanias says that there ought to be a law against the love of boys, "for the end of boys is unclear, whether the result will be virtue or vice as regards both soul and body." τὸ γὰρ τῶν παίδων τέλος ἄδηλον οἷ τελευτᾷ κακίας καὶ ἀρετῆς ψυχῆς τε περὶ καὶ σώματος.

are right to think that Socrates is talking about a criterion with reference to which we call actions "good" and "evil," but it is the *telos*, in the sense of the issue or outcome of our actions, that serves as this criterion. Translators who opt for "result" get it exactly right.[39] Traces of this idea can be seen in Cicero's use of the formula in connection with the Epicurean position, according to which people never err about the ends of goods and evils, but only go wrong regarding them when they are ignorant of the things by which they are brought about (*efficiantur*) (*Fin.* 1. 55).

IX

I suggest that it is the idea of a *telos*, in the sense of issue or outcome, by having which, and therefore when viewed as a standard of assessment by reference to which, things qualify as good or evil, as we see it in the *Protagoras*, that is ultimately behind Cicero's formula, *fines bonorum et malorum*, and its Greek original. But before pursuing this suggestion, I want to linger a little longer on Plato. For if this argument is on the right lines, we have not only found the sense of *telos* that explains the formula, but also one that is or lies close to the root of the dominant sense of *telos* as that for the sake of which; and if this is right, we should be able to see how the senses could have been close enough to complement rather than clash with each other.

Plato does not use *telos* in the sense of end or issue in the *Gorgias*, but the idea, which finds expression in the *Protagoras*, is, I suggest, presupposed by the use of *telos* in the dominant sense, which seems to make its first appearance there. The passage in the *Gorgias* where the *telos* figures is the immediate sequel to Callicles' concession that some pleasures, namely those that produce (ποιεῖν) health, strength, or some other virtue of the body, are good while those doing the opposite are evil (499b–d), and it refers back to an earlier discussion between Socrates and Polus, which was set in train by Socrates' charge that rhetoric is merely a form of flattery and not a true art at all. Polus had there defended rhetoric by appealing to the orator's tyrant-like power to kill, expel, or expropriate whomever he wishes (466cd).

The burden of Socrates' reply is, in part, that it is not these acts, or others like them, that we wish or want (βούλεσθαι) but that for the sake of which we take them (467de, 468b). This point is developed in service of another, namely, that it is always the good that we wish and for whose sake we take every action that we take, so that the orators whose power Polus extols turn out never to get what they wish and therefore not to have any real power at all (468e, 469e). The good that everyone wishes or wants is, of course, the end of all actions (πράξεις) that Socrates introduces later in his conversation

---

[39] Taylor 1991; Schofield and Griffith 2009.

with Callicles (499e). Early in the argument, however, in arguing for the first of these points, namely that it is not the actions that we perform on each occasion that we wish, but rather that for whose sake we perform them, Socrates could have said, and is implicitly relying on the idea, that our reason for acting or that for whose sake we act must be something that occupies the place of the end, in the sense of the issue or outcome, of what we do (cf. Aristotle, *EE* 2. 1. 1219a 8 ff.).[40]

It is but a step from the end, seen as what occupies the place of the issue or outcome of what we do, and do precisely because it has this as its issue, to the idea of the end as that for the sake of which we act. The capacity that allows us to evaluate actions with reference to their end or issue and to classify them as good or evil accordingly can be applied to the actions of others or to our own past actions, but its most important application is to the potential actions in our power that we contemplate as we deliberate. These too will be good or bad with reference to their end or issue, or rather their expected end or the end to which they conduce, and if all goes well, the end for the sake of which we choose an act *will be* the end in which it issues.

Without being sure of the details, or precisely when or by whom the critical steps were taken, I suggest that it was attention to the end, in the sense of issue or outcome, that we pursue and which is our reason for action, that lies behind the sense of *telos* meaning that for the sake of which or goal. Once in circulation, the latter sense spread quickly and soon gained a lasting ascendancy. Meanwhile, however, the sense of issue or result, remained available and was put to work in the idea of the end or ends by resulting in or conducing to which, actions qualify not only as good, but also as evil, and if I am right, it is this idea that is enshrined in the formula, ends of goods and evils.

If this proposal is on the right lines, we can see how authors who use the formula were able to shift without strain between talk of the end of goods and the end as that for the sake of which. The good by bringing about or conducing to which an action qualifies as good and the good in order to obtain which I choose and take that action are, after all, the same thing viewed under two intimately related aspects. If you will, we choose actions whose end or outcome is our end or goal.[41] A parallel development setting out from the end or ends, in the sense of issue or outcome by bringing about or conducing to which actions qualify as evil, and are therefore to be shunned, and

---

[40] Cf. *Rep.* 10. 613a ff., where Socrates says the time has come to restore to the just man the honors and rewards of which he was deprived for the sake of argument. Human beings are compared to runners, all of whom, to be sure, reach the end of the race (τελευτάω; 613a6, b12; τέλος; 613c3, d7), but whereas the bad ones are seen to be ridiculous at the end, the good ones are crowned and rewarded with prizes. So it is he says at the end (τέλος) of every action (πρᾶξις) and of life itself.
[41] "The relation of means to end is the relation of cause to effect regarded by someone who intends the effect.... The effect becomes an end when someone introduces the cause with the intention of producing that effect" (Robinson 1964, 30).

yielding a sense of *telos* meaning something like that with a view to avoiding which we avoid other things and, which stands in the same relation to the end of evils as the end for whose sake stands to the end of goods, is perhaps not inconceivable. For whatever reasons, this did not happen. As a result, there is an asymmetry: the end of goods has a counterpart, namely the end as that for whose sake, where the end of evils does not.

X

The evidence from Plato does not contain the formula, "ends of goods and evils," but if the argument made here is correct, the formula is an expression of the same understanding of ends that we have found in the *Protagoras*. Potentially more troubling than the simple gap in testimony between Plato's time and that of Cicero and his Epicurean contemporaries, however, is an apparent conceptual gap between the idea of ends of goods and evils as I have argued it should be interpreted and some of the positions to which it is applied by Cicero, notably that of the Stoics, which figures so prominently in the *De finibus*. Concerns on this score can only be exacerbated by the dearth of evidence, which leaves it unclear whether and by whom apart from Cicero the idea was applied to positions like the Stoa's.

The hedonist position put forward in the *Protagoras* is a form of consequentialism, and all the goods apart from pleasure itself are instrumental goods. The role of instrumental goods, however, is much reduced if it does not disappear entirely in the ethics of Plato, Aristotle, and the Stoa, where virtuous actions worthy of choice for their own sake come to the fore. Yet if Cicero is to be believed, every properly constituted ethical system lays down ends of both goods and evils (*Div.* 2. 2; *Lucullus* 129, 132). How can the formula understood along the lines proposed here accommodate views like these, especially the Stoa's?

One way of resolving the problem is to suppose that the meaning of the "ends" in the formula, like the familiar meaning of *telos* as that for the sake of which, underwent a development of the kind for which Aristotle provides evidence in *EN* 1. There he tells us that some ends are products apart from the activity by which they are produced; others are identical to the activities themselves, which are undertaken for their own sake (1. 1, 1094a3 ff.). Ends of the second type may nevertheless also be chosen for the sake of further ends and ultimately happiness, to which they are related not as instrumental means producing it but components that make up or compose it. In straightforwardly productive cases, as we have seen, the end for the sake of which actions are chosen is the end by resulting in which they are worthy of choice and therefore good. As long as we restrict our attention to instrumental goods, this is what it means to be the end of goods on my account.

The relation being-for-the-sake-of that holds between activity and end when the end is not distinct from the activity also presupposes a relation between the same terms analogous to production, something like constituting or realizing, in which the item that is the end, in the sense of that for the sake of which, also plays a part analogous to that of the end, in the sense of issue or result. By a natural extension of the idea of an end, it should be possible to conceive the end of goods as happiness, or the distinctive characteristic of the happy life, by giving rise to which goods are good, where "giving rise to" covers not only the relation of producing but also that of constituting or realizing. The end of evils will be *mutatis mutandis* the same, namely unhappiness, or the distinctive characteristic of the life of unhappiness, by giving rise to which evils are evil. In this way, the two opposed ends can serve as standards of good and evil.

The idea of ends of goods and evils is not attested for the Stoics. We do, however, know that they made a place in their system for an account (a *logos* or *ratio*) of goods and evils, and that this contains traces of ideas like those we have been examining (SVF 3. 68, 69). Thus we find a distinction, indebted to a similar distinction of Plato's, between goods that are final, those that productive and those that are both final and productive (Stobaeus 2. 71 15 ff. = LS 60 M; DL 7. 96–7; Cicero, *Fin*. 3. 55; cf. Plato, *Rep*. 2. 357b–d). Two things about it are especially important for our present purpose. It distinguishes two ways in which goods contribute to happiness: goods are productive (ποιητικά) by producing or generating happiness (ἀποτελεῖν); final (τελικά) by filling out or completing it (συμπληροῦν), so becoming parts of happiness. And there is a division of evils on precisely the same lines. Evils are productive by producing unhappiness; final by filling out or completing unhappiness, so becoming parts of it. If happiness and unhappiness were viewed as ends to which goods and evils give rise in this way and by reference to which they qualify as good and evil, the idea of ends of goods and evils need not have been alien to Stoic thought.

The idea of filling out or constituting happiness figures prominently in Cicero's account of the disagreement between the Stoa and the Peripatos, on the one hand, and between the so-called Old Academy of Antiochus and the Stoa, on the other, especially when the issue in contention is whether happiness is constituted by goods of the body and external goods in addition to goods of the soul or by goods of the last type alone.[42] Cato, Cicero's Stoic spokesman in *De finibus* 3, says that the Peripatetics think that everything that they style good "pertains" to the happy life—*pertinere* being the verb Cicero uses to characterize the relation between final goods and happiness (*Fin*. 3. 55)—while the Stoics do not accept that everything worthy of estimation, that is,

---

[42] See in this vol. B. Inwood, Ch. 11 "Ancient Goods."

so-called preferred items, is constitutive of (*complere*) the happy life (*Fin.* 3. 41; cf. 32, 43; 2, 42; 4. 31, 35; 5. 25, 37, 47; *Tusc.* 5. 39).

To be sure, the use of the idea of ends of goods and evils by the Stoics themselves is a mere possibility. The gap in between Plato's testimony and the appearance of the formula in the work of Cicero and his Greek contemporaries remains troubling. Cicero uses it constantly, assigns it a place of central importance, and treats it as the common property of every philosopher with an ethical theory. Yet outside his works, the formula is found only two or three times in out-of-the-way places (where, however, it also seems to be viewed as common property so far as one can tell). Perhaps though not guilty of inventing the formula, *fines bonorum et malorum*, Cicero was guilty of applying it to theories to which their own authors had not applied it. He certainly gives it a prominence that has no counterpart in any surviving Greek evidence.

On any view of its meaning, the formula must have achieved currency as a technical term in time to be taken up by Cicero and his Epicurean contemporaries. I was inclined to dismiss Hirzel's view that the formula originated as a piece of Cyrenaic terminology. Perhaps too hastily. The idea of ends of goods and evils, as I have interpreted it, lends itself to the purposes of hedonism especially well as we have seen. And it is noteworthy that a high proportion of the tiny number of testimonies that seem to hint at the idea concern the Cyrenaics or Epicureans.[43] Perhaps there is even room for a theory of a now unfashionable kind, according to which the hedonist theory of the *Protagoras* reflects the influence of Aristippus the elder, whose doctrines reenter Plato's school with Carneades. Though the possibility cannot be excluded, I remain doubtful.

XI

Hirzel's views about Cicero's proximate sources are another matter, however. I shall conclude by trying to make it plausible that the formula and the ideas it expresses go

---

[43] The Cyrenaic, Theodorus (4th c. B.C.), held that joy (χαρά) and distress (λύπη) are the *telos* (DL 2. 98; cf. 93). PHerc 1251, likely by Philodemus according to its most recent editors, refers to a plurality of ends three times (Schmid 1939; Indelli and Tsouna-McKirahan 1995). The first is in a polemical section directed against opposing views including that of those—apparently Cyrenaics—who make the affections of the soul ends that stand in need of no further judgment so, the author maintains, granting us unlimited license (col. III.6–14). These are presumably pleasure and pain (Schmid 1939, 55, 57; Indelli and Tsouna-McKirahan 1995, 124). Later, in the exposition of the correct, Epicurean view, the author says that choices and avoidances are measured against the ends of nature (XI. 17–20) and that the measurement of choices and avoidances is by the congenital ends, which afford the most manifest evidence (XIII. 8–12). Both sets of editors take the reference to be to items on the good side of the scale, ἀπονία and ἀταραξία (Schmid 1939, 66; Indelli and Tsouna-McKirahan 1995, 165, 171), but perhaps they are opposed as ends of goods and evils?

back to Antiochus and through him to Carneades. The focus on Antiochus should not imply that there was necessarily a single route of transmission to Cicero. If Carneades employed the formula, then so almost certainly did Clitomachus, Philo of Larissa, and other Academics, and the Epicurean testimonies suggest that it was in still wider circulation. It merely reflects the evidence that we have, the nature of which also means that the case for Antiochus' familiarity with ends of goods and evils is inevitably stronger than that for Carneades'. But if the case for Carneades can be made plausible, the case that these ideas were applied to Stoic ethical theory, either by the Stoics themselves or in a way they could at least have recognized, will be strengthened as well. What is more, it will also become easier to think that, though hardly the peculiar property of the Academy, the idea of ends of goods and evils was not an alien intrusion, but very much at home there. Just possibly, though we shall in all probability never know, it had a continuous history in Academic philosophy stretching back to the roots that we have identified in Plato himself.

Appeals to the idea of ends of goods and evils are especially thick on the ground in passages where Cicero is closely engaged with Antiochus' philosophy. The *Academica priora*, though chiefly occupied with epistemology, ends with an extended speech by Cicero speaking on behalf of the New Academy (64–148). Its object is to exhibit the extent and seriousness of the unresolved disagreement among the philosophers about the main issues in their discipline, so lending support to the Academy's commitment to cautious, open-minded skeptical inquiry while challenging Antiochus' pretensions to dogmatic certainty. A subsection is devoted to each of the three main divisions of philosophy: physics (116–28), ethics (129–41), and logic (142–6).

Before proceeding to document the numerous disagreements in these areas, Cicero takes strong exception to the way in which Antiochus combines adherence to the stringent standards the Stoics impose on assent with reckless eagerness to lay down doctrines about matters of the gravest importance and utmost difficulty, among them the ends of goods and evils (114). Cicero, who knew Antiochus' writings well and was personally acquainted with their author, apparently took it for granted that Antiochus employed the idea of ends of goods and evils. When a short time later he takes up ethics, Cicero begins by asking whether anything has been securely established in the matter of goods and evils and observes that the fundamental desideratum in ethical theory is to lay down ends to which the totality of goods and evils can be referred (129). In the course of exhibiting the dissension among the philosophers, he makes use of the famous *Carneadea divisio* (131), Carneades' systematic classification of actual and possible theories of the end or highest good, which he also employs elsewhere in different forms and to different argumentative purposes.[44]

---

[44] Illuminating discussion in Algra 1995, Annas 2007, 187–22, Lévy 1992, 353–60.

Though these views are presented as different responses to the requirement that an ethical theory lay down ends of goods and evils, they are views about the end identified with the highest good. If Cicero is to be believed, however, this is not a problem. According to him, "it is plain that there is an end of evils opposed to each of the ends of goods that I have expounded" (132). A simple operation, then, transforms an account of the end of goods into an account of ends of both goods and evils and by implication an equally simple operation effects the reverse transformation.

This suggests that the idea of ends of goods and evils may be even more pervasive in Cicero, and therefore possibly in the authorities on whom he relied, than we had already supposed. As we have seen, there is already a puzzle about what the relation between goods and their end is supposed to be even before we consider evils and theirs. The relation—that of giving rise to on the view defended here—is the essential thing. Once one has this, its application to evils is easy and can, depending on the context, be taken as implied by a reference to the end of goods. For example by the Antiochean view, reported by Lucullus, that the two most important things in philosophy are the criterion of truth and end of goods, a pairing which also suggests that the end of goods also played a criterial role (29). These considerations, I submit, lend support to the idea that Antiochus, at least, made use of ends of goods and evils.

The case is far from conclusive, and could hardly be given the evidence. The highest good, the end as that for the sake of which, and the end of goods as I have interpreted it are so related that one can usually be substituted for the other without difficulty. An author like Cicero could, then, have favored one at the expense of another in a way that does not accurately reflect the way in which the position he is describing was presented by its authors or even introduce one into the description of a view whose authors did not use it themselves. If Cicero's accounts are in the main accurate, however, the testimony that we have been considering may contain an important clue with a bearing not only on Antiochus but also on the likelihood that Carneades was familiar with the idea of ends of goods and evils.

The views classified by Carneades' division in the *Academica priora* are, of course, views about the end for the sake of which everything is to be done, but this is not the aspect that Cicero emphasizes. Rather it is as views about the end of goods, each of which implicitly contains, and is easily transformed into, a view about the end of evils as well, that they are put forward by Cicero, in response to the need for ends or standards to which goods and evils are referred. And on some other occasions on which Cicero turns to the *Carneadea divisio*, the question at issue is framed in the same way. Thus in *De finibus* 2, where the case against the Epicurean position is presented, he emphasizes as he does elsewhere, the importance of starting from the consideration of the natural, uncorrupted behavior of infants—the issue in contention in the famous cradle argument. This, he says, is the source from which the whole account of goods and evils must flow (*ratio bonorum et malorum*), immediately before setting out the views classified by Carneades' division, which he therefore plainly regards as accounts of goods and evils.

If the emphasis on display in these passages belonged to the original context of argument in which the *divisio* was introduced by Carneades, that is, if that debate was conceived, in the first instance, as a debate about systems of goods and evils, the *ratio* or *notio bonorum et malorum* as Cicero calls it, it becomes that much more plausible to suppose that the idea of ends of goods and evils was at home in it.

The discussion of the *divisio* in *De finibus* 5, which furnishes the fullest account that we have of it and is the only one that explicitly credits Carneades, also views matters in this way, making this plain, among other ways, by frequent appeals to ends of goods and evils. The same cautions apply. The idea of a *ratio bonorum et malorum* implied by talk of ends of goods and evils can be expressed without them. The presence of ends of goods and evils may be due to Cicero, or if not to him to Antiochus, to the defense of whose views the passage belongs. Even the section that is explicitly concerned with Carneades' views has long been suspected of containing at least one clear Antiochean intrusion.[45] There may be others that are less clear, and in any case there are other problems as well.[46]

We can distinguish between an Antiochean frame, which begins at 5.15, and an account of the *Carneadea divisio*, which begins at 5.16 but the end of which is harder to specify. At no point are we dealing with something that deserves to be called a fragment of Carneades in any except the loosest sense. Piso, the Antiochean spokesman, first treats the question at issue as about the *summum bonum*, but immediately goes on to treat its resolution as equivalent to the discovery of the ends of things, and this as the same thing as knowing what the extremes of both goods and evils are. And on the resolution of this question, he continues, depends an understanding of the best way of life and the complete system of our duties (15). Here he turns to the *Carneadea Divisio* for help understanding the dissension over this issue among the philosophers.

Carneades began with the idea that, like other arts, prudence or the art of life must be occupied with an object other than itself. This object must be one towards which we have an original natural impulse. Three such objects are possible: pleasure, the absence of pain, or the so-called first natural things. Still meaning to report Carneades' views, Piso says "the source of the whole question about ends of goods and evils, when we seek to discover what is the extreme or ultimate of goods and evils, is to be found in

---

[45] Madvig 1876, 633, 815–25.
[46] Annas 2007, Striker 1986.

the first natural impulse," a sentiment that he repeats after he has finished expounding Carneades (22).

The first natural impulse and its object are, however, only the point of departure for moral development. Reflection gives rise to a system of duties referred to the object of the first natural impulse. These duties are both towards that object and away from its corresponding opposite, by which we are naturally repelled (18). The idea made explicit here, that an object of attraction is always paired with an object of repulsion, is implicit throughout, and it is plausible to connect it with the different conceptions of the end that the *divisio* classifies, by taking these, at least implicitly, always to be views about goods and evils.

Though Piso does not put it this way, moral development can stop here with the emergence of prudence and the system of duties governing prudent conduct. The object with which prudence is occupied will then also be the object of the art of life in the sense of being its goal and the good by obtaining which one is happy. Prudence and any other virtues there may be and the duties we perform in exercising them will be of merely instrumental value, and there are three views of the end conceived in this way: it will consist in either pleasure, the absence of pain, or the possession of the first natural things.

Moral development need not end here, however. A further phase is possible in which arises a conception of the honorable (τὸ κάλον, honestum), which attaches to virtue. The honorable is good in its own right and not, or not merely, as an instrument (cf. *Fin.* 2.45). Corresponding to each view of the first natural impulse, then, there will be a view of the honorable, namely, as doing everything for the sake of its object, whether pleasure, freedom from suffering or the first natural things, regardless of whether one obtains it (19). The Stoics, of course, insist that only the honorable is good, which yields the view that virtue and virtuous activity alone are good, where the virtuous activity in question is occupied with the first natural things. Although the same move is available with regard to the other two conceptions of the honorable, only the position taken by the Stoa has actual adherents.

These three possible views are the first mentioned by Piso, who says in connection with them that "the difference among the ends of goods and evils is as great as that among initial natural principles" (19). This is misleading as there are other factors, namely whether one recognizes the honorable and takes it to be a good among others or the sole good, but it is true if we restrict our attention to views presupposing the same stage of moral development. Only now does Piso return (*rursum*) to the simple views that identify the highest good with the objects of the first natural impulses (19), before going on to describe a further three views which take the highest good to be a combination of one of the objects with virtue, one of which views, namely, that the highest good combines virtue with the first natural things, is Antiochus', which it is Piso's object to vindicate.

To summarize the case for Carneades' familiarity with ends of goods and evils: They feature prominently in the exposition of the *divisio*, which is presented by Cicero as concerned, in the first instance, with accounts of goods and evils. Because the end for the sake of which one chooses an action is inseparable from the end by conducing to which the action one chooses for its sake is good, we cannot be sure this emphasis belonged to the original context of the *divisio*, but the evidence strongly suggests that it did. There is, then, a good fit between the ends of goods and evils, on the one hand, and the *divisio* and the question about goods and evils that it seems to have been meant to address, on the other, and though their presence may be explained in other ways, one explanation is that they belonged with the *divisio* from the start.

A special merit of the idea of ends of goods and evils, on the interpretation defended here, is that it provides a link between standards of goods and evils and the end, conceived as the goal or that for the sake of which. The latter conception was not only of central importance in ancient ethical theory quite generally, but figured elsewhere in the debate between Carneades and the Stoa: in the controversy about whether the Stoics' peculiar conception of the goal as doing everything with a view to obtaining items the possession of which was no part of it did not commit them to postulating two ends of life. For unlike a pair of ends, one of goods, the other of evils, two ends for the sake of which would be a fatal defect in an ethical theory (Plutarch, *Comm. not.* 1070 F; Cicero, *Fin.* 3. 22).[47]

Acknowledgments

I owe more to Gisela Striker as a mentor and a friend than I can say; I'm grateful for the chance to help honor her here. I'm obliged for exceptionally stimulating comments to audiences at the Southern Association in Cambridge, Berlin, Budapest, Kings College London, Harvard, and Pittsburgh; to Jessica Moss, who called my attention to a vital passage in the *Protagoras*; and to Brad Inwood, Stephen Menn, and Mitzi Lee for extremely helpful written comments.

Bibliography

Algra, K. 1995. "Chrysippus, Carneades, Cicero: The Ethical *Divisiones* in Cicero's *Lucullus*." In *Assent and Argument: Studies in Cicero's Academic Books*, ed. B. Inwood and J. Mansfeld. Leiden. 107–39.

Allen, J. 2006. "Dialectic and Virtue in Plato's *Protagoras*." In *The Virtuous Life in Greek Ethics*, ed. B. Reis. Cambridge. 6–31.

Ambrose, P. 1965. "The Homeric Telos." *Glotta* 43: 38–62.

---

[47] See Striker 1986. Plutarch refers to τέλη, Cicero speaks of two *ultima bonorum*.

Annas, J. 2007. "Carneades' Classification of Ethical Theories." In *Pyrrhonists, Patricians, Platonizers: Hellenistic Philosophy in the Period 155-86 BC*, ed. A. M. Ioppolo and D. N. Sedley. Naples. 187-223.

Antoniadis, E. 1916. *Aristipp und die Kyrenaiker*. Diss. Göttingen.

Ast, F., 1835-9. *Lexicon Platonicum*. Leipzig.

Bett, R. trans. 2005. *Sextus Empiricus: Against the Logicians*. Cambridge.

Bonitz, H. 1870. *Index Aristotelicus*. Berlin, repr. Darmstadt, 1960.

Broadie, S. 2005. "On the Idea of the summum bonum." In *Virtue, Norms, and Objectivity:, Issues in Ancient and Modern Ethics*, ed. C. Gill. Oxford. 41-58.

Bury, R. G. trans. 1933-49. *Sextus Empiricus*. 4 vols. Cambridge, Mass.

Chantraine, P. 1968. *Dictionnaire étymologique de la langue grecque, histoire des mots*. Paris.

Cooper, J. M. 1999. "Pleasure and Desire in Epicurus." In *Reason and Emotion*, id. Princeton. 485-514.

Croiset, A. and Bodin, L. ed. 1948. *Platon oeuvres completes. Tome iii. pt. 1: Protagoras*. Paris.

Crönert, W. 1906. *Kolotes und Menedemos*. Leipzig.

Davies, J. ed. 1741. *Cicero: De finibus bonorum at malorum*, 2nd edn. Cambridge.

Décarie, V. trans. 1978. *Aristote: Éthique à Eudème*. Paris.

Diano, C. 1933. "Il Titolo 'De finibus bonorum et malorum.'" *Giornale critico della Filosofia italiana* 14: 167-9.

—— ed. 1946. *Epicuri Ethica*. Florence.

Dodds, E. R. ed. 1959. *Plato: Gorgias*. Oxford.

Dirlmeier, F. trans. 1963. *Aristoteles: Eudemische Ethik*. Berlin.

Döring, A. 1893. "Doxographisches zur Lehre vom τέλον." *Zeitschrift für Philosophie und philosophische Kritik 101*: 165-203.

Fischer, U. 1965. *Der Telosgedanke in Dramen des Aischylos: Ende, Ziel, Erfüllung Machtvollkommenheit*. Hildesheim.

Frisk, H. 1960-70. *Griechisches Etymologisches Wörterbuch*. Heidelberg.

Giannantoni, G. ed. 1990. *Socratis et Socraticorum Reliquiae*. 4 vols. Naples.

Giusta, M. 1964. *I Dossografi di Etica*. Turin.

Glucker, J. 1978. *Antiochus and the Late Academy*. Göttingen.

Guthrie, W. K. C. trans. 1956. *Plato: Protagoras and Meno*. London.

Hadot, P. 1994. "Liste commentée des oeuvres de Chrysippe (D.L. VII 189-202)." In *Dictionnaire des philosophes antiques*, ed. R. Goulet. Paris. vol. 2. 336-56.

Hartung, H.-J. 1970. *Ciceros's Methode bei der Uebersetzung griechischer philosophischen Termini*. Diss. Hamburg.

Hirzel, R. 1882. *Untersuchungen zu Cicero's philosophischen Schriften, Teil II: De finibus. De officiis*. Leipzig.

Holwerda, D. 1963. "ΤΕΛΟΣ." *Mnemosyne* 16: 337-63.

Indelli, G. and Tsouna-McKirahan, V. ed. 1995. [Philodemus] [*On Choices and Avoidances*]. Naples.

Jowett, B. trans. ed. 3 1892. *The Dialogues of Plato*. 5 vols. London.

Lévy, C. 1992. *Cicero Academicus: Recherches sur les Académiques et sur la philosophie cicéronienne*. Rome.

Lieberg, G. 1958. "Aristippo e la Scuola Cirenaica." *Rivista Critica di Storia della Filosofia* 13: 3-11.

Liscu, M., 1939. *Étude sur la langue de la philosophie moral chez Cicero*. Paris.

Lombardo, S. and Bell, K. trans. 1992. *Plato: Protagoras*. Indianapolis.

Lörcher, A. 1911. *Das Fremde und das Eigene in Cicero's Büchern De finibus bonorum et malorum und den Academica*. Halle.
Madvig, N. ed. 1876. *Cicero: De finibus bonorum et malorum*, 3rd edn. Copenhagen.
Mannebach, E. ed. 1961. *Aristippi et Cyrenaicorum fragmenta*. Leiden.
Martha, J. ed. 1928-30. *Ciceron: Des termes extrémes des biens et des mals*. Paris.
Merguet, H. 1887-94. *Lexicon zu den philosophischen Schriften Cicero's*. Jena.
——. 1905-6. *Handlexicon zu Cicero*. Leipzig.
Muret ["Muretus"], Marc-Antoine. 1791-1828. *Variarum lectionum libri XVIIII*. ed. F. A. Wolf and J. Fasi. Halle.
Philippson, R. 1913. Review of Lörcher, *Berliner philologische Wochenschrift* 33: 598-617.
—— 1939. "M. Tullius Cicero, Die Philosophische Schriften." *RE VII A*: 1104-92
Puglia E. ed. 1988. *Demetrio Lacone Aporie Testuali ed Esegetiche in Epicuro*. Naples.
Rackham, H. trans. 1931. *Cicero: De finibus*, 2nd edn. Cambridge, Mass.
——. trans. 1933. *Cicero: De natura Deorum, Academica*. Cambridge, Mass.
Reid, J. S. ed. 1885. *M. Tulli Ciceronis Academica*. London.
Robinson, R. 1964. *An Atheist's Values*. Oxford.
Schäublin, C. et al. trans. 1995. *Cicero Akademische Abhandlungen*. Hamburg.
Schiche, T. ed. 1915, *Cicero: De finibus bonorum et malorum*. Leipzig.
Schmid, W. ed. 1939. *Ethica Epicurea*. Leipzig.
Schofield, M. and Griffith, T. ed. and trans. 2009. *Plato: Gorgias, Menexenus and Protagoras*. Cambridge.
Striker, G. 1986. "Antipater, or the Art of Living." In *The Norms of Nature*, ed. M. Schofield and G. Striker. Cambridge. 185-204.
——. 1991. "Following Nature: A Study in Stoic Ethics." *OSAP* 9: 1-73.
——. 1995. "Cicero and Greek Philosophy." *Harvard Studies in Classical Philology* 97: 53-61.
——. 1996. *Essays on Hellenistic Epistemology and Ethics*. Cambridge.
Taylor, C. C. W. trans. 1991. *Plato: Protagoras*, 2nd edn. Oxford.
Tsouna, V. 1998. *The Epistemology of the Cyrenaic School*. Cambridge.
Usener, H. 1977. *Glossarium Epicureum*. Rome.
Warren, J. 2002. *Epicurus and Democritean Ethics: An Archaeology of Ataraxia*. Cambridge.
Woods, M. trans. 1992. *Aristotle: Eudemian Ethics Books I, II, and VIII*, 2nd ed. Oxford.
Woolf, R. trans. 2001. *Cicero: On Moral Ends*. Cambridge.

11

ANCIENT GOODS
THE *TRIA GENERA BONORUM* IN ETHICAL THEORY

Brad Inwood

I've given this paper the title "Ancient Goods," but my interest is somewhat narrower. Its focus will be the common Greek, and later Roman, way of classifying good things into three basic kinds: goods of the mind (or soul), goods of the body, and goods located outside the person, external goods. Examples are familiar: courage, intelligence, the virtues generally, but also attributes like a good memory and quick-wittedness; good health, physical integrity, athletic ability; wealth, high social status, the respect of others. Even a fleeting familiarity with ancient ethics will reveal how often this kind of classification arises. What is not so clear is how much this classification matters, how it is used, and what it contributed to debate about important problems in ethics. Though my concern is with the history of this classification, I think there is something of more than merely historical interest to observe, a kind of moral about moral theorizing which we can draw from the experience of the ancients.

In outline, here is the story I want to tell. The notion that human goods fall into these three kinds was an obvious one in Greek culture. Even non-philosophers thought of the human person as being a combination of soul and body, and it is obvious that things outside the boundaries of the person can be good or bad for him, at least in a loose sense of good. This notion was tidied up by philosophers, starting with Plato, who recognized it as a common-sense starting point for substantial ethical theorizing. Aristotle had a useful term for such generally held views that supply good inputs to philosophical debate—these are *endoxa* (views held by the many or the wise). Aristotle acknowledged Plato's use of this endoxic classification, and he used it himself. Plato and Aristotle both had substantial claims to make about the good and its role in ethics and metaphysics, but my view is that although they used the three-genus division of goods frequently it never became a decisive factor in the formation of their doctrines.

A much larger role was played by the so-called "use argument" and the closely related conditionalization thesis—about which there is a large literature. Here the idea is that things like money, physical health, even mental traits like excellent memory or quickness of wit, can be good or bad depending on how they are used—any "good" which can be misused or used to the disadvantage of the agent is not unconditionally good (and some, such as the Stoics, said that any such thing is not good at all) but only good when used well. Virtue turns out to be the only good which is free of this conditional status.

The Stoic view, that conditional goods aren't goods at all, narrowed the scope of good considerably: only virtue and actions or agents characterized by virtue could be considered good. This view had its roots in the Stoic reaction to some of the more Socratic parts of Plato's corpus, and once they had argued that good should be understood in this narrower sense they had to find a place for the goods of the body and external goods. These they recategorized as non-good advantages, the so-called "preferred indifferents" (DL 7.102–106). Such things as health and wealth are indifferent (since they are not good) in the sense that possession of them does not give us a greater share in *eudaimonia*—for they argued that success in a human life was determined by the way we *use* circumstances and resources, both favorable and unfavorable. But only one rather peculiar Stoic (Ariston of Chios) was prepared to claim that something that is indifferent to happiness is thereby normatively neutral. Stoics introduced a second scale of value, preferred-ness or dispreferred-ness, in order to capture the intuitions which their theory called into question and re-evaluated.

Despite this narrowing of the sense of good, which eventually had classificatory consequences, even the great Stoic Chrysippus, who worked in the third century BC, made allowance for the usefulness of the traditional endoxic way of talking about goods. That is, the Stoics did not make such a big deal about the categories of good (that is, that there would now in substance only be one) until later. And later on we do see an obsessive concern with the classification of goods as a principal focus of philosophical debate. I'm going to argue that we can identify *why* the endoxic classification used unapologetically by Plato and Aristotle and tolerated by Chrysippus became, rather suddenly, a vital issue to philosophers, a major locus of disagreement that served to define schools of thought one from another. We can identify the dialectical moment when the question of the number of kinds of good became central, and eventually far too central, to the conduct of ethical debate. It eventually helped to set a kind of intellectual fashion for categorizations and divisions into kinds which often distorted and rendered arid some areas of moral theorizing. It's not that careful analytical categorization is a bad thing—subtle distinctions are vitally useful. But even the ancients themselves saw, in the end, that technical categorization had gone beyond the bounds of intellectual utility to become a kind of obscurantism. And they protested, rightly in my opinion.

Here is one such voice of protest. Many centuries after Plato, perhaps around 175 AD, the polemical Platonist Atticus roared in outrage: "Go on, then, if you want, make your classifications and lay out your fancy distinctions of goods into three or four[1] or many kinds! These categorizations have no bearing on the issue [the issue in question is whether the most just man is happiest or not] and *this* isn't the way to bring us over to Plato."[2] He then castigates not only the three-way division I'm focusing on, but several other categorizations which he thinks of as equally misguided.[3]

His targets were the dividers and classifiers of ancient value theory, whom he thought had fallen into pettiness in their approach to classifications of the good. That he was not merely being crabby can be seen by considering not just the worst of the examples he cites—he is right to complain that working out a classification of the goods mapped onto the ten categories of Aristotle's *Organon* won't really help us to understand Plato's moral thought—but also some of the other divisions from later antiquity.

One place to look is in the curious handbooks of Stoic and Peripatetic moral theory from the first century BC or AD preserved in Stobaeus' *Eclogae* (*Ecl.*) or *Selections*.[4] After expounding Peripatetic moral theory, hanging the whole discussion on the three kinds of good (body, soul, externals), the Peripatetic author adds a curious appendix: at *Ecl.* 2.134–137 we are given a set of alternative divisions of the good; in fact, at least eight such divisions under the later heading "How many senses of good are there?" It would be tedious to go through them all (one paragraph after another begins "Here's another division..."). None of these distinctions is utterly useless, but modern discussions of ancient ethics typically ignore this material—not without cause. Here classification seems to be an end in itself.

And not just in the Peripatetic school. The later Stoics were also affected by this habit. One might think, after all, that since they held that there is really only one *genos* of the good we would be hard pressed to find Stoic classifications of the good along these lines. But the Stoic handbook also preserves for us a number of divisions of the good.[5] One of the strangest emulates the overworked tripartition Atticus complained about. At *Ecl.* 2.70.8 ff. a formal Stoic tripartition is set out,[6] and we learn that goods

---

[1] Although I won't discuss fourfold divisions of goods, Atticus isn't merely generalizing. See DL 3.101, [Aristotle] *Divisiones* ch. 23.

[2] Fr. 2, ch. 17 lines 122–125 Des Places.

[3] He mentions the division of goods into the honorable, the praiseworthy, those which are powers, those which are instrumentally useful; the division into "ends" and "non-ends"; and several others.

[4] On this, see Sharples (1983) and Hahm (1983).

[5] It is a reflection of their Socratic origins that the exposition of Stoic ethics opens with a reiteration of the division in the *Lysis* of all things into goods, bads, and things which are neither (*Ecl.* 2.57.18–20). Compare DL 7.61.

[6] The form of the partition was a matter of logical interest. At DL 7.62 it is suggested that the Stoic Krinis illustrated a *merismos* (partitioning) with an example from the division of goods: "A partitioning is an ordering of a genus into topics, as Krinis says; for example, of goods, some are

are divided into three groups: those of the soul, those that are external, and those that are neither of the soul nor external.[7]

> Of good things, some are in the soul, some external, and some neither in the soul nor external. In the soul are the virtues and virtuous conditions and in general praiseworthy activities. External are friends and acquaintances and things like that. Neither in the soul nor external are virtuous men and in general those who have the virtues.

This tripartition is reported elsewhere. Sextus Empiricus (*PH* 3.180–181) reports the Stoic tripartition (he actually called it a *trigeneia*, the technical term used elsewhere for the Peripatetic theory) of goods into those of the soul (virtues), externals (such as the good man who is also a friend), and those which are neither in the soul nor external (such as the good man in relation to himself). Unsurprisingly, Sextus presents this as a rejoinder to or counterpart of the Peripatetic tripartition into goods of the body, soul, and externals.[8] A distinct Stoic tripartition given just a few pages earlier (at *PH* 3.171)[9] is more integrally Stoic, in that all three senses turn on the distinctive Stoic and Socratic definition in terms of utility.

> In one sense they say that the good is that by which one can be benefited (this is the most ultimate sense of good and is virtue); in another sense it is that with respect to which one happens to be benefited (for example virtue and virtuous actions); and in a third sense it is that which is able to be of benefit, i.e., virtue and virtuous action and the good man and one's friend and gods and good *daimones*. So the second meaning of good includes the first and the third includes the second.

But it is hard not to recognize in this forced subordination to a tripartite division the kind of "scholastic" presentation that Atticus complains about.

I have picked out a couple of Peripatetic and Stoic examples, but this kind of classification was important enough in the Platonist tradition that another expositor of Plato, Alcinous, an approximate contemporary of Atticus, devoted a chapter (27) of his *Handbook of Platonism* for teachers of Platonism to discussing Plato's classifications of

---

of the soul and some are bodily." We cannot be certain that the example came from Krinis. It is likely that the illustration is endoxic rather than a statement of Krinis' own view.

[7] Similarly put at DL 7.95.
[8] Compare *M* 11.46.
[9] See also *M* 11.25–27.

the good.[10] There are many passages in Plato that could be mustered to support the view that Plato was a divider and classifier of goods, as many later Platonist philosophers noticed[11]—but at the same time Plato was most famous for the idea that there was a single Form of the Good.

It is necessary to step back and ask why this was such an important issue for the Platonists. The key lies in another remark that Atticus makes. He complains that treating all three kinds of goods as necessary for happiness *ruins* Plato's theory, "stripping away the sufficiency of virtue" for happiness.[12] This is an allusion to the most important fact about ancient theories of the good—the relationship of the good to happiness. I think it is safe to say that we moderns have relatively broad notions of what kinds of values contribute to a flourishing life, but the ancients tended to regard everything that goes into the good life as being a good or being closely related to *a* or *the* good.

This is perhaps clearest in the branch of ancient moral theory that I am neglecting in this paper, hedonism. Epicureans and other hedonists held that the only good is pleasure and that maximization of that good is the key to a happy life. This foreshadows some forms of consequentialism. Although the goal of pleasure maximization became a nonstarter for mainstream ancient ethics (despite Plato's flirtation with it in the *Protagoras* and Aristotle's evident sympathies in *EN* 10) it is perhaps the clearest example of the widespread ancient notion that the ultimate state of personal fulfillment and success, *eudaimonia* or happiness, was the result of maximizing our hold on the good. The particular identification of the good was debatable, but the idea that possession of the good is the key to happiness became so pervasive that it was almost universally taken for granted.[13]

Sometimes this assumption emerges almost incidentally, as in Plato's *Symposium* at 205a1, where it is uncontroversial that happy people are happy in virtue of *possessing* good things.[14] At other times it is a striking programmatic assumption, as in the initial stages of the protreptic argument in the *Euthydemus*.[15] In 278e the young Clinias is asked whether it isn't the case that being happy, doing well (the goal of all human

---

[10] According to Alcinous, Plato acknowledged that the various things considered good by us humans are good in virtue of their *participation* in the "highest and most honorable good." The view he takes deserves consideration in its own right; see Annas (1999) 43–44, and below.

[11] See Dillon (1977) 9. Philo of Alexandria also took the doctrine that there are three kinds of good for granted (see *Quod Det.* 7). At *Quaestiones in Genesim* 3.16 Philo claims that the doctrine of three kinds of "perfections" or goods had its origin in scripture and then was picked up with approval by philosophers; Aristotle and the other Peripatetics are singled out.

[12] Ch. 20, p. 45, 129–142 Des Places.

[13] See *De Finibus* 5.83.

[14] I thank Ákos Brunner for the reminder.

[15] I have learned a great deal from Julia Annas' extensive discussion of this text in Annas (1999), especially ch. 2 and pp. 35–43, and from John Cooper's discussion in "Aristotle and the Goods of Fortune," chapter 13 in Cooper (1999) (originally published in *Philosophical Review* 94 [1985] 173–196). Cooper's discussion has a significantly different aim than mine and makes several

beings), depends on the possession of many good things. He agrees, of course, and in what follows Socrates induces the youth to agree that it is not just the possession of "good things" that assures happiness but rather the proper use of them; his argument culminates at 281d–282a. This is the main text (the other important text is at *Meno* 87–89) in which Plato's Socrates develops the "use argument" which determines so much of the substantial ancient theorizing about goods.

Aristotle too reveals the centrality of the connection between goods and happiness at *Eudemian Ethics* 1214a30–33: "being happy and living a blessed and noble life would consist most of all in three things, those which seem to be most worthy of choice. For some people say that *phronēsis* is the greatest good, some say that virtue is, and some that pleasure is." The debate about happiness, as Aristotle sets it out, makes a quick transition to a debate about the comparative magnitude of goods.[16] To us that may seem a hasty transition, but it illustrates how debates about the nature and classification of the good came to be so central in mainstream ancient ethics.[17]

This persistent idea turns up again centuries later in the work of the anthologist Stobaeus, who made sure to have the following text copied into the collection of useful extracts which he compiled for his son in the fifth century AD. It may have been taken from the work of a late first century BC Platonist named Eudorus, who worked in Alexandria.[18] At one point (*Ecl.* 2 p. 46) "Eudorus" said:

> The Stoics say, by way of definition, that the *telos* [the goal of life achievement of which is termed happiness] is that for the sake of which everything is done appropriately but which itself is not done for the sake of anything else;[19] and they put the point this way too, that it is that for the sake of which other things

---

important philosophical and exegetical claims. I do not agree with his claim on p. 305 that these passages of the *Euthydemus* and *Meno* seem "to be the origin of Aristotle's and later Greek philosophy's tripartition of (so-called) goods." One aim of the present paper is to show that the situation, even in Plato and Aristotle, is considerably more complicated.

[16] See 1214a34–b6.

[17] The obviousness of this position is illustrated by the fact that even Aristotle's rival Speusippus shared it: Clement reports (*Strom.* 2.22.133) that one of his definitions of happiness was simply "the possession of good things." The other definition reported here is more subtle: a complete or perfect condition with respect to things which are according to nature. (See on Xenocrates below.) In Aristotle the issue about how various kinds of goods contribute to happiness sometimes appears as a discussion of the relative choiceworthiness of various things, but this way of addressing the question seems distinct.

[18] Göransson (1995) 188 challenges the received opinion reflected in Dillon (1977) 122–126, that this stretch of text should be attributed to Eudorus. Though sympathetic to Göransson's trenchant historical skepticism, I think that if the author was not Eudorus it was someone else of that era rather than a much later writer.

[19] This is a Stoic recasting of Aristotle's position in *EN* 1.

are done but itself for the sake of nothing else; and again, that it is that to which everything that is done appropriately in life has reference but itself to nothing else. But the more recent Peripatetics, followers of Critolaus, say that the goal is that which is compounded of[20] all the goods (and this means of all three kinds of goods). But this is not correct. For it is not the case that all goods are components of the *telos*. For bodily goods are not and neither are the goods which come from external things, but only [goods which are] activities of the virtue of the soul. It would have been better to say "exercised" in place of "compounded" in order to indicate that it is virtue's capacity to *use* things which is at stake.[21]

Critolaus, the key figure in the text just cited, was head of the Peripatetic school in the mid-second century BC; his opinion on happiness was striking, influential, and often reported.[22] It was repeated by Clement of Alexandria (*Strom.* 2.21.129) in blunter form: "Critolaus, himself also a Peripatetic, said that the *telos* is the completion of a life which flows smoothly according to nature [a Stoic-sounding characterization of the *telos*], indicating thereby the three-kind completeness [*tēn ek tōn triōn genōn sumplēroumenēn trigenikēn teleiotēta*] composed of the three kinds [of goods]." This was surely not actually Aristotle's considered view,[23] but Critolaus' success in imposing this interpretation on his school is clear. In Diogenes Laertius' life of Aristotle (at DL 5.30), we read that Aristotle:

took the view that the goal is the use of virtue in a complete life. And he said that happiness is a completion [*sumplērōma*] made up of three goods: goods of the soul, which he also says are first in their impact; second, from bodily goods

---

[20] Literally: filled up with, *sumpeplērōmenon*. For the criticism of Critolaus, see below on *Ecl.* 2.126.12–127.2.

[21] The conception of virtue as that which *uses* other alleged goods is found in Plato's *Meno* (87–89) and *Euthydemus*. In the *Euthydemus* Socrates concludes at 281de that the things initially called good are not actually good, but rather that only the wisdom that uses them well is good (see above). See Annas (1991) and Annas (1999) ch. 2. See also Reshotko (2006) ch. 5.

[22] At *TD* 5.51 Cicero reports that Critolaus was concerned with the relative weightings of the three goods in one's life, using the metaphor of a scale; Critolaus is being criticized for his arbitrary assignment of "weights" to the various goods, and it is clear that his crucial contribution was the inclusive doctrine that one should fill out one's life with all three kinds of good in some proportion or other. The best recent survey of later Peripatetic views of happiness can be found in Sharples (2007) esp. pp. 627–633. There is no doubt that the debate within the Peripatetic school was stimulated by reflection on Aristotle's own ambivalent position (see *EN* 1.10, 1100b25 ff.). For further discussion see Russell (2010), White (1990), White (2002), Inwood (2002).

[23] That the goods are "parts" (*merē*) of happiness was hinted at as an *endoxon* in Aristotle's *EE* 1214b24–27.

(health and strength and good looks and so on); third, from external goods, wealth and good birth and reputation and similar things. And he said that virtue is not sufficient for happiness, since it needs in addition bodily and external goods, given that the wise man will be unhappy both if he suffers physical hardship and if he is impoverished, and also in similar situations. But vice is sufficient for unhappiness, even if he has the best possible supply of bodily and external goods.[24]

Note that here the idea that *use* is the goal reflects, perhaps rather weakly, Aristotle's ideas about activity according to virtue, but it is occluded by the simpler idea of filling up or possession of goods in the three categories. This move is Critolaus' handiwork and much of what follows below is an attempt to understand what Critolaus was up to and the impact of his claim on succeeding generations of philosophers.[25] To put the matter crudely, we will have three positions: Plato and his followers, Aristotle and the Peripatetics, and Stoicism.

These three Socratic schools defined the field of debate in ethics, at least from the time of Carneades and Critolaus as well as the Stoic Antipater (mid-second century BC). On the question of goods, the Stoics took one extreme position: there is only one basic kind of good, virtue and what "participates" in it.[26] Aristotle's school took the other sharply defined position; there are three kinds of good, those of the body, those of the soul, and external goods. And Plato seems to have been up for grabs.[27] Sometimes

---

[24] As Mansfeld (1992) 147–149, esp. n. 48, documents, this view had become the stereotyped Aristotelian position by the time of Cicero and Seneca. But he does not establish that this was already the standard Peripatetic view in Chrysippus' day, as he claims on p. 149. At SVF 3.474 = Origen *Contra Celsum* 8.51, Chrysippus certainly refers to the competing and false view that there are three kinds of goods, but there is no reason to think that he treated this as a *Peripatetic* view. (Cf. Cicero *TD* 4.62.) For all we know he regarded this as the common property of Plato, Aristotle, and their followers. See also the extended discussion of Peripatetic doxography about the good attributed to Arius Didymus in Moraux (1973).

[25] Note the impact of Critolaus' way of framing the issues (in terms of *sumplērōma*) on Stoic discussions. Even when the debate with Peripatetics is not obviously at issue, this terminology appears in discussions of Stoic ethics. See, for example, Sextus *M* 11.30 = SVF 3.73, *Ecl.* 2.72.5 = SVF 3.106, and DL 7.97 = SVF 3.107. Critolaus' impact on Stoicism was complex. In SVF 3.73 it is the good which is said to fill up happiness. In SVF 3.106 and 107 the virtues are said to fill up happiness by producing and completing it, and by being its parts; they are *telika* goods. Since there seem to be several ways for the Stoics to indicate the special role of virtue in producing happiness, the adoption of a term otherwise known as distinctive of Critolaus is striking.

[26] See Sextus *M* 11.76 and 184; compare the definition of *kalon* at DL 7.101 (remembering that only the *kalon* is *agathon*). Decisively: *Ecl.* 2.101.5–7. The most "official" Stoic definitions of good all turn on the Socratic concept of "benefit." See, e.g., DL 7.94, *M* 11.22, 40, and *Ecl.* 2.69.

[27] Modern interpreters differ on this point. Annas (1999, ch. 2), for example, argues forcefully that Plato should be read in essentially the Stoic manner; someone concerned more centrally

he is treated as a one-essential-good theorist (as in the eyes of Eudorus, Atticus, or indeed of Antipater the Stoic, who wrote a work entitled *That only the honourable is good according to Plato*) and sometimes as a three-kinds theorist.[28] Plato's dialogues are sufficiently variegated that there was ample opportunity to find and defend any number of "opinions" or *doxai* in his works. Let me illustrate this briefly with a text from "Eudorus" (see above) recently put in the spotlight by Julia Annas.[29]

> Plato has many voices, but not, as some think, many opinions. He divided the good in many ways. Into two by genus: some goods are divine and some are human. He called the virtues in the soul divine goods, and he called good conditions in the bodily part and prosperity from external sources human goods. He divided it into three by location. For you might say that of goods, some are virtues in the soul, some are virtues in the body, and some are virtues in externals (i.e., good conditions and prosperity). And into five by species. For first he says that the good is the form itself, which is divine and separable. Second it is the compound of *phronēsis* and pleasure, which some think that Plato holds to be the goal of human life. Third is *phronēsis* itself by itself; fourth is the compound of knowledge and the crafts; and fifth is pleasure itself by itself. He uses these distinctions especially in book 1 of the *Laws* and in the *Philebus*.
>
> Otherwise: only the honorable is good, in so far as nothing which exists is good unless it participates in virtue (just as a torch and iron participate in fire, without which nothing is said to be hot unqualifiedly);[30] but in conjunction with the other goods, the three kinds, two (bodily goods along with externals) [are good] insofar as they participate in virtue. For just as the substance of the moon is unillumined by itself but is illuminated by participation in the light from the sun, in this way only that which participates in virtue is good. For the ability to benefit comes to be present in human things because of the divine. (*Ecl.* 2.55.5–21)[31]

---

with, say, moral psychology (such as Lorenz 2006) will probably bracket Plato more closely with Aristotle than the Stoics. My concern here is only with the range of interpretive possibilities open in the ancient context, and on this point the disagreement between Antipater and Antiochus is decisive; see also the following note.

[28] See the remarks at Dillon (1977) 9 and above. He identifies Eudorus and Atticus as proponents of the view that only goods of the soul are needed for happiness and Antiochus and Plutarch as exponents of the more Peripatetic interpretation of Plato; see also pp. 123–125 on Eudorus, 197 and 360 on Plutarch. Alcinous (in *Handbook* ch. 27) also has a complicated and nuanced view.

[29] Annas (1999) ch. 1.

[30] Compare DL 7.103 and *PH* 3.179.

[31] See also 2.49.25–50.1 and Annas (1999) 13.

This seems to be an attempt to explicate Plato's views, especially those of the *Laws* and *Philebus*, in terms of the standard Stoic definitions of good as virtue or what participates in virtue[32] or as that which is such as to provide benefit. How accurate an account of Plato's views it gives us remains debatable.

It is interesting that in the earlier Eudoran text the author defended a complex view (there are three kinds but only one is a *component* of the *telos*) but does so by drawing on an Aristotelian formulation about the virtuous life, one which exploits the notion of "activities." And he does so after reporting a Stoic view which he does not feel he needs to criticize. Similarly, the Stoic Seneca a few decades later reports (at *Ep.* 85.18) that both Speusippus and Xenocrates *denied* the proposition that only the *kalon* is good, which is the strict notion of good associated with Stoicism and which Antipater, at least, claimed was also Plato's view. This is the landscape of later ancient moral theory—more fluid than you would expect if you assume that school loyalty straightforwardly determines people's philosophical positions. Especially so when Plato's doctrines are at issue,[33] but even in the case of Aristotle and his school.

Both the tight connection of the good with happiness and the enthusiasm for classification of goods which seems characteristic of later ancient thought had roots in the fourth century BC; so did the basic idea that goods fall into three kinds, for in one form or another it is adumbrated in both Plato and Aristotle. To illustrate this, we can turn to a few more texts which tell us in a formal way about the "divisions" of many kinds of things.[34] There are two curious texts, the first of unknown authorship but transmitted in the Aristotelian corpus, called the "Aristotelian Divisions', and the second a chapter from Diogenes Laertius' *Life of Plato*. Chapter 1 of the Aristotelian text gives us clear doctrine:

> Of goods, some are in the soul, some in the body, and some are external. For example, justice and practical wisdom and courage and self-control and such

---

[32] The language of participation is, of course, originally Plato's. But the Stoic adoption of it altered its sense and we see this here. The case of Alcinous ch. 27 perhaps reflects Stoic *and* Platonic influences, and is worthy of fuller treatment.

[33] It is worth recalling that the early Academic Crantor got people to think about the relative value of various goods with a kind of parable (Sextus *M* 11.52–59). We are to picture a public theater where various goods come forward to make speeches on their own behalf, each arguing that it provides the greatest benefit to human beings. The reported order, in Greek eyes, was courage, health, pleasure, wealth. (That wealth came last in line was also the view in Plato's *Laws*; see 697b, 743de, 870ab.) Sextus contrasts this Academic view with that of the Stoics who deny that any of these candidates is a genuine good, on the strength of the "use" argument (*M* 11.61) which the Stoics had learned from Socratic dialogues (such as the *Euthydemus* and *Meno*).

[34] Perhaps this philosophical activity was encouraged by Plato's own emphasis late in his career of the importance of collection and division. But it was certainly a pervasive and (to me, at any rate) often irritatingly formalistic genre of philosophical analysis.

things are in the soul. And beauty and good condition and health and strength are in the body. And friends and the happiness of one's fatherland and wealth are among the externals. So there are three forms of good, some in the soul, some in the body and some external.

Diogenes Laertius, at 3.80–81, begins as follows, "According to Aristotle, Plato divided things in the following manner" and continues with a verbatim quotation of the text we know from the Aristotelian *Divisions*. It is, I think, more than an interesting quirk of later ancient philosophical scholarship that an identical division is given by an anonymous Peripatetic source for Aristotle (and the same doctrine is attributed to the Peripatetics at *Ecl*. 2.124 ff and 136) and by Diogenes Laertius (on Aristotle's authority) for Plato. But what exactly was going on?[35] A number of possibilities suggest themselves. But the obvious one, to my mind, is that someone in the early Academy[36] settled on this bit of doctrine as one shared by Plato and Aristotle.[37]

Despite his own tendency to classify and divide, Aristotle himself never put the point about three kinds of goods as crisply as the later reports about his views suggest. Nevertheless, we find indications of what inspired this bit of historical tidiness.[38] There are two important passages in Aristotle's treatises: First, in the *Nicomachean Ethics* at 1.8 and second in the *Politics* at 7.1. Here is what Aristotle himself has to say:

> EN 1098b9–16 One must investigate happiness not only on the basis of the conclusion and the premises of the argument, but also on the basis of what is *said* about it. For all facts agree with what is true, but they[39] quickly come into disharmony with falsehood. Well then, good things are distributed into three, and some are said to be external, some of the body and some of the soul; so we say that those of the soul are most important and are especially good, and we align the actions and activities of the soul with the soul....
>
> *Pol*. 1323a21–35. Supposing, then, that much of what is said about the best life is well said, even some of what is said in exoteric works, it is also at this point proper to make use of these claims. Really, no one would make any objection to

---

[35] This oddity is noted but not discussed by Mansfeld (1992) 61.
[36] Possibly Xenocrates, a hunch based on his proneness to the use of divisions and on the information provided by Clement at *Strom*. 2.22.133 (see below).
[37] See Karamanolis (2006).
[38] Note that Clement claims that the doctrine of three kinds of good was introduced into philosophy (perhaps from the civic realm) by the Peripatetics (see *Strom*. 2.7.34), a point perhaps anticipated by Philo at *Quod Det*. 7.
[39] Omitting the words *t'alethes*.

one division, at least; there are three parts of the best life (external things, bodily things, and things in the soul) and blessedly happy people must have them all. For no one would say that someone is blessedly happy if he has no portion of courage or temperance or justice or wisdom but is afraid of bugs that fly at him, stops at nothing if he desires to eat or drink, and will ruin his dearest friends for the sake of a nickel; and similarly if with regard to his intellectual capacities he is as mindless and erroneous as a child or a madman. But virtually everyone would concede these claims, though they differ over the degree or about which factor is more important.

Apparently this tripartition is an *endoxon*—"everyone would concede these claims"—and it is accordingly found in *exōterikoi logoi*[40] and not necessarily Aristotle's own settled view.[41]

Whatever we make of such "exoteric" *logoi*, it is clear that Aristotle's own theory cannot be reduced to such a simple classification.[42] Not only does it gloss over the crucial role of activity in his conception of happiness, but even the threefold classification

---

[40] Its status as an *endoxon* is confirmed by the way the notion is adopted in Plato's *Laws* and by the use of the tripartition of goods as an organizing principle in rhetorical handbooks. See, e.g., Theon *Progymnasmata* 109–110, Cicero *Topica* 83, *Part. Orat.* 38, 74, *De Inventione* 2.177, *De Oratore* 3.116 (by implication); also Aristotle *Rhet.* 1360b19–30; book 3 of Aristotle's *Topics* (see esp. 118a31–33) makes it clear that similar topics about kinds and degrees of choiceworthiness and the good were part of dialectical discussion in the fourth century BC.

[41] In fact, we do not know what works are referred to here, so it is difficult to know how committed Aristotle himself is to the classification as stated. It is worth comparing *EN* 1.13, 1102a26–27: "in the *exōterikoi logoi* too some things are said about the soul sufficiently well, and we must put them to use." In both passages the theory in question (nature of the soul, classification of the goods) is being applied to politics; *some* things are said well enough in the exoteric *logoi*, and so they are to be put to use. In both passages Aristotle avoids full endorsement of the view he exploits; so too with allusion to exoteric *logoi* elsewhere in the *EN* (1140a3). However, at *Metaphysics* 1076a28 he may, as Annas (1976) 136 notes ad loc., be referring to his own work or to that of others; the term *tethrulētai* suggests the latter, to me at least. It is similarly unclear at *Physics* 217b31. Yet sometimes Aristotle implies that the exoteric *logoi* do represent his own views (as at *Politics* 1278b31–32). The fact that exoteric as well as philosophical works are mentioned together at *EE* 1217b22, in connection with Plato's Form of the Good, suggests that the division may have been used as a dialectical premise in an argument against the sort of univocity which a Form of good would demand; cf. Plutarch at *Adv. Colotem* 1115bc.

[42] The simplification which turns this into an Aristotelian doctrine rather than an *endoxon* may be under way already at *Magna Moralia* 1.3 (1184b1–6): it is difficult to tell how the *MM* (here inspired by *EN* 1098b10–16) intends the description of the *diairesis* into three to be taken. See also *MM* 1202a30–35 where the author adds trigeneric language to a point made without it at the corresponding part in *EN* (7.4). Note too that in the discussion of luck at *MM* 2.8 the author claims that external goods are *necessary* for happiness (1206b33, 1207b17–18). This is clearly a development of the weaker position taken by Aristotle himself in *EN* 1; the process of firming up

of goods is not his only "official" position. In the opening sentences of book 2 of his *Eudemian Ethics* (*EE* 1218b31–37) Aristotle announces a fresh starting point and says:

> All goods are either external or in the soul, and the more choiceworthy of these are those in the soul, according to the division we make also in the exoteric works. For *phronēsis* and virtue and pleasure are in the soul and *everyone thinks* that some or all of these are the *telos*. Of goods in the soul, some are conditions or capacities and others are activities and changes.

Here the division is twofold; the significance of omitting bodily goods from the classification is not clear. This is presented as an endoxic classification, but Aristotle does not distance himself from it; nevertheless his commonest division is the threefold division into goods of the body, soul, and externals. And it is this threefold division of good things that, according to Diogenes Laertius, Aristotle attributed to Plato.

One economical way of accounting for all these facts is to suppose that Aristotle knew that this view about good things was widely accepted in his place and time and believed as well that it was shared by Plato himself. And not perhaps unreasonably.[43] In book 1 of the *Laws* (631b–d) divine and human goods are distinguished, and elsewhere in that sprawling work the division into body, soul, and externals appears.[44] At *Laws* 697b the notion comes closest to being a "doctrine"; here the speaker ranks valuable things in the order soul (virtues), body, externals (those "said to be about" property and money); the endoxic character of the classification and ranking is evident—which does not, of course, mean that Plato would not himself in some measure endorse it.[45]

---

exploratory remarks by Aristotle into doctrines is clearly under way. Cf. Cooper (1999) 293–294 and n. 5.

[43] Though Atticus would surely have disagreed. See Karamanolis (2006) 154–163.

[44] It appears as a virtually formal doctrine in the *Laws* at 697a–c, echoed at 743c–e and 870ab; this may have guided the reading of *Laws* 631b–d. Moreover, as Ryan Balot points out, in the proem to *Laws* 5 things of value are rank-ordered into the soul and its states, the body, and external advantages (such as money and other possessions). See Annas (1999) 48. In earlier works too there are places where Plato or his spokesman advances views which seem to presuppose the validity of some such division, even though it is not presented as a settled doctrine. For example, at *Republic* 491c wealth, good connections, beauty, and physical strength are referred to as *legomena agatha*—language similar to that used by Aristotle.

[45] The Athenian is discussing the policy of assigning honors and dishonors as a strategy for ensuring civic success. The most honorable or valuable things are called *ta peri tēn psuchēn agatha*, second place is held by *ta peri to sōma kala kai agatha*; third place goes to *ta peri tēn ousian kai chrēmata legomena*. Although the classification into body, soul, externals is clear, it is not clear that what is being divided are just goods, as is the case when the *endoxon* settles down as a firm school doctrine.

Moreover, the ubiquity of the body/soul polarity and of the idea, most prominent in the *Gorgias*,[46] that there are parallel crafts that care for the interests of the soul and the body (together with the recognition that *oikonomikē* is the craft of household, i.e., wealth management); and the salience of Socrates' claim in the *Alcibiades* 132bc[47] that there are three things people should care for (soul, body, and possessions such as money)—these facts make it, at the very least, highly plausible that Plato agreed with the *endoxon* that there are distinguishable goods of the body, the soul, and things outside the body-soul compound.

Whatever texts were drawn on, it seems clear that one line of Platonic interpretation, a very early one at that, did group Plato with Aristotle as a proponent of the *tria genera* doctrine. This historical claim is clearly behind the statement at *Ecl.* 2.56.8–9 that "Aristotle himself also adopted a triad of goods, just as Plato does in some places."[48]

A more complicated view about Plato is attributed to Xenocrates (Clement *Strom.* 2.22.133):

> Xenocrates of Chalcedon says that happiness is the possession of one's proper virtue and the ability which serves this virtue. Next, as regards what it is in, he says plainly that this is the soul. As regards what produces this state, it is the virtues. As regards its component parts, it is noble actions and excellent conditions, dispositions, movements, and relationships [of the soul]. As regards its necessary conditions, it is bodily and external things. For Xenocrates' associate Polemo plainly means that happiness is self-sufficiency in all good things or in the greatest number and most important of them. At any rate, he holds the doctrine that without virtue one would never be happy, but without bodily and external things virtue is self-sufficient for happiness.

Xenocrates and Polemo presupposed the doctrine of three kinds of goods but still preserved a special role for goods of the soul. The less pluralistic way of interpreting

---

[46] Which also contains a passage (467e) in which Socrates induces Polus to agree that wisdom (soul), health (body), and wealth (external) are good—an uncontroversial view easily agreed to by Socrates' conventional-minded interlocutor. The endoxic character of this list is noted (not in these terms) by Reshotko (2006) 97. At *Euthydemus* 281 that wisdom, health, beauty, and wealth are on the list of goods.

[47] I am grateful to Gábor Betegh for pointing out the pertinence of this passage.

[48] Wachsmuth's notes suggest that he thinks that *kata tous topous* refers to various places where Aristotle holds this position. But word order and general sense suggest that the reference is to Plato.

Plato is also found in later texts, such as the ecclesiastical writer Hippolytus (*Refutation of All Heresies* 1.20.5):

> Anyway, Plato says that in reality [*ontōs*] the only goods are those in the soul and that these are sufficient for happiness. But Aristotle introduces the "trigeneric" nature [*trigeneia*] of the goods and says that the wise man is not complete if he does not also have the goods of the body and external goods. And these are beauty, strength, good perception, sound physical condition. Externals are wealth, high birth, reputation, power, peace, and friendship. The internal goods of the soul, as Plato too thought, are intelligence, self-control, justice, and courage.

Hippolytus does go on to allude to the Stoics, but in his view the protagonists in debate are Plato and Aristotle. Hippolytus, then, should be grouped with unifiers like Atticus. Note that by the time Hippolytus came to write, the doctrine that goods came in three *genera* was so familiar and so standard a part of debate that a distinct tag had been coined for it: the *trigeneia* of goods.[49]

In later antiquity, then, the doctrine of the three kinds of goods was either treated as a doctrine common to the two great exponents of the Socratic tradition (in contrast to the Stoics who denied it) or as a distinctive feature of the Peripatetic tradition.[50] The differences of opinion about Plato's view are shaped by the interests of those reporting them: if what is at stake is a listing of things *called* good or *treated as* good in any sense whatsoever, then there is no difficulty in putting Plato[51] in the camp of those who recognize three broad kinds of goods. But if the focus is on the role of genuine goods as components of the happy life, then it is more plausible and attractive to distinguish Plato's view from that of Aristotle and his followers and to argue that the

---

[49] It is also used by Sextus at *PH* 3.181; also Eusebius *P.E.* 11.4.1. Other shorthand expressions had been used as well, such as the *trias tōn agathōn* in Arius Didymus at *Ecl.* 2.56 or the simpler *to ek tōn triōn genōn* at *Ecl.* 2.46; cf. Clement *Strom.* 2.129.10. For all of this material see Mansfeld (1992) 147–149 and Moraux (1973).

[50] That Peripatetics were strongly associated with the *tria genera* view is also confirmed by the almost casual remark of Seneca at *Ep.* 88.5, which shows that by the mid-first century AD the notion that goods fell into these *tria genera* was a signature doctrine that established Peripatetic credentials all by itself, just as the doctrine that "all things are uncertain" was the brand label for Academics and *lathe biōsas* was for Epicureanism. The evidence of Cicero (see below) shows that Antiochus held this view of the Peripatetics, though he also thought that Plato and the rest of the so-called Old Academy shared the Peripatetic view.

[51] This may also apply to Philo, who says (*Quod. Det.* 7) that Moses embraced the doctrine *pros...politeian mallon ē pros alētheian* and that the only truly perfect good is one composed of a fusion of the three interdependent kinds of good (bodily, psychic, external).

correct Platonic view is that the only *true* good (that is, the only good that makes a difference to human happiness) is an optimal condition of the soul. Either he shares the Stoic position that there is only one good and that possession of this good makes you happy; or he holds a version of the Peripatetic view, that there are three kinds of goods and that all are needed for complete happiness, at least in some degree; or he acknowledges the *endoxon* that there are three kinds of good but thinks that only goods of the soul contribute to human perfection and happiness, while the other goods are merely instrumental, in fact dispensable. Plato's philosophical position can always be located within the debate between Peripatetics and Stoics, though of course it is always open to a reader of Plato to revert directly to his texts and present a fresh appraisal of the situation. This is what the Platonist Alcinous *claims* to have done in chapter 27 of the *Handbook*. Let me take just a brief moment to consider how he does this.[52]

Alcinous begins with the claim that the greatest good is difficult to discover (alluding to the introduction of the Form of the good in the *Republic*, esp. 504e–505b) and therefore treated as esoteric (alluding to the lost lecture on the good). His claim, though, is that careful study of his writings will show that the good for human beings lies in "knowledge and contemplation of the primal good, which one may term God and the primal intellect" (tr. Dillon).[53] Things that are merely opined to be good by human beings are not truly good, but are called so because they participate in the primary good. This ought to mean that they are derivatively and defectively good, as are the participants in any Form, but an even stricter limitation on their goodness is imposed when Alcinous adds the claim that things like health, beauty, wealth, and so on are only good insofar as their use is connected to virtue—this is a clear allusion to the "use" doctrine of the *Euthydemus*, a text also admired and used by Stoics. When Alcinous insists that human, mortal goods (the term from *Laws* 631b) do not produce happiness, he aligns himself with the stricter view about Plato, the one invoked by the Stoics who enlisted Plato on their side in the "happiness" debate of the late Hellenistic period. After invoking *Phaedrus* 248b and *Republic* 7's doctrines on education, including the simile of the cave, Alcinous again insists that the true good, the only thing sufficient for happiness, is knowledge and contemplation of the divine (which seems to be equated somehow with virtue in general).[54]

---

[52] See also Annas (1999) 42–45.

[53] Alcinous seems to fall into the very trap that Socrates warns about in *Republic* 505bc, that the good can scarcely be knowledge of the good. But he hedges, specifying that human good is knowledge of primary good, i.e., of god in his identity as the primary intellect (a hint at the Platonist identification of Platonic god and the unmoved mover, which is hardly something one could learn from Plato's writings directly).

[54] Alcinous seems to get a bit muddled when he adds that the goods by participation fall into two groups, the human and the divine (*Laws* 631b), since the divine goods should be the true goods while only the merely mortal goods should be deemed human goods.

Alcinous is not, obviously, just expounding what one can see in or construct out of Plato's writings, but rather struggling to square the doctrine of the good with the idea that the human *telos* is likeness to god. For only thus can one make sense of the notion that human happiness can be achieved only through divine goods, while human good on its own does not yield human happiness. The "commonly accepted goods, such as wealth and monarchy on a grand scale and bodily health and physical strength and beauty," do not yield happiness, which is only possible when human beings have the knowledge that constitutes virtue. Alcinous is unclear, I think, on whether these "commonly accepted goods" or goods of opinion are to be identified with those which are "separated from" and have "no participation in the essence of the first principle," but he is squarely on the side of those who hold that there is only one kind of *genuine* good. The reconciliation of this unitary conception of the good with the *tria genera* doctrine comes by way of a rather fuzzy invocation of the notion of participation juxtaposed with the *Laws*' distinction of human and divine goods and with the "use" argument of the *Euthydemus*. Despite his claims to be working directly with Plato's writings alone Alcinous is still focused on locating Plato along the continuum defined by Stoics and Peripatetics at either end.

And that, of course, is just what we see in the Hellenistic period too, when ethical debate was dominated by the issue of the sufficiency of virtue for happiness and the need to fit the doctrine of the goods into that framework. Let us turn back to that discussion, which was in my view decisive for the shaping of the debates in later antiquity.

Any account of the philosophical debates in the first century BC turns on the evidence of Cicero, a self-described Academic who had studied at length with a professional Stoic and was deeply influenced by the Academic Antiochus of Ascalon.[55] In theory of knowledge Cicero himself pulled back from Antiochus to a more authentically "sceptical" Academic view that he learned from his teacher Philo of Larisa, but in ethics Cicero was particularly interested in the Peripatetic contribution.[56] In the

---

[55] Antiochus was an innovative Academic who claimed to revive and uphold the doctrines of the Old Academy, that is, a set of doctrines shared by Plato and his early followers (including the Peripatetics) as well as by the Stoics. He accused the Stoics of needlessly complicating the philosophical landscape by changing terminology even though they shared the views of the Old Academy.

[56] The impact of Critolaus and his notion of *sumplērōma* is reflected in the pro-Peripatetic account in Cicero. At *Fin.* 5.14, in his critical review of Peripatetic philosophy after Theophrastus, Piso finds that the only successor worthy of the school's name is Critolaus (for he respected and emulated the ancients) and grants him a distinction second only to Antiochus. Hence I suggest that Critolaus, in addition to his impact on his own school, had considerable influence over the framing of ethical questions by Antiochus. And the language of "filling" is found (in Latin) at, e.g., 2.21, 3.41, 3.43, 4.31, 5.37, 5.40, 5.45, 5.47, 5.68–69, and 5.71–72. The prominence of the term in the Peripatetically influenced account of Piso in book 5 tends to confirm the influence of

introduction to book 5 of the *De Finibus*, for instance, the spokesman for the general Antiochean viewpoint[57] is in fact a Peripatetic sympathizer, Piso.[58]

From Cicero's works we may conclude that Antiochus himself adopted the doctrine of the *tria genera bonorum*. This is the overt message of *Acad.* 1.19–22. Varro is the speaker and the climax of his remarks at 1.22 reflects both a clear Peripatetic association with the doctrine and Antiochus' own characteristic claims about the Old Academy:

> These are the "three kinds of good" most people ascribe to the Peripatetics.[59] Nor are they wrong about that—this division *does* belong to them. The mistake is to think that the "Academics" of that time differed from the "Peripatetics." They shared this theory, and both groups believed that the ethical end was to obtain all or the greatest of the primary objects nature recommends (i.e., the objects sought for their own sake). But the greatest primary objects are precisely the ones in the mind and in virtue. So the unanimous view of that ancient system of philosophy was this: while the happy life depends on virtue alone, it isn't the happiest life without the addition of bodily goods and of the other

---

Critolaus; Cicero's use of the notion in books 2 and 3 reflects the broadly Antiochean conceptual framework of *De Finibus* as a whole.

[57] See Moraux (1973) 218–219. He regards Staseas' emphasis on the contribution of bodily and external goods (which is what *fortuna* refers to here, as in Seneca at *Ben.* 5.3.1–2) as typical of late Hellenistic Peripatetic views. See Moraux n. 9. References include *Acad.* 1.33, *Fin.* 5.12, 84, *TD* 5.85, Plutarch *Pericles* 33; for Critolaus see *Ecl.* 2.46, *Strom.* 2.21.129 (=fr. 20 Wehrli). For the value of goods of the soul see *TD* 5.50 (=fr. 21 Wehrli), *Fin.* 5.91–92, 95 (=fr. 22 Wehrli); also relevant are *Ecl.* 2.126–127 and 130.

[58] Piso's credentials as a spokesman are doubly asserted. He spent some months in Athens learning Antiochean doctrine and also had Staseas the Peripatetic from Naples living in his house for several years. Cicero in his authorial voice appeals to his dedicatee Brutus for confirmation that Piso's account of Antiochean doctrine is reliable (*Fin.* 5.8). Nevertheless Cicero is careful to clarify later on in the book (*Fin.* 5.75) that the Peripatetic Staseas' views differed from those of Antiochus; the way Staseas differed was characteristically Peripatetic: he "agreed with those who put a lot of weight on good or bad fortune and also on good or bad bodily conditions."

[59] Other texts indicating this view are readily available. In book 5 of the *Tusculan Disputations* the doctrine of *tria genera* is assigned to Theophrastus (5.24); he is criticized for some features of his ethics but not for this division of goods. Compare *Fin.* 5.12. At *TD* 5.76 and 5.84–85 the doctrine is claimed for both the Peripatetics and the Old Academy (a sign that the passage was inspired, at least, by Antiochus; the latter of these texts points strongly to Carneadean influence in the development of Antiochus' synthesizing view) and marked off from the Stoic view that there is only one kind of good. From the Stoic viewpoint the doctrine of *tria genera* is Peripatetic, the main opposing view in ethics (*Fin.* 3.41–48) which played a pivotal role in the debate between Stoics and Old Academics. See *Fin.* 5.14 on the agreement of Aristotle and Polemo, according to Antiochus.

category described above, i.e., goods conducive to the exercise of virtue. (tr. Brittain)

Antiochus maintained that the Academy and the Peripatetics both held that there are three kinds of goods; in his view only the Stoics rejected the doctrine. We have seen earlier that the Peripatetic position is clear, but that the claim becomes highly contentious when made for Plato. And of course, to claim the doctrine for the Old Academy as such is to attribute it to the master, Plato, as well.

Although Stoic doctrine about the uniqueness of the good is clear—only virtue is good and the other "goods" are actually preferred indifferents—as late as the time of Chrysippus Stoics could be refreshingly relaxed about the terminology. Chrysippus conceded that for some purposes the external and bodily advantages strictly classified as indifferent might be designated as "good" without doing any philosophical harm, providing that one remained clear about the meaning of one's terms (Plutarch *St.Rep.* 1048a). Similarly, he granted that in a practical and therapeutic context one could "heal" the passions even if one held the erroneous view that there are three kinds of good, i.e., that bodily and external advantages are genuinely good (SVF 3.474 = Origen *Contra Celsum* 8.51).[60] Chrysippus is the philosopher who effectively defined Stoic orthodoxy and is usually regarded as a dedicated defender of Zeno's doctrines. If he could be slack about terminology, any Stoic would be allowed the license. It is hard to imagine this kind of liberality about key ethical terms in the first century BC, when the lines of debate had hardened with regard to the classification of goods.[61] Something clearly happened to raise the stakes with regard to the classification of the good.

Just when this "something" happened is not certain, but the difference between Chrysippus' liberal approach and the hard lines drawn in Cicero's day points to the second century BC. It is hard to resist the speculation that the burst of polemical activity associated with Carneades played an important role in shaping the debate.[62] He was, after all, the contemporary of the Peripatetic Critolaus, who frankly asserted that the *telos* just consisted in the possession of all three kinds of goods. After that, a Stoic (or indeed a Platonist) who wished to assert the exclusive role of virtue in the constitution of the happy life (and the complete dispensability of the bodily and external

---

[60] Cf. Cicero *TD* 4.62.

[61] There is no reason to think that the remarks directed against Chrysippus at *Fin.* 5.89 (that he is willing to call preferred things good in his daily life) reflects the stance Chrysippus is taking in the passages discussed in this paragraph. The Antiochean spokesman in *Fin.* 5, Piso, is making exactly the point against Chrysippus that he (and Cicero in book 4) make against all Stoics, from Zeno to their own day.

[62] This is suggested by the reference to "primary natural things" in *Acad.* 1.22. It would be a long but not difficult story to connect this issue with the *Carneadea divisio*.

advantages) would find it natural to do so by denying them the label "good." And immediately after Critolaus the Stoic Antipater went on the offensive by claiming that Plato himself held that only the *kalon* is good. It seems, then, that, in the period after Carneades and Critolaus and because of the debate they sparked, the classificatory aspect of Stoic value theory became more important dialectically than it had previously been. Getting one's terms right, getting the classification straight, and sticking to one's guns about such matters had become vital to the conduct of ethical debate.

This is the situation to which Antiochus was reacting when he accused the Stoics of merely altering the terminology inherited from the Old Academy without changing the substance. As he saw it, preferred indifferents are just goods under another label. From his standpoint, the Stoic denial of the *tria genera bonorum* was bogus. He held that, like the Old Academy, the Stoics substantially accepted the categorization of goods into the standard three types embraced by Peripatetics ever since Aristotle and foisted on Plato by Aristotle or Xenocrates or someone else of that generation. All the Stoics did, in his eyes, was to fiddle the terminology so that they could pretend to be innovative.

In fact, the Stoic denial of the *tria genera* was substantive; it reflected their conviction about the nature of the *telos* and enabled them to assert the sufficiency of virtue for happiness and the ultimate irrelevance of bodily and external (including social) conditions. They could no more accept the standard *tria genera* as the truth about goods than they could abandon their conception of the *telos*. More and more, the substantial disagreement about the nature of the good life was brought back to a debate which on its surface was merely classificatory. We see the signs of this in Cicero *De Finibus* books 3–5. In book 3 the Stoic speaker Cato casts the debate over the nature of the good as a disagreement between Peripatetics and Stoics brought to a head by the influence of Carneades; Cato, of course, is certain that this is no merely verbal dispute but rather one that goes to the heart of the disagreement between Peripatetics and Stoics about the happy life (3.41–45). To this Piso, the Peripatetic, gives a response along Antiochean lines in book 5 (*Fin.* 5. 71–72). He reasserts, in a form so subtle as to be unclear about whether the bodily and external goods are necessary for happiness, the Peripatetic view represented as Old Academic by Antiochus. Cicero gives himself the last word in response to this, on behalf of the more rigorous Stoic position, for which he claims Socrates and Plato as allies against the Peripatetics (*Fin.* 5.84 tr. Woolf (2001)):

> Your exposition bounds easily along: "There are three classes of goods." But when it reaches its conclusion it gets stuck in the mud. It wants to say that the wise person lacks nothing needed for a happy life—a discourse based on morality, in the style of Socrates and Plato too. "This is the position I have the courage to uphold," it is claimed. But you cannot uphold it, unless you unravel your

earlier statements. If poverty is an evil, then no beggar can be happy, however wise. Zeno, by contrast, was bold enough to claim that such a person is not just happy but rich. Pain is an evil: then no one can be happy in the throes of crucifixion. Children are good: then childlessness is miserable. One's homeland is a good: then exile is miserable. Health is a good: the sick are miserable. Bodily soundness is a good: the disabled are miserable. Keen eyesight is a good: the blind are miserable. Perhaps the consolation of wisdom can alleviate each of these evils taken singly. But surely it will not be able to rise above them all taken together.

Now imagine a wise person who is blind, disabled, suffering the gravest illness, in exile, childless, needy, and being tortured on the rack for good measure. Zeno, what do you call this person? "Happy." Even completely happy? "Absolutely," he will reply. "I have shown that happiness no more admits of degrees than does virtue, in which happiness itself consists."

In this way, then, the classification question about goods became a central issue of moral debate—we have come a long way from the *endoxon* of the fourth century BC. Antiochus took a harmonizing line about Plato's position on the topic, but this remained controversial—here Cicero himself as a character in the dialogue brings Socrates and Plato over to the Stoic side of the debate—whereas the Peripatetics are the standard-bearers for the doctrine. Platonists who held the one-genus interpretation of Plato would have Cicero and the Stoics on their side, but Antiochus firmly in opposition.

Out of this complicated but still substantive debate was born the approach to ethics which I discussed at the outset, the one which Atticus complained about.[63] All schools were involved, but I'd like to conclude with a look at two texts which take on special interest when viewed in this context. First, yet another text from the midst of the Peripatetic orgy of classification. In the midst of it (at *Ecl.* 2.126.12–127.2) we see clearly that even within the Peripatetic school there were voices of resistance; the author of this summary reworks the school doctrine in such a way as to pull it back from the relatively lax position on the role of external and bodily goods which we find in the first century BC and moves it back towards what we might rather expect of a Platonist or a Stoic—or at least to what we actually do find in book 1 of the *Nicomachean Ethics*.[64]

Since virtue greatly surpasses bodily and external goods with regard to producing [happiness] and being desirable for its own sake, it follows that the goal is

---

[63] See Sedley (2005).
[64] Compare Eudorus at *Ecl.* 2.46, discussed above.

not a compound [*sumplērōma*] of bodily and external goods nor is it the attainment of all of them, but rather that it is living according to virtue amid bodily and external goods, either all of them or most of them and the most important of them. Hence happiness is an activity in accordance with virtue in actions which are outfitted as one would wish. And bodily and external goods are said to be productive of happiness because they contribute to it *when they are present*. But those who believe that they make up [*sumplēroun*] happiness are ignorant of the fact that happiness is a *life* and that a life is made up of action. And none of the bodily or external goods is in itself an action nor, generally, an activity.

There is debate and even dissension within the Peripatetic school, but the interesting point is that the issues of this debate had to be cast in terms of the three kinds of good.[65]

The last text I want to look at is from Seneca, number 66 of the *Moral Epistles*.[66] Seneca tells of paying a visit to an old friend from his school days, one Claranus, who is now old and feeble in body though vigorous in mind. They spend several days in philosophical discussion (rather like a Ciceronian philosophical dialogue, though it is not fully developed) and on the first day they devote themselves to the topic: "how all goods can be equal if they come in three different types [*triplex eorum condicio est*]" (66.5). The main theme of the letter is indeed the equality of all goods and it turns out to be a thoroughly familiar doctrine, developed in an interesting and novel way. But for us the interesting thing is the three-way classification of goods which he invokes to set up his discussion. Several things are striking. First, he did not need to invoke the categorization to motivate his discussion. The equality of all goods could be introduced without the formal move of distinguishing kinds or types of goods. Second, the division he invokes into *three* rather than any other number is a clear reflection of what had become by his day a settled tradition of dividing goods. Finally, the actual division into three which he proposes is unique. That is, although Seneca is so often accused of being an eclectic thinker, he does not here adopt the Peripatetic division into body,

---

[65] Note that immediately following this long discussion in Stobaeus we find a curious appendix: at *Ecl.* 2.134–137 we are given a set of alternative divisions of the good; in fact, at least eight such divisions under the later heading "How many senses of good are there?" The habit of classificatory philosophy is well and truly entrenched.

[66] Letter 66 is Seneca's only exploration of the idea that there are *tria genera bonorum*; but it is worth keeping in mind letter 118, which is devoted to the question of the definition of the good and presents reliable information on technical definitions of the good. But *divisiones* are not mentioned there, and it is clear that freedom from the classificatory framework that hangs over 66 has enabled him to be more faithful to his Stoic sources.

soul, external which has dominated the tradition since the fourth century BC and which Antiochus claimed as common to the entire Socratic tradition; of course Seneca knew this doctrine well through his deep familiarity with Cicero's major philosophical works (*De Finibus* and *Tusculan Disputations* most of all) and indeed he refers to it elsewhere in an almost casual fashion (at *De Beneficiis* 5.3.1–2), invoking the goods "of the mind, of the body and of fortune" when contrasting his own Stoic views with those of Peripatetic opponents.[67]

Perhaps it is not surprising that Seneca should not allude to the by now hackneyed idea that there are three kinds of goods when he is working out his own Stoic views. After all, it was a non-Stoic division and Seneca's main philosophical opponents are Peripatetics rather than Platonists or even Epicureans. But he also does not adopt the most common Stoic tripartition of goods (those of the soul, those that are external and those that are neither of the soul nor external), though it had almost certainly already been developed by that time. The division he does use is this:

> 5. On the first day our question was how all goods can be equal if they can occur in three different kinds of situation. Certain goods, as our school thinks, are primary (e.g., joy, peace, the salvation of the fatherland); certain goods are secondary, being manifested in unfortunate circumstances (e.g., the endurance of torture and self-control when seriously ill). We will wish the former goods for ourselves straightforwardly and the latter only if necessary. There are in addition tertiary goods (e.g., a decorous gait, an expression which is sedate and proper, and a posture which is suitable for a man of good sense).

This is certainly not a standard Stoic tripartition; nor indeed is it any other known tripartition. Insofar as it is a reflection of Stoic doctrine, it seems to includes elements of two different classifications. The third type of good, if it is a good at all, must refer to the external manifestations of good character, that is, virtue, that we see associated with *to prepon* or *decorum* in Cicero's *De Officiis*;[68] it picks out something which participates in virtue by being its overt social manifestation. The first two kinds, though, are different. They are goods as recognized in unconstrained and constrained circumstances.[69] Virtue is always beneficial, but the virtue displayed when life is going well is different from the virtue displayed in times of hardship. The courage of a political leader at the height of his powers is different in some ways from the courage of a saint

---

[67] Even here Seneca's point is that the alleged *bona* are not genuinely good.
[68] The form of the doctrine there owes a good deal to Panaetius.
[69] This is reminiscent of the distinction among *kathēkonta* into those which are *kata peristasin* and those which are *aneu peristaseōs* (DL 7.109).

facing torture and martyrdom for his convictions. Yet both are courage and so goods. This is a genuine and Stoic distinction among goods, though not actually of much use for classificatory purposes. Put together, the three-way division here is simply weird.

Why did Seneca deploy it, then? Authorial intentions are elusive, but it would fit well with Seneca's approach, as I understand it, if he were introducing this new and unusual three-way distinction of goods as a response to what *he saw* as the needless technicality and "scholasticism" of the current philosophical scene. In the letter immediately preceding he had done just this for "cause"—too many kinds of cause had been bandied about and he preferred to return to the simplicity of Stoic theory, which admitted only one cause. But even there he made a point of *avoiding* the complex Stoic doctrines of kinds of causes which emerged from the debates about determinism and which Seneca would have known, if from no other source, from Cicero's *De Fato*. He did something similar in letter 58, where the overanalyzed concept was "being." This is a theme that repeats itself often in Seneca's letters, the dismissal of highly technical doctrines or distinctions which, in his view, add little or nothing to the philosophical substance of the question at hand. In letter 66, then, he is probably doing the same for "good." Being, causation, and goodness are (and were then) three standard high-profile philosophical topics. That all of them had been analyzed to death (in Seneca's view) led him to select them as examples to show how philosophy should really be done: with one's sight firmly fixed on substantial issues rather than needless classificatory debates.

Even without this letter there is abundant reason to suppose that the doctrine of kinds of good had become sterile,[70] so Seneca's reaction to that situation is not a surprise. And yet this issue had not always been overspecialized. If the story of this classification that I have developed here is even roughly right, the alleged founder of the *trigeneia*, Plato, may never have held the doctrine as his own (though he certainly used it in the *Laws* and agreed with all the propositions which might be needed to express it). Aristotle recognized the distinction of goods into those of the soul, those of the body, and external goods as a valuable and constructive *endoxon* to be used in developing moral and political theory. He or another early Academic such as Xenocrates pointed out that Plato also "held" this view—it could be extracted from the dialogues with minimal effort and its presence there

---

[70] One could argue that many philosophers of the early imperial period became impatient with what they saw as pointless technicality and reacted sharply against it. We see this spirit to some extent in physics, when Seneca ridicules Platonic and Aristotelian analyses of causes and senses of being in letters 58 and 65 (similar to his irritation with Stoic metaphysical scholasticism in 117). With regard to the situation in logic, see Barnes (1997). I think we also see it in Epictetus, who not only reshapes Stoic ethics into a fresh and more direct form of discourse but even reworks the three-part categorization of philosophy shared by Platonists and Stoics (logic, physics, ethics) into his more substantive three *topoi* (*Discourse* 3.2).

confirmed the usefulness of the *endoxon* in ethical debate. As a conceptual point, then, about the way good is regarded by the many and the wise, this became a feature of the early Academy. Its Platonic status, however, was never as secure as its Aristotelian credentials, a situation made even more clear when Critolaus used the division to formulate *actual Peripatetic doctrine*. From that point on the Stoics *had to* formulate their disagreement with Peripatetics in terms of this distinction about goods and Plato's views became a matter for debate. The Stoic Antipater claimed Plato for his own school, while Antiochus kept him firmly in the Old Academy and argued that even the Stoics *really* held this view, if only they had been willing to admit it. In second half of the last century BC and in the early imperial period various categorizations of the good ran rampant (our sketchy story has only scratched the surface), sometimes drawing attention to productive distinctions, but often not. Eventually voices of protest were heard. I don't think that Peripatetics ever gave up their commitment to this classificatory approach, but at least one Stoic did (if my understanding of Seneca's letter 66 is right); and he was right to complain, since Stoic views about the good did not in fact benefit from this extraneous bit of theoretical apparatus. And so too did the odd Platonist, like Atticus. It is appropriate, then, to close by recalling his zealous expostulation, a fitting but ultimately futile last word in protest against the rising tide of analytical scholasticism that burdened so much of the philosophy of late antiquity. In the words of Atticus, then: "Go on, then, if you want, make your classifications and lay out your fancy distinctions of goods into three or four or many kinds! These categorizations have no bearing on the issue and *this* isn't the way to bring us over to Plato."

Acknowledgments

I am grateful to members of several audiences for critical challenges to the main argument of this paper in earlier versions and many constructive suggestions. For written comments I would like to thank Julia Annas, Gábor Betegh, Ákos Brunner, Robert Wardy, and Jennifer Whiting. Even more, though, I would like to thank Gisela Striker for leading and inspiring by example, and for supportive encouragement over many years. It is an honor and a pleasure to dedicate this paper to her as a small, indeed inadequate, expression of friendship and gratitude.

References

Annas, J. (1976) *Aristotle's Metaphysics M and N*, Oxford: Oxford University Press.
Annas, J. (1991) "Virtue as the Use of Other Goods" *Apeiron* 26: 53–66.
Annas, J. (1999) *Platonic Ethics Old and New*, Ithaca: Cornell University Press.
Annas, J. and R. Woolf (2001) *Cicero: On Moral Ends*, Cambridge: Cambridge University Press.
Barnes, J. (1997) *Logic and the Imperial Stoa*, Leiden: Brill.

Brittain, C. (2006) *On Academic Scepticism*, Indianapolis: Hackett.
Cooper, J. (1999) *Reason and Emotion: Essays on Ancient Moral Psychology and Ethical Theory*, Princeton: Princeton University Press.
Dillon, J. (1977) *The Middle Platonists*, London: Duckworth.
Dillon, J. (1993) *Alcinous: The Handbook of Platonism*, Oxford: Oxford University Press.
Göransson, T. (1995) *Albinus, Alcinous, Arius Didymus*, Göteborg: Acta Universitatis Gothoburgensis (= Studia Graeca et Latina Gothoburgensia LXI).
Hahm, D. (1983) "The Diaeretic Method and the Purpose of Arius' Doxography" pp. 15–37 in *On Stoic and Peripatetic Ethics: The Work of Arius Didymus* ed. W.W. Fortenbaugh, New Brunswick NJ: Transaction Books.
Inwood, B. (2002) "Comment on Stephen White, 'Happiness in the Hellenistic Lyceum'" pp. 95–101 in *Eudaimonia and Well-Being: Ancient and Modern Conceptions* edd. L.J. Jost and R.A. Shiner = *Apeiron* 35.4.
Karamanolis, G. (2006) *Plato and Aristotle in Agreement?* Oxford: Oxford University Press.
Lorenz, H. (2006) *The Brute Within: Appetitive Desire in Plato and Aristotle*, Oxford: Oxford University Press.
Mansfeld, J. (1992) *Heresiography in Context*, Leiden: Brill.
Moraux, P. (1973) *Der Aristotelismus bei den Griechen* volume 1, Berlin: De Gruyter.
Reshotko, N. (2006) *Socratic Virtue: Making the Best of the Neither-Good-Nor-Bad*, Cambridge: Cambridge University Press.
Russell, D. (2010) "Virtue and Happiness in the Lyceum and Beyond" *Oxford Studies in Ancient Philosophy 38*: 143–185.
Sedley, D. (2005) "Stoics Metaphysics at Rome" ch. 6 of *Metaphysics, Soul and Ethics in Ancient Thought* ed. R. Salles, Oxford: Oxford University Press.
Sharples, R.W. (1983) "The Peripatetic Classification of Goods" pp. 139–159 in *On Stoic and Peripatetic Ethics: The Work of Arius Didymus* ed. W.W. Fortenbaugh, New Brunswick NJ: Transaction Books.
Sharples, R.W. (2007) "The Peripatetics on Happiness" ch. 35 in vol. 2 of *Greek and Roman Philosophy 100 BC—200 AD* edd. R. W. Sharples and R. Sorabji; 2 voll., *Bulletin of the Institute of Classical Studies. Supplement* 94. London: Institute of Classical Studies, University of London.
White, S. (1990) "Is Aristotelian Happiness a Good Life or the Best Life" *Oxford Studies in Ancient Philosophy 8*: 103–143.
White, S. (2002) "Happiness in the Hellenistic Lyceum" pp. 69–93 in *Eudaimonia and Well-Being: Ancient and Modern Conceptions* edd. L.J. Jost and R.A. Shiner = *Apeiron* 35.4.

12

THE PHILOSOPHICAL AMBITIONS OF SENECA'S *LETTERS*

John Schafer

One of the perennial questions about Seneca's *Letters* is whether, and to what extent, the collection forms a coherent unity. This is of course related to, and largely presupposes a certain answer to, the question of their "genuineness" or "literarity"; one wouldn't naturally expect to find a robust "thematic unity" in, say, Cicero's correspondence with his brother Quintus. I mention this issue only to pronounce on it dogmatically and move on: of course Seneca's *Letters* are "literary," of course they are intended to be read and judged by *us*, their third-party onlookers, regardless of the reality (or otherwise) of their recipient, Seneca's friend Lucilius.[1]

Even among readers who share this assumption, however, some will be unsympathetic to attempts to descry too much structure, let alone unity, in the collection. In particular, there is an enduring tradition of seeing them as a collection of (more or less freestanding) "essays"—a tradition which surely gains much of its purchase from the *Letters*' crucial importance as generic model for Montaigne's *Essays*, and hence, of course, for the essay itself as a distinct literary mode.[2] Indeed, staying within Seneca's corpus, the works which are misleadingly (to us) called *Dialogi* are often, and not unreasonably, rendered as "Moral Essays"; and it is true both that these works share many affinities with the *Letters*, and that they are discrete works, whose possible connections one to another fall far short of an overarching unity.

On the contrary, as many critics nowadays urge, the *Letters* can be shown to be a single, literary whole.[3] Put briefly, I see the collection as the dramatization of Seneca's friendship with and tutelage of a less-progressed fellow-progressor toward virtue, a

---

[1] See Mazzoli 1989: 1846–55 for a review of critical opinions on the genuineness of the *Letters*; Griffin 1976: 416–19 is the classic (and widely accepted) argument for their fictional status.
[2] Pire 1954.
[3] Noteworthy recent literary interpretations of the *Letters* are Wilson 1987, Hachmann 1995, Schönegg 1999, and Henderson 2004.

detailed exposition of moral reform and guidance, a master *exemplum* of the value of exemplarity in that guidance.[4] Also: a self-conscious intervention in Latin literature, responding closely to poets such as Virgil and Horace; a wistful commentary, part apology and part *apologia*, on Seneca's turbulent career in politics; and its author's public, extroverted *meditatio mortis*, his rehearsal of the death which, as he well knows, either his age and ill health or Nero's savagery will soon bring about.

One possible outcome of this interpretive project is that in emphasizing Seneca's artistic and personal ends it will marginalize the portion of the *Letters* that is most intensely philosophical. This would be a disappointing result, especially for the following reason: in the worst case, the work's failure to integrate its philosophical content with its literary agenda would fatally undermine that agenda: the resulting disunity would, by ancient lights no less than modern, represent an artistic failure, like the painting of the hybrid human/animal monster ridiculed by Horace in the *Ars Poetica*.[5]

On the other hand, there are advantages to a reading that privileges the literary over the philosophical; for one, it posits a helpful affinity between Senecan tragedy and Senecan prose. More importantly, though, for many readers it will render the *Letters* more interesting: for all that the rehabilitation of post-Aristotelian philosophy is now an established fact, questions undoubtedly remain about Seneca, about his place in the tradition: if we are now less likely to use him merely as a problematic witness to early Stoicism, to doubt whether he counts as a philosopher at all, still we rightly continue to ask what kind of philosopher he was, how good a philosopher he was. If our efforts vindicate his greatest work as respectable philosophy in productive dialogue with exceptional literary acumen, his net reputation will surely not have fallen.

To proceed, then, I assume, on grounds that will have to go largely unstated, the organic unity adumbrated above. I will first cast an eye on some of the formal and thematic heterogenies which are obvious to any reader of the work, and ask how (and against what) we are to characterize the content that strikes us as "most philosophical" in the *Letters*. Next I will focus on what I take to be clues about how that side of the collection interacts with its other aspects, about what Seneca takes himself to be doing. It will turn out that Seneca has his own answer to our question about his status and significance, and it is one that I think is in fact quite defensible.

On the first of these problems, two related issues are of central importance: the sequentiality of the collection and the length of individual letters. These are the first things a reader notices: the early letters are largely personal, chatty, accessible, and short; as the series progresses, as Lucilius progresses, they become denser, more

---

[4] For the larger picture, see Schafer 2011.
[5] *Ars Poetica* 1–9.

ambitious, and longer. The correlation between longer, more philosophical, and later letters is very strong. To illustrate, Brad Inwood's recent volume on Seneca is a translation of and commentary on seventeen of the most philosophically interesting letters.[6] Of the 124 extant letters, the first he includes is number 58. He omits the longest two (94 and 95) on grounds of limited space and because they have already attracted a significant body of modern scholarship.[7] Nonetheless, his collection includes four of the ten longest letters, and ten of his letters are selected from the last twenty in the extant collection.[8]

The way this dynamic works, however, is not simple or mechanical. There are indeed short, personal letters toward the end of the collection (letters 103, 112). There are also short letters which are fully devoted to philosophical argument (106, 116); by the same token, there are long letters (24, 78) which are less philosophical, and at least one long, philosophical letter which comes early (9). The best thing to say about all of this is that it is deliberate and artful: Seneca establishes a basic pattern which is both easy to discern and clearly meaningful; in turn, the pattern creates expectations, which Seneca can meaningfully subvert. In different ways, both the shortest and the longest letters are marked, and invite extra attention. To make good this claim, I turn first to letter 38, which at 162 words is the second shortest in the collection; and then to 94 and 95, each of which comprises roughly 4,100 words, by far the longest. Here is 38 in its entirety:

Merito exigis ut hoc inter nos epistularum commercium frequentemus. Plurimum proficit sermo, quia minutatim inrepit animo: disputationes praeparatae et effusae audiente populo plus habent strepitus, minus familiaritatis. Philosophia bonum consilium est: consilium nemo clare dat. Aliquando utendum est et illis, ut ita dicam, contionibus, ubi qui dubitat inpellendus est; ubi vero non hoc agendum est, ut discere velit, sed ut discat, ad haec submissiora verba veniendum est. Facilius intrant et haerent; nec enim multis opus est sed efficacibus. Seminis modo spargenda sunt, quod quamvis sit exiguum, cum occupavit idoneum locum, vires suas explicat et ex minimo in maximos auctus diffunditur. Idem facit ratio: non late patet; si aspicias, in opere crescit. Pauca

---

[6] Inwood 2007.
[7] Inwood 2007: xxii. Bellincioni 1979 is a translation and commentary; Schafer 2009 is the most recent study, which argues against the widespread assumption in Anglophone scholarship that these letters are about the role of rules in Stoic deliberation (Annas 1993: 94–108, Mitsis 1993, Inwood 1999).
[8] Statistics on the length of individual letters are helpfully collected in Mazzoli 1989: 1823–25 and Lana 1991: 292–304.

sunt quae dicuntur, sed si illa animus bene excepit, convalescunt et exsurgunt. Eadem est, inquam, praeceptorum condicio quae seminum: multum efficiunt, et angusta sunt. Tantum, ut dixi, idonea mens rapiat illa et in se trahat; multa invicem et ipsa generabit et plus reddet quam acceperit. Vale.

You're right to urge that we speed up this traffic in letters between us. The conversational style is very helpful, because it creeps into the soul bit by bit: set-piece speeches poured out to a large audience have more bombast, less familiarity. Philosophy is good advice; nobody gives advice at a yell. Sometimes it is appropriate to use harangues, so to speak, when someone is hesitant and needs to be pushed; but when you're not trying to make someone want to learn, but rather learn, it's time for words of this sort, gentler ones. These go in and stick on more easily; what's needed isn't many words, but effective ones. They should be scattered like a seed, which, however tiny it is, in the right place will unfurl its strength and spread from least to greatest. Reason does the same thing: it isn't broad and obvious: if you look, it grows in its work. The words spoken are few, but if the soul has received them well, they grow strong and rise up. What I'm saying is that precepts are exactly like seeds: extremely productive, and small. Like I said, just let the right mind snatch them and draw them into itself: it will conceive a large brood in turn and give back more than it took in. Farewell.

This letter offers a very clear example of Senecan self-referentiality and programmaticity. The words spoken are few: *this is a very short letter*. But if the soul has received them well (the verb *excipere* is also normal Latin for "interpret"),[9] *there's a lot to this letter, if you catch my meaning*. Reason isn't broad and obvious; if you look, it grows in its work: *ratio* also means "plan, rationale"; *opus* is a literary work: *my intention in this work becomes clear if you read carefully*. Sometimes it is appropriate to use harangues: *but not here; that isn't the sort of instruction I am exploring*. And finally, the sexual metaphor in the final sentence is the perfect comment on, defense of Seneca's sententious style: a condensed apothegm is received by a fertile mind and then grows in the mind's interpreting of it. The image is likewise also an instruction to the reader.

In different ways, the longest letters provoke similar reflections. Letter 94, uniquely in the collection, begins without any of the customary epistolary touches: no mention of a previous letter from Lucilius, no first-personal remarks from Seneca, no banter. Instead the topic comes immediately: there is a historic dispute about the credentials

---

[9] *OLD* s.v. 9c; Seneca memorably uses the word in this sense at *Letters* 12.7.

of a certain "part of philosophy," namely the one that gives specific instructions or *praecepta* to people in virtue of their various social roles. Aristo of Chios, the associate of Zeno's usually styled as a "dissident" or "heterodox" Stoic, denied the utility of precept-giving, asserting that only training in what Seneca calls *decreta*, or the actual doctrines of philosophy along with their justifications, will reliably motivate a person to become good. Cleanthes, as representative of normative or "orthodox" Stoicism, argued on the contrary that precepts are effective, but only when combined with doctrinal instruction (94.1–4).

Having established this opposition, Seneca reports a variety of related arguments against precept-giving (94.5–17), which he then responds to *ad singula*, point by point (94.18–51). I can only very hastily sketch the nature of the various arguments and counterarguments here. In general the arguments against precept-giving spring from classically Stoic ideas and concerns, and are hence signaled to constitute a formidable critique. The source of moral error is false opinion: merely telling someone what to do doesn't reform her opinions (94.5–8). If asked why we should follow precepts, the preceptor will say "because it's just"; but the truth and the force of *that* claim depend on what justice is (94.11).

Seneca's responses in general work to deepen and complicate the objector's implicit picture of moral experience. A person may indeed have a strong commitment to a good moral principle: a timely precept may *remind* him of that commitment (94.21, 26–27). Following a good precept itself strengthens an agent's sense of the precept's rightness; right action is a positive feedback loop (94.34, 45–51). But most importantly, perhaps, the defense of precepts is connected to the value of the preceptor, the exemplary model: the *authority* of a trusted and respected figure leads us away from the corruption of prevailing values and back towards our own natures (94.40–41, 52–60).

The next letter then defends *decreta*, doctrinal philosophy, against unnamed opponents who argue that precept-giving alone is sufficient for wisdom. The structure and length of this letter closely parallel the previous one; however, while the philosophical adversary in 94 was the famous Aristo (even if his name seems to have been a byword for philosophical extremism),[10] the opponents in 95 seem to correspond to no actual philosophers, and their critique does not amount to anything like a philosophical *stance*.[11] Instead, the objections of theirs to which Seneca devotes the most attention are populist, even anti-philosophical: many people are good without the benefit of philosophical study, and in general people in the distant past were better than they are now, when simple and homespun "wisdom" prevailed, before the advent of ethical

---

[10] Certainly this is how Cicero saw matters: *De Finibus* 2.35, 5.23; *Disputationes Tusculanae* 5.85; *De Officiis* 1.6.
[11] Schafer 2009: 80–83.

systems. If these systems are the cure, why are we sicker now than we were before? (95.13, 36). Seneca's answer concedes that the times are bad; but precisely for that reason we now need a compelling narrative, an intellectually respectable justification for digging in our heels and resisting the allure of vice. Even before we fully understand our doctrines and come to have intellectual confidence in their truth, the outline of the system provides an emotional commitment, like a soldier's love for the legionary standards (95.29–35). In perhaps the purplest passage in the *Letters*, Seneca depicts that vision: a revisionist cult of the gods, shorn of superstitious fear and simple-minded anthropomorphism, in which the gods are propitiated by our goodness alone; a humanism grounded in our kinship as rational beings sprung from a common origin, parts of a single body; and a rational contempt for mere "things," the Stoic indifferents (95.47–54). In our current state, we need not only the guidance of precepts and preceptors, but also the guidance of this vision, to stiffen our moral spines; as we reach rational perfection, precepts fall away, and our emotional commitment to *decreta* or doctrines is replaced with our knowledge of their truth (95.44–46, 55–59, *et passim*).

As mentioned earlier, letters 94 and 95 are clearly unique: while there are sequential connections between other letters, they are in general much looser; no other pair forms such a diptych; each one is almost half again as long as the next longest letter (66), and no letter other than 94 is completely lacking in Seneca's I and Lucilius' You. All of this by itself amounts at the least to a prima facie case for their having a special hermeneutic status. This case is then clinched, I take it, by applying the same interpretive strategy used earlier for the shortest letter, 38, namely testing for their self-referentiality or self-applicability within the collection.

Before doing so, however, I want to make a few general remarks about the issue of programmaticity in the interpretation of classical literature. Although the word itself has only recently become a term of art, there is a longstanding and well-grounded tradition of reading remarks in classical authors—especially poets—along lines that classicists nowadays call "programmatic," that is, as commenting on their own texts, revealing their literary goals, and hinting at the right way to read them. It would be a venturesome critic indeed who would doubt the relevance of this approach to the first line of Catullus poem 1 (*to whom do I dedicate this charming, novel little book?*) or Apollo's instruction at the beginning of Virgil's sixth *Eclogue* (*a shepherd should graze fat sheep, but sing a slender poem*). Now Seneca is a Latin poet, and even by the lights of his most energetic critics he is remarkable for his generic versatility.[12] It would be no surprise if he affected so common a literary gesture in the *Letters*.[13]

---

[12] Cf. Quintilian 10.1.125–131.
[13] See Batstone 2007 for an excellent discussion of this issue as it relates to Catullus.

There is no criterion of truth in literary criticism, of course; the closest thing is the slippery test of explanatory power. But for program a good place to look is the beginning of a work. Letter 1 begins: *do thus, my Lucilius: vindicate yourself for yourself*. Seneca's role as teacher or guide is asserted in the opening command; and then the *content* of that command notably features self-reflexivity: Lucilius is subject, direct object, and indirect object of the verb *vindica*. The basic meaning of "vindicate" is "to assert a claim of ownership"; it is a term from the judicial sphere: "I vindicate X for Y" means "I assert [in court] that X belongs to Y." (Other important connotations: "rescue from danger or harm" and "free from blame.") With a *person* as direct object the context is one of slavery; but with the same person as the *indirect* object, the phrase comes to mean "assert your freedom" or "set yourself free."[14] In Roman law there is a formal action called the *causa liberalis*, in which an intercessor argues on behalf of a slave that he, the slave, is in fact legally free; Seneca's instruction here calls on Lucilius to do metaphorically what is not actually possible in court, to be his *own* advocate for his freedom. The opening, then, announces that moral reform and moral progress are its subject, and simultaneously situates the relevant (Greek) intellectual background within a Roman cultural context while making a novel contribution to the famous Stoic paradox: "only the wise person is free, but only the unwise slave can free herself."

The letter continues by urging Lucilius to gather up and save his time, to "embrace every hour," to reflect that we die a little every moment, that most of our dying has already taken place: "death holds whatever portion of our life is in the past." And then an abrupt shift, as Seneca turns his own advice upon himself, puts into practice the reflexivity he advises at the beginning, makes himself both subject and object of his text. "You ask what I do that I should give you this advice. I will confess frankly: as happens with a spendthrift but hardworking person, my accounts balance. I can't say I waste nothing, but I will say what I waste and why and how: I will report the causes of my poverty." And then the letter quickly wraps up with a return to the theme of time.

Examples can be given for the thematic or programmatic relevance of every line in this letter; for my purposes the basic movement of the letter is the most crucial element.[15] A flurry of precepts gives way to a reflection on the preceptor's qualifications to give them; commenting on and justifying what the *Letters* do is an essential part of their project. Sometimes this point is understood only as the narrower point that a putative moral teacher risks alienating his student—"so, I guess *you're* perfect, then?" In fact that point is undoubtedly present, and reappears elsewhere in the *Letters* as well (27.1). But that is only one feature of the passage. The *Letters* call constantly for

---

[14] Maurach 1970: 26.
[15] This ground is covered in more detail in Schafer 2011: 36–37.

self-scrutiny, for testing whether one's actions are internally consistent and also consistent with one's moral commitments.[16] They are also conducted under the auspices of the friendship between Seneca and Lucilius; and friendship, as letter 3 specifies, demands complete disclosure: "speak as boldly with a friend as you do with yourself.... share with your friend all your concerns, all your thoughts" (3.2–3). By simultaneously applying these thematic instructions, we emerge with the expectation that Seneca's tutelage of his friend will not only *have* pedagogical principles, but it will also explicitly *examine* and justify those principles.

Finally, before leaving letter 1 I will advert to two phrases whose programmatic relevance, I will argue, is of crucial significance to the central issue of this paper: "I will confess frankly" and "I will report the causes of my poverty."

Having seen how this sort of reading works, let us return to the longest letters, 94 and 95. These divide the teaching of philosophy into precept-giving and doctrinal training, or, we may say, "nontechnical" and "technical" instruction. Each sort of instruction has its proper sphere and each has its own sort of motivational efficacy, but they are not of equal importance, and over the course of a philosophical education the former yields gradually to the latter. There is an obvious convergence between this picture of moral education and the moral education that the *Letters* as a whole depict. If we press these letters for programmatic significance, then, we have an explanation of what Seneca takes himself to be doing with his shifts in philosophical register, as well as his justification for doing so.[17]

Furthermore, in defending precepts by likening them to high-sounding maxims, especially in verse, exhortations, consolations, and above all examples (94.42–49), Seneca signals that the role vindicated for precepts also applies to the literary form of the letters, especially to such characteristic features as their progressive construction of an authorial persona, frequent quotations from poetry, and constant use of metaphor.

The upshot of this is that Seneca's justification of his overall project is a problematized and limited one. Precept-giving is a respectable and worthwhile part of philosophy, but it is insufficient by itself *ad consummandam sapientiam*, for completing wisdom (95.1). Of course the collection contains *decreta*, doctrinal teaching, but it does so in a deliberately non-systematic way, within an artistic framework that functions the way precepts do; further, many of the issues that are actually discussed are forthrightly signaled as philosophically marginal. Now that fact is very revealing: it is precisely in virtue of their comprehensiveness that *decreta* are capable of producing wisdom. This is troubling, and requires an explanation.

---

[16] Edwards 1997.
[17] Schafer 2009: 67–77.

Here and there there are hints in the *Letters* of Lucilius' reading of philosophical works other than the *Letters* themselves. In letter 6 Seneca represents Lucilius as writing, "send to me too the things you have found so effective." Seneca muses sententiously that "the possession of no good is pleasant without a friend" and then happily agrees to the request: "and accordingly I'll send you the books themselves [their authors are unspecified], and so you don't invest a lot of effort in hunting out helpful material here and there, I'll add notes, so you can straightaway get to the stuff I like and admire" (6.5). Of course we understand this charming detail in the light of Lucilius' early stage in his philosophical training; consonant with this is Seneca's practice at the beginning of the collection of ending every letter with a pithy *bon mot* or "thought of the day." In letter 33 Seneca declines Lucilius' request to continue this practice. He instead encourages his friend to progress to continuous Stoic writings, in which, Seneca polemically claims, there are fewer noteworthy passages because everything is noteworthy: "a single tree doesn't provoke wonder when the whole forest reaches the same height" (33.1). Next, in letter 39 Seneca agrees to a request for a different sort of text: "the *commentarii* that you ask for, carefully arranged and forced into a small space, I will indeed compose; but consider whether perhaps *ratio ordinaria*[18] is more useful than what we nowadays call a *breviarium*, but back when we really spoke Latin was called a *summarium*" (39.1).

Then there is the interesting case of letter 45. Lucilius has complained that he doesn't have access to a wide range of books at his official post in Sicily. He has asked Seneca for his, Seneca's, writings. "I am indeed ready to send you whatever ones I have, and to empty out my whole storehouse" (45.2). But then his tone changes:

> Ceterum quod libros meos tibi mitti desideras, non magis ideo me disertum puto quam formonsum putarem si imaginem meam peteres. Indulgentiae scio istud esse, non iudici; et si modo iudici est, indulgentia tibi inposuit. Sed qualescumque sunt, tu illos sic lege tamquam verum quaeram adhuc, non sciam, et contumaciter quaeram. Non enim me cuiquam emancipavi, nullius nomen fero; multum magnorum virorum iudicio credo, aliquid et meo vindico.

> But as to the fact that you wish my books to be sent to you, that doesn't make me think myself eloquent any more than I would think myself handsome, if you asked for a picture of me. I know this is a matter of your indulgence of me, not of your judgment of me; but even if it's your judgment, your indulgence gave it to you. But of whatever quality they are, read them as if I'm still seeking the truth, not as if I know it, and indeed that I'm aggressively seeking it. For

---

[18] The phrase can be plausibly translated either as "the regular manner" or "systematic exposition."

I'm nobody's ex-slave, I carry nobody's name; much of what I believe relies on the judgment of great men; some of it I lay claim to by my own judgment, too. (45.3–4)

Seneca suspects Lucilius of flattery, and his response is very nearly rude (especially later in the letter: at 45.7 he is ostensibly discussing the problem of differentiating between good things and their counterfeits, and picks a rather stinging example: "how similar flattery is to friendship!...a coaxing enemy comes to me in the guise of a friend") Nonetheless, he should not be read as merely deflecting the putative flattery with false modesty. His attitude toward his own writings is more complicated than that: *my books have their limitations, true. Don't read them as the last word on the matter, because they're not. But it's not all cut-and-paste philosophy, either; I can and do form my own attitudes and defend them.*

By contrast, in letter 64 Seneca himself has been reading (or listening to) another philosopher. He tells Lucilius how friends came to visit, philosophy was discussed, and then a book of Quintus Sextius, the founder of what was reputedly the only Roman philosophical school, was read (64.1–2). Seneca's enthusiastic recollection gives way to a reflection on the richness of the philosophical tradition as a whole:

Veneror itaque inventa sapientiae inventoresque; adire tamquam multorum hereditatem iuvat. Mihi ista adquisita, mihi laborata sunt. Sed agamus bonum patrem familiae, faciamus ampliora quae accepimus.... Multum adhuc restat operis.... sed etiam si omnia a veteribus inventa sunt, hoc semper novum erit, usus et inventorum ab aliis scientia ac dispositio. Puta relicta nobis medicamenta quibus sanarentur oculi: non opus est mihi alia quaerere, sed haec tamen morbis et temporibus aptanda sunt.... Animi remedia inventa sunt ab antiquis; quomodo autem admoveantur aut quando nostri operis est quaerere.

And therefore I honor the discoveries of wisdom and its discoverers; it pleases me to approach them as if they were the inheritance of many people. Their ideas were sought out and elaborated for me. But let's play the good paterfamilias: let's increase what we have received.... There still remains a lot of work to do.... but even if everything was discovered by the ancients, the following will always be new, namely how to make use of, know, and arrange the things discovered by others. Suppose that medications for treating the eye have been left to us: I needn't look for others, but yet the ones we have must be fitted to particular diseases and particular circumstances.... Remedies for the soul were invented by the ancients, but how to apply them or when is our task to seek. (64.7–8)

It is here in 64, I think, that we have the fuller and more reliable statement of Seneca's philosophical agenda in the *Letters*. The tone is certainly different from letter 45, and we seem to be invited to scrutinize the differences in context. The letter gives us a rather tetchy Seneca—and it bears emphasis that his Roman audience is much more highly attuned to this anxiety than we might be. Elite friendship is a fraught issue; friendship with the more powerful is a requisite for social advancement, and the more powerful rarely forget this. Striking the right balance—how friendly should I be? how much independence should I assert?—is a familiar issue in Latin literature, most memorably focalized in Horace's depiction of his relationship with his patron Maecenas.[19] The Senecan ideal of the philosophical friendship is surely conditioned by the unmentioned specter of false political friendship, and in particular by Seneca's own career in the poisonous environment of the Julio-Claudian court. When Seneca, then, detects the odor of flattery within the philosophical friendship he has been cultivating precisely to avoid the disheartening problematic of conventional friendship, he quite visibly overreacts, lays bare anxieties one typically tries to conceal, and comes off not so well for it: *I do too have my own opinions!*

In 64, on the other hand, Seneca relates a highly successful interaction with both his living friends and a philosophical predecessor. His enthusiastic reading of Sextius frees him, at least for the moment, from his anxiety about his own standing in the tradition, allows him to make a much more constructive evaluation of his own role. His ambition is perhaps more modest, certainly better focused; whereas in 45 he had insisted merely that his own judgment had *some* independent value, here in 64 he is confident about what his achievement will consist in: practical ethical reflection, the modalities of moral reform, the transplanting (an important Senecan metaphor) of an old plant in new literary and cultural soil.[20]

Now it is certainly possible to read these two letters as directly reflecting Seneca's attitude towards his own output, to say that sometimes he is defensive about, at other times at peace with, its quality and significance. My claim, of course, is that Seneca, qua author of this literary unity, *depicts* himself reacting differently, invites our scrutiny of his reactions. In different ways, both letters fulfill the programmatic promises in letter 1: "I will confess frankly.... I will report the causes of my poverty." Seneca uses his own reaction to show us the causes of his relative poverty, as well as how he comes to term with this poverty.[21]

---

[19] Maecenas is a notable target of Senecan polemic in letter 114.
[20] see especially Henderson 2004: 150–153 *et passim* on letter 86.
[21] Reflecting another line in letter 1: "I don't consider him a pauper who has *enough*, however little is left to him" (1.5).

Looking forward again to 94 and 95, Seneca locates his own contribution as a philosopher on the precept-giving side. This produces an interesting tension or instability. Precept-giving is a stage on philosophy's way; it is not self-sufficient; but neither is it the case that doctrinal training only starts after the precepts end. The *Letters* then must have their doctrinal aspect, but by Seneca's admission they might not be capable of carrying out that project in full; the value of the *Letters* is not meant to consist in that achievement.

Several later letters confirm this expectation. Number 72 begins with a candid demurral:

> Quod quaeris a me liquebat mihi—sic rem edidiceram—per se; sed diu non retemptavi memoriam meam, itaque non facile me sequitur. Quod evenit libris situ cohaerentibus, hoc evenisse mihi sentio: explicandus est animus.... ergo hoc in praesentia differamus.
>
> What you ask me for was once clear to me (I had really learned the matter) on its own; but I hadn't exercised my memory for a long time, and so it's not coming to me easily. What happens to papyrus rolls that stick together from long disuse: that's what I sense has happened to me: my mind needs to be disentangled.... so let's put this matter off for now.

We never find out what the "matter" was; the point is surely Seneca's ostentation of modesty.

Particularly a bit later in the series, Lucilius' increasingly probing questions seem to put Seneca a bit off balance; his control over the curriculum, so to speak, is a little less firm. At 102 Lucilius complains that Seneca had not adequately settled a particular matter; Seneca replies that he had intended to defer the question on the grounds that it involves a tricky intersection of ethical and logical problems; but since Lucilius insists, he agrees to discuss it. And then a few letters later, at 106, something similar happens. Seneca is late in replying to Lucilius' question, which turns out to be "is the good a body?" His explanation is:

> Id de quo quaerebas veniebat in contextum operis mei; scis enim me moralem philosophiam velle conplecti et omnes ad eam pertinentis quaestiones explicare. Itaque dubitavi utrum differrem te donec suus isti rei veniret locus, an ius tibi extra ordinem dicerem: humanius visum est tam longe venientem non detinere. Itaque et hoc ex illa serie rerum cohaerentium excerpam et, si qua erunt eiusmodi, non quaerenti tibi ultro mittam.
>
> what you asked about was going to find a place in the fabric of my work: for you know that I intend to encompass moral philosophy and explicate all the questions

associated with it. And so I wasn't sure whether to put you off until the matter found its proper place, or to grant you this as a special privilege: I decided it was more human not to keep waiting someone who came from so far away. And so, I will excerpt this too from that self-coherent series, and if anything else of the same sort comes up, I'll send it to you on my own, without your asking for it. (106.1–3)

This project reemerges two letters later. Letter 108 begins:

Id de quo quaeris ex iis est quae scire tantum eo, ut scias, pertinet. Sed nihilominus, quia pertinet, properas nec vis expectare libros quos cum maxime ordino continentis totam moralem philosophiae partem.

What you ask about is one of those things which is relevant to know only for the bare fact of knowing it. But nonetheless, because it does have that relevance, you're in a hurry and you don't want to wait for the books I'm just now arranging which will contain the entire moral branch of philosophy. (108.1)

These two references tell us most of what we know about this apparent project of Seneca's. Most of our questions about this work are insoluble. Unfortunately, the matter is also of significant relevance to my argument here.

Briefly, the discernible facts are as follows: the *Letters*, or at least parts of them, are firmly datable to the last few years of Seneca's life, to the period after his withdrawal from the Neronian court in 62 CE; letter 91 mentions a catastrophic fire at Lugdunum, modern Lyon, which according to Tacitus occurred after the Great Fire at Rome, in 64.[22] Seneca's forced suicide comes after the uncovering of the Pisonian conspiracy in the spring of 65. The *Natural Questions*, also dedicated to Lucilius (though never mentioned or alluded to in the *Letters*), likewise date from this period.[23] It would seem to pose an immense burden on Seneca for him also to be composing such an ambitious work at the same time. On the other hand, the fourth-century Christian author Lactantius preserves a few quotations from a work he calls the *Moralis Philosophiae Libri* (henceforth = *MPL*).[24] So unless Lactantius' source is spurious, it would appear that by the time of his death Seneca had assembled some sort of text; how long it was, how it was arranged, and in what sense it was intended to "embrace all of moral philosophy" are unrecoverable. Compounding this problem is the fact that our text of the *Letters* is also incomplete: we have twenty books,

---

[22] *Annals* 16.13.
[23] See Griffin 1976: 395–411 for the dating of Seneca's prose works.
[24] Collected in Vottero 1998 as fragments 93–96.

but Aulus Gellius would later quote a passage from the twenty-second book.[25] And it is quite likely that both projects were left incomplete at Seneca's death.[26]

In the light of this uncertainty, it seems that in judging the relevance of the *MPL* to the *Letters* the safest course is to restrict our attention to what the *Letters* say about them. A few things stand out: it seems that other letters may be "excerpts," both before and after the two that are signaled as such: *And so, I will excerpt this too from that self-coherent series, and if anything else of the same sort comes up, I will send it to you on my own, without your asking for it.* Letters 94 and 95 would be a natural suggestion, as has been observed.[27] Yet it seems unlikely that a large portion of the later letters should be suspected to belong to this category, since there is not much appreciable increase in their thematic coherence (at any rate, no sequence of letters aside from 94/95 seems likely to reflect the sequence of such a "systematic" work).

The claim I want to make about the *MPL* is that their function in the *Letters* is as a foil for the more doctrinal letters that *are* found in the collection. The *Letters* depict Seneca as judging that his student Lucilius is progressing past the sort of instruction that they provide. The *MPL*, meanwhile, are explicitly signaled as aspirational: "you know that I *wish to* embrace all of moral philosophy." Perhaps we are to understand this as the Seneca-character's admirable, albeit implausible, hope that he is progressing to the level of near-wisdom which would allow him to produce a fully systematic and freestanding account of virtue, impulse, *oikeiosis*, the passions, and the rest of the Stoic ethical apparatus. Or perhaps he more modestly envisages a work with fully discrete sections, each dealing with a related *quaestio*, perhaps as follows: "some people think the virtues are mutually entailing, others don't: here are the arguments on each side"; roughly the compositional model of the *Natural Questions*. Either way, my point stands: the *Letters* point beyond themselves, and—though this will depend on one's view of the *MPL*—very likely beyond their author: if you'll pardon the literary anachronism, Seneca is perhaps Lucilius' *Virgilio*, but he will never quite make it as his *Beatrice*.

Letter 108 reveals the causes of Seneca's poverty in another way, too. The issue Lucilius had asked about is deferred in 108 and will be dealt with in 109. Letter 108 instead contains a long personal meditation, really the only letter in the collection that says much about Seneca's earlier life. His official justification for the letter, in which he recalls his early training from his teachers Attalus and Sotion (108.13–21), is that his own example should be a model for how Lucilius' "burning" enthusiasm might be

---

[25] *Noctes Atticae* 12.2.2 ff.
[26] See Leeman 1953 and Vottero 1998: 64–75 for more on the *MPL*.
[27] Lana 1991: 289.

focused (108.1). Seneca tells how deeply he fell in love with philosophy, eagerly adopting ascetic habits (108.13–16) and even, under the influence of the neo-Pythagorean vogue at the time, a vegetarian diet: perhaps spilling blood for pleasure creates habits of cruelty, and perhaps metempsychosis is true; if one or both of those is right, abstention is morally required; if they're wrong, one hasn't really lost anything by abstaining. How did Seneca lose this habit? Under Tiberius there was a witch-hunt against foreign cults, and avoiding certain kinds of meat could start rumors; Seneca's father "easily persuaded [him] to begin a better diet" (108.17–22). Seneca fairly winks at us: "principle, you see," says the notorious alleged hypocrite.

The point of all this? Lucilius' not-so-youthful enthusiasm for philosophy shouldn't be diverted from the core ethical concerns: "some mistakes are made by the teachers' fault, who teach us how to argue, not how to live, and some by the learners' fault, who go to their preceptors with the goal of cultivating not their soul but their cleverness. And thus what was *philosophia* is turned into *philologia*" (108.23). He then demonstrates with examples from Virgil and Cicero how the same text can be scrutinized differently by a *philosophus, philologus,* and *grammaticus*; I take it his preference for his own reception is clear.

Now of course this is a problem too; if Seneca is a first-class man of letters and a business class philosopher, is he not being slightly masochistic, not to say self-negating, here? Yes and no. The defense of his own practice goes by way of locating it in *pars praeceptiva*, the precept-giving part of philosophy. Precepts work like *exempla* do; perhaps the biggest result of all the literary virtuosity in the *Letters* is their production of the master *exemplum*, the depiction of an alternative mode of doing philosophy, of leading a philosophical life, in which the power of intimate exchange between teacher and student, friend and friend, writer and reader, is both asserted and (many will feel) pragmatically demonstrated. Yet all of that ingenuity is subject to a strict means-end test of its value: if and only if it conduces to virtue is it justified. And in turn the kind of philosophy that Seneca both practices and thinks he has vindicated is itself a limited one: it leads somewhere Seneca probably cannot go.

So what do the technical or doctrinal letters do? What they can; which is to say, rather a lot: if Lucilius is ready and willing to go further, he will do so with a firm grounding. For all their eye-rolling when discussing, say, Zenonian syllogisms, they do discuss them; Seneca knows one really does need a keen dialectical wit to get anywhere in philosophy.[28] They discuss the ideas of other schools (especially letters 58, 65, and 66, which are quite important) in a sympathetic and open-minded way: no good to train Lucilius to be a sectarian fanatic. Many of them, like 94 and 95, are reflections on

---

[28] Inwood 2007: 218–219 *contra* Cooper 2004: 317–320.

didactic method: what role for logic? What role for "liberal studies"? They represent Stoic ideas faithfully and in some depth, all the while making a more than plausible case against a cramped, rote-learning approach to philosophy, an approach we may well suppose to have been widespread enough to merit Seneca's polemical attention. And recall that doctrines too have a protreptic role: before fully understood, while coming to be understood, they exert a pull on the learner: and, judging personally—I don't see how else can we judge *this* issue—a letter like 120, which discusses how we come to have a notion of the good, is very successful in this regard: go, read. And of course there's much more to say; I will close by saying they show how Seneca simultaneously vindicates himself to himself and reports the causes of his poverty: no less than Plato's *Apology*, Seneca's *Letters* present their hero striving to heed the command of the Delphic god.

Acknowledgments

In deep gratitude and with sweet nostalgia I dedicate this piece to my *Doktormutter* Gisela, *sine qua non*:

ἕτερος ἐξ ἑτέρης σοφὸς τό τε πάλαι τό τε νῦν·
οὐδὲ γὰρ ῥᾷστον ἀρρήτων ἐπέων πύλας
ἐξευρεῖν.

Literature Cited

Annas, J. 1993. *The Morality of Happiness*. Oxford.
Batstone, W. 2007. Catullus and the Programmatic Poem: The Origins, Scope, and Utility of a Concept. In Skinner, M. (ed.) *A Companion to Catullus*: 235–253. Oxford.
Bellincioni, M. 1979. *Lettere a Lucilio, Libro XV: Le lettere 94 e 95*. Brescia.
Cooper, J. 2004. *Knowledge, Nature, and the Good: Essays on Ancient Philosophy*. Princeton.
Edwards, C. 1997. Self-Scrutiny and Self-Transformation in Seneca's *Letters*. *Greece & Rome* 44: 23–38.
Griffin, M. 1976. *Seneca: A Philosopher in Politics*. Oxford.
Hachmann, E. 1995. *Die Führung des Lesers in Senecas "Epistulae Morales."* Münster.
Henderson, J. 2004. *Morals and Villas in Seneca's "Letters": Places to Dwell*. Cambridge.
Inwood, B. 1999. Rules and Reasoning in Stoic Ethics. In Ierodiakonou, K. (ed.) *Topics in Stoic Philosophy*: 95–127. Oxford.
Inwood, B. 2007. *Seneca: Selected Philosophical Letters*. Oxford.
Lana, I. 1991. Le *Lettere a Lucilio* nella letteratura epistolare. In *Sénèque et la Prose Latine*: 254–311. Vanoeuvres-Geneva: Fondation Hardt.
Leeman, A. D. 1953. Seneca's Plan for a Work "Moralis Philosophiae" and Their Influence on His Later Epistles. *Mnemosyne* 6: 307–13.
Maurach, G. 1970. *Der Bau von Senecas "Epistulae Morales."* Heidelberg.
Mazzoli, G. 1989. Le *Epistulae Morales ad Lucilium* di Seneca: Valore letterario e filosofico. *Aufstieg und Niedergang der Römischen Welt* 2.36.3: 1823–77.

Mitsis, P. 1993. Seneca on Reason, Rules, and Moral Development. In Brunschwig, J. and Nussbaum, M. (eds.) *Passions and Perceptions:* 285–312. Cambridge.

Pire, G. 1954. De l'Influence de Sénèque sur les Essais de Montaigne. *Les Études Classiques* 22: 270–86.

Schafer, J. 2009. Ars Didactica: *Seneca's 94th and 95th "Letters."* Göttingen.

Schafer, J. 2011. Seneca's *Epistulae Morales* as Dramatized Education. *Classical Philology* 106: 32–52.

Schönegg, B. 1999. *Senecas* Epistulae Morales *als Philosophisches Kunstwerk.* Bern.

Vottero, D. 1998. *Lucio Anneo Seneca: I frammenti.* Bologna.

Wilson, M. 1987. Seneca's *Letters* to Lucilius: A Revaluation. In Boyle, A. J. (ed.) *The Imperial Muse,* vol. 1, 102–21. Berwick, Victoria.

PART FIVE
Hellenistic Epistemology

13

THE EPISTEMOLOGY OF PTOLEMY'S *ON THE CRITERION*

Mark J. Schiefsky

1.

Among the works of the ancient Greek mathematician and astronomer Ptolemy of Alexandria (fl. second century AD) is a short text on philosophical topics entitled *On the criterion and commanding faculty* (περὶ κριτηρίου καὶ ἡγεμονικοῦ).[1] The two-part title reflects a basic division in the text between a longer first section primarily concerned with epistemology (chapters 1–12) and a second, shorter part devoted to psychological issues (chapters 13–16). Ptolemy's main goal in the first section is to set out a detailed account of the κριτήριον—"the mechanics of making a judgment," in the trenchant formulation of John Dillon[2]—drawing a close analogy with the process of legal judgment as practiced in the lawcourt or δικαστήριον. By means of a detailed elaboration of this analogy he is able to explain how the various faculties and activities of the soul—especially sense perception (αἴσθησις), intellect (νοῦς), and reasoning (λόγος)—work together to produce scientific knowledge. My aim in this paper is to offer an interpretation of the epistemological theory set out in the first part of *On the criterion* and to relate it both to the philosophical tradition and to Ptolemy's investigations in the ancient exact sciences, particularly astronomy, harmonics, and optics.

Ptolemy's decision to address the topic of the κριτήριον should be viewed as a deliberate effort to engage with the philosophical tradition.[3] By the second century AD the term had long been a touchstone of epistemological discussion. Works *On the*

---

[1] I refer to the text as *On the criterion* throughout; references are to the chapter number, page, and line of the standard modern edition (Lammert 1961). Translations are my own and are based on Lammert's text unless otherwise indicated. For an English translation of the entire text see Huby and Neal 1989. The most thorough and incisive commentary (in Latin) is Bullialdus 1663, which also includes a Greek text and Latin translation.

[2] Dillon 1993: 61.

[3] Such a concern fits very well with what we know of Ptolemy's intellectual orientation from his principal scientific works; see for example the opening chapter of the *Almagest* (I.4–7 Heiberg),

criterion (περὶ κριτηρίου) are attributed to both Epicurus and Posidonius, and Alcinous begins his exposition of Platonic epistemology in the *Didaskalikos* with an account of the κριτήριον.[4] A brief rundown of the various uses of the term will help to situate Ptolemy's account against the philosophical background.[5] In its most general sense the term κριτήριον refers to an instrument or means of judgment, with no implications about what kind of instrument or how it is to be used. In Plato and Aristotle the term is used of an ability or capacity to judge.[6] By a natural extension of this sense, κριτήριον came to be used of specific faculties of the soul such as sense perception or reason, conceived of as instruments of judgment. This usage is not associated with any particular epistemological theory insofar as it implies nothing about the reliability of the faculties in question or how they should be employed. More specialized uses of κριτήριον emerged in Hellenistic epistemology, particularly in connection with the debates about the "criterion of truth" (κριτήριον τῆς ἀληθείας) between the Stoics, Epicureans, and Skeptics. The participants in these debates shared the notion that a criterion of truth was a means of distinguishing with certainty between true and false opinions. The Epicureans and Stoics proposed various candidates for a criterion of truth in this sense, while the Skeptics denied that such a criterion can be found. Epicurus arguably introduced this notion of a criterion of truth by means of an analogy between the κριτήριον and the κανών (the carpenter's rule or straightedge), suggesting the idea of a κριτήριον as something which is itself true (just as the straightedge is itself straight) and so can be used as a means for assessing the truth and falsity of opinions.[7] Yet another sense of κριτήριον emerges in the course of the debate between the Stoics and the Academic Skeptics, namely, the idea of a criterion as a piece of evidence that warrants belief in the truth of a claim without serving as an indubitable guarantee. This notion is associated with the development of a conception of fallible knowledge by later Academics such as Philo of Larissa.[8]

If we turn to *On the criterion* with this Hellenistic background in mind, a striking difference that emerges is Ptolemy's lack of explicit concern with skepticism. He does

---

which presents mathematics in general (and mathematical astronomy in particular) as one of the three branches of theoretical philosophy, alongside physics and theology. On Ptolemy and philosophy the most complete account is still Boll 1894, though Feke and Jones 2010 sets the agenda for a reexamination of Ptolemy's philosophy in light of contemporary scholarship.

[4] Diogenes Laertius (D.L.) 10.27, 7.54; Alcinous, *Didaskalikos* 4, pp. 154.10–156.23 Hermann (for the text see Whittaker and Louis 1990). As Dillon remarks (1993: 61), a discussion of the κριτήριον was "the accepted preliminary to any systematic exposition of logical theory."
[5] On the various uses of κριτήριον see Striker 1974: 23–33.
[6] Pl. *Tht.* 178b6, *Rep.* 582a6; Arist. *Metaph.* 1063a3.
[7] For Epicurus' analogy between κριτήριον and κανών see Striker 1974: 31–3.
[8] On these Academic theories see Striker 1990: 155–60 and Brittain 2001.

not confront any skeptical arguments in the text; rather, he assumes throughout that knowledge is possible and attempts to explain how it can be achieved. On the whole, Ptolemy uses κριτήριον in its general sense of "means of judgment" or "faculty." Yet in giving an account of what he calls "the criterion of the things that are" (τὸ κριτήριον τῶν ὄντων; ch. 1, 3.1), Ptolemy presents a five-part analysis that includes not only the cognitive faculties and processes involved in judgment—νοῦς, αἴσθησις, and λόγος—but also the object that is being judged (identified as "what is," τὸ ὄν) and the aim of judgment (truth or ἀλήθεια). For Ptolemy, then, an account of the κριτήριον is an account of all the elements involved in the process of judgment as well as their interaction; Dillon's "mechanics of making a judgment" captures the idea very well.[9] As for "what is" (τὸ ὄν), the object of judgment, Ptolemy explains that it plays the role of "subject" (ὑποκείμενον) and "what is judged" (τὸ κρινόμενον), since it is "the clearest (δηλώτατον) and most generic (γενικώτατον) of the things that come under examination" (ch. 2, 4.16–18). Some examples of judgment in the text include: recognizing that a certain perceptible thing is a man or a horse, or an example of health or disease (ch. 11, 17.9–10); judging that "man is the same as horse, qua animal, but different, qua rational" (ch. 11, 17.10–12); grasping "the forms as separated from perceptible things" (ch. 12, 18.1–4); and ascending from particular objects to genera, species, and being (τὸ ὄν) itself (ch. 12, 18.17–19.6). In general, then, Ptolemy's concern is to explain the process by which the human mind can grasp the formal features of perceptible objects and the relations between them.

These features of Ptolemy's account indicate that it has closer affinities to the Platonic and Aristotelian traditions as represented by texts such as the *Didaskalikos* of Alcinous or the description of Peripatetic epistemology in Sextus Empiricus (*Adv. math.* 7.214-7) than to any of the distinctively Hellenistic schools. The similarities with the Peripatetic account are particularly close, as we shall see. This is of course not to say that Ptolemy was ignorant of developments in Hellenistic epistemology. As far as skepticism is concerned, A. A. Long has drawn attention to the way in which

---

[9] The phrase περὶ κριτήριον is probably best rendered as "On judgment"; cf. Alcinous, *Didask.* 4, p. 154.10-13 Hermann: "Since there is something that judges (τὸ κρῖνον), and there is something that is judged (τὸ κρινόμενον), there must also be something that results from these, and that may be termed judgment (κρίσις). In the strictest sense (κυρίως), one might declare "criterion" (κριτήριον) to be the act of judgment (τὴν κρίσιν), but more broadly that which judges (τὸ κρῖνον)" (transl. Dillon, slightly modified). In two passages of *On the criterion* (ch. 12, 17.17 and 18.10) Ptolemy refers to sense perception (αἴσθησις) and intellect (νοῦς) as κριτήρια. This should be understood in light of the widespread use of κριτήριον to refer to faculties of the soul, even though these faculties are strictly speaking only elements of the "universal and unqualified κριτήριον" (τὸ καθόλου καὶ ἁπλοῦν κριτήριον; ch. 1, 3.17-8) whose structure is explained by Ptolemy's five-part analysis.

Ptolemy pursues a strategy of "optimum agreement" in *On the criterion*, emphasizing the common ground between different views and arguing that apparent disagreements concern terminology rather than substance.[10] Such a strategy can be seen as a response to the Skeptics' efforts to appeal to the allegedly irreconcilable disagreement (διαφωνία) between different schools to attack the possibility of knowledge. It should also be viewed against the background of the attempt of later Academics such as Philo of Larissa to identify principles that enjoyed widespread agreement as starting points for (fallible) knowledge in the arts and sciences.[11] Nonetheless, it is clear that Ptolemy's explicit purpose in *On the criterion* is not to establish that knowledge is possible, but to explain how it can be attained.

This emphasis may be disappointing if one is interested in the history of skeptical arguments, but it makes good sense if *On the criterion* is viewed in relation to Ptolemy's scientific works. As a practicing scientist who made fundamental contributions across the entire range of the ancient exact sciences, Ptolemy was naturally more concerned with how one goes about judging truth than with the abstract issue of whether or not such judgment is possible. This point has also been emphasized by Long, who characterizes *On the criterion* as offering an "epistemology for the practicing scientist."[12] From this perspective *On the criterion* should be viewed as setting out a basic position on epistemological issues—such as the relative contributions of sense perception and reasoning to scientific knowledge—that are relevant to the methodology employed by Ptolemy in his scientific works. As Long has pointed out, this reading is supported by close parallels between the epistemology of *On the criterion* and the *Harmonics*.[13] In the opening chapter of the *Harmonics* Ptolemy explains that the two κριτήρια in harmonics are reason (λόγος) and perception (αἴσθησις); the proper use of these two "means of judgment" is a constant theme throughout the work.[14] He distinguishes his approach to the analysis of harmonic intervals from that of the excessively "rationalist" Pythagoreans—for whom rationally justifiable theories should be accepted even when they are directly contradicted by clear evidence of the senses—and that of the overly "empirical" Aristoxeneans, for whom audible harmonies are not subject to rational mathematical analysis at all.[15] This attempt to strike a balance between rationalism

---

[10] Long 1989: 165, 171–2.
[11] Tarrant 1981.
[12] Long 1989: 163–4.
[13] Long 1989: 168–70; cf. Bullialdus 1663: 33–5 and Boll 1894: 94–100.
[14] *Harm.* 1.1, p. 3.3–5 Düring: "The means of judgment (κριτήρια) in harmonics are hearing (ἀκοή) and reason (λόγος), but not in the same way: rather, hearing is concerned with matter (ὕλη) and modification (πάθος), reason with the form (εἶδος) and the cause (τὸ αἴτιον)." The chapter goes on to discuss the relationship of αἴσθησις in general to λόγος (below, n. 19).
[15] *Harmonics* 1.1–2; esp. 1.2, p. 5.24–6.13 Düring. Cf. Long 1989: 168–70 and Barker 2000.

and empiricism corresponds *mutatis mutandis* to the position that Ptolemy advocates in a key passage of *On the criterion*: one should neither dismiss sense perception as irrelevant, nor prefer its conclusions to those of thought (ch. 10, 15.5–8). *On the criterion*, then, may be considered a sort of epistemological prelude to Ptolemy's scientific works.[16]

If this view is correct, we should expect the details of the epistemological theory advanced in *On the criterion* to have implications for the understanding of Ptolemy's scientific methodology. I shall return to this point in the conclusion. Before turning to a detailed examination of the text, however, I would like to point out that this view can also help to explain a number of features of *On the criterion* that may seem puzzling at first glance. In particular, *On the criterion* makes no reference to mathematics or demonstration (ἀπόδειξις), a fact which is surprising in light of the central importance of mathematics throughout Ptolemy's scientific work. But the reason for this fact, and for the text's concern with the mind's grasp of forms, becomes clear upon consideration of Ptolemy's general approach to the mathematical sciences as described in the *Almagest* and *Harmonics*. Both texts show that Ptolemy conceives of astronomy and harmonics as attempting to explain the observable behavior of perceptible objects in terms of the relationships between their quantitative, formal features, as expressed in mathematical models (ὑποθέσεις).[17] The forms (εἴδη) do not belong to a separated, Platonic realm, but are underlying features of the objects of study.[18] Thus the harmonicist explains the audible harmonies by reference to the formal, quantitative relationships between different pitches, while the astronomer explains the movements of the observable heavenly bodies by reference to the formal features of the spheres or other bodies on which they are carried (as set out in the mathematical models of epicycles and deferents). Grasping the formal relationships studied by mathematics requires the use of reason (λόγος), which is described in the *Harmonics* as autonomous and orderly (αὐτοτελής, τεταγμένος) in contrast

---

[16] For argument on partly independent grounds that *On the criterion* is an early work of Ptolemy's, see Feke and Jones 2010.

[17] For ὑπόθεσις in the sense of "model" in Ptolemy see Toomer 1984: 23–4. The term of course has a range of meanings, including "assumption" and "basic principle" on which something else is constructed; cf. Barker 2000: 23–7.

[18] For the analysis of existing things (τὰ ὄντα) into form (εἶδος), matter (ὕλη), and motion (κίνησις) see *Almagest* 1.1, I 5.10–13 Heiberg; *Harm.* 3.3, p. 92.9–11 Düring. The *Almagest* passage states that none of the three can be observed (θεωρηθῆναι) in isolation, though each can be *conceived* (νοηθῆναι) independently of the others. Ptolemy goes on to contrast the subject matter of mathematics with that of theology and physics: while theology is concerned with the first cause of the primary motion of the universe and physics with "material and ever-changing quality" (τῆς ὑλικῆς καὶ ἀεὶ κινουμένης ποιότητος) such as white and sweet, the subject matter of mathematics is "quality with respect to form and change of position (τῆς κατὰ τὰ εἴδη καὶ τὰς μεταβατικὰς κινήσεις ποιότητος)," such as shape, place, time, and motion (*Almagest* 1.1, I 5.13–6.4 Heiberg).

to sense perception (αἴσθησις), which is inexact and unreliable insofar as it is bound up with unstable matter.[19] Because of the fallibility and imprecision of sense perception, a mathematical model such as the division of the scale by the harmonic "canon" (κανών) or monochord can serve as a "rational criterion" (λογικὸν κριτήριον), that is, a standard which can assist the senses in making fine discriminations.[20] But the primary goal of both the astronomer and the harmonicist is to develop a theory that agrees with the observable phenomena, and it is the "concord" or "agreement" (συμφωνία) between theory and observation that serves as the main criterion of a theory's truth.[21] This has the important consequence that theories in astronomy and harmonics cannot be known with demonstrative certainty. To be sure, once a mathematical model has been developed, exact consequences

---

[19] *Harm.* 1.1, p. 3.1–20 Düring; for the beginning see above, n. 14. Ptolemy goes on to say that λόγος is capable of discovering what is exact (ἀκριβής), while αἴσθησις is limited to the discovery of what is approximate (σύνεγγυς); just as matter is defined (ὁρίζεται) and limited (περαίνεται) only by form, so the apprehensions (διαλήψεις) of sense perception are limited and defined by those of reason. Because of the instability (τὸ ἄστατον) of matter, "neither the perception of all people, nor even that of the very same people, remains the same when directed repeatedly to objects in the same condition" (p. 3.17–9 Düring; transl. Barker 1989). The instability of matter is also cited as one reason for the limited reliability of physics in the *Almagest* (τὸ τῆς ὕλης ἄστατον καὶ ἄδηλον, I 6.15 Heiberg).

[20] *Harm.* 1.1–2, p. 5.6–13 Düring: "Since similar things occur in relation to sounds and to the hearing, there is needed to help them, just as there is for the eyes, some rational criterion (κριτήριον λογικόν) working through appropriate instruments (διὰ τῶν οἰκείων ὀργάνων), as the plumb line (σταθμή) is needed to deal with straightness, for instance, and the compasses for the circle and the measurement of its parts. For the ears…. there is needed some method derived from reason, to deal with the things that they are not naturally capable of judging accurately, a method against which they will not bear witness, but which they will agree is correct. The instrument (ὄργανον) of this kind of method is called the harmonic canon (κανών), a term adopted out of common usage, and from its straightening (κανονίζειν) those things in sense perception that fall short with respect to truth" (transl. Barker 1989, slightly modified).

[21] Cf. *Harm.* 1.2, p. 5.13–9 Düring: "The aim of the harmonicist would be to preserve (διασῶσαι) in every way the rational hypotheses (ὑποθέσεις) of the canon as never in any way conflicting with sense perceptions according to the judgment of most people, just as the aim of the astronomer (ἀστρόλογος) is to preserve the hypotheses of the heavenly movements in agreement (συμφώνους) with their carefully observed (τηρουμέναις) courses, these [hypotheses] themselves being taken from the evident (ἐναργῶν), rough and ready (ὁλοσχερέστερον) appearances, but discovering the particulars (τὰ κατὰ μέρος) by reason as accurately as possible." Whether the astronomer's project is defined as "saving the hypotheses" (as here) or "saving the phenomena" (the formulation traditionally ascribed to Plato), the goal is to develop theories that will agree with observation. For the idea of confirmation see *Almagest* 1.8, I 26.9–12 Heiberg: the ὑποθέσεις that have been set out so far will be "completely confirmed and attested (βεβαιωθησομένας καὶ ἐπιμαρτυρηθησομένας τέλεον) by the agreement with the phenomena (τῆς…πρὸς τὰ φαινόμενα συμφωνίας) of the things that will be demonstrated sequentially in what follows." That agreement with observation is a more important criterion of the truth of a theory than derivability from rational principles is apparent from *Almagest* 9.2 (II 211–12 Heiberg), where Ptolemy indicates that his planetary theories will feature "basic assumptions which we arrived at not from some readily apparent principle, but

can be drawn from it using the indisputable methods of arithmetic and geometry. But the process of building the model involves a significant empirical component; hence its accuracy is necessarily affected by the imprecision of sense perception. Moreover, deciding when a theory qualifies as agreeing with observation is a delicate matter that involves judgment and requires assessing whether observations fall within an acceptable margin of error.[22] Finally, Ptolemy explicitly recognizes that there may be more than one model that agrees with the observable phenomena; hence agreement with observation does not *imply* the model's truth.[23] The upshot is that Ptolemy's conception of method in the exact sciences gave him good reason to conceive of theories in disciplines such as astronomy and harmonics as fallible, even though they make as much use as possible of deductive methods.[24] The agreement between theory and observation is a criterion in the sense of being a reliable indication of the theory's truth; it is not an indubitable guarantee.[25]

The close connection between reason, form, and mathematics in Ptolemy's thought explains the emphasis on form and the apparently puzzling lack of any reference to mathematics or demonstration in *On the criterion*. What the text addresses is the

from a long period of trial and application" (κατὰ τὴν συνεχῆ διάπειραν καὶ ἐφαρμογήν, II 212.3–5 Heiberg; transl. Toomer 1984). The paradigm example is the introduction of the equant point, according to which the center of uniform rotation is assumed to be different from the geometrical center of some of the circles in the planetary models. The justification of such features consists precisely in the fact that their consequences agree with the phenomena.

[22] On the question of observational error in Ptolemy see Lloyd 1982; cf. Grasshoff 1990: 211.

[23] See, for example, Ptolemy's proof of the empirical equivalence of the epicyclic and eccentric models of the solar motion in *Almagest* 3.3, I 219–32 Heiberg. The idea that agreement with observation does not serve as a demonstration of a theory's truth has a long subsequent history; cf. Aquinas, *Summa Theologica* 1.32. As Musgrave has shown (1991), Ptolemy's recognition of this point in no way commits him to an instrumentalist position along the lines set out by P. Duhem (1969).

[24] At *Almagest* 1.1, I 6.11–21 Heiberg Ptolemy says that both physics and theology should properly be called "conjecture" (εἰκασία) rather than knowledge, and that there is no hope that philosophers will ever agree about them; mathematics, however, can provide firm (βέβαιαν) and unshakable (ἀμετάπιστον) knowledge, "for its kind of proof (ἀπόδειξις) proceeds by indisputable (ἀναμφισβητήτων) methods, namely arithmetic and geometry." But while Ptolemy obviously prizes the reliability of mathematical demonstration and makes extensive use of deductive methods in his scientific works, those works are not organized to conform to the ideals of either Aristotelian demonstration or Euclidean axiomatics (cf. Suppes 1980). In general, Ptolemy's position seems to be that sciences such as astronomy and harmonics should make use of arithmetic and geometry as tools (they are "instruments of indisputable (ἀναμφισβητήτοις) authority"; *Harm.* 3.3, p. 94.16–17 Düring), while also recognizing the limits of what they can reveal about the physical world. Barker (2000: 15) emphasizes Ptolemy's recognition of the fallibility of his scientific theories.

[25] Although Ptolemy does not say that συμφωνία is a κριτήριον, his position amounts to a recognition that it serves as a criterion of truth of scientific theories in the weaker sense that emerges from the Stoic/Academic debate (above, n. 8).

general issue of how the mind grasps forms and uses its cognitive faculties in the judgment of truth. Its concern is to explain the contributions of the senses and the intellect to this process, without going into the details of the nature of reasoning in a discipline such as geometry or arithmetic, or the method of building a mathematical model from empirical data in astronomy or harmonics. The emphasis is not on the certainty that can be achieved through demonstration, but on the issues involved in developing theories from observations and assessing their truth. In sum, what *On the criterion* provides is not a scientific method as such, but an epistemological theory on the basis of which scientific methods can be developed. By understanding the way in which the human mind grasps truth and the epistemological basis of reliable judgment, Ptolemy suggests, the scientist will better be able to develop suitable methods to reach the truth about the world in particular areas of investigation.

With these considerations in mind, I turn to a close examination of the epistemological theory set out in *On the criterion*. My principal goal is to show how Ptolemy draws on the philosophical tradition to formulate a theory of knowledge that addresses the issues raised by his work in the exact sciences. In the conclusion I will summarize some of the distinctive aspects of Ptolemy's epistemology and briefly consider some of its implications for the understanding of his scientific method.

2.

The most striking feature of Ptolemy's procedure in *On the criterion* is the extended analogy he draws in chapters 1–3 between the κριτήριον and the lawcourt or δικαστήριον—where this is understood not as a place, but as a body of individuals (the assembly or the jury) that renders judgment. The analogy was supported by the fact that the term κριτήριον was regularly used to refer to the lawcourt in Hellenistic Greek.[26] As far as we know, however, Ptolemy is the first thinker to develop the analogy in detail. He frames his approach in terms of an Aristotelian progression from particulars to universals:

> We would investigate the means of judging the things that are (τὸ κριτήριον τῶν ὄντων) in the necessary way if we were to compare it to some of the means of judgment (κριτηρίοις) that are specifically arranged under it. For the most natural preliminary approach to all universals is through the particulars which fall under the same genus. (ch. 1, 3.1–5)

---

[26] E.g. Polybius 9.33; cf. Debrunner 1954: 56. Plato, *Laws* 767b seems to be the only pre-Hellenistic example of the use of the term in this sense.

That the universal is grasped by starting from the particular is of course well-established Aristotelian doctrine.[27] But Ptolemy's procedure is interesting in that he takes the lawcourt to be both an example of the genus κριτήριον and an analog for the general class. Moreover, the analogical approach is not just an expository device; it is in fact how Ptolemy thinks one can best grasp the structure of the κριτήριον. With this opening Ptolemy signals that an understanding of the κριτήριον is to be reached not by deduction from first principles but by reflecting on examples of how judgment is actually carried out.

Ptolemy begins his exposition of the lawcourt analogy by presenting a general picture of legal judgment: a judge or magistrate (ὁ ἄρχων) renders judgment on a matter of dispute, for example, an act (πρᾶξις), which is "made manifest in a certain way" (δηλωθεῖσάν πως) during the court proceedings. The magistrate judges by "following the law" (ἀκολουθῶν νόμῳ), and with the goal of civic association (κοινωνία) in mind.[28] From this example Ptolemy derives a five-part analysis of the elements of judgment, which is applied to judgments with technical instruments and to the case of judgment in general (Table 13.1). As set out in column 1 of Table 13.1, these elements are: (1) what is judged (τὸ κρινόμενον), (2) that through which (δι' οὗ) it is judged, (3) that which judges (τὸ κρῖνον), (4) that by which (ᾧ) it is judged, (5) and that for the sake of which (οὗ ἕνεκεν) it is judged. Applying this schema to the case of legal judgment yields the correspondences set out in column 2 of the table: what is judged (τὸ κρινόμενον) is the act (πρᾶξις), that "through which" (δι' οὗ) it is judged is the "presentation" (δήλωσις) of the case, that which judges (τὸ κρῖνον) is the magistrate (ὁ ἄρχων), that "by which" (ᾧ) it is judged is the law (νόμος), and that "for the sake of which" (οὗ ἕνεκα) judgment is rendered is civic association (κοινωνία).[29] In the general case of judgment by the human mind (column 4), intellect (νοῦς) is the judge; it seeks to grasp "what is" (τὸ ὄν) for the sake of truth (ἀλήθεια), and it does so "through" sense perception (αἴσθησις) and "by" reasoning (λόγος).

The relationship between the first, third, and fifth elements in Ptolemy's scheme is clear enough. Any act of judgment involves a judge (τὸ κρῖνον) and something that is

---

[27] See e.g. A. Po. B 19, 100a 4—b 5; Metaph. A 1, 980a 27–981a 12.

[28] Ptolemy's model of the judicial process—involving a single magistrate, the reading of legal documents, courtroom speeches, and examination of witnesses—corresponds reasonably well to what we know of legal practices in Greco-Roman Egypt in the second century AD. On these see Taubenschlag 1916; Kelly 2011: 170–77 and *passim*.

[29] Ch. 1, 3.10–14.3. The tabular arrangement is a convenient way to present Ptolemy's criterial scheme, though the text makes no reference to a table. In some manuscripts, however, the text of *On the criterion* is followed by a table that sets out various ways of filling out Ptolemy's scheme for different types of judgment (Lammert 1961: 24–5; Huby and Neal 1989: 227–30).

Table 13.1 Ptolemy's analysis of the elements of judgment

Elements of judgment	Legal judgment	Judgments with technical instruments	Judgment in general
1 what is judged (τὸ κρινόμενον)	act (πρᾶξις)	magnitude (μέγεθος)	what is (τὸ ὄν)
2 that through which (τὸ δι' οὗ)	presentation of case (δήλωσις)	cubit-rule (πῆχυς)	sense perception (αἴσθησις)
3 that which judges (τὸ κρῖνον)	magistrate (ἄρχων)	surveyor (ἀναμετρητής)	intellect (νοῦς)
4 that by which (τὸ ᾧ)	law (νόμος)	application of rule (ἐπιβολή, παραβολή)	reasoning (λόγος)
5 that for the sake of which (τὸ οὗ ἕνεκα)	civic association (κοινωνία)	size (πηλικότης)	truth (ἀλήθεια)

judged (τὸ κρινόμενον); it can also be said to aim at some goal (τὸ οὗ ἕνεκα).[30] The main difficulty is understanding the roles of the second and fourth elements; since these correspond to sense perception (αἴσθησις) and reasoning (λόγος) in the general case, it is crucial to define their roles precisely. One way to approach this problem is to try to understand the semantic value of the two expressions that Ptolemy uses to designate these elements, the "through which" (διά + genitive) and "by which" (dative) locutions.[31] The preposition διά followed by the genitive case can be taken in a spatial or temporal sense (as when something moves "through" a distance or period of time) but also as expressing the means or instrument "through which" something is done (LSJ s.v. I, III). In the legal case, the advocates' presentation of the case provides the judge with access to events that he has not witnessed; it thus conveys information "through" distances in time and space. But the case of measurement (column 3) emphasizes the instrumental role of the second element, since that element corresponds to the measuring instrument (the πῆχυς or cubit-rule). As for the fourth element, that "by which"

---

[30] That Ptolemy identifies civic association (κοινωνία) as the goal of legal judgment reflects the role of the lawcourt as a forum for settling disputes and sustaining the civic order. For a view of the social function of the legal system in Greco-Roman Egypt see Kelly 2011.

[31] This approach is inspired by Burnyeat's analysis of the distinction between that "through which" (διά + genitive) and that "by which" (dative) we perceive in Pl., *Tht.* 184–86 (Burnyeat 1976). The passage is an obvious model for Ptolemy's usage, whether directly or via the Platonic tradition.

(ᾧ) judgment is rendered, the dative can also express the idea of means or instrument. But Ptolemy's picture of legal judgment, in which the judge judges by "following the law" (ἀκολουθῶν νόμῳ), suggests interpreting the dative as modal, that is, as expressing the character of the action that is involved in judgment. This is supported by the example of measurement (col. 3), in which the fourth element corresponds to the way in which the rule is applied (by being placed alongside or on top of what is to be measured). Now in one sense, "following the law" might be understood as the application of procedures for evaluating the evidence presented in court. But the law can also be conceived of as a standard or norm, that is, as something by comparison with which the rightness of actions is assessed.[32] This suggests understanding the fourth criterial element as that "by reference to which" one judges, where the operation of "referring" is understood as comparison to a standard or norm.[33]

Ptolemy gives two additional instrumental examples to illustrate his scheme, involving judgments of weight and judgments of perpendicularity or straightness (ch. 1, 4.3–14; Table 13.2). Taken together with the measurement example, these support the interpretation of the fourth element as expressing both the mode or manner of judgment and, more specifically, the comparison to standards. In the case of the cubit-rule, the straightedge, and the plumb line, the fourth element corresponds to the application of the instrument (e.g., placing the rule alongside the object to be measured). But in the case of the balance, the fourth element is not its application but rather the result of that application, the inclination (ῥοπή) of the balance one way or another. It is by reference to this inclination that one can decide which of the two weights is greater. In fact the application of the other instruments also involves a similar comparison. A wall, for example, is assessed for straightness or perpendicularity by comparison to the straightedge or plumb line; similarly, measurement by the cubit-rule involves comparison between the length to be measured and the length of the standard rule. The difference between these instruments and the balance is simply that the former are themselves standards (of length, straightness, or perpendicularity) while the balance is not. In sum, then, the fourth element refers to the use of the second to yield a result, by reference to which a reliable judgment is made.[34]

---

[32] For the analogy between law (νόμος) and κανών as rule or norm see Oppel 1937: 51–7. Cf. Dio Chrysostom 75.1: law is "the just straightedge (κανὼν δίκαιος), against which (πρὸς ὅν) each person must straighten (ἀπευθύνειν) his own character."

[33] For the dative cf. Pl. *Rep.* 582a (cited by Smyth [1956: sec. 1512] as an example of the "dative of standard of judgment") and Gal. *De opt. doctr.* 1.43.21–44.2 Kühn: some have taught that man has no κριτήριον "by comparison with which he will discern each of the things that are with precision" (ᾧ παραβάλλων ἕκαστον τῶν ὄντων ἀκριβῶς διαγνώσεται).

[34] If Ptolemy's fourth element expresses the idea of a standard of judgment, it might seem puzzling that the κανών and σταθμή are identified with the *second* element. But I take it that they are

Table 13.2 Ptolemy's elements of judgments illustrated by analogies with measuring instruments

Elements of judgment	Magnitude	Weight	Perpendicularity, straightness
1 what is judged (τὸ κρινόμενον)	magnitude (μέγεθος)	weight (βάρος)	state, placement (σχέσις, θέσις)
2 that through which (τὸ δι' οὗ)	cubit-rule (πῆχυς)	balance (ζυγόν)	plumb line, straightedge (σταθμή, κανών)
3 that which judges (τὸ κρῖνον)	surveyor (ἀναμετρητής)	weigher (ζυγοστάτης)	builder, carpenter
4 that by which (τὸ ᾧ)	laying alongside/on (παραβολή, ἐπιβολή)	inclination (ῥοπή)	placing alongside, extending (παράθεσις, ἀπότασις)
5 that for the sake of which (τὸ οὗ ἕνεκα)	quantity of magnitude (ἡ πηλικότης τοῦ μεγέθους)	excess of weight (ἡ ὑπεροχὴ τοῦ βάρους)	perpendicularity, straightness (ὀρθότης, εὐθύτης)

A similar appeal to the instrument analogy to express a distinction between agent, instrument, and use is found in Sextus Empiricus' presentation and refutation of theories of the criterion in *Adv. math.* 7. At 7.35-7 Sextus explains that the term κριτήριον as applied to a means of judging truth can be understood in several senses, which he explains by analogy to the use of technical instruments such as the balance. Just as the process of weighing involves a weigher, a balance, and the application of the balance, so the κριτήριον can be understood as (a) that "by the agency of which" (ὑφ' οὗ) judgment takes place (e.g. man), (b) that "through which" (δι' οὗ) it takes place (e.g. αἴσθησις or διάνοια), and (c) "application and mode" (προσβολὴ καὶ σχέσις). An example of the third sense is the application of an impression (προσβολὴ τῆς φαντασίας), "according to which" (καθ' ἥν) the man judges. The same division is found in *Pyrr. hyp.* 2.15, except that the phrase "according to which" (καθ' ὅ) is used in place of προσβολὴ καὶ

---

identified with this element qua instruments, not qua standards; i.e. it is irrelevant to the the role of the κανών as that "through which" judgment is reached that the straightedge is itself straight. For the idea of the κανών and σταθμή as instruments whose use provides a standard of assessment cf. *Harm.* 1.1-2, p. 5.6-13 Düring (above, n. 20).

σχέσις. The distinctions that Sextus draws correspond closely to those that underlie the second, third, and fourth elements in Ptolemy's criterial scheme. Like Ptolemy, Sextus distinguishes between criterial instruments (expressed by the phrase δι' οὗ) and their application to yield a result "according to which" or "in virtue of which" judgment is made. For Sextus the result of applying the instruments is an impression (φαντασία). In Ptolemy's picture, the result of applying the instrument is (e.g.) the inclination (ῥοπή) of the scales, or the correspondence/lack of correspondence between a standard length and a length to be measured.

I shall return to the significance of the parallel with Sextus at the end of this section. But we can now pause to offer a preliminary analysis of the contrast between the second and fourth elements in Ptolemy's scheme. The example of legal judgment suggests a contrast between the source of information (the presentation of evidence in court) and the methods and standards for evaluating it (the law). The instrument analogy suggests a contrast between instruments and their use to reach results on which secure judgment can be based. This perspective can readily be applied to the legal case: the evidence is "used" by considering it in light of the law, which yields a result in virtue of which the decision is made; the whole process can be described as "following the law." Thus, Ptolemy's identification of αἴσθησις with the second criterial element and λόγος with the fourth (col. 4 in Table 13.1) can be understood as follows: sense perception functions as a source of information (like the evidence provided in court) and λόγος as a way of using that information to reach a result "by reference to which" judgment can be made. In other words, αἴσθησις supplies the raw information, while λόγος provides the methods of assessment and standards of judgment.

Now since in Ptolemy's scheme the agent of judgment (τὸ κρῖνον) is the intellect (νοῦς), both sense perception and λόγος can also be viewed as instruments that the intellect uses in different ways. Ptolemy builds this perspective into his exposition of the lawcourt analogy as well. In chapter 2 he explains that the first and fifth elements of his criterial scheme are "extremes" (ἄκρα), which can immediately be identified with "what is" (τὸ ὄν) (as "the most generic subject of investigation") and with truth (since all investigation aims at truth; 4.15–5.3). The middle position between the extremes is occupied by the third element, the agent of judgment, which is a source or principle (ἀρχή); surrounding it are the second and fourth, "like instruments" (περιοχὴ δὲ καὶ ὥσπερ ὄργανα, 5.4–6). Later in the chapter (5.15–18) Ptolemy offers another characterization in which the first, third, and fifth elements are said to be "limits" (ὅροι) and "extremities" (ἀκρότητες) which are "simple" and "unmixed in their nature," while the second and fourth are the "interval" (διάστημα) and "means" (μεσότητες), "like conveyors in their transmissions to the extremes" (ὥσπερ πορισταὶ κατὰ τὰς πρὸς τὰ ἄκρα διαδόσεις). Sense perception (αἴσθησις) mediates between τὸ ὄν and the intellect (presumably by providing sensory evidence that reveals information about the objects of judgment) while reasoning (λόγος) mediates between the intellect and truth (presumably by making use of the evidence of the senses in such a way as to reveal the truth). The upshot of these characterizations is that the contrast between the second and fourth elements—and so between αἴσθησις and λόγος—can be described as a contrast between different kinds of instrumentality. This of course is supported by the fact that both the "through which" (δι' οὗ) and "by which" (ᾧ) locutions can express the idea of means or instrument.

Ptolemy goes on to provide a more detailed account of the operation of both αἴσθησις and λόγος, based on a division between the perceptive and rational elements of the soul (ch. 2, 5.18–6.11). The perceptive faculty (αἰσθητικὴ δύναμις) includes the sense organs (τὰ αἰσθητήρια), which are "the instruments (ὄργανα) of the body through which (δι' ὧν) it grasps (ἅπτεται) perceptible things"; φαντασία, the "impression (τύπωσις) and transmission (διάδοσις) to the intellect"; and ἔννοια or "conception," the intellect's retention (κατοχή) and memory (μνήμη) of what has been transmitted to it (τῶν διαδοθέντων). These abilities are shared by other animals as well as human beings. The principal activity of the rational part of the soul (τὸ λογικόν), which is distinctive to humans, is thought (διάνοια), defined as "internal reason (ὁ λόγος ὁ ἐνδιάθετος), a kind of exposition (διέξοδος) and recalling (ἀναπόλησις) and discrimination (διάκρισις) of what has been remembered" (6.3–5). The identification of λόγος with thought conceived of as a kind of internal conversation echoes Platonic formulations in the *Sophist* and *Theaetetus*, and shows that what Ptolemy means by λόγος is not a faculty but a process of rational discourse.[35] Corresponding to the internal λόγος of thought is external or "expressed" (προφορικός) λόγος, which is conveyed in speech (διάλεκτος). Ptolemy further distinguishes between the "simple and undifferentiated" (ἁπλῆ καὶ ἀδιάρθρωτος) use of internal λόγος, which becomes opinion (δόξα, οἴησις), and its "systematic and unshakeable" (τεχνική, ἀμετάπειστος) application, which becomes knowledge (ἐπιστήμη).

This highly compressed account of the various stages on the path from sense perception to knowledge leaves many issues open, but several points at least are clear. (1) The senses are viewed as providing access to the external world "through" the sense organs (διά in its spatial sense), thus supporting the assignment of αἴσθησις to the second element in the criterial scheme. (2) The conception of λόγος as a process rather than a faculty clarifies the way in which the intellect can be said to "use" sensory evidence by means of λόγος: the impressions (φαντασίαι) of the senses are retained in memory and analyzed through the process of discursive reasoning. (3) The senses are portrayed simply as conveyors of information—"impressions" or φαντασίαι—which

---

[35] Pl. *Soph.* 263e, *Tht.* 189e–190a; cf. Alcinous, *Didask.* 4, p. 155.17–20 Hermann.

are passed along to the intellect through a process of "transmission" (διάδοσις). There is no suggestion that the formation of φαντασίαι might involve anything more than the "stamping" (τύπωσις) of an external object on the sense organs; similarly, the genesis of ἔννοιαι from φαντασίαι is apparently identified with their "retention" (κατοχή) in memory. As Boll noted, there is a close parallel to Ptolemy's account of concept formation in Sextus' account of Peripatetic philosophy at *Adv. math.* 7.217-26.[36] But unlike Ptolemy, the Peripatetics distinguish between ἔννοια and μνήμη; the former is described as the "collection of impressions (φαντάσματα) of the intellect (νοῦς)" and a "summing up of particulars towards the universal" (συγκεφαλαίωσις τῶν ἐπὶ μέρος εἰς τὸ καθόλου; *Adv. math.* 7.224). In this picture ἔννοια corresponds roughly to what Aristotle calls "experience" or ἐμπειρία in his own accounts of concept formation.[37] There is reason to suppose that Ptolemy held a similar view, which might have emerged in a fuller account.[38] Nonetheless the effect of his abbreviated description is to emphasize the role of the senses as conveyors of information that is not altered in the process of transmission. (4) Finally, despite the fact that Ptolemy assigns ἔννοια to the perceptive rather than the rational part of the soul, his account also suggests that the content of ἔννοιαι can be expressed in language via λόγος. At 6.6-9 he draws a striking analogy: as νοῦς stands to φθόγγος ("sound"), so ἔννοια stands to φωνή ("voice"), and διάνοια to διάλεκτος ("speech"). φωνή ("the sound of the voice, whether of men or animals," LSJ s.v.) is distinct from both undifferentiated sound (φθόγγος) and articulate speech (διάλεκτος). Similarly ἔννοια is distinct from from both νοῦς (here conceived of as potential rather than active intellect) and from the articulate, rational discourse that is Ptolemy's internal λόγος.[39] By situating ἔννοια along a spectrum of increasing differentiation and

---

[36] Boll (1894), 79-82. Both Ptolemy and Sextus discuss αἴσθησις, φαντασία, νοῦς, ἔννοια, μνήμη, διάνοια, δόξα, and ἐπιστήμη. Further parallels include the identification of αἴσθησις and νοῦς as "primary criteria" (πρῶτα κριτήρια; cf. ch. 12, 17.17) and an appeal to the instrument analogy in which νοῦς plays the role of craftsman (τεχνίτης) and αἴσθησις that of instrument (ὄργανον) (*Adv. math.* 7.226).

[37] *Metaph.* A 1, 980a27-981a12; *A. Po.* B 19, 100a4-b5.

[38] For a Stoic (or Stoicizing) account associating ἔννοια with ἐμπειρία see SVF 2.83 (= Aetius 4.11). Dillon (1993: 68) notes that Alcinous sometimes identifies memory with the result of the preservation of sense impressions (e.g. *Didask.* 4, p. 154.39-40 Hermann) and sometimes treats it as a synonym of φυσικὴ ἔννοια, "natural concept" or "natural concept-formation" (ch. 4, p. 155.34 Hermann). This is no contradiction, however, since "For A., memory's activity in preserving and 'collating' sense impressions also serves to give us an intuition of the forms as they are manifested in matter." Similarly, Ptolemy says that it is "through the memory extended from perceptible things" (κατὰ τὴν διατεινομένην ἀπὸ τῶν αἰσθητῶν μνήμην) that one comes to grasp the forms as separated from particulars (ch. 12, 18.1-4; see the discussion of this passage below).

[39] Cf. Arist. *HA* 535a26-31: φωνή is ascribed to animals while διάλεκτος is defined as "the articulation of voice by the tongue" (ἡ τῆς φωνῆς τῇ γλώττῃ διάρθρωσις); both are distinguished from mere sound (ψόφος).

articulation, Ptolemy's analogy suggests that an ἔννοια has the potential to be expressed in language. And since an ἔννοια on the present account is simply the retention of φαντασίαι in memory, the analogy suggests that the content of sense impressions can be expressed in language as well. This will be confirmed in the sequel.

In chapter 3 Ptolemy returns to the lawcourt analogy and extends it to include the cognitive faculties, processes, and states described in chapter 2 (6.12–7.6). αἴσθησις is now said to correspond to the advocates, while the sense organs correspond to the memoranda or petitions (ὑπομνήματα) filed by the litigants,[40] φαντασία to the speeches given in court (αἱ ῥητορεῖαι), and ἔννοια to the "memory and writing down of what has been said" in court (μνήμη καὶ ἀναγραφὴ τῶν ῥηθέντων). Just as the faculty of sense perception makes use of the sense organs to fashion its impressions (φαντασίαι) on the intellect, so the advocates make use of ὑπομνήματα in fashioning their speeches in court. The distinction between ὑπομνήματα and complete speeches might be a hint that φαντασία involves a certain amount of embellishment;[41] similarly, the analogy between ἔννοια and the writing down of the speeches could suggest that the process of forming ἔννοιαι involves a certain amount of summary or generalization. In any case, the comparison of φαντασία with courtroom speeches suggests that φαντασίαι are rich representations of perceptible objects, the contents of which can be expressed in language by λόγος. Finally and most importantly, the comparison of sense perception to the advocates and φαντασία to their speeches conveys the partisan character of sensory evidence: the reports of the senses are like representations fashioned by the advocates to support a certain point of view.[42]

For all its complexity, Ptolemy's lawcourt analogy is an effective means of clarifying the relationship between the different aspects of human judgment. In this picture intellect or νοῦς is the authoritative judge; it pronounces judgment by assessing the evidence of the senses in the light of rational discourse (λόγος). The senses provide the evidence that gives the intellect access to what is to be judged. But the impressions they produce

---

[40] ὑπόμνημα is regularly used of a petition addressed to a magistrate in Greco-Roman Egypt; cf. LSJ s.v. IV. In a legal context such petitions typically detailed the complaints of the petitioner and so could serve as the basis of the advocates' speeches. Kelly (2011: 172–5) draws attention to the significant overlap of terminology and rhetorical *topoi* between the text of petitions and courtroom speeches.

[41] φαντασία is said to involve representation or depiction (ἀναζωγράγησις) in Alcinous (*Didask.* 4, p. 155.13–17 Hermann); cf. ἀναζωγραφῇ at Sextus, *Adv. math.* 7.222.

[42] At 6.19–7.1 internal λόγος is likened to "the consultation and achievement of the judgment (τὸ συμβούλιον καὶ τέλος τῆς γνώμης)" and expressed λόγος to "the sentence and announcement of the judgment (τῇ ἀποφάσει καὶ ἀνακηρύξει τῆς κρίσεως)." This seems inapposite, insofar as expressed λόγος (i.e. language) seems to be a medium of deliberation as much as internal λόγος. But Ptolemy consistently emphasizes the superiority of internal to expressed λόγος; the latter, he claims, can easily lead to distraction and error (e.g. ch. 5, 8.13–20). The restriction of external λόγος to the

on the intellect, like the speeches of advocates in court, are partisan and not objective. The intellect must evaluate or "use" them by a process of reasoning (λόγος), just as the judge must evaluate the speeches of the advocates by following the procedures of the law (νόμος). Like the law, λόγος supplies the methods of evaluation and standards by which the evidence is assessed. Thus both αἴσθησις and λόγος are instruments employed by the intellect, though they function in different ways—the first as providing information, the second as a means of evaluating it. The various contrasts that Ptolemy draws between the second and fourth elements of the criterial scheme—between source of information and means of evaluation, instrument and use, or different kinds of use—are all captured by the "through which" (δι' οὗ) and "by which" (ᾧ) locutions. Finally we may note that the lawcourt analogy suggests that both sense perception and reasoning are essential for gaining knowledge of the nature of things: without the senses the intellect has no access to the world, and without reasoning, it has no means of assessing what the senses report. But the power of judgment lies with the intellect and its use of λόγος rather than the senses.

Before turning to the further development of these ideas in chapters 4–12 of the text, I would like to return to the comparison between Ptolemy and Sextus. While a number of roughly contemporary authors advocate criterial schemes that correspond to elements of Ptolemy's, Sextus' tripartite division between agent, instrument, and mode of application is by far the closest parallel.[43] This is potentially significant for the understanding of Ptolemy's argumentative strategy. There is reason to think that Sextus' tripartite division originated in a Skeptical context, since a passage in Diogenes Laertius suggests that the three aspects of judgment that Sextus identifies were discussed by certain skeptics as alternative candidates for being the criterion of truth.[44] It is certainly the case that the scheme functions in this way in Sextus' text. In his refutation of the existence of a criterion of truth he proceeds systematically through the three aspects as though they were alternatives: neither can man be the criterion (Adv. math. 7.263–342); nor can sense perception and intellect, whether working separately or together (7.343–69); nor can φαντασία, whether "cognitive" or only "plausible"

---

announcement of the decision may be meant to emphasize that the only true deliberation is the internal deliberation of thought. In any case the characterization of internal λόγος confirms the role of the fourth criterial element as including both the process of reaching a judgment (the deliberation or consultation, συμβούλιον) and the result (τέλος) of that process.

[43] According to D.L. 1.21, the "eclectic" philosopher Potamon of Alexandria distinguished between the criterion of truth "by the agency of which" (ὑφ' οὗ) judgment comes about (the commanding faculty or ἡγεμονικόν) and that "through which" (δι' οὗ) it comes about, identified as "the most exact impression (τὴν ἀκριβεστάτην φαντασίαν)." Alcinous distinguishes between the agent (ὑφ' οὗ) of judgment (the human intellect, νοῦς), and that "through which" (δι' οὗ) judgment comes about, viz. a "natural instrument of judging" (ὄργανον φυσικὸν κριτικόν) that is identified with natural or innate reason (λόγος φυσικός) (Didask. 4, p. 154.10–18 Hermann).

[44] D.L. 9.95; cf. Striker 1974: 69–70.

(7.370–439). The tripartite division thus serves Sextus as a means of organizing his refutation of many different theories of the criterion. Ptolemy adopts the same division but for the opposite purpose: to show that his theory of the κριτήριον captures the key elements of judgment common to other views, and so rests on a basis of wide agreement. In this way, Ptolemy turns a strategy of refutation to a strategy for commanding assent.[45]

3.

The remainder of the epistemological section of *On the criterion* (chapters 4–12) is concerned with clarifying the relative contributions of intellect (νοῦς), sense perception (αἴσθησις), and rational discourse (λόγος) to scientific knowledge. Ptolemy builds on the picture developed in the lawcourt analogy, although he largely drops the analogical mode of exposition. The basis of the account is the traditional distinction between sense perception and intellect. At the beginning of chapter 4 Ptolemy remarks that νοῦς and αἴσθησις are "principles of a kind, and elements" (ἀρχαί τινες καὶ στοιχεῖα), while the other aspects of the soul involved in judgment are "faculties (δυνάμεις) and organs (ὄργανα) and activities (ἐνεργήματα)"; hence a grasp of the similarities and differences of perception and intellect will be sufficient to clarify all the relevant issues (7.7–11).[46]

After a largely methodological interlude that emphasizes the need to avoid empty terminological disputes (ch. 4–8, 7.12–13.3) Ptolemy returns to epistemology proper. In chapters 8 and 9 (13.4–15.4) he offers a detailed comparison between sense perception and intellect that emphasizes the superiority of the latter. The key points of this comparison are as follows. (1) Ptolemy draws a sharp distinction between the functions of sense and intellect. Sense perception is conceived of as a messenger (ἄγγελος) that grasps perceptible things (αἰσθητά) through the sense organs and "transmits to the intellect by way of impression the affections that arise in it" (διαδίδωσι κατὰ τὴν φαντασίαν τὰ γινόμενα περὶ αὐτὴν πάθη τῷ νῷ). The intellect adds (ἐπισυνάπτει) the activity of thought and critical judgment (τὴν διανοητικὴν καὶ κριτικὴν ἐνέργειαν; ch. 8, 13.5–10). The senses judge (κρίνειν) how they themselves are affected (i.e. their πάθη), while the intellect judges both the external objects (ὑποκείμενα) that produce the affections and

---

[45] The fact that Potamon was known for "selecting his doctrines from each of the schools" (ἐκλεξαμέου τὰ ἀρέσκοντα ἐξ ἑκάστης τῶν αἱρέσεων, D.L. 1.21) suggests that one motivation for the introduction of such criterial schemes was to clarify the common basis of apparently divergent theories.

[46] For αἴσθησις and νοῦς as principles or "primary criteria" (πρῶτα κριτήρια) see Sextus, *Adv. math.* 7.217–8, 226; Alcinous, *Didask.* 4, p. 154.32–4 Hermann.

the faculty of sense perception itself (ch. 8, 13.12–16).[47] (2) At the same time, perception and intellect need to work together: "there is perception and thought of the same things, but not in the same way" (ch. 8, 13.10–12). The picture of sense perception as a messenger implies that the intellect can receive and work on the message; for Ptolemy, therefore, the category of the intelligible (νοητόν) includes the transmissions of αἴσθησις once they have been received and processed by the intellect.[48] (3) The senses can grasp their objects independently of the intellect, but only when those objects are actually present or at slight remove. By contrast, the intellect is dependent on the senses for its first impressions of things in the world; once it has received those impressions, however, it retains them in memory even when they are no longer present, to such an extent that it might seem to have generated its initial conception (τὴν πρώτην ἔννοιαν) of things on its own (ch. 8, 13.16–14.3). (4) Even if the intellect's first encounter with things in the world takes place through the senses, it has an independent power of thought and judgment. Sense perception, by contrast, needs to be affected (παθεῖν) in order to perceive the same things; moreover it is often affected in opposite ways by the same things, and in the same way by opposite things (ch. 9, 14.23–15.4). (5) Finally, in chapter 9 Ptolemy offers a teleological argument in support of the superiority of the intellect and its characteristic activity of rational thought (τὸ διανοεῖσθαι) to sense perception (14.4–21). In potentiality (δυνάμει), intellect is neither prior nor posterior to sense perception; but in actuality (ἐνέργειᾳ) sense perception is prior. This is because it is present in imperfect (ἀτελής) creatures which cannot engage in rational thought at all, and develops first in those which can (14.4–16). But precisely because it is the first to develop, and because the capacity for sense perception is shared more widely among living things than the capacity for rational thought, Ptolemy infers that the latter is more honorable (τιμιώτερον; 14.16–21).

Throughout this account Ptolemy's emphasis is on the greater autonomy and reliability of thought in contrast to sensation; his sole concessions to the senses are that they develop before the intellect (which is in any case not a mark of honor in his view) and that the intellect is dependent on them for its initial grasp of objects in the world. Just as we would expect from the lawcourt analogy, the senses are conceived of as a source of information about external objects, but the power of judgment belongs to

---

[47] The distinction between ὑποκείμενα and πάθη is traditional in Hellenistic epistemology; cf. Sextus, Adv. math. 7.195, 7.365; Gal. De dignos. puls. 1.5, 8.793 Kühn (= SVF 2.79). For τὸ ἐκτὸς ὑποκείνενον = αἰσθητόν see Adv. math. 9.352 (= SVF 2.80).
[48] Noted by Boll (1894: 80 and n. 1), who cites the reference to "things cognized through the senses" (τῶν δι' αἰσθήσεως νενοημένων) at Harm. 1.1, p. 3.13 Düring. Cf. the phrase "things in no way cognized through the senses" (τῶν μηδ' ὅλως δι' αἰσθήσεων νενοημένων) at Crit. 12, 18.5.

the intellect. And the relative weakness and unreliability of the senses in comparison to the intellect matches the view set out in the *Harmonics* (above, nn. 19–20). Ptolemy goes on in chapter 10 to explain the implications of this picture for understanding the proper uses of sense perception and intellect:

> Thus we must neither dismiss sense perception as contributing little or nothing to the knowledge (ἐπίγνωσις) of the things that are (τῶν ὄντων), nor prefer its conclusion to that of thought (διάνοια), but rather distribute to each its proper work and make use of each for the things which it is naturally able to grasp infallibly (ἃ πέφυκε διαλαμβάνειν ἀδιαψεύστως). (ch. 10, 15.5–9)

As I noted in section 1 above, this passage anticipates Ptolemy's effort in the *Harmonics* to distinguish his own method from both an a priori rationalism (whereby sensory evidence would be "dismissed" in favor of rational theories) and from an uncritical reliance on the senses. Both the senses and the intellect are to be used for what they can grasp infallibly (ἀδιαψεύστως); Ptolemy goes on to explain what this amounts to in the case of the senses:

> That is, we must make use of sense perception (αἴσθησις) for the presentation (δήλωσις) of the affections (παθήματα) that it undergoes—for it tells the truth (ἀληθεύει) about these and states just what it has suffered, without qualification (φησιν αὐτὸ μόνον ἁπλῶς ὃ πέπονθεν); but that what has affected it is of such a kind (τὸ διαθὲν δ' ὅτι τοιοῦτον), it sometimes errs. And we must make use of the intellect (διάνοια) for the judgment (κρίσις) of both the affections (παθήματα) themselves and the things that give rise to them (τῶν διαθέντων). (ch. 10, 15.9–14)

I suggest that the doctrine that sense perception "tells the truth" (ἀληθεύει) about how it is affected should be understood in light of an idea with a long history in Greek epistemology: namely, the notion that the subjective experiences of the senses are veridical and cannot be questioned. For example, if the sense of sight conveys to the intellect the impression of a round tower, the statement "That looks like a round tower" cannot be questioned; for the statement is nothing more than an expression of the sense's report. Epicurus' doctrine that "all perceptions are true"—which Ptolemy here echoes—has also been interpreted along these lines.[49] This interpretation presupposes

---

[49] Striker 1977. For the irrefutability of the affections of the senses see Pl. *Tht.* 179c (acknowledging that there may be something to the claim that reports of "present affections" [τὸ παρὸν ἑκάστῳ πάθος] are instances of knowledge); Arist. *Metaph.* Γ 4, 1010b19–26 (even if the same wine may

that it is possible to express the content of sense impressions in linguistic form; but that is exactly what Ptolemy's picture of sense perception as a messenger leads us to expect (cf. the discussion of ch. 2 in section 2 above). Note that Ptolemy's view is not that the senses are *limited* to grasping their own πάθη. As in the lawcourt analogy—recalled here by the use of the term δήλωσις for the "presentation" of sensory evidence to the intellect—the senses are thought of as grasping external objects (αἰσθητά, ὑποκείμενα) and providing a rich representation of them; the point is that their reports, like the statements of advocates in court, are partisan and nonobjective. In other words, all that one can be certain about on the basis of the senses is the way things *appear* to be, not the way they are. This, Ptolemy suggests, provides a reliable basis for inferences about the nature of things in the world when it is combined with the intellect's power of critical judgment.

Next Ptolemy sketches a picture of the intellect's critical examination of the senses' reports:

For by joining to what is transmitted [by the senses] its memories of the properties (συμβεβηκότα) of each thing, it exposes (ἀπελέγχει) in a progressive examination (ἀνάκρισις) both the things that have produced an appropriate affection (τὸ οἰκεῖον πάθος) in the senses, and those that have produced an inappropriate one. If the affection is inappropriate to what produces it, [it exposes] whether such a thing has come about by sense perception itself or by something external, sometimes making its examination through sense perceptions again— either those that are similar and unaffected (ἀπαθῆ), when the cause concerns the senses, or through dissimilar [perceptions] of the same object (ὑποκείμενον), when this is not the case. But many cases it submits, by itself, to reasoning (λόγος), and discovers what is appropriate to the nature of each thing (τὸ οἰκεῖον ἑκάστῃ φύσει) through a continuous movement divorced from the senses, in progressive contemplation. (ch. 10, 15.5–16.4)

The essential procedure is the comparison of sense impressions to those that have been stored in memory, presumably as ἔννοιαι. For example, repeated sense impressions lead to a conception (ἔννοια) that swans are white, so if sight reports the presence of a black swan, the intellect has reason to suspect that something has gone awry. In such a case,

---

taste sweet to some but not to others, there is no change in the sensation (πάθος) of sweetness, and the sense of taste always reports the truth (ἀληθεύει) about whether something *tastes* sweet); and Sextus, *Adv. math.* 7.191 (on the Cyrenaics): "that we feel whiteness or sweetness can be said infallibly (ἀδιαψεύστως) and incontrovertibly (ἀνεξελέγκτως); but that the object productive of the affection (πάθος) is white or is sweet it is impossible to affirm."

the intellect's task is to determine whether the cause lies in the sense itself or in something external to it. If the cause lies in a particular sense (i.e. because the sense organs are in an abnormal state), the intellect compares perceptions of the same sense when in its normal state. For example, a jaundiced person will compare his (alleged) impressions that the world is yellow with the impressions he had when healthy.[50] If the senses are not themselves in an abnormal state, there must be some external cause of the error, such as a distortion in the air caused by an object's being viewed from a great distance. In such cases the intellect will try to circumvent the problem by considering "dissimilar [perceptions] of the same object," for example, perceptions of touch or hearing as well as vision. But in keeping with his general emphasis on the autonomy of the intellect, Ptolemy concludes by saying that in many cases the intellect will resort to reasoning (λόγος) and so discover "what is appropriate to the nature of each thing through a continuous movement divorced from the senses, in progressive contemplation."[51]

So far, then, Ptolemy has suggested that the basis of the senses' reliability lies in their reports of how they are affected by external objects. But he now goes on to identify a second source of reliability in the "simple" or "proper" judgments of the faculties of both sense and intellect:

> One must, however, pay special attention to the simple and unmixed judgments (τοῖς ἁπλοῖς καὶ ἀμιγέσι κρίμασιν), whenever the transmissions of the impressions are unaffected and clear (ἐναργής), as being as unerring (ἀψευδής) as human power permits. For it is clear that some judgments (κρίματα) of the senses and the intellect (τῶν αἰσθησέων καὶ διανοιῶν) are proper (ἴδια), while others are common (κοινά). (ch. 10, 16.4–9)

The faculties in question include the five senses as well as the theoretical and practical intellect. As Ptolemy puts it, each of these faculties (δυναμέων) "naturally tells the truth (ἀληθεύειν πέφυκεν) whenever it considers (ἐπισκοπῇ) only what is peculiar and proper to it (τὸ ἴδιον καὶ οἰκεῖον μόνον), when it is undistracted (ἀπερίσπαστος) by combinations

---

[50] My example; see Bullialdus (1663: 139–40) for examples involving the appearances of the planets and the moon.

[51] For examples of the critical examination of the reports of the senses along these lines we can turn to book 2 of Ptolemy's *Optics* (extant only in a Latin translation [made from an Arabic version] edited by Lejeune 1989), which provides explanations of a wide variety of optical illusions in which the sense of sight fails to report the true nature of its objects. The distinction between errors arising from the sense of sight itself and those arising from external factors plays an important role in Ptolemy's account (cf. *Optics* 2.83, p. 55 Lejeune and 2.102, p. 64 Lejeune). These parallels are further evidence for the link between the epistemology of *On the criterion* and Ptolemy's scientific methodology.

[sc. with other faculties]" (ch. 11, 16.13–15). Ptolemy gives examples of simple judgments involving (a) the senses (when sight perceives color, or hearing sound), (b) the theoretical intellect (when it considers same or different, equal or unequal, and "in general the differences and similarities of forms [εἰδῶν]"), and (c) the practical intellect (when it considers "the appropriate and inappropriate (τὸ οἰκεῖον καὶ ἀνοίκειον), and in general, the emotions (πάθη)" (ch. 11, 16.15–17.1). These contrast with the complex or common judgments that are made when different faculties combine with one another (συμπλακεῖσαι) and share in (κοινωνήσασαι) the judgment of external objects. Ptolemy suggests that such judgments arise in two kinds of case (ch. 11, 17.1–12). First, certain properties may be grasped by more than one faculty, as is the case with perceptible qualities such as bulk (ὄγκος), magnitude, number, shape, position, order, and motion, and intelligible qualities such as truth, choiceworthiness (αἱρετόν), and their opposites. Perceptible qualities such as magnitude, shape, and position can be grasped by more than one of the senses; similarly, judgments of what is true or choiceworthy may involve the cooperation of the senses and the intellectual faculties. A second class of complex judgments arises in the case of objects that are "multiform" (πολυειδής) by virtue of sharing in several "primary and unmixed properties," for example, the judgments that "this thing is a man or a horse" (in the case of perceptibles), or "man is the same as horse, qua animal, but different, qua rational" (in the case of intelligibles). Both "rational" and "animal" are predicated of "man"; therefore "man" cannot be grasped by a single act of either perception or intellect.[52] In all such cases the faculties admit doubt and error.

Ptolemy's distinction between simple/proper and complex/common judgments is obviously based on the familiar Aristotelian distinction between proper and common sensibles.[53] In setting out this doctrine Aristotle makes the point that perception of the proper sensibles is always (or nearly always) accurate, while the perception of things that can be grasped by more than one sense (i.e. the common sensibles) is subject to error.[54] Aristotle's common sensibles—which include shape, size, and especially motion—correspond closely to Ptolemy's list of perceptible properties that involve complex judgments (ch. 11, 17.4–5).[55] Moreover it is exactly these kinds of properties

---

[52] Cf. Bullialdus 1663: 149–50.
[53] E.g. *De anima* 418a7–25, 428b18–30, 430b29–31.
[54] E.g. at *De anima* 428b18–30 Aristotle says that perception of proper sensibles is always accurate "or shares as little as possible in error" (ἢ ὅτι ὀλίγιστον ἔχουσα τὸ ψεῦδος); by contrast, the senses can be wrong about the objects that produce the sensations, and are even less accurate where the common sensibles are concerned.
[55] For lists of the common sensibles in Aristotle see e.g. *De anima* 418a17–8 (κίνησις, ἠρεμία, ἀριθμός, σχῆμα, μέγεθος); 425a15–7 (adding the remark that the common sensibles are all grasped by motion, κίνησις).

that are said to be the special concern of the mathematical sciences in the *Almagest*.⁵⁶ This is significant for the evaluation of the place of observation in Ptolemy's scientific practice. For Ptolemy there is no question of the senses having an infallible grasp of quantitative properties such as shape and size; hence mathematical models that depend on grasping such properties are inevitably subject to error and uncertainty.⁵⁷

The idea that the intellect has a natural capacity to make certain simple judgments accurately also has a clear Aristotelian pedigree. In both *De anima* 3.6 (430a26-b31) and *Metaph.* Θ 10 (1051a34-1052a11) Aristotle argues that a certain class of intellectual judgments are free from error, and he draws an explicit analogy between the senses' grasp of their proper objects and the intellect's simple cognitions at *De anima* 430b26-31. These passages are somewhat obscure, but one contrast that does emerge reasonably clearly is between the intellect's grasp of "indivisible" (ἀδιαιρετόν) concepts or essences (where it either grasps a concept or does not, and there is no question of error) with cases where it predicates one thing of another (and so can be either correct or incorrect in doing so). Ptolemy's theory is *prima facie* different in that it is not concerned with the grasp of concepts or essences in general; rather, it attributes to the theoretical intellect the ability to judge particular basic concepts such as similarity, difference, equality, and the like. Still, the idea that there is a class of simple or intuitive judgments of the intellect that are free of error is common to both Ptolemy and Aristotle, and a further indication of the Aristotelian background to Ptolemy's theory.

Ptolemy offers no justification for his theory of the natural reliability of the simple or proper judgments of the senses and the intellect. But the important role played by the notion of faculties (δυνάμεις) in his account, combined with the appeal to the idea of the senses' *natural* reliability (ἀληθεύειν πέφυκεν, 16.15) and the teleological considerations invoked in the comparison of intellect and sensation in chapter 9, suggests a teleological justification. The argument would be that whatever can be grasped by one faculty *alone* must be the particular activity or actualization of that faculty.⁵⁸ On the assumption that faculties are correlated with specific activities *by nature*, there would then be a reason to conclude that the ability to grasp the proper objects of sense and intellect is also present in human beings by nature.

If the foregoing analysis is correct then Ptolemy's epistemology rests on two foundations: the veridical character of subjective experience, and the natural capacity of

---

⁵⁶ I 6.1-4 H; above, n. 18.

⁵⁷ The theory of proper sensibles figures in both the *Harmonics* (3.3, p. 93.14-20 Düring) and the *Optics* (e.g. 2.13, p. 17 Lejeune). In the latter work Ptolemy explains several errors in visual perception as being due to the difficulty that sight has in grasping objects other than color (2.134-6, pp. 80-82 Lejeune).

⁵⁸ Cf. ch. 9, 14.20-21: rational thought is the "proper faculty" (τὴν οἰκείαν δύναμιν) of "more perfect" (τελειότερα) creatures.

the intellectual and sensory faculties to judge correctly about the matters that are distinctive to them. The distinction between the two ideas is clearest in the case of sense perception. When Ptolemy says that the senses report their παθήματα truly, there is no reason to suppose that these παθήματα are *restricted* to reports of proper qualities (so that sight, for example, would report only on an object's color). The lawcourt analogy suggests that the senses offer rich representations of objects via φαντασία. Furthermore, what makes the Aristotelian common sensibles "common" is of course just the fact that they can be grasped by more than one sense; hence Ptolemy in the *Optics* quite correctly describes sight as grasping both proper and common sensibles, for example, both color and shape.[59] The doctrine that the senses naturally tell the truth about their proper objects is a separate idea, based on teleological considerations, that establishes a clear connection between mind and world: color actually exists in the world, independently of the human mind, and the sense of sight is naturally suited to grasp it. In the case of the practical intellect, the distinction between the veridicality of subjective experience and the natural reliability of the faculties' proper judgments is blurred insofar as Ptolemy gives πάθη (i.e. emotions) as examples of judgments proper to the practical intellect. This suggests the veridical character of subjective experience: one either feels angry or one does not, and there is no arbiter in the matter other than the reaction of the practical intellect. But the practical intellect also has as its distinctive objects the "appropriate and inappropriate" (οἰκεῖον καὶ ἀνοικεῖον), and such judgments are not necessarily a matter of subjective feeling. As far as the theoretical intellect is concerned, Ptolemy surely cannot mean to say that just because we *think* we grasp the differences between forms, therefore we *do*, in the same way that because we *feel* angry, we *are* angry. Something more is needed to ensure that the mind is grasping real differences in the world; this connection is secured by appeal to the Aristotelian idea that the human intellect possesses faculties that can reliably make the kinds of judgments that are distinctive to them.

The remainder of Ptolemy's epistemological account (ch. 12) is concerned with clarifying the contributions of λόγος. First Ptolemy summarizes what αἴσθησις and νοῦς are able to do *independently* of λόγος:

Now the absolute and primary criteria (τὰ ἀπολελυμένα καὶ πρῶτα κριτήρια)[60] are immediately capable of grasping (καταληπτικά) apart from reasoning (χωρὶς λόγου), and need no other principle (ἀρχή) at least insofar as their activity itself

---

[59] *Optics* 2.2, p. 12 Lejeune: *Dicimus ergo quod uisus cognoscit corpus, magnitudinem, colorem, figuram, situm, motum, et quietem.*

[60] I.e. the intellect (νοῦς) and sense perception (αἴσθησις).

is concerned (κατά γε τὴν ἐνέργειαν αὐτήν).⁶¹ They grasp (ἀντιλαμβάνεται), first of all, themselves and their special movements, according to the inner consciousness (συναίσθησις); then, the primary sense organs, and those external objects which are stable and share in forms; and, by virtue of the memory which is extended from perceptible things, the forms themselves as things separated and divorced from the existence of particulars (ὡς κεχωρισμένων τινῶν καὶ ἀπηλλαγμένων τῆς τῶν καθ' ἕκαστον ὑποστάσεως). (ch. 12, 17.17–18.4)

From this passage it emerges that sense perception and intellect can do quite a bit without λόγος. Not only are they aware of their own activity; they also have the ability to grasp objects in the world (the things that "share in forms"), and the forms themselves as separate from their instantiations in sensible particulars.⁶² Thus, λόγος is not required for a preliminary grasp of forms; for this, memory (and the associated ἔννοιαι) are sufficient.⁶³ That it is only a *preliminary* grasp is suggested by the fact that Ptolemy goes on immediately to remark that without using λόγος the intellect can easily go wrong by conceiving "images" (εἴδωλα) and "apparitions" (φαντάσματα) of things that are "not at all cognized through the senses" (τῶν μηδ' ὅλως δι' αἰσθήσεων νενοημένων), for example, evil spirits or giants (ch. 12, 18.4–9). The implication is that λόγος is needed to avoid such error and secure true beliefs, as well as a reliable grasp of forms.

Furthermore, a certain kind of λόγος is also needed in order to move from true belief to knowledge:

When the internal reasoning (ἐνδιάθετος λόγος) of thought is joined with these simple and non-inferential (ἀσυλλογίστοις) criteria in independent application (κατὰ τὴν ἀπολελυμένην ἐπιβολήν), it too still only forms opinions (δοξάζει); but when in clear (ἐναργής), skillful (τεχνική) discernment, it takes on the condition of knowledge, by separating and combining the differences and absences of difference between existing things (τῶν ὄντων), and moving up from particulars to universals and all the way up to the genera and species (εἴδη) of objects (ὑποκείμενα). (ch. 12, 18.9–17)

---

⁶¹ Lammert emends the MSS' reading ἐνέργειαν ("activity") to ἐνάργειαν ("clarity"), but I do not think this is necessary given Ptolemy's emphasis on the Aristotelian distinction between δύναμις and ἐνέργεια elsewhere in the text (e.g. ch. 9, 14.4–9).
⁶² The qualification "*as* separated" (ὡς κεχωρισμένων) is of course crucial: these are Aristotelian forms that are separable from particulars only in thought.
⁶³ For Alcinous' similar view see above, n. 38.

Ptolemy picks up his earlier remark that the "simple and undifferentiated" application of internal λόγος becomes opinion, while its "skilled and unshakeable" application becomes ἐπιστήμη and γνῶσις (ch. 2, 6.9–11). As the term τεχνική suggests, the contrast between the two applications of λόγος lies in the systematic character of the latter: ἐπιστήμη results from the application of reasoning that is integrated into a larger system and therefore "unshakable" (ἀμετάπειστος). This is of course a notion that can be traced back to Plato and Aristotle; notably, however, Ptolemy shows no hint of the Platonist idea that belief is distinguished from knowledge by its different objects.[64] The chapter concludes with an example illustrating the progression from sense perception to knowledge:

As whenever from encountering Plato and Dion and the similarity of particular form (τῆς καθ' ἕκαστον τοῦ εἴδους ὁμοιότητος) it thinks of a common genus, man, and from encountering man and horse it thinks of animal, and from encountering animal and plant, what is (τὸ ὄν) itself, and in this way it passes back downwards distinguishing and dividing always what is divided in species as indivisible in genus until, passing to things that are entirely indivisible and have no common genus, it finds that the individual particulars (τὰ καθ' ἕκαστον) are consistent (σύμφωνα) with the principles that have been derived [from them], making a circuit and revolution that is unchangeable and incontrovertible. (ch. 12, 18.17–19.6)

The methodology of ascending from particulars to universals is exactly that which Ptolemy follows in his investigation of the κριτήριον. What is new here is the idea that one must also descend from the universal to the particular to ensure that the initial observations are in agreement (σύμφωνα) with the theories derived from them. This recalls the importance of συμφωνία in Ptolemy's scientific methodology as noted in section 1 above. What Ptolemy is presenting here is an analog not of mathematical demonstration but of the process of building mathematical models and assessing their predictions in light of observations. The reliability of one's grasp of universals and the distinctions between them—the "theory" that is being described in this passage—is dependent on the ability to show that it matches the initial observations. The idea of a "circuit" (περίοδος) and "revolution" (ἀνακύκλησις) is an appropriate analog for the iterative process of developing a mathematical model from initial observations and assessing it against further observations until agreement (συμφωνία) has been achieved.

---

[64] Alcinous, *Didask*. 4, p. 154.29–32 Hermann: "scientific reason" (ἐπιστημονικὸς λόγος) is reliable and stable (βέβαιος, μόνιμος) because it is concerned with principles that are themselves reliable and stable.

It is this *circuit* that Ptolemy calls "unshakeable and incontrovertible," and its reliability depends ultimately on agreement with observation.

4.

I have argued that *On the criterion* sets out an epistemological theory that answers to the distinctive problems and emphases of Ptolemy's work in the exact sciences. The theory explains how the human intellect can grasp the kinds of formal properties that are studied by mathematics as Ptolemy conceives of it. It clarifies the roles of sense perception and intellect and suggests guidelines for how the two should be used to develop scientific theories. The overall emphasis in both the lawcourt analogy and the subsequent discussion is on the relative limitations of sense perception in comparison to the intellect and the need for the intellect to judge the evidence of the senses via λόγος. The infallibility of the senses in reporting how they are affected, and their natural ability to grasp their proper objects, is sufficient to secure an empirical basis for the mathematical sciences. The intellectual faculties, like the senses, are naturally able to grasp the truth concerning matters that are distinctive to them. But judgments about quantitative properties relevant to the mathematical sciences, and of properties such as truth, involve different faculties working together and so are susceptible to error. By using reasoning or λόγος the mind can avoid error and move from true belief to knowledge; but scientific knowledge in fields such as astronomy and harmonics depends on agreement with observation and so is fallible.

In framing this epistemological theory for his scientific work, Ptolemy draws on a wide range of philosophical theories. His appeal to the infallibility of the senses' reports of their affections (πάθη, παθήματα) echoes Epicurus' famous dictum that "all perceptions are true," while the doctrine of the reliability of the senses and intellectual faculties when judging their proper objects is Aristotelian in inspiration. On the whole the theory's closest affinities are with the Peripatetic tradition. But Ptolemy's epistemology has a number of distinctive features within this tradition, including (1) the idea that the senses' reports of their παθήματα are a reliable source of empirical evidence; (2) the attempt to ground the natural reliability of the faculties of both sense and intellect on the doctrine of simple or proper judgments; and (3) the comparatively minor role played by the notion of "clarity" or "vividness" (ἐνάργεια) in his account.[65]

---

[65] ἐναργής occurs only twice in the text. At ch. 10, 16.5–6, ἐναργῆ is paired with ἀπαθεῖς ("unaffected"), referring to the senses' transmissions (διαδόσεις) of impressions of their proper objects; at ch. 12, 18.18.12–3 it is paired with τεχνική and refers to the discrimination (διάκρισις) that is carried out via λόγος. A third instance in Lammert's text is ἐνάργειαν at ch. 12, 17.19, but this rests on an unnecessary emendation of the MS reading ἐνέργειαν (above, n. 61). By contrast, the notion

As I have noted, Ptolemy's appeal to the Aristotelian doctrine of proper judgments could provide him with a neat teleological argument for his theory: each faculty is naturally constructed to grasp what is distinctive to it. Moreover, Ptolemy viewed his mathematical theories as providing powerful evidence for the teleological order and underlying rationality of nature; as he puts it in the *Harmonics*, "in everything it is the proper task of the theoretical scientist to show that the works of nature are crafted (δημιουργούμενα) with reason and with an orderly cause."[66] Thus the success of his mathematical theories themselves could provide a reason to adopt an epistemological theory based on the idea that human beings have the natural ability to make reliable judgments about the world.

I conclude with some very brief reflections on the implications of *On the criterion* for the understanding of Ptolemy's scientific method. The consistent emphasis on the role of intellect as the authoritative judge (via λόγος) of sense impressions in *On the criterion* suggests that Ptolemy was profoundly aware of the importance of theoretical considerations in driving the selection and evaluation of empirical data. This may help to shed light on his practice in cases where he has been accused of being rather cavalier—if not dishonest—in his handling of such data. Two notorious examples are the star catalog in books 7–8 of the *Almagest*—where Ptolemy's claim to have carried out detailed observations has been called into question in light of similarities between his results and the earlier work of Hipparchus—and the analysis of refraction in book 5 of the *Optics*, where what is presented as observational data seems to have been derived from a theoretical model. In both cases, close study of the methodological assumptions that govern Ptolemy's practice reveals that they conform quite well to the emphasis on the priority of intellect and λόγος in *On the criterion*.[67] In this way the study of Ptolemy's foray into epistemology may help us gain a better perspective on his methods in those works on which his intellectual reputation chiefly, and rightly, rests.

Acknowledgments

I am grateful to audiences at Caltech, the University of Chicago, and Harvard University for their comments on oral presentations of some of this material; special thanks are

---

of ἐνάργεια figures prominently in both Sextus' report on the Peripatetics (*Adv. math.* 7.217–8) and in Galen's Peripatetic-inspired epistemological discussions (e.g. *De opt. doctr.* 1.49 Kühn; *De plac. Hipp. et Plat.* 9.7.3–5, 5.778–9 Kühn); cf. Tarrant 1981.

[66] *Harm.* 1.2, p. 5.19–21 Düring; transl. Barker 1989.

[67] On the basis of a close study of the star catalog Grasshoff (1990: 209–16) characterizes Ptolemy's methodological perspective as one of "holistic rationalism," in which observations are subject to radical evaluation and revision in light of theoretical considerations. Similarly, Smith (1982) explains Ptolemy's handling of refraction as an understandable attempt to apply a theoretical framework to guide empirical investigation in a particularly difficult case.

due to Mitzi Lee for her patience and for an extremely helpful set of comments on an earlier draft. It is an honor to have the opportunity to contribute to a volume dedicated to Gisela Striker, who as advisor, colleague, and friend has done more than anyone to guide and inspire my approach to ancient philosophy. With deep gratitude and affection, I offer this paper to her as a small token of thanks for all her advice and support over the years.

Works Cited

Barker, A. 1989. *Greek musical writings, vol. 2: Harmonic and acoustic theory.* Cambridge: Cambridge University Press.
Barker, A. 2000. *Scientific method in Ptolemy's Harmonics.* Cambridge: Cambridge University Press.
Boll, F. 1894. *Studien über Claudius Ptolemäus: Ein Beitrag zur Geschichte der griechischen Philosophie und Astrologie.* Leipzig: Teubner.
Bullialdus, I. 1663. *Claudii Ptolemaei tractatus de iudicandi facultate et animi principatu.* Paris: Cramoisy. Online at http://gallica.bnf.fr.
Burnyeat, M. F. 1976. "Plato on the grammar of perceiving." *Classical Quarterly* n. s. 26.1: 29–51.
Debrunner, A. 1954. *Geschichte der griechischen Sprache II.* Berlin.
Dillon, J. 1988. *The question of "eclecticism": Studies in later Greek philosophy.* Berkeley: University of California Press.
Dillon, J. 1993. *Alcinous: The handbook of Platonism.* Oxford: Clarendon Press.
Duhem, P. 1969. *To save the phenomena: An essay on the idea of physical theory from Plato to Galileo.* Chicago: University of Chicago Press.
Düring, I. 1930. *Die Harmonielehre de Klaudios Ptolemaios.* Göteborg: Elanders.
Feke, J. and A. Jones. 2010. "Ptolemy." In L. Gerson, ed., *The Cambridge history of philosophy in late antiquity.* Cambridge: Cambridge University Press.
Grasshoff, G. 1990. *The history of Ptolemy's star catalogue.* New York: Springer-Verlag.
Heiberg, J. 1898–1903. *Claudii Ptolemaei opera quae extant, vol. 1.* Leipzig: Teubner.
Huby, P. and G. Neal, eds. 1989. *The criterion of truth: Essays written in honour of George Kerferd.* Liverpool: Liverpool University Press.
Kelly, B. 2011. *Petitions, litigation, and social control in Roman Egypt.* Oxford: Oxford University Press.
Lammert, F. 1961. *Claudii Ptolemaei opera quae extant, vol. 3, 2.* Leipzig: Teubner.
Lejeune, A. 1989. *L'Optique de Claude Ptolémée, dans la version latine d'après l'arabe de l'émir Eugène de Sicile.* Leiden; New York: Brill.
Lloyd, G. E. R. 1982. "Observational error in later Greek science." In J. Barnes, J. Brunschwig, M. Burnyeat, and M. Schofield, eds., *Science and speculation: Studies in Hellenistic theory and practice.* Cambridge: Cambridge University Press.
Long, A. 1989. "Ptolemy on the criterion: An epistemology for the practicing scientist." In Huby and Neal 1989 and Dillon 1989.
Musgrave, A. 1991. "The myth of astronomical instrumentalism." In G. Munévar, ed., *Beyond reason: Essays on the philosophy of Paul Feyerabend.* Dordrecht: Kluwer.
Oppel, H. 1937. Kanôn. *Zur Bedeutungsgeschichte des Wortes und seiner lateinischen Entsprechungen (regula-norma).* Leipzig: Dieterich.

Smith, A. M. 1982. "Ptolemy's search for a law of refraction: A case study in the classical methodology of 'saving the appearances' and its limitations." *Archive for history of exact sciences 26*: 221–40.

Smyth, H. W. 1956. *Greek grammar.* Cambridge, MA: Harvard University Press.

Striker, G. 1974. "Κριτήριον τῆς ἀληθείας." *Nachrichten der Akademie der Wissenschaften in Göttingen, phil.-hist. Kl. 2*: 47–110. Cited as reprinted in English translation in Striker 1996.

Striker, G. 1977. "Epicurus on the truth of sense impressions." *Archiv für Geschichte der Philosophie 59*: 125–42. Cited as reprinted in Striker 1996.

Striker, G. 1990. "The problem of the criterion." In S. Everson, ed., *Epistemology.* Cambridge: Cambridge University Press.

Striker, G. 1996. *Essays in Hellenistic epistemology and ethics.* Cambridge: Cambridge University Press.

Suppes, P. 1980. "Limitations of the axiomatic method in ancient Greek mathematical sciences." In J. Hintikka, D. Gruender, and E. Agazzi, eds., *Pisa Conference Proceedings, vol. 1.* Dordrecht: Reidel.

Tarrant, H. 1981. "Agreement and the self-evident in Philo of Larissa." *Dionysius 5*: 66–97.

Taubenschlag, R. 1916. *Das Strafrecht im Rechte der Papyri.* Leipzig: Teubner.

Toomer, G. 1984. *Ptolemy's Almagest.* London: Duckworth.

Whittaker, J. and P. Louis. 1990. *Alcinoos: Enseignement des doctrines de Platon.* Paris: Les Belles Lettres.

14

THE COMPULSIONS OF STOIC ASSENT

Charles Brittain

1. INTRODUCTION

Assent is a fundamental notion in the novel theory of reason introduced by Zeno and filled out by Chrysippus and his successors in response to Academic criticism. It plays a key role in Stoic epistemology, psychology, and ethics, since belief and rational action are caused by assent, and happiness depends on regulating it effectively. But, although the Academic objections to it have received a lot of attention in recent years, much about the Stoic conception of assent remains unclear.[1]

The central problem, in my view, is that the Stoic theory often looks like an attempt to combine two incompatible models of assent: a naturalistic model, in which assent is an automatic response to impressions determined by the degree of fit between their content and the agent's antecedent beliefs; and something closer to a voluntaristic model, in which, despite the deterministic framework of Stoic psychology, the rational agent retains a degree of control over his or her individual assents. My aim here, however, is not to describe and solve this wider problem by offering a general theory of Stoic assent, but to examine a much narrower question about assent to *cataleptic* impressions, in the hope that this might shed some light on the larger problem. The question at issue is just this: do the Stoics think that assent to cataleptic impressions is, in some sense, *necessary* for rational agents?

The standard view, I think, is that it is: cataleptic impressions "cause" or "force" us to assent, or are "irresistible" or "inevitable" for rational agents.[2] On this view, the idea is that our minds are naturally structured to assent automatically to cataleptic impressions

---

[1] On the Arcesilaus' and Carneades' appropriation of the Stoic notion of assent, see the classic essays by Striker (1980) 54–83 and Frede (1987) 201–22. The later Academic uses of the notion are elaborated in Brittain (2001).

[2] Proponents of the "standard" view include Görler (1977) 83–92 at 91 and n. 29 (resistance to cataleptic impressions is "aussichtlos"); Frede (1983) 65–93 at 84 (they "cause the mind to accept them"); Striker (1990) 143–60 at 153 (they are "irresistible, such that they force our assent");

in virtue of a cognitive discriminatory mechanism triggered by their self-evident character. And the fact that this mechanism is an automatic one, and unconscious, or at least, not necessarily conscious, explains why the cataleptic impression can serve as the "criterion of truth"—that is, as the self-warranting basis for developing systematic knowledge—despite our readiness to succumb to false or unwarranted impressions.

I hope to undermine this view, by arguing that, while it is natural to assent to cataleptic impressions, there are cases in which we don't assent to them, and some in which it is right not to. If this is right, it is not necessary to assent to cataleptic impressions.[3] It doesn't follow that cataleptic impressions don't have a significant causal effect on us, or that we can't use them as criteria of truth; but it does mean that the mechanisms of assent are more complicated than the standard view supposes. On this account, then, we might say that reason retains a degree of control over its individual assents. But if we do say that, it won't be because the faculty of assent is the locus of an indeterminist freedom, but because some of our beliefs can interfere with the natural response to cataleptic impressions by causing us to withhold assent from them.[4]

2. ASSENT

Before turning to our question about cataleptic impressions, however, it will be useful to start with a few general considerations about assent. Since the outlines of the Stoic theory are fairly familiar, I will restrict myself to noting two basic points about it, followed by two comments on some more controversial issues that concern us here.

The first point is that to assent to a rational impression—that is, to a perceptual or non-perceptual thought that something is the case—is to take it to be true and thus to believe it. The Stoic distinction between thought and belief is grounded on a view about causation: our impressions are, in the first instance, passive alterations of our minds, or bits of cognitive input imposed on us by the world, whereas our response to them is a mental activity, something that depends on ourselves. And, in their view, that response consists either in assent, resulting in an occurrent belief, or in the suspension of assent, which amounts to waiting for further input.[5]

Ioppolo (1990) 433–49 at 437 (assent is a "necessary concomitant" of their reception); Allen (1994) 85–113 at 105 (they "cannot fail to win assent").

[3] The adequacy of the standard view has been put in question, especially by Sandbach (1971) 9–21 at 14–5, Inwood (1985) 76–7, and Annas (1990) 184–203 at 196–203, but it has rarely been flatly rejected. A notable exception is the implicit recantation of the standard view by Michael Frede in his (1999) 295–322, at 313–6.

[4] Traces of an indeterminist interpretation are found in Long (1991) 102–20 at 118–20.

[5] See Cicero, *Acad.* 1.40: primum de sensibus ipsis quaedam dixit nova, quos iunctos esse censuit e quadam quasi impulsione oblata extrinsecus, quam ille *fantasian*, nos visum appellemus

The second point is that the way in which our assent depends causally on ourselves is in virtue of our rationality, that is, roughly, the set of our prior assents and dispositions to assent (including our natural and common conceptions). It is this that distinguishes us from non-rational animals and pre-rational children, whose actions or responses to impressions are triggered automatically or instinctively by the content of those impressions. For in our case rationality allows us to play active and individual causal roles in the world on the basis of the beliefs it generates via assent.[6]

The two comments I want to make both concern the *mechanisms* of assent and the ways in which we discriminate between impressions in virtue of our rationality. The first is about the **activity** of assent. The Stoics used the model of a balance or scale to describe the dynamic process of the mind involved in coming to assent (or not).[7] One of the functions of this model is to point to a level of passivity and automaticity in the process by illustrating the causal effects on the mind that certain kinds of impression have per se; thus merely receiving or forming an impression of a certain kind causes the mind to incline in one direction or the other, just as the imposition of weights inclines a balance. The implied passivity of assent is initially rather surprising, given that it is introduced as the active response to our passive reception of impressions. But it shouldn't worry us for two reasons. First, even the passivity of *impressions* is relative to other psychological operations and serves primarily to mark their function in the reception of information; they remain states of the mind formed by itself in virtue of its faculty of impression.[8] Second, the idea is that it is in virtue of its *content* that the formed impression has the causal effect of inclining our mind towards or against assent: that is, the mind *reacts* to the content it has formed. Further, the Stoics take that content to come in two forms, which I will call "perceptual" or "representational" and

---

licet.... sed ad haec quae visa sunt et quasi accepta sensibus assensionem adiungit animorum, quam esse vult in nobis positam et voluntariam. ("Zeno considered perceptions to be compounds of a kind of externally induced 'impact'—he called this a *phantasia*, but we can call it an 'impression.'... But, as I was saying, he conjoined these, the impressions received, as it were, by the senses, with the assent of our minds, which he took to be voluntary and have its source in us.") Cf. Sextus *M.* 7.240-1, which defines impressions as "passive conditions" (*peiseis*) and assent as a psychological activity (*energeia*).

[6] See e.g., DL 7.85-6, cf. 7.51, and Hierocles *St. Eth.* 1.31-3. The Stoic conception of reason is examined in Frede (1994). See also n. 35 below.

[7] See Cicero *Acad.* 2.38, cited in n. 40 below, which has a balance "sinking down." Plutarch has "turns" of a scale (*rhopê*) at *Adv. Col.* 1122c and *Virt. Mor.* 447a, and "inclination" (*epiklisis*) at *St. Rep.* 1045c. The balance model is also used by Carneades in Sextus—see *M.* 7.166-89; cf. *PH.* 1.226-30—and by Plutarch in his own (non-Stoic) right—see *Gen. Soc.* 580f, 588f.

[8] This is clear in the relevant case of rational impressions, since their conceptualization is necessarily a function of the subject's mind (see DL 7.51); but it is also implicit in all impressions, as Sextus suggests when explaining that a cataleptic impression is one produced "with skill" (*technikōs*) in *M.* 7.248 and 250.

"propositional" content.⁹ Both sorts seem to have certain immediate causal effects. The precise effects of the *representational* content of *cataleptic* impressions are, of course, a point at issue here. But, whether or not cataleptic impressions compel assent, we know that the detail, clarity, and distinctness of their representation makes them "striking" (*M.* 7.257, 405), while non-cataleptic ones have weaker effects (see *Acad.* 2.52–3, n. 16 below). The *propositional* content of impressions also has an immediate effect in virtue of which they are categorized in Sextus' account of the older Stoics as "plausible" or not, depending on whether they "produce a smooth motion in the soul... <or> turn us away from assent" (*M.* 7.242).¹⁰ The ascription to the Stoics of this sort of psycho-physical reaction to propositional content is not unique to Sextus' account of their epistemology: we find the same mechanism in the case of the emotions, where impressions that strike a sage may cause her to blush or blanch although she doesn't assent to them.¹¹ Here too it seems clear that the sage's immediate reaction to the propositional content of the impression must constitute an initial inclination to assent to it, albeit one she resists.

So far we have seen how the balance model suggests that the process of assent involves the mind's passive affection on receiving an impression, without any sign of an active or critical response. But the model also serves to point out that the natural inclination to the content of, for example, plausible impressions is something that the mind might actively *resist* (as the sage does in the emotional case), by a countervailing inclination in the opposite direction. One sign that the Stoics intended this implication is furnished by the notion of "yielding" to impressions (*eixis*). The evidence for the Stoic use of this notion is slight, and it is often supposed that yielding is a sub- or pre-rational initial inclination that precedes assent.¹² But in the cases preserved in our sources yielding to an impression is always conjoined with assenting to it, whether it

---

⁹ This use of the term "representational" derives from Frede (1983) 65–93 at 66–71, who distinguished between the proposition represented in a rational impression and the way in which it is represented, i.e. detail and accuracy of its representation. In his terms, the former is the propositional and the latter the representational content of the impression. See further, Brennan (2003) 257–94 at 260–3 and esp. his n. 8.

¹⁰ Sextus *M.* 7.242: τούτων <i.e. φαντασιῶν> γὰρ αἱ μέν εἰσι πιθαναί, αἱ δὲ ἀπίθανοι, αἱ δὲ πιθαναὶ ἅμα καὶ ἀπίθανοι, αἱ δὲ οὔτε πιθαναὶ οὔτε ἀπίθανοι. πιθαναὶ μὲν οὖν εἰσιν αἱ λεῖον κίνημα περὶ ψυχὴν ἐργαζόμεναι, ὥσπερ νῦν τὸ "ἡμέραν εἶναι" καὶ τὸ "ἐμὲ διαλέγεσθαι" καὶ πᾶν ὃ τῆς ὁμοίας ἔχεται περιφανείας, ἀπίθανοι δὲ αἱ μὴ τοιαῦται ἀλλ' ἀποστρέφουσαι ἡμᾶς τῆς συγκαταθέσεως, οἷον "εἰ ἡμέρα ἐστίν, οὐκ ἔστιν ἥλιος ὑπὲρ γῆς· εἰ σκότος ἐστίν, ἡμέρα ἐστίν."

¹¹ See e.g. Seneca, *De Ira* 2.3–4 and Gellius, *Noct. Att.* 19.1 on "preliminary passions." The nature of the content of the impressions involved in emotion remains controversial; see Frede (1986) 93–110 and, *contra*, Brennan (1998) 21–70 at 44–52.

¹² See Inwood (1985) 72–81.

is a true, cataleptic impression (DL 7.51), or a false or non-cataleptic impression (see Plutarch *Virt. Mor.* 447a, *St. Rep.* 1057a, and *Adv. Col.* 1122c). It thus seems likely that yielding is also a rational activity. Its significance for our purpose is that the *vice* of yielding seems to be defined as *non-resistance* to a (plausible) non-cataleptic impression (see e.g. Plutarch *St. Rep.* 1057a).[13] A natural way to take this is as implying that every assent, whether to a cataleptic impression or not, is eventually a case of yielding, so that resistance is suspending assent at least *pro tem*. But, in any case, the connection between yielding and the "turns" and "inclinations" of the balance model certainly suggest that an active resistance to impressions is possible. This doesn't tell us, of course, what makes the mind yield or resist when it does, or whether it can resist cataleptic impressions. Nor does it explain what resistance consists in. No doubt when the mind receives impressions that are plausible in virtue of the fit between their propositional content and the subject's other beliefs and expectations, but are non-cataleptic because they represent that proposition with insufficient perceptual detail or accuracy, it resists them in the sense of automatically inclining against assent. But presumably it can also resist impressions whose initial causal impact stems from their relative perceptual or representational accuracy and detail when their propositional content fails to fit with some of our other beliefs.

My second comment concerns the **effects** of assent (or assents qua states as opposed to activities). The Stoics categorize the beliefs resulting from the activity of assent according to various *objective* cognitive features. The most familiar category depends on the cognitive character of the *impressions* one assents to. So assent to a cataleptic impression produces a case of cognition (*catalêpsis*), while assent to a non-cataleptic impression—at least on one account—produces an opinion (*doxa*) which is either rash or a mistake (see Cicero *Acad.* 1.40–1 and Plutarch *St. Rep.* 1056f).[14] A second categorization depends on the overall *disposition* or tension (*tonos*) of the mind giving its assent: that disposition is either weak or strong, in that it is either reversible, in the sense that the beliefs it gave rise to may later be given up as a result of rational considerations, or irreversible;[15] and individual assents and beliefs caused by these states are

---

[13] Plutarch, *St. Rep.* 1057a: οὐκ οἶδα γὰρ ὅπως ἀνέγκλητός ἐστι τοιαύτας ποιοῦσα φαντασίας, αἷς τὸ μὴ μάχεσθαι μηδ' ἀντιβαίνειν ἀλλ' ἕπεσθαι καὶ εἴκειν ἐγκλητόν ἐστι. Cf. Cicero *Acad.* 2.66, [Chrysippus?] *P.Herc.* 1020 = *SVF* 2.131 lines 8–16, and Clement *Strom.* 2.17.76.

[14] This definition of "opinion" and its consequent distinction from "folly" are controversial. They are defended in Görler (1977) 83–92 and Arthur (1983) 69–78 and rejected in Brennan (1998) 21–70 at 26–7 and Meinwald (2005) 215–31.

[15] See Cicero *Acad.* 1.41: Quod autem erat sensu comprensum id ipsum sensum appellabat, et si ita erat comprensum ut convelli ratione non posset scientiam, sin aliter inscientiam nominabat; ex qua existebat etiam opinio, quae esset imbecilla et cum falso incognitoque communis. ("Zeno called an impression that had been grasped by one of the senses a 'perception'; and if it had been grasped in such a way that it couldn't be dislodged by reason, he called it 'scientific knowledge,' if

accordingly either weak or strong (Sextus *M.* 7.151, DL 7.46 and Stobaeus *Ec.* 2.74). A key difference between these two states is that the strong disposition of knowledge (*epistêmê*) consists entirely of prior cognitions, while the weak disposition of folly (*agnoia*) does not. This shows that these dispositions qualify our individual assents, because, except in pathological circumstances, we can lose our grasp on a cognition— for example, by assenting to a false impression—only if we already have false beliefs (cf. Plutarch *St. Rep.* 1036e). So, in normal circumstances, the strong disposition of knowledge rules out weak assents and makes individual assents strong.

It is fairly clear, I think, how these categories support the Stoics' normative constraint on assent, that one should assent only to cataleptic impressions. But it is less obvious whether these categories are also designed to point to *subjective* differences between assents. One might think that from the subject's point of view, all beliefs have the same status: they all *seem* true—that's why the subject assented to them. But there is some evidence that the Stoics think that there are subjective differences, not just between our immediate reactions to the impressions to which we assent (*supra*), but also in the resulting beliefs. One bit of evidence is from Zeno's hand-simile, which suggests that an assent constituting a cognition is more secure than one that isn't (*Acad.* 2.145). Another is from Cicero's account of the Stoic views on dreams, drunkenness, and other abnormal states, where he suggests that assent in such conditions is weaker than ordinary assent (i.e., on the Stoic view, cognition), because beliefs acquired in these conditions are ones that we readily give up once we have recovered (*Acad.* 2.52).[16] If these reports are correct, they might go some way towards explaining why the Stoics are relatively optimistic about the possibility of moral and cognitive progress, since our weak cognitions would still be *stronger* assents than our opinions. What they don't explain, however, is the mechanism(s) that might bring this about. One candidate is something analogous to the automatic causal mechanism for discriminating cataleptic impressions that operates in non-rational animals. But these subjective differences in

not, 'ignorance.' The latter was also the source of opinion, which was a weak condition covering false as well as non-cataleptic impressions.")

[16] Cicero *Acad.* 2.52: illud enim dicimus, non eandem esse vim neque integritatem dormientium et vigilantium nec mente nec sensu. ne vinulenti quidem quae faciunt eadem adprobatione faciunt qua sobrii: dubitant haesitant revocant se interdum iisque quae videntur inbecillius adsentiuntur, cumque edormierunt illa visa quam levia fuerint intellegunt. ("... the mind and senses of people who are asleep and people who are awake do not have the same force or integrity. Not even intoxicated people do what they do with the same approval as the sober: they doubt, they hesitate, they sometimes recollect themselves, and they assent more weakly to their impressions—and when they have slept it off, they understand how light those impressions were.")

our assent may instead be the products of a less automatic mechanism governed by the level of certainty or commitment to the belief the subject has.[17]

So much for my general considerations about assent. The interim conclusion I hope to draw is modest: the mechanisms of assent are, as one might expect, quite complicated. Our minds respond in varying degrees to the various kinds of content our impressions have.

3. UNCOMPELLING CATALEPTIC IMPRESSIONS

With this caveat in mind, we can now turn to the question at issue: do cataleptic impressions compel our assent? I will argue in three stages that they don't: first, I will set out the central evidence for my nonstandard position, which is an interpretation of the view Sextus ascribes to the "Younger Stoics" in *M.* 7.253-60; then I will give two arguments to show that the Younger Stoic position is one that the "Older Stoics," including Chrysippus, are committed to as well; and finally, I will deal with two objections to my account based on the standard view.

The Younger Stoics are introduced by Sextus as proponents of a qualification of the older Stoic view that the cataleptic impression is the "criterion of truth":

> But while the older Stoics say that the cataleptic impression is the criterion of truth, the younger Stoics added the qualification "when it doesn't have an obstacle." For there are cases when one gets a cataleptic impression, but it is incredible owing to the external circumstances.[18] (*M.* 7.253-4)

Although Sextus doesn't identify their motivation for making this qualification, it is fairly clear from parts of his report and the Antiochian echoes of this view in Cicero's *Academica* that the Younger Stoics' purpose was to defend Chrysippus' theory of the criterion against Carneades' criticisms. So what we should expect from them is an argument against the Academic view that assent is conditioned primarily by considerations of coherence between impressions, and its corollary that impressions constitute at best *evidence for* judgments rather than autonomous "criteria" per se (cf. *M.* 7.166-89).

---

[17] The Stoics probably addressed levels of certainty under the rubric of the cognitive vice of "suspicion" (*huponoia*); but our evidence for this concept is meager—see Stobaeus *Ec.* 2.7.11m (*fin.*) [= *SVF* 3.548] and [Chrysippus?] *P. Herc.* 1020 [= *SVF* 2.131, p. 41.16].

[18] Sextus *M.* 7.253-4: Ἀλλὰ γὰρ οἱ μὲν ἀρχαιότεροι τῶν Στωικῶν κριτήριόν φασιν εἶναι τῆς ἀληθείας τὴν καταληπτικὴν ταύτην φαντασίαν, οἱ δὲ νεώτεροι προσετίθεσαν καὶ τὸ μηδὲν ἔχουσαν ἔνστημα. ἔσθ' ὅτε γὰρ καταληπτικὴ μὲν προσπίπτει φαντασία, ἄπιστος δὲ διὰ τὴν ἔξωθεν περίστασιν.

The argument we get from the Younger Stoics comes in two stages (inverted by Sextus). The first explains why the cataleptic impression is the criterion of truth:

> For this [the cataleptic impression] is so evident and striking that it all but grabs us by the hair, dragging us to assent, and it needs nothing else to strike us like that or to establish its difference from other impressions.[19] (*M.* 7.257b)

An impression is cataleptic if it has three features: (1) it is evident (*enargês*); (2) it is striking (*plêktikos*); and (3) it is, so to speak, "autonomous." The first and third of these clearly echo the standard, "old Stoic" definition of the cataleptic impression. The first corresponds to its second part: because they are accurately "stamped and impressed" (*M.* 7.255, cf. DL 7.50, *M.* 7.248: *tranê*), cataleptic impressions have maximal perceptual or representational detail. And the third feature draws on the third part of the standard definition: cataleptic impressions can't be false, because their distinctive perceptual or representational detail only occurs under the appropriate causal conditions (*M.* 7.258). Hence, the Younger Stoics note, cataleptic impressions are "autonomous" in the sense that they don't need corroboration from further impressions to guarantee their truth. The second feature—their virtual compulsion of assent—doesn't correspond to part of the standard definition, presumably because it doesn't mark an intrinsic property of cataleptic impressions, but rather notes their causal effect on *rational* agents. But the view that cataleptic impressions are conducive to assent in those agents is also a standard one (see DL 7.51 and Sextus *M.* 7.405, cited in n. 38).

The first stage of the argument against Carneades, then, on my reading, is an orthodox defense of the Chrysippian theory of cataleptic impressions. Cataleptic impressions serve as the criterion because their propositional content is guaranteed by their perceptual or representational detail, and we are naturally structured to assent to them. Hence, when our perceptual impressions aren't cataleptic, we normally change the conditions until they are (*M.* 7. 258). Further, their nature is such that no additional considerations of coherence are required to warrant them: they constitute, as it were, conclusive evidence of the proposition they represent.

The second stage of the argument aims to disarm an Academic objection to this orthodox Stoic account. It doesn't follow from Chrysippus' theory, the Younger Stoics allow, that coherence conditions can never interfere with this natural process. There are, as Carneades pointed out, rare cases in which a rational agent receives a cataleptic impression, but fails to assent to it, despite its strikingness, owing to an antecedent

---

[19] Sextus *M.* 7.257b: αὕτη γὰρ ἐναργὴς οὖσα καὶ πληκτικὴ μόνον οὐχὶ τῶν τριχῶν, φασί, λαμβάνεται, κατασπῶσα ἡμᾶς εἰς συγκατάθεσιν, καὶ ἄλλου μηδενὸς δεομένη εἰς τὸ τοιαύτη προσπίπτειν ἢ εἰς τὸ τὴν πρὸς τὰς ἄλλας διαφορὰν ὑποβάλλειν.

belief (see *M.* 7.253–4, cited in n. 18). However, these cases don't show that the cataleptic impression isn't the criterion of truth, but only that there are some circumstances in which we can't use it. Or, to put it another way, the cataleptic impression doesn't serve as the criterion of truth universally, but only "when it doesn't have an obstacle" (*M.* 7.254).

This interpretation of the Younger Stoics gives them, I think, the beginnings of a respectable argument, although there's more to learn about the kinds of obstacles involved in the rare cases. The crucial point for the moment, however, is the implication that the supposed innovation of the Younger Stoics—their admission that cataleptic impressions don't *compel* assent—is something presupposed by Chrysippus' theory. For, if this is correct, the Younger Stoic qualification of the role of the cataleptic impression as the criterion of truth is a clarification or restatement of Chrysippus' position, rather than a revision of it.

On my reconstruction this follows from two controversial claims about the sentence "For this is so evident and striking that it all but grabs us by the hair, dragging us to assent" in *M.* 7. 257 (cited in n. 19). One is the way I interpret the phrase "all but grabs us by the hair, dragging us to assent": I take this to mean that they *all but* drag us to assent, that is, they strongly incline us to assent, or drag us so that we are almost, but not in fact, compelled to assent to them. This is not the standard way to take this adverbial unit here, but it is possible, and I think, natural.[20] And the second is that I take "this" (*hautê*), the demonstrative pronoun that introduces the subject of the sentence, to refer to the cataleptic impression in general, rather than to the species of cataleptic impressions without an obstacle. This is a slightly strained reading, I admit, because the pronoun is most readily taken to refer to the last relevant antecedent, which is the cataleptic impression without an obstacle. But my reading allows for a plausible reconstruction of the second part of the passage, which doesn't in fact appeal to the lack of obstacles of the kind mentioned in the first part; and it prevents the Younger Stoics from saying that cataleptic impressions compel assent except in cases when they don't, that is, when they have obstacles.

Still, however we read the passage, the Younger Stoics are clearly committed at least to the view that cataleptic impressions don't *always* compel assent, and hence don't always serve as the criterion. To see exactly why their use as the criterion is limited in this way, we need to look a bit more closely at the kinds of obstacles they can have. The

---

[20] The construction is clearly used in this way by Demosthenes in *Olynthiaca* 1.2: Ὁ μὲν οὖν παρὼν καιρός, ὦ ἄνδρες Ἀθηναῖοι, μόνον οὐχὶ λέγει φωνὴν ἀφιεὶς ὅτι τῶν πραγμάτων ὑμῖν ἐκείνων αὐτοῖς ἀντιληπτέον ἐστίν, εἴπερ ὑπὲρ σωτηρίας αὐτῶν φροντίζετε· ("The present crisis, fellow Athenians, *all but* calls aloud to you to take control of their affairs yourselves, if you are really concerned about their safety.")

two cases Sextus offers show that what intervenes to disrupt the normal causal effect of a cataleptic impression is a prior belief that is inconsistent with its propositional content. One case is that of Menelaus, who,

> during his return from Troy, saw the real Helen in Proteus' palace, after leaving in his ship the phantasm <of Helen> for which the 10-year-long war had taken place. So he received an impression from what is, and stamped and impressed according to what is, but didn't yield to it [or: didn't find it credible].[21] (*M.* 7.255)

Menelaus didn't assent to his cataleptic impression, Sextus explains, because:

> He was aware that he had left Helen under guard in his ship, and that it wasn't implausible that the one he found at Pharos wasn't Helen, but rather some sort of phantasm or something supernatural.[22] (*M.* 7. 256)

Thus, in Sextus' account, Menelaus *couldn't believe his eyes*, as it were: in this context, the propositional content of his impression—"This is Helen"—was just too implausible to be overcome by the perceptual or representational detail that made it cataleptic. And his impression was implausible because it was inconsistent with a host of false beliefs Menelaus had formed about Helen over the course of 10 years, and, in particular, a few minutes before when he thought he left her on his boat. (Sextus' other case in *M.* 7.254-6 is the very similar one of Admetus, who is unable to believe that his wife is back from the dead when he sees her, owing to his very well-grounded belief that the dead don't come back to life.)[23]

A notable feature of Sextus' cases is that both involve *false* beliefs. This looks a bit problematic for the Younger Stoics, since one might think that the scope of the criterion shouldn't be limited by failures of rationality—fools, after all, clearly fail to apply the criterion when they acquire their false beliefs, but this doesn't tell us anything about the criterion as such. But there is good reason to be suspicious of Sextus

---

[21] Sextus *M.* 7.255: καὶ ὅτε ἀπὸ Τροίας ὁ Μενέλαος ἀνακομισθεὶς ἑώρα τὴν ἀληθῆ Ἑλένην παρὰ τῷ Πρωτεῖ, [καὶ] καταλιπὼν ἐπὶ τῆς νεὼς τὸ ἐκείνης εἴδωλον, περὶ οὗ δεκαετὴς συνέστη πόλεμος, ἀπὸ ὑπάρχοντος μὲν καὶ κατ' αὐτὸ τὸ ὑπάρχον καὶ ἐναπομεμαγμένην καὶ ἐναπεσφραγισμένην ἐλάμβανε φαντασίαν, οὐκ εἶχε δὲ αὐτήν <...>. Bekker's emendation for the textual crux at the end of this sentence—οὐκ εἶχε δὲ αὐτὴν <πιστήν>, "he didn't find it credible"—is easier but ascribes an otherwise unknown idiom to the Stoics. So I prefer Lachelier's οὐκ εἶκε δὲ αὐτῇ—"he didn't yield to it," which provides an attested Stoic technical phrase and fits the context perfectly.

[22] Sextus *M.* 7.256: ὅ τε Μενέλαος συνεώρα ὅτι ἀπολέλοιπεν ἐν τῇ νηὶ φυλαττομένην τὴν Ἑλένην, καὶ οὐκ ἀπίθανον μέν ἐστιν Ἑλένην μὴ εἶναι τὴν ἐπὶ τῆς Φάρου εὑρεθεῖσαν, φάντασμα δέ τι καὶ δαιμόνιον.

[23] See *M.* 7.254: τότε ὁ Ἄδμητος ἔσπασε μὲν καταληπτικὴν φαντασίαν ἀπὸ τῆς Ἀλκήστιδος, ἠπίστει δ' αὐτῇ. ("Admetus got a cataleptic impression from Alcestis, but didn't believe it.")

here, since both his examples seem to be drawn directly from Carneades' objections to Chrysippus (cf. *M.* 7. 180, *PH* 1.228). So we might suspect that the Younger Stoics offered various cases, some of them involving true prior beliefs, and some even involving sages. And if that were the case, their full response to Carneades, on my reconstruction, would be to point out that his alleged counterexamples show us something vital about the providential structuring of our minds: the application of the criterion is limited precisely due to a design feature that is fundamental to our rationality, namely, the fact that our beliefs can override the default mechanisms leading to assent.

4. THE UNYIELDING SAGE

To substantiate this reconstruction of the Younger Stoics, then, we need to find some cases, ideally from Chrysippus himself, in which a sage refrains from assenting to cataleptic impressions. And given that the Stoics need such cases to be extremely rare—since cataleptic impressions must normally trump any prior beliefs we have that are inconsistent with them, if we are to make any cognitive progress—we should expect these cases to be somewhat far-fetched.

My first case is from situations in which the sage is undergoing a temporary bout of *illness, melancholy, or madness*. This case is rather underdetermined by the evidence, and only implicitly tied to Chrysippus, but it gives some indication of what we are looking for. The evidence is exhausted by two short fragments. The first, from Cicero, shows that the Stoics and Academics debated what happened in these situations:

> "But the wise person restrains himself in madness so as not to approve falsehoods in the place of truths." And he often does at other times, too, if his senses happen to be slow or heavy in some way, or if his impressions are too obscure, or if he is prevented from discerning by lack of time. Nevertheless this point—that the wise person sometimes restrains his assent—tells entirely against you Academics: for if there were no difference between impressions, he would either always restrain his assent, or never.[24] (*Acad.* 2.53; the speaker is Lucullus, the Antiochian with Stoic epistemological views.)

---

[24] Cicero *Acad.* 2.53: At enim ipse sapiens sustinet se in furore ne adprobet falsa pro veris." Et alias quidem saepe, si aut in sensibus ipsius est aliqua forte gravitas aut tarditas, aut obscuriora sunt quae videntur, aut a perspiciendo temporis brevitate excluditur. Quamquam totum hoc, sapientem aliquando sustinere adsensionem, contra vos est. si enim inter visa <nihil interesset>, aut semper sustineret aut numquam.

And the second, from Diogenes Laertius, shows that Chrysippus was interested in them too:

Chrysippus thought that virtue could be lost owing to drink or melancholy, but Cleanthes that it could not because <it is constituted by> strong cognitions.[25] (DL 7.127)

The scenario, then, is this. A sage feels the onset of a bout of severe illness that will disturb the condition of her mind. But when the mind is severely disturbed or weakened, it tends to produce mostly, sometimes even only, non-cataleptic impressions, which are nonetheless hard to resist in this weakened condition. Yet the sage must resist, if she is to preserve her virtue or wisdom, so she decides that she will avoid assent for the duration. If we look at the impressions the sage receives from this moment on, it seems clear that they will form a series, beginning with cataleptic impressions—"The aspirin are over there," "I really am getting ill"—passing though a stage of non-cataleptic impressions while the bout is severe, and ending up with cataleptic impressions again—"I am better," "It's time to get up." So the first of these are cataleptic impressions to which the sage doesn't assent owing to an antecedent belief—in this case, a true practical belief (that she should avoid all assent for the moment) that is incompatible with *any* assent, rather than with the specific content of her current impressions.

If this scenario seems rather implausible, we can refine it by imagining our sage reflecting on the cognitive character of her impressions (since sages are more capable of being aware of this character than the rest of us). At the beginning of the earlier sequence, it will be obvious to her that her impressions aren't non-cataleptic, so she can assent to them. But, as the illness or melancholy comes on, we can presume that it becomes progressively harder and harder to tell that they have the requisite objective features of evidence and distinctness. So on this picture, too, she will need to begin to suspend her assent as her awareness of their cognitive features runs out, that is, I think, before she has reached the last of the actually cataleptic impressions.

There are some problems with this hypothetical scenario—for instance, how the sage knows when to resume assent (see case 2 below). But I think that something like this scenario must be presupposed by the Academic objector in *Acad.* 2.53 (above) and conceded by the Stoicizing respondent. For the point can't be just that sages don't assent to individual non-cataleptic impressions, as Lucullus tries to make out, because

---

[25] DL 7.127: καὶ μὴν τὴν ἀρετὴν Χρύσιππος μὲν ἀποβλητήν, Κλεάνθης δὲ ἀναπόβλητον· ὁ μὲν ἀποβλητὴν διὰ μέθην καὶ μελαγχολίαν, ὁ δὲ ἀναπόβλητον διὰ βεβαίους καταλήψεις.

this is too obvious: it goes without saying that the sage doesn't assent to vague impressions, such as the intimation that someone in the distance is her friend (although it seems unlikely that sages can avoid *having* such familiar impressions, given that they can't avoid impressions that would constitute emotions *if* they assented to them).

So much for case 1. My second case, from a sage in the midst of a *sorites argument*. This is described in two sources and explicitly tied to Chrysippus. The first source is a passage from the *Academica*, where Cicero in his Academic *persona* uses Chrysippus' views on the sorites to show the inefficacy of Stoic logic (*Acad.* 2.92–4). The idea is simple: Chrysippus claimed that the correct way to deal with a sorites argument was to answer the questions up to a certain point, and then "be silent" (*hêsuxazein*) to avoid falling into error (*Acad.* 2.93). But, Cicero argues:

> if the point is just that you're not *saying* anything, you aren't achieving anything. For what does someone trying to catch you out care whether he traps you when you're silent or speaking? If, on the other hand, you specify without any doubt that it is "few" as far as, let's say, 9, but halt before 10, then you're suspending your assent from cases that are certain and evident as well. But that's just what you don't let me [the Academic skeptic] do in obscure cases!²⁶ (*Acad.* 2.94)

So Chrysippus thinks that sometimes we can and should suspend assent to cataleptic impressions. There are two problems, here, however. The first concerns what Chrysippus meant when he advised "being silent," since some scholars have denied that it implies refraining from assent. But I will ignore this, since it is hard to see what else it could imply in this context, even if dialectical falling silent should turn out to imply something else in other texts.²⁷ The second problem is that Cicero seems to *argue* here for the conclusion that Chrysippus thinks that we (or the sage) should suspend assent to evident cases, that is, to cataleptic impressions, in these conditions; but that suggests that this wasn't his position, or, at least, that this wasn't clear or explicit. This is a bit troubling, but is perhaps due just to the rhetoric of the immediate passage, since

---

²⁶ Cicero *Acad.* 2.94: si id tantum modo ut taceas, nihil adsequeris; quid enim ad illum qui te captare vult, utrum tacentem inretiat te an loquentem? sin autem usque ad novem verbi gratia sine dubitatione respondes pauca esse, in decumo insistis, etiam a certis et inlustrioribus cohibes adsensum; hoc idem me in obscuris facere non sinis.

²⁷ Here I agree with the arguments of Bobzien (2005) 239–73 at 264–71 against Atherton (1993) 419–24. Cf. *Acad.* 2.94, where Chrysippus seems to characterize his remedy for the *sorites* as a suspension of assent: ut agitator callidus…equos sustinebo ("I will *restrain* my horse…like a skilled charioteer").

the point of the argument as a whole is a different one, namely, that the Stoics can't *solve* the sorites.[28]

At any rate, Sextus, our second source, seems to confirm Cicero's claim about the sorites, and also to offer something like an explanation for Chrysippus' view. The gist of Sextus' report is given in the introduction of his wider skeptical argument, which is again reassuringly to a quite different conclusion (in this case about the universality of "*aparallaxia*," i.e. the indiscernibility of cataleptic from non-cataleptic impressions in general):

> For in the sorites, <the puzzle> when the last cataleptic impression is next to the first non-cataleptic one and is almost indistinguishable from it, Chrysippus claims that the sage will come to a halt and fall silent in the case of impressions where the difference is this small, but that he will assent to one <of the pair> in the case of impressions where the difference is greater.[29] (*M.* 7.416)

Sextus' exposition of the problem is hard to grasp, but in the light of Susanne Bobzien's work on it, I can suggest this sketchy reconstruction.[30] Imagine a sage looking at a sequence of 10,000 heaps of grain containing from 1 to 10,000 grains, where—irrespective of whether there is a last *true* impression of fewness or not—the last *cataleptic* impression of fewness she can in principle get is that "50 is few." If she compares the pile of 50 with the pile of 10,000, she will be able to assent to the cataleptic impression that "50 is few." But if she compares the pile of 50 with the pile of 51, it will no longer be clear to her that "50 is few." Hence, when the sage is answering a sorites series of questions, what she ought to do, on Chrysippus' view, is fall silent shortly before—or, in principle, one heap before—she reaches the last case in which she could have a cataleptic impression.

The point of comparing the two cases—50 versus 10,000 with 50 versus 51—is presumably to show that one's reaction to an impression is partially dependent on the

---

[28] The back reference to this passage in *Acad.* 2.107 supports this reading of the rhetoric. For here again the Stoic point that the sage can suspend assent to cataleptic impressions in the very defined circumstance of a sorites argument is just *assumed* by Cicero and used to press a very different Academic point, that one can refrain from assent quite universally—which was clearly not part of Chrysippus', or the Younger Stoics', view.

[29] Sextus *M.* 7.416: ἐπὶ γὰρ τοῦ σωρίτου τῆς ἐσχάτης καταληπτικῆς φαντασίας τῇ πρώτῃ ἀκαταλήπτῳ παρακειμένης καὶ δυσδιορίστου σχεδὸν ὑπαρχούσης, φασὶν οἱ περὶ τὸν Χρύσιππον, ὅτι ἐφ' ὧν μὲν φαντασιῶν ὀλίγη τις οὕτως ἐστὶ διαφορά, στήσεται ὁ σοφὸς καὶ ἡσυχάσει, ἐφ' ὧν δὲ πλείων προσπίπτει, ἐπὶ τούτων συγκαταθήσεται τῇ ἑτέρᾳ ὡς ἀληθεῖ.

[30] See Bobzien (2002) 217–38, esp. 233–7. The earlier treatments of the two passages by Barnes (1982) 24–68 esp. 49–56 and Burnyeat (1982) 315–58 esp. 333–8 remain useful.

context in which one receives it. But given Chrysippus' theory of cataleptic impressions, he can't think that our contextual beliefs or expectations make any difference to the objective features of the impressions, since that would be to surrender to the coherentist view Carneades espoused. So Chrysippus must think that it is possible to become unclear or confused about whether or not a particular impression is cataleptic; and for that reason he recommends falling silent, or suspending assent, before one reaches the end of the sequence of cataleptic impressions that "n is few."[31]

So here are two cases in which it looks like Chrysippus is committed to the view that the sage can suspend assent to cataleptic impressions, that is, that not only is it not necessary to assent to them, but it is also sometimes wrong to. A notable difference between these two cases and the Younger Stoic examples is that there seem to be two ways to construe the sage's suspension of assent in the new cases: either as the result of practical judgment not to assent to any impression for a time, formed prior to the relevant cataleptic impression, or as a reaction to the subjective unclarity of the sage's cataleptic impressions. The first description looks heroic: the sage's mental strength seems to allow her to resist cataleptic impressions *ad libitum*, in a way that would be quite impossible for the rest of us. But perhaps the second description is not an alternative to the first, but an explanation of it, so that what the sage decides or resolves— and carries through with unlike the rest of us—is not to assent when things become unclear to her. At any rate, the theory I am proposing is not that we can just *decide* not to believe our senses when they are in perfect working order, but rather that we *fail* to assent to cataleptic impressions when we are *certain* that our senses couldn't be right.

5. OBJECTIONS

So far, I hope to have given some reason to think that the Younger Stoic view is an accurate restatement of the older, Chrysippian theory that we are naturally set up to assent to cataleptic impressions, but our beliefs can override this natural mechanism in certain circumstances. A positive defense of this view would need to show how it coheres with the Stoic model of cognitive progress—for instance, by showing that our natural or automatic cognitive mechanisms are defensive, that is, designed to allow us to resist non-cataleptic impressions.[32] But since this is a rather large task, I will instead

---

[31] Bobzien (2002) 217–38 at 223 n. 25 points to support for this interpretation in Sextus' exposition of the Stoic views about plausible impressions in *M*. 7.243, where the category of "both plausible and implausible" is constituted by impressions "that are now thus, but now thus, according to their relata" and exemplified by "aporetic arguments" like the sorites.

[32] There is evidence, I think, to support this, e.g. in the lists of the cognitive virtues of the sage at DL 7.46, *P.Herc.* 1020 (= *SVF* 2.131), and in Stobaeus *Ec.* 2.7.11m and the other texts collected in *SVF* 3.548–56.

defend it negatively, by trying to defuse the objections to it from proponents of the standard view that cataleptic impressions (always) compel assent.

These objections come in two kinds. The **first**, sketched by Gisela Striker in her groundbreaking work on the criterion, argues that *the Younger Stoics were just wrong*: their agreement that there are rare cataleptic impressions one doesn't assent to amounts to a significant revision of Chrysippus' theory and a major concession to the Academics.[33] This objection is supported by four arguments.

The first argument concerns the *propositional content of cataleptic impressions*. The suggestion is that the Younger Stoics ought to have denied that Menelaus, in their example, received a cataleptic impression: what he saw was not "This is Helen," but rather something like "That's a ghost" or "That can't be Helen." One could spell out this argument in various ways, but the most interesting one relies, I think, on what we can call a quasi-internalist theory of cataleptic impressions. The idea here is roughly that your impressions are cataleptic just because of the way in which they depend on and fit with your concepts, beliefs, and dispositions to believe: assent to them is automatic precisely because their content fit, so their *self*-evidence can't come apart from their obviousness or clarity *to their recipient*. Thus, in the Menelaus case, his false beliefs about Helen affect the kinds of thoughts he can have, making it impossible for him to have a cataleptic impression that "This is Helen."

The quasi-internalist theory is attractive because our concepts and beliefs clearly do affect the nature of our impressions. But it can't be right in this extreme form, because it implies, I think, that ordinary people will end up with very few cataleptic impressions, which is contrary to the basic Stoic idea that normal perception typically provides cognition. First, there is no reason to deny that Menelaus could have an impression with the propositional content "This is Helen." It is true, of course, that Menelaus can't think "This [the person now here on land] is the person now on the ship [Helen]." But we can imagine, if necessary, that he takes her back to the ship, puts her next to the phantasm, and asks himself: "Is this one Helen?" Perhaps he oscillates, initially, between impressions that each is Helen, and opts for the phantasm; but then he does have impressions from Helen that "This is Helen." So the question isn't about the propositional content, but whether the perceptual or representational content could be "evident" or cataleptic under normal perceptual conditions given that Menelaus has many false beliefs. But it is clear that the mere *possession* of false beliefs doesn't alter our mental condition in a

---

[33] See Gisela Striker (1990) 143–60 at 152–3 (with n. 14). (The ground was first broken in her original work in German in 1974.) Arguments 1 and 4 below are drawn from her criticism of the Younger Stoics in her note 14; arguments 2 and 3 are taken from her exposition of the orthodox Stoic view on her pages 152–3. Versions of arguments 2 and 4 are also found in Allen (1994) 85–113 at 105–6.

way that prevents us from getting cataleptic impressions, since otherwise fools couldn't ever have them. Nor could the mere possession of *false beliefs in the same semantic domain*, that is, here, about Helen, since all of us presumably have some false beliefs about our friends, but these don't prevent us from being able to recognize them properly. Nor, in general, will the possession of false beliefs in the same semantic domain *that are inconsistent with the propositional content of an impression*. For if they did, we would never be able to correct our beliefs on the basis of new perceptual information, so that meeting Socrates in Megara would never suffice to correct an antecedent belief that he never leaves Athens.

So it looks like we need to reject or revise the quasi-internalist theory. Our beliefs and general mental condition clearly have significant effects on our impressions, since our beliefs influence the kinds of propositional contents we usually entertain and our condition can render them non-cataleptic (though disease or mental malfunction). But the primary effect of our beliefs and conditions is on our assent, not on our impressions. So the features that make our true impressions cataleptic—their evidence or accurate and detailed stamping and impressing—are objective features, and, as it were, relatively indifferent to our current beliefs. For the Menelaus case implies, I think, that there must be a degree of independence between the concepts we apply in perception (e.g. of Helen) and our specific and occurrent beliefs about perceptual objects—though I am not in a position to generalize this suggestion into a satisfying quasi-externalist theory.

The remaining arguments to show that the Younger Stoics were wrong concern the connection between cataleptic impressions and assent elsewhere in the Stoa. One, our second argument, derives from the Stoic theory of *natural conceptions or preconceptions*. Although the theory remains rather controversial, the gist of it is that human beings naturally develop certain conceptions, in virtue of which (or some of which) they eventually become rational beings.[34] But in order for these conceptions to constitute reason and to serve as criteria of truth (DL 7.54, Alex. *Mixt.* p. 217.2–4), they must be the result of a natural and automatic causal process immune to distortion by faulty or vague perceptual input and proto-reasoning. Thus there *must* be an automatic mechanism that singles out the cataleptic impressions that eventually yield these conceptions. And, since all of us form natural conceptions, it must be necessary to assent to these cataleptic impressions.

But, while this interpretation of the theory of natural conceptions, or something like it, must be roughly right, the conclusion doesn't follow. For, as noted in section

---

[34] The basic texts are Aetius 4.11 and Plutarch fr. 215f; for some recent work on the theory, see Brittain (2005) 164–209 and Dyson (2009).

2, pre- and non-rational animals don't have a faculty of assent.[35] Rational beings are different from children or animals precisely by their distinctive ability to give and suspend assent to their impressions. So the generation of natural conceptions doesn't work through assent, but rather through an automatic non-rational mechanism of the kind that moves animals to action, which is superseded by assent in rational adults.

An apparent difficulty for this view, however, is that part of the evidence for it ascribes to Zeno the claim that:

> another motive [for thinking that we should trust the senses] was that nature had given <cognition> as a standard and foundation for knowledge of the world: it was the source from which our conceptions of things were later stamped on our minds, which in turn give rise not just to the starting points but to certain broader paths for discovering reason.[36] (*Acad.*1.42)

Since Zeno defines cognition as assent to a cataleptic impression (*Acad.* 1.40), this looks awkward. But this problem can be resolved in one of two ways. First, by supposing that Cicero has lost track of the subject of this long sentence—the grammar makes "cognition" (*comprehensio*) the subject, but the semantics suggest that it should be "the cataleptic impression" (*visum comprehendible*), an unwieldy phrase Cicero tries to avoid. Or, second, by positing a notion of quasi-assent in children, to go along with their well-attested quasi-speech and quasi-emotions.[37] The second option is tempting, since the Stoics need some way of explaining why children develop reason while animals don't. But, in either case, it is plain, I think, that children can't have the faculty of *rational* assent because they don't have reason; and if they do have quasi-assent, it will necessarily be automatic, because they don't have conceptualized beliefs that could override it. So this argument tells us nothing about the mechanisms of assent in rational agents.

The third argument to show the error of the Younger Stoics, is derived from other accounts of the *strikingness* of cataleptic impressions. The evidence in this case comes primarily from an Academic "indiscernibility" (*aparallaxia*) argument against the

---

[35] See Hierocles *St. Eth.* 1.31–3, Clement *Strom.* 2.20.111 (= *SVF* 2.714), Philo *Alleg.* 1.30 (= *SVF* 2.844); cf. nn. 6 and 12 above.

[36] Cicero *Acad.* 1.42: quodque natura quasi normam scientiae et principium sui dedisset unde postea notiones rerum in animis imprimerentur; e quibus non principia solum sed latiores quaedam ad rationem inveniendam viae reperiuntur.

[37] See Varro *Ling. Lat.* 6.56, Seneca *De Ira* 1.3.7, Plutarch *Soll. An.* 960f, 961e–f, Porphyry *Abst.* 3.21–2. The underlying Stoic theory of non-rational cognition is examined in Brittain (2002) 253–308 at 256–74.

cataleptic impression, set out in detail in Cicero *Acad.* 2.88–90 and in Sextus *M.* 7.402–8. The structure of the Academic argument is given by the conclusion in *M.* 7.405:

> So if some impressions are cataleptic in virtue of leading us to assent and to going on to the action appropriate to them, given that false impressions like this also occur, we ought to say that non-cataleptic impressions are indiscernible from cataleptic impressions.[38]

That is, given that the Academics can show cases in which the causal effects of non-cataleptic impressions are identical to those of cataleptic impressions—for instance in the famous case of Heracles shooting his own children, but also in the more mundane cases of Catulus' crazy neighbor Tutidanus, or our ordinary dreams—the Stoics can't identify cataleptic impressions as those that motivate us to action. Or, as Cicero puts it, "there's no difference between true and false impressions with respect to the mind's assent" (*Acad.* 2.90). The objection to the Younger Stoic view, then, is that this Academic argument presupposes that the older Stoics thought that cataleptic impressions are essentially assent-inducing.

But this seems too strong a conclusion to draw from the Academic argument. It's true, of course, that all the Stoics think that cataleptic impressions are normally and naturally conducive to assent (see DL 7.51 and Sextus *M.* 7.257). But it doesn't follow that we necessarily assent to them. First, as we have seen, the extreme causal effect of compelling assent can't be part of the definition, since animals and child don't assent. Nor, however, should we expect to find it in a definition of rational cataleptic impressions, since it isn't an intrinsic feature of the impressions (unlike their truth, evidence, and "autonomous" distinctiveness). At most, if there is an intrinsic feature here that differs from their evidence, it will be that of "strikingness," not assent-compulsion—as Sextus' more careful phrasing at the introduction of this argument suggests, where he starts from the clearly Stoic premise that cataleptic impressions are "striking and evident" (*M.* 7.403). And it doesn't immediately follow from this feature that one necessarily reacts to it with assent. Second, the Stoic response to this Academic argument shows that what they wanted to claim was not that cataleptic impressions compel assent, but rather that there is a *difference* in our reactions to cataleptic and non-cataleptic impressions (see *Acad.* 2.52, cited in n. 16): our assent to non-cataleptic impressions is weaker than it is to cataleptic impressions. This difference can most obviously be seen in the fact that we normally assent to cataleptic impressions and

---

[38] Sextus M. 7.405: εἰ οὖν καταληπτικαί τινές εἰσι φαντασίαι παρόσον ἐπάγονται ἡμᾶς εἰς συγκατάθεσιν καὶ εἰς τὸ τὴν ἀκόλουθον αὐταῖς πρᾶξιν συνάπτειν, ἐπεὶ καὶ ψευδεῖς τοιαῦται πεφήνασι, λεκτέον ἀπαραλλάκτους εἶναι ταῖς καταληπτικαῖς φαντασίαις τὰς ἀκαταλήπτους.

refrain from assent to non-cataleptic ones. This doesn't imply, of course, that we can't assent to non-cataleptic ones; but nor does it imply that we must always assent to cataleptic ones. It just means that cataleptic impressions have a stronger causal effect on our minds than other impressions: they are extremely conducive to assent.[39]

The fourth and last argument comes from *Antiochus*. This offers the most intriguing evidence, but also the least persuasive argument, so I will deal with it briefly. The argument is simple: in the course of his evidently Stoic arguments against the Academic pretension to suspend assent universally, Lucullus, Antiochus's spokesman, claims that assent to cataleptic impressions is necessary:

> In fact, by not allowing people to perceive or assent, there's a sense in which the Academics actually rob them of their minds. For just as the balance of a scale must sink down when weights are placed on it, so the mind must yield to perspicuous impressions; just as an animal can't fail to have an impulse towards something that appears suited to its nature (what the Greeks call *oikeion*), it can't fail to approve a perspicuous thing it is presented with.[40] (*Acad.* 2.38.)

There are two basic problems with the argument that this shows that assent to cataleptic impressions is necessary in the Stoic view. The first is that the passage probably doesn't mean to claim more than that it is our *nature* to assent to cataleptic impressions, which is compatible with the Younger Stoic view Antiochus otherwise follows rather closely.[41] A good reason to think this is provided by the parallel Antiochus uses and its helpfully specific gloss. For it isn't in fact strictly speaking necessary for an animal to have an impulse towards something it perceives as "suited to its nature" (*oikeion*). What is *suited* to an animal's nature is a general class of things, e.g. dog food for dogs. But, while it *is* necessary for animals to have impulses for suitable things (*oikeia*) when getting

---

[39] The Stoics used the verbs to express the notion of "conduciveness" to assent, including σπάω (*M.* 7.254), περισπάω (Plutarch *St. Rep.* 1036e), and κατασπάω (*M.* 7.257)—all based on the metaphor of "pulling"—and ἐπάγω (*M.* 7.405)—using the metaphor of "leading." Note that -σπάω forms aren't compelling in Plutarch *St. Rep.* 1056–7, or in Sextus' account of Carneades at *M.* 7.179–80. Where περισπάω is compelling in Plutarch 1036d, it is because it refers to beliefs, not impressions.

[40] Cicero *Acad.* 2.38: et vero animus quodam modo eripitur iis quos neque sentire neque adsentiri volunt. ut enim necesse est lancem in libram ponderibus inpositis deprimi *sic* animum perspicuis cedere. nam quo modo non potest animal ullum non adpetere id quod adcommodatum ad naturam adpareat (Graeci id *oikeion* appellant), *sic* non potest obiectam rem perspicuam non adprobare.

[41] See Brittain (2012) 104–30 for a review of Antiochus' epistemology, including his somewhat heterodox ideas about assent. The parallels between Antiochus and the Younger Stoics include *Acad.* 2.19—*M.* 7.258; *Acad.* 2.33—*M.* 7.269; further cases are noted *ad loc.* in Brittain 2006.

them is appropriate or befitting (*kathêkon*), getting them isn't always appropriate—if it were, animals at pasture would burst from overfeeding. According to the analogy, then, it is natural for the mind to yield to evident impressions, and perhaps necessary that it yields to some of them, but it isn't necessary in every case. And this interpretation of the passage is supported by Cicero's apparent reply to Antiochus' argument in *Acad.* 2.107, which characterizes it as the claim that "it is impossible for anyone to assent to nothing."

The second problem is that Antiochus' views on assent are anyway heterodox, since he ascribed assent to all animals. This isn't very clear from the passage above (where the reference of the penultimate "it" is ambiguous between the mind and the animal); but the preceding sentence includes the ill-phrased claim that we must either remove the senses from animals in general, or allow them assent, "which is in our power" (*Acad.* 2.37). And the depth, if not the precise nature, of his heterodoxy on this issue is confirmed by the Antiochian Piso's claim in *De finibus* 5.38 that some of the larger mammals are capable of mental activities that produce states analogous to virtue. So, Antiochus either overstates the Younger Stoic position or fails to confirm the alleged Older Stoic position. I conclude from this review of four arguments for it that the first objection, that the Younger Stoics mistakenly abandoned the orthodoxy under pressure from Carneades, isn't warranted by the evidence.

The **second** objection I will consider comes in the form of a rival interpretation of the Younger Stoic position proposed by James Allen in his excellent study of Academic "probabilism."[42] On his interpretation, *the Younger Stoics aren't in error, because they accept the* (alleged) *older Stoic view that assent to cataleptic impressions is necessary*. The apparent concession the Younger Stoics make to Carneades' examples of Menelaus and Admetus is thus not that our beliefs can interfere with the causal effects that incline us to assent to a cataleptic impression (as I have argued), but rather that our beliefs or reasoning can undermine its criterial function by causing us to reject almost immediately the cognition it provides. So, on Allen's interpretation, Menelaus did in fact assent to the cataleptic impression "This is Helen"; but, because he then reasoned that it couldn't really be her since she was on his ship, he immediately gave up his belief.

This is an ingenious interpretation of the passage, and one that offers the Younger Stoics a view they could have held, if they had thought that assent to cataleptic impressions was necessary: the Stoic model of *acrasia* certainly shows, as Allen argues, that we can oscillate wildly between incompatible beliefs. I don't think it fits the text, however, because the distinction it requires between assenting to a cataleptic impression and forming a settled belief is one that Sextus can't be making here. For in Sextus'

---

[42] Allen (1994) 85–113 at 108–13.

terminology—and the Stoics'—the difference between getting an impression (*prospiptei*) and trusting it or finding it incredible (*apistos*) in *M*.7.254 can only refer to the distinction between having a thought and assenting to it.[43] But the more important point, I think, is to see that the basic motivation for this rival interpretation is something that both Allen and I accept. For Allen's main purpose is to provide the Younger Stoics with a position that guarantees the autonomy of cataleptic impressions by isolating our assent to them from reasoning: Carneades has won if the Stoics concede that assent is the product of a reflective judgment we arrive at *about* our impressions. But, as I hope I have made clear, the view I am urging doesn't make this concession. On my view, Menelaus doesn't *decide* to reject the evidence of his senses owing to considerations of coherence; rather, his false beliefs about Helen just *override* the automatic causal effect of receiving a cataleptic impression.[44] In such cases, the mind is moved to assent by the perceptual detail of an impression, but this motion is checked by the exceptional inconsistency between its propositional content and the subject's antecedent beliefs. So the self-evident or self-warranting nature of the cataleptic impression does ensure that it serves as the criterion of truth—except in rare cases, like Menelaus'.

6. CONCLUSION

To sum up: I have argued that the melancholy and sorites cases show that Chrysippus thought that we can suspend assent to cataleptic impressions, that the Younger Stoic position that we sometimes do suspend assent to them can be plausibly interpreted as a clarification of Chrysippus' view, and that the standard reasons for denying that this was Chrysippus' view are inadequate. If these arguments work, it isn't necessary to assent to cataleptic impressions on the Stoic view. And it isn't necessary because the Stoics thought that the mechanisms of assent are complex in various ways: for instance, one works through the representational or perceptual character of our impressions, and another through their propositional content and hence our individual beliefs. Since these two mechanisms can, in principle, conflict, it is possible, in the case of cataleptic impressions, for their objective perceptual features or evidence to come apart, as it were, from the normal subjective reactions to their propositional content as plausible

---

[43] This distinction is found *passim* in Sextus' report on the Stoic criterion: see *M.* 7.244–5, 247, 249, 257–8, and 260.

[44] This is compatible with Sextus' phrasing in *M.* 7.256, despite his explanation of Admetus' and Menelaus' failure to assent in terms of reasons, because Sextus is careful about the tenses he uses here: in both cases he uses the imperfect—Admetus "reckoned that" (ἐλογίζετο ὅτι) and Menelaus "was aware that" (συνεώρα ὅτι). The tenses indicate that these aren't thoughts or arguments the heroes made at that moment, but rather the underlying beliefs that made them resist their respective cataleptic impressions.

or obvious. And when this happens, a rational agent will suspend assent to a cataleptic impression, because a rational agent is essentially one whose assents are conditioned by his or her beliefs.

Acknowledgments

It is a delight to dedicate this essay to Gisela Striker, *prima inter pares* in the renaissance of philosophical scholarship on Stoicism and ancient skepticism, its most fearless critic, and the most generous and amused mentor of its students. Though I was never formally her student, she has sometimes been amused, I think, and certainly always done for me *quae salva fide facere possit* (*Off.* 3.34).

I am very grateful to Tad Brennan for his help and criticism of this paper in its several forms.

Bibliography

Allen, J. 1994. "Academic Probabilism and Stoic Epistemology," *Classical Quarterly 44*, 85–113.
Annas, J. 1990. "Stoic Epistemology," in S. Everson (ed.), *Epistemology* (Cambridge) 184–303.
Arthur, E. 1983. "The Stoic Analysis of the Mind's Reactions to Presentations," *Hermes 111*, 69–78.
Atherton, C. 1993. *The Stoics on Ambiguity* (Cambridge).
Barnes, J. 1982. "Medicine, Experience and Logic," in J. Barnes, J. Brunschwig, M. Burnyeat, and M. Schofield (eds.), *Science and Speculation: Studies in Hellenistic Theory and Practise* (Cambridge) 24–68.
Bobzien, S. 2002. "Chrysippus and the Epistemic Theory of Vagueness," *Proceedings of the Aristotelian Society 102*, 217–38.
———. 2005. "The Stoics on the Fallacies of Equivocation," in B. Inwood and D. Frede (eds.), *Language and Learning* (Cambridge) 239–73.
Brennan, T. 1998. "The Old Stoic Theory of Emotions," in J. Sihvola and T. Engberg-Pedersen (eds.), *The Emotions in Hellenistic Philosophy* (Dordrecht) 21–70.
———. 2003. "Stoic Moral Psychology," in B. Inwood (ed.), *The Cambridge Companion to the Stoics* (Cambridge) 257–94.
Brittain, C. 2001. *Philo of Larissa* (Oxford).
———. 2002. "Non-rational Perception in the Stoics and Augustine," *OSAP 22.1*, 253–308.
———. 2005. "Common Sense. Concepts, Definition, and Meaning in and out of the Stoa," in B. Inwood and D. Frede (eds.), *Language and Learning* (Cambridge) 164–209.
———. 2006. *Cicero: On Academic Scepticism* (Indianapolis).
———. 2012. "Antiochus' Epistemology," in D. Sedley (ed.), *The Philosophy of Antiochus* (Cambridge) 104–30.
Burnyeat, M. 1982. "Gods and Heaps," in M. Schofield and M. Nussbaum (eds.), *Language and Logos* (Cambridge) 315–38.
Dyson, H. 2009. *Prolepsis and Ennoia in the Early Stoa* (Berlin).
Frede, M. 1983. "Stoics and Skeptics on Clear and Distinct Impressions," in M. Burnyeat (ed.), *The Skeptical Tradition* (London) 65–93 (= Frede, *Essays in Ancient Philosophy* [Oxford, 1987] 151–76).

———. 1986. "The Stoic Doctrine of the Affections of the Soul," in M. Schofield and G. Striker (eds.), *The Norms of Nature* (Cambridge) 93-110.
———. 1987. "The Skeptic's Two Kinds of Assent," in his *Essays in Ancient Philosophy* (Oxford) 201-22.
———. 1994. "The Stoic Conception of Reason," in K. Boudouris (ed.), *Hellenistic Philosophy*, vol. ii (Athens) 50-63.
———. 1999. "Stoic Epistemology," in K. Algra, J. Barnes, J. Mansfeld, and M. Schofield (eds.), *The Cambridge History of Hellenistic Philosophy* (Cambridge) 295-322.
Görler, W. 1977. "*Asthenes sunkatathesis* zur stoischen Erkenntnistheorie," *Würzburger Jahrbücher für die Altertumswissenschaft* NF 3, 83-92.
Inwood, B. 1985. *Ethics and Human Action in Early Stoicism* (Oxford).
Ioppolo, A.-M. 1990. "Presentation and Assent: A Physical and Cognitive Problem in Early Stoicism," *Classical Quarterly* 40, 433-49.
Long, A.A. 1991. "Representation and the Self," in S. Everson (ed.), *Companions to Ancient Thought 2: Psychology* (Cambridge) 101-20 (= Long, *Stoic Studies* [Cambridge, 1996] 264-85).
Meinwald, C. 2005. "Ignorance and Opinion in Stoic Epistemology," *Phronesis* 50.3, 215-31.
Sandbach, F. 1971. '*Phantasia kataleptike*', in A. Long (ed.), *Problems in Stoicism* (London, 1996²) 9-22.
Striker, G. 1974. Κριτήριον τῆς ἀληθείας. *Nachrichten der Akademie der Wissenschaften zu Göttingen*, I. Phil.-hist. Klasse, 2, 48-110 (= G. Striker, *Essays on Hellenistic Epistemology and Ethics* [Cambridge, 1996] 22-76).
———. 1980. "Sceptical Strategies," in M. Schofield, M. Burnyeat, and J. Barnes (eds.), *Doubt and Dogmatism* (Oxford) 54-83 (= G. Striker, *Essays on Hellenistic Epistemology and Ethics* [Cambridge, 1996] 92-115).
———. 1990. "The Problem of the Criterion," in S. Everson (ed.), *Epistemology* (Cambridge) 143-60 (= G. Striker, *Essays on Hellenistic Epistemology and Ethics* [Cambridge, 1996] 150-65).
von Arnim, H. 1903-5. *Stoicorum Veterum Fragmenta*, vols. i-iii, Stuttgart (1964²) [= *SVF*].

15

SEXTUS EMPIRICUS ON PERSUASIVENESS AND EQUIPOLLENCE

Svavar Hrafn Svavarsson

1. INTRODUCTION

Much has been written about the notion of appearance in Sextus Empiricus and its status as a skeptical kind of belief, distinct from dogmatic belief.[1] Less attention has been paid to the notion of *persuasiveness*, although it promises some insight into the skeptical mind.[2] The role of this notion is twofold. On the one hand Sextus suggests that the skeptic suspends belief because he experiences contrary accounts (λόγοι) for appearances (i.e. accounts that purport to establish the truth of particular appearances) as *equal with regard to being persuasive and unpersuasive*.[3] The equipollence (ἰσοσθένεια) of contrary accounts consists in this kind of equality. This claim can be and has been taken to mean the following: being *equally persuaded* by both accounts, the skeptic suspends belief.[4] And this

---

[1] For the influential arguments that set the terms for the debate, see Burnyeat and Frede (1998).
[2] But see Machuca (2009). The terms Sextus usually employs when discussing persuasiveness are of two kinds. On the one hand he uses the adjective πιστός, noun πίστις, and verb πιστεύω. On the other, he uses the adjective πιθανός, nouns πιθανότης and πειθώ, and verb πείθω/πείθεσθαι. According to my search on *Thesaurus Linguae Grecae*, the former is more commonly used. Something is πιστόν if it is trustworthy, credible, convincing, plausible, believable, persuasive, and thus generates πίστις. Sextus seems to use πιστόν and πιθανόν interchangeably. In *PH* 1.10 Sextus explains equipollence as equality of conflicting accounts with regard to πίστις and ἀπιστία, while in *PH* 1.190 he explains it referring to the equality of what appears πιθανόν. In *PH* 1.183 and 2.79 he refers to equal πιθανότης. In *PH* 1.222 he uses both terms. The terms are variously translated, but I have opted for uniformity: when something is πιστόν or πιθανόν, it is *persuasive*.
[3] *PH* 1.10, 203: κατὰ πίστιν καὶ ἀπιστίαν. *PH* 1.196: πρὸς πίστιν καὶ ἀπιστίαν. *PH* 1.198, 202, 222, 227, 232: κατὰ πίστιν ἢ ἀπιστίαν.
[4] See most recently Pellegrin (2010: 126): "This equal strength is *experienced* by the sceptic, in that he is equally convinced by opposing arguments. Thus, early in *PH* 3, Sextus concludes that 'it is also necessary to suspend assent about the existence of cause, saying that cause no more is anything than it is not, as far as what the dogmatists say is concerned' (3.29), because he has laid out one by one the arguments for and against and has found them equally plausible. 'Plausible' renders the Greek term *pithanon*, which comes from the verb *peithô*, 'convince, persuade'; the point, then, is that the plausibility of the opposed arguments carries equal conviction for the sceptic

might mean that he is not persuaded by either account.[5] On the other hand, Sextus does allow the skeptic to be persuaded of something being the case just in the sense of experiencing the appearance that such is the case, so long as this appearance does not consist in being persuaded by one account rather than another, since that would presumably violate the equipollence of the contrary accounts. Thus there are two kinds of persuasion, one of which the skeptic may have, and another which he may not have. This is analogous to two kinds of belief, one of which the skeptic may have, and another which he may not have. But here we encounter a problem, for Sextus also suggests that what appears to the skeptic to be the case may appear so to him *precisely because he is persuaded* at some point by one account of that's being the case rather than by an account for the contrary. If that is what Sextus has in mind, the equal persuasiveness of contrary accounts that the skeptic experiences evidently need not mean that his experience consists in *his* being equally persuaded by contrary accounts. The skeptic could be persuaded by one account rather than another and still experience the equal persuasiveness of both accounts. I shall suggest—and this is the aim of my paper—that the equal persuasiveness of contrary accounts rather means that contrary accounts persuade different people differently or the same person at different instances. This equal persuasiveness is apparent to the skeptic and he cannot opt for either account. He has no means to determine by which account *he ought to be persuaded*, even as he as a matter of fact may be persuaded by one of the accounts. The skeptic might even find it impossible to decide whether he ought to be persuaded by one account because of the thought that one day a better account might be advanced and he might be persuaded by that (see *PH* 1.33–34, 89, 96–97; 2.38–41; 3.233–34). In this case his suspension, based as always on equal persuasiveness, does not arise because he actually is equally persuaded by contrary accounts; he just thinks that he might be persuaded at a later point. This interpretation of equipollence does not entail that the skeptic cannot suspend belief because he is equally persuaded by both accounts; it just entails that he need not be so persuaded.

In section 2 below, I argue that, according to Sextus, the skeptic can indeed be persuaded of many things, and that he can be so persuaded through the force of some argumentative account, or, to put it bluntly, a philosophical argument for something's being the case. I shall concentrate on one passage, namely *M* 8.473–78, and discuss its implications. In section 3, I suggest that the effect of equipollence on the skeptic does not consist in *his* finding contrary accounts, including arguments, equally persuasive in the sense of being equally persuaded by both accounts. Although this can happen,

---

who listens to them." A similar view on equipollence seems implicit in Hankinson (1995: 27), Thorsrud (2009: 128), Woodruff (2010: 211). Burnyeat (1998 [1980]: 54) is careful: the opposed claims are "equally worthy and equally unworthy of belief."

[5] As Bailey (2002: 126–27) suggests.

as it can happen to all of us, the effect of equipollence consists in the skeptic's being unable to determine by which account he ought to be persuaded, irrespective of which account in fact persuades him. To elucidate my account, I discuss Sextus' contrast between skeptics and Academics, who do think that some appearances are persuasive in the sense that one ought to be persuaded of them.

2. ARGUMENTS AND PERSUASIVENESS

Sextus acknowledges that the skeptic's appearances—what he is left with after suspending belief—can be based on reasoned arguments, even on the skeptic's own reasoned arguments. Or so I maintain.

In his depiction of the skeptical practice of opposing appearances, paradigmatically as in the modes of Aenesidemus, the skeptic may compare his own appearance to that of another, who experiences a contrary appearance. He invariably finds them equipollent after having studied the different accounts of the contrary appearances. These accounts attempt to establish the truth of either appearance, but the skeptic cannot prefer one account to the other. The equipollence of the appearances stems from the equipollence of the accounts that purport to establish their truth. Then the skeptic suspends belief as to the truth of these appearances.

At this point one might ask the skeptic why he experiences the appearance that he does, after having suspended belief. In answer, Sextus will characterize the skeptic's appearance as an experience or affection (just like he characterizes the effect of equipollence itself); the skeptic's appearance "lies in feeling and unwilled affection" (*PH* 1.22).[6] One way for him to answer is simply to say that this just happens to be his experience and he would not want to venture an explanation. But often he suggests an answer, explaining the skeptic's experiences and appearances. It is necessary for him to do so if he wants to contrast contrary accounts for appearances. In a natural state, Sextus says, he experiences honey as sweet. His being in a natural state explains why honey persuades him that it is sweet (*M* 8.53); whether honey is really sweet is another issue (*PH* 1.101). He also says that it is an unclear matter whether honey is sweet "as far as the account goes" (ὅσον ἐπὶ τῷ λόγῳ: *PH* 1.20), referring to the equipollence of opposed accounts. One would then think that accounts of appearances were not something that persuaded the skeptic. But appearances are not only perceptual. Sextus also says that he was raised in such a way that he believes in the gods; the explanation for his appearance that there are gods is his upbringing (*PH* 3.2). And he says (most clearly in *M* 8.473–78), that he can be persuaded by an argumentative account so that

---

[6] ἐν πείσει γὰρ καὶ ἀβουλήτῳ πάθει κειμένη.

it appears to him that something is the case; he can even change his mind, discarding one appearance for a contrary one, because he is persuaded by an account. Consider the passage *M* 8.473–78.

In it Sextus discusses the persuasiveness of skeptical arguments against demonstration, which he has just recounted. As he eventually points out (476–77), the skeptic pits argument against argument, both strong, and suspends belief as to the truth of their conclusions. This is his procedure in all cases, whether he is discussing demonstration or something else: "attaching ourselves neither to one set nor to the other, let us agree to suspension of belief" (477).[7] He is evidently referring to the equipollence, or equal persuasiveness, of the arguments for and against demonstration. As indicated at the outset of the paper, equipollence has been explained as contrary accounts equally persuading the skeptic. It may therefore be surprising that Sextus has in fact just conceded (in *M* 8.473) that the skeptic might after all be persuaded *by one of the accounts*, as opposed to the other. For in answer to the dogmatists' charge that skeptical arguments against demonstration are self-refuting, Sextus offers one as being "safe" (ἀσφαλῶς), presumably implying that it is consistent with skeptical procedure: "They [the skeptics] will say that the argument against demonstration is *merely persuasive, and that for the moment it persuades them and induces assent*, but that they do not know whether it will also be like this in the future because of the multifariousness[8] of human thought" (473).[9] Sextus acknowledges that the skeptic can be *persuaded* by an argumentative account, which he has himself introduced; he even repeats this assertion (474).[10]

Being persuaded in this skeptical way by an account, Sextus goes on to suggest, amounts to suffering an affection, like being glad or grieving (475). Even if the process involves an argument, and one of the skeptic's own making at that, the effect is like

---

[7] μήτε ἐκείνοις μήτε τούτοις προσθέμενοι τὴν ἐποχὴν ὁμολογῶμεν. Translations of *M* 7 and 8 are (with occasional changes) those of Bett (2005).

[8] The term, πολύτροπον, famously used of Odysseus, has been variously translated; for Sextus' use, cf. *M* 8.241, 333a; 9.29.

[9] φήσουσι γὰρ τὸν κατὰ τῆς ἀποδείξεως λόγον πιθανὸν εἶναι μόνον καὶ πρὸς τὸ παρὸν πείθειν αὐτοὺς καὶ ἐπάγεσθαι συγκατάθεσιν, ἀγνοεῖν δέ, εἰ καὶ αὖθις ἔσται τοιοῦτος διὰ τὸ πολύτροπον τῆς ἀνθρωπίνης διανοίας.

[10] Sextus seems to make the same claim (although not as clearly) in his discussion of the criterion in *M* 7.444: "... even if we do seem to join in doing away with the criterion, we can use the currently available appearance for this purpose, but not as a criterion. In putting forward by way of this [currently available appearance] the persuasive arguments that strike us in favor of there being no criterion, we do put them forward, but we do not do this with assent, given the fact that the opposing arguments are equally persuasive" (εἶτα κἂν τῷ ὄντι συναναιρεῖν δοκῶμεν τὸ κριτήριον, δυνάμεθα εἰς τοῦτο οὐχ ὡς κριτηρίῳ χρῆσθαι τῇ προχείρῳ φαντασίᾳ, καθ' ἣν τοὺς προσπίπτοντας ἡμῖν πιθανοὺς λόγους τιθέντες εἰς τὸ μηδὲν εἶναι κριτήριον ἐκτιθέμεθα μέν, οὐ μετὰ συγκαταθέσεως δὲ τοῦτο ποιοῦμεν διὰ τὸ καὶ τοὺς ἀντικειμένους λόγους ἐπ' ἴσης εἶναι πιθανούς).

that of a physical affection. We see that the scope of skeptical affections is wide. The skeptic is, at least for the moment, knocked down by the skeptical argument. And if the skeptic is affected (and persuaded by argument) in this way, he cannot be persuaded by (another) argument that he is in fact not affected in this way: "For as no one can persuade the glad person by argument that he is not glad, or the grieving person that he is not grieving, neither can one persuade the persuaded person that he not persuaded" (475).[11] So, the skeptic is persuaded by an account that there is no demonstration. The skeptic, then, can be persuaded by an argument, and suspend belief because of the equal persuasiveness of that argument and another argument for the contrary.

What are the implications of this passage? First, the skeptic's affections, which are the basis of the skeptical life, can have their sources in arguments as well as elsewhere. Second, one and the same argument can affect the skeptic differently "because of the multifariousness of human thought" (473). He may find one argument persuasive this year, but find an argument to the contrary persuasive next year. Third, the persuading argument can be of the skeptic's own making.

The first point above, namely that arguments can be the sources of the skeptic's affections, is clear from other passages. In one passage Sextus explicitly refers to the possibility that arguments may affect the skeptic so as to cause his appearances. He opens his second book of the *Outlines of Pyrrhonism* by answering the question whether the skeptic can have thoughts (νόησις) of what dogmatists discuss. He suggests that they can. In one part of his explanation of the suggestion he says: "For the skeptic is not barred, I think, from thought, if it both arises from arguments that passively/affectively[12] strike him appearing evidently to him and does not at all imply the reality of the things thought" (*PH* 2.10).[13] It appears that arguments can passively/affectively strike the skeptic. Sextus continues and submits that the skeptic "assents to those things that strike him in accordance with a passive/affective appearance, insofar

---

[11] καθὰ γὰρ τὸν χαίροντα οὐθεὶς δύναται λόγῳ πεῖσαι, ὅτι οὐ χαίρει, καὶ τὸν λυπούμενον, ὅτι οὐ λυπεῖται, οὕτως οὐδὲ τὸν πειθόμενον, ὅτι οὐ πείθεται. Striker (1996 [1981]: 146) has pointed out this character of skeptical affections, referring to the same passage in *M* 8.473–75: "Even the Pyrrhonists occasionally claim the right to find an argument or a thesis convincing; but this does not mean that they think such a thesis, rather than its opposite, corresponds to the truth concerning the nature of things. Conviction is, for them, a state of mind, comparable to a physical sensation."

[12] I find the adverb παθητικῶς difficult to translate, so I give the two most common translations.

[13] νοήσεως γὰρ οὐκ ἀπείργεται ὁ σκεπτικός, οἶμαι, ἀπό τε τῶν παθητικῶς ὑποπιπτόντων <καὶ> κατ' ἐνάργειαν φαινομένων αὐτῷ λόγων γινομένης καὶ μὴ πάντως εἰσαγούσης τὴν ὕπαρξιν τῶν νοουμένων. The reading of the main manuscripts is λόγων, while λόγῳ is also attested. In their translation Annas and Barnes omit the word, while other translators retain it: Bury has "reason" and Mates "discussions."

as they appear to him."[14] One infers that the skeptic acquiesces in appearances, when they strike him in the appropriate way arising as they do from arguments.

This status of arguments need not come as a surprise. Sextus has explained that opposing appearances consists in juxtaposing objects of perception and objects of thought in any which way (PH 1.9). Both of these objects appear to one, according to Sextus; they supply one with appearances. What he says in PH 2.10 is that arguments can supply one with appearances in the form of thoughts, as opposed to perceptions. The skeptic then acts on his appearances, and would therefore seem to act on appearances that arise from arguments.[15] In another passage, Sextus makes the following suggestion: "But when the subject matter is unclear and hidden away from us, then, since the reference of the argument to this can no longer be secure, it is left for thought to deal in persuasiveness and be drawn into assent by what is reasonable. But since different people make different judgments of reasonableness and persuasiveness, disagreement arises, with neither the person who has missed the target knowing that he has missed it, nor the one who has hit it knowing that he has hit it" (M 8.324).[16] In unclear matters, that is, matters on which the skeptic suspends belief—as always because of equipollence—arguments affect people differently because people, including the skeptics, are differently persuaded. And because of this disagreement, no one knows whether what he is persuaded of is true or not.

The second implication of the passage above, that is, that the skeptic may change his mind, reveals how Sextus understands the equal persuasiveness that leads the skeptic to suspension of belief. He is persuaded of the claim that there are no demonstrations, but because he might be differently persuaded later, given the "multifariousness of human thought," he is led to suspend belief. Being persuaded by an argument in this manner should be understood as an example of passively suffering affections; this is evidently what Sextus has in mind. But if so, that might be understood as a fault in Sextan skepticism. The reason would be the following.

---

[14] τοῖς κατὰ φαντασίαν παθητικὴν ὑποπίπτουσιν αὐτῷ, καθὸ φαίνεται αὐτῷ, συγκατατίθεται.

[15] Sextus expresses the same sentiment in very general terms in his description of the first of the fourfold criterion of action: "By nature's guidance we are naturally capable of perceiving and thinking" (PH 1.24: ὑφηγήσει μὲν φυσικῇ καθ' ἣν φυσικῶς αἰσθητικοὶ καὶ νοητικοί ἐσμεν).

[16] ὅταν δὲ ἄδηλον καθεστήκῃ τὸ πρᾶγμα καὶ ἀποκεκρυμμένον ἡμῖν, τότε μηκέτι δυναμένης ἐπὶ τοῦτο βεβαίως γίνεσθαι τῆς τοῦ λόγου ἀναπομπῆς λείπεται τὸ καταπιθανεύεσθαι καὶ ἐκ τῶν εἰκότων ἐπισπᾶσθαι τὴν διάνοιαν εἰς συγκατάθεσιν. ἄλλου δὲ ἄλλως εἰκάζοντος καὶ διαπιθανευομένου φύεται ἡ διαφωνία, μήτε τοῦ ἀποτυχόντος εἰδότος ὅτι ἀπέτυχεν, μήτε τοῦ ἐπιτυχόντος εἰδότος ὅτι ἐπέτυχεν. It is interesting that Sextus here alludes both to what is reasonable and to what is persuasive, since the former is Arcesilaus' and the second Carneades' criterion of action.

A distinction has been made between phenomenological and epistemic appearances, where the latter are identical with tentative beliefs, while the former are non-judgmental appearances.[17] To work for Sextus, phenomenological appearances have to cut across the distinction between perceptual and non-perceptual appearances. One might find this conflation faulty in cases of philosophical arguments: "In the philosophical case, the impression...simply *is* my assent to the conclusion of an argument, assent to it as true."[18] The objection, to my mind, is forceful. But others reject this distinction as alien to Sextus and conceptually flawed; there are no phenomenological appearances.[19] Interpreting skeptical appearances as epistemic, however, seems to require that the skeptic suspends belief just insofar as the appearance is based on particular arguments, construed as philosophical or theoretical, since there are equally persuasive arguments that contradict these. As I have suggested, Sextus concedes that the skeptic may as a matter of fact be persuaded by such arguments even as he suspends belief. But as far as I can see, that consideration does not undermine the interpretation of appearances as epistemic.

The third implication of the passage above complicates matters further. According to it, the skeptic can himself be the source of the argument that for the moment persuades him; he can argue his way to a conclusion of which he is persuaded. He can be so persuaded by an argument of his own concoction for the claim that there is no demonstration, as we have seen. It then appears to him that there is no demonstration. This appearance is supposed to be affective/passive, since it "lies in feeling and unwilled affection" (*PH* 1.22). But granting the skeptic the ability to reflect in this manner, and experience an appearance in accordance with his reflection, seems even less in tune with his passivity than simply suffering the arguments of others. Is there at all room for original reflection as a source of appearances in the skeptic's life? The affective/passive character of the skeptic's life, which Sextus time and again tries to convey, seems to tell against that possibility. One would think that reflection is a mark of an active mind that results in a judgment, which would seem beyond the Pyrrhonist. As Gisela Striker says: "Following appearances...never requires a decision as to what is true or false, nor endorsement of what appears to be the right way of proceeding. Such decisions the Sceptic feels unable to make.... Sextus is thus drawing a distinction between what we might call judgements—the voluntary and reason-based acceptance of something as true—and mere beliefs that we find ourselves having involuntarily and without any

---

[17] This distinction has often been made, but see in particular Annas and Barnes (1985: 22–24), Burnyeat (1998 [1980]).

[18] So Burnyeat (1998 [1980]: 56–57).

[19] The issue is discussed in Burnyeat and Frede (1998), elucidated in Barney (1992) and Thorsrud (2009: 172–83).

critical reflection."[20] But—and this is the problem—according to my interpretation of the passage above, the skeptic's appearances may be based on his reasoning and critical reflection.

Sextus offers an account of the skeptic's fourfold criterion (*PH* 1.21–24) that is intended to describe the sources of the skeptic's appearances and give an idea of the basis of his actions. The skeptic can perceive and think. He can suffer all kinds of affections that lead him to act (being hungry he is led to seek food). He follows the laws and customs that have happened to inform him. He is employed in all kinds of endeavors that demand expertise. Prima facie nothing in this enumeration rules out the possibility that the skeptic may be persuaded by arguments and even change his mind because of them.[21] But *if* Sextus' point is that these skeptical beliefs, the appearances, do not originate in the reflection of the skeptic himself (being unwilled and passive/affective), then it is impossible for him to be affected by his own argument so that he changes his mind. In *M* 8.473–78, however, Sextus explains that the skeptic can be persuaded by his own argument that there is no demonstration. There is some tension here. Sextus could suggest that arguments that persuade him are just examples of appearances that happen to persuade him. They would not be different from other appearances in that regard. And that would mean that argumentative accounts for appearances— argumentative accounts that persuade the skeptic (e.g. for the claim that there are no demonstrations)—were to be seen as sets of appearances by which the skeptic can be persuaded in his affective/passive way.

We may gauge the explanation of the skeptic's affection/passivity by examining Sextus' description of the skeptic's route to suspension of belief in his account of the Aenesideman modes. Appearances are not only perceptual, but include thoughts, preconceptions, and conclusions to arguments. He conceives of non-perceptual appearances as analogous to and interchangeable with perceptual ones. The latter do not have any special status. They do not seem to be more affective/passive than other appearances. In offering his accounts of contrary perceptual appearances, Sextus compares for example the different effects of one and the same thing on different perceivers or on perceivers in different circumstances. The accounts themselves are found to be equipollent and lead the inquirer into suspension of belief as to their truth and the truth of the appearances. It nevertheless can be the case that the inquirer himself suffers one of

---

[20] Striker (2010: 203).
[21] Nevertheless some proclamations Sextus makes are suspiciously final, such as that there are gods and providence. He also claims that the skeptic finds piety good and impiety bad. If this claim is not offered as an analytic truth (which is hardly the case), Sextus can be taken to make the skeptic completely resigned to custom. Against this, Sextus can point out that every skeptical proclamation is qualified by something like "as it appears to me now."

the appearances. And his appearance can change for all sorts of reasons, for example because of changed circumstances. The account of the appearance can only suggest why he suffers it when he suffers it. It cannot, according to the skeptic, establish its truth. He thinks that honey is sweet because he is in a certain state when he tastes it. If he were no longer in this state, his experience of the honey might change. Because he does not distinguish perceptual and non-perceptual appearances, Sextus gives an account of non-perceptual appearances analogous to that of perceptual ones. He clearly attempts this in his tenth Aenesideman mode.[22] The inquirer suffers non-perceptual appearances, for whatever reasons. And as they match perceptual appearances, an account can be given of them that could include reflection as a causal factor, reflection that persuades the skeptic and causes him to change his mind. Sextus thus seems to open up to the possibility of the skeptic's being persuaded by his own argument, rather than just being persuaded by the arguments of others, when he treats reasoning on a par with perceiving.

Sextus elsewhere touches upon what may persuade the skeptic, and *a fortiori* on the causes of at least some of his non-perceptual appearances. Before we consider that, it is worth pointing out that Diogenes also offers an account of persuasion: "One ought not to suppose that that which persuades us is true. For the same thing does not persuade everyone nor does it persuade the same people constantly. Persuasiveness sometimes arises on the basis of externals, the reputation of the speaker or his intellectual eminence or wiliness, or on the basis of his familiarity or charm" (9.94).[23] Whether the skeptic (or anybody else) is persuaded that something is the case depends on external conditions, apart from depending on his own constitution. These external conditions are analogous to external conditions in cases of perceptual appearances.

Sextus makes the same point as Diogenes, namely that we should not call what persuades us true (*M* 8.51–54), because "the same thing does not persuade everyone, nor the same people all the time" (52).[24] Here, the assumption seems to be that, if the

---

[22] Elsewhere he explicitly addresses the question: "Those who are in agreement about someone as having discovered the truth either have a differing condition in virtue of which they agree, or one that is not differing at all but one and the same. But they could not possibly have a differing condition, since that will undoubtedly require them to disagree" (*M* 7.333: οἱ περί τινος ὡς εὑρηκότος τἀληθὲς συμφωνοῦντες ἤτοι διάφορον ἔχουσι διάθεσιν καθ' ἥν συμφωνοῦσιν, ἤ διάφορον μὲν οὐδαμῶς μίαν δὲ καὶ τὴν αὐτήν. ἀλλὰ διάφορον μὲν οὐδαμῶς ἂν ἔχοιεν, ἐπεὶ πάντως αὐτοὺς δεήσει διαφωνεῖν).

[23] Τό τε πεῖθον οὐχ ὑποληπτέον ἀληθὲς ὑπάρχειν· οὐ γὰρ πάντας τὸ αὐτὸ πείθειν οὐδὲ τοὺς αὐτοὺς συνεχές. γίνεται δὲ καὶ παρὰ τὰ ἐκτὸς ἡ πιθανότης, παρὰ τὸ ἔνδοξον τοῦ λέγοντος ἤ παρὰ τὸ φροντιστικὸν ἤ παρὰ τὸ αἱμύλον ἤ παρὰ τὸ σύνηθες ἤ παρὰ τὸ κεχαρισμένον. Translations from Diogenes are those of Inwood and Gerson (1997).

[24] οὐ τὸ αὐτὸ πάντας πείθει οὐδὲ διὰ παντὸς τοὺς αὐτούς.

same thing were to persuade everyone all the time, one should accept it; then the thing would be really persuasive. Sextus argues, however, that the mere possibility of reasonable dissent suffices to establish equipollence. Diogenes also reports, seemingly on the authority of Aenesidemus himself but in a way that brings to mind the fourfold criterion: "For they [the skeptics] say that we are persuaded when things are consistently perceived, when they never or at least rarely change, when they become familiar to us, and when they are determined by custom and when they are delightful and marvelous" (9.78).[25] This rather mysterious passage at least makes the same point as the previous one about the sources of persuasion. Insofar as the skeptic can be persuaded that something is the case, in the sense of experiencing that appearance, by argument, he does seem capable of experiencing reason-based appearances. These beliefs are affective/passive and unwilled; such are all the skeptic's beliefs. But because of equipollence they are different from both dogmatic and Academic beliefs.

I submit that the skeptic can, according to Sextus, be persuaded by argument (even his own) that something is the case. And this can happen to the skeptic while he suspends belief because of equipollence. Consider now the role of persuasiveness in equipollence.

3. EQUIPOLLENCE AND PERSUASIVENESS

The skeptic, being aware that things appear differently to others than they appear to him, and being unable to prefer his own appearance to those of others, resists believing that things really are as they appear to him, although he cannot but acquiesce in his own appearance. His inability to prefer his own appearance to its contrary as being true stems from the equipollence of the contrary accounts for these contrary appearances. Sextus presents the effect of equipollence as the skeptic's experience or affection (*PH* 1.203): "Thus when I say 'Opposed to every account there is an equal account,' I am implicitly saying this: 'To every account I have scrutinized which purports to establish something in dogmatic fashion, there appears to me to be opposed another account, purporting to establish something in dogmatic fashion, equal to it in persuasiveness or lack of persuasiveness.' Thus the utterance of this remark is not dogmatic but a report of a human affection which is apparent to the person who feels it."[26] Most

---

[25] πείθειν γὰρ τά τε κατ' αἴσθησιν συμφώνως ἔχοντα καὶ τὰ μηδέποτε ἢ σπανίως γοῦν μεταπίπτοντα τά τε συνήθη καὶ τὰ νόμοις διεσταλμένα καὶ <τὰ> τέρποντα καὶ τὰ θαυμαζόμενα.

[26] ὅταν οὖν εἴπω "παντὶ λόγῳ λόγος ἴσος ἀντίκειται," δυνάμει τοῦτό φημι "παντὶ τῷ ὑπ' ἐμοῦ ζητουμένῳ λόγῳ, ὃς κατασκευάζει τι δογματικῶς, ἕτερος λόγος κατασκευάζων τι δογματικῶς, ἴσος αὐτῷ κατὰ πίστιν καὶ ἀπιστίαν, ἀντικεῖσθαι φαίνεταί μοι,' ὡς εἶναι τὴν τοῦ λόγου προφορὰν οὐ δογματικὴν ἀλλ' ἀνθρωπείου πάθους ἀπαγγελίαν, ὅ ἐστι φαινόμενον τῷ πάσχοντι. In *PH* 1.196, likewise, equal persuasiveness is something that appears to the skeptic. Translations from the *Outlines* are by Annas and Barnes

commentators would agree that Sextus has the following in mind when discussing the effects of equipollence: in the skeptic's experience there is no more reason to believe that x is really F rather than that x is really not-F.[27] While this is surely a correct understanding, these are not the terms Sextus employs when explaining equipollence, as can be surmised from the quotation above. Rather, he refers to persuasiveness, as in his explanation of the term early in the *Outlines of Pyrrhonism*: "By 'equipollence' we mean equality with regard to being persuasive or unpersuasive: none of the conflicting accounts takes precedence over any other as being more persuasive" (*PH* 1.10).[28] He makes similar claims several times.[29] It appears to the skeptic that contrary accounts are equally persuasive.

As indicated at the outset of the paper, this explanation may be taken to mean that the skeptic is equally persuaded by both accounts. But we have seen that he is not; he can be persuaded by just one of the accounts. I suggest another way to understand Sextus' explanation of equipollence in terms of equal persuasiveness. He means that the skeptic cannot decide by which account *he ought to be* persuaded. Indeed, Sextus says explicitly in one of his explanations of suspension of belief (*PH* 1.196): "We use 'I suspend belief' for 'I cannot say which of the things proposed *I should find persuasive* and which I should not find persuasive,' making clear that objects appear to us equal in respect of persuasiveness and lack of persuasiveness."[30] The persuasiveness of an account does not give it the status of a standard which a reasonable person ought to follow. Understood thus, Sextus' explanation is compatible with the claim that the skeptic may nevertheless happen to be persuaded by an account. This explanation of

(2000), with occasional changes. Commentators have explained this affection in broadly two ways, on the one hand as causal, indicating psychological compulsion (e.g. Burnyeat [1998 (1980): 43–44], Barnes [1990: 2610, 2649–50], Hankinson [1995: 30]), and on the other as also hypothetical, indicating rational inference (Perin [2010: ch. 2]).

[27] See e.g. Striker (1996 [1980]: 95–96), Burnyeat (1998 [1980]: 44), Perin (2010: 38).

[28] "ἰσοσθένειαν" δὲ λέγομεν τὴν κατὰ πίστιν καὶ ἀπιστίαν ἰσότητα, ὡς μηδένα μηδενὸς προκεῖσθαι τῶν μαχομένων λόγων ὡς πιστότερον.

[29] *PH* 1.196: "We use 'I suspend belief' for 'I cannot say which of the things proposed I should find persuasive and which I should not find persuasive,' making clear that objects appear to us equal in respect of persuasiveness and lack of persuasiveness" (Τὸ δὲ "ἐπέχω" παραλαμβάνομεν ἀντὶ τοῦ "οὐκ ἔχω εἰπεῖν τίνι χρὴ τῶν προκειμένων πιστεῦσαι ἢ τίνι ἀπιστῆσαι," δηλοῦντες ὅτι ἴσα ἡμῖν φαίνεται τὰ πράγματα πρὸς πίστιν καὶ ἀπιστίαν); 202: "we say 'equal' with reference to persuasiveness and lack of persuasiveness" ("ἴσον" δέ φαμεν κατὰ πίστιν ἢ ἀπιστίαν); 227: "we say that appearances are equal in persuasiveness and lack of persuasiveness (as far as the account goes)" (τάς τε φαντασίας ἡμεῖς μὲν ἴσας λέγομεν εἶναι κατὰ πίστιν ἢ ἀπιστίαν ὅσον ἐπὶ τῷ λόγῳ); cf. *PH* 1.198 (explaining ἀόριστα), 222 (on Plato accepting persuasive accounts), 232 (on Arcesilaus being a proper skeptic). He refers to "equal persuasiveness" in *PH* 1.183 and 2.79. The text of *PH* 1.190 is uncertain: "By 'equipollence' we mean equality in what appears persuasive to us" (ἰσοσθένειαν μὲν λεγόντων ἡμῶν τὴν <ἰσότητα τὴν> κατὰ τὸ φαινόμενον ἡμῖν πιθανόν).

[30] For the Greek text, see last note.

equal persuasiveness stands in contrast to the thesis Sextus attributes to the Academics that some accounts really are persuasive, that is, that reasonable persons ought to be persuaded by them.

We find this thesis explained in Sextus' discussion of the difference between Academics and Pyrrhonists in *PH* 1.220-35 (and *M* 7.159-89, 435-38), where an account of persuasiveness is central. This is to be expected since the persuasive was Carneades' criterion, from which Sextus wanted to distance himself while at the same time allowing the skeptic to be persuaded.[31] Here, then, we have Sextus' account of two kinds of persuasion, Pyrrhonian and Academic. It should be kept in mind that his account of the Academic notion is polemical. Since my interest here is confined to what Sextus meant, I leave aside the question how accurate his account of the Academic notion is.

In his account, Sextus begins by pinpointing two crucial differences between Pyrrhonists and Academics. One is the familiar distinction between two kinds of skeptical philosophies. Unlike the Pyrrhonists, the Academics claim that nothing can be apprehended (*PH* 1.226, cf. 1.3). The other is this: "For the Academics say that things are good and bad not in the way we do, but *after having been persuaded that it is persuasive* that what they call good rather than its contrary really is good (and similarly with bad), whereas we do not call anything good or bad with the judgment that what we say is persuasive—rather, without holding opinions we follow ordinary life in order not to be inactive. Further, we say that appearances are equal in persuasiveness and lack of persuasiveness as far as the account goes, while they say that *some [appearances] are persuasive and others unpersuasive*" (*PH* 1.226-27).[32] Sextus here confines the persuasive appearances of the Academics to good things and bad no doubt because they served as the criterion of action for the Academics (cf. *PH* 1.231; *M* 7.166, 435-36).

For the Pyrrhonists, contrary appearances are equal in persuasiveness. This equality of their persuasiveness refers to the accounts for them, which include arguments,

---

[31] Indeed, the emphasis Sextus places on equal persuasiveness when explaining equipollence is surely explicable by the Pyrrhonist aversion to the mitigated skepticism of the New Academy, which was presented in terms of persuasive appearances; see Burnyeat (1998 [1980]: 33-34), cf. Striker (2010: 204-5). I translate Carneades' πιθανόν and (in Cicero's translation) *probabile* with "persuasive."

[32] ἀγαθὸν γάρ τί φασιν εἶναι οἱ Ἀκαδημαϊκοὶ καὶ κακὸν οὐχ ὡς ἡμεῖς, ἀλλὰ μετὰ τοῦ πεπεῖσθαι ὅτι πιθανόν ἐστι μᾶλλον ὃ λέγουσιν εἶναι ἀγαθὸν ὑπάρχειν ἢ τὸ ἐναντίον, καὶ ἐπὶ τοῦ κακοῦ ὁμοίως, ἡμῶν ἀγαθόν τι ἢ κακὸν εἶναι λεγόντων οὐδὲν μετὰ τοῦ πιθανὸν εἶναι νομίζειν ὅ φαμεν, ἀλλ' ἀδοξάστως ἑπομένων τῷ βίῳ, ἵνα μὴ ἀνενέργητοι ὦμεν. τάς τε φαντασίας ἡμεῖς μὲν ἴσας λέγομεν εἶναι κατὰ πίστιν ἢ ἀπιστίαν ὅσον ἐπὶ τῷ λόγῳ, ἐκεῖνοι δὲ τὰς μὲν πιθανὰς εἶναί φασι τὰς δὲ ἀπιθάνους.

and are intended to establish their truth.[33] Sextus marks a distinction between the Academics and the Pyrrhonists in terms of this persuasiveness. The distinction seems to be the following. As we have seen, the Pyrrhonists can be persuaded so that something appears to them to be the case; but they do not, as do the Academics, additionally think that some appearances really are persuasive, that is, that they ought to be persuaded by them. Even though one should in general be persuaded by the persuasive appearance, according to the Academics, one ought in complex circumstances to be persuaded by appearances that are "persuasive, scrutinized and undistractable" (*PH* 1.229).[34] Take for example the appearance that virtue is good. According to Sextus, the Academics and the Pyrrhonists might both be persuaded that virtue is good. For the Pyrrhonists this just means that it appears to them that virtue is good. It might even do so on account of an argument. The Academics think that this appearance (that virtue is good) is such that they ought to be persuaded that virtue is good. The Pyrrhonists may find the appearance persuasive, and be persuaded that virtue is good. But at the same time they suspend belief because they cannot decide whether they ought to be so persuaded.

It should be emphasized that, as we saw in section 2 above, Pyrrhonists are not debarred from being persuaded by accounts for appearances, just like the Academics. Sextus even finds his account of the number of the Aenesideman modes persuasive (*PH* 1.39). What is more, he clearly makes the same point in this discussion of the

---

[33] As explained above, the equipollence of appearances stems from the equipollence of the accounts for the appearances in question. That is how I understand Sextus' explanation of equipollence in *PH* 1.10. The phrase used in the passage under discussion (in *PH* 1.227), "as far as the account goes" (ὅσον ἐπὶ τῷ λόγῳ), has been the subject of some discussion (see especially Brunschwig [1994]). I understand it in this context to affirm the source of the equipollence of appearances in the equipollence of accounts for those appearances. (In *PH* 3.48 and 72 the phrase does seem to refer to arguments for particular claims.) Others take it differently. Frede, whose understanding has perhaps been dominant, says: "Sextus often qualifies his remark that we have to withhold assent as far as this is a matter of reason or philosophical reason" (Frede 1998 [1984]: 133). This understanding allows him to distinguish one kind of assent (namely to a claim based on philosophical reasoning), which the skeptic withholds, and another kind (not based on philosophical reasoning), which the skeptic embraces. Although I agree, as do most commentators, that there are two kinds of assent, to one of which the skeptic is entitled, I do not think that the skeptic withholds assent to a claim insofar as that claim is based on an argumentative account. In section 2 above I argued that the skeptic can be persuaded and (in his skeptical affective/passive way) assent to a claim even *because* of some argumentative account. The point of my argument in the present section is that the reason the skeptic withholds assent is the equal persuasiveness of contrary accounts, which consists in contrary accounts persuading different people differently.

[34] In *M* 7.175 he says that, according to Carneades, "... one should not distrust the one that for the most part tells the truth" (οὐ μέντοι... ἀπιστητέον ἐστὶ τῇ ὡς <ἐπὶ> τὸ πολὺ ἀληθευούσῃ), i.e. the persuasive appearance.

distinction between Academics and Pyrrhonists: "Even if both Academics and Skeptics say that they are persuaded by some things, the difference even here between the two philosophies is clear. For 'being persuaded' is used in different senses. It means not resisting but simply following without strong inclination or adherence (as a boy is said to go along with his chaperone); and it sometimes means assenting to something by choice and, as it were, sympathy (as a dissolute man goes along with someone who urges extravagant living)" (*PH* 1.229–30).[35] The difference between them does not lie in what persuades them, but in the manner of their persuasion.

Leaving aside the moralizing tone of Sextus' explanations (obedient innocent versus impressionable glutton), the Pyrrhonist can be persuaded just in the sense of having an affective/passive appearance. And this, as we have seen, can happen through the force of some argumentative account. The Academic, however, according to Sextus, believes in a different sense what he is persuaded of, namely that he ought to be so persuaded.

As we know, Sextus has nothing against appearances. He embraces them. They are the skeptic's lifeline. The skeptic, in a famous example derived from Timon (DL 9.105), concedes that honey appears sweet, but suspends belief as to its being by nature or really sweet (*PH* 1.20; the example is repeated in the account of the fourth Aenesideman mode, in *PH* 1.101; cf. 211, 213, 2.51, 63). For him this means that honey simply tastes sweet; it "sweetens" him, as Sextus says. Analogously, we have found out, arguments may appear persuasive in that they simply persuade. In this respect, the persuasiveness of arguments is like the sweetness of honey; the skeptic is persuaded that x is F iff x appears F to the skeptic. Persuasion is relegated to the level of appearances. Indeed, using the same example of honey, Sextus speaks of people being persuaded that it is (or is not) sweet (*M* 8.53).

Sextus emphasizes the above distinction between Pyrrhonists and Academics in the conclusion of the same passage concerning persuasiveness: "Hence, since Carneades and Clitomachus say with a strong inclination both that they are persuaded and that something is persuasive, whereas we say so in the sense of simply yielding without adherence, in this respect too we differ from them" (*PH* 1.230).[36] Persuasiveness may

---

[35] εἰ δὲ καὶ πείθεσθαί τισιν οἵ τε ἀπὸ τῆς Ἀκαδημίας καὶ οἱ ἀπὸ τῆς σκέψεως λέγουσι, πρόδηλος καὶ ἡ κατὰ τοῦτο διαφορὰ τῶν φιλοσοφιῶν. τὸ γὰρ πείθεσθαι λέγεται διαφόρως, τό τε μὴ ἀντιτείνειν ἀλλ᾽ ἁπλῶς ἕπεσθαι ἄνευ σφοδρᾶς προσκλίσεως καὶ προσπαθείας, ὡς ὁ παῖς πείθεσθαι λέγεται τῷ παιδαγωγῷ· ἅπαξ δὲ τὸ μετὰ αἱρέσεως καὶ οἱονεὶ συμπαθείας κατὰ τὸ σφόδρα βούλεσθαι συγκατατίθεσθαί τινι, ὡς ὁ ἄσωτος πείθεται τῷ δαπανητικῶς βιοῦν ἀξιοῦντι.

[36] διόπερ ἐπειδὴ οἱ μὲν περὶ Καρνεάδην καὶ Κλειτόμαχον μετὰ προσκλίσεως σφοδρᾶς πείθεσθαί τε καὶ πιθανὸν εἶναί τί φασιν, ἡμεῖς δὲ κατὰ τὸ ἁπλῶς εἴκειν ἄνευ προσπαθείας, καὶ κατὰ τοῦτο ἂν αὐτῶν διαφέροιμεν.

appear to belong to things, so that something may appear persuasive, not simply in the sense of persuading by appearing to be the case, but by having the property of being such that one ought to be persuaded by it. The Academics believe, Sextus claims, that some appearances really are persuasive in this way. For them, but not for the Pyrrhonists, persuasive appearances are a criterion. In *M* 7.435–38 Sextus finds fault with the Academic criterion of the persuasive. This passage is complicated, but Sextus' central claim is that accepting the persuasive appearance as a criterion (whether of action or truth), that is, accepting that some appearances are such that one ought to be persuaded by them, requires just as much of a dogmatic commitment as accepting a Stoic apprehensive appearance, that is, accepting that some appearances are such that one ought to assent to them.

The Pyrrhonist, on the other hand, cannot agree with the Academic that there are such persuasive appearances. In his explanation of the phrase "I suspend belief," Sextus says: "We use 'I suspend belief' for 'I cannot say which of the things proposed *I should find persuasive and which I should not find persuasive*,' making clear that objects appear to us equal in respect of persuasiveness and lack of persuasiveness. Whether they are equal, we do not affirm: we say what appears to us about them when they make an impression on us" (*PH* 1.196).[37] Sextus makes the same point elsewhere: "If [we find] some [appearances persuasive], how shall we judge that it is right to find these appearances persuasive and those unpersuasive?" (*PH* 2.77).[38] This is why Sextus' point against the Academics is this: they claim that some appearances really are persuasive, while the skeptic cannot decide which appearances are persuasive, even if he is persuaded of some and not others. He just doesn't know whether he should be so persuaded.

How does this distinction between Pyrrhonists and Academics help to explain that the skeptic may be persuaded by an account even as he suspends belief because of the equipollence of accounts? Sextus can say that a particular account appears persuasive to the skeptic in the sense of persuading him. First, Sextus can (and does) ponder the various ways in which people (including the skeptics) may be persuaded by particular accounts of various things. But second, at the same time as the skeptic is persuaded, he finds himself unable to determine whether the persuading account really is persuasive because the contrary account appears just as persuasive to, *not necessarily the skeptic at that point*, but someone else or the skeptic at another point (even only hypothetically),

---

[37] Τὸ δὲ "ἐπέχω" παραλαμβάνομεν ἀντὶ τοῦ "οὐκ ἔχω εἰπεῖν τίνι χρὴ τῶν προκειμένων πιστεῦσαι ἢ τίνι ἀπιστῆσαι," δηλοῦντες ὅτι ἴσα ἡμῖν φαίνεται τὰ πράγματα πρὸς πίστιν καὶ ἀπιστίαν. καὶ εἰ μὲν ἴσα ἐστίν, οὐ διαβεβαιούμεθα· τὸ δὲ φαινόμενον ἡμῖν περὶ αὐτῶν, ὅτε ἡμῖν ὑποπίπτει, λέγομεν.

[38] εἰ δέ τισιν, πῶς ἐπικρινοῦμεν ὅτι ταῖσδε μὲν ταῖς φαντασίαις πιστεύειν προσήκει, ταῖσδε δὲ ἀπιστεῖν.

whose *authority* is equal to the originally persuaded skeptic.[39] He has no reason to think that he ought to be persuaded by what persuades most people, including himself, or normal people (cf. *PH* 1.88–89, 102–103, *M* 8.51–54; cf. *PH* 1.112–13). Discussing the Stoic sage, or the cleverest person imaginable, as the one by whom we should be persuaded, Sextus suggests that we *should not find him persuasive* (*PH* 2.38–43). We should not give him our assent as judging objects truly, Sextus says, even while we think that he is speaking the truth, because he is not such that we ought to be persuaded by him (42).

This is the sense in which accounts are equally persuasive; different accounts persuade different people or the same people at different instances. The Academics do not find accounts equally persuasive in this manner, according to Sextus. The equal authority of the accounts then forces the skeptic to report that the contrary accounts appear to him equally persuasive, and obliges him to suspend belief in the truth of either one, even if he is actually (for the moment at least) persuaded by one of them. In a way he believes (just insofar as he is persuaded) and suspends belief at the same time (because the accounts are equally authoritative).

We see this procedure most clearly in Sextus' description of the modes of Aenesidemus. When comparing contrary accounts for contrary appearances Sextus readily grants that the skeptic can have one of the appearances that something is the case. In that sense he is persuaded that this is the case, as we have seen. When he has this appearance, he evidently does not have the contrary appearance and is not persuaded of the contrary. This holds good both for perceptual and non-perceptual appearances. Only in this way can the skeptic have his own appearance, that is, find something persuasive in the skeptical sense, without accepting it as being such that a reasonable person ought to be persuaded of it. Now the skeptic suspends belief about this being the case or not. He expresses this reaction in terms of persuasiveness, by saying that the accounts for this being the case or not are equally persuasive. As we have seen, that need not mean that he at that instance is equally persuaded by both accounts, although that can also happen, but rather that he cannot choose between what happens to persuade him and what may persuade others. What prompts the skeptic to suspend belief in the truth of particular appearances is *this kind* of equal persuasiveness of accounts for and against the truth of these appearances.

I have argued for the claim that when the skeptic is faced with the equipollence of contrary accounts he need not be equally persuaded by both accounts. He can be persuaded by one of them for all sorts of reasons. But others can be persuaded by the

---

[39] For an account of suspension of belief because of equipollence as equal authority, see Striker (1996 [1983]: 121–25).

other account. They are equally persuasive, not in the sense of persuading the skeptic equally, but in equally persuading different people or the same people in different circumstances. Equipollence consists in the equal authority of the two accounts. The skeptic cannot decide whether the account that persuades him is true or the contrary account that persuades someone else, or indeed the skeptic himself under different circumstances. I submit that such is the notion of equal persuasiveness that Sextus uses to explain equipollence.

Acknowledgments

My thanks to Mitzi Lee for patiently clarifying my argument, as well as to Eyfi Emilsson, and an anonymous referee. Most of all I thank the dedicatee of this collection, Gisela Striker, whose expert instruction and rigorous supervision I was fortunate enough to receive as a graduate student.

References

Annas, Julia and Jonathan Barnes (1985), *The Modes of Scepticism: Ancient Texts and Modern Interpretations* (Cambridge: Cambridge University Press).
Annas, Julia and Jonathan Barnes (2000), Sextus Empiricus: *Outlines of Scepticism* (Cambridge: Cambridge University Press).
Bailey, Alan (2002), *Sextus Empiricus and Pyrrhonean Scepticism* (Oxford: Clarendon Press).
Barnes, Jonathan (1990), "Pyrrhonism, Belief, and Causation: Observations on the Scepticism of Sextus Empiricus," *Aufstieg und Niedergang der römischen Welt 36.4*: 2608–95.
Barney, Rachel (1992), "Appearances and Impressions," *Phronesis 37.3*: 283–313.
Bett, Richard (2005), *Sextus Empiricus: Against the Logician* (Cambridge: Cambridge University Press).
Brunschwig, Jacques (1994 [1990]), "The ὅσον ἐπὶ τῷ λόγῳ Formula in Sextus Empiricus," in *Papers in Hellenistic Philosophy* (Cambridge: Cambridge University Press), 244–58. First published in French as "La formule ὅσον ἐπὶ τῷ λόγῳ chez Sextus Empiricus," A.-J. Voelke (ed.), *Le Scepticisme antique* (Geneva: Cahiers de la *Revue de Théologie et de Philosophie* 13), 107–21.
Burnyeat, Myles (1998 [1980]), "Can the Sceptic Live His Scepticism?," in M. Burnyeat and M. Frede (eds.), *The Original Sceptics. A Controversy* (Indianapolis: Hackett), 26–57. First published in M. Schofield, M. Burnyeat, and J. Barnes (eds.), *Doubt and Dogmatism* (Oxford: Clarendon Press), 20–53; later in M. Burnyeat (ed.), *The Skeptical Tradition* (Berkeley: University of California Press, 1983), 117–48.
Burnyeat, Myles and Michael Frede (eds.) (1998), *The Original Sceptics: A Controversy* (Indianapolis: Hackett).
Frede, Michael (1998 [1984]), "The Skeptic's Two Kinds of Assent and the Possibility of Knowledge," in M. Burnyeat and M. Frede (eds.), *The Original Sceptics: A Controversy* (Indianapolis: Hackett), 127–51. First published in R. Rorty, J.B. Schneewind, and Q. Skinner (eds.), *Philosophy in History: Essays on the Historiography of Philosophy* (Cambridge: Cambridge University Press), 255–78; later in *Essays in Ancient Philosophy* (Minneapolis: University of Minnesota Press, 1989), 201–22.

Hankinson, R.J. (1995), *The Sceptics* (London: Routledge).
Inwood, Brad and L.P. Gerson (1997), *Hellenistic Philosophy: Introductory Readings*. 2nd ed. (Indianapolis: Hackett).
Machuca, Diego E. (2009), "Argumentative Persuasiveness in Ancient Pyrrhonism," *Méthexis* 22: 101-26.
Pellegrin, Pierre (2010), "Sextus Empiricus," in R. Bett (ed.), *The Cambridge Companion to Ancient Sceptisicm* (Cambridge: Cambridge University Press), 120-41.
Perin, Casey (2010), *The Demands of Reason: An Essay on Pyrrhonean Scepticism* (Oxford: Oxford University Press).
Striker, Gisela (1996 [1980]), "Sceptical Strategies," *Essays in Hellenistic Epistemology and Ethics* (Cambridge: Cambridge University Press), 92-115. First published in M. Schofield, M. Burnyeat, and J. Barnes (eds.), *Doubt and Dogmatism* (Oxford: Clarendon Press), 54-83.
Striker, Gisela (1996 [1981]), "On the Difference between the Pyrrhonists and the Academics," *Essays in Hellenistic Epistemology and Ethics* (Cambridge: Cambridge University Press), 135-49. First published as "Über den Unterschied zwischen den Pyrrhoneern und den Akademikern," *Phronesis* 26: 153-71.
Striker, Gisela (1996 [1983]), "The Ten Tropes of Aenesidemus," *Essays in Hellenistic Epistemology and Ethics* (Cambridge: Cambridge University Press), 116-34). First published in M. Burnyeat (ed.), *The Skeptical Tradition* (Berkeley: University of California Press, 1983), 95-115.
Striker, Gisela (2010), "Academics versus Pyrrhonists, reconsidered," in R. Bett (ed.), *The Cambridge Companion to Ancient Scepticism* (Cambridge: Cambridge University Press), 195-207.
Thorsrud, Harald (2009), *Ancient Scepticism* (Stocksfield: Acumen).
Woodruff, Paul (2010), "The Pyrrhonian Modes," in R. Bett (ed.), *The Cambridge Companion to Ancient Sceptisicm* (Cambridge: Cambridge University Press), 208-31.

BIBLIOGRAPHY FOR GISELA STRIKER

Books and Monographs

Peras und Apeiron. Das Problem der Formen in Plato's Philebus, Hypomnemata 30 (1970), Göttingen.

"Κριτήριον τῆς ἀληθείας," Nachrichten der Akademie der Wissenschaften zu Göttingen, I. Phil.-hist. Klasse, 2 (1974), 48–110; published in English translation in Striker, *Essays on Hellenistic Epistemology and Ethics*, 1996, 22–76.

Essays on Hellenistic Epistemology and Ethics, Cambridge: Cambridge University Press 1996.

Aristotle, *Prior Analytics Book I*, Translation, introduction and commentary by Gisela Striker, Oxford: Clarendon Press 2009.

Books Edited

M. Schofield and G. Striker (eds.), *The Norms of Nature*, Cambridge: Cambridge University Press 1986.

M. Frede and G. Striker (eds.), *Rationality in Greek Thought*, Oxford: Clarendon Press 1996.

Papers and Articles

"Zur Frage nach den Quellen von Boethius' *De Hypotheticis Syllogismis*," *Archiv für Geschichte der Philosophie* 55 (1973), 70–75.

"Epicurus on the Truth of Sense Impressions," *Archiv für Geschichte der Philosophie* 59 (1977), 125–142; reprinted in Striker, *Essays on Hellenistic Epistemology and Ethics*, 1996, 77–91.

"Aristoteles über Syllogismen 'aufgrund einer Hypothese,'" *Hermes* 107 (1979), 33–50.

"Sceptical Strategies" in M. Schofield, M. Burnyeat, and J. Barnes (eds.), *Doubt and Dogmatism*, Oxford: Oxford University Press 1980, 54–83; reprinted in Striker, *Essays on Hellenistic Epistemology and Ethics*, 1996, 92–115.

"Über den Unterschied zwischen den Pyrrhoneern und den Akademikern," *Phronesis* 26 (1981), 153–171; "On the Difference between the Pyrrhonists and the Academics" (English translation), in Striker, *Essays on Hellenistic Epistemology and Ethics*, 1996, 135–149.

"The Ten Tropes of Aenesidemus" in M. Burnyeat (ed.), *The Skeptical Tradition*, Berkeley: University of California Press 1983, 95–115; reprinted in Striker, *Essays on Hellenistic Epistemology and Ethics*, 1996, 116–134.

"The Role of *oikeiôsis* in Stoic Ethics," *Oxford Studies in Ancient Philosophy* 1 (1983), 145–167; reprinted in Striker, *Essays on Hellenistic Epistemology and Ethics*, 1996, 281–297.

"Notwendigkeit mit Lücken," *Neue Hefte für Philosophie* 24–25 (1985), 146–164.

"Antipater, or the Art of Living," in M. Schofield and G. Striker (eds.), *The Norms of Nature*, Cambridge University Press 1986, 185–204; reprinted in Striker, *Essays on Hellenistic Epistemology and Ethics*, 1996, 298–315.

"Origins of the Concept of Natural Law" in J. Cleary (ed.), *Proceedings of the Boston Area Colloquium in Ancient Philosophy* 2 (1987), 79–94; reprinted in Striker, *Essays on Hellenistic Epistemology and Ethics*, 1996, 209–220.

"Greek Ethics and Moral Theory," *The Tanner Lectures on Human Values* 9 (1988), 181–202; reprinted in Striker, *Essays on Hellenistic Epistemology and Ethics*, 1996, 169–182.

"Comments on John Cooper's 'Some Remarks on Aristotle's Moral Psychology'", *The Southern Journal of Philosophy* 27 (Supplement) (1988), 43–47.

"Commentary on Mitsis' "Epicurus on Death and the Duration of Life'", *Proceedings of the Boston Area Colloquium in Ancient Philosophy* 4 (1988) 323–328.

"*Ataraxia*: Happiness as Tranquillity," *The Monist* 73 (1990), 97–110; reprinted in Striker, *Essays on Hellenistic Epistemology and Ethics*, 1996, 183–195.

"The Problem of the Criterion" in S. Everson (ed.), *Epistemology* (*Companions to Ancient Philosophy* I), Cambridge: Cambridge University Press 1990, 143–160; reprinted in Striker, *Essays on Hellenistic Epistemology and Ethics*, 1996, 150–165.

"Comments on Irwin", in G. Patzig (ed.), *Aristoteles' Politik: Akten des XI. Symposium Aristotelicum*, Göttingen: Vandenhoeck & Ruprecht 1990, 99–100.

"Following Nature: A Study in Stoic Ethics," *Oxford Studies in Ancient Philosophy* 9 (1991), 1–73; reprinted in Striker, *Essays on Hellenistic Epistemology and Ethics*, 1996, 221–280.

"Epicurean Hedonism" in J. Brunschwig and M. Nussbaum (eds.), *Passions and Perceptions*, Cambridge: Cambridge University Press 1993, 3–17.

Commentary on David Furley, "The Originality of Stoic Cosmology," *Proceedings of the Boston Area Colloquium in Ancient Philosophy* 9 (1993), 76–81.

"Plato's Socrates and the Stoics" in P. A. Vander Waerdt (ed.), *The Socratic Movement*, Ithaca: Cornell University Press 1994, 241–251; reprinted in Striker, *Essays on Hellenistic Epistemology and Ethics*, 1996, 316–324.

"Assertoric vs. Modal Syllogistic," *Ancient Philosophy* 14 (1994), 39–51.

"Cicero and Greek Philosophy," *Harvard Studies in Classical Philology* 97 (1995), 53–61.

"Emotions in Context" in A. O. Rorty (ed.), *Essays on Aristotle's Rhetoric*, Berkeley: University of California Press 1996, 286–302.

"Methods of Sophistry," in *Essays on Hellenistic Epistemology and Ethics*, Cambridge: Cambridge University Press 1996, 3–21.

"Perfection and Reduction in Aristotle's Prior Analytics," in M. Frede and G. Striker (eds.), *Rationality in Greek Thought*, Oxford: Clarendon Press 1996, 203–220.

"Academics Fighting Academics" in B. Inwood and J. Mansfeld (eds.), *Assent and Argument*, Leiden: Brill 1997, 257–276.

"Aristotle and the Uses of Logic" in J. Gentzler (ed.), *Method in Ancient Philosophy*, Oxford: Clarendon Press 1998, 209–226.

"Why Study the History of Philosophy?", *The Harvard Review of Philosophy* 7 /1 (1999): 15–18.

"Scepticism as a Kind of Philosophy," *Archiv für Geschichte der Philosophie* 83 (2001), 113–129.

Commentary on Margaret Graver, "Managing Mental Pain: Epicurus vs Aristippus on the Pre-rehearsal of Future Ills," *Proceedings of the Boston Area Colloquium in Ancient Philosophy* 17 (2001), 178–182.

"Historical Reflections on Classical Pyrrhonism and Neo-Pyrrhonism" in W. Sinnott-Armstrong (ed.), *Pyrrhonian Skepticism*, Oxford: Oxford University Press 2004, 13–24.

"Aristotle's Ethics as Political Science" in B. Reis and S. Haffmans (eds.), *The Virtuous Life in Greek Ethics*, Cambridge: Cambridge University Press 2006, 127–41.

"Comments on Lennox, 'Aristotle's Natural Science: The Many and the One', in J.H. Lesher (ed.), *From Inquiry to Demonstrative Knowledge: New Essays on Aristotle's Posterior Analytics'*, Kelowna, BC: Academic Printing & Publishing, 25–30.

"Academics versus Pyrrhonists, Reconsidered" in R. Bett (ed.), *The Cambridge Companion to Ancient Scepticism*, Cambridge: Cambridge University Press 2010, 195–208.

"A Note on the Ontology of Aristotle's *Categories*, Chapter 2", in B. Morison and K. Ierodiakonou (eds.), *Episteme, etc.: Essays in honour of Jonathan Barnes*, Oxford: Oxford University Press 2011.

Articles in Encyclopedic Works

"Epikur" in O. Höffe (ed.), *Klassiker der Philosophie I*, Munich: Beck 1981, 95–115.

"Epictetus," "Marcus Aurelius," "Stoicism" in L. C. Becker and C. B. Becker (eds.), *Encyclopedia of Ethics*, New York: Garland 1992.

"Clitomachus," "Antiochus," "Olympiodorus," "Ariston of Alexandria," "Carneades," "Arcesilaus," "Philon," "Agrippa," "Charmadas," "Aenesidemus," "Timon," "Pyrrhon," "Sextus Empiricus," "Sceptics," in Simon Hornblower and Anthony Spawforth (eds.), *Oxford Classical Dictionary*, 3rd edn., Oxford: Oxford University Press 1996.

"Ancient skepticism", in S. Hetherington (ed.), *Epistemology: The Key Thinkers*, London: Continuum 2012.

Selected Book Reviews

Mignucci, M., Aristotele: Gli analitici primi, Archiv für Geschichte der Philosophie LII (1970) 200–203.

Giannantoni, G., *Lo scetticismo antico*, Ancient Philosophy 5/1 (1985) 145–151.

Inwood, B., *Ethics and Human Action in Early Stoicism*, Canadian Journal of Philosophy 19/1 (1989) 91–100.

Tarrant, H., *Scepticism or Platonism?: The Philosophy of the Fourth Academy*, Ancient Philosophy 11/1 (1991) 202–206.

Irwin, T.H., *Aristotle's First Principles*, Journal of Philosophy 88/9 (1991) 489–496.

Sorabji, R., *Aristotle Transformed: The Ancient Commentators and their Influence*, The Philosophical Review 101/4 (October 1992) 847–849.

Cicero: On Stoic Good and Evil. De Finibus 3 and Paradoxa Stoicorum, edited, translated and with an introduction and commentary by M.R. Wright. Philosophical Books 34/1 (1993) 11–12.

Williams, Bernard, *Shame and Necessity*, London Review of Books 15/16 (19 August 1993) 17–18.

Tarrant, H., *Thrasyllan Platonism*, Philosophical Review 104/2 (1995) 263–265.

Long, A.A. *Stoic Studies*. Ethics 109/1 (1998), 172–174.

Erler, M. et al., *Grundriß der Geschichte der Philosophie. Begründet von Friedrich Ueberweg. Völlig neuarbeitete Ausgabe. Die Philosophie der Antike, Band 4: Die hellenistische Philosophie*, Gnomon 71/2 (1999) 101–105.

Tsouna-McKirahan, V., *The Epistemology of the Cyrenaic School*, Mind 110/437 (2001) 274–277.

Graver, M., *Stoicism and Emotion*, Philosophical Books 49/4 (2008) 372–373.

INDEX OF NAMES

Academics 272, 304, 342, 347, 350, 367–70
Academy 236, 273
 early 60, 62, 279
 New 248, 367n31
 Old 231, 269n50, 271n55, 272, 272n59, 274, 279
Acerbi, Fabio 226
Ackrill, John ix, 85n5, 103
Adam 72n30
Admetus (example in Sextus) 341, 352, 353n44
Aenesidemus 358, 365, 371
Albinus 219
Alcinous xv, 201, 219–20, 258, 259n10, 263n28, 264n32, 270, 270n53, 270n54, 271, 302–3, 314n35, 316, 317n43, 326n63, 327n64
Al Farabi 201n14
Alexander of Aphrodisias xiii, 137–8, 158, 163, 164n37, 166, 170n48, 175n1, 180n13, 183, 183n18, 184, 188, 193n32, 199, 200, 200n6, 201–26
Algra, K. 248n44, 252
Allen, James xiii, 231, 235n17, 252, 333n3, 347n33, 352–4
Ambrose, P. 239n30, 240n31, 241, 242n37, 252
Americans 93
Ammonius 155n16, 158n23, 170n48, 175, 176, 177, 179, 193n32, 201n14, 209n33
Annas, J. 83n1,103, 248n44,250n46, 253, 259n10, 259n15, 261n21, 262n27, 263, 263n29, 263n31, 266n41, 267n44, 279, 270n52, 279, 283n7, 296, 333n3, 354, 360n13, 362n17, 372
Anonymus *IN SE* 161n29, 161n30
Antiochus of Ascalon 231, 248–50, 269–75, 277, 279, 351–2
Antipater (Stoic, mid-2nd c. BC) 262–4, 274, 279
Antiphon 108
Antoniadis, E. 236n18, 238n26, 253
Apelt, O. 60n2, 78
Apuleius (?) 183n18, 233
Aquinas, Thomas 307n23

Arcesilaus 332n1, 361n16, 366n29
Archelaus 55
Aristippus of Cyrene 234, 247
Ariston (Aristo) of Chios 256, 285
Aristotle ix–xv, 17, 21, 37–9, 51, 61–5, 74, 76, 83–102, 104–15, 117–22, 124–44, 149–66, 168–81, 184–5, 187–92, 196, 199–207, 209–13, 215–22, 226, 231–2, 235, 238, 239n28, 241, 244–5, 255–7, 259–2, 264–69, 272, 274, 278, 302, 315, 321n49, 32–4, 327
Arius Didymus 262n24, 269n49
von Arnim, H. 355
Arthur, E. 336n14, 354
Ast, F. 253
Atherton, C. 344n27, 354
Attalus 294
Atticus (Cicero) 231n4
Atticus (2nd c. AD Platonist) 25–8, 263, 267n43, 269, 275, 279
Aulus Gellius 294, 335n11
Avicenna 201n13

Badawi, A. 178n8, 178n, 198
Badham, C. 10, 19
Bailey, Alan 357n4, 372
Bailey, D. 122
Balot, Ryan 267n44
Baltes, M. 61n4, 78
Barker, A. 304n15, 305,307n24, 329n66, 330
Barnes, Jonathan xii, 130n20, 144, 150n1, 151n3, 152n6, 158n20, 158n22, 160n28, 163n32, 165n42, 166n43, 171, 173, 175n2, 181n15, 187n23, 188n24, 189n25, 191n27, 193n31, 193n32, 198, 199n5, 200n7, 220n62, 224n72, 226, 278n70, 279, 345n30, 354, 360n13, 362n17, 366n26, 372
Barney, R. 362n19, 372
Batstone, W. 286n13, 296
Beere, J. 173
Bekker, I. 341n21
Bell, K. 235, 253
Bellincioni, M. 283n7, 296
Bengson, J. 143n34, 144

Betegh, Gábor 62n8, 78, 268n47, 279
Bett, R. 236n19, 253, 359n7, 372
Bobonich, C. 12n25, 19
Bobzien, Susanne xiii, 158n23, 164n36,
    173, 199, 199n5, 200n6, 200n7, 200n9,
    206n26, 207n29, 211n36, 213n40,
    213n41, 213n43, 215n48, 215n49,
    217n56, 218n59, 219, 220n62, 220n64,
    223n70, 223n71, 224n73, 225n74, 226,
    227, 344n27, 345, 345n30, 346n31, 354
Bocheński, I. 177n7, 198
Bodin, L. 235, 253
Bodnár, István 226
Boethius 175n1, 177, 199, 223
Boethus xii, 175, 177-8, 180-6, 189n26,
    190-3, 196-7, 200, 216n51
Bok, H. 125, 125n3, 144
Boll, F. 302n3, 304n13, 315, 315n36,
    319n48, 390
Bolzano, B. 166-7, 173
Bonitz, H. 253
Boyle, M. 38n27, 58
Brennan, T. 335n9, 335n11, 336n14, 354
Brittain, Charles xv 280, 331, 332n1, 348n34,
    354, 349, 351n41
Broadie, Sarah xi 21, 60, 60n1, 68n20, 69n23,
    72n31, 78, 100n33, 103, 115, 116n18,
    122, 125n4, 135n26, 144, 237n24, 253
Brown, L. 106n3
Brunner, Ákos 259n14, 279
Brunschwig, J. 112n15, 368n33, 372
Bullialdus, I. 301n1, 304n13, 322n50, 323n52
Burnyeat, M. 18n33, 19, 62n8, 67n17, 78,
    103, 109, 310n31, 330, 345n30, 354, 356,
    357n4, 362n18, 362n19, 366n26, 366n27,
    367n31, 372
Bury, R.G. 236n19, 253, 360n13

Callard, A. 173
Callias 130-1
Callicles 22, 31, 34, 35, 50, 56, 239, 243, 244
Cambridge University ix
Carneades 247-52, 262, 273-4, 332n1,
    334n7, 338-9, 342, 346, 351n39, 352,
    361n16, 367, 368n34, 369
Carroll, Lewis 197
Cato (Cicero) 246, 274
Catullus 287
Chantilly ix
Chantraine, P. 240n32, 253
Charles, D. 38, 58
Cherniss, H. 61n4, 62n9, 63n14, 66n16, 78
Chrysippus x, 216n51, 232n5, 256, 262n24,
    273, 273n61, 332, 339-40, 342-7, 353

Cicero xiii, xiv, 231, 231n1, 23n1n4,
    23-4, 237-8, 243, 245-50, 252, 261n22,
    262n24, 266n40, 269n50, 271-5, 277-8,
    281, 285n10, 295, 333n5, 334n7, 336-8,
    342, 344-5, 349, 350, 352, 367n31
Clay, D. 60n2
Cleanthes 285, 343
Cleitophon 108n6
Clement of Alexandria 232, 241, 260n17,
    261, 265n36, 265n38
Clinias (*Euthydemus*) 259
Clitomachus 248, 369
Colli, G. 160n27, 161n29, 173
Columbia University ix, 122
Cooper, John M. 11n18, 16n28, 17n29,
    19, 122, 125, 125n2, 129n18, 144, 253,
    259n15, 267n42, 280, 295n28, 296
Cornarius 32, 33
Crantor (early Academic) 264n33
Critias 67
Critolaus 261-2, 271n56, 262b56, 273-4, 279
Crivelli, P. 154n9, 155n15, 162n31, 173
Croiset, A. 253, 235
Crönert, W. 234n15, 253
Cyrenaics 236, 321n49
Cyrene 236

David 177n5
Davies, John 232-3, 237n22, 253
Debrunner, A. 330
Décarie, V. 253
Delcomminette, S. 8n11, 16n28, 20, 33n19, 58
Demetrius of Laconia 234
Demiurge 60, 63n12, 65n15, 66,
    69n23, 70, 74
Democritus 241
Demosthenes 121n25, 340n20
Devereux, D. 129n18, 144
Diano, C. 236n21, 237n22, 238n27, 253
Diès, A. 10, 20
Dillon, J. 66n16, 76n39, 78, 259n11,
    260n18, 263n28, 280, 301, 302n4, 303,
    315n38, 330
Dio Chrysostom 311n2
Diogenes Laertius 86n9, 231n3, 261, 264,
    265, 267, 302n4, 317, 343, 364, 365
Diogenes of Apollonia 69
Dirlmeier, F. 233n10, 253
Dodds, E.R. 231n2, 253
Dorion, L.-A. 150n1, 151n3, 151n4, 152n6,
    153n8, 155n18, 159n24, 161n29, 162n31,
    169n46, 173
Döring, A. 232n5, 253
Duhem, P. 307n23, 330

Düring, I. 330
Dyson, H. 348n34, 354

Ebbesen, S. 152n5, 174
Ebert, T. 165n39, 165n41, 174
Ebrey, D. 173
Edlow, R.B. 151n4, 174
Edwards, C. 288n16, 296
Emilsson, E. 372
Empedocles 69
Epicureans xiv, 247, 259, 277, 302
Epicurus x, 231, 302
Eubulides 186–7
Euler, L. 197
Euripides 241
Eusebius 234, 269n49
Evans, Matthew 11n19, 20, 22, 40n29, 41, 41n30, 42, 51–3, 58
Eudemus 188, 193
Eudorus (1st c. BC Platonist) 260, 263, 275n64
Everson, S. 126n7, 144

Fait, P. 150n1, 151n3, 152n5, 152n7, 155n18, 159n24, 162n31, 169n46, 174
Feke, J. 302n3, 305n16, 330
Fischer, U. 240n33, 253
Fletcher, E. 24n5, 58
Forster, E.S. 150n1, 151n4, 160n27, 161n29, 174
Freddoso, A. 74n34, 78
Frede, Dorothea ix, xi, 8n10, 9n12, 10n14, 10n16, 20, 22, 23, 23n3, 23n4, 24, 24n7, 28, 28n14, 29, 29n15, 30, 30n16, 33, 33n20, 42, 42n32, 47, 58, 83, 100n33, 103, 122, 128n11, 128n12, 129n14, 144
Frede, Michael ix, 132n23, 145, 154n13, 164n37, 165n41, 165n42, 170n48, 174, 184n20, 189n25, 189n26, 198, 199n5, 200n7, 227, 332n1, 332n2, 333n3, 334n6, 335n9, 355, 356, 362n19, 368n33, 372
Frege, G. 217
Frisk, H. 253

Galen 24, 24n8, 181, 183, 200, 204, 208n32, 215, 216, 216n51, 219, 220, 221n65, 224, 232n5, 319n47, 329n65
Gauthier, R.A. 84n3, 103
George Martin Lane Professor of Philosophy and Classics ix
Germany ix
Gerson, L. 364n23, 373
Giannantoni, G. 237n22, 253

Giusta, M. 234n16, 253,
Glucker, J. 232n5, 253
Goldman, A. 143n34, 145
Göransson, T. 260, 280
Gorgias 50n38, 240, 240n33, 241
Görler, W. 332n2, 336n14, 354
Gosling, J. 9n12, 10n17, 20, 23n3, 41n29, 44n34, 58
Göttingen ix
Gottlieb, P. 85n5, 103
Goulet, R. 199n5, 227
Grasshoff, G. 307n22, 329n67, 330
Greeks 62
Gregoric, P. 126n7, 127n9, 128n10, 130n21, 130n22, 145
Grgic, F. 126n7, 130n21, 130n22, 145
Gregory, A. 60n3, 78
Griffin, M. 281n1, 293n23, 296
Griffith, T. 243n39, 253
Guthrie, W.K.C. 235, 253

Hachmann, E. 281n3, 296
Häcker, K.F. 84n3, 103
Hadot, P. 232n5, 253
Hahm, D. 280
Hankinson, R.J. 357n4, 366n26, 373
Hardie, W.F.R. 115
Harte, Verity x, 3n1, 20, 22, 26, 27n11, 40n29, 41n29, 43n33, 53n40, 57, 58, 67n17, 78, 122
Hartung, H.-J. 234n16, 253
Harvard University ix, 122
Hasper, P.S. 150n1, 159n25, 161n29, 169n47, 173–4
Hecaton 232
Heiberg, J. 330
Henderson, J. 281n3, 291n20, 296
Hermias 177
Herminus 183
Hermocrates 67
Herodotus 119, 241
Hipparchus 329
Hippolytus 269
Hirzel, R. 235–7, 247, 253
Hobbes, T. 108n6
Holland, J.H. 144n37, 145
Holwerda, D. 239n29, 240n33, 253
Homer 239, 241
Horace 282, 291
Huby, P.M. 177n7, 193n32, 198, 301n1, 309n29, 330
Hume, D. 21, 129, 129n16, 145
Hunt, P.A. 122
Hursthouse, R. 87n11, 103

Iamblichus 177
Ibn Sina (Avicenna) 201n13
Ierodiakonou, K. 199n5, 227
Indelli, G. 247n43, 253
Inwood, Brad xiii, xiv, 57, 246n42, 252, 261n22, 280, 283,283n6, 283n7, 295n28, 296, 333n3, 335n12, 355, 364n23, 373
Ioppolo, A.-M. 333n2, 355
Irwin, T. 11n18, 12n23, 20, 84n3, 103, 106n2, 110n11, 117n21, 123

Johansen, T. 127n9, 145
John Ackrill Memorial Lecture x
Jolif, J.Y. 84n3, 103
Jones, A. 302n3, 305n16, 330
Jowett, Benjamin 4n3, 235, 253
Julian, Emperor 177, 177n5, 178, 179, 197, 197n36

Kahneman, D. 144n35, 145
Kant, I. 83, 84
Karamanolis, G. 265n37, 267n43, 280
Kellman, P.J. 144n36, 145
Kelly, B. 309n28, 310n30, 316n40, 330
Keyt, D. 123
von Kirchmann, J.H. 161n29, 161n30, 174
Kirwan, C. 159n25, 174
Kosman, A. 88n15, 103
Kraut, R. 108n5, 108n6, 109n8, 110n11, 112, 113n16, 122, 123
Krinis (Stoic) 257n6, 258n6
Kvanvig, J. 74n34, 75n36, 78

LaBarge, S. 126n7, 129n17, 145
Lachelier, J. 341n21
Lactantius 293
Lammert, F. 301n1, 309n29, 326n61, 328n65330
Lana, I. 283n8, 294n27, 296
Laurence Professor of Ancient Philosophy ix
Lavin, D. 38n27, 58
Lear, G. 11n21, 12n23, 17n29, 17n30, 20, 117n21, 123, 173
Lear, J. 164n35, 174
Lee, H.D.P. 60n2, 78
Lee, Mi-Kyoung (Mitzi) xii, 57, 104, 144, 252, 330, 372
Lee, S. 74n34, 78
Lee, T.-S. 177n6, 181n17, 188n24, 197n35, 198
Leeman, A.D. 294n26, 296
Lejeune, A. 322n51, 330
Lévy, C. 232n5, 248n44, 253
Lieberg, G. 237n22, 253
Lipton, P. 144n35, 145

Liscu, M. 234n16, 253
Lloyd, G.E.R. 307n22, 330
Lombardo, S. 235, 253
Long, A.A. 303-4, 330, 333n4, 355
Lörcher, A. 232n8, 254
Lorenz, H. 38n26, 58, 128n11, 128n12, 145, 280
Louis, P. 302n4, 331
Lovibond, Sabina 22, 43n33, 51-5, 58
Lucilius (Seneca) 281-2, 284, 286-90, 292, 294-5
Lucullus 249, 351
Lugdunum (Lyon) 293

Machuca, Diego 356n2, 373
Madvig, N. 233, 237n22, 250n45, 254
Maecenas 291
Malink, Marko xii, 149
Mannebach, E. 237n22, 254
Mansfeld, J. 262n24, 265n35, 269n49, 280
Maroth, M. 199n4, 216, 219n, 227
Martha, J. 232n8, 254
Maurach, G. 287n14, 296
Maximus 177-82, 184, 186-97
Mazzoli, G. 281n1, 283n8, 296
McCabe, M.M. 9n13, 12, 12n22, 20
McCann, H. 74n34, 78
McTaggart, J.M.E. 67n19
Meinwald, C. 336n14, 355
Menedemus 187n23
Menelaus (or Menedemus?) 186, 187
Menelaus (example in Sextus) 341, 347-8, 352-3
Menn, S. 136n28, 145, 252
Merguet, H. 254
Metcalf, R. 122
Michael of Ephesus 161-2
Middle Platonists 200
Mignucci, M. 193n31, 198, 199n5, 227
Miller, Dana xii, 122, 124
Millgram, E. 145
Mitsis, P. 283n7, 297
Moffett, M. 143n34, 144
de Montaigne, Michel 281
Mooradian, N. 32n18, 58
Moraux, P. 177n7, 181n15, 198, 262n24, 269n49, 272, 280
Morison, B. 166n43, 174
Moss, J. 38n26, 58, 127n9, 129n15, 136n27, 145, 252
Mueller, I. 165n38, 165n42, 174, 199n5, 202n16, 227
Muret ["Muretus"], Marc-Antoine 232, 237n22, 254
Musgrave, A. 307n23, 330

Neal, G. 301n1, 309n29, 330
Nellie Wallace Lectures ix
Nero 282
North, Helen 96, 103
Nortmann 165n38, 165n41, 174
Nussbaum, M. 12n24, 20

Oakes, R. 74n34, 78
Oppel, H. 311n32, 330
Oxford ix

Panaetius 277n68
Parmenides 61n5
Pasnau, R. 122
Patzig, Günther ix, 175n2, 177n7, 180n13, 181n15, 197n36, 198
Pellegrin, P. 356n4, 373
Perin, Casey 366n26, 366n27, 373
Peripatetics 181, 183, 188, 199n4, 205–6, 213, 217–19, 221, 223, 225–6, 246, 262, 265, 270–4, 277, 279, 315
Peripatos 246
Pfeiffer, C. 173
Philebus 3, 4, 6, 7, 12, 13, 15, 25, 57
Philippson, Robert 232n9, 233, 237n22, 254
Phillips, J. 74n34, 78
Philo of Alexandria 259n11, 269n51
Philo of Larissa 248, 271, 302, 304
Philodemus 233, 234, 235, 247n43
Philoponus 164n37, 180n13, 199
Pire, G. 281n2, 297
Piso 250, 251, 272, 272n58, 273n61, 352
Plato ix–xi, xiii–xv, 18, 21–4, 35, 41, 43, 47n37, 49, 52, 55, 57, 60–5, 67, 69, 71–3, 75–7, 84, 90, 92, 96, 97n29, 99, 107n4, 108, 201, 213, 231, 235–6, 238, 242–8, 255–60, 262–74, 278–9, 296, 302, 306n21, 314n35, 327, 366n29
Platonists 61, 221, 225, 275, 277, 278n70
Platonists, Middle 200
Plotinus 63
Plutarch 241, 252, 266n41, 334n7, 336–7, 351n39
[Plutarch] 201, 234
Polemo 268, 272n59
Polus 25, 243, 268n46
Polybius 309
Porphyry 177
Posidonius 302
Poste, E. 160, 160n28, 162n31, 174
Potamon of Alexandria 317n43, 318n45
Pradeau, J.-F. 33n19, 58
Princeton ix
Proclus 63, 177

Protarchus 4–15, 17, 22, 25–6, 29–32, 36–7, 39–40, 42–6, 48, 53, 55–6
Ptolemy of Alexandria xiv–xv, 201, 301–29
Puglia, E. 234n15, 254
Punch 90, 91
Pyrrhonian skeptics 231
Pyrrhonists 367–70

Quinn, P. 74n34, 79
Quintilian 286n12
Quintus (Cicero) 281
Quintus Sextius 290

Rackham, H. 237, 254
Rapp, C. 87n11, 103, 173
Rashed, Marwen 178n8, 180n14
Rawls, J. 123
Receptacle 63n12, 72
Reeve, C.D.C. 110n10
Reid, J.S. 237n22, 254
Reshotko, N. 261n21, 280
Robinson, R. 244n41, 254
Rogers, Kelly 117n21, 118, 123
Rolfes, E. 161n29, 161n30, 174
de Romilly, J. 112n15, 123
Roman philosophers xiv
Rosen, Jacob 173
Ross, W.D. 106n3, 110n11, 140n32, 145
Russell, D. 261n22, 280

Sachs, D. 107n4, 123
Sandbach, F. 333n3, 355
Santos, F.D. 179n10, 198
Scaliger the elder 232
Schafer, John xiv, 281, 282n4, 283n7, 285n11, 287n15, 288n17, 297
Schäublin, C. 237n22, 254
Schiche, T. 254
Schiefsky, Mark xiv–xv, 201n11, 227, 301
Schmid, W. 247n43, 254
Schneider, J.-P. 181n15, 198
Schönegg, B. 281n3, 297
Schofield, M. 110n10, 243n39, 254
Schreiber, S. 150n1, 151n3, 151n4, 155n18, 159n24, 159n25, 160, 160n28, 169n46, 174
Scythians 134
Sedley, D. 60n3, 61n5, 63n14, 69n22, 79, 275, 280
Seneca xiv, 233, 262n24, 269n50, 272n57, 276, 276n66, 277 9, 281–96, 335n11
Sextus Empiricus xv, 183, 236, 258, 262n25, 262n26, 264n33, 269n49, 303, 312–13, 315, 316–19, 321n49, 334n5, 334n7, 334n8, 335, 335n10, 337-9, 341, 345, 346n31, 350, 352, 353n43, 353n44, 356–71

Sharples, R.W. 261n22, 280
Sherman, N. 89n16, 103
Siebel 166n44, 167n45, 174
Simplicius 179n10
Siwecki, J. 124n1, 145
Skeptics 302
  academic 302
Smith, A.M. 329n67, 331
Smyth, H.W. 311n33, 331
Socrates 3–13, 15–16, 18–19, 22–50, 52–67,
  130–1, 235, 239, 243–4, 260, 261n21,
  268, 275
Sophocles 241
Sorabji, R. 60n3, 74n34, 79
Sotion 294
Spartans 134
Speca 199n5, 203n20, 227
Speusippus 260n17, 264
Stanford ix
Staseas (Peripatetic) 272n57, 272n58
Stoa 231, 245, 246, 251, 252
Stobaeus 257, 260, 276n65, 337
Stoics xiv, xv, 199n4, 204–8, 211, 213, 216–17,
  219, 222n66, 223, 225, 231, 238, 245–6,
  251–2, 256–7, 260, 264n33, 269–75,
  278n70, 279, 302, 334–7, 342, 345,
  350–2
  'Younger' 338–42, 345n28, 346–53
  'Older' 338
Street, T. 201n13, 227
Striker, Gisela v, ix–x, xiv–xvi, 21, 22, 28n14,
  57, 58, 78, 88n13, 103, 105n1, 106n2,
  117n19, 120, 122–3, 131, 144–5, 154n13,
  165n39, 165n41, 173–4, 177n3, 185,
  188n24, 193n31, 197n35, 197n36, 198–9,
  203n18, 217n55, 227, 250n46, 252, 254,
  279, 296, 302n7, 302n8, 317n44, 320n49,
  330–2, 347, 354–5, 360n11, 362–3,
  366n27, 367n31, 371n39, 372, 373,
  375–8
Suppes, P. 307n24, 331
Susemihl, F. 84n4
Svavarsson, Svavar Hrafn xv, 356
Symposium Hellenisticum ix
Syrianus 177
Szaif, J. 122

Tacitus 293
Tanner Lectures ix
Tarán, L. 61n5, 66n16, 70n24, 79
Tarrant, H. 304n11, 331
Tarski 166, 166n44, 167, 168, 174
Taubenschlag, R. 309n28, 331
Taylor, A.E. 28n14, 58

Taylor, C.C.W. 41n29, 44n34, 94n27, 103,
  243n39, 254
Thein, Karel 33n19, 59
Themistius 39n28, 177–97
Theodorus the Cyrenaic 247n43
Theon 266
Theophrastus 177, 177n7, 188, 193n32, 272n59
Thirty, The 110–11
Thorsrud, H. 357n4, 362n19, 373
Thrasymachus 108
Tiberius 295
Timaeus 60–2, 64–7, 72
Timon 369
Toomer, G. 305, 331
Tsouna-McKirahan, V. 247n43, 236n19,
  253, 254

United States 93
Urmson, J.O. 87n11, 103
Usener, H. 254

Varro (Acad.) 272
Velleman, D. 38n27, 59
Venn 197
Virgil 282, 295
Vlastos, G. 61n4, 63n14, 66n16, 70n24,
  71n29, 79
Vottero, D. 293n24, 294n26, 297

Wachsmuth, C. 268n48
Wallies, M. 202n15
Walter C. Klein Professor of Philosophy and
  Classics ix
Wardy, Robert 279
Warren, J. 232n5, 254
Weidemann, H. 155n19, 174
White, S. 261n22, 280
Whittaker, J. 302n4, 331
Whiting, Jennifer x, xi, 24n6, 38n26, 39n28,
  54n41, 59, 279
Williams, Bernard 22, 59, 123
Wilson, M. 281n3, 297
Woodruff, P. 357n4, 373
Woods, M. 254
Woolf, R. 254

Xenocrates 61, 63, 63n13, 76n37, 77, 260n17,
  264, 265n36, 268, 274, 278

Young, C. 112, 123

Zeno of Citium 273, 273n61, 275, 285, 332,
  334n5, 337, 349
Zeyl, D. 34n22

INDEX LOCORUM

References are listed by author and work; passages within each work are listed in order following the standard paginations. Wherever possible we have preserved the citation format used by the author within whose chapter the reference appears.

The following abbreviation is used in this index:
SVF *StoicorumVeterum Fragmenta*, von Arnim, H. (ed.) (Leipzig: 1903–24)

Aëtius
4.11 348n34

Alcinous
Didaskalikos
Ch. 4, p. 154.10–18 Hermann 317n43
Ch. 4, pp. 154.10–156.23
  Hermann 302n4, 303n9
Ch. 4, p. 154.29–32 Hermann 327n64
Ch. 4, p. 154.32–4 Hermann 318n46
Ch. 4, p. 154.39-40 Hermann 315n38
Ch. 4, p. 155.13-17 Hermann 316n41
Ch. 4, pp. 155.17-20 Hermann 314n35
Ch. 4, p. 155.34 Hermann 315n38
Ch. 6 200n8, 220
Ch. 11.15 215n46
Ch. 27 263n28, 264n32

Alexander of Aphrodisias
de Fato
165.14–171.17 201n10

in Analytica Priora (=*in AnPr.*)
6.22 183n18
11.6–9 158n20
11.17–20 215
11.18 214n44, 215n47
17.5–10 158n23
17.7–8 215
17.8–9 217n54
18.12–22 211n37
18.14–18 170n48
19.4 218n60
19.4–5 217
20–1 215
21.28–30 164n37
24.2–12 217n52
29.23–29 188

31.4–10 193n32
69.26–29 175n1
77.6–9, 26–28 180n13
84.15–17 163
100.14–18 184n21
113.7–9 180n13
177.21 214n45
177.31 214n45
178.28 214n45
179.32 214n45
180.2 214n45
262–4 223
262–5 205
262.6–9 217
262.7 215
262.9 202n16
262.28 202n16
262.28–31 202
262.28–264.31 202n16
262.28–265.5 202n15, 221
262.31 222, 222n66
262.31–2 218n59
263.22–5 206n25
262.32 214n44
263.26–33 217n57
264.14–31 222
264.15 223n69
264.26 223n69
264.32–265.13 206n25
265.1–24 217n53
324.7 215
325.37–326.1 202n15
326.3–5 202
326.4–5 202n15
326.6–7 217n54
327.2–3 215
336.13–20 208
336.18–20 208n31

344.9–345.12 164n37
346.27–8 164n37
347.5–7 165n39
348.29–32 158n23
350.16–18 158n23
372.29–30 163
373.16–17 163
373.18–20 204n21
373.28–35 204n21
386.22–3 202n15, 203
386.27–8 218
386.27–30 202n15, 203
389.31–390.1 202n15, 203
390.3–5 218
390.3–6 202n15, 203, 221
390.4–5 215
in Met.
318.23 215
490.33–491.5 137–8
in Top.
8.8–14 158n23
10.6–12 170n48
11–12 218n60
12.11–15 163n33
63.25 217n54
165–6 206, 208
165.6–7 207n28, 218
165.12–13 207
166.11–13 207
174–5 206, 208
174–6 211, 212
174.5–6 218
174.6–7 218
174.7 208
175 218n60
175.2–10 209
175.21–6 210
191.18 215, 217n54
218.3–5 184
Mixt.
p. 217.2–4 348

Ammonius
in Analytica Priora (=*in AnPr.*)
14.28–33 176
17.26–9 158n23
27.6–14 158
27.14–16 176
27.35–28.8 170n48
28.13–20 158
31.11–15 177
31.25–29 175
31.38–32.3 177
32.33–33.1 177

32.33–37 176
33.18–21 176
in Categoriae (=*in Cat.*)
95.8 209n33
in de Interpretatione (=*in Int.*)
7.32–3, 10.1–17 155n16
73.35–74.1 158n23
84.13–27 155n16

[Ammonius]
AnPr.
68.23–41 220n64

Anonymous
In Sophistici Elenchi
18.16–17 161n29
18.8–18 161n30

Anonymous
*Log.etQuadr.*38 224n72

Antiphon
On Truth
DK 87 B44 108

5. 89 240n33

Apuleius
Apologia 15, 10 233n11

[Apuleius]
de Interpretatione
191.6–11 200n8
201.4–11 200n8
ix. 205.21–206.6 183n18
209.9–14 200n8
212.10–12 200n8

Aquinas
Summa Theologica
1.32 307n23

Aristotle
Categories
Ch. 10 209
11b17–23 209n33
11b38–12a25 *209n33*
13a37–b35 209n33
De Anima
I 1. 403a17–18 89n18
II 6. 418a7–25 323n53
II 6. 418a17–18 323n55
III 1. 425a15–17 323n55
III 3 129n14

III 3. 427b24–27 130n20
III 3. 428a12–15 38
III 3. 428b2–5 39
III 3. 428b18–30 323n53, 323n54
III 3. 429a4–6 127
III 6. 430a26–b31 324
III 6. 430b29–31 323n53
III 7. 431a8–17 38
III 7. 431a14–17 128n11
III 7. 431b2 128
III 7. 431b6–10 128
III 7. 432a7–10 128
III 10. 433b28–29 128
III 11. 434a11 129
III 11. 434a7–10 129n15
De Int.
4. 16b26 155n14
5. 17a8–9 155a14
5–6. 17a23–6 155n14
5–6. 17a20–6 158a20
6. 17a33–7 154, 155n16
8. 18a12–13 158n21
10. 19b6–7 159n21
11. 20b12–15 158n21
De Motu
7. 701a20–22 138n30
HA
535a26–31 315n39
Magna Moralia
I 2. 1184a14 233n10
I 3. 1184b1–6 266n42
I 3. 1184b8 233n10
II 6. 1202a30–35 266n42
II 8. 1206b33 266n42
II 8. 1207b17–18 266n42
Mem.
1. 449b30–a7 128
Eudemian Ethics
I 1. 1214a30–33 260
I 1. 1214a34–b6 260
I 2. 1214b24–27 261n23
I 8. 1217b2–5 237n24
I 8. 1217b22 266n41
I 8. 1218b7–12 237n24
II 1. 1218b31–37 267
II 1. 1219a8 ff. 244
II 1. 1219a10–11 239n28
II 3. 1220b38–1221a12 84n4
II 3. 1221a3 93n25
II 10. 1227a18–22 232
III 7 93n25
VII 10. 1242a19–28 121n26
VIII 3 117
VIII 3. 1248b17–25 119

VIII 3. 1248b18 233n10
Mechanics
I 26. 857a5–6 141n33
Metaphysics
A 1. 980a27–981a12 309n27, 315n37
A 1. 980b29–981a1 126
A 1. 981a1 127
A 1. 981a5–7 127, 130n20, 141
A 1. 981a7–9 130
A 1. 981a7–12 131–2
A 1. 981a12–13 131
A 1. 981a13–15 129
A 1. 981a15–16 129
A 1. 981a16–17 139
A 1. 981a17–18 130
A 1. 981a29–30 132
α 2. 994a8ff. 239n28
Γ 4. 1010b19–26 320n49
Δ 16. 1021b16–1022a3 177n3
Δ 17. 1022a6–8 239n28
E 1. 1025b22–24 133
E 1. 1025b22–24 135n27, 140n32
Z 7 137
Z 7. 1032a28–30 126n5
Z 7. 1032b6–9 137
Z 7. 1032b13–14 138n29
Z 7. 1032b15–16 137
Z 7. 1032b19–20 139
Z 7. 1032b23 138
Θ 10. 1051a34–1052a11 324
K 6. 1063a3 302n6
Λ 6 62n10
M 1. 1076a28 266n41
Nicomachean Ethics
I 1. 1094a3 ff. 245
I 2. 1094a18–21 239n28
I 2. 1094a22–24 83n2
I 2. 1094a22–b11 101
I 2. 1094b7–10 119
I 4. 1095a16 237
I 4. 1095b10–14 104
I 7. 1097a18–19 232n9
I 7. 1097a22 238
I 8. 1098b9–16 265
I 8. 1098b10–16 266n42
I 9. 1099b29–32 112
I 10. 1100b25 ff. 261n22
I 11. 1100b35 90n22
I 12. 1101b31–2 119
I 12. 1102a3–4 237n24
I 13. 1102a7–12 112
I 13. 1102a26–27 266n41
I 13. 1102a30 88
II 1. 1103a16–20 88

II 1. 1103a32–34 141
II 2. 1104a3–4 139
II 1. 1104a6–9 139n31
II 2. 1104a20–2 89
II 2. 1104a21–24 99
II 3. 1104b5–8 100
II 3. 1104b8–14 99
II 2. 1104b14 88
II 3. 1104b31 117
II 3. 1105a10–12 99
II 4. 1105a21–23 89
II 4. 1106a6–8 89
II 5 89n19, 90, 95, 97, 99
II 5. 1106b17 88
II 5. 1107a4–5 88
II 6. 1106b36–1107a6 87
II 6. 1107a8 91
II 6. 1107a3–8 98
II 7 89n17, 90, 95, 97
II 7. 1107b31 98
II 7. 1108a30–b6 92
II 7. 1108a26–28 95
II 7. 1108a30–35 92
II 7. 1107a33–4 84
II 7. 1108a6 93
II 7. 1108b7–9 84
III 1 112
III 3 133, 134, 137, 38
III 3. 1112a26–27 134
III 3. 1112a28–29 134
III 3. 1112a30–31 134
III 3. 1112a34–b2 134
III 3. 1112b2–8 133
III 3. 1112b3 135
III 3. 1112b4 125
III 3. 1112b4–5 134n25
III 3. 1112b4–6 135
III 3. 1112b8–9 135
III 3. 1112b12 135
III 3. 1112b13–14 136
III 3. 1112b15 135, 136
III 3. 1112b15–20 135
III 3. 1112b16–17 136
III 3. 1112b17–20 143
III 3. 1112b17–24 136
III 5. 1115a4–5 86
III 6. 1115a17–19 94
III 6. 1115a19 96n28
III 8. 1115b12 117n20
III 7. 1115b35–b6 95
III 8. 1116a10–12 117
III 8. 1116a18–21 117
III 8. 1116a27–9 117
III 8. 1116a28 117n20

III 8. 1116b2–3 117n20
III 8. 1117b9 117n20
III 8. 1117b14 117n20
III 10. 1117b29 98
III 10. 1118a1–10 97n29
III 11. 1118b25 90n22
III 11. 1119a18 117n20
III 12. 1119a25–27 94n27
IV 1. 1120a11 117
IV 1. 1120a12 117n20
IV 1. 1120a17–18 100n32
IV 1. 1120a23 117n20
IV 1. 1121a27–30 117
IV 2. 1122b6 117n20
IV 2. 1122b19–23 120
IV 2. 1123a24 117n20
IV 2. 1123a31–2 117
IV 5. 1125b30 98n31
IV 6. 1126b22–25 99n31
IV 8. 1128a3–4 152n4
IV 8. 1128a28 90n22
IV 9. 1128b15–21 92
IV 9. 1128b26–29 93
V 9. 1136b22 117n20
V 1. 1129a32–b1 106
V 1. 1129b11–25 109
V 1. 1129b14–19 110
V 1. 1129b19–25 111
V 1. 1129b25–7 114
V 1. 1129b25–1130a10 114
V 1. 1130a8–13 115
V 2. 1130b10–16 107
V 2. 1130b22 113n17
V 7 109n8, 113
VI 2 51
VI 2–9 133
VI 4. 1140a2 133
VI 4. 1140a3 266n41
VI 4. 1140a16–17 133
VI 4. 1140a20–23 140
VI 7. 1141b16–21 129
VI 8 122
VI 8. 1141b23–5 110
VI 8. 1141b34–1142a11 110
VI 9. 1142b5 137
VI 13. 1144b3–6 101
VI 13. 1144b32–1145a6 83n2
VII 4. 1148a22–b14 97
VII 4 266n42
VII 11. 1152b1–3 235
VIII 1. 1155a3–5 95
VIII 1. 1155a28–31 119
VIII 9. 1160a13–14 111
VIII 12. 1162a16–19 121n26

IX 8. 1169a3–15 121
IX 8. 1169a6 117
IX 8. 1169a18–26 117n20
IX 9. 1169b16–22 121n26
X 9 112
X 9. 1179b29–32 120
X 9. 1179b31–1180a5 105
X 9. 1180a5–8 120
X 9. 1181a19–21 132n23
On the Heavens [De Caelo]
I 3. 270a12–b25 62n10
I 10 64
I 10–12 62n10
I 10. 279b4–12 64
I 10. 279b12 62
I 10. 279b33–280a10 64
I 10. 280a1 61, 63n12
I 10. 280a28–31 62
I 10. 280a30–32 64
I 12. 283a11 61n5
II 1 62n10
II 10–11 62n10
III 2. 300b17–18 62, 63n12

Physics
I 1. 184a16–17 143
I 1. 184a20–21 144
II 2. 194a27 241
II 2. 194a31–2 241
II 8. 199b28 133n24
II 8. 199b30 134n24
IV 10. 217b31 266n41
VII 3. 246b4–5 172n50
VIII 1 62n10
Politics
I 2. 1253a7–18 121n26
1 4. 1254a5 133
II 8 112, 112n15
II 8. 1268b38–1269a3 109
II 8. 1269a12 130n19
III 4 112, 122
III 4. 1259b31–1260a25 96n28
III 4. 1276b27–30 112
III 4. 1277b25–30 110n10
III 6. 1278b15–30 121n26
III 6. 1278b31–2 266n41
III 6. 1279a17–19 111
III 9 113
III 11. 1282b8–13 109
III 12. 1282b16–18 111
III 13. 1283b35–42 111
IV 10 112
IV 13–14 112
VII 1. 1323a21–35 265

VII 9. 1328b37–41 126n6
VII 13–17 112n14
VIII 112n14
VIII 3. 1337b8–11 126n6
VIII 3. 1337b36 241
Posterior Analytics (=AnPo)
I 1. 24b18–20 154n12
I 12. 77b27–33 162n31
I 13. 78b21–3 171
I 13. 78b15–20 171
I 18. 81b6 129
I 31. 88a5–6 131
II 2. 90a14–18 172
II 19. 100a4–6 126
II 19. 100a4–b5 309n27
II 19. 100a4–b5 315n37
Prior Analytics (=AnPr)
I 1. 24a16–17 158n20
I 1. 24b20 165n40
I 1. 24b20–2 165
I 1. 24b22–26 176
I 1. 24b28–30 190
I 4. 25b39–40 190
I 4. 26a24 190
I 4. 26a27–28 190
I 4. 26b28–30 175, 190
I 5. 28a4–7 175
I 6. 28a15–16 175
I 6. 29a30–31 175
I 23 203n19, 204, 205
I 23. 40b20–2 166
I 23. 41a22–37 203n19, 204
I 23. 41a37–41 203n19, 204
I 23. 41a40 202
I 23. 41b1–5 166
I 27. 43b17 216n50
I 29 203n19, 204, 205
I 29. 45a23–b15 203n19, 204
I 29. 45b15–16 203n19, 204
I 29. 45b15–19 203n19, 204
I 32. 47a22–35 164n37
I 32. 47a26–8 165
I 32. 47a31–5 165
I 44 203n19, 204, 205
I 44. 50a16–28 203n19, 204
I 44. 50a29–38 203n19, 204
I 44. 50a33–5 203n19, 204
I 44. 50a39–b2 203n19, 204
II 1. 53a11–12
II 5. 58a27 29 189n25
II 7. 59a10–11 189n25
II 20. 66b11 154n9
Rhetoric
I 2. 1356b16 165n40

I 2. 1356b16–18 154n12
I 2. 1356b17 165n40
I 2. 1356b28–29 139
I 2. 1356b28–32 131–2
I 3. 1358b38 117
I 5. 1360b19–30 266n40
I 5. 1362a2 126n5
I 9 117
I 9. 1366a33–6 119
I 9. 1366b3–4 117
I 9. 1367b28 119
II 1 89n19
II 2–11 89n19
II 4. 1382a6–7 90n22
II 4. 1382a15 90
II 5–11 87n10
II 5. 1382a21–22 128
II 6. 1384b4–5 93n25
II 9. 1386b10–15 93n25
II 11 90n21
II 12. 1389a32–5 117
II 13. 1389b35 117
II 19. 1393a17–18 130n19
Sophistici Elenchi
1 157
1. 164a20–2 150
1. 164b27–165a2 154
1. 165a2 165n40
1. 165a2–3 153
1. 165a4 156
1. 165a6–13 156
1. 165a18 156
4 149, 151
4. 165b23–30, 151n2
4. 166b20–7 151n2
5 149, 151, 155, 156, 157
5. 167a21–2 151
5. 167a22 151n4
5. 167a23–7 155
6 149, 150, 151, 153, 168, 172
6. 168a24 159
6. 169a6–12 157
6. 169a6–18 149
6. 169a12–18 157
6. 168a17–20 153
6. 168a19–23 164n34
6. 168a26–8 159n24
6. 168a26–33 150, 159, 161, 162, 162n31
6. 168a30–1 160n28
6. 168a30–3 161, 164
6. 168a36–7 154n9
6. 168b4–5 154n10
6. 168b24 165n40
6. 169a18–21 162n31

7. 169a25–9 169n46
8. 170a9–11 151n2
9. 170b1–2 154n9
10. 171a5–7 152
10. 171a2–3 154n10
10. 171a6 152n6
10. 171a9–11 162n31
17. 175b39–176a18 164n36
20. 177a33–5 169n46
20. 177b1–4 169n46
20. 177b1–9 159n25
21. 177b37–178a3 159, 162n31
Top
I1. 100a25–7 154n12, 165n40
I 7. 103a9–10 160
I 7. 103a25–7 160
II 4 206
II 4. 111b17–23 207
II 6. 112a24–31 208
III 3. 118a31–33 266n40
VI 2. 139b20–1 172n50
VI 6. 145b7–8 172n50
VIII 11. 161b28–30 165, 165n40

[Aristotle]
Divisiones
Ch. 23 257n1

Atticus
Fr. 2, ch. 17 lines 122–125 Des
    Places 256–7
Ch. 20, p. 45, 129–142 Des
    Places 259n12
Augustine
De civitate Dei 19.1 233n12

Aulus Gellius
NoctesAtticae
XII.2.2 ff. 294n25
XIV 1 335n11
XVI.8.1–8 200n8

Boethius
syll cat
823A 175n1

Catallus
Poem 1 286

Cicero
Academici Libri Book 1 (*Acad. post.*, Varro)
1.19 235, 238
1.19–22 272
1.22 273n62

1.33 272n57
1.40 333n5, 349
1.40–1 336
1.41 336n15, 337n15
1.42 349, 349n36
Academica Book 2 (*Acad. pr., Lucullus*)
2.19 351n41
2.29 249
2.33 351n41
2.37 352
2.38 334n7, 351, 351n40
2.52 337n16, 350
2.52–3 335
2.53 342, 342n24, 343
2.64–148 248
2.66 336n13
2.88–90 350
2.90 350
2.92–4 344
2.93 344
2.94 344, 344n26, 344n27
2.107 345n28, 352
2.114 232n4, 248
2.116–28 248
2.129 232n4, 232n5, 235, 237, 245, 248
2.129–41 248
2.131 248
2.132 232, 232n4, 232n5, 245, 249
2.142–6 248
2.145 337
De Beneficiis
5.3.1–2 277
Div.
2. 2 245
Inv.
1. 6 231n1
2.177 266n40
Fin.
1. 11 232, 235, 238
1. 29 235
1. 42 231, 235
1. 55 243
2. 19 251
2. 21 271n56
2. 45 251
3. 22 252
3. 26 231, 235
3. 32 247
2. 35 285n10
3. 41 247, 271n56
3. 41–45 274
3.41–48 272n59
3.43 247, 271n56
3.55 246, 246

4.54–5 200n8
4.19 231n1
4.31 247, 271n56
4.32 238
4.35 247
5.8 272n58
5.12 272n57, 272n59
5.14 271n56, 272n59
5.15 232, 235, 250
5.15–17 235
5.18 251
5.22 251
5.23 235, 285n10
5.24 272n59
5.25 247
5.27 238
5.37 238, 247, 271n56
5.38 352
5.40 271n56
5.45 271n56
5. 47 247, 271n56
5.68–69 271n56
5.71–72 271n56, 274
5.75 272n58
5.83 259n13
5.84 272n57, 274
5.89 273n61
5.91–2 272n57
5.95 272n57
De Officiis
1.6 285n10
3.34 354
De Oratore
3.116 266n40
Part. orat.
3 231n1
9 231n1
38 266n40
74 266n40
Topica
12.53–14.57 200n8
83 266n40
TD
4.62 262n24, 273n60
5. 39 247
5. 50 272n57
5. 51 261n22
5.76 272n59
5.84–85 272n59
5. 85 272n57, 285n10

Clement of Alexandria
Stromateis
2.7.34 265n38

2.17.76 336n13
2.20.111 349n35
2.21.129 261, 272n57
2.22.133 260n17, 265n36, 268
2. 127 ff. 232n5
2.129.10 269n49
21. 130, 2 241

David
In AnPr
xi 1 177n5

Demetrius of Laconia
PHerc 1012, col XIII 234

Democritus
Frag. 269 241

Demosthenes
Against Leptines
20.5 121n25
Olynthiaca
1.2 340n20

Dio Chrysostom
75.1 311n32

Diogenes Laertius
Lives of the Philosophers
I 21 317n43, 318n45
II 93 247n43
II 98 247n43
III 80–81 265
III 101 257
V 30 261
V 31 86n9
VII 46 337, 346n32
VII 50 339
VII 51 334n6, 334n8, 336, 339, 350
VII 54 302n4, 348
VII 61 257n5
VII 62 257n6
VII 76 217n58
VII 77 208n30
VII 80 216
VII 81 212n38
VII 85–6 334n6
VII 87 232n5
VII 94 262n26
VII 95 258n7
VII 97 262n25
VII 96–7 246
VII 101 262n26
VII 102 232n5

VII 102–6 256
VII 103 263n30
VII 109 277n69
VII 127 343, 343n25
IX 95 317n44
IX 105 369
IX 107–8 231n3
X 27 231n3, 302n4

Epictetus
Discourse
3.2 278n70

Epicurus
Men. 128 231n3
131 231n3

R.S.
22 231n3
25 231n3

Euripides
Electra 956 241
Hipp. 867 241

[Euripides]
fr. 1110 Nauck 240n33

Eusebius
Praeparatio Evangelica 1.8.9 = Diels,
  Doxographi graeci, 581, 21–582,
  1 = Mannebach fr. 159A = Giannantoni
  IV A 166 234
11.4.1 269n49

Galen
De dignos. puls.
1.5, 8.793 Kühn (=SVF 2.79) 319n47

De libris propriis
13 24n8
XV. 4 232n5
De opt. doctr.
1.43.21–44.2 Kühn 311n33
1.49 Kühn 329n65
De plac. Hipp. et Plat.
9.7.3–5, 5.778–9 Kühn 329n65
Institutiologica
2.2 215n46
5.1 220n63
6.2 215n46
6.6 200n8, 212n38
7.2 183, 200, 200n8, 216n51,
  221n65

[Galen]
hist phil
XV 200n8
XIX 239 183n18

Gorgias
Helen
8 240
Palamedes
35 241
36 240n33

Herodotus
1. 30 2421n35
1. 82 241
1. 155 241
9. 2 241

Hesiod
Op.
669 241

Hierocles
St. Eth.
1.31–3 334n6, 349n35

Hippolytus
Refutation of All Heresides
1.20.5 269

Homer
Il.
7.16 241n35
7.104 241n35
7.787 241n35
16.630 241
18.378 240
20.101 242

Odyssey
22.479 240

Horace
Ars Poetica
1–9 282

Lucianus
Vitarum Auctio 24 200n8

Michael of Ephesus
in Sophistici Elenchi (=*in SE*)
57.15–31 161n30
57.25–31 161n29
65.25–66.1 162n31

Muretus
Variae Lectiones
XVII.1 232n6

Parmenides
Frag. B8. 8–10 61n5

Philo
Alleg.
1.30 349n35
De Plantatione
115 200n8
Quaestiones in Genesim
3.16 259n11
Quod Det.
7 259n11, 265n38, 269n51

Philodemus
IV col. XXXVIIa, 4–17 233
PHerc 1251 247n43
Philoponus
in Analytica Priora (=*in AnPr*)
114.16–20 180n13
244.1– 246.14 224n72
245.3–23 220n64
320.16–322.18 164n37
323.18–27 164n37

Plato
Alcibiades
132bc 268
Cratylus
420a 90n20
Euthydemus 278e 259
281 268
281d–282a 260
291d–e 261n21
Gorgias
452e 50n38
466c–d 243
467d–e 243
467e 268n46
468b 243
468e 243
469e 243
471ff. 55
474b 25n9
479e–481c 31
484c 50n38
492e3–494c7 27n13
494a6 34
494c6–e6 34
497e3 33
499b–d 243

499e 231, 239, 244
Laches
191d–e 96n28
Laws
631b 270, 270n54
631b–d 267, 267n44
697a–c 267a44
697b 264n33, 267
743ce 267n44
743de 264n33
767b 308n26
870ab 264n33, 267n4
X. 896e8–899b9 76n38
Lysis
220b 242
Meno
72a 84
87–89 260, 261n21
Parmenides
151e3–152e3 61n7
141a5–d3 61n7
Phaedo
97c6–d3 19
99c9–d1 18–19
Phaedrus
248b 270
Philebus
11b4–5 4
11b7–c2 4
11d4–6 3, 4n5
11d8 4n5
11d11–12a4 5, 5n7
11e2 4n5, 5n7, 5n8
12a1 5n8
12c8–d6 33, 35
13b3–5 5
13b6–c2 5, 14, 43
13b7 4n4
14b5–7 5
19b2–4 6
19c2–3 18
20a5–9 6
20b 8
20b–22c 3
20b7–9 13
20b8 11n19
20b9–c5 13
20c2 11n19
20c4–6 8, 15
20c8 6
20d 56
20d8–10 6, 19, 38
20e6 15
21a4 6, 8

21a8–12 10
21a8–22b1 26
21a9 11
21a11 15
21a14–b1 10
21b–c 40n29
21b3–4 11
21b6–9 6, 10
21c 27
21c–d 25, 26
21c1–4 6, 10
21c5–6 10, 10n16
21d3 16
21d4–5 6, 12
21e4 16
22a5 16
22a9–b2 16
22b1 6
22b3–4 11n19
22b3–6 16
22c1–2 13, 13n26, 15
22c3 19n34
22c5 19n34
22e3 19n34
26a4 17n31
31a8–10 17n31
32b–c 26
32b9–c2 27
32c3–5 26
32e 31
36b8–9 27
36c–41b 36–39
36e 29, 30
38a8 33
38b2 54
38b12–13 37
38c–e 37
39a4–7 37n23
39d1–e5 40
40a9–12 22n1, 40
40a9–c6 39–44
40b 54–6
40b2–c6 42
40b7 37n23
40c1–6 52
40c4–6 22
40c8–d10 23
41a1–4 43
41a5–6 43
41a8 44
41b–42c 44–47
41b3 44
42a5 44
42a7–9 52

42b2–c3 46
42c–44b 47–48
42c–43d 27n13
43b 28n14
43b–c 26
43d 28n14, 31
44a 31
44b 28n14
44b–50c 48–50
45c 36
46d 35
47a6–9 35
47a23–25 39
47b2–7 35
48c–49e 33, 33n21
53c–55b 27n13
58a7–b3 50n38
59e7–61a3 7
60a7–b1 4n4
60d3–e7 7
63d2–64a1 34
66b2 17n31

Protagoras
349a6 ff. 235
353e8 242
354a ff. 242
354b–d 235
354b7 242
354b8 235
354d2 235
354d8 235
354e8 242
355a5 242
356–7 46

Republic
I. 338d–339a 108
I. 340b 108n6
II. 357b–d 246
IV. 442d–443a 107n4
V. 475d 97n29
VI. 491c 267n44
VI. 504e–505b 270
VII 270
IX. 582a 311n33
IX. 582a6 302n6
X. 613a ff. 244n40
X. 613b12 244n40
X. 613c3 244n40
X. 613d7 244n40

Soph.
263e 314n35

Symp.
181e 242n38

Theaetetus
178b6 302n6
179c 320n49
184–6 310n31
189e–190a 314n35

Timaeus
17a2 67n18
19a7 67n18
20b1 67n18
20c6 67n18
25e2 67n18
26a3 67n18
26a7 67n18
26b4 67n18
26c8 67n18
28c2–29a6 61
28c2–29b1 71
29b4–5 62n8
29c1–d3 62
29c4–d3 73n32
29d7–47e3 73n32
30a3–6 60
30a4 66
34a1–5 70
34a8–9 60
34b1–9 69
34b10–35a1 66n16
37a6–39e4 60
37c6–d7 61
37c6 74
38a3–4 61n7
39e3–40a2 71
39e3–40d5 69
41a3–7 69
41a7–b2 74
41c2–6 70n25
42b5–7 74
42b5–c4 71n27
47e3–68d7 73n32
48a7–b3 73n32
48d2–3 73n32
48d5 63n12
48e2–53a7 72
53a8–b5 66
53c1–2 63n12
68ae1–92c 73n32
68e1–4 60
68e3 66
69b3–4 66
69c1 66
90d 231
90e6–91a1 71n27
90e6–91d6 71n28
91d5–92c3 71n27
92a4–9 61

92c6–7 69
106a1–b7 60n2
106a3–4 60, 60n2

Plutarch
Adv. Colotem
1115bc 266n41
1122c 334n7, 336
Comm. not. 1070F 241, 252
De E apud Delphos 386E–387C 200n8
fr. 215f 348n34
Gen. Soc.
580f 334n7
588f 334n7
Pericles
33 272n57
Soll.An
960f 349n37
961e–f 349n37
St. Rep.
1036d 351n39
1036e 337, 351n39
1045c 334n7
1048a 273
1056–7 351n39
1056f 336
1057a 336, 336n13
Virt. Mor.
447a 334n7, 336

[Plutarch]
On Fate 568b–574e 201n10

Polybius
9.33 308n26

Porphyry
Abst.
3.21–2 349n37

Ptolemy of Alexandria
Almagest
1.1, I.4–7 Heiberg 301n3
1.1, I 5.10–13 Heiberg 305n18
1.1, I 5.13–6.4 Heiberg 305n18
1.1, I 6.1–4 Hermann 324n56
1.1, I 6.11–21 Heiberg 307n24
I 6.15 Heiberg 306n19
1.8, I 26.9–12 Heiberg 306n21
3.3, I 219–32 Heiberg 307n23
9.2, II 211–12 Heiberg 306n21
II 212.3–5 Heiberg 307n21
Harmonics
1.1, p. 3.1–20 Düring 306n19
1.1, p. 3.3–5 Düring 304
1.1–2, p. 5.6–13 Düring 306n20, 312n34
1.1, p. 3.13 Düring 319n48
1.2, p. 5.13–9 Düring 306n21
1.2, p. 5.19–21 Düring 329n66
1.2, p. 5.24–6.13 Düring 304n15
3.3, p. 92.9–11 Düring 305n18
3.3, p. 93.14–20 Düring 324n57
3.3, p. 94.16–17 Düring 307n24
On the criterion and commanding faculty
ch. 1, 3.1 303
ch. 1, 3.1–5 308
ch. 1, 3.10–14.3 309n29
ch. 1, 3.17–8 303n9
ch. 1, 4.3–14 311
ch. 2, 4.15–5.3 313
ch. 2, 4.16–18 303
ch. 2, 5.4–6 313
ch. 2, 5.15–18 313
ch. 2, 5.18–6.11 314
ch. 2, 6.6–9 315
ch. 2, 6.9–11 327
ch. 3, 6.12–7.6 316
ch. 3, 6.19–7.1 316n42
ch. 4, 7.7–11 318
ch. 4–8, 7.12–13.3 318
ch. 5, 8.13–20 316n42
chs. 8–9, 13.4–15.4 318
ch. 8, 13.5–10 318
ch. 8, 13.10–12 319
ch. 8, 13.12–16 319
ch. 8, 13.16–14.3 319
ch. 9, 14.4–9 326n61
ch. 9, 14.4–16 319
ch. 9, 14.4–21 319
ch. 9, 14.16–21 319
ch. 9, 14.20–21 324n58
ch. 9, 14.23–15.4 319
ch. 10, 15.5–8 305
ch. 10, 15.5–9 320
ch. 10, 15.5–16.4 321
ch. 10, 15.9–14 320
ch. 10, 16.4–9 322
ch. 10, 16.5–6 328n65
ch. 11, 16.13–15 323
ch. 11, 16.15 324
ch. 11, 16.15–17.1 323
ch. 11, 17.1–12 323
ch. 11, 17.4–5 323
ch. 11, 17.9–10 303
ch. 11, 17.10–12 303
ch. 12, 17.17 303n9, 315n36
ch. 12, 17.17–18.4 325–6
ch. 12, 17.19 328n65

ch. 12, 18.1-4 303, 315n38
ch. 12, 18.4-9 326
ch. 12, 18.5 319n48
ch. 12, 18.9-17 326
ch. 12, 18.10 303n9
ch. 12, 18.17-19.6 303, 327
ch. 12, 18.18.12-3 328n65
Optics
2.2, p. 12 Lejeune 325n59
2.13, p. 17 Lejeune 324n57
2.83, p. 55 Lejeune 322n51
2.102, p. 64 Lejeune 322n51
2.134-6, pp. 80-82 Lejeune 324n57

Quintilian
10.1.125-131 286n12

Scholium in Arist.
156b43-47 177n5
157a13-18 194
157a18-21 194
157a24-28 194n34

Semonides
1. 12 240n33

Seneca
Ben.
5.3.1-2 272n57
De Ira 2.3-4 335n11
1.3.7 349n37
Epistulae Morales (=*Ep.*)
1 287-8, 291n21
3.2-3 288
6.5 289
9 283
12.7 284n9
24 283
27.1 287
33 289
38 283, 286
39 289
45 289-91
58 278n70, 283, 295
64 290-1
65 278n70, 295
66 278, 286, 295
66.5 276-7
72 292
78 283
78.25 233n11
86 291n20
88.5 269n50
91 293

94 283, 284, 286, 288, 292, 294, 295
94.1-4 285
94.5-8 285
94.5-17 285
94.11 285
94.18-51 285
94.21 285
94.26-27 285
94.34 285
94.40-41 285
94.45-51 285
94.52-60 285
95 283, 286, 288, 292, 294, 295
95.1 288
95.13 286
95.29-35 286
95.36 286
95.44-46 286
95.47-54 286
95.55-59 286
103 283
106 283, 292-3
108 293, 294-5
112 283
114 291n19
116 283
120 296

Sextus Empiricus
PH
I 3 367
I 9 361
I 10 356n2, 356n3, 366, 368n33
I 20 358, 369
I 21-24 363
I 22 358, 362
I 24 361n15
I 25 231n3
I 33-34 357
I 39 368
I 88-9 371
I 89 357
I 96-7 357
I 101 358, 369
I 102-3 371
I 112-113 371
I 183 356n2, 366n29
I 190 356n2, 366n29
I 196 356n3, 365n26, 366, 366n29, 370
I 198 356n3, 366n29
I 202 356n3
I 203 356n3, 365
I 211 369
I 213 369

I 215 231n3
I 220–35 367
I 222 356n2, 356n3, 366n29
I 226 367
I 226–7 367
I 226–30 334n7
I 227 356n3, 366n29, 368n33
I 228 342
I 229 368
I 229–30 369
I 230 369
I 231 231n3, 367
I 232 356n3, 366n29
II 10 360, 361
II 15 312
II 38–41 357
II 38–43 371
II 51 369
II 63 369
II 77 370
II 79 356n2, 366n29
II 136 206n27
II 156 183n18
II 157–59 200n8
II 158 212n38, 216
III 2 358
III 29 356n4
III 48 368n33
III 72 368n33
III 171 258
III 179 263n30
III 181 269n49
III 233–4 357
adv. Math.
VII 35–7 312
VII 151 337
VII 159–89 367
VII 166 367
VII 166–89 334n7, 338
VII 175 368n34
VII 179–80 351n39
VII 180 342
VII 191 321n49
VII 195 319n47
VII 199–200 236
VII 214–17 303
VII 217–18 318n46, 329n65
VII 217–26 315
VII 222 316n41
VII 224 315
VII 226 315n36, 318n46
VII 240–1 334n5
VII 242 335, 335n10
VII 243 346n31

VII 244–5 353n43
VII 247 353n43
VII 248 334n8, 339
VII 249 353n43
VII 250 334n8
VII 253–4 338, 338n18, 340
VII 253–60 338
VII 254 341n23, 351n39, 353
VII 255 339, 341, 341n21
VII 256 341, 341n22, 353n44
VII 257 335, 339, 339n19, 340, 350, 351n39
VII 257–8 353n43
VII 258 339, 351n41
VII 260 353n43
VII 263–342 317
VII 269 351n41
VII 301–2 206n27
VII 333 364n22
VII 343–69 317
VII 365 319n47
VII 370–439 318
VII 402–8 350
VII 403 350
VII 405 335, 339, 350, 350n38, 351n39
VII 416 345, 345n29
VII 435–6 367
VII 435–8 367, 370
VII 444 359n10
VIII 51–4 364, 371
VIII 53 358, 369
VIII 223 183n18
VIII 226 216
VIII 241 359n8
VIII 324 361
VIII 333a 359n8
VIII 473–8 357, 358, 359, 360, 360n11, 363
IX 29 359n8
IX 78 365
IX 352 319n47
XI 22 262n26
XI 25–7 258n9
XI 30 262n25
XI 40 262n26
XI 46 258n8
XI 52–59 264n33 XI 61 264n33
XI 76 262n26
XI 184 262n26

Simplicius
in Cat
1.13–16 179n10

Sophocles
Oed. Col. 1721 241

Stobaeus
Ecl.
2.7.11m 338n17, 346n32
2.46 260, 269n49, 272n57, 275n64
2.49.25–50.1 263n31
2.55.5–21 263
2.56 269n49
2.56.8–9 268
2. 57.18–20 257n5
2.69 262n26
2.70.8 ff. 257
2.71.15 ff. = LS M 246
2.72.5 262n25
2.74 337
2.101.5–7 262n26
2.124ff. 265
2.126–127 272n57
2.126.12–127.2 261n20, 275
2.130 272n57
2.134–7 257, 276n65
2.136 265

SVF
2.83 315n38
2.131 336n14, 338n17, 346n32
2.714 349n35
2.844 349n35
3.2 231n3
3.3 238
3.16 231n3
3.68 246
3.69 246
3.73 262n25
3.106 262n25
3.107 262n25
3.474 262n24, 273
3.548 338n17
3.548–56 346n32

Suda
s.v. Ἰουλιανός 177n5
s.v. Μάξιμος 179n10

Tacitus
Annals
16.13 293n22

Themistius
In libros Aristotelis de anima paraphrasis
47a23–5 39n28
In reply to Maximus on the reduction of the second and third figures to the first

180.5–10 178
180.5–184.37 178
180.10–12 178
180.15–16 178
180.17–23 187
180.23–26 186
181.4–6 180n13
184.13–16, 24–27 188
184.29–30 188
184.38–185.1 180
184.38–190.38 178
185.1–3 186
185.3–5 181
185.5–8 186
185.30–33 189
185.38–39 189
185.38–40 190
185.40–43 190
186.3–5 190
186.8–10 182
186.9 189n26
186.14–18 191
186.15 195
186.18–20 191
186.22–26 193
186.26–20, 35–37 194
187.1–3 195
187.30–32 196
187.35–38 196
189.36–40 185
190.38–191.1 180
190.38–191.3 181
190.38–39 180n14
190.39–193.20 178
191.4–6 184
192.9–12 191
192.15–22 192
192.15–29 182
193.9–11 183
193.21–194.26 178
192.33–40 195

Theon
Progymnasmata
109–110 266n40

Varro
de Lingua Latina (=*Ling.Lat.*)
6.56 349n37

Virgil
Eclogue 6 286